Striking Through Clouds

The War Diary of No. 514 Squadron, RAF

Striking Through Clouds

The War Diary of No. 514 Squadron, RAF

Simon Hepworth and Andrew Porrelli

The 514 Squadron badge is used and reproduced under licence from the MOD

Mention The War Publications

First published 2014 by Mention The War Publications, a division of Airworx GmbH, Zug, Switzerland.

Copyright 2014 © Simon Hepworth and Andrew Porrelli.

The right of Simon Hepworth and Andrew Porrelli to be identified as Authors of this work is asserted by them in accordance with the Copyright, Designs and Patents Act 1988.

The original Operational Record Book of 514 Squadron is Crown Copyright and stored in microfiche and digital format by the National Archives. The authors acknowledge with gratitude the permission of the National Archives to use their material for the transcripts in this book.

All rights reserved. No part of this publication may be reproduced, stored in a retrieval system, transmitted in any form or by any means, electronic, mechanical or photocopied, recorded or otherwise, without the written permission of the copyright owners.

The 514 Squadron badge is used and reproduced under licence from the MOD.

Cover design: Topics - The Creative Partnership www.topicsdesign.co.uk

A CIP catalogue reference for this book is available from the British Library.

ISBN-13: 978-1495440489
ISBN-10: 1495440486

Cover photograph: 514 Squadron Lancasters operating against Wesseling on 30th October 1944. NG121, JI-H was flown on this occasion by F/O Stan Wright, RCAF and his crew. The photograph was taken by F/O 'Art' Wark, flying 514 Sqn. Lancaster, PD325 A2-L. Unlike too many of their colleagues, F/O Wright, F/O Wark and their crews survived their tour of operations. Photo courtesy of F/O Ken Ridley, Navigator in the Wright crew. Thanks to Garth Ridley.

Dedication

Sgt 1594519 John Porrelli, RAFVR, and crew. Failed to return from Valenciennes on 16th June 1944. Grandfather of Andrew Porrelli.

Sgt 1891510 Peter Andrew Gosnold, RAFVR, and crew. Failed to return from Homberg on 21st November 1944. Great Uncle of Simon Hepworth.

Flight Lieutenant Ron Pickler DFC, 514 Sqn pilot and author, passed away 19th April 2014. Ron was tireless in preserving the memory of the squadron.

In total, 435 members of 514 Squadron lost their lives in the service of their country. This book is gratefully dedicated to their memory and to all those who also served in 514 Squadron, Royal Air Force 1943 to 1945.

I Will Remember

by Sarah Atchison
(Granddaughter of Sgt Ross Flemming RCAF, 514 Sqn Navigator)

As I stand here today,
I look around at those who have come,
To Remember all of the spirits and souls
Lost to battle
Fighting for our freedom.
Each person has a memory,
A memory that contains love and triumph
A memory for a friend, or,
A memory for a loved one.
A memory that will last a lifetime.
As I look into the Veteran's faces,
I can see the pain.
The pain of seeing a friend,
Knowing he's right behind you,
And when you turn to him,
He's gone.
In his memory he sees his family,
His friends.
Wishing he wasn't there.
Not knowing if he will survive.
But as I look deeper into their faces,
I can find those memories,
Hidden in their eyes.
All of us weep,
Some not knowing the real pain,
But those who do,
Weep with triumph and glory,
Knowing that all is Remembered,
On this Remembrance Day.
I will Remember.

Contents

Foreword..10
Authors' Notes 12
Acknowledgements...15
A Brief History of 514 Squadron............................17
The Leaders of 514 Squadron.................................24
514 Squadron Operational Record..........................31
War Stories
    Sgt Ernest 'Sunny' Gledhill..........................449
    Sgt Bill Saddler..456
    Sgt Peter Gosnold..460
    P/O Bob Langley... 466
    Sgt John Porrelli and F/L Arnold Morrison............471
    Sgt Ross Flemming..................................... 498
Move of 514 Squadron to RAF Waterbeach..........505
Glossary..535

Foreword

By Flight Lieutenant EA 'Alex' Campbell, RCAF, DFC

Thank you, Simon and Andy, for trusting me with the 'Foreword' for your upcoming history of 514 Squadron.
As for myself, Good Luck has followed me throughout these volatile times with human greed at its ugliest.
Being happily married, with a wonderful caring family, good health interspersed with setbacks of maturing age, are some of the blessings bestowed on me.
Some 10,000 Canadian airmen died during WW2 and within the Commonwealth, the numbers reach 22,000. Every one of those young folk has been denied the amenities of life that we enjoy.

Cheers to All,

Alex Campbell
Skipper of Lancaster A2C

The following are bits of 'patter' heard during a bombing run:

Bomb Aimer: *"Crossing enemy coast."*

Navigator: *"Alter course to 130 degrees in 10 seconds... 5,4,3,2,1 NOW!"*

"Altitude 12,500 feet"

Flight Engineer: *"Port Outer running hot Skipper"*

Mid Upper Gunner: *"Weird light zero four five degrees up...Heavy Flak and searchlights, Starboard beam"*

Rear Gunner: *"Fighter! Port! Go!"*
"He broke away Skipper."

Wireless Operator: *"Leaving Monica now Skipper."*

Flight Engineer: *"Navigator, How long to landfall?"*
Navigator: *"46 minutes."*
Flight Engineer: *"Make it 20 minutes, we're short on petrol."*

Skipper: *"Cut the chatter."*

Alex Campbell (left) with fellow 514 Sqn veterans Ron Pickler, Don Gardner, Jack Gillespie, Earl Jones, Fred Goodman, Ed Commeford and Ken Ridley, at the squadron reunion, Hamilton, August 2003. Source: Alex Campbell.

Authors' Notes

Striking Through Clouds is the day-by-day contemporaneous account of the operations of 514 Squadron. Recorded sometimes diligently, often in brief and occasionally with a bare minimum of detail, this was a dispassionate but comprehensive account of the war effort of the squadron and its members.

The account is taken directly from the Operational Record Book (ORB) of the squadron, now held in the National Archives. Until now this was retained in microfiche form, from which a print could be made. These are, naturally enough, often lacking clarity and definition, sometimes to the point of illegibility. The authors have made their best efforts to read the records and write them up in documentary form. Where there have been errors, we can only apologise, particularly where names have been incorrectly spelt. A considered decision was taken to convey the information represented by the ORB entries, rather than simply transcribe them complete with the inevitable grammatical and spelling errors. Where necessary such mistakes, made by hard-pressed staff under considerable pressure, have been rectified. However, every effort has been made to ensure that absolutely nothing of substance has been omitted. The format of the ORB entries evolved over time, and this has been reflected in their appearance in this book. For the most part, the contents should be considered a record rather than a narrative. Wherever possible, the personal style of the compiling officer has been retained. Every day, the compiling officer would record the weather conditions as these affected the squadron's ability to operate. Non-operational flying was then detailed, along with notable events on the ground, such as the visit of King George VI and Queen Elizabeth, awards ceremonies and other events. Operations were recorded in summary form, and in the ORB a paragraph is added following the debriefing of each crew. These were usually similar so a representative example is given for each operation, with notable comments from other pilots. All ranks used are those applicable at the time of the ORB entry. In 1944 a decision was apparently taken to commission as officers all sergeant pilots, as it was felt that a commission as, initially, Pilot Officer or Flying Officer was more befitting their responsibilities as captains of heavy bombers. The crew lists appear in the order in which they are listed in the ORBs.

The Appendices to the ORB include a large number of combat reports, compiled after the return of the crew. The combat reports have been transcribed and are entered on the date of the operation to which they relate. These were, of course, from incidents in which the aircraft and crew survived the encounter.

The Diaries would, the authors felt, benefit immensely from the inclusion of later information about losses and notes concerning the context of particular raids. To distinguish these from the ORB entries, such notes are shown in italics.

Missing Aircraft

When an aircraft failed to return from ops, information about its fate, and that of its crew, was almost always totally absent. Occasionally, the loss of an identified Lancaster would be witnessed and reported on return to base. This was, however, exceptional. Usually it was weeks, months or even years before the picture became clear. Even now, seventy years or so later, a number of 514 Squadron aircraft remain simply 'lost without trace'. Word was gradually received of crews taken prisoner, evading capture and returning to England. After the war, wreckage was recovered and war graves registered, particularly by the admirable Commonwealth War Graves Commission. Much useful information has been collated and recorded in the definitive *'RAF Bomber Command Losses'* by WR Chorley (Midland Counties Publications / Ian Allan Publishing 1997). This work has been the starting point for detailing the circumstances of each loss, being considered the authoritative source. Bill Chorley's permission to the authors to refer frequently to his material is very much appreciated.

Attribution of specific losses of squadron aircraft to German night fighters has relied heavily on the excellent and comprehensive *'Nachtjagd War Diaries'*, by Dr. Theo EW Boiten and Roderick J. Mackenzie (Wing Leader Books 2011, www.wingleader.co.uk). Where necessary, additional research was undertaken to establish the time and place of the Lancaster being brought down, and these have been cross-referenced with claims by Luftwaffe crews of the destruction of an unidentified heavy bomber. The authors are grateful to the publishers of *'Nachtjagd War Diaries'* for allowing extensive reference to be made to the two volumes of the work.

Because of the uncertainty surrounding the circumstances of many of the losses, the wording has been chosen with care. Where the loss was witnessed, or is stated as fact by one of the authoritative sources checked, a confident statement is entered for each Missing Aircraft entry. Losses to German night fighters, as detailed in *'Nachtjagd War Diaries'*, are sometimes clearly attributed. In other cases, the shooting down is attributed as 'probably' or 'possibly' and these words appear as appropriate. In other cases, there has been no claim made for a 514 Squadron aircraft and it is necessary to speculate against all the evidence. Again, this is made clear in each case. Out of the 66 operational losses there remain two that cannot be definitively or reasonably explained.

Raid Notes

Supplementary information about the context of the raids has been gathered from a number of sources, much of which is available in the invaluable reference book *'The Bomber Command War Diaries'* by Martin Middlebrook and Chris Everitt (Midland Publishing / Ian Allan Publishing 1996). As with Bill Chorley's *'Bomber Command Losses'* series, this work is regarded as authoritative. Relevant observations from local reports, noted by the authors of those works, have provided invaluable additional information. Additional material has been gleaned from numerous open sources on the internet, most of it published anonymously or with dated links. Where it has not been possible to contact the original authors personally, the authors of this work wish to extend their appreciation.

Photographs

Most of the photos in this book have been shared with the authors by veterans and their families. To all of these people we are very grateful, and they are each credited where appropriate. The quality of many photographs is not exceptional, due to their age and the transfer between media. The authors have decided that it is appropriate to share a usable image, albeit of less than top quality, rather than miss the opportunity to show a particular photo.

Finally…

Today we are left, fortuitously, with a few resilient survivors, many more having, inevitably, passed away in the intervening decades. Some have left written records, others have passed on their recollections to their families. There is still interest, even three generations removed from those who served, and a genuine desire to know what the crews did, and what they went through. The following history, taken from the official Operational Record Books, tells, day by day, op by op and loss by loss, the story of all those who served in 514 Squadron. Andrew Porrelli and I separately became interested in the history of 514 Squadron as we tried to find out the stories of our relatives who lost their lives in 1944. The story of 'our' crews is inextricably linked to the squadron itself, and it was clear that a single source detailing its brief history would, perhaps, be useful to others who wondered what their family members or friends had been through. 435 members of the squadron did not come back and, for many of those who did, the whole experience was not something they felt comfortable reliving. We hope this record proves of use and interest.

Acknowledgements

The authors are also very grateful to the following people and sources of information about 514 Squadron's operations:

The National Archives without whose records and permission to reproduce them, this book would not have been possible.

Wendy Flemming, 514 Squadron Association in Canada.

Clive Hill, 514 Squadron Association in the UK, for his work with keeping the squadron reunions going.

The families of F/O Geoff France, Sgt Pete Gosnold, Sgt William Meredith, F/O Frederick Eisberg, and Sgt John Porrelli for their long-standing support for this work.

Garth Ridley and Robert Guy, and other relatives of squadron members, for their observations, contributions, and photos.

Linda Miles for sharing photos relating to DS816 and crew, especially her father, F/Lt. AH Morrison DFC, RAAF.

514 Squadron veterans Joe Dibley, Ron Pickler, Bob Chester-Masters, Ted Key and Bernard Yeomans for pointing me, at various stages, in the right direction.

Oliver Merrington, Waterbeach Military Heritage Museum.

The Bomber Command History Forum whose members have helped with various detailed queries. The site is well worth a visit at the following location:
www.lancasterbombers.net/BomberCommandHistoryForum/

Facebook groups, especially 'RAF Bomber Command' and 'Lincolnshire Bomber Command Memorial' for their help with publicising my requests for information.

Roger Guernon, for his help in the circumstances surrounding the loss and recovery of DS822 as well as his additional research, photographs and fact-checking.

Auckland War Memorial Museum.

Our partners and children for putting up with the pair of us, on opposite sides of the world, constantly tapping on our keyboards.

Readers are invited to visit the website, www.514squadron.co.uk or join the Facebook community, www.facebook.com/514SquadronRaf

A Brief History of 514 Squadron

In 1943, 3 Group had fallen behind some of the other groups, primarily operating the obsolescent Short Stirling heavy bomber compared with the later models of the Handley Page Halifax and, of course, the Avro Lancaster which equipped the rest of Bomber Command. Eventually the Group re-equipped, the plan being to switch from Stirlings to Lancasters. Along with 115 Sqn, already in existence, 514 Sqn was equipped with Mk.II Lancasters, the aircraft being powered by four 1650hp Bristol Hercules radial engines rather than the iconic Rolls-Royce Merlin. The rationale behind the modification of the Lancaster was a concern in 1942 / 43 that there might be a shortage of the Merlins. Some 300 Lancaster airframes were equipped with the air-cooled Hercules; 67 such aircraft passed through 514 Sqn's hands with 59 being lost through enemy action or accident before the type was withdrawn in September 1944. With an operational strength of thirty aircraft, the squadron's fleet was to be lost, along with the crews, nearly twice over in the next eleven months with a total of eighty aircraft destroyed or written off by the end of the war.

3 Group itself was moving towards specialisation in blind bombing techniques, in an attempt to improve the concentration of bombs on specific targets. Cloud cover being a regular feature over targets in Northern Europe, a means was needed to ensure that this did not result in wasted effort. The requirement had resulted, by 1943, in the wider use of H2S radar and the Gee navigation system. Both systems had their known shortcomings; H2S could distinguish only certain specific features of the ground beneath the aircraft, whilst its signals could be detected and tracked by enemy night fighters. Gee, based on a number of radio transmitters in England, was limited by the Earth's curvature and was susceptible to jamming.

Towards the end of 1943, a new location system was being trialled. With an accuracy of 150 feet at 300 miles range from a transmitter in England, Gee-H could effectively place an aircraft over a relatively small target, such as a large factory, an oil plant or railway yard. The system did not require the bomb aimer to see either the target or markers, and so bombing through ten-tenths cloud cover with sufficient accuracy to hit a high-value target was feasible. The system could handle, in theory, up to 100 aircraft at the same time, though in practice rarely more than 70 would use it simultaneously. By late 1943 this would constitute a relatively small force however, so the 'GH Leader' tactic evolved. This entailed a GH-equipped aircraft bombing when its receiver said it was over the target; up to four other aircraft would formate on the leader, releasing their own weapons when they saw bombs falling from the leader. The system really came into its own when the Allies enjoyed sufficient air superiority to allow Bomber Command to attack in daylight as well as at night.

Having developed the GH tactics to a degree that impressive results were regularly being achieved, 3 Group was allowed the latitude to operate independently of other Bomber Command groups when required, although the group's aircraft participated in major raids until the end of hostilities.

514 Sqn was born on 1st September 1943, though the Adjutant was the first member of its staff to arrive at RAF Foulsham in Norfolk on 6th September.   Five days later the squadron's first Lancaster Mk.II, DS735, arrived. Nearly two months' hard work led to the squadron making its operational debut, to the Mannesheim Works at Düsseldorf, on a raid to trial GH bombing on November 3rd 1943. 514 Squadron was thus fully operational by the start of the winter-long Battle of Berlin, which started in earnest on 18th November 1943. The sixteen operations in which 514 Sqn took part cost seven aircraft through enemy action along with another which over-ran the runway on its return, fortunately without casualties on that occasion.

Midway through November 1943, 514 Sqn received orders to move from its Norfolk base to RAF Waterbeach, four miles north of Cambridge, where it remained for the rest of its existence. The move was shrouded in secrecy, the official reason being that the runway needed resurfacing. The truth was that RAF Foulsham had been transferred to 100 Group, whose aircraft operated counter-measures against German defences. The movement was organised and carried out in just over a week. Three of the squadron's aircraft travelled from Foulsham to Waterbeach via Berlin, carrying out a bombing raid en route. The crew's kit, including bicycles, was stowed on board for the trip.

The strength of the squadron was soon increased to three flights of ten aircraft. 514 Squadron aircraft bore two means of identification; the serial number, unique to each aircraft and which stayed with it permanently along with the squadron code, which was often changed, particularly when individual aircraft were transferred between Flights. This was in the form JI- followed by a single letter (for aircraft of 'A' and 'B' flights) and A2- (for 'C' Flight). The ORB usually shortened this to the single letter itself, e.g. JI-B was shortened to 'B' whilst A2-B was shortened to 'B2'. 'A' Flight used the codes JI-A to JI-K (omitting JI-I), 'B' Flight JI-L to JI-U and 'C' Flight A2-B to A2-L (again omitting A2-I). It has been suggested that this was to confuse German Intelligence. Each flight was commanded by a Squadron Leader, these changing periodically as the individual officer reached the end of his tour, was transferred elsewhere or, in the sad case of S/Ldr Ernest Sly, lost on operations. A decorated veteran of previous tours, S/Ldr Sly was the highest-ranking officer lost by 514 Squadron on ops.

(Above) Avro Lancaster B Mk.II DS816, JI-O of 'B' Flight. 514 Sqn was one of the few to be equipped from the outset with the Bristol Hercules-powered Mk.II Lancaster. The variant was intended to solve the concern that a shortage of Rolls-Royce Merlin engine might hamper the supply of Lancasters in 1943 / 44. In the event, the shortage did not materialise and the surviving Mk.IIs were withdrawn in Autumn 1944, the final operational deployment being 23rd September 1944 to Neuss. Some 300 were produced. The Mk.II occasionally featured a ventral machine gun (not on DS816 however), as the variant was not fitted with H2S. Other features included the bulged bomb bay. The aircraft climbed more quickly than other variants, though not quite as high. It could carry a lower bomb weight but the Hercules engine, being air-cooled, was more resistant to damage than the Merlin. DS816 was one of the first aircraft to be assigned to 514 Sqn on its formation and took part in the Battle of Berlin. She failed to return from her 41st sortie, an operation against Valenciennes on 15/16th June 1944, being shot down at Croisilles, Pas de Calais. Only her navigator, P/O AH Morrison RAAF, survived. Image by Aviation Design Studio.

Survival was partly a matter of skill, but mostly of luck, as demonstrated by the loss of the highly experienced and decorated S/Ldr Sly on the same operation as the crew of Flight Sergeant PE Mason, on their first op. One pilot, continually riding his luck, was Flying Officer Lou Greenburgh. F/O Greenburgh ditched his aircraft in the North Sea at the end of December 1943, his crew surviving to tell the tale. On another raid, two of his crew baled out of their out-of-control Lancaster before F/O Greenburgh regained control and made a safe return to England. Undeterred, F/O Greenburgh returned again to ops and was shot down again in June 1944, with the loss of his Wireless Operator and the capture of his gunners and Flight Engineer. The intrepid F/O Greenburgh evaded capture, and having had his aircraft shot down twice and damaged twice in 22 operations, survived the war.

As winter wore on, the emphasis of Bomber Command's operations switched from Berlin to targets linked to aircraft production, this becoming predominant from mid-February 1944 onwards. Following 'Big Week', the combined RAF / US Eighth Air Force assault on aircraft production, a brief return to Berlin was followed by sporadic attacks against other German cities. In early spring, the strategy of Bomber Command moved from destroying the industrial infrastructure to paving the way for the Allied landings on D-Day. This played to the strength of GH-equipped squadrons, targets being smaller and, being in the territory of our occupied allies, requiring precision if friendly casualties were to be avoided. Through April and May most such ops were against the railway infrastructure in Occupied France, primarily marshalling yards and repair depots. The targeting of maintenance facilities was to ensure that the rail network could no longer be easily patched up after the final raids before D-Day itself. German officials commented after the war that crippling the railway network had been the most significant factor in preventing German forces from fighting off the Allied invasion.

The Luftwaffe, recognising the switch in focus from Germany to more tactical targets in France, lost no time in moving its night fighters in response. This resulted in continuing losses to the squadron's aircraft and crews, though greater support was available on the ground to aircrew who managed to escape from their crippled Lancasters, including the irrepressible F/O Greenburgh, shot down over France in June 1944.

As D-Day approached, a variety of targets offered themselves, particularly coastal gun batteries posing a very real threat to the invasion fleet. Most of these were in the Pas de Calais area. These attacks also supported the intention to deceive the Germans into believing that the imminent invasion would be in that location, rather than on the Normandy beaches.

Bomber Command had, by now, demonstrated its capabilities as a tactical force, capable of the precision bombing of entrenched German forces even whilst in close proximity to Allied troops.   There were occasional, nonetheless tragic, errors; a number of Canadian ground troops were killed by bombs when they had, for an unknown reason, used yellow flares which were confused with target indicators of the same colour, in use that day. Civilian casualties were also, regrettably, inevitable though these were much lower than might have been anticipated. With air supremacy established over the Normandy bridgehead, and most targets within range of supporting fighter cover, Bomber Command was now able to operate over France by day as well as night.

(Above) Avro Lancaster Mk.I PD265, JI-G. Mk.I and Mk. III Lancasters gradually replaced the Mk.II from June 1944 onwards. The first operational sortie by Mk. I Lancs were on 21st June 1944 to Domleger, having been beaten into 514 Sqn service by Mk.III PB143, JI-B, which attacked Montdidier on 17th June 1944. Whilst the Mk.I Lancaster was powered by Rolls-Royce Merlins, the Mk.III aircraft, whilst built in England, were powered by Packard Merlins, built in the USA under licence. The yellow stripes on the fin denote a G-H Leader aircraft. PD265 was lost on her 38th operation, shot down by flak on 21st November 1944 having just bombed the Rhein-Preussen synthetic oil plant at Homberg. Her pilot, F/O Geoff France, and Navigator, F/O Frederick Eisberg were the only survivors. Image by Aviation Design Studio.

The flexibility of the bomber force was admirably shown when, for six weeks in July and August 1944, the South East of England was menaced by V1 and V2 flying bombs. An intensive campaign to eradicate the construction sites and storage depots was effective in eradicating the threat. Other targets at this time included the German E-Boat light naval strike force at Le Havre, which was decimated in a spectacularly successful attack, in which 514 Sqn played a full part, whilst other raids were made against beleaguered German forces dug into fortified defences in the Channel Ports, particularly Boulogne and Calais.Northern France having been secured by the Allies, the next campaign for Bomber Command was 'The Oil Plan', targeting German oil production and storage. Whilst Air Chief Marshal Sir Arthur Harris, Air Officer Commander in Chief of Bomber Command, famously had little time for 'panacea' targets, he did accept that the continuing availability and supply of fuel was of fundamental importance to the German war effort, and to the Luftwaffe in particular. Attacking the transport infrastructure in Germany went hand-in-glove with attempts to destroy fuel storage and, especially, the synthetic oil production facilities. Naturally these were vigorously defended, most notably the Rhein-Preussen facility at Meerbeck, Homberg, where an attack on July 20th 1944 saw four of the squadron's aircraft lost. 514 Sqn would ultimately lose as many Lancasters attacking that single facility as it did during the sixteen raids the squadron conducted against Berlin.

As the war approached its conclusion, operations continued against oil facilities, as well as communications lines and troop concentrations as the Allied ground forces moved towards, and eventually into, Germany itself. The squadron took part in the controversial raid on Dresden, this being seen at the time as a routine operation to a communications target. In the prevailing circumstance of total war, morals and ethics could not be a key concern for the squadron as an organisation. It must never be forgotten that this was a fight for national, as well as personal, survival. The atrocities of the Nazi regime, now so clear, mean that the endeavours of the squadron and its crews were never anything less than absolutely necessary.

The war's end meant a few short months of more rewarding activity for 514 Sqn. Operation Manna, the dropping of desperately needed food parcels for the Dutch, was followed by a long series of flights to collect prisoners of war from France and Italy. Tragedy was still not finished with the squadron when a Lancaster carrying 24 POWs and six crew crashed on leaving Juvincourt in France with the loss of all on board.

In the course of its two-year operational life, 514 Sqn flew 3675 sorties on 218 bombing raids, in the course of which it dropped 14,650 tons of bombs. A further four mining operations were also undertaken, with 70 sea mines being dropped. 426 aircrew and nine ground crew lost their lives whilst serving with the squadron. 66 Lancasters were lost on operations with a further fourteen crashing either on ops or local flying. Twelve were brought down by flak, 38 by night fighters (other unaccounted losses are considered as most likely to have been shot down by night fighters, due to intense enemy activity on the occasion in question), one collided with another aircraft, and at least three were brought down by bombs from higher-flying aircraft whilst six were lost without trace. Of these it is possible that two 514 Sqn aircraft collided over the North Sea whilst en route to or from Leipzig, and another aircraft possibly collided with another squadron's Lancaster which crashed near Caen. None of these aircraft ever having been found, it is impossible to know for certain.

Whilst most losses occurred singly, it was inevitable that some raids saw heavier losses, Magdeburg and Leipzig costing three Lancasters each, an ill-starred trip to Homberg four aircraft whilst the worst occasion was the attack on Nuremberg. The raid on the night of 29th / 30th March 1944 saw four Lancasters from 514 Sqn shot down by night fighters whilst a further two crash landed on their return. The night was the bloodiest of Bomber Command's entire war, as well as 514 Sqn's worst raid.

On 22nd August 1945, the ORB simply noted '514 Squadron disbanded'. The written record suggests no fanfare or fuss to mark the end of the two-year life of the unit. There was a Farewell Dinner in the Officers' Mess, and on that note 514 Squadron passed into history.

(Above) A line up of Lancaster Mk.II aircraft of 'A' Flight at Waterbeach, late 1943 or early 1944. The aircraft in the foreground is JI-H, DS813, originally flown by F/S (later P/O) E Greenwood and crew, including Sgt George Henry. DS813 failed to return from Stuttgart on 28th / 29th July 1944, with the loss of F/L AF Fowke and crew. Behind JI-H is JI-B, LL624, eventually to be struck off charge on 28th September 1944 following her fourth crash landing, having left 514 Sqn by that time. JI-J (serial unknown) is third in line. Source: Tracy Holroyd-Smith / Sgt George Henry.

The Leaders of 514 Squadron

In its two-year existence, 514 Squadron was commanded by three experienced pilots.

8th September 1943 – 15th May 1944:
Wing Commander Arthur James Samson DFC

Born in Newfoundland but settling in Barrow-in-Furness, W/Cdr Samson oversaw the first eight months of the squadron's operations, including the Battle of Berlin and the run-up to D-Day. The ORB notes that, following the reported ditching of one of the squadron's Lancasters he put together a scratch crew and personally flew a search mission, locating the downed aircraft some 70 miles out in the North Sea. The crew all survived their 16-hour ordeal thanks to this inspiring piece of leadership by their squadron commander.

W/Cdr Samson survived the war itself, only to be killed on 8th September 1945 when flying a Dakota carrying sick POWs recently released from Japanese captivity. The aircraft exploded just off the coast of Burma with the loss of all 4 crew and 24 passengers.

W/Cdr Samson's courage and leadership were not in any doubt. The citation for his DFC, awarded in 1942, read:

'For the last three months Squadron Leader Samson has been employed as a flight commander. One night in July 1942, he attacked Saarbrucken, despite intense anti-aircraft fire, and on another occasion in August he flew a very badly damaged aircraft safely back to base. One night in September 1942, when approaching Munich, his aircraft was caught in a cone of searchlights and subjected to very heavy fire from the ground defences. Nevertheless, Squadron Leader Samson proceeded and attacked his objective. On the return journey he was again heavily attacked by anti-aircraft fire and the second pilot and flight engineer were wounded. Despite great difficulties, this officer flew his aircraft home and effected a forced lading without damage. Squadron Leader Samson has proved to be a cool, courageous captain with a fine sense of leadership.'

16th May 1944 to 7th February 1945:
Wing Commander Michael Wyatt DFC

Arthur Samson would have been a hard act for any successor to follow, but Mike Wyatt was certainly well-placed to step into his predecessor's shoes. A veteran of both XV and 75(NZ) Squadrons, the latter as Squadron Commander, Mike Wyatt had crash-landed his Stirling in Spain returning from a raid on Turin. W/Cdr Wyatt was in the habit of accompanying new crews on their first operation, a risky venture given the odds faced by inexperienced crews. He was, by all accounts, a popular commander. W/Cdr Mike Wyatt DFC left 514 Sqn on 7th February 1945, to take up a new post as Assistant Director in the Air Ministry's new Directorate of Navigation. It is fair to say that, by then, Mike Wyatt had done his bit. He survived the war, leaving the RAF as a Group Captain.

(Above) Wing Commander Michael Wyatt DFC.
Source:75nzsquadron.com

7th February 1945 – Squadron Disbanded:
Wing Commander Peter Morgan

There is little information available about the squadron's third and final Commanding Officer, save that he was to sign the final entry in the Operational Record Book when 514 Sqn was disbanded.

'A' Flight Commanders:

11/11/43 to 1/5/44	S/Ldr Ernest Reid
22/4/44 to 10/6/44	S/Ldr William Devas
23/6/44 to 6/11/44	S/Ldr Philip Clay
January 1945 to Disbandment	S/Ldr Kenneth Condict

'B' Flight Commanders:

3/11/43 to 9/5/44	S/Ldr Alan Roberts
22/5/44 to 7/7/44	S/Ldr Ralph Chopping
15/8/44 to 15/11/44	S/Ldr Marcus Dods
16/11/44 to Disbandment	S/Ldr HCG Wilcox

'C' Flight Commanders:

29/12/43 to 14/1/44	S/Ldr Ernest Sly
15/2/44 to 18/4/44	S/Ldr C Payne
31/5/44 to 18/7/44	S/Ldr DWA Stewart
26/8/44 to 2/12/44	S/Ldr John Timms
January 1945 to Disbandment	S/Ldr Ernest Cozens

All the above dates are approximate and are as indicated in the ORB, either by mention or by the rank and aircraft on specific sorties showing that the pilot concerned was acting as Flight Commander.

Individual Details

Arriving with his crew at 514 Sqn on 18th April 1944, **S/Ldr William Devas** had a relatively short stay, being posted to No. 115 Squadron in June 1944 as squadron commander. His original crew remained in 514 Sqn, flying with W/O WD Brickwood. The Bomb Aimer, F/O H Crampton RNZAF was killed over Lens on 11th August 1944 when the nose of the aircraft was struck by a bomb from another aircraft. W/O Brickwood and his crew were subsequently shot down on the night of

12th/13th September 1944 operating to Frankfurt. The replacement Bomb Aimer and the crew's Flight Engineer were the only survivors. William Devas AFC, is believed to have left the RAF in the sixties, as a Group Captain.

Squadron Leader Philip Clay took over command of 'A' Flight in June 1944, he and his crew completing 29 ops with the squadron. His DFC citation read:
'As captain and pilot this officer has completed a large number of sorties, involving attacks on a variety of targets both at night and by day. On one occasion, when detailed to attack the railway sidings at Chalons-Sur-Marne, the air speed indicators in his aircraft became unserviceable soon after taking off. Despite this Squadron Leader Clay continued to the target. Before the objective was reached, one of the starboard engines caught fire and the propeller had to be feathered. Nevertheless Squadron Leader Clay held to his course and executed a successful bombing attack. This officer is a very determined and gallant leader, whose ability has been outstanding.'

S/Ldr Alan Lestocq Roberts was born in 1916 in Teddington, Middlesex. He was awarded the DFC (1942) and Bar (1944), and was also Mentioned in Despatches (1944). His DFC was awarded following a number of long-distance raids, including Stettin and Genoa in three nights. Alan Roberts survived the war and passed away in Guildford in 1980. The Bar to his DFC was awarded in early 1944 following 514 Sqn's operation to Schweinfurt. The citation read:
'One night in February, 1944, this officer captained an aircraft detailed to attack Schweinfurt. Early on the outward flight it was discovered that, owing to a broken pipe-line, the whole of the oxygen supply had been lost. Nevertheless Squadron Leader Roberts came down to a lower altitude and flew on to the target. Whilst over the area the aircraft was set on fire but the flames were extinguished and Squadron Leader Roberts flew back to base to complete his mission successfully. This officer displayed great determination throughout, setting a high example of devotion to duty.'

After his tour with 514 Sqn, **S/Ldr Ralph Campbell Chopping** transferred to 7 Sqn, part of the Pathfinder Force, stationed at RAF Oakington. On 26th August 1944 he was flying Lancaster NE123, MG-J when he failed to return from an attack on gun batteries at Brest. He and his crew are commemorated on the Runnymede Memorial. The citation for his DFC read:

'This officer has completed very many sorties as pilot and captain of aircraft. He has displayed a high standard of skill and his determination to achieve success has been most commendable. On one occasion in May, 1944, he piloted an aircraft detailed to attack Dortmund. Early on the outward flight severe icing conditions were encountered, causing the aircraft to vibrate violently. Control was temporarily lost and the bomber fell towards ground at an alarming rate. Squadron Leader Chopping ordered his crew to leave by parachute but himself remained at his post and struggled to regain control. He succeeded in doing so when down to some 2,000 feet and went on to jettison his bombs in the sea. He afterwards flew the aircraft to an airfield and effected a safe landing. His coolness and resolution on this occasion was typical of that he has shown throughout his tour.'

The citation for **S/Ldr Marcus Dods**' DFC read:
This officer has completed a tour of operational duty during which he has displayed skill, courage and resolution of a high standard. In November 1944, Squadron Leader Dods piloted an aircraft detailed to attack Dortmund. Soon after crossing the English coast one engine became completely unserviceable. This did not deter Squadron Leader Dods who went on to attack the target with his usual determination. His devotion to duty has been outstanding.

S/Ldr Ernest Frank Sly, DFC, AFM lost his life, along with his crew, on 14th January 1944 when they were shot down during an operation to Brunswick. He was the most senior officer lost by 514 Sqn. during the war. He was awarded the Air Force Medal in 1940, after nursing a crippled Airspeed Oxford to a safe forced landing, the aircraft having lost the outer portion of its starboard wing. The following account was published in a newspaper at the time:

'*A twenty-three year old Royal Air Force flying instructor, who when his plane was damaged in a collision with a pupil's aircraft, landed in a field with one wing off and the other damaged, and with his undercarriage retracted, has been awarded the Air Force Medal. He is Sergeant. Frank Sly, a flying instructor in the advanced training squadron of a flying training school. His award is for 'exceptional valour, courage and devotion to duty whilst flying, though not in active operations against the enemy.' Sergeant. Sly was carrying out formation flying practice in a twin-engined training aircraft with a pupil in another aircraft of the same type.*

'On reaching 900 feet his passenger noticed that the pupil's aircraft was approaching from practically dead astern, and was just about to cause a collision. Sergeant. Sly immediately banked his aircraft to the left, but was unable to prevent the other aircraft coming into a collision with his starboard wing and severing it just beyond the engine. By using full left aileron and full starboard engine - his right aileron having dropped off complete with the torn off wing - Sergeant. Sly succeeded in regaining control of his aircraft. He flew straight for two miles. Meanwhile the starboard wing continued to break up. But at last the Sergeant got his damaged aircraft down and landed.'

His DFC was awarded whilst serving with No.218 Squadron in 1943. His citation read:

'In November 1942, while on operations against Stuttgart, one engine of this officer's aircraft became unserviceable while over the target area. Despite this, he pressed home his attack in a daring manner, and returned safely to base. On another occasion, while minelaying in the Baltic, Squadron Leader Sly was forced to bring his aircraft down to 300 feet owing to damage sustained in combat with an enemy fighter. By superb airmanship and determination a safe return was made. Squadron Leader Sly has, at all times, displayed high courage and devotion to duty.

S/Ldr Ernest Brazier Cozens RCAF was awarded the DFC on 9th Jan 1943 whilst in 218 Sqn.

'Pilot Officer Cozens has participated in a large number of operational sorties. One night in December 1942, he was captain of an aircraft detailed to attack a target in northwest Germany. When approaching the objective his aircraft was held in a cone of searchlights and badly damaged by anti-aircraft fire. Despite this, Pilot Officer Cozens, displaying great determination, flew on and bombed the target from a very low level. On the return journey the bomber was again hit by anti-aircraft fire and the starboard inner engine caught alight. Descending to one hundred feet a fuel tank was jettisoned and the fire extinguished. Pilot Officer Cozens then flew his aircraft safely back to base. He is an outstanding officer whose only desire is to get at grips with the enemy. His quiet determination and courage have been a fine example to other members of his crew.'

514 Squadron
Operational Record

September 1943

Headquarters No. 3 Group, administration instruction No. 78, received by RAF Station, Foulsham, covered the formation of 514 Squadron, this formation to take place at the 1st of September, 1943 at RAF Station Foulsham.

1st September 1943.
The official formation of 514 Squadron on the authority of Bomber Command letter BC/S.21717/13/Org dated 1st September, 1943, at RAF Station Foulsham, under establishment scale War/B1/336 to carry out the special duties of a Heavy Bomber Squadron armed with 16 ic plus 4 ir Lancaster II aircraft. Aircrew of 514 Squadron to be provided by 1678 Heavy Conversion Flight. Acting Wing Commander AJ Samson DFC is appointed Commanding Officer of 514 Squadron.
Note: There are no ORB entries from 2nd to 6th September 1943 inclusive.

7th September 1943.
The first officer to arrive was the Squadron Adjutant Flight Lieutenant M. Stevens, who reported to RAF Station, Foulsham, on the afternoon of the 6th September 1943, A block of offices allotted to the Squadron had been taken over by the Flight Sergeant Discip, prior to the arrival of the Adjutant, with what few men that had arrived the time was spent in cleaning up offices, crew room etc. Two living sites were also allotted to the Squadron.

8th September 1943.
As all offices were absolutely stripped of furniture even to shelves being removed by the outgoing units a systematic search was started to find the necessary office furniture required. The Officer Commanding the Squadron W/Cdr AJ Samson, DFC who is still employed by Headquarters No. 3 Group paid a visit to Squadron Headquarters; the Adjutant visited 226 Squadron at Swanton Morley, this Squadron was kind enough to supply him with a small quantity of the necessary forms etc. urgently needed.

9th September 1943.
Sites two and five sleeping quarters allotted to the Squadron were thoroughly cleaned and bedded up in preparation for the intake of the

non-flying personnel now arriving in goodly numbers daily. W/Cdr AJ Samson, DFC again paid a flying visit to see how things were progressing.

10th September 1943.
Weather conditions very bad, pouring with rain all day. A considerable quantity of Aircraft Equipment and spares arrived by road from RAF Station, Mildenhall. This kept the ground staff very busy all day, unloading. Another section of the ground staff was employed on cleaning out and rearranging the aircrew locker room.

11th September 1943.
Weather conditions still very bad raining heavily on and off all day. Working parties continued to unload and sort out the Aircraft spares and equipment. A second party continuing their work in the Crew Locker Room, and cleaning out the adjoining lecture rooms. The Adjutant paid a visit to the Adjutant of 115 Squadron at Little Snoring. The first Lancaster II aircraft DS735 arrived in the afternoon.

12th September 1943.
Weather dull, heavy and still inclined to rain. The W/Cd paid a visit to the Squadron together with Group Captain E.P. Mackay the new Station Commander and inspected Squadron offices, Crew Room, Locker Room, etc. The erection of a hut as a Squadron Intelligence Library was discussed and a spot selected. They also toured the perimeter and Aircraft dispersal areas. The Wing Commander took off by air to return to No. 3 Group Headquarter but found visibility very bad and had to return and do his journey by road. The Group Gunnery Leader S/Ldr. D. Keary DFC and the Group Bombing Leader S/Ldr. Stowe DFM paid a visit to the Squadron. The second aircraft DS785 arrived.

13th September 1943.
Following a night of thunder storms the weather has been dull with showers all day. The Squadron Adjutant visited RAF Station, Oulton, to obtain office furniture. The third aircraft DS783 arrived. The ground personnel are now working with their own trade sections preparing stores and spares in readiness for the incoming aircraft. Typewriters and a selection of Stationery was collected from A.P.F.S. London.

14th September 1943.
The weather was generally brighter and much warmer. Working parties continued unloading and sorting out aircraft equipment that had arrived. W/Cdr. AJ Samson DFC reported to take command of the Squadron. The fourth aircraft DS784 arrived.

15th September 1943.
Weather continued clear and warm. The thanks giving service was held in the open to commemorate the Battle of Britain. All ranks that could possibly be spared attended and the service was taken by the Station padre S/Ldr. W Rees. The Squadron dispersal areas were selected. The advance party of 1678 Conversion Flight from RAF Little Snoring moved in. The fifth aircraft DS786 arrived.

16th September 1943.
Heavy and cloudy with occasional showers. All sections continue working on incoming Stores. F/O T. Angus a Canadian arrived to take up the duties of Bombing Leader of the Squadron. The main body of 1678 Conversion Flight together with aircraft arrived. This Conversion Flight will supply a number of crews for the Squadron after converting to Lancaster Mark II.
The Wing Commander accompanied by the Squadron Adjutant inspected dispersal huts being taken over by the Squadron and arrangements were made with the Station Administration Officer to have these distempered and cleaned before taking over. The sixth aircraft DS787 arrived. There was an ENSA concert in the evening. The room provided for these concerts is inadequate for the size of the Station; those who were lucky enough to see the show enjoyed it very much, after the performance the visitors were entertained by the Sergeants in the Sergeants Mess.

17th September 1943.
Weather: Fair, cloudy, improved during the afternoon. Work continued on all new aircraft in preparation for air tests. F/Lt Dodwell from No. 3 Group Headquarters, an Operational Specialist, visited the Squadron Commander to talk over special training of the aircrew of this Squadron.

18th September 1943.
Weather: Cloudy with local showers. W/Cdr AJ Samson DFC gave a tactics lecture to aircrew undergoing training with the conversion

flight. S/Ldr AL Roberts DFC who will be Flight Commander of 'B' Flight arrived from Westcott in a Wellington Mk.II to pay a visit prior to his being posted to the squadron. Two more aircraft DS813 and DS736 arrived. A/G/C HE Hills OBE of No. 3 Group Headquarters visited the Squadron to talk over the general situation with the Squadron Commander. F/O T Angus proceeded on a Bombing Leader's course to RAF Station Manby.

19th September 1943.
Weather: Local fog early morning becoming brighter with showers at intervals during the day. F/O PR Thompson DFC arrived to take over the duties of Signal Leader of the Squadron. Three aircraft arrived, DS706, DS814 and DS815. The first two crews arrived, one from 115 Squadron, the other one from 1678 Conversion Flight. S/Ldr Hildyard and S/Ldr McCaffery, Group Tactic Officer and Group Navigation Officer respectively, paid a short visit to the Squadron to have a look round and see the set up. It was confirmed that out of 21 fitters II E and FMEs posted to the Squadron from Group resources 12 had never seen a Hercules engine. F. staff of Group were informed and requested to extract and replacements posted.

20th September 1943.
Weather: Rather cold with occasional showers. All sections working at high pressure on modifications of the new aircraft. The two new crews joined in the work of the departmental organisation of the Squadron. Sun-ray treatment commenced, both crews reported to the Station sick quarters together with the Signals Leader and Squadron Commander for treatment.

21st September 1943.
Weather: Fine, but very cold. Aircraft DS816 arrived and DS735 was air-tested, meaning that at last the Squadron was airborne. 'A' Flight pilot P/O GJ Chequer became airborne at 1650 hours and completed an hour's test flight. The Radar Officer flew with him to test GH which proved to be perfect. W/Cdr Matthews, the Group Engineer Officer, paid a visit to the Squadron Commander to explain the intake of a large percentage of fitters with little or no experience of the Hercules engine. The Wing Commander paid a visit to No. 3 Group Headquarters about the outstanding postings to the Squadron.

22nd September 1943.
Weather: Fair but cold with occasional showers, the freezing level being only 4000'. The second aircraft piloted by F/Sgt GS Hughes had a very successful air test. S/Ldr Reid reported from 1678 Conversion Flight to this Squadron to take up the duties of Flight Commander of 'A' Flight. Six complete crews reported including S/Ldr Reid's crew. The Wing Commander had a gathering of all crews and gave them a pep talk. Another aircraft DS817 arrived.

23rd September 1943.
Weather: Fair but cloudy. Visibility improved towards the afternoon. Strong winds in the North making it still very cold. All ground staff still working very hard to get the aircraft allotted serviceable for further air tests. F/O H Beckett DFC arrived from RAF Station Little Snoring to take up his duties as Squadron Navigation Officer. P/O H Hall reported to take up his duties a Flight Engineer Leader. F/O PR Thompson DFC the Signal Leader together with P/O H Hall visited RAF Station Downham Market, in hopes of picking up aircraft spares from crashed aircraft. F/O JN Pollock arrived from 1483 BG Flight to take up his duties as Gunnery Leader of the Squadron. Two more aircraft DS784 and DS787 became airborne.

24th September 1943.
Weather: Fair, much warmer with good visibility. The Squadron Commander took (to) the air in a Lancaster II with 1678 Conversion Flight., Pilot F/Lt Thomas, remained in the air for an hour and a half. S/Ldr AL Roberts DFC reported from ECDU Westcott to take up his duties as Flight Commander of 'B' Flight. Arrangements were made with No. 3 Group Headquarters to post a crew in for him. Two more aircraft DS818 and DS820 arrived making 15 aircraft now on the Squadron strength. DS786 and DS706 were air tested.

25th September 1943.
Weather: Fair with occasional showers. F/O GJ Chequer in aircraft DS706 'G' took part in Fighter Affiliation. The Squadron Doctor F/O ME Lemerle reported from RAF Station Oakington, as his leave had previously been cancelled permission was granted for him to go on leave immediately. Three more aircraft, DS821, DS822 and DS738 arrived.

26th September 1943.
Weather: Fair with heavy showers, local thunder. Air Commodore Kirkpatrick DFC, Senior Air Staff Officer at Headquarters No. 3 Group, visited the Squadron to see how we were getting on and was very pleased with the plans already outlined for the Squadron. F/O KH Dodwell, a Group Specialist Officer, accompanied him.

27th September 1943.
Weather: Cold North Westerly wind, heavy scattered showers, clearing up during the afternoon making visibility good. More aircrew arrived making the strength up to 13 complete crews. Members of aircrew continued good work under their respective Section Leaders. P/O GJ Chequer did a three hour cross-country trip in DS735 'A'. F/Sgt DCC Crombie and crew air tested DS736 'L', 'B' Flight's first aircraft to be tested. Weather became very bad late evening and poured with rain throughout the night.

28th September 1943.
Weather: Cloudy with heavy continuous rain. S/Ldr Reid took to the air in 'B' DS783 and had a successful trip except for minor snags. A certain amount of turret trouble developed. The Armament Officer investigated and arranged for a special maintenance party from the makers to check up. A stand down was arranged in the afternoon and a pre-payment bus was organised for a selection of the aircrew to visit Norwich. There being no decent town near this Station within 10 miles. The Adjutant F/Lt M. Stevens was detailed as Station Security Officer, the district RAF Security Officer paid him a visit in the afternoon.

29th September 1943.
Weather: overcast, light drizzle, making visibility poor. It became generally warmer during the day. Balance of crews from other Squadrons arrived making 17 complete crews all told. The crews still continued good work with their respective Section Leaders and were given special training about DR navigation. The Group Electrical Engineer Officer S/Ldr Easton with Mr. Able of the Bristol Engineering Coy. paid a visit to the Squadron

30th September 1943.
Weather: Still overcast with local drizzle and fog patches, visibility less than 1000 yards but improved late afternoon. An attempt was made to remove some branches of the tree overhanging the training centre

Astrodome, but owing to it being oak and provided with a saw that would not cut it, the attempt was given up as a bad job. All crews available attend special lecture in the Intelligence Briefing Room during the afternoon. A programme was prepared to start special training with available serviceable aircraft on the 1st October. The late Met forecast requested proved (such) continual bad weather through the night that the early portion of special training arranged was cancelled.

October 1943

(Above) 514 Squadron 'A' Flight, October 1943. Photo courtesy of V Reith (sister of F/O WL McGown) via J and S Ronald and Roger Guernon.

1st October 1943.
Weather: Cloudy, low drizzle, visibility not very good. Strict and special training commenced. Owing to bad visibility the early morning programme had to be cancelled.
1315 hrs: Two aircraft detailed for GH training, DS815 was air tested. The afternoon training proved very good and without any major snags.

2nd October 1943.
Weather: Fair and much warmer. Four aircraft with eight pilots and navigators of 'A' Flight took off at 0745 hours for special training, continued until 1115 hours 'Up with the lark' is our catch-word and everybody made the grade cheerfully. The Conversion Flight was somewhat shaken by the Squadron's enthusiasm and complained that the roar of our engines was disturbing their morning rest. Four more aircraft were airborne at 1330hrs for the afternoon training.
DS814 was air-tested. DS823 and DS824 arrived.

3rd October 1943.
Weather: Mainly fair with a cold wind. 'Up with the lark' again which, in a few cases, was a bit hard, owing to a certain amount of recreation the previous evening, even the Squadron Adjutant turned out to make sure the crews had their flying rations. 'A' returned owing to G trouble. *(Note: This possibly refers to the Gee navigation equipment).* The crew transferred to 'F' to complete their detail. The take-off for the afternoon detail was delayed for nearly an hour as one of the two bowsers available was in use with the Conversion Flight and the other had to be emptied into a Stirling which had landed short of petrol. Steps were immediately taken to ensure that a similar delay did not occur again in the future. The remainder of 'A' Flight crews attended a lecture given by the Squadron Navigation Officer F/O H Beckett on Special High Level Training.

4th October 1943.
Weather: Mainly fair and good visibility, local showers late in the day. Early morning training had to be cancelled owing to Fairwood Common being unfit for landing. Four aircraft took off at 1130hrs to be on target from 1300hrs to 1700hrs giving two hours per navigator. This being our first High Level Training. Some photographs taken on Low Level Training became available showing that a reasonable standard had been achieved.

5th October 1943.
Weather: Cloudy with occasional drizzle. Early detail became airborne but had to be recalled owing to weather conditions. Wing Commander Wyatt DFC, the GTI 3 Group and Squadron Leader Keary GGC visited the Squadron and after a general tour were quite pleased with the Squadron's progress.
DS818 was air tested. DS828 arrived.

6th October 1943.
Weather: Heavy, low clouds with rain, strong winds and cold. Special training detailed had to be cancelled owing to weather conditions. The crews attended lectures by their respective Section Leaders. The Squadron Commander with Navigation Officer visited RAF Station, Oulton in the morning. In the afternoon the Squadron Commander and Signal Leader visited Wing Commander Corry at Bircham Newton and were shown the Air Sea Rescue equipment. Wing Commander Corry

agreed to take three crews of the Squadron at a time when available to give them all details of Air Sea Rescue work. DS816 was air-tested.

7th October 1943.
Weather: Mainly fair, very good conditions for flying. An early start was made and owing to weather conditions resulted in a good and record training day, with seventeen hours on GH training. Wing Commander AJ Samson DFC flying 'C' for Charlie.

8th October 1943.
Weather: Fair but cold wind. Four aircraft continued on Special Training and two aircraft from 'B' Flight carried out a height and load test. Generally it proved to be another record day.

9th October 1943.
Weather: Mainly fair with cloud and occasional rain towards the end of the day. Navigation training proceeded according to plan and 'B' Flight did some fighter affiliation. 'B' Flight started on their special training. The Squadron Commander undertook some special navigation training with Flying Officer JD Trick, an assistant instructor loaned to us by 115 Squadron.

10th October 1943.
Weather: Conditions very bad for flying owing to thick fog, even the birds were walking. Flying commenced at noon with fighter affiliation and the weather became worse towards the afternoon and two of the aircraft were directed to RAF Station, Stradishall.

11th October 1943.
Fog persisting in local district hampered flying. This prevented the two aircraft returning from Stradishall. Three crews visited Bircham Newton on Air Sea Rescue training.

12th October 1943.
Weather: Wide spread fog making visibility very bad, becoming clearer later in the day, enabling the two aircraft stranded at Stradishall to return to base. Wing Commander Watkins, DFC, DFM, in charge of Operations (2), Headquarters 3 Group visited the Squadron.

13th October 1943.
Weather: Cloudy wide spread fog making visibility very poor. Owing to weather conditions training was curtailed. Crews were lectured by

their respective Section Leaders. Three crews visited Bircham Newton for Air Sea Rescue training.

14th October 1943.
Weather: Overcast with bright intervals and much warmer. Aircraft became airborne 1145 hours for special training. Three further crews visited Bircham Newton on Air Sea Rescue work. The Station Commander Group Captain GP Mackay flew in 'G' for George with the Squadron Commander. The Air Officer Commanding No. 3 Group accompanied by the Station Commander visited a special training centre and viewed the Training Record of the Squadron and was well satisfied with the progress.

15th October 1943.
Weather: Cloudy, dull with local fog and mist. 'B' Flight continued with the special training. Three aircraft detailed for an 'Eric'. Wing Commander Burnett with Wing Commander Watkins flew in 'T' for Tommy. Squadron Commander piloted 'F' for Freddy. It was a good exercise generally. The Wing Commander in 'F' for Freddy was attacked by fighters over base and had a twenty minutes running fight with the Thunderbolts.

16th October 1943.
Weather: fair, cloudy with slight haze. Low level training was continued throughout the day. Air Commodore Kirkpatrick, DFC, the SASO of No. 3 Group arrived by air to take part in the exercise. He flew in 'E' for Edward as Second Pilot to the Squadron Commander.
The following Section Leaders were promoted to Acting Flight Lieutenants: Flying Officer H Beckett, Flying Officer JN Pollock, Flying Officer R Thompson.
Flying Officer TA Angus reported back from his Bombing Course. Flying Officer TA Angus passed out of the course with an 'A' and heading the list; a very good show.

17th October 1943.
Weather: Conditions bad, pouring with rain all day. Owing to weather conditions there was no flying and as the Squadron had worked exceedingly well with their training to date crews were given a stand-down.

18th October 1943.
Weather: Fair with scattered showers. Special training continued. Out of the twenty two aircraft which had arrived fourteen had been made serviceable.

19th October 1943.
Weather: Fair but cloudy with cold winds. All 'A' Flight crews with aircraft available did fighter affiliation with Hurricanes from the Group Circus. F/O GHD Hinde and F/O RS Clements were detailed for an operational flight as second pilots to 115 Squadron. Remainder of crews continued their special training. The operation for which 115 Sqdn. had been detailed was cancelled.

20th October 1943.
Weather: Fair and much warmer. Four aircraft were detailed for a Command Bullseye, which proved very successful. F/O GHD Hinde and F/O RS Clements detailed for second Pilot trip with 115 Squadron.

21st October 1943.
Weather: Very bad raining heavily, cold with high winds. F/O RS Clements who was second Pilot to F/Lt. Anderson in 'F' for Freddie of 115 Squadron had been reported as missing, nothing has been heard of this aircraft after take-off. Two aircrew from 'A' Flight visited Bircham Newton. 'B' Flight had lecture on Beam Approach Training.
Note: F/O RS Clements is listed on the 514 Squadron Roll of Honour as having lost his life on 20th October 1943. He was flying in DS725, KO-F, shot down at 2000 hours by Lt. Paul Fehre of 5./NJG3 at Engersen, near Gardelegen. There were no survivors from the crew.

22nd October 1943.
Weather: Mainly fair still cold. 'B' Flight continued their special training, 'A' Flight on routine tests, compass swinging etc. with six aircraft detailed for night Command Bullseye. Five aircraft took off in filthy weather and saw nothing on route, landing back at Base in heavy rain. The exercise was useful in a sense that it gave the crews practice in bad weather flying at night.

23rd October 1943.
Weather: Heavy rain throughout night, cloudy, rainy periods throughout the day. Fighter affiliation was arranged but had to be cancelled owing to bad weather. Aircrew continued training under their

respective Section Leaders. Aircraft DS825 was transferred to 115 Sqdn., Little Snoring.

24th October 1943.
Weather: Fair, generally misty and fog patches. A number of Aircrew and Headquarters Officers practiced rifle shooting on the 25 yds range for selection of the Squadron team for the Group Shoot.

25th October 1943.
Weather: General mist and fog clearing towards afternoon. A number of aircraft were detailed for Cross Country and loaded climbs. The Wing Commander proceeded on the Cross Country and loaded climb in 'T' for Tommy.

26th October 1943.
Weather: Wide spread fog and rain. Seven aircraft were offered for a gardening trip but owing to bad weather refused. Ground training continued. Wing Commander AJ Samson reported to Bomber Command for a special conference.
Note: Although there are no details, it is entirely possible that the Bomber Command conference was about the forthcoming Battle of Berlin, in which the squadron was to play a full part.

27th October 1943.
Weather: Still wide spread fog. Lectures for crews under their respective Section Leaders.

28th October 1943.
Weather: Wide spread fog. Ground work continued.

29th October 1943.
Weather: Fog still very bad. Aircrew officers reported to the range for rifle shooting.

30th October 1943.
Weather: Fair with fog patches. The first Squadron Battle Order was issued. Two aircraft being detailed for gardening, this was unfortunately cancelled owing to weather conditions.

31st October 1943.
Weather: Cloudy with rain, fog patches. Two aircraft were detailed for gardening, but were again cancelled owing to bad weather. The

Squadron and Station rifle teams proceeded to Stradishall for Group Shoot, unfortunately, through being misled in training the team did very badly. Lectures by respective Section Leaders continued. As the Squadron is newly formed a photograph was taken of Headquarters Staff Officers.

(Above) 514 Sqn senior officers, 31st October 1943. Back Row: P/O Croston (Electrical Officer), F/O Angus (Bombing Leader), F/Lt Wand, Engineer), F/Lt Hall (Engineering Leader), F/Lt Thomson (Signals Leader), F/O Trick (Specialist / Instruments), F/O Bowen (Specialist / Instruments). Front Row: F/Lt Beckett (Navigation Officer), F/Lt Stevens (Adjutant), S/Ldr Reid ('A' Flight Commander), W/Cdr Samson (Squadron Commander), S/Ldr Roberts ('B' Flight Commander), F/O Lemerle (Medical Officer), F/Lt Pollock (Gunnery Officer). Source - National Archives.

November 1943

1st November 1943.
Weather: Very dull, slight rain persisting throughout the day. No operational details asked for. Aircrew continued under their respective Section Leaders.

2nd November 1943.
Weather: Early mist clearing towards afternoon remained dull and cloudy. General training continued during the day. Four details on long cross country.

3rd November 1943.
Weather: Local fog clearing during the day, generally fair. Five details on cross-country, two of these on height and load test. Eight aircraft called for the Squadron's first Operational trip. The effort was a mining also a bombing trip. Owing to technical snags only two aircraft took off on the bombing raid. The four detailed for mining all got away. All aircraft returned safely, a very satisfactory result for the Squadron's first operation. Six new aircraft arrived from AWA Coventry. Squadron Leader Shipric, Bomber Command Navigation Officer, Squadron Leader Brown, Group Navigation Officer and Flight Lieutenant Dodwell, Group Specialist Officer visited the Squadron to see take-off.
GARDENING – FRISIAN ISLANDS
4 Lancasters were detailed from 514 Squadron for gardening operations and took off, the first becoming airborne at 1805 hrs.
P/O Hinds in DS738, JI-J reported: Aircraft carried 2 x B218, 4 x 200. Primary area Frisian Islands. No cloud, visibility good. 6 vegetables planted successfully in ordered position.
Note: Sgt R Langley in DS787, JI-F commented in his log book 'Wizard night. Never saw a thing.' Although the time the mines were dropped is not recorded, the sorties took approximately two hours and the mining operation therefore occurred before the first 514 Sqn bombs were dropped on Düsseldorf.
The crews taking part in this first operation were those of S/Ldr AL Roberts, F/O GH Hinde, Sgt R Langley and F/S WL McGown.
BOMBING – DÜSSELDORF - MANNESMANN WORKS.
One Lancaster from 514 Squadron attacked the works dropping 1 x 400, 720 x 4lb incendiaries, 32 x 30lb incendiaries (including 60 x 4lb) between 1943 -2003 hours from 26,000/20,000 feet. *(NB: Typing errors deliberately included: see P/O Payne's report below).* One Lancaster from 514 Squadron was unable to pinpoint the works, joined

the main attack on DÜSSELDORF dropping 1 x 4000, 720 x 4lb incendiaries, 32 x 30lb incendiaries (including 60 x 4lb). A good concentration of fire was seen in the DÜSSELDORF area with thick smoke up to 10,000 feet, and the attack appears to have been a good prang. No results were seen on the attack on the works.

F/S GS Hughes in DS785, JI-D reported: Aircraft carried 1 x 4000, 720 x 4 lb incendiaries (including 60 x 4 lb) x LB. Attacked target at 1945 hours, height 20,000 feet. 032 Degs. Industrial haze. No cloud. Report combat with enemy aircraft.

P/O C Payne in DS786, JI-E reported: Aircraft carried 1 x 4000, 720 x 4 lb incendiaries, 32 x 30 lb incendiaries (including 60 x 4 lb). Attacked target at 1951 hours, height 20,600 feet 040 Degs. 150 MPH. Good visibility. Ground markers seen to the South. Large fires seen in Main target area and some fires seen on out leg. Photos attempted but no flash. Very satisfactory raid.

Combat Report:
Aircraft: DS785 – 'D'
Captain: F/S GS Hughes.
Target: Düsseldorf

Outward bound for target, flying on a course of 115 degrees, height 20,000 feet, IAS 150(mph). 1st Encounter: At 1925 hours Bomb Aimer reported a twin engined aircraft, identified as an Me210 approaching from dead ahead about 50-100 feet below. As E/A passed under Lancaster, Rear Gunner opened fire at point blank range and held it for approximately 3 seconds. Strikes were observed on centre portion and E/A was last seen flying away astern but appeared to be losing height. There was no return fire from E/A. Visibility was good above cloud with 1/4 moon up. There was no flak, searchlights, track lights or flares.

2nd Encounter: At 2007 hours homeward bound, course 285 degrees, height 19,500feet. Rear Gunner Reported twin engined aircraft about 1,000 yards away, which he soon identified as a Ju88 flying parallel course slightly down on starboard quarter in the dark part of the sky but silhouetted against the white cloud tops. E/A closed range on the beam to 500 yards and was still flying parallel course when MU Gunner and Rear Gunner opened fire. Both Gunners claimed hits on E/A, which quickly broke away on starboard beam and was not seen again. There was no return fire from Ju88 and no flak, searchlights or flares. Visibility was good.

MU Gunner – Sgt Moorhouse – 60 rounds.
Rear Gunner- Sgt Thornton - 500 rounds.

Target: *Mannesmann Steel Tubing Works*
Aircraft deployed total: *589*
514 Squadron: *2*
Aircraft lost total: *18 (2 Lancasters)*
514 Squadron: *Nil*

Comments: This was the first time GH was tested on a large scale. 38 Lancasters were fitted with GH but with returned Aircraft and GH faults, only 15 managed to bomb the steel tubing factory in Mannesmann. This was 514 Squadron's first bombing mission. F/S GS Hughes in DS785, JI-D had the honour of dropping the squadron's first bombs at 1945 hours from 20,000 feet.

(Above) Ju88 R-1 night fighter. With a crew of three and armed with various combinations of 20mm cannon and 7.92mm machine guns, the Ju88 was a deadly foe, accounting for several 514 Sqn aircraft. The Ju88 could also be configured to carry two vertically-mounted 20mm cannon, code-named 'Shrage Musik' (Jazz Music) which enabled the aircraft to position itself unseen under the belly of a bomber, firing upwards into the fuel tanks. This tactic remained unrecognised by Bomber Command until late into the war. Source: Airworx GmbH Archive.

4th November 1943.
Weather: Dull and cloudy, bright periods. No operational efforts were called for. Five aircraft were out on Special Training detail. Other aircraft took part in Fighter affiliation.

5th November 1943.
Weather: Dull and cloudy with fairly good visibility. Several aircraft on Height and Load Test. Early afternoon a practice take-off and landing by thirteen aircraft. Practice take off was very good. Landing only a qualified success. Further training necessary.

6th November 1943.
Weather: Cloudy and drizzle continued throughout the day. Four aircraft were called for an operation effort but was eventually cancelled. Twelve aircraft were detailed for a Bullseye on special training, eleven reported their duty carried out.

7th November 1943.
Weather: Heavy showers with bright periods with strong wind.
GARDENING – LA ROCHELLE
Two aircraft were detailed for a mining trip to La Rochelle. 6 veg. 1500-4000 feet. 0411 hours. 10/10 cloud from English coast out. No fighter seen. Both returned safely after carrying out their mission.
F/S E Greenwood in DS813 JI-H reported: Aircraft carried 3 G714 (11, 10 and 8). Primary area: LA ROCHELLE. 10/10 cloud. Base about 4000 feet. Very quiet route. No troubles, successful pin point. No opposition.

8th November 1943.
Weather: Fine with sunny periods. One aircraft was detailed for a long bombing trip. This was cancelled. Local flying with practice bombing and training was carried out by eleven aircraft.

9th November 1943.
Weather: Foggy, clearing with sunny periods. Local training continued by all available crews.

10th November 1943.
Weather: Early mists later clearing with bright periods. 14 aircraft engaged on special training. Four aircraft took part in a night Bulls Eye exercise.

11th November 1943.
Weather: Fair and cold with good visibility. Ten aircraft were detailed for a mining effort. One aircraft returned and nine reported their duty carried out. One aircraft landed at Hixon. Accounted to be a good show.
GARDENING – LA TRANCHE 1 aircraft returned owing to Navigational errors.
Weather good with good visibility. All aircraft pin-pointed on LA TRANCHE. Defences at the western end of Ils de Re were quite active for the last aircraft and consisted of 2S/L 4/5 light guns and 2 Heavy guns.
F/S FCV Steed in DS786 JI-E reported: Aircraft carried 3 x G714, 2 x H802. Primary area LA TRANCHE. No cloud. Visibility good. Hole in rear gunner's turret. TR 1196 aerial shot away. Route satisfactory.

12th November 1943.
Weather: Fair becoming cloudy with scattered showers. Wing Commander AJ Samson DFC visited Hixon by air but found it impossible to land so returned. Local training flights by six aircraft.

13th November 1943.
Weather: Cloudy, slight rain with bright periods. Eight aircraft on local flying and special training. Wing Commander AJ Samson, DFC, together with Squadron Navigation Officer and the Squadron Adjutant visited RAF Station Waterbeach.

14th November 1943.
Weather: Cloudy with occasional showers, cold wind. Eight aircraft were detailed to give trips to ATC Cadets. Information was received by Headquarters 3 Group Administration Instructions No. 89 that owing to the re-organisation of 3 Group this Squadron would move from RAF Station, Foulsham to RAF Station Waterbeach. This move to be carried out by road and air on November 23rd 1943 with minimum of interference to the operational effort of the Squadron. The Squadron to move under War Establishment War/BC/336. The movement to be carried out and completed by 25th November 1943.

Note: The move from RAF Foulsham to RAF Waterbeach was part of the reorganization of 3 Group. RAF Foulsham became home to 192 Sqn, part of 100 Group, with 462 Sqn RAAF, of the same electronic warfare group, joining them later. As with all such wartime unit movement, the logistical process was expected to take place with the absolute minimum effect on operations. A copy of the Movement Order, listing all members of the squadron on this date is attached at the end of this book.

15th November 1943.
Weather: Fair, strong winds with occasional showers. A number of aircraft carried local training flights, others on fighter affiliation.

16th November 1943.
Weather: Cloudy, strong cold wind with occasional showers. Ten aircraft were called for an operational effort. Owing to weather conditions had to be cancelled.

17th November 1943.
Weather: Wintry showers, rain and sleet. Crews continued training under their respective Section Leaders.

18th November 1943.
Weather: Fair with occasional wintry showers. The Squadron Advanced Party proceeded by road to RAF Station, Waterbeach. An effort of twelve aircraft was called for bombing operations. Two detailed for BERLIN took off, six took off for the second target MANNHEIM. Three did not take off owing to major snags. A reserved aircraft was not required. One aircraft unfortunately failed to return, making the first missing aircraft from the Squadron.
BOMBING - BERLIN.
F/S GS Hughes in DS787 JI-F reported: Bomb load 1x4000, 16x30, 270x4. Primary target: BERLIN. Visibility was poor with 10/10 low cloud. Red TIs were well separated and there were no Green TIs visible so the bombs were aimed at the centre of the Reds at 2101 hours, Ht. 20,000 feet. A scattered raid with PFF late over the target area.

Target: Berlin Area
Aircraft deployed total: 444 (440 Lancasters, 4 Mosquitoes)
514 Squadron: 2
Aircraft lost total: 9 (Lancasters)
514 Squadron: Nil

Comments: The target was cloud covered and scattered results were later reported, with 4 industrial buildings being destroyed.

BOMBING – MANNHEIM
Sgt KF Samuels in DS706, JI-G reported: Bomb load 1 x 400(0) 16 x 30 720 x 4. Primary target MANNHEIM. Visibility good, no cloud. TIs were well concentrated with 20 large fires burning and many incendiaries. Bombed centre of green TIs.

Target: *Mannheim Area (Diversionary Raid)*
Aircraft deployed total: 395
514 Squadron: 6
Aircraft lost total: 23
514 Squadron: 1

Comments: Target was cloud covered so scattered results were reported. The Daimler-Benz factory was damaged. DS784, JI-C was 514 Squadron's first operational loss.

Missing Aircraft:

DS784, JI-C. The aircraft left Foulsham at 1724hrs and was detailed to attack Mannheim. The aircraft was attacked, apparently by two night-fighters, exploding at or over Assesse, 16 km SE of Namur, Belgium. The loss is credited to Lt. Erhard Peters, 1./NJG4 but was also claimed by Hptm. Franz Evers, Stab 1./NJG6. The crew had previously carried out one sortie, a mining trip. This was their first bombing raid.

P/O SPL Thomas	*Pilot*	*KIA*
Sgt R Fontaine	*Bomb Aimer*	*KIA*
Sgt JL Brent	*Navigator*	*KIA*
Sgt F Thomas	*WOP/AG*	*KIA*
Sgt HA Lucas	*MU Gunner*	*Evaded*
Sgt H Stagg	*Flight Engineer*	*KIA*
F/S BS Haines RAAF	*Rear Gunner*	*POW*

Sgt Lucas remained hidden in Brussels until Liberation.

19th November 1943.
Weather: Fair with local mist and fog. A number of aircraft took off on a long cross-country trip on special training, one aircraft was

detailed for a sea search. This aircraft returned late afternoon without sighting anything.

20th November 1943.
Weather: Widespread fog. Crews continued training under their respective Section Leaders.

21st November 1943.
Weather: Widespread fog dispersing slightly during the afternoon. Crews were given an afternoon stand-down.

22nd November 1943.
Weather: Widespread fog with rain clearing towards late afternoon. Six aircraft were detailed for bombing operations, later one was cancelled. Four aircraft took off, the fifth had to be cancelled at the last moment owing to sickness. The mission was carried out successfully and all returned safely.
BOMBING - BERLIN.
Four aircraft detailed and four aircraft attacked the primary area BERLIN. The target was obscured by 10/10 cloud. Sky markers concentrated and numerous explosions were seen through the clouds. Flak intense but searchlights ineffective, very few enemy aircraft sighted.
F/L C Payne in DS786, JI-E reported: Bomb load 1 x 4000, 360 x 4 incendiaries, 90 x 4 incendiaries. Primary target BERLIN. 10/10 cloud tops 10/12,000 feet. PFF flares. Very large glow beneath cloud. An exceptionally big explosion at 2022 hours. Think it must have been a good PRANG as so many Lancs could be seen in target area.

Target:	*Berlin Area*
Aircraft deployed total:	*764*
514 Squadron:	*4*
Aircraft lost total:	*26*
514 Squadron:	*Nil*

Comments: Localised firestorms meant that approximately 2000 people were killed and another 175,000 affected by loss of homes in this raid.

23rd November 1943.
Weather: Fair throughout the day with cold winds. The main body of the squadron moved by road and air to RAF Station, Waterbeach. An effort of four aircraft was called for a bombing operation. One was

cancelled and the remaining three took off, and returned safely, one to Waterbeach, the other two to RAF Station, Cranfield. The main body arrived at RAF Station Waterbeach early afternoon where a hot meal awaited them and all arrangements were made for their comfort.

BOMBING - BERLIN.

3 aircraft took off to attack the target Berlin. 8/10 - 10/10 cloud along whole route to Berlin. 10 / 10 cloud over Berlin tops estimated 8 / 10,000 feet, visibility above good. Many white fighter flares seen in form of circle around Berlin, with lane of red flares to port and white to starboard on route out from Berlin. Aircraft seen falling in flames and explode with red and green flares falling from it.

F/L GRD Hinde in DS738, JI-J reported: Bomb load 1x4000 HC, 32x30 incendiaries, 450 x 4 incendiaries, 90 x 4. 10/10 cloud, tops 8/10,000 feet. Visibility good. Bombed target at 2013 hours at 20,000 feet. Glow of fires visible under cloud for considerable distance on return route. Camera operated.

Target:	*Berlin Area*
Aircraft deployed total:	*383*
514 Squadron:	*3*
Aircraft lost total:	*20 (Lancasters)*
514 Squadron:	*Nil*

Comments: Fires were still burning from the raid of the previous night, and many of these were bombed in error, lessening the effectiveness of this raid. 514 Squadron's DS738 landed at RAF Waterbeach on 24th November 1943 at 0001 hours, making it the first operational aircraft to land at the squadron's new home.

24th November 1943.
Weather: Dull throughout the day with occasional showers. Most sections spent the day in taking over offices allotted to them sorting and checking all their stores that had arrived the previous day.

25th November 1943.
Weather: Fair at first, occasional showers developing to steady rain. An effort of ten aircraft was called for, eight on a bombing trip and two for gardening. The bombing operation was called off in late afternoon owing to weather conditions. One aircraft took off on a gardening operation, he completed his mission and returned having to land away from base.

GARDENING – SW FRANCE

1 aircraft took off to attack the target, SW France. Bomb load 4 Veg.
F/S NW Thackray in DS824, JI-U, reported: Bomb load 4 Veg. Primary area SW FRANCE. 10/10 cloud, tops 17000 feet along whole route. Came down to 24000 feet. (Note: This is probably meant to read 2400 feet). 4 Veg planted as ordered. Diverted to Exeter.

26th November 1943.

Weather: Early mist with fog patches dispersing early afternoon. A bombing effort was called for and as it was a target for long crews only, the crews were gathered together under cover of security; the target was mentioned with the result that all short crews available volunteered. Eight crews took off, one owing to engine trouble returned early, one unfortunately is missing but the remainder returned and landed at base safely. A good show.

BOMBING – BERLIN

Eight aircraft took off to bomb the target Berlin. 1 aircraft failed to return. Very little cloud over the target. Visibility was good marred by ground haze. Defences were particularly busy. Bombing was good and fires soon sprang up. Fighters very active in the Frankfurt area.

F/L DAA Gray in JI-Q DS818 reported: Bomb load 1 x 4000 HC, 24 x 30 incendiaries, 405 x 4 incendiaries, 45 x 4 X. Primary target: BERLIN. Weather clear. Target attacked at 2127 hours at 21,000 feet. Target area appeared to be a mass of flames. Controls stiff with ice. All route markers were seen.

Target:	*Berlin Area*
Aircraft deployed total:	450
514 Squadron:	8
Aircraft lost total:	28 (Lancasters)
514 Squadron:	1

Comments: Berlin Zoo was damaged on this raid, allowing many dangerous animals to escape. These included a number of big cats, all of which had to be hunted and shot by the German authorities.

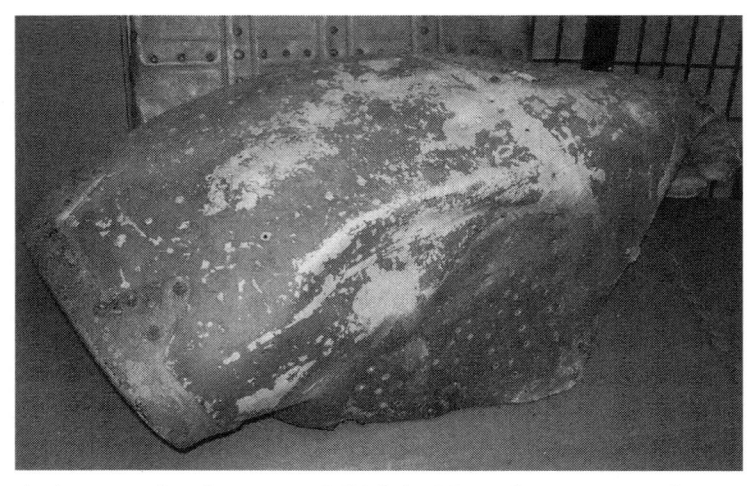

(Above) An air inlet from one DS814's Hercules engines, later salvaged by German aviation archaeologists. Source: Mario Schultze / John Saddler.

Missing Aircraft:

DS814, JI-M shot down at 21.43 hours by flak of 1.-4./Schw.Abt.148 leaving the target area, tragically with the loss of its whole crew, who were on their first op.

F/O MR Cantin RCAF	*Pilot*	*KIA*
Sgt SE Smith	*Bomb Aimer*	*KIA*
Sgt WGF Saddler	*Navigator*	*KIA*
Sgt WE Mitchell	*WOP/AG*	*KIA*
Sgt LF Eyre	*MU Gunner*	*KIA*
Sgt RN Walne	*Rear Gunner*	*KIA*
Sgt KG King	*Flight Engineer*	*KIA*

27th November 1943.
Weather: Generally foggy, clearing slightly early afternoon, intermittent rain, sleet. As weather conditions were bad for flying crews continued training under their Section Leaders. Squadron Leader EF Sly, DFC, AFM and crew arrived and were attached to 1678 Conversion Flight for Conversion. Squadron Leader EF Sly takes over command of the 'C' Flight.

28th November 1943.
Weather: Widespread fog with intermittent rain becoming fair later afternoon. A night BULLS-EYE exercise was called for. Four crews took part and all returned safely.

29th November 1943.
Weather: Clear and bright most of the day with strong cold wind. Most crews took part in flying exercise in special training. Wing Commander M Wyatt DFC, 3 Group, visited the Squadron. All crews not flying continued special training under their Section Leaders.

30th November 1943.
Weather: Fair with thundery showers at intervals and hail locally. Ten aircraft were called for operations but owing to weather conditions had to be cancelled.

Monthly Totals for November 1943
Total sorties for November 1943:   44

(Above) A foe that was to feature prominently in 514 Sqn's war: a Messerschmitt Bf110 night fighter. The radar aerials are prominent on this as on other night fighters. Although largely ineffective as a fighter / bomber in the Battle of Britain, the Bf110 came into its own in the night skies over Occupied Europe, especially in the hands of skilled pilots such as Hptm Martin Drewes, who claimed at least two 514 Sqn Lancasters. Source: Airworx GmbH Archive.

December 1943

1st December 1943.
Weather: Fine, no cloud, light wind.
Air tests took place in the morning. Ten aircraft were called for Bombing Operations, but the effort was cancelled at a late hour owing to the weather conditions.

2nd December 1943.
Weather: Wet in the morning and overcast, but clearing later. Air tests took place in the morning. Ten aircraft were detailed for Bombing Operations. All aircraft took off successfully but three returned early. One aircraft failed to return and two reported combats in one of which a Rear Gunner was killed and the aircraft badly 'shot up'. Aircraft LL679 arrived. BOMBING -BERLIN.
Ten aircraft took off to bomb the target. Three returned early and one failed to return. 5-7/10 cloud over the target. Considerable fires and smoke up to 1500 feet. Fires seen 120 miles away on way home. Little trouble from searchlights. Heavy Flak, fairly intense, decreasing as attack progressed. Considerable fighter activity over target. One Lancaster attacked from astern, the enemy aircraft firing several bursts, the Rear Gunner was killed and the aircraft damaged.
F/S FCV Steed, DS815, JI-E reported: 'Bomb load 1 x 4000, 40 x 30 incendiaries, 650 x 4 incendiaries, 70 x 4 incendiaries. Primary target BERLIN. 4/10 cloud. Bombed on green TIs at 2023 at 20300 ft. 4 lbs inc. bomb, presumably from another aircraft fell through Perspex behind Nav table, thrown overboard. Port aileron holed by, presumably, 30 lb inc. Log blown through hole in aircraft. Encounter with enemy aircraft reported.
P/O GS Hughes in DS783, JI-B reported: 'Bomb load 1 x 8000, 160 x 4 incendiaries, 20 x 4 incendiaries. Primary target BERLIN. 5-6/10 cloud. Bombed on green TIs 2025 at 20,000 ft. Attacked by fighter in target area and Rear Gunner (Sgt L Wilton) killed. Aircraft sustaining severe damage. Hydraulics, rear turret, mid-upper turret, oxygen u/s. Port tyre, port inner engine damaged. Landed safely on 3 engines.

Combat Reports:
Aircraft: DS783 – 'B'
Captain: P/O GS Hughes.
Target: BERLIN
Homeward bound on a course of 360 degrees, height 20,000 feet, IAS 155. At 2030 hours, Lancaster was attacked from the port fine quarter,

slightly down, by an E/A later recognised by WOP/A.G. as ME210. The one and only burst fired by E/A killed Rear Gunner instantly, put mid upper turret u/s and caused fires in the bomb racks, and inside fuselage which lasted about 30 seconds, setting alight to Mid Gunners clothing, compelling him to vacate the turret momentarily. E/A broke away to starboard quarter up and made a second attack immediately from 400 yards. Lancaster 'B' effectively corkscrewed to starboard on the instructions of WOP/A.G. Controlling from Astro-dome, and E/A was soon lost to sight. Attempts were made to extricate Rear Gunner whose turret was jammed with gun pointing starboard, but broken parts prevented effective use of external rotation valve. Visibility was slightly hazy with 1/2 moon, Lancaster 'B' had just left fighter flare path but there was no flak during combat and aircraft was not held in searchlights.
MU Gunner – Sgt Moorhouse - Nil.
Rear Gunner- Sgt L Wilton (RCAF) - Nil.

Aircraft: DS815 'N'
Captain: F/S FCV Steed.
Target: BERLIN
Homeward bound, height 20,000 feet, on a course of 105 degrees, IAS 165. At 20.23 hours Mid Upper Gunner reported an Me109 on port beam about 500 yards range attacking another Lancaster, shots were observed from E/A but no return fire from Lancaster. E/A however appeared to break off attack and passed over Gunner's aircraft from port to starboard beam and turning closed range to 400 yards without attacking, when Mid Upper Gunner opened fire and held it for 2 seconds. E/A immediately broke away on the port quarter down and was not seen again. Hits were claimed on E/A. At the time of combat, searchlight activity was slight and there was no predicted flak, track lights, or flares. Visibility with half-moon was good.
MU Gunner – Sgt Sweet - 100 rounds.
Rear Gunner- Sgt CA Forsythe RCAF – Nil.

Target:	*Berlin Area.*
Aircraft deployed total:	*458*
514 Squadron:	*10 (3 returned early)*
Aircraft lost total:	*40*
514 Squadron:	*1 plus 1 crew member KIA: Rear Gunner Sgt L Wilton in DS783, JI-B.*

Comments: The bombing was scattered over south Berlin. One of the aircraft lost was carrying members of the press, Captain Grieg for the Daily Mail and Norman Stockton, Sydney Sun.

Missing aircraft:

DS738, JI-J. Shot down by a night fighter over Potsdam approaching target area. Possibly the Lancaster claimed by Lt. Alfred Koerver of Stab.II or 7/JG302 at 2011 hours. According to the Bomb Aimer, F/S JD Alford RAAF, the port fin and rudder were shot away, port wing tank set on fire, undercarriage hydraulics damaged and there was possibly damage to the rear turret. It is thought that the Rear Gunner, Sgt R. Curle, was killed as he did not respond to the order to bale out. The port wing was on fire and the aircraft entered a dive. It is thought that the pilot, F/L Hinde from Rhodesia, was thrown clear. All crew survived as POW except for Sgt Curle. His body was not recovered and he is commemorated on the Runnymede Memorial.

F/L GHD Hinde	*Pilot*	*POW*
F/S JD Alford	*Bomb Aimer*	*POW*
P/O MSC Emery	*Navigator*	*POW*
Sgt W Muskett	*WOP/AG*	*POW*
Sgt R Galloway	*MU Gunner*	*POW*
Sgt R Curle	*Rear Gunner*	*KIA*
Sgt WJ Stephen	*Flight Engineer*	*POW*

3rd December 1943.
Weather: Fog all day until late. Air tests took place in the morning. Five aircraft were detailed for bombing operations. Two failed to take off. The other three successfully completed their mission and returned safely.
BOMBING – LEIPZIG.
3 aircraft set out to bomb the target. There was 10/10 cloud over the target with tops about 5000 – 6000 feet. Markers well concentrated and were bombed. The glow of fires was seen on the clouds and a column of smoke seen above the clouds.
P/O E Greenwood, JI-R DS820 reported: 'Bomb load 1 x 2000 HC, 48 x 30 incendiaries, 800 x 4 incendiaries, 100 x 4 incendiaries. Primary target LEIPZIG. Quiet trip. 10/10 clouds obscuring target area. Fire reflection through clouds. Bombed total load on release flares. If flares were in right position they had it down below.'

Target: *Leipzig Area*
Aircraft deployed total: *527 (Halifax and Lancasters)*
514 Squadron: *3*
Aircraft lost total: *24*
514 Squadron: *Nil*

Comments: After feinting towards Berlin, the group diverted to the intended target leaving few fighters to provide opposition, although the stream was coming under sporadic attack. The T.Is were well positioned making this a most successful raid. However this was marred by extra casualties incurred when many aircraft in the stream mistakenly flew over the Frankfurt defences.

4th December 1943.
Weather: Fine and sunny throughout the day. Air tests, navigational training flights and fighter affiliation were carried out. Some crews were given an afternoon's stand-down.

5th December 1943.
Weather: Widespread fog all day. No flying took place. Ground training continued.

6th December 1943.
Weather: Widespread fog all day. No flying took place. Aircrew were given a 'pep-talk' by Wing Commander AJ Samson DFC in the afternoon. The funeral of Sgt Wilton, L. killed on operations on the night of 2.12.43 took place at Cambridge and was attended by the Gunnery Leader and several other from the Squadron in addition to the funeral party.

7th December 1943.
Weather: Fog thick as ever. No flying took place. Sections continued their training under their respective leaders.

8th December 1943.
Weather: Fog again all day. No flying took place. Stand-down for some of the older hands, others continued their ground training.

9th December 1943.
Weather: Slight improvement, after the usual foggy morning. Airborne at last to the extent of one aircraft on a weather test in the

afternoon, which was lost to sight immediately on leaving the ground. Ground training continued.

10th December 1943.
Weather: Fine and sunny all day, but very cold. Air tests and air firing exercises took place in the morning. One crew took part in an 'Eric' exercise. Two crews were detailed for a 'Bullseye' but one of these failed to take off as their aircraft was unserviceable. The other crew successfully carried out the duty and returned to base. In the afternoon the Station was visited by HRH the Duke of Gloucester, who was conducted round the Squadron by Wing Commander AJ Samson DFC. Aircraft LL681, LL683 and LL684 arrived.

11th December 1943.
Weather: Overcast with some sleet showers and bitterly cold. Air tests, Navigational Training and cross country flights were carried out by all available crews. Clay pigeon shooting for Air Gunners and some others not flying took place in the afternoon.

12th December 1943.
Weather: Overcast all day and very cold. Navigational training, practice bombing and air-firing flights were carried out. Notification of the immediate award of the DFC to Pilot Officer GS Hughes (Pilot) was received for his fine show on the night of 2.12.43 when he brought his badly damaged aircraft back from the raid on Berlin. This is the first award obtained since the formation of the Squadron.

13th December 1943.
Weather: Fine and sunny all day. Eleven details of fighter affiliation were carried out, in addition to air tests, practice bombing and air firing flights.

14th December 1943.
Weather: Widespread fog all day. No flying took place. A 'stand-down' was given to 'A' and 'B' Flights.

15th December 1943.
Weather: Fog, increasing in afternoon. Air tests, navigation and bombing flights in the morning. One crew carried out an Air Sea Rescue search, without result. Flying cancelled in afternoon. Sections continued with their ground training, Air Gunners getting in some clay pigeon shooting. The Squadron was visited by the Group Gunnery

Leader, Squadron Leader DH Keary, DFC and the Group Bombing Leader, Squadron Leader D Stowe, DFM.

16th December 1943.
Weather: Overcast. Twelve aircraft were detailed for bombing operations. Eleven of these took off in good time, and one (which subsequently went on to complete the mission successfully) took off late. One aircraft returned early owing to engine trouble and the remaining eleven, after successfully completing their mission, we're diverted from Base, two to Little Snoring, the remainder to Downham Market.
BOMBING – BERLIN.
12 aircraft took off to bomb the target, one returned early owing to Port undercarriage could not be raised. 10/10 cloud over target. It is known that parts of the Capital were hit. Lancaster 'R' reports combat with an FW190 over the city and claim to have damaged it.
F/S DCC Crombie, DS820 JI-R reported: Bomb load 1x 2000, 40 x 30 incendiaries, 630 x 4 incendiaries. Primary target: Berlin. 10/10 cloud over target. Bombed at 2006 at18500 feet. Fires appeared to be burning well from glow seen through cloud. Returned on 3 engines. Good trip for the weather conditions. Had combat over Berlin with FW190 which was claimed and damaged. No damage to our aircraft. Landed at Downham Market 0015.

Combat Reports:
Aircraft: DS820 'R'
Captain: F/S DCC Crombie
Target: BERLIN
Flying over target (bombs not dropped), flying on a course of 111 degrees, height 21,000 feet, IAS 170. At 2002 hours Rear Gunner reported an E/A recognised as an F.W.190 flying on starboard quarter down and on a parallel course, range 300 yards and on the point of making an attack. He immediately gave the order for corkscrew to starboard and opened fire holding it for approximately 3 seconds, E/A attacked following Lancaster on first part of manoeuvre closing in to 150 yards on starboard quarter up. Rear Gunner and Mid Upper Gunner both opened fire for 2 seconds. At this stage E/A opened fire but shots appeared to pass under Lancaster and E/A broke away to port up. E/A now about 400 yards port quarter up makes second attack. Lancaster was still corkscrewing when Mid Upper Gunner opened fire, immediately E/A closed to 200 yards but did not open fire and broke away quickly underneath to starboard and was not seen again. Many

hits were seen by both gunners and E/A claimed as damaged. Lancaster sustained no damage.
MU Gunner – Sgt Jenner - 150 rounds.
Rear Gunner - Sgt Hill - 250 rounds.

Aircraft: LL627 'U'
Captain: F/S NW Thackray
Target: BERLIN
Homeward bound (bombs dropped), 8 minutes from target, flying on a course of 320 degrees, height 22,000 feet, IAS 160. At 2016 hours with enemy flare path on port side Mid Upper Gunner reported twin engined aircraft about 700 yards on the port quarter slightly down preparing to attack. He immediately gave order to corkscrew to port and Rear Gunner opened fire with 2 second burst at the same time, E/A closed range to 500 yards but did not open fire and immediately broke off attack and disappeared below and was not seen again. There was no flak or searchlights at the time of combat and visibility was good.
MU Gunner – Sgt CH Henn RAAF - Nil.
Rear Gunner - Sgt RE Bromley RAAF - 100 rounds.

Aircraft: DS815 'N'
Captain: F/L CW Nichol
Target: BERLIN
Outward bound (bombs not dropped), flying on a course of 120 degrees, 5240N 0535E, height 20,000feet, IAS 155. At 18.15 hours with searchlights on cloud-base and some enemy flares on each side, Mid Upper Gunner reported single engined aircraft on starboard quarter level, range 500 yards and immediately gave order to corkscrew to starboard opening fire at the same time and holding it for 2-3 seconds. E/A did not open fire and promptly broke off attack to port quarter down and was not seen again. There was some light flak in the vicinity during combat and visibility was good.
MU Gunner – Sgt AR Bird – 100 rounds.
Rear Gunner - Sgt GC Fearman – Nil.

Target: *Berlin Area*
Aircraft deployed total: *493 (10 Mosquitoes, 383 Lancasters)*
514 Squadron: *12 (1 returned early)*
Aircraft lost total: *55 (54 Lancasters)*
514 Squadron: *Nil*

Comments: This raid had mixed results. Railway facilities were destroyed which subsequently affected the transportation of supplies to the Russian Front. Also, by the raid's end, approximately 25% of all housing in Berlin had been destroyed. 1 Stirling and 25 Lancasters were lost due to deplorable flying conditions of thick fog and low cloud upon return. The conditions resulted in many crashing or being abandoned on return to England with the tragic loss of around 150 aircrew. 514 Squadron's aircraft managed to return unscathed.

17th December 1943.
Weather: Fog all day. No flying took place. The eleven aircraft diverted after last night's operations were unable to be flown back to base. The Bomb Aimers and Air Gunners of the crews from these aircraft returned by road in the evening. A lecture on Mining by Commander MacDonald, RN, was given in the afternoon and was found most interesting.

18th December 1943.
Weather: Overcast with poor visibility. Only one of the eleven aircraft diverted on the night of 16.12.43 was flown back to Base. The remainder of the crews returned to Base by road.

19th December 1943.
Weather: Fair, visibility good. Air tests, navigation training and practice bombing flights and air/ground firing (Rushford Range) took place. Skeleton crews proceeded by road to collect diverted aircraft. Six crews were detailed for a 'Bullseye', of these three took off and successfully completed the detail.

20th December 1943.
Weather: Fine and sunny. Four details of fighter affiliation, 'C' Flight. One 'C' Flight crew successfully carried out a 'Bullseye'. Twelve aircraft were detailed for bombing operations. Eleven took off but one returned early. One aircraft failed to return. The remainder successfully completed their mission and (with the exception of one which landed on two engines at Woodbridge) returned to base. No combats were reported.
BOMBING - FRANKFURT AM MAIN.
Twelve aircraft were detailed to attack the target. One did not take off. One returned to base owing to engine trouble. One returned early and landed at Woodbridge. One is missing. There was 5/10 cloud over Frankfurt. The area within 20 miles of the target reflected many

incendiaries on the cloud. Opposition was moderate. Numerous searchlights were ineffective owing to cloud, and there was only a fair amount of heavy Flak. Very few fighters were seen though numerous fighter flares are reported. There was one indecisive combat with a Ju88 North of the target on the way home.

F/S W Henry in DS823, JI-M reported: Bomb load 1 x 4000, 48 x 30 incendiaries, 950 x 4 incendiaries, 100 x 4 incendiaries. Primary target FRANKFURT. 5-7/10 cloud, visibility over cloud good. Bombed target at 1950 at 20,000. 16 x 30 hung up, brought back to Base. Effort appeared to be too widespread and fires burning short of target. Shortage of TIs may have had a lot to do with this.

Target:	*Frankfurt am Main Area*
Aircraft deployed total:	*650*
514 Squadron:	*11 (1 returned early)*
Aircraft lost total:	*41*
514 Squadron:	*1*

Comments: Many aircraft were attacked by fighters on the outbound leg of the raid. On approaching the target, the Germans set off dummy TIs and lit a fire as a diversion. This failed a little however, as a wind change forced the smoke to reverse direction and it ended up over Frankfurt by mistake. By the end of the raid, over 23,000 people had been rendered homeless.

Missing Aircraft:

DS817, JI-P. The aircraft exploded in midair after an attack by a night fighter flown by Hptm. Wilhelm Herget, 8./NJG3. DS817 crashed at Rettert, WNW of the target, at approx. 2015hrs on 20/12 1943.

F/S GF Davies	*Pilot*	*POW*
Sgt EJ Roberts	*Navigator*	*KIA*
Sgt RJ Seddon	*Air Bomber*	*KIA*
Sgt H Morris	*WOP/AG*	*KIA*
Sgt AR Bird	*MU Gunner*	*KIA*
Sgt WDB O'Dea RAAF	*Rear Gunner*	*KIA*
Sgt J Smethurst	*Flight Engineer*	*KIA*

Note: The ORB lists Sgt O'Dea as O'Dean. However, all other records including the Commonwealth War Graves Commission list him as Sgt O'Dea, so that is presumed to be the correct spelling.

21st December 1943.
Weather: Dull, visibility poor. Air tests took place in the morning, and the crew diverted to Woodbridge after last night's operation returned to Base. In the afternoon the Medical Officer gave a lecture to all aircrew on the subject of Oxygen and High Flying.

22nd December 1943.
Weather: Fair, visibility good. 'C' Flight becomes operational. Air tests, Air/Ground firing at Rushford Range and an acceptance test took place. Two crews were on Air/Sea Rescue.

23rd December 1943.
Weather: fair, visibility poor but improving later. Air tests, Acceptance Test and Air/Ground firing at Rushford Range were carried out.
BOMBING – BERLIN.
19 aircraft were detailed to bomb the target. 4 failed to take off, 2 returned early and 1 is missing. One landed at Foulsham on return owing to petrol shortage. There was considerable cloud over the target. Good fires were started and seen 100 miles away. Several fighters were seen. Two indecisive combats just North of Berlin reported by one Lancaster. Opposition was moderate.
F/S W Henry in DS823 JI-M reported: Bomb Load 1 x 4000, 32 x 30 incendiaries, 450 x 4 incendiaries, 90 x 4 incendiaries. Primary target BERLIN. 5/10 cloud. Bombed at 0409 at 20,000 ft. Many good fires seen on leaving, reflected through clouds. Quite concentrated. Good attack. Route OK though a bit long.
F/O LT Kingwell in LL625, JI-C reported: Bombed at 0413 hours at 19,000 feet. Huge orange coloured fire blazing. Had three encounters with enemy aircraft.

Combat Report:
Aircraft: LL625 – 'C'
Captain: F/O LT Kingwell
Target: BERLIN
1st Encounter: Nearing target area, flying on a course of 014 degrees, at 20,000 feet, IAS 150. At 0405 hours Bomb Aimer reported a twin engined aircraft identified as a Ju88 approaching almost head on but slightly on the port bow up. As E/A passed over Lancaster to starboard quarter Rear Gunner opened fire with a short burst of approximately 1

second at a range of 100 yards. E/A was quickly lost to view and was not seen again. S/L on cloud base, visibility fair.

2nd Encounter: At 0416 hours about 7 miles north of target, course 358 degrees at 19,500 feet IAS 160 (bombs dropped). Bomb Aimer reported a twin engined aircraft identified as a Ju88 approaching from the port bow slightly up about 600 yards away. Bomb Aimer immediately gave order to corkscrew to port as E/A opened fire which passed over Lancaster. Mid Upper Gunner replied with a short burst as E/A passed overhead. E/A broke away astern and was not seen again.

3rd Encounter: At 0420 hours homeward bound, course 358 degrees, height 21,000, IAS 160, Mid Upper Gunner sighted E/A identified as an FW190 on the starboard quarter up at 800 yards slowly closing in. At 600 yards Mid Upper Gunner opened fire with a short burst, at the same time giving the order to corkscrew to starboard. E/A which was almost immediately lost to view did not reply and was not seen again.

MU Gunner – Sgt H Taylor – 80 rounds.
Rear Gunner - W/O HS Fidge RAAF – 120 rounds.

Target:	*Berlin Area*
Aircraft deployed total:	*379 (364 Lancasters)*
514 Squadron:	*15*
Aircraft lost total:	*16*
514 Squadron:	*1*

Comments: The PPF (Pathfinders) experienced H2S problems resulting in the TIs being scattered. On a positive note, a clever diversion by Mosquitoes, temporarily tricked the German Fighter controllers which reduced the amount of fighter opposition. According to 'Nachtjagd War Diaries', a Ju88 G-6 of 6.NJG3 was shot down and credited to the rear gunner of a 514 Sqn. Lancaster over Berlin. Fw. Frank and his BF (Radar Operator) Uffz. Schierholz, an ace crew with 27 victories, baled out unharmed.

Missing aircraft:

LL671, A2-B. According to F/S Maloney, the only survivor, it is believed that F/O Whitting, the pilot, was killed during an attack on the aircraft. The aircraft crashed at Catheim, approximately 10 miles North of Frankfurt. This location has been difficult to verify; however it is likely that LL671 was attacked by Ofw. Walter Mackens of 1./JG300 at 0250 hours or Oblt. Hans-Heinz Augenstein of 7./NJG1 at

0300 hours, both of these unidentified claims being in the Frankfurt area. The crew were on their first operation.

(Left) This photo from the ORB Appendices is marked 'Sgt Whitting'. The squadron records mention only F/O KG Whitting RAAF and it is believed that the photo is of him. Source: Crown Copyright / National Archive.

F/O KG Whitting RAAF	Pilot	KIA
F/S D Edwards	Navigator	KIA
F/S RW Basey	Air Bomber	KIA
Sgt WA Casey	WOP/AG	KIA
F/S JE Maloney	MU Gunner	POW
Sgt PAT Nelson	Rear Gunner	KIA
Sgt LF Rostock	Flight Engineer	KIA

24th December 1943.
Weather: Fair, visibility moderate. The aircraft which landed at Foulsham after last night's operations returned to base. Two crews proceeded on Air/Sea Rescue Search otherwise there was a general squadron stand-down. The Squadron Adjutant was confined to bed with Bronchitis, and as the Assistant Adjutant was on a Discip. Course, the duties of Adjutant were assumed by the Gunnery Leader F/Lt JN Pollock till he should recover.
Note: The operation referred to as 'last night' actually took place very early on 24th with aircraft taking off a few minutes after midnight. This caused some confusion in the ORB Summary of Events.

25th December 1943.
Weather: Overcast, some fog, visibility poor. No flying took place. There was a stand-down for the Squadron after the completion of daily inspections, and football matches (of a not very serious nature) were played in the morning which were well supported by members of the Squadron.

26th December 1943.
Weather: Fog in morning with poor visibility improving later. No flying took place. There was a Squadron stand-down in the afternoon.

27th December 1943.
Weather: Fine and sunny all day. A very full day's flying programme was carried out with air tests, beam sorties, acceptance tests, loaded climb, cross countries, GH practice, Bomb Aimer flying and fighter affiliation. In the afternoon there was clay pigeon shooting for Air Gunners not flying in which some other aircrew joined in.

28th December 1943.
Weather: Fair, visibility improving. Air tests and high and low level bombing practices took place and ground training was carried out by the various sections.

29th December 1943.
Weather: Fine and sunny, visibility fair. The Squadron Adjutant resumed his duties after his illness. Air tests took place in the morning and there were some cross countries. Nineteen aircraft were detailed for bombing operations of which two failed to take off. The remainder successfully completed their mission and returned safely to base with the exception of one which was last heard of over the North Sea reporting shortage of petrol and was presumed to have 'ditched'. No combats were reported.
BOMBING – BERLIN.
19 aircraft were detailed to bomb the target. Two did not take off, 1 returned early and 1 is missing. Markers were considered good and 10/10 cloud seems to have hampered the defences. Fires were large and seen from 70 miles. One large explosion is reported. One combat is reported and the Lancaster forced to 'Ditch' owing to petrol shortage. The crew rescued unhurt.
P/O WHJ Vizer in LL653, A2-F, reported: Bomb load 1 x 4000, 24 x 30 incendiaries, 54 x 4 incendiaries, 90 x 4 incendiaries. Primary target BERLIN. There was 10/10 cloud well below. Bombed at 2017 hours at 19,000 ft. in centre of about 12 concentrated red and green sky markers. Glow of fires seen below. All route markers on way to target seen in correct positions and effective. Route markers not seen on return journey. Monica not used. Would have been a good raid if PFF were right. One or two fighter flares either side of target were seen.

Combat Report:
Aircraft: DS821 – 'S'
Captain: F/O L Greenburgh
Target: BERLIN

1st encounter: Outward bound, flying on a course of 090 degrees at 20,000 feet, IAS 155. At 1815 hours when in the Meppen area Rear Gunner saw exhaust of aircraft on port quarter down at range of about 700 yards, closing in. At 400 yards range on port quarter down this aircraft opened fire on Lancaster and was recognised by Rear Gunner as a Ju88, and Rear Gunner gave order to corkscrew to port and returned E/A's fire with a very long and almost uninterrupted burst of 6 seconds as E/A closed in slowly passing under Lancaster and finally breaking away on the starboard quarter down. MU Gunner did not see E/A but fired some short bursts in the direction of Rear Gunners trace. In the corkscrew Rear Gunner saw what appeared to be a rocket projectile fired at Lancaster from E/A and the Pilot and WOP saw an orange glow or explosion close under Lancaster's port wing. During this attack Lancaster's petrol tank was presumably damaged causing the petrol leak which ultimately resulted in Lancaster's ditching. No S/L, Flak, or flares were observed.

2nd Encounter: At 2200 hours homeward bound, with bombs dropped, in approximately the same position as during the outward bound encounter, flying on course of 270 Degrees IAS 175 at 21,000 feet, M/U Gunner reported and identified a Ju88 climbing on the fine starboard quarter level not firing but manoeuvring for attack at a range of 200 yards. MU Gunner immediately gave order to corkscrew to starboard at which moment Rear Gunner also sighted E/A and both Gunners of Lancaster opened fire on E/A simultaneously, MU Gunner with 3 very short bursts and Rear Gunner with a large number of short bursts many of which appeared to be hitting E/A. As E/A broke away to starboard quarter up, Rear Gunner saw it wobble as if out of control and MU Gunner saw a red glow from the centre of the fuselage, and it is claimed as probably destroyed. About half a minute prior to this attack a bright yellow flare had been observed about half a mile to starboard. There were no S/Ls or flak.

3rd Encounter: At 2215 hours while in the Enkhuizen area homeward bound and shortly after a serious shortage of petrol had been noticed, Lancaster was flying on a course of 270 Degrees IAS 210 at height of 17,000 feet when Rear Gunner reported and identified a Ju88 on the starboard quarter up at a range of 400 yards, closing in and firing on Lancaster. Rear Gunner ordered corkscrew starboard and MU Gunner saw E/A just after the dive had commenced. Both Gunners of Lancaster opened fire simultaneously when E/A was at a range of 300 yards. E/A broke away to port quarter up, repeated a similar attack from there to starboard quarter, and again a similar attack from starboard to port quarter. During each of these attacks MU Gunner was

firing a series of short bursts and Rear Gunner a long burst at E/A which was firing at Lancaster. There were no S/L or Flak but 3 orange flares were observed to starboard about a mile away just prior to this encounter.
MU Gunner – Sgt Carey - 500 rounds.
Rear Gunner – F/S Drake - 1240 rounds.

(Above) F/O Greenburgh's Lancaster DS821, JI-S still afloat in the North Sea the morning after ditching. Source: Victoria RSL.

Target: Berlin Area
Aircraft deployed total: 712
514 Squadron: 17 (1 returned early)
Aircraft lost total: 20
514 Squadron: 1

Comments: Berlin's defences were hampered by Bomber Command's tactics and bad weather, resulting in relatively low losses.

Missing Aircraft:

DS821, JI-S, flown by F/O L Greenburgh, ditched in the North Sea after it ran out of fuel following combat with a night fighter flown by Ofw. Karl-Heinz Scherling of 12./NJG 30 km South of Texel.

F/O L Greenburgh	*Pilot*	*Survived*
Sgt PG Butler	*Navigator*	*Survived*
Sgt DL Bament	*Air Bomber*	*Survived*
Sgt GH Stromberg	*WOP/AG*	*Survived*
Sgt FJ Carey	*MU Gunner*	*Survived*
F/S CA Drake	*Rear Gunner*	*Survived*
Sgt L Weddle	*Flight Engineer*	*Survived*

(Above) Aircrew train in ditching techniques at RAF Waterbeach. Such training paid dividends for the Greenburgh crew, who survived sixteen hours in the North Sea, 70 miles off the East Coast of England. Source: Airworx GmbH Archive.

30th December 1943.
Weather: Fine and sunny, visibility fair. Air tests, a loaded climb and cross countries were carried out. Early in the morning, just after dawn, W/Cdr AJ Samson DFC with a 'scratch' crew set out to search for the Squadron crew who were presumed to have 'ditched' after last night's operations. On the first leg of the search a Verey Light was seen and a dinghy in which there appeared to be six men was shortly afterwards sighted. This was kept in sight for three hours during which time other

aircraft on Air/Sea Rescue duties appeared and remained on the scene. Finally a Rescue Launch appeared in the vicinity and was guided to the dinghy and all the occupants were taken on board. It was subsequently ascertained that the dinghy contained all seven of the crew of the Squadron aircraft which had 'ditched' last night, and that none of them was injured. This is the first known case of a 'ditching' in the Squadron and the circumstances of the rescue caused great satisfaction. The aircraft itself was observed still afloat, after nearly twelve hours in the sea.

31st December 1943.
Weather: Fine and sunny, visibility fair. Air tests were carried out in the morning. Nineteen aircraft were detailed for bombing operations, but the operation was cancelled during briefing shortly after 1500 hours.

Monthly Totals for December 1943
Total sorties: 65

January 1944

1st January 1944.
Weather: Fine and Sunny, visibility fair. Air Tests were carried out in the morning.
BOMBING- BERLIN.
Seventeen aircraft were detailed to bomb the target. Two were withdrawn and one returned early. The remainder successfully completed their mission and returned to base. There was 10/10 cloud over the target. Bombing appears to have been somewhat scattered, but explosions were seen and columns of smoke were reported above the cloud tops at 20,000 feet. Flak was moderate over the target, but a number of fighters were seen and 3 combats reported.
S/L EP Sly, LL685 A2-G, reported: Bomb load 1 x 4000, 24 x 30, 450 x 4, 90 x 4 lbs incendiaries. Primary target: BERLIN. There was 10/10 cloud with tops at 20,000 feet. Sky markers with red and green stars seen. Bombed at 0313 hours at 20,000 feet. Very few sky markers scattered over 5 miles. Photo attempted.

Target: *Berlin Area*
Aircraft deployed total: *421 (Lancasters)*
514 Squadron: *15 (1 returned early)*
Aircraft lost total: *28 (Lancasters)*
514 Squadron: *Nil*

Comments: Generally the bombing was considered fairly scattered. Shipping infrastructure on an important waterway was destroyed causing shipping in the area to be disrupted for several days.

2nd January 1944.
Weather: Fine and sunny, visibility good. Air Tests were carried out in the morning and Low Flying Practice.
BOMBING – BERLIN.
17 Aircraft were detailed for Bombing Operations. 4 Aircraft failed to take off and 3 returned early. The remainder successfully completed their mission and returned to Base. There was 10/10 cloud over the target.

P/O JK Williams in DS824, JI-K, reported: Bomb load 1 x 4000, 24 x 30, 450 x 4, 90 x 4 incendiaries. Primary target: BERLIN. There was 10/10 cloud. Bombed at 0248 hours at 21,000 ft. Route satisfactory. PFF appeared concentrated. Had encounter with enemy aircraft.

Combat Reports:
Aircraft: DS824, 'K'
Captain: P/O JK Williams.
Target: BERLIN
Homeward bound (bombs just dropped), 10 miles South of Berlin, flying on a course of 270 degrees at 20,000 feet, IAS 180. At 0254 hours homeward bound, 10 miles south of Berlin (bombs dropped), Engineer saw twin engined aircraft well below and on the starboard bow silhouetted against the cloud and climbing under Lancaster to port quarter, and almost immediately after Mid Upper Gunner saw aircraft identified as Ju88 dead astern at a range of 150 yards and immediately gave order to dive. As he did so E/A opened fire on Lancaster and broke away above and was not seen again.
Immediately prior to encounter Rear Gunner was keeping observation on 2 other E/A on port quarter and giving commentary on their movements and did not see attacking E/A during encounter except for brief glimpse of trace. Lancaster did not return E/As fire. On return hits were discovered on Lancaster's port tailplane. At time of encounter there were searchlights on cloud base, unpredicted flak, and four fighter flares on each side of Lancaster.
MU Gunner – Sgt Pratt - Nil.
Rear Gunner – F/S. EA Lane (RCAF) - Nil.

Aircraft: LL672, A2-C
Captain: F/O JMJ Bourke
Target: BERLIN
1st Encounter: Nearing target area and about to commence bombing run, flying on a course of 096 degrees, at 20,000 feet, IAS 160. At 0313 hours Rear Gunner reported twin engined aircraft identified as Me110 on starboard quarter slightly down at a range of 300 yards firing at Lancaster with trace passing below. Rear Gunner immediately gave order to corkscrew starboard and opened fire as E/A closed in. Rear Gunner firing 2 bursts of 2 seconds each, experiencing stoppages in 2 guns and trace appeared to be hitting E/A which broke away on port quarter down and was not seen again. At the time there were no effective searchlights or predicted flack but a number of flares were burning in the vicinity.
2nd Encounter: At 0340 hours homeward bound about 25 miles E of Leipzig flying on a course of 210 degrees at 22,000 feet IAS 160 (bombs dropped) Rear Gunner reported a twin engined aircraft believed to be a Ju88 on port quarter level at a range of 350 yards. Rear

Gunner gave order to corkscrew to port and fired a burst of 4 seconds at E/A again experiencing stoppages in 2 guns. E/A closed in and opened fire at Lancaster his trace passing well above. E/A was lost to view in corkscrew while still attacking and was not seen again. No searchlights, flak or flares were observed.
MU Gunner – Sgt H Brewer - Nil.
Rear Gunner – Sgt A Williston - 300 rounds.

Target: *Berlin Area*
Aircraft deployed total: *383*
514 Squadron: *13 (3 returned early)*
Aircraft lost total: *27 (Lancasters)*
514 Squadron: *Nil*

Comments: Bombing was again scattered, and regarded as fairly ineffective. 156 Squadron suffered badly with the loss of 5 of its 14 aircraft and 10 Pathfinders were also lost.

3rd January 1944.
Weather: Dull, some rain, visibility fair. Strong wind. Air Tests took place in the morning, and there was a Squadron stand-down in the afternoon.

4th January 1944.
Weather: Fine and sunny. Strong wind. A very full days flying program was carried out with Air Tests, Bombing Practice, Low Flying Practice, Height and Load Test.

5th January 1944.
Weather: Fine, visibility fair. Air Tests were carried out in the morning. 21 crews were detailed for Bombing Operations which were cancelled shortly after Main Briefing at 22.30 hours.

6th January 1944.
Weather: Fair, visibility good. Air Tests, Practice Bombing, Air/Sea Firing and Cross Countries were carried out. In the afternoon Squadron Crews not flying took part in football matches and other sports.

7th January 1944.
Weather: Dull, visibility fair, some rain. Two crews were detailed for a 'Bullseye' but this was cancelled. Air Tests, air/ground firing at

Rushford Range, GH Tests and Bombing Practice at Elmdon Range took place. Some crews not flying did Physical Training in the afternoon.

8th January 1944.
Weather: Dull, cloud low, visibility improving later. A 'Bullseye' for which 1 crew was detailed, was cancelled. Air Tests, Bombing Practice at Rushford Range, Special Navigational Exercises, and a Height and Load Test were carried out.

9th January 1944.
Weather: Dull, some rain, visibility poor. Air Tests, Fighter Affiliation, Loaded Climb, Cross Country and Navigational Exercises were carried out.

10th January 1944.
Weather: Fine and sunny all day. Air Tests, Air/Ground Firing at Lakenheath Range, Air/Sea Firing, Low Flying Practice and Special Navigational Exercises took place.

11th January 1944.
Weather: Dull, with some rain and snow, Visibility poor. Air Tests, Air/Sea Firing, Formation Practice and Special Navigational Exercises were carried out.

12th January 1944.
Weather: Dull and overcast, visibility poor. Bombing Practice and Special Navigational Training was carried out.

13th January 1944.
Weather: Dull and overcast, visibility poor. An 'Eric' Exercise for which all available Aircraft were detailed was cancelled. A Prisoner-of-War Lecture was given to all Air Crews in the morning by Flight Lieutenant C. Keen, Intelligence Officer. Air Tests, Air/Sea Firing and Navigational Exercises were carried out.

14th January 1944.
Weather: Fine and sunny all day. Air Tests and a Height and Load Test took place in the morning. Main Briefing took place for the first time in the New Briefing room. The Group Gunnery Leader - S/Ldr. DHK Keary, DFC - paid a visit to the Squadron in the afternoon. The Group Intelligence Officer - S/Ldr EE Colquhoun, the Group Engineering

Leader - F/L R Holmes, DFC, the Public Relations Officer - S/L LA Nickolle also visited the Station and were present at the Briefing and Interrogation of crews.

BOMBING – BRUNSWICK.

23 aircraft were detailed for Bombing Operations. 3 failed to take off, 4 returned early and 2 aircraft failed to return. The remainder carried out their mission successfully and returned to Base. Believed to be a good raid. Ju88s were seen firing rocket projectiles. Photos of Brunswick are largely cloud. No results observed.

P/O GS Hughes RAAF in DS785, JI-D reported: Bomb load 1x 4000 bomb. Primary target: BRUNSWICK. There was 10/10 cloud. Bombed at 1920 hours from 20000 feet. Fires visible through cloud. Well concentrated fires below cloud. Broadcast winds good. Fighters appeared to drop red flares and flak opened up on these. Photo flash hung up.

Target: *Brunswick Area*
Aircraft deployed total: *471 (469 Lancasters and 2 Halifax)*
514 Squadron: *20 (4 returned early)*
Aircraft lost total: *38*
514 Squadron: *2*

Comments: The first major attack on Brunswick of the war. It was a much smaller target and the attack was considered scattered and ineffective. Opposition from fighters caused heavy losses.

Missing Aircraft:

LL685, A2-G. Intercepted at 0105 hours by a night-fighter flown by Hptm. Walter Barte of Stab III./NJG3 West of Bennebostel and crashed 5km S of Celle. The crew are now buried in Hannover War Cemetery.

S/L EF Sly DFC	*Pilot*	*KIA*
F/O JL Martin RCAF	*Navigator*	*KIA*
P/O EH Thomas DFM RCAF	*Bomb Aimer*	*KIA*
P/O WL Harvey DFM RNZAF	*WOP/AG*	*KIA*
F/O JA Sneddon DFM RCAF	*MU Gunner*	*KIA*
P/O FG Rosher DFM	*Rear Gunner*	*KIA*
F/O PF Boulter	*Flight Engineer*	*KIA*

S/L Sly DFC was Flight Commander, 'C' Flight. He was the most senior officer to lose his life whilst serving with 514 Squadron.

LL679, A2-J. Probably victim of a night-fighter, crashing at Lauenburg, SE of Dassel. It is possible that LL679 fell victim to Hptm. Erhardt Peters of 9./NJG3 who is credited with an unidentified Lancaster at 1933hrs, approximately the time that LL679 was in the area. There were no survivors from the crew, on their first operational sortie, who are buried in Hannover War Cemetery.

F/S PE Mason RNZAF	*Pilot*	*KIA*
F/S AE Dimock	*Air Bomber*	*KIA*
F/S JS Gallagher RNZAF	*Navigator*	*KIA*
F/S L Kell RNZAF	*WOP/AG*	*KIA*
Sgt EJ Oakley RCAF	*MU Gunner*	*KIA*
Sgt JW Hennis	*Rear Gunner*	*KIA*
Sgt RF Laishley	*Flight Engineer*	*KIA*

15th January 1944.
Weather: Fog all day. No flying took place all day. There was a Squadron stand-down in the afternoon. Several Aircrew took part in Football Matches and other Sports.

16th January 1944.
Weather: Fog all day. No flying took place all day. Ground Training continued in the respective Sections. Squadron Leader B Wallis, DFC and Bar, the Group Training Inspector (2) paid a visit to the Squadron.

17th January 1944.
Weather: Fog all day. No flying all day. There was a Squadron Stand-down in the afternoon.

18th January 1944.
Weather: Dull and overcast. Visibility poor. Some limited Navigational Training flights, but mostly ground training.

19th January 1944.
Weather: Fair early, fog and rain later. Air Tests and Air/Ground Firing were carried out.

20th January 1944.
Weather: Thick fog in morning, clearing at 14.00 hours.
BOMBING – BERLIN.
20 aircraft were detailed to bomb the target. 1 was withdrawn, 1 jettisoned and 5 returned early. The take-off of the remainder, which was witnessed by the Group Engineering Leader F/Lt. R. Holmes, DFC, was the most successful to date, being completed in 14 minutes. 5 Aircraft were forced to turn back and the rest returned to Base after completion of their mission. There was 10/10 cloud over the target, but sky markers were well concentrated and if these were on target the attack should be a success. Reflection of fires could be seen from 130 miles.
F/L GJ Chequer in JI-A, DS735, reported: Bomb load 1 x 4000, 32 x 50, 540 x 4, 60 x 4 incendiaries. Primary target: BERLIN. There was haze and 8/10 cloud. Bombed at 1929 hours at 21,000 ft. Bombed on ETA arriving before Pathfinders. Saw TIs on leaving target and believed to have dropped bombs approx. 3 miles S of TIs.

Combat Reports:
Aircraft: LL677- 'E2'
Captain: F/Sgt A Winstanley
Target: BERLIN
1st Encounter: Outward bound, bombs not dropped, 1 mile S of Henstedt, height 22,700 feet, course 120 degrees. At 19.01 hours Mid Upper Gunner reported unidentified twin engined A/C on starboard quarter level at a range of 100 yards which immediately opened fire, and shots appeared to be hitting starboard wing of Lancaster which had commenced to corkscrew to starboard. Owing to violent nature of manoeuvre, Gunners were unable to bring sights to bear on E/A, which broke away to starboard up, and turned to make another attack at range of 600 yards, opening fire again immediately with shots hitting starboard inner engine and rendering Mid Upper Turret Unserviceable. Before Mid Upper Gunner could hand manipulate the turret, E/A had broken off attack and was lost to sight. During the encounter, no flak or searchlights were in evidence but 2 fighter flares were to port. Visibility clear with 10/10ths cloud.
2nd Encounter. At 20.55 hours Lancaster was homeward bound (bombs dropped) flying at 18,000 feet, immediately after 'Monica' warning, Mid Upper Gunner reported tracer coming from starboard bow to port quarter, and Lancaster commenced corkscrew movement to starboard.

A few seconds later on a 'Monica' warning, Lancaster commenced a corkscrew and Rear Gunner reported a Ju88 at a range of 200 yards on fine port quarter up, and immediately opened up holding it for 2 seconds, E/A broke away quickly to starboard without returning fire. Hits were observed by Gunners on E/A. Visibility fair with 9/10ths cloud.
MU Gunner – Sgt E Buckley - Nil.
Rear Gunner – Sgt WF Sutherland - 150 rounds.

Aircraft: DS816 'O'
Captain: P/O GS Hughes RAAF, DFC
Target: BERLIN.
Combat Report: Outward bound (bombs not dropped), flying on a course of 100 true, at 20,000 feet, IAS 160. At 1904 hours (bombs not dropped), Rear Gunner who had just given warning of 2 flares astern reported, silhouetted against cloud, an unidentified twin engined aircraft dead astern and slightly down at a range of 1200 yards, closing in and climbing to starboard quarter. At 800 yards this aircraft appeared to be commencing a curve of pursuit and Rear Gunner gave order to weave preparatory to taking more violent evasive action. E/A immediately broke off attack and held off at 800 yards on the starboard quarter up for about 5 minutes after which it came in to attack again from that direction. When it had closed to 600 yards, Rear Gunner gave order to corkscrew to starboard and E/A immediately broke off attack to port quarter up, there being no exchange of fire.
E/A then made another attack from port quarter up and at 600 yards range, Rear Gunner gave order for diving turn to port. During this manoeuvre Rear Gunner could not get sights to bear on E/A but Mid Upper Gunner got in 3 short bursts. At the 3rd burst which appeared to be hitting or passing very close to the target, E/A broke off attack as Lancaster dived into cloud, and E/A was lost to view and not seen again. There was no fire from E/A during this or the previous attack. No searchlights or flak were observed. Visibility was hazy. 10/10ths cloud.
MU Gunner – Sgt EG Moorhouse - 80 rounds.
Rear Gunner – Sgt LJH Whitbread – Nil

Target:	*Berlin Area*
Aircraft deployed total:	769
514 Squadron:	*19 (1 jettisoned and 5 returned early)*
Aircraft lost total:	35
514 Squadron:	*Nil*

Comments: Again Bomber Command suffered stiff opposition, with fighters harassing the stream until it was well into the return journey. The target was cloud covered so assessing the success of the operation was impossible. Sky marking was good. Crews using H2S felt their bombs landed in eastern Berlin.

21st January 1944.
Weather: Fine and sunny all day. Air Tests were carried out and an Air/Sea Rescue Search. Wing Commander AJ Samson, DFC resumes command of the Squadron vice Squadron Leader EGB Reid.
BOMBING – MAGDEBURG.
18 Aircraft were detailed for Bombing Operations. 1 of these turned back, and 4 failed to return - the heaviest loss in the Squadron to date. The remainder returned to Base after completing their mission. There was 5-7/10 cloud.
F/L DAA Gray in LL703, JI-L reported: Bomb load 1 x 4000, 90 x 4, 32 x 30 incendiaries. Primary target: MAGDEBURG. There was 5/10 cloud. Bombed at 2304 at 20,000 ft. TIs very scattered in length over target area. Well lit up. No red markers seen – one green with yellow stars. More cloud than anticipated.

(Above) A 4000 lb 'Cookie' bomb sits in front of Lancaster Mk.II JI-L (serial not known) as the aircraft performs an engine test. 4000 lb Medium (MC) and High Capacity (HC) bombs were the weapon of choice for industrial targets, usually mixed with an assortment of smaller General Purpose (GP) bombs or incendiary. Source: Airworx Gmbh Archive.

Combat Report:
Aircraft: LL681 'J'
Captain: F/O LJ Kingwell.
Target: MAGDEBURG

Having overshot the target, Lancaster 'J' was returning back to get into position for bombing run flying at a height of 20,500 feet on a course of 300 degrees IAS 170. At 23.01 hours, with no 'Monica' warning, tracer was seen coming from dead astern slightly above and Rear Gunner gave order to corkscrew to port. Attacking A/C followed the Lancaster in the corkscrew firing continuously, but only its tracer could be seen. Rear Gunner (who had stoppages in 2 inner guns) and Mid Upper Gunner (who had stoppages on 1 gun) fired long bursts in direction of attacking A/Cs tracer until on the roll from down port to up starboard, the attacking A/C appeared to have been shaken off, as no more tracer was seen. Lancaster sustained extensive damage in this attack including damage to the port inner engine, port right hand undercarriage, port bomb door, starboard main-plane and starboard outer oil tanks. No searchlights, flares or flak were observed at the time. E/A attacked from dark part of sky with Lancaster silhouetted against the target area.

MU Gunner – Sgt Taylor - 180 rounds
Rear Gunner – W/O HS Fidge (RAAF) - 360 rounds

Target: *Magdeburg Area*
Aircraft deployed total: *648*
514 Squadron: *18 (1 returned early)*
Aircraft lost total: *57*
514 Squadron: *4*

Comments: The first major raid on Magdeburg was plagued by enemy night fighters. Opposition was fierce causing havoc and many losses. Some crews arrived ahead of Pathfinders and bombed using H2S. Marking was sparse which resulted in a scattered attack. Most of the bombs are believed to have fallen outside the city. 514 Sqn suffered its biggest single losses on operations so far, 4 aircraft failing to return.

Missing Aircraft:

LL680, A2-H. Outbound at 21,000 feet, intercepted and shot down by a night fighter. As aircraft disintegrated, P/O Vizer was thrown clear through the Perspex canopy and survived though badly injured. There were no other survivors from the crew.

P/O VHJ Vizer	Pilot	POW
Sgt ES Lowe	Navigator	KIA
Sgt CJ McLaughlin	Bomb Aimer	KIA
Sgt EJ Pitman	WOP/AG	KIA
Sgt JD Barker	MU Gunner	KIA
Sgt LT Gardiner	Rear Gunner	KIA
Sgt K Foyle	Flight Engineer	KIA

DS824, JI-K. Shot down by Oblt. Martin Drewes, 11./NJG1. Crashed in the Ijsselmeer. Four of crew including P/O Williams, were on second tour. There were no survivors from the crew.

P/O JK Williams	Pilot	KIA
P/O DP Henshaw	Bomb Aimer	KIA
Sgt LN Millis	Navigator	KIA
F/S WH Chapman	WOP/Air	KIA
Sgt A Pratt	MU Gunner	KIA
F/S EA Lane	Rear Gunner	KIA
Sgt JR Koenen	Flight Engineer	KIA

LL672, A2-C. Shot down outbound from 21,000 feet over Perleberg and credited as 'possibly Ofw. Heinz Vinke, 11./NJG1'. Sgts McQueeney and Williston were killed, the other crew members survived as POW

F/L JMJ Bourke RCAF	Pilot	POW
F/O ES Clare RCAF	Bomb Aimer	POW
Sgt SE Cuttler	Navigator	POW
Sgt RI Smith	WOP/Air	POW
Sgt J Brewer	MU Gunner	POW
Sgt A Williston RCAF	Rear Gunner	KIA
Sgt P McQueeney	Flight Engineer	KIA

LL627, JI-U. Lost in the same area (Ijsselmeer) as DS824, with the loss of the entire crew. Possibly this aircraft was also shot down by Ofw. Heinz Vinke at the same time as DS824 was shot down by Oblt. Drewes.

F/S RAJ Bennett RCAF	Pilot	KIA
Sgt WL Baker RCAF	Bomb Aimer	KIA
F/S TW Dodd RCAF	Navigator	KIA
F/S PW Upton	WOP/Air	KIA
Sgt A Brettell	MU Gunner	KIA
W/O DJ Hughes	Rear Gunner	KIA
Sgt KA Lowery	Flight Engineer	KIA

22nd January 1944.
Weather: Dull, overcast all day, strong winds. Air Tests and Special Navigational Training were carried out in the morning. There was a stand-down in the afternoon.

23rd January 1944.
Weather: Fine, strong winds. The award of the Distinguished Flying Cross to Flight Lieutenant C Payne on 22.1.44 was published. Air Tests, Bombing Practice and a Height and Load took place. Fighter Affiliation which had been arranged was cancelled due to the unserviceability of the Fighter Aircraft. 5 Aircraft were detailed for a 'Bullseye' which was cancelled.

24th January 1944.
Weather: Fine in morning, rain storms in the afternoon. Air Tests and Fighter Affiliation took place in the morning, but the Fighter Affiliation arranged for the afternoon was cancelled due to weather conditions. Some crews not flying took part in Physical Training and others attended some Prisoner of War films in the Station Cinema, which were excellent.

25th January 1944.
Weather: Fair early, high winds and storms later. Air Tests were carried out in the morning. 9 Aircraft were detailed for Bombing Operations, but the effort was cancelled shortly after Briefing at 16.30 hours.

26th January 1944.
Weather: Fair in morning, rain storms in the afternoon. Air Tests, Air/Sea Firing, Navigational Training and 2 details of Fighter Affiliation were carried out.

27th January 1944. Weather: Fair, visibility good. Air Tests and Air/Sea Firing were carried out in which 'Flak Suits' were tested for the first time.

BOMBING – BERLIN.
21 Aircraft were detailed for Bombing Operations. 1 failed to take off and 5 returned early, 1 of which overshot the landing, the crew being unhurt. The remainder successfully bombed the target and returned to Base. 2 Russian Army Officers, Major-General Sharapov and Lt. Col. Roudor who were visiting the Station attended the interrogation of the Crews on their return. There was 6-8/10 cloud encountered as far as Hannover increasing to 10/10. As the target was approached sky markers were well concentrated and all crews identified the target by these. Cloud prevented any accurate assessment of the raid, but the glow of fires on the cloud was visible for 150 miles on the return trip. The target was encircled by fighter flares and there was considerable fighter activity, but only four combats have been reported and one Ju88 is claimed as damaged.

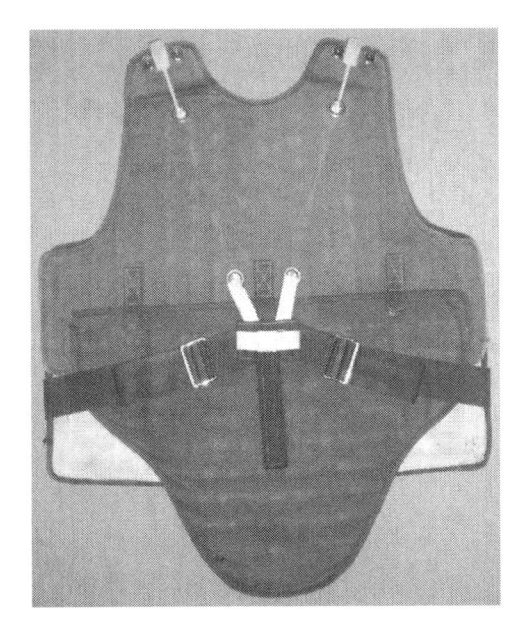

(Above) Flak suits were armoured vests designed to protect the torso from shrapnel. They were, however, cumbersome, heavy and uncomfortable and, crucially, had to be discarded before the parachute could be attached to its harness. The red toggle, when pulled, allowed the flak suit to be discarded quickly. However, they were not widely used by Bomber Command. Source: Ric Bond

F/S CG Miller in 'B2' reported: Bomb load 1 x 4000, 7 cans incendiaries. Primary target: BERLIN. There was 10/10 cloud, tops

10,000 ft. Bombed at 2045 at 21,000 ft. Enemy fighters in target area. 1 canister incendiaries hung up. Owing to fuel shortage landed at Manston.

Combat Report:
Aircraft: DS785 'D'
Captain: P/O GS Hughes RAAF, DFC
Target: BERLIN.
Outward bound (bombs not dropped), flying on a course of 055 degrees, height 20,000 feet IAS 130. At 1904 hours on a 'Monica' warning Lancaster commenced a slight weaving manoeuvre. A few seconds after this warning Mid Upper Gunner reported a twin engined aircraft recognised quickly as a Ju88 on the port quarter well down at a range of 500 yards commencing an attack. He immediately gave order to corkscrew to port. E/A opened fire with 1 short and 1 long burst, shots passing underneath Lancaster. Rear Gunner fires almost simultaneously with E/A and held it for approximately 4 seconds until E/A closing in to approximately 100 yards, broke away on starboard quarter up, and was soon lost to view. Many hits were claimed on E/A. Lancaster sustained no damage. During combat there was no flak, searchlights or fighter flares. Visibility was slightly hazy.
MU Gunner – Sgt EG Moorhouse – Nil.
Rear Gunner – Sgt LJH Whitbread – 250 rounds.

Target:	*Berlin Area*
Aircraft deployed total:	*530 (515 Lancasters and 15 Mosquitoes)*
514 Squadron:	*20 (5 returned early)*
Aircraft lost total:	*33*
514 Squadron:	*Nil*

Comments: Cloud cover obscured the target so sky marking was used, which resulted in fairly scattered bombing. Later reports of significant damage to some important infrastructure, and approximately 20,000 people being displaced. Night fighters took their toll again although this time less affectively than the previous operation. LL674 A2-D returned early and touched down at 2020hrs, overran the runway and finished up in a boundary ditch. The crew was named as F/S HJ Symmons and F/O N Hall.

28th January 1944.

Weather: Dull, visibility fair. Air Tests were carried out in the morning. Air Vice Marshal RD Oxland, CB, CBE, Senior Air Staff Officer Bomber Command attended the Briefing and gave a short talk on Enemy RDF Methods and Counter-Measures. He was also present at the take-off and interrogation of returning Crews.

BOMBING – BERLIN.

19 Aircraft were detailed for Bombing Operations, of these 3 failed to take off and 1 was cancelled and 1 returned early. The remainder successfully carried out their mission and returned to Base. Crew encountered 9-10/10 cloud on the way which thinned out somewhat over the target. Sky markers were well concentrated, and the reflections of many fires could be seen from the German coast on the homeward journey. Explosions were reported over the target. There appeared to be less fighter opposition than previously.

S/L EGB Reid in LL624, JI-B reported: 'Bomb load 1 x 4000 lb bomb, 16 x 30, 750 x 4 incendiaries. Primary target: BERLIN. There was 10/10 cloud with tops 5000 ft. Bombed at 0319 hours at 21,000 ft. Very good Attack. Good concentration of fires.

Combat Report:
Aircraft: LL625 'C'
Captain: F/O JR Laing.
Target: BERLIN

At 0424 hours approx. 90 miles North of Berlin Rear Gunner reported a twin engined aircraft recognised later as a Ju88 on the starboard quarter up, at a range slightly over 1000 yards, and preparing to make an attack. When E/A had closed range to 600-700 yards and commenced attacking. Rear Gunner instructed Pilot to dive starboard and both Gunners opened fire, the Rear Gunner with bursts of 2 or 3 seconds and Mid Upper Gunner with one burst lasting 2 seconds. E/A seemed to close to approx. 150 yards but did not fire, and was last seen breaking away on the port quarter down, weaving violently to avoid fire from Lancaster which was hitting the front portion of fuselage. E/A is claimed as Badly Damaged. During combat there was no flak or searchlights, but a few fighter flares in the distance. Visibility was good.

MU Gunner – Sgt RB McAllister RCAF – 100 rounds.
Rear Gunner – Sgt CA Salt – 400 rounds.

Target: Berlin Area
Aircraft deployed total: 677
514 Squadron: 15 (1 returned early)
Aircraft lost total: 46
514 Squadron: Nil

Comments: Despite diversionary tactics, night fighters were again providing stiff opposition for Bomber Command resulting in many losses over the target. With more favourable weather conditions, some ground marking was possible, the result being widespread destruction. Approximately 180,000 people were displaced. Bomber Command claimed it as their most concentrated attack so far.

29th January 1944.
Weather: Dull, visibility fair. Air Tests, Height and Load Tests, Cross Country and Low Flying Practice was carried out. There was a stand-Down for most crews in the afternoon.

30th January 1944.
Weather: Fine and sunny. Air Tests and Height and Load Tests were carried out.
BOMBING – BERLIN.
17 Aircraft were detailed to bomb the target. 1 was withdrawn, 2 returned early and 2 are missing. The remainder landed at Base. There was 10/10 cloud over the target. Numerous combats were reported.
F/O E Greenwood in DS813, JI-H reported: 'Bomb load 1 x 8000 lb bomb. Primary target: BERLIN. There was 10/10 cloud. Bombed at 2022 hours at 20,000 ft. There was good concentration of sky markers. Monica u/s. Route too hot – Attack not as good as previous night.

Combat Reports:
Aircraft: DS785 'D'
Captain: P/O K Penkuri
Target: BERLIN
Homeward bound (bombs dropped), flying on a course of 296 degrees, at a height of 23,000 feet, IAS 155. At 2125 hours, 25 miles S.W. Of Brunswick Mid Upper Gunner reported an unidentified twin engined aircraft on starboard quarter up at an estimated range of 400 yards coming in on a curve of pursuit and firing at Lancaster. Rear Gunner and Mid Upper Gunner opened fire at E/A with bursts of 3 to 4 seconds, and Rear Gunner gave order to corkscrew to starboard. E/A broke away very near to Lancaster on the port quarter and was not seen

again. No hits or Damage were sustained by Lancaster. A flare had been reported on starboard quarter just prior to the attack. There were no searchlights or flak.
MU Gunner – Sgt KE Peake – 160 rounds.
Rear Gunner – Sgt J Crawford. – 400 rounds.

Aircraft: LL625 'C'
Captain: P/O JR Laing.
Target: BERLIN
Outward bound (bombs not dropped) flying on a course of 155 degrees, height 20,000 feet, IAS 165. At 2002 hours approx. 80 miles north of Berlin Rear Gunner reported a twin engined aircraft which he was able to recognise later as a Ju88 on the starboard quarter well down at a range of 1000 yards, silhouetted against the white cloud tops and appeared to be 'shadowing' Lancaster which had been keeping up a banking search. E/A closing range to 800 yards began a weaving action from starboard to port quarter and back again which lasted about two or three minutes, the Gunners of the Lancaster controlling in turns reporting its movements while keeping a normal 'search' going.
When E/A now between 700-800 yards dead astern almost level seemed to be on the point of attacking, Rear Gunner ordered a corkscrew to port. The pilot very effectively 'tightening' the manoeuvre on his instruction as E/A opened fire with one short burst which went wide to starboard. At this stage with range about 600 yards and E/A dead astern slightly up, both Gunners opened fire, the Rear Gunner with two 4 second bursts and Mid Upper Gunner with one lasting 2 seconds. E/A tried to press home the attack, but seemed unable to bring guns to bear on Lancaster, the accurate fire from which, set alight to its port engine immediately enveloping it in flames. E/A was last seen by both Gunners and Wireless Operator diving out of control in flames on the starboard quarter.
An object, assumed to be a parachute was observed leaving E/A as it went down. The crew of another Lancaster of the Squadron confirmed 'the kill' by reporting a twin engined aircraft seen going down in flames at 2010 hours. During the combat there was no flak or searchlights, but Lancaster was flying between two lines of fighter flares. Visibility was very good with a bright quarter moon up. E/A only fired once during the encounter. Lancaster sustained no damage.
MU Gunner – Sgt RB McAllister RCAF - 80 rounds
Rear Gunner – Sgt CA Salt - 500 rounds

Aircraft: LL678 'L2'
Captain: F/S HS Delacour RAAF
Target: BERLIN
1st Encounter: Outward bound(bombs not dropped), position 55.10N 06.30E flying at a height of 20,000 feet IAS 150 and altering course from 098 to 080. At 02.12 hours while Lancaster was changing course Rear Gunner saw unidentified twin engined aircraft coming in from port quarter up at a range of 300 yards appearing to overshoot to starboard and endeavouring to get into attacking position. Rear Gunner opened fire with a burst of 2 seconds and E/A (which did not return fire) disappeared to starboard and was not seen again. No S/Ls, flak or flares observed.
2nd Encounter: At 03.28 hours homeward bound with bombs just dropped 7 miles S.E. Of target area, flying on a course of 117 degrees at a height of 20, 000 feet IAS 180. Rear Gunner saw twin engined aircraft believed to be a Ju88 on port quarter up at range of 400 yards holding off. When E/A appeared to be commencing attack, Rear Gunner opened fire with burst of 3 to 4 seconds and Mid Upper Gunner fired 2 bursts as Lancaster went into diving turn to port. Wireless Operator and both Gunners saw trace appearing to hit E/A which did not return fire. There were numerous flares in the target area but no searchlights or flak.
MU Gunner – Sgt S.F. Williams (RCAF) – 120 rounds.
Rear Gunner – F/S GD Savage – 400 rounds

Aircraft: DS822, 'T'
Captain: F/S PM Ashpitel
Target: BERLIN.
About to commence bombing run, flying on a course of 155 degrees, at a height of 19,000 feet, IAS 170. At 2024 hours Wireless Operator saw a twin-engined aircraft identified as a Ju88, (painted light brown and apparently a day-fighter) silhouetted against the target fires on the starboard bow down, passing under Lancaster to port quarter. The Rear Gunner saw E/A on port quarter down at range of 200 yards approaching, about to get into attacking position, and he did a burst of 2 to 3 seconds as E/A was closing in from 200 to 150 yards. At 150 yards when Rear Gunner had momentarily stopped firing, E/A made as though to break away and Rear Gunner opened up again with another burst of 3 to 4 seconds at which E/A rolled over on its back and disappeared below. During the Rear Gunners second burst the Wireless Operator saw pieces flying off E/A and it is claimed as damaged. E/A

did not fire at Lancaster during encounter. No S/L, flak or fighters were observed in the vicinity.
MU Gunner – F/O HC Bryant – Nil
Rear Gunner – W/O R Hall – 500 rounds

Target: *Berlin Area*
Aircraft deployed total: *534*
514 Squadron: *16 (2 returned early)*
Aircraft lost total: *33*
514 Squadron: *2*

Comments: There was less opposition on this occasion, although unfortunately for Bomber Command, again the city was obscured by cloud. Major concentrations of bombs fell on the south-west and centre of the city causing severe fire damage. Over 1000 casualties were later reported. Josef Goebbels' Propaganda Ministry was heavily damaged.

Missing Aircraft:

DS706, JI-G. Lost without trace. Possibly one of two Lancasters shot down over the North Sea by Lt. Guido Krupinski and Ofw. Heinz Vinke, both of 11./NJG1. No survivors amongst crew.

F/L GK Boyd DFC	*Pilot*	*KIA*
Sgt LSJ Adkin	*Navigator*	*KIA*
F/S PD Martindale	*Bomb Aimer*	*KIA*
Sgt J Downing	*WOP/Air*	*KIA*
Sgt RAD Mirams	*MU Gunner*	*KIA*
Sgt A Nicholson	*Rear Gunner*	*KIA*
Sgt PW Webb	*Flight Engineer*	*KIA*

DS735, JI-A. Aircraft was shot down approximately 10 miles North of Brandenburg. There were numerous unidentified aircraft shot down by night fighters in the Berlin area on this op and it is probable that DS735 was one such. KIA crew members buried in Berlin War Cemetery. F/S Mortimer was subsequently killed on 19/4/45 when Typhoons shot up a POW column near Boizenburg. F/S Robertson survived the war and was discharged from the RAAF as a Warrant Officer.

F/L GJ Chequer RCAF	Pilot	KIA
F/S K Mortimer	Navigator	POW
F/S EJ Wallington	Bomb Aimer	POW
Sgt R Montgomery	WOP/Air	KIA
F/S JL O'Brien RAAF	MU Gunner	KIA
F/S AJ Robertson RAAF	Rear Gunner	POW
Sgt J Carey	Flight Engineer	POW
F/S RL Gulliford	Second Pilot	POW

31st January 1944.
Weather: Dull and overcast all day. Air Tests and Navigational Training were carried out.

(Above) Uffz. Heinz Vinke may have accounted for up to three Lancasters of 514 Sqn in January 1944. A highly successful night fighter pilot, latterly with 11./NJG1, Uffz. Vinke was credited with 52 victories. He was posted missing on 26th February 1944 after his aircraft was shot down by two RAF Typhoons. Source: Airworx GmbH Archive.

Monthly Summary for January 1944

Operational: (Compiled by F/Lt. JN Pollock)

Enemy Aircraft Destroyed:	2
Enemy Aircraft Damaged:	4
Operational Flying Hours for January 1944:	785hrs 15mins.
Non-Operational Flying Hours for January 1944:	201hrs 05mins.
Total tons of bombs dropped in January 1944:	350 tons.
Number of Sorties for January 1944.	129

Strength of Squadron as at 31st January 1944.

Aircrew:
    50 Officers
    242 SNCOs

Ground:
    2 Officers,
    33 SNCOs,
    307 other ranks
    12 WAAFs

February 1944

Compiled by Flight Lieutenant JN Pollock

Note: The change of compiling officer saw a change in style, which is reflected below.

1st February 1944.
Weather: Fine, some cloud in the morning. Very mild.
Non-Operational Flying: Air Tests, Nav. Exercises and SBAs were carried out.
Movements: Flight Lieutenant H. Hall Squadron Engineer Leader proceeds on Engineer Leaders' Course at St. Athans lasting one month.

2nd February 1944.
Weather: Fair, still mild but rather cloudy.
Non-Operational Flying: Air Tests, Low and High Level Nav. Exercises, H and L Tests, Air Firing, SBA, Beam Flying and Cross Country took place and 4 details of Fighter Affiliation were carried out.
Visits: Wing Commander AJ Samson DFC flew to Wellesbourne and back in the afternoon.

3rd February 1944.
Weather: Fine, but strong wind.
Non-Operational Flying: Air Tests and Special Nav. Exercises were carried out.
Ground Training: All available crews attended a Cine Lecture on 'H2S' in the morning.
Visits: Wing Commander AJ Samson, DFC visited 3 Group H.Q. in the afternoon. Pilot Officer C.H. Simon, Assistant Adjutant, returned to the Squadron from his Admin. Course.

4th February 1944.
Weather: Clear and sunny with slight touch of frost. Wind still strong.
Non-Operational Flying: Air Tests, Air/Sea Firing, Bombing Practice at Rushforth, Cross Countries and Nav. Exercises were carried out. The fighter from Newmarket due to arrive for Fighter Affiliation Practice was cancelled owing to strong wind.
Visits: Press Representatives visited the Station and Squadron in the afternoon with the Group Public Relations Officer Squadron Leader LA Nickolls.

5th February 1944.
Weather: Fine, some cloud and very cold wind.
Non-Operational Flying: A very full day's programme was carried out with Air Tests, Cross Country, High and Low Level Nav. Exercises, Day and Night Bombing at Rushforth and Lakenheath, Local Practices, 2 Engine Flying, 3 Engined Overshoot, Beam flying, Bomb Aimer Flying, Low Flying and 4 details of Fighter Affiliation.
Visits: Wing Commander AJ Samson, DFC flew to RAF Warboys and back in the afternoon.
Movements: Flight Lieutenant H. Beckett, DFC, Squadron Navigation Leader, proceeded to Upwood on a Navigation Course.

6th February 1944.
Weather: Fine morning but clouded over later in afternoon.
Non-Operational Flying: 11 crews took part in an 'Eric' Exercise taking off at approximately 11.00 hours and landing 14.30 hours. Nav. Exercises and SBA were also carried out.
Defence: Group Captain CLL Saye, OBE, AFC, Station Commander, held a parade for Defence Squadrons and Flights in the afternoon. The Squadron Gunnery Leader, Flight Lieutenant JN Pollock commenced a series of lectures on Aircraft Recognition to Defence Personnel.

7th February 1944.
Weather: Cloudy but milder.
Non-Operational Flying: Air Tests, Air/Sea Firing, Bombing at Lakenheath, Nav. Exercises and Cross Country were carried out.
Movements: Wing Commander AJ Samson, DFC proceeded to Bomber Command, High Wycombe for Tactics Course lasting four days.
Policy: Flight Lieutenant JN Pollock, Squadron Gunnery Leader made arrangements with American Fighter Squadron for future Fighter Affiliation in addition to the Hurricane provided by Newmarket.

8th February 1944.
Weather: Clear and sunny with fairly strong and rather cold wind.
Non-Operational Flying: Air Tests, H and L Tests, Nav. Exercises, Low Flying Practices, Compass Check and four details of Fighter Affiliation were carried out. A conference was held at which Squadron Leader EGB Reid presided and which was attended by Flight Commanders and Section Leaders to discuss a comprehensive Bombing and Air Gunnery program to take place on the 10th inst.

Policy: A Squadron Self-Help Scheme was instituted and parties were detailed to work on runways and to clean and distemper Squadron Buildings etc.

Visits: Air Vice Marshall R. Harrison, CBE, DFC, AFC, the Air Officer Commanding 3 Group visited the Station in the afternoon and was conducted round the Squadron by the Station Commander Group Captain GI.L Saye, OBE, AFC and Squadron Leader EGB Reid.

Administration: Squadron Leader EGB Reid assumes command of the Squadron vice Wing Commander AJ Samson, DFC.

9th February 1944.
Weather: Fine, fairly strong wind.
Non-Operational Flying: An offer was obtained from an American Unit at Steeple Morden to supply two Thunderbolts for Fighter Affiliation at any time if not required for Operations.
Administration: The Squadron was given a complete stand-down.

10th February 1944.
Weather: Rather cloudy with very strong wind. Intermittent snow storms.
Non-Operational Flying: The Thunderbolts which it was hoped would come over for Fighter Affiliation were unable to do so owing to Operational requirements, but a Hurricane was provided by RAF Newmarket and seven details of Fighter Affiliation were carried out in the morning. In addition, Air Test and Bombing Practices at Elmdon and Nav. Exercises were carried out, but the programme arranged had to be curtailed in the afternoon due to weather conditions. No. 3 Group Controller gave Flight Lieutenant JN Pollock assurance that one Hurricane, possibly two, would be available for a big training arranged for the 11th.

11th February 1944.
Weather: Clear, with little cloud and freezing. Intermittent showers later.
Non-Operational Flying: 10 details of Fighter Affiliation were carried out in addition to Air Tests, Practice Bombing, Nav. Exercises, Cross Country and Compass Check.

12th February 1944.
Weather: Cloudy. Milder.
Non-Operational Flying: Air Tests, SBAs, H and L Tests, Beam Flying and 2 details of Fighter Affiliation were carried out.

Visits: The Squadron Gunnery Leader Flight Lieutenant JN Pollock and Squadron Leader EGB Reid flew over to the American Fighter Station at Bottisham to make arrangements for Fighter Affiliation and met Captain Tod of the USAAF at Group Operations to discuss details.
Administration: A sports afternoon was arranged for crews not flying.
Movements: Wing Commander AJ Samson, DFC returned from Bomber Command after attending a Course on Tactics.

13th February 1944.
Weather: Fine and sunny.
Non-Operational Flying: Air Tests were carried out.
Operational Flying: 19 Aircraft were detailed for Bombing Operations which were cancelled at 16.30 hours.
Administration: Wing Commander AJ Samson, DFC resumed command of the Squadron.

14th February 1944.
Weather: Overcast all day. Visibility bad.
Non-Operational Flying: Only one Air Test was carried out, the weather being too bad for general flying.
Ground Training: A lecture was given to all aircrew personnel on Tactics by the Squadron Commander, Wing Commander AJ Samson, DFC.
Movements: The Squadron Bombing Leader, Flight Lieutenant T.A. Angus, DFC proceeded on a Night Vision Instructors Course at Upper Heyford.

15th February 1944.
Weather: Fine and sunny all day. Very mild.
Non-Operational Flying: Air Tests, and H and L Tests were carried out.
Operational Flying: 22 Aircraft were detailed for Bombing Operations of which all took off. One Aircraft returned early and landed on three engines, and the remainder carried out their mission and returned to Base. This is a Squadron record to date, for the number of successful sorties on any one mission.
BOMBING – BERLIN.
22 aircraft were detailed to bomb the Target. One returned early, the remainder successfully carried out their mission and returned to Base. There was 10/10 cloud over the target with tops 10/12,000 feet. Sky marking was rather scattered but concentration of aircraft over the target was good and crews reported glow beneath cloud in the target area, and some fighter activity, particularly to North of the target.

Searchlights were ineffective. Numerous fighter flares were seen from Danish coast to target. Though results were difficult to assess owing to cloud, the operation should prove to have been successful.

F/O PJK Hood in DS820, JI-A reported: Bomb load 1 x 4000 Bomb. 32 x 30, 540 x 4, 90 x 4x incendiaries. Primary target: BERLIN. There was 10/10 cloud with tops 10,000 ft. Bombed at 2130 hours at 20,000 ft. Quiet Route. Flak over Berlin fairly heavy, otherwise 'no bother'. Explosion seen over Berlin at 2126 hrs.

Combat Report:
Aircraft: LL684 'B2'
Captain: P/O ABL Winstanley.
Target: BERLIN
Outward bound (bombs not dropped), flying on course of 160 degrees height 20, 000 feet, IAS 155. At 2045 hours in position 54.30N 13.08E. Rear Gunner reported trace passing Lancaster from starboard side and ordered corkscrew to starboard. Neither Gunner was able to see attacking aircraft, but both fired in the general direction of the trace with bursts lasting approximately 2 seconds. E/A appeared to fire only 1 short burst and although not seen, was effectively shaken off. 5 minutes previously Mid Upper Gunner had reported twin engined aircraft well below and climbing rapidly to intercept Lancaster and had shaken it off by a corkscrew manoeuvre. Visibility was very poor below on top of 10/10ths cloud. No flak, no searchlights or fighter flares were observed. Lancaster sustained no damage.
MU Gunner – Sgt JS Johnson – 80 rounds.
Rear Gunner – F/S SJ Everitt RCAF – 150 rounds

Target:	*Berlin Area*
Aircraft deployed total:	*891 (561 Lancasters)*
514 Squadron:	*22 (1 returned early)*
Aircraft lost total:	*43*
514 Squadron:	*Nil*

Comments: A record raid at the time, with 2462 tons of bombs being dropped. Although the target was cloud covered as usual, the massive force caused severe damage with over 1100 fires reported along with heavy damage to important infrastructure in Siemensstadt. It is considered this raid marked the end of the 'Battle of Berlin' as the city was not attacked for over a month afterwards.

16th February 1944.
Weather: Rain and fog. Visibility very bad.
Operational Flying: 22 Aircraft were detailed for Bombing Operations which were cancelled at 1530 hours.

17th February 1944.
Weather: Wet and Overcast.
Non-Operational Flying: No flying took place.
Operational Flying: 23 Aircraft were detailed for Bombing Operations which were cancelled at 1630 hours.

18th February 1944.
Weather: Overcast with sleet and snow. Very cold.
Non-Operational Flying: Air Tests and Air/Sea Firing were carried out.
Operational Flying: 22 Aircraft were detailed for Bombing Operations which were cancelled at 1630 hours.
Movements: Flight Lieutenant T.A. Angus returned to unit from Night Vision Instructors Course.

19th February 1944.
Weather: Overcast with some sleet. Visibility fair. Very cold.
Non-Operational Flying: Air Tests and Air/Ground Firing at Lakenheath were carried out.
Visits: Squadron Leader DH Keary, DFC Group Gunnery Leader visited the Squadron and accompanied the Squadron Gunnery Leader, Flight Lieutenant JN Pollock on inspection of Aircraft marshalled for take-off.
Administration: Squadron Leader EGB Reid assumed command of the Squadron in place of Wing Commander AJ Samson, DFC who undertook the duties of Station Commander.
Operational Flying: BOMBING – LEIPZIG
23 aircraft were detailed to bomb the target. Four were withdrawn, three returned early and 3 are missing. 1 landed at Mepal on return. There was 10/10 cloud over the target. Many large fires are reported, and late crews say there was smoke up to 20,000 ft. on leaving the area. The PFF think it was a reasonably successful attack despite the strong winds.
P/O E Greenwood in DS813, JI-H reported: Bomb load 1 x 2000, 1 x 500 lbs bomb. 40 x 30, 900 x 4 incendiaries. Primary target: LEIPZIG. There was 10/10 cloud. Bombed at 0412 hours at 20,000 ft. One large fire noticed spreading out around. Should be OK if PFF were correct.

Northern route satisfactory. Had encounter with enemy aircraft, but no damage is claimed. Lancaster suffered no damage.

Combat Report:
Aircraft: LL645 'H2'
Captain: F/O ICS Hay
Target: LEIPZIG
At 0408 hours, 5 miles S.W. Of Leipzig, Rear Gunner saw a rocket projectile coming towards Lancaster on port quarter up which died away before reaching Lancaster, and immediately after saw a twin-engined aircraft identified as a Ju88 on port quarter up at a range of 1500 yards silhouetted against a fighter flare. Rear Gunner gave order to corkscrew to port. During the corkscrew, E/A fired another rocket projectile at Lancaster from range of approx. 1200 yards which passed well below Lancaster on port quarter. Shortly after E/A was lost to view and was not seen again. No searchlights or flak were experienced at the time and only one fighter flare.
MU Gunner – Sgt WE Baldwin – Nil
Rear Gunner – Sgt WH Tate – Nil

Target:	*Leipzig – Aircraft Factories.*
Aircraft deployed total:	*823*
514 Squadron:	*19 (3 returned early)*
Aircraft lost total:	*78*
514 Squadron:	*3*

Comments: This attack marked the start of 'Big Week', a combined night and day assault on aircraft factories by, respectively, Bomber Command and the USAAF. The strategy was to destroy the Luftwaffe in combat, particularly in daytime, whilst also wrecking the aircraft industry, thus preventing replacement aircraft reaching the front line. The goal was to so weaken the Luftwaffe that air superiority would be achieved over the landing grounds of the forthcoming invasion. Cloud covered the target so sky markers were used. Night fighters attacked for the whole operation, taking a massive toll on allied aircraft resulting in the second highest loss to hit Bomber Command in the entire war. Poor weather predictions caused some allied aircraft to arrive ahead of the Pathfinders, and go into a holding pattern. This proved costly as the fighters and flak from ground defences took its toll. Some 20 aircraft fell to flak and 4 were lost in collisions with most of the rest being claimed by the night fighters. This raid, the last in which Halifax IIs and Vs were deployed to Germany, saw the heaviest loss of bombers to date, a toll that would only be surpassed by the Nuremberg raid of 30/31st March 1944.

Missing Aircraft:

DS736, A2-D. Lost without trace. No survivors from the crew, who are commemorated on the Runnymede Memorial. The aircraft was probably the victim of an unidentified night fighter.

F/S N Hall	Pilot	KIA
Sgt KL Cragg	Bomb Aimer	KIA
Sgt JR Williams	Navigator	KIA
Sgt FR Lewis	WOP/Air	KIA
Sgt WK Watkins	MU Gunner	KIA
Sgt TS Woodford	Rear Gunner	KIA
Sgt AR Hodson	Flight Engineer	KIA

LL681, JI-J. Lost without trace. No survivors from the crew, who are commemorated on the Runnymede Memorial. The aircraft was probably the victim of an unidentified night fighter.

F/L LJ Kingwell	Pilot	KIA
Sgt WA Bates	Bomb Aimer	KIA
Sgt GE Knight	Navigator	KIA
Sgt HM Whichelow	WOP/Air	KIA
Sgt H Taylor	MU Gunner	KIA
W/O HS Fidge RAAF	Rear Gunner	KIA
Sgt DW Newbury	Flight Engineer	KIA
W/O JD Dodding	(2nd Pilot)	KIA

DS823 JI-M. Shot down by night fighter, crashing at 0230hrs at Essern-Osterloh with the loss of all the crew. Possibly attributable to Lt. Hans Raum, 9./NJG3.

F/S W Henry RCAF	Pilot	KIA
F/S WS Ball	Bomb Aimer	KIA
Sgt SW Ricketts	Navigator	KIA
Sgt FH Vallance	WOP/Air	KIA
Sgt D Kenny	MU Gunner	KIA
Sgt W Lannigan	Rear Gunner	KIA
Sgt AE Bennett	Flight Engineer	KIA

20th February 1944.
Weather: Overcast and very cold. Visibility fair.
Non-Operational Flying: Air Tests were carried out during the day.
Operational Flying: BOMBING – STUTTGART
15 aircraft were detailed to bomb the target. 2 were withdrawn, 1 returned early and landed at Mepal. There was 3-10/10 and some clear patches in the target area and visibility was good. Most crews arrived early in the target area and had to wait for the markers to drop. The attack is considered as being well concentrated, falling mainly to the North of the town with scattered fires burning from East to West. Fires gained a good hold as the attack developed and smoke was seen rising to several thousands of feet and the glow was visible from 150/200 miles on the return trip.

S/L EGB Reid in LL728, JI-B reported: Bomb load 1 x 8000 lbs, 16 x 30, 300 x 4 incendiaries. Primary target: STUTTGART. There was 6/10 cloud. Bombed at 0410 hours at 20,000 ft. No visual details. Incendiaries over a wide area. Ground snow covered. Route OK.

Combat Report:
Aircraft: DS785 'D'
Captain: F/S E.A Kingham.
Target: STUTTGART.
Approaching Stuttgart at a height of 21,000 feet on a course of 040 degrees M. IAS 160. At 0406 hours on commencement of bombing run, Rear Gunner saw a twin engined aircraft later identified as an Me210, on starboard quarter fine (level), at a range of 400-500 yards, which opened fire on Lancaster, the trace passing well to port. Rear Gunner immediately gave order to corkscrew starboard and opened fire with a 3 second burst. E/A made no attempt to press home the attack and immediately broke away on port quarter level and was lost to view. Mid Upper Gunner was waiting to get in a burst on the breakaway but was unable to do so owing to the range and speed of E/As disengagement. There were no fighter flares, searchlights at the time, but some flak. Lancaster suffered no damage.
MU Gunner – Sgt FN Ansell - Nil.
Rear Gunner – Sgt A Davies – 200 rounds

(Above) 'A' Flight Lancaster Mk.IIs at their dispersal at Waterbeach. Second in line, behind the tractor, is LL728, JI-B, the mount of S/Ldr EGB 'Barney' Reid DFC, 'A' Flight Commander. Source: Tracy Holroyd-Smith / Sgt George Henry.

Target: Stuttgart – Aircraft Factories
Aircraft deployed total: 598
514 Squadron: 13 (1 returned early and landed at Mepal)
Aircraft lost total: 14
514 Squadron: Nil

Comments: Again, cloud cover hampered the attack. Although bombing was scattered, the Bosch factory along with other important public buildings were badly damaged or destroyed. The success of the raid was marred somewhat, by 5 allied aircraft crashing on return to England.

21st February 1944.
Weather: Fair. Visibility good. Warmer

Non-Operational Flying: Air Tests and Height and Load tests were carried out.

22nd February 1944.
Weather: Dull. Visibility fair.
Non-Operational Flying: Air Tests, Air/Sea Firing and Height and Load Tests were carried out during the day.
Operational Flying: 20 Aircraft were detailed for Bombing Operations but the effort was cancelled at 18.30 hours.

23rd February 1944.
Weather: Dull and cold. Visibility fair.
Non-Operational Flying: An Air Test and Air/Sea Firing were carried out.
Administration: Wing Commander AJ Samson, DFC resumed command of the Squadron.

24th February 1944.
Weather: Fine and sunny all day.
Non-Operational Flying: Air Tests and 1 detail of Fighter Affiliation were carried out.
Operational Flying: BOMBING – SCHWEINFURT.
21 aircraft were detailed to bomb the target. One returned early and one is missing. The attack was in two phases. 8 took off in the first phase and 13 in the second phase. First phase aircraft reported that markers may have slightly undershot but later were plentiful. Good fires were started and smoke was seen to several thousand feet. Second phase aircraft report seeing fires for 200 miles before reaching target. Target could not be identified because of smoke. There was some heavy flak. The route was considered good.
F/S R Langley in DS842, JI-F reported: Bomb load 1 x 8000 lb bomb. Primary target: SCHWEINFURT. Weather was perfect. Bombed at 2311 hours at 20,000 ft. Saw large explosion to South. Seemed a very good attack. Barrage of HF moderate. Large factory seen to be hit and set on fire by showers of incendiaries.

Combat Reports:
Aircraft: DS816 'H2'
Captain: F/O ICS Hay.
Target: SCHWEINFURT
Just leaving the target (bombs dropped), flying at a height of 20,000 feet, IAS 170. Course 032 degrees T. At 23.15 hours 2 miles north of

Schweinfurt, Mid Upper Gunner saw twin engined aircraft believed to be a Ju88 crossing underneath Lancaster from port bow to starboard beam and fired 1 burst at it for 2 seconds, but no hits were observed. E/A did not alter course and disappeared from view. Visibility was very bad and there were no searchlights, fighter flares or flak.
MU Gunner – Sgt .E Baldwin – 40 rounds.
Rear Gunner – Sgt WH Tate. – Nil.

Aircraft: LL733 'G'
Captain: F/Lt RC Chopping
Target: SCHWEINFURT.
At approx. 0117 hours, 10 miles N.E. Of Schweinfurt, Rear Gunner reported Me210 at 200 yards range slightly up on the starboard fine quarter. Rear Gunner immediately opened fire with a 3 second burst and simultaneously gave order to corkscrew starboard. E/A did not open fire but broke away quickly to port up giving Mid Upper Gunner a chance to get in a good 2 second burst. Rear Gunner saw many strikes on rear portion of fuselage – E/A is claimed as damaged. During combat there was no flak, or searchlights on aircraft or fighter flares, but visibility was excellent.
MU Gunner – F/O HW May – 50 rounds.
Rear Gunner – Sgt PJ Fox RCAF – 150 rounds.

Target:	*Schweinfurt Ball-bearing Factories*
Aircraft deployed total:	*734*
514 Squadron:	*21 (1 returned early)*
Aircraft lost total:	*33*
514 Squadron:	*1*

Comments: Following a USAAF day raid, this night attack formed two waves, with lighter losses to the second. The attack was on ball-bearing factories, still part of the assault on aircraft manufacturing and component production. Of 392 aircraft of the first wave, 22 aircraft were lost, compared to 11 losses of 342 aircraft in the second wave. Crews reported only normal damage, due mainly to under-shoots.

Missing aircraft:

DS785, JI-D. Crashed at 0114 hours at Heidingsfeld, near Würzburg. Cause of crash unknown, but possibly a victim of Lt. Hans Raum, 9./NJG3, who claimed a 4-engined aircraft West of Wurzburg; however it is equally possible that the aircraft was a victim of flak. No survivors from the crew, who are buried in Dürnbach War Cemetery. This was Sgt Kay's second sortie.

F/S A Kay	*Pilot*	*KIA*
Sgt JHD Fenwick	*Navigator*	*KIA*
Sgt JJ McKeown	*Bomb Aimer*	*KIA*
Sgt JP McCormick RCAF	*WOP/Air*	*KIA*
F/S BW Bargquist	*MU Gunner*	*KIA*
Sgt R Harrison	*Rear Gunner*	*KIA*
Sgt EC Marchant	*Flight Engineer*	*KIA*

25th February 1944.
Weather: Fair early. Dull and overcast later.
Non-Operational Flying: Air Tests were carried out during the day.
Operational Flying: BOMBING – AUGSBURG.
21 Aircraft were detailed for Bombing Operations of which 5 failed to take off. 1 returned early and the remainder carried out their duty and (with the exception of 2 which landed at Oakington) returned to Base. The crews of the 2 Aircraft which landed at Oakington returned by coach to Base. Crews report several fires and black smoke over the target.
F/O JR Laing in DS842, JI-F reported: Bomb load 1 x 8000 lb bomb, 8 x 30, 90 x 4 incendiaries. Primary target: AUGSBURG. Weather, thin patchy cloud. Bombed at 0127 hours at 19,000 ft. Northern part of target solid mass of fire. Monica u/s. Route very good. Pretty good effort. Total S/Ls (searchlights) about 60, mostly S and N of the target. Solid concentration of fires seen from 200 miles.

Combat Report:
Aircraft: LL733 'G'
Captain: F/Lt RC Chopping.
Target: AUGSBURG
1st Encounter: At 2321 hours in the Aachen area, Engineer reported unidentified aircraft on the starboard quarter down. A few seconds later Rear Gunner reported an Me109 on the starboard quarter up at a range of 350 yards, and on the point of making an attack. He immediately ordered Pilot to corkscrew to starboard and opened fire at the same time with a burst lasting 2 seconds, followed by Mid Upper with a 2-3 second burst as E/A broke away on the port quarter up. Rear Gunner saw many strikes on the port wing of E/A which did not return

Lancaster's fire. Visibility was good. There was no flak or searchlights or fighter flares during encounter.

2nd Encounter: At 0040 hours Lancaster, which was a few minutes early was orbiting 20 miles N/E Friedrichshafen, when Rear Gunner reported a Ju88 on the port quarter down at a range of 500 yards. E/A which was flying a parallel course apparently had not spotted Lancaster. Rear Gunner taking deliberate aim opened fire holding it for 3-4 seconds, and ordered Pilot to corkscrew to port. E/A quickly increased speed pulling ahead to the beam and disappeared below without returning Lancaster's fire. His were seen on E/A which is claimed as damaged. Visibility was very good with 3 large groups of searchlights in the target area, but no fighter flares or flak.

3rd Encounter: - At 0222 hours 12 Miles N/E of St. Dieder, on course of 297 degrees, at 20.000 feet, IAS 160., homeward bound, bombs dropped, Rear Gunner reported a single engined aircraft recognised as an Me109 on the port quarter up, range 400 yards, just about to commence an attack. He immediately gave order to corkscrew to port and opened fire with a burst lasting 3 seconds. Hits were seen on E/A which did not fire but attempted to break away astern and was thrown over on its back apparently out of control as it passed through Lancaster's slip-stream. Mid Upper Gunner, who was waiting for break away, saw another Me109 at a range of 30 yards on the port quarter up, closing in to attack. Lancaster was still corkscrewing, and Mid Upper Gunner opened fire immediately holding it for 3 seconds. E/A did not fire as the Gunner saw both E/A quickly break away and almost colliding in their efforts to avoid accurate fire from the Lancaster. Visibility was good. There was no flak, searchlights or fighter flares. In the 3 encounters Lancaster was not fired at and the E/A were unable to press home their attacks. All attacks were proceeded by a 'Monica' warning.

MU Gunner – F/O HW May – 150 rounds.
Rear Gunner – Sgt PJ Fox RCAF – 400 rounds

Target: *Augsburg–Aircraft Component Manufacturing*
Aircraft deployed total: 594
514 Squadron: 16 (1 returned early).
Aircraft lost total: 21
514 Squadron: Nil

Comments: Again the stream split into two, which proved successful as losses were considered relatively low. Bombing caused the damage or destruction of approximately 8000 buildings and nearly 90 000 people became suddenly homeless. A successful raid in which again, important infrastructure was damaged or destroyed including the MAN engineering company's buildings and an aircraft component factory. Artwork estimated to be worth approximately £80 million was also believed destroyed in civic buildings.

26th February 1944.
Weather: Dull and overcast.
Non-Operational Flying: 'C' Flight carried out an Air Test and Air/Sea Firing, otherwise no flying took place.

27th February 1944.
Weather: Dull and overcast. Visibility very poor.
Non-Operational Flying: The Aircraft that landed at Oakington after Operations on the night of 25/26th. February, 1944 was collected and brought back to Base. No other flying took place
Ground Training: A lecture on Engine Handling was given to Pilots and Engineers in the morning by Squadron Leader A.L. Roberts. Another lecture (with Epidiascope Slides) on P.F.F. Target Indication Methods was given to Aircrews in the morning by Squadron Leader W.E. Clarkson, Senior Station Intelligence Officer.

28 February 1944.
Weather: Fine and sunny early. Overcast later with snowstorms.
Non-Operational Flying: Air Tests were carried out.
Operational Flying: 22 Aircraft were detailed for Bombing Operations which were cancelled at 18.30 hours.

29 February 1944.
Weather: Fine and sunny.
Non-Operational Flying: Air Tests, Local Practices, Formation Practices and 8 details of Fighter Affiliation were carried out.
The Squadron Bombing Competition was won by Pilot Officer G.S. Hughes, DFC and crew who collect the prize.
Visits: A visit was paid to the Squadron by Mr. L. Taylor the Press Representative of the A.T.C. Gazette and Mr. W.S. Masters, Public Relations Officer (A.T.C.) Air Ministry, with particular regard to the Flight Engineers.

Monthly Summary for February 1944

Operational: (Compiled by F/Lt. JN Pollock.)

Enemy Aircraft Destroyed:	Nil
Enemy Aircraft Damaged:	4
Operational Flying Hours for February 1944:	584.20
Non-Operational Flying Hours for February 1944:	283.50
Total tons of bombs dropped in February 1944:	260
Cumulative tons of bombs dropped:	920
Number of Sorties for February 1944:	86

Strength of Squadron as at 29th February 1944.

Aircrew: 60 Officers
271 SNCOs

Ground: 3 Officers
34 SNCOs
315 other ranks
(including 12 WAAFs)

March 1944

1st March 1944.
Weather: Fine and sunny. Cold Wind.
Non-Operational Flying: Air Tests were carried out.
Movements: Flight Lieutenant H. Hall, DFC, Squadron Engineer Leader returned from his Engineering Course.
Awards: The immediate award of the DFC to Flying Officer L. Greenburgh was promulgated for his conduct on the night of 29/30th December 1943, when his Aircraft was 'ditched' during an Operational Flight.
Operational Flying: BOMBING – STUTTGART.
22 aircraft were detailed to bomb the target, one was withdrawn and three returned early. Weather was 10/10ths in the target area and on most of the route. Reports vary as to markers accuracy, but it is not the general opinion that this raid was an unqualified success. However the route was liked and more or less trouble free, fighters being few and far between.
F/O GS Hughes in LL733, JI-G reported: Bomb load 1 x 8000 lb. bomb, 8 x 30, 90 x 4 incendiaries. Primary target: STUTTGART. There was 10/10 cloud. Bombed at 0309 hours at 20,000 ft. Glows seen from wide area as aircraft was leaving.

Target:	*Stuttgart Area*
Aircraft deployed total:	*557*
514 Squadron:	*21 (3 returned early)*
Aircraft lost total:	*4*
514 Squadron:	*Nil*

Comments: A change of fortune as this time heavy cloud cover hampered enemy defences and allied losses were very few (only 4). Despite the thick cloud, the bombing effort was considered reasonably effective with the destruction of many houses and key industrial Infrastructure including the Daimler-Benz and Bosch factories.

2nd March 1944.
Weather: Fine and sunny.
Non-Operational Flying: Air Tests and Bombing Practices were carried out.

3rd March 1944.
Weather: Fine and sunny. Very cold with strong wind.
Ground Training: Flight Lieutenant R. Thompson, DFC, Squadron Signals Leader gave a talk to Station Operations Watchkeepers on Operational Signals procedure.
Non-Operational Flying: Air Tests, Air/Sea Firing, Bombing Practices and Local Flying took place and 2 crews took part in a 'Bullseye' Exercise. 8 details of Fighter Affiliation were carried out.

4th March 1944.
Weather: Fine and sunny. Cold wind.
Non-Operational Flying: Bombing Practices were carried out and 14 details of Fighter Affiliation.

5th March 1944.
Weather: Fine and sunny
Ground Training: Clay Pigeon Shooting for Air Gunners and others took place in the afternoon. Flight Lieutenant R. Thompson DFC Squadron Signals Leader gave another talk to Squadron Operational Watchkeepers on Operational Signals procedure.
Non-Operational Flying: Local Practices, Cross Countries, Air/Sea Firing and Night Bombing Practices were carried out, and 4 details of Fighter Affiliation.

6th March 1944.
Weather: Fine and sunny all day. Much warmer.
Non-Operational Flying: Air Tests, Bombing and Local Practices and 6 details of Fighter Affiliation were carried out.

7th March 1944.
Weather: Fine and sunny.
Non-Operational Flying: Air Tests were carried out.
Operational Flying: BOMBING – LE MANS.
Eighteen aircraft were detailed to bomb the target. All aircraft took off and returned to Base. 10/10ths cloud prevented visual identification of the target and made assessment of the attack difficult. A few markers were seen and a glow of fires could be seen on the clouds. One large explosion was reported at 2159hours. About 6 HF guns were reported and a little tracer was seen in the target area.
P/O NW Thackray RAAF in LL734 JI-U reported: Bomb load 10 x 1000, 4 x 500 lb bombs. Primary target: LE MANS. There was 10/10 cloud with tops 6000 feet. Gee fix and fires reflected through cloud.

Bombed at 2159 hours from 13,000 ft. Large explosions seen from own bombs. Orange glows seen and occasional bombs bursting.

Target:	*Le Mans Railway Yards*
Aircraft deployed total:	*304*
514 Squadron:	*17*
Aircraft lost total:	*Nil*
514 Squadron:	*Nil*

Comments: The stream concentrated its bombing on the railway yards with overall success. Despite prior planning and the best efforts of crews, a few bombs fell outside the railway yards and 31 French residents were unfortunately killed. No aircraft were lost on this mission.

8th March 1944.
Weather: Fine and sunny. Overcast later.
Non-Operational Flying: Air Tests were carried out.
Recreation: A very successful party and sing-song was given in the evening by all Air Aircrews to the Ground Crews in the Briefing Room.

9th March 1944.
Weather: Overcast. Fine periods.
Non-Operational Flying: 2 'Eric' Exercises were carried out.
Visits: Flight Lieutenant T. Angus, DFC, Squadron Bombing Leader and Flight Lieutenant G. Greenfield, Station Armament Officer proceeded to Watford to inspect construction of Mk. XIV Bomb Sights.

10th March 1944.
Weather: Overcast. Poor visibility.
Non-Operational Flying: Air Tests, SBAs, Height and Load Tests and Air/Sea Firing were carried out and 4 'Bullseyes'.
Operational Flying: 21 Aircraft were detailed for Bombing Operations, but the effort was cancelled at 12.30 hours.
Awards: The immediate award of the DFC to Pilot Officer JM Hydes, Wireless Operator/Air, for his conduct on the night of 24/25th February, 1944, when putting out incendiaries in an Aircraft during an Operational Sortie, was promulgated.

11th March 1944.
Weather: Clear and sunny.
Non-Operational Flying: Air Tests, Air/Sea Firing, Practice Bombing, Height and Load Test and 8 details of Fighter Affiliation were carried out.

12th March 1944.
Weather: Overcast. Visibility very poor.
Non-Operational Flying: Physical Training was given to Aircrew personnel in the morning.
Operational Flying: No flying took place. There was a stand-down in the afternoon.

13th March 1944.
Weather: Sunny, some cloud and fairly strong wind.
Non-Operational Flying: Air Tests, Air/Sea and Air/Ground Firing were carried out. 1 Aircraft took off for Photography and Photo-Flash Test with Flight Lieutenant T. Angus. DFC, Squadron Bombing Leader, Flying Officer J. Nicol, Squadron Armament Officer and Sergeant J Bishop of the Photography Section on board. Unfortunately, heavy shower clouds prevented experiments being carried out at Rushford Bombing Range.

14th March 1944.
Weather: Cloudy early but clear later. Slight wind.
Non-Operational Flying: Air Tests, Air/Sea and Air/Ground Firing and Height and Load Tests were carried out.
Recreation: A sports program for Aircrew Personnel was arranged for the afternoon.

15th March 1944.
Weather: Clear with little cloud and some slight haze.
Non-Operational Flying: Air Tests and Air/Sea Firing were carried out.
Operational Flying: BOMBING – STUTTGART.
23 Aircraft were detailed for Bombing Operations. All took off but 1 returned early. 1 Aircraft failed to return, 2 landed at Newmarket and the remainder returned to base. Sergeant JJ McNeill, Mid Upper Gunner, was killed by enemy action.
F/S JB Underwood in DS786, A2-F reported: Bomb load 10 x 1000 lb. bomb, 1050 x 4, 90 x 4 incendiaries. Primary target: STUTTGART. There was 5/10 thin cloud. Bombed at 2321 hours at 16,000 ft. There was a good concentration of Tis, red and green with fires around. Port

outer engine airscrew blades and exhaust manifold wiped off in collision with FW190. Cannon shell through rear turret. We were attacked by FW190.

Combat Report:
Aircraft: DS786 'F2'
Captain: F/S JB Underwood
Target: STUTTGART
At 2320 hours a few seconds before dropping bombs, Rear Gunner reported an FW190 on the fine port quarter level at a range of 300 yards. E/An opened fire at Lancaster and Rear Gunner returned it with a 4 second burst and ordered Pilot to corkscrew to port. E/A closed in almost dead astern slightly up within 30 yards and Mid Upper Gunner firing between the fire, gave it a burst lasting 1-2 seconds. Many hits were seen on E/A which at this stage was within a few yards of the tail and tried to break away underneath, and in the attempt, collided with Lancaster carrying away most of the air-screw and exhaust manifold on the port outer engine. The Bomb Aimer was the last to see it spiralling down out of control on the starboard bow. The E/A is claimed as destroyed. During encounter there was no flak or searchlights but a few fighter flares in the vicinity. Visibility was good. On examination later it was found that Lancaster had sustained severe damage on port side and round rear turret due to a cannon shell. Parts of the E/A airscrew and Perspex cockpit were found embedded in the engine nacelles on the port side.
MU Gunner – Sgt Sime – 50 rounds.
Rear Gunner – Sgt John – 240 rounds

'Nachtjagd War Diaries' records: One Wild Boar attacked a 514 Squadron Lancaster at 2330 hours at 20000 feet over Stuttgart. The German pilot opened fire on the Lancaster from the port quarter level at a range of 300 yards. Both the Lancaster's gunners returned fire, and hits were registered on the fighter, which they identified as an FW190. The FW190's aim, however, was also accurate, the Lancaster receiving numerous strikes. So determined was the attack that the German pilot collided with the Lancaster resulting in damage to the rear turret and port rudder, and wrecking the port outer engine. On the Lancaster's return, part of the fighter's canopy Perspex and fuselage was found embedded in the engine. The crew reported the German fighter as destroyed. The incident probably concerns the loss of Ofw. Fritz Nimmisch of 1./JG300, who was killed flying an Me109 G-6 near Boblingen and which was the only Wild Boar loss that was

reported (other than a second 1./JG300 pilot who was injured by 'friendly' Flak fire).

P/O EA Greenwood RCAF in DS813, JI-H reported: Bomb load 1 x 1000 lb. bomb, 1050 x 4, 90 x 4, 64 x 30 incendiaries. Primary target: STUTTGART. There was 7/10 cloud. Bombed at 2329 hours from 20,000 feet. Many fires burning when we left. Mid Upper turret blown off. Attacked over Stuttgart by enemy aircraft resulting in death of Mid Upper Gunner.

Combat Report:
Aircraft: DS813 'H'
Captain: P/O E.A Greenwood RCAF
Target: STUTTGART
At 2328 hours approx. 1 minute before dropping bombs, trace was observed passing close to Lancaster on the starboard side. Immediately after this, Rear Gunner saw return fire from Mid Upper Gunner who had not given the Pilot a combat manoeuvre, presumably through lack of time in dealing with the E/A. The Pilot however, started corkscrewing to starboard. At this stage Rear Gunner reported an Me109 (with green under surface) on the port quarter up and gave it a burst lasting 1-2 seconds as it was banking steeply to break away. Hits were observed as it broke off the attack and it was last seen flying away on the port quarter with smoke coming from its engine. Immediately after E/A had fired at Lancaster, the Navigator in his compartment saw a brilliant purple flash from the Mid Upper turret. As no response had come from Mid Upper Gunner to numerous enquiries, the Wireless Operator and Engineer proceeded to the turret to render assistance, and found the Gunner had been killed instantly by the burst of fire from E/A. Numerous attempts were made to extricate him, but without success. Visibility was good due to light from the target. There was no flak, searchlights or aircraft during this encounter. Lancaster sustained damage to the Mid Upper Turret, round the astro-dome and the main spar.
MU Gunner – Sgt McNeill - KIA
Rear Gunner – P/O Bourne – 100 rounds.

Aircraft: DS820 'A'
Captain: F/O PJK Hood
Target: STUTTGART
At 2314 hours approx. 15 miles South of Stuttgart Rear Gunner reported an FW190 at a range of 500 yards almost dead astern slightly

down. E/A which was silhouetted against light from the ground seemed to be preparing for attack. Immediately after this had been reported Lancaster was fired at by an E/A on the starboard full quarter which was spotted and recognised by Rear Gunner as Ju88 at a range of about 100 yards. He immediately gave the order for corkscrew to starboard and opened fire with a burst lasting 4 seconds. Hits were observed near cockpit of E/A which was last seen diving steeply through the clouds. The FW190 did not make an attack. Lancaster suffered no damage. At the time of encounter visibility was good. There was no flak, fighter flares or S/Ls.
MU Gunner – Sgt CDF McKenzie – Nil
Rear Gunner – Tech/Sgt MC Lanthier USAAF – 300 rounds.

Target: *Stuttgart Area.*
Aircraft deployed total: *863*
514 Squadron: *23 (1 returned early)*
Aircraft lost total: *37*
514 Squadron: *1*
Comments: After heading towards Switzerland, the stream turned for Stuttgart. This diversionary tactic worked somewhat, delaying the night fighter attack until just before the target. Pathfinder markings fell short, possibly because of strong winds, resulting in a scattered attack.

Missing aircraft:
LL653, JI-E. Probably shot down by a night fighter flown by Hptm. Eckart-Wilhelm von Bonin, Stab II./NJG1, exploding and crashing between Blondefontaine and Villars-le-Pautel. No survivors from the crew, who are buried in Villars-le-Pautel Communal Cemetery.

F/O K Penkuri RCAF	*Pilot*	*KIA*
F/S K Drummond RNZAF	*(2nd Pilot)*	*KIA*
W/O LA Wry RCAF	*Navigator*	*KIA*
Sgt DJ Kilner	*Bomb Aimer*	*KIA*
Sgt TY Owen	*WOP/Air*	*KIA*
Sgt KE Peake	*MU Gunner*	*KIA*
Sgt WF Sutherland RCAF	*Rear Gunner*	*KIA*
Sgt G Cosgrove	*Flight Engineer*	*KIA*

(Above) P/O Kaiho Penkuri at Sywell, showing off a pair of flying boots, after arriving from his native Canada. Source: Jerome Thibault.

16th March 1944.
Weather: Overcast.
Non-Operational Flying: Air Tests and Air/Sea Rescue were carried out.
Operational Flying: 19 Aircraft were detailed for Bombing Operations, but the effort was cancelled just before take-off.

17th March 1944.
Weather: Foggy, clearing towards noon.
Non-Operational Flying: In the afternoon Air Tests and Cross Countries were carried out, and a number of Flapless Landing Practices

at Woodbridge, on which 1 Aircraft crashed but without casualties.
Note: In fact, it appears that two aircraft crashed.
DS820, JI-R, flown by F/S Shearing, crash-landed at Martlesham Heath.
LL669, JI-S, flown by F/S CJ Medland, crash-landed at Woodbridge.

18th March 1944.
Weather: Fair and sunny. Cloudy later.
Non-Operational Flying: Air Tests were carried out.
Operational Flying: BOMBING – FRANKFURT.
19 aircraft were detailed to bomb the target. 2 were withdrawn, 3 returned early and the remainder (with the exception of 1 which landed at Newmarket) returned to Base after completion of the duty. Green TIs were dropped as being well concentrated, but fires appeared to have been rather scattered. Some explosions were reported. Flak was moderate, S/Ls were numerous.
F/L CW Nichol in LL703, JI-L reported: Bomb load 1 x 4000 lb. bomb, 1350 x 4, 90 x 4, 32 x 30 incendiaries. Primary target: FRANKFURT. Weather, wispy cloud much haze. Bombed at 2205 hours from 20,000 ft. Some fires seen coinciding with position of Red Tis. Cookies seen bursting in area. Built up area seen. Aircraft arrived early and orbited waiting for the markers. Route OK.

Combat Report:
Aircraft: LL727 'C2'
Captain: F/O L Greenburgh
Target: FRANKFURT
Outward bound (bombs not dropped), flying at 18,000 feet. At 23.50 hours Rear Gunner reported unidentified twin engined aircraft on starboard quarter up at a range of 800 yards. Enemy persisted in following Lancaster in same position and at same range for considerable time. Mid Upper Gunner and Rear Gunner finally fired 2 or 3 short bursts each at E/A and Rear Gunner gave order to corkscrew to starboard. Enemy aircraft which did not open fire was lost in the corkscrew and not seen again. Visibility was poor. Numerous fighter flares were in evidence but no searchlights or flak directed at Lancaster. No 'Monica' warning.
MU Gunner – Sgt RJ Woosnam – 200 rounds.
Rear Gunner – F/S CA Drake RAAF – 400 rounds.

Target: Frankfurt Area
Aircraft deployed total: 864
514 Squadron: 17 (2 returned early)
Aircraft lost total: 22
514 Squadron: Nil

Comments: Tactics helped the allies again and the night fighters were split. Pathfinders marked the target accurately and extreme damage to most of the city was the result. Nearly 100 industrial buildings and 5500 homes were destroyed.

19th March 1944.
Weather: Fine and sunny.
Non-Operational Flying: Air Tests, Height and Load Tests and Cross Country were carried out.
Movements: Flight Lieutenant JN Pollock, Squadron Gunnery Leader proceeded on a Night Vision Course at Upper Heyford.
Operational Flying: 19 Aircraft were detailed for Bombing Operations, but the effort was cancelled.
20th March 1944.
Weather: Overcast. Visibility fair.
Non-Operational Flying: Air Tests and Height and Load Tests were carried out.
Operational Flying: 21 Aircraft were detailed for Bombing Operations, but the effort was cancelled.

21st March 1944.
Weather: Overcast, visibility fair.
Non-Operational Flying: Air Tests were carried out.
Operational Flying: 23 Aircraft were detailed for Bombing Operations, but the effort was cancelled at 1915 hours.

22nd March 1944.
Weather: Fine and sunny.
Non-Operational Flying: Air Tests were carried out.
Operational Flying: BOMBING – FRANKFURT.
22 aircraft were detailed to bomb the target. 1 returned early and 2 are missing. 1 landed at Mildenhall badly damaged (with 2 Gunners killed and 2 of the Crew having abandoned Aircraft). Sergeant B.P. Le Neve Foster, Flight Engineer (LL645, JI-R) was killed by Flak. Sergeant L.H.D. Warren, Mid Upper Gunner and Sergeant L.D. Blackford (both LL703, JI-L) were killed by fire from enemy aircraft. The target was

covered by a broken layer of thin cloud but the PFF are reported as being good and TIs were well concentrated. Many crews were able to identify the river main and some ground detail. Bombing was concentrated and good fires have been reported. The glow of fires could be seen from 200 miles.

F/S PM Ashpitel in DS822, JI-T, reported: Bomb load 1 x 1000 lb. bomb, 64 x 30, 1161 x 4, 129 x 4 incendiaries. Primary target: FRANKFURT. There was 5/10 thin cloud. Bombed at 2154 hours from 19,000 ft. 2 incendiaries from another aircraft fell into Mid Upper Turret, severing oxygen mask of Mid Upper Gunner (F/O HC Bryant). There were many S/Ls. Wireless Operator counted 127.

F/S CF Prowles in DS826, JI-L reported: Bomb Load 1 x 2000 lb. Bomb, 1050 x 4 lb incendiaries. Primary Target: DÜSSELDORF. There was no cloud. Bombed at 0121 hours from 19,000 feet. Many fires seen surrounding the TIs. Very good attack. Searchlights numerous, accurate flak, too accurate for comfort. Route good. Large explosion seen 0138 hours.

F/S BW Windsor RNZAF in LL703, JI-L, reported: Bomb load 1 x 1000 lb. bomb, 64 x 30, 1161 x 4, 129 x 4 incendiaries. No attack. Attacked by fighter. 2 long bursts from level astern, Rear Gunner fired and said 'Dive', went into almost vertical dive, when 2nd burst from fighter killed Rear Gunner (Sgt LD Blackford) and Mid Upper Gunner (Sgt LHD Warren) setting fire to aircraft in bomb bay. Bombs jettisoned. Bomb Aimer and Navigator baled out after orders.

Combat Reports:
Aircraft: LL703 'L'
Captain: F/S BW Windsor RNZAF
Target: FRANKFURT

At 2205 hours and without warning from the oral Monica, Engineer suddenly saw trace coming over the 'glasshouse' from dead astern and the Rear Gunner was heard to order the Pilot to dive. During the dive, which became uncontrolled (due to damage caused to elevators by E/A fire) a very long burst of fire was heard from the rear turret, but it transpired that both Gunners must have been killed instantaneously by E/A burst of fire and presumably the Rear Gunners grip was still on the controls. The Pilot with the assistance of the Engineer resumed control of the aircraft, but meanwhile the Bomb Aimer and Navigator had 'Baled Out' on Captain's orders.
MU Gunner – Sgt LHD Warren – KIA
Rear Gunner – Sgt LD Blackford - KIA

Aircraft: LL728 'B'
Captain: F/S JG Hudson RNZAF
Target: FRANKFURT
Homeward bound (bombs dropped), flying on a course of 333 degrees T, IAS 160, height 20,000 feet. At 2217.hours when 10 miles South of Luxembourg, Mid Upper Gunner reported unidentified twin engined aircraft on the starboard beam slightly up at a range of approximately 400-500 yards apparently closing in to attack. Mid Upper Gunner immediately opened fire with a short burst of about 1 second and gave order to corkscrew to starboard. E/A was lost to view as soon as corkscrew was commenced and was not seen again. E/A which was not seen by any other member of the crew, and upon which, no hits were observed, did not fire on Lancaster.
No searchlights, flak or fighter flares were in evidence at the time. Visibility was fair with bright starlight.
MU Gunner – Sgt CA Campbell RCAF – 50 rounds
Rear Gunner – Sgt WL Granbois RCAF - Nil.

Aircraft: LL727 'C2'
Captain: F/O L Greenburgh.
Target: FRANKFURT
Homeward bound (bombs dropped), flying at 19,000 feet. At 2220 hours, after 'Monica' warning, Rear Gunner reported a Ju88 on port quarter level at range of 800-900 yards. E/A followed Lancaster in this position and range for 2 to 3 minutes dropping a number of flares and firing 2 bursts at Lancaster, the trace passing close to tailplane. Rear Gunner gave order to corkscrew to port and further trace was observed during this manoeuvre, but not near Lancaster. After 2 or 3 minutes of violent evasive action E/A was lost to view and was not seen again. Neither the Lancaster's Gunners replied to E/As fire as it never approached within effective range.
Visibility was very good. No flak or searchlights directed at Lancaster.
MU Gunner – Sgt FJ Carey. – Nil.
Rear Gunner – F/Sgt CA Drake RAAF – Nil.

Aircraft: LL620 'G2'
Captain: F/S JB Topham.
Target: FRANKFURT.
1st Encounter: Outward bound (bombs not dropped), flying at 20,000 feet. At 21.40 hours in position 15 miles N of Marburg, Mid Upper Gunner saw and reported an FW190 on starboard quarter up at range of 150 yards. Mid Upper Gunner gave order to corkscrew to starboard and

opened fire with a short burst as E/A broke away underneath. There were no searchlights, flak or fighter flares.

2nd Encounter: At 21.50 hours in position 25 miles North of Frankfurt at 20,000 feet, Mid Upper Gunner reported a Ju88 on port quarter up, range 150 yards. Mid Upper Gunner ordered corkscrew to starboard and opened fire on E/A with short bursts as it broke away to starboard quarter up. There were some searchlights and fighter flares but no flak.

3rd Encounter: At 21.58 hours on bombing run over target, just about to bomb, Flight Engineer saw a fighter flare very close to the starboard beam up and then a single engined unidentified aircraft lit up by it. He immediately gave order to corkscrew to starboard and Mid Upper Gunner fired a short burst at E/A as it broke away below Lancaster. 'Monica' warning of E/As approach was given in each case. Enemy did not open fire in any of the 3 cases.

MU Gunner – Sgt J Scully – 500 rounds.
Rear Gunner – Sgt P Anstey – Nil

Aircraft: LL698 'J2'
Captain: F/S CJ Johnson.
Target: FRANKFURT

1st Encounter: Outward bound (bombs not dropped), flying on a course of 185 degrees M, IAS 170, height 20,000 feet. At 21.47 hours when in position 5054N. 0845E Mid Upper Gunner reported an FW190 on port fine quarter up at a range of approximately 300 yards coming in on curve of pursuit, and immediately gave order to corkscrew to port when E/A was quickly lost to view and was not seen again. No fire was exchanged.

2nd Encounter: At 21.52 hours still outward bound in position 5038 N. 0845E. On same course height and speed, Mid Upper Gunner saw an unidentified twin engined aircraft on starboard quarter level at range of 400 yards in attacking position with Lancaster silhouetted against glare of target and fighter flares, and gave order to corkscrew to starboard. Immediately after commencement of this manoeuvre, E/A fired what appeared to be 2 rocket projectiles at Lancaster which passed fairly close underneath. Mid Upper Gunner and Rear Gunner attempted to reply but all guns were apparently frozen up and Mid Upper Gunner could only get in a 2 second burst and Rear Gunner could only fire 1 round from each of the 4 guns. Meanwhile, E/A followed Lancaster through 2 complete corkscrews but without firing and broke away underneath, climbing to port bow up where it was finally lost to view. No searchlights but some flak and numerous fighter flares were in evidence.

3rd Encounter: At 21.57 hours still outward bound in position 5018N. 0835E on same course, height and speed, both Gunners saw simultaneously an unidentified twin engined aircraft on port beam slightly up coming in to attack. Mid Upper Gunner gave order to corkscrew to port and both Gunners attempted to open fire but unsuccessfully except for 1 very short burst in case of the Mid Upper Gunner. E/A which did not open fire, was lost to view almost immediately after commencement of corkscrew and was not seen again. No searchlights were visible through the glare of the target, but there were numerous fighter flares and some flak.

MU Gunner – Sgt J Poad – 30 rounds
Rear Gunner – Sgt RA Dymott RCAF - 4 rounds.

Target: *Frankfurt Area*
Aircraft deployed total: *816*
514 Squadron: *22 (1 returned early)*
Aircraft lost total: *33*
514 Squadron: *2 aircraft plus 2 Gunners (LL703, JI-R) and 1 Flight Engineer (LL645, JI-R)*

Comments: Diversionary tactics were again successful, the Germans mistaking Hannover as the target. TIs were accurate and damage to the city was even worse than the previous raid. Many Nazi Party buildings were destroyed. The three raids on Frankfurt, added to the raids of the Americans, led to the city being almost obliterated.

Missing aircraft:

DS815, JI-N. Intercepted on return leg at 0015 hours by night-fighter flown by Hptm. Ludwig Meister of 1./NJG4, which opened fire, killing F/S Elliott and injuring F/O Deans. On fire and with port engines faltering, F/L Nichol skilfully landed the aircraft 400 metres west of la Californie (Pas de Calais).

F/L CW Nichol	*Pilot*	*POW*
Sgt PS Hoare	*Navigator*	*POW*
F/O KD Deans	*Bomb Aimer*	*POW*
F/S AJ Elliott	*WOP/Air*	*KIA*
F/S AV Jackson	*MU Gunner*	*Evaded*
Sgt GC Fearman	*Rear Gunner*	*Evaded*
Sgt F Townshend	*Flight Engineer*	*POW*

LL684, A2-B. Shot down at 2130 hours by a Ju88 flown by Oblt. Heinz Rökker of 2./NJG2. The aircraft crashed 8 km SE of Emmen, Holland.

F/S T JB Underwood	Pilot	KIA
F/O IJF Rich	Navigator	KIA
F/O WD McPhee RCAF	Bomb Aimer	POW
Sgt RJ Day	WOP/Air	KIA
Sgt RC Sime RCAF	MU Gunner	POW
Sgt H John	Rear Gunner	KIA
Sgt AW Johnson	Flight Engineer	KIA

23rd March 1944.
Weather: Overcast.
Non-Operational Flying: Navigation Exercises and an 'Eric' Exercise were carried out.
Operational Flying: There was a Squadron stand-down for Aircrew in the afternoon.

24th March 1944.
Weather: Overcast. Clear later.
Non-Operational Flying: Air Tests were carried out.
Operational Flying: BOMBING – BERLIN.
Nineteen aircraft were detailed to bomb the target. One returned early and one is missing. The remainder carried out their mission and returned to Base. Sergeant L Moorhouse, Mid Upper Gunner (LL738, JI-D) was wounded by fire from enemy aircraft. There was 5-8/10 cloud over the target and winds were stronger than anticipated. The attack is believed to have been rather scattered.
F/O L Greenburgh in LL727, A2-C reported: Bomb load 1 x 8000 lb. bomb. Primary target: BERLIN. There was 7-8/10 cloud over the target. Bombed at 2230 hours from 20,000 feet. Medium concentration of fires seen. Caught in searchlights over Denmark. Attacked by Ju88. Engineer and Bomb Aimer baled out after orders.

Combat Report:
Aircraft: LL727 'C2'
Captain: F/O L Greenburgh
Target: BERLIN
On the night of 24th March 1944, Lancaster II 'C2' of 514 Squadron was homeward bound, bombs dropped flying 20000 feet on a course 217 deg, IAS 175. At 2235 hours approx. 15 miles south of target Mid Upper Gunner reported a Ju88 on the starboard quarter down 300 yards

range closing in to attack. He immediately gave order to corkscrew starboard opening fire with 3 short bursts followed by Rear Gunner with 2 bursts. E/A opened fire almost simultaneously with 2 or 3 bursts and quickly broke away to port up and was soon lost to view. No Claim. Lancaster sustained no damage.

2nd Encounter: - At 2237 hours on the same heading Rear Gunner reported Ju88 on the port quarter up at 400 yards range coming in quickly. He gave E/A a 2 second burst followed by Mid Upper Gunner with 4 short bursts and ordered corkscrew to port. E/A fired a series of long bursts during encounter but Lancaster suffered no damage. Mid Upper Gunner saw strikes on centre section of E/A. No claims. No flak, searchlights or fighter flares were seen.

3rd Encounter: - At 2245 hours Engineer reported aircraft making an attack from starboard bow down and immediately ordered Pilot to corkscrew to starboard. As Lancaster made first part of manoeuvre by diving to starboard E/A fired a burst putting Lancaster's starboard engine out of action causing aircraft to turn over into a vicious spiral and it became uncontrollable. All the instruments were completely unserviceable and aircraft was losing height rapidly, completely out of control. At 10,000 feet Pilot gave order to abandon aircraft. The Engineer and Bomb Aimer jumped immediately and the Pilot was half way out of his seat but decided to have another attempt to control aircraft when he realised that the Navigator's chute had been thrown out of the Escape Hatch during the spin, and at about 7,000 feet managed to get aircraft on more or less an even keel. At 9,000 feet Lancaster returned to base and Pilot made a safe landing. The Mid Upper Gunner and Wireless Operator were standing by the Rear Hatch almost on the point of jumping when they realised that the aircraft was now by this time under control and returned to their posts. E/A was lost after the Lancaster started spinning and Gunners were unable to get any shots at it. Visual Monica gave warning of approach of E/A on all astern attacks but not from the bow. The Monica caught fire during the spin. No flak was directed at the aircraft, but there were some searchlights and fighter flares in the vicinity. Visibility was very good.

MU Gunner – Sgt PJ Carey – 200 rounds.
Rear Gunner – F/S CA Drake RAAF – 350 rounds

Aircraft: LL738 'D'
Captain: P/O GS Hughes RAAF DFC
Target: BERLIN
On the night of 24 / 25th March, 1944 Lancaster 'D' of 514 Squadron was on the bombing run, bombs not dropped. At 2239 hours over

Berlin proper both Gunners reported a fighter flare on fine starboard quarter slightly up about 200 yards away. Instantaneously Pilot commenced to corkscrew in this direction, and at the same moment, trace appeared coming towards Lancaster from behind the flare seriously wounding the Mid Upper Gunner in the arm. Rear Gunner and Mid Upper Gunner (The latter manipulating his turret and guns with one hand) immediately opened fire in the direction of the trace and continued firing as a Ju88 became visible trying to press home an attack and finally breaking away above Lancaster. Since this encounter the crew of this aircraft (with the exception of the Mid Upper Gunner, now in Hospital) are unfortunately missing after an Operational Sortie.
MU Gunner – Sgt L Moorhouse – 120 rounds.
Rear Gunner – Sgt GH Thornton. – 400 rounds.

Aircraft: LL697 'E'
Captain: F/S NR Wishart.
Target: BERLIN
Homeward bound (bombs dropped), flying at 20,000 feet, on a course of 325 degrees, IAS 165. At 23.05 hours in a position 51.40N 10.00E. Engineer reported a single engined aircraft flying above from the starboard bow to the port quarter and ordered Pilot to commence a corkscrew manoeuvre to starboard, as he gave it a burst lasting 2 seconds. It (E/A) was last seen flying away on the port quarter without altering course or firing at Lancaster. No claims. Visibility was good. No flak or fighter flares, but just prior to encounter 1 searchlight had been indicating Lancaster's course.
MU Gunner – Sgt TJ Saint – 70 rounds.
Rear Gunner – Sgt F Fairbrass – Nil.

Aircraft: LL670 'K2'
Captain: P/O E Protheroe
Target: BERLIN
1st Encounter: Flying on a course of 035 degrees T. IAS 190, height 18,000 feet. At 22.45 hours Mid Upper Gunner saw and reported a single engined aircraft believed to be an FW190 on starboard beam up at range of 250 yards, and ordered corkscrew to starboard at the same time opening fire with a burst of 3 to 4 seconds on E/A. E/A did not return fire and broke away to starboard quarter down and was not seen again. Visibility was good and there were no searchlights, flak or fighter flares.
2nd Encounter: At 00.04 hours homeward bound with bombs dropped, flying on a course of 300 degrees T. IAS 180, height 17,000 feet,

Lancaster had been coned by searchlights for about 7 minutes and had just cleared searchlights by evasive action, when Rear Gunner saw and reported Me109 in the beam of searchlight on port quarter up at range of 700 yards, coming in to attack. At about 600 yards Rear Gunner gave order to corkscrew to port as E/A fired what appeared to be a rocket projectile at Lancaster. Both Gunners returned E/As fire, the Rear Gunner with a burst of 3 to 4 seconds and Mid Upper Gunner with a burst of about 2 seconds. E/A was lost in the corkscrew and was not seen again. Just before E/A attacked, there had been several very accurate bursts of medium, heavy flak. Visibility was good and there were no fighter flares in the immediate vicinity. No warning from visual Monica was obtained in either encounter.
MU Gunner – Sgt SW Bires – 100 rounds.
Rear Gunner – Sgt RM Collins – 250 rounds

Aircraft: LL698 'J2'
Captain: F/S CJ Johnson.
Target: BERLIN
Homeward bound (bombs dropped), flying on a course of 290 degrees 'T', IAS 186, height 20,000 feet. At 22.44 hours in position 52.02N. 12.30E. Mid Upper Gunner saw and reported a Lancaster on starboard beam about 1000 feet below being attacked by a Ju88. Mid Upper Gunner fired a burst of about 2 seconds at E/A at a range of about 700 yards on the starboard beam down and E/A immediately broke off attack on other Lancaster and was not seen again. The Lancaster and E/A were silhouetted against a fighter flare. No searchlights or flak in evidence.
MU Gunner – Sgt J Poad – 60 rounds.
Rear Gunner – Sgt RA Dymott RCAF – Nil.

Target:	*Berlin Area*
Aircraft deployed total:	*883*
514 Squadron:	*19 (1 returned early)*
Aircraft lost total:	*72*
514 Squadron:	*1*

Comments: This was to be the last major attack on Berlin for the RAF. Around five important military locations were hit, including the Waffen-SS Leibstandarte Adolf Hitler barracks. Strong winds scattered the stream of allied bombers on return, leaving them to the mercy of enemy radar guided flak batteries and night fighters. The losses were accordingly very heavy.

Missing aircraft:

LL625, JI-C. Crashed on homeward leg, at Wörlitz, 12 km ENE of Dessau. Possibly shot down by Hptm. Heinz-Horst Hissbach of 5./ NJG2, who claimed a '4-motor' in the rough vicinity of Dessau at 2250hrs, approximately the time that LL625 would have been in the area.

(Above) F/O John Laing was killed along with five of his crew when their Lancaster Mk.II LL625 JI-C was shot down returning from Berlin on 24th March 1944. This photo shows the aircraft and crew after LL625 had completed eleven ops, the most recent being another visit to the German capital in the care of F/O Laing and crew. The Laing crew were lost on their fifteenth op and LL625's eighteenth. Source: Courtesy of Valerie McAllister-Roy, daughter of F/S Bayne McAllister.

F/O JR Laing	Pilot	KIA
Sgt A Vickers	Navigator	KIA
F/S J Knights	Bomb Aimer	KIA
F/S GE Scott	WOP/Air	KIA
F/S RB McAllister RCAF	MU Gunner	POW
Sgt CA Salt	Rear Gunner	KIA
Sgt PCK Bennett	Flight Engineer	KIA

25th March 1944.
Weather: Fine and sunny.
Non-Operational Flying: Air Tests and a Cross Country were carried out.
Movements: Flight Lieutenant JN Pollock, Squadron Gunnery Leader returned from his Night Vision Course at Upper Heyford.

26th March 1944.
Weather: Fine and sunny.
Non-Operational Flying: Air Tests were carried out.
Operational Flying: BOMBING – ESSEN.
Sixteen aircraft were detailed to bomb the target. One returned early. 10/10 cloud covered the whole outward route and the target and to 5 deg. E. on return. Red TIs were difficult to distinguish early in the attack but greens were seen later. The glow of fires and bomb flashes were seen through the cloud and smoke was reported up to 20,000 feet. Flak was slight to moderate and very few fighters were seen.
F/S JG Hudson RNZAF in LL690, JI-J reported: Bomb load 1 x 2000 lb. bomb, 56 x 30, 1080 x 4, 120 x 4 incendiaries. Primary target: ESSEN. There was 10/10 cloud with broken patches. Bombed at 2209 hours from 20,000 feet. Nothing seen. Uneventful trip. Route OK.

Combat Reports:
Aircraft: LL698 'J2'
Captain: F/S CJ Johnson
Target: ESSEN
Homeward bound (bombs dropped), flying on a course of 284 M. IAS 170, height 20,500 feet. At 22.30 hours in position 50.32 degrees N. 0612 degrees 30 minutes E. both gunners simultaneously saw and reported a Ju88 coming in fast to attack on starboard quarter down at a range of 500 yards. Rear Gunner immediately gave order to corkscrew to starboard and at commencement of corkscrew E/A, which by this time was dead astern down at range of 250-300 yards, opened fire on Lancaster (the trace passing well underneath). To which Rear Gunner

replied with a long burst of 5 seconds. Mid Upper Gunner was unable to get guns to bear. Trace was observed by Rear Gunner to strike E/A which broke off combat to port beam down and was not seen again. Lancaster suffered no damage. Visibility was very good. Lancaster was probably silhouetted against searchlight glow on cloud base. There was some fighter flares but no flak in vicinity.
MU Gunner – Sgt J Poad – Nil.
Rear Gunner – Sgt RA Dymott RCAF – 400 rounds.

Aircraft: LL728 'B'
Captain: F/S EHJ Shearing.
Target: ESSEN
Homeward bound (bombs dropped), flying at 20,000 feet on a course of 157 M. IAS 160. At 22.15 hours in a position 5105N 0715E Rear Gunner reported an Me210 making an attack on another Lancaster on the port quarter down at a range of approximately 600 yards. Both Gunners bought guns to bear and gave E/A a good 2-3 seconds burst each. E/A promptly broke away from the other aircraft and turned to attack Lancaster. Rear Gunner gave corkscrew manoeuvre to port, and both Gunners fired continuously at E/A which followed Lancaster without opening fire during the first phase of the manoeuvre and finally broke away to starboard down and was not seen again. Visibility was clear above the cloud base which was lit up by the target. No flak or searchlights were directed at Lancaster at the time, but there were fighter flares in the distance.
MU Gunner – Sgt JL Masson RCAF – 400 rounds.
Rear Gunner – Sgt MH Smart RCAF – 800 rounds.

Aircraft: DS669 'C'
Captain: F/S CJ Medland
Target: ESSEN
On the night of 26 / 27th March, 1944 Lancaster 'C' of 514 Squadron was homeward bound bombs dropped flying at 20,000 feet on a course of 275 T, IAS 170. At 2234 hours in a position 50.30 N 06.50 E Rear Gunner reported a single engined aircraft, recognised later as an Me109 with amber light on the nose, on the fine starboard quarter level at a range of 800 yards. He immediately prepared Pilot for corkscrew to starboard and when E/A closed to 500 yards gave the order for the manoeuvre to commence, firing at the same time a burst lasting 3 seconds which appeared to pass above E/A. E/A followed Lancaster into corkscrew closing range to approx. 300 yards and Rear Gunner fired a second burst 2-3 seconds, observing strikes on the port wing. E/

A was trying hard to press home the attack and Rear Gunner fired a third burst, trace appearing to enter the centre section. The light in the nose was extinguished at this stage. As E/A broke away quickly down on the starboard quarter Mid Upper Gunner reported flames coming from its engine which increased in intensity as it disappeared through the clouds. A glow was observed by both Gunners and Engineer, a few seconds later through the cloud and apparently a mid-air explosion. Immediately after the Mid Upper Gunner, who was unable to bring guns to bear on E/A during encounter reported what was believed to be Me210 attacking from the port beam at a range of 200 yards. He promptly gave the order for corkscrew to port and E/A was soon lost to view. During encounters neither E/A fired at Lancaster. Visibility good. No flak or fighter flares in the vicinity. E/A is claimed as destroyed.
MU Gunner – Sgt CE Rose RCAF – Nil
Rear Gunner – Sgt BR Williams – 450 rounds

Target: *Essen industrial target (probably Krupps)*
Aircraft deployed total: 705
514 Squadron: 16 (1 returned early)
Aircraft lost total: 9
514 Squadron: Nil

Comments: An effective attack overall, the change of target fooled the enemy and even though cloud-covered, TIs were well placed over the target to good effect.

27th March 1944.
Weather: Overcast. Fair later.
Non-Operational Flying: Local Flying took place.

28th March 1944.
Weather: Overcast.
Non-Operational Flying: Air Tests were carried out.
Funeral: Sergeant LHD Warren, the Air Gunner killed on the night of 22/23rd March, 1944 was buried at Mildenhall. The Squadron Gunnery Leader, Flight Lieutenant JN Pollock, Pilot Officer HCA Chapman and Flight Sergeant RW Windsor, the Captain, attended the funeral.

29th March 1944.
Weather: Overcast, rain in the afternoon.

Non-Operational Flying: Air Tests and Air/Ground Firing were carried out.
Operational Flying: 21 Aircraft were detailed for Bombing Operations, but the effort was cancelled at 14.30 hours.

30th March 1944.
Weather: Fine in the morning, cloudy later.
Funeral: Sergeant LD Blackford, the Air Gunner killed on the night of the 22/23rd. March, 1944, was buried at Chadwell Heath. The funeral was attended by Pilot Officer PAS Twinn and Flight Sergeant BW Windsor, the Captain.
Operational Flying: BOMBING – NUREMBURG. *Note: The squadron ORB consistently uses the spelling shown here, rather than the correct 'Nuremberg'.*
Twenty-one aircraft were detailed to bomb the target. Two did not take off, four failed to return, three landed at Woodbridge on return, one landed at 137 Aerodrome on return, one landed at Tangmere on return, two crash-landed on return, one at RAF Sawbridgeworth, Herts, the other two miles south west of Waterbeach. 4 returned early. There was 6-8/10 cloud on route and over the target with tops at 22,000 feet. There was severe fighter and flak activity south of the Ruhr. Markers appeared scattered.
S/L AL Roberts in DS816, JI-O reported: Bomb load 1 x 1000 lb. bomb, 80 x 30, 900 x 4 incendiaries. Primary target: NUREMBURG. Weather was cloudy with 8/10 – 10/10 cloud. Bombed at 0123 hours from 20,000 feet. Red flares and yellow stars, concentrated. Many good fires. Badly chosen route. Attack good.
P/O DA Woods RAAF in LL739, JI-M reported: Bomb load 1 x 1000 lb. bomb, 96 x 30, 810 x 4, 90 x 4. Returned early and landed at Woodbridge. Attacked by Me210 five times. Wing damaged. Rear guns frozen, Mid Upper guns would only fire 4 rounds at a time. Saw 15 to 20 aircraft shot down by fighter on outward route S. of Ruhr.
P/O WE Chitty RAAF in LL645, JI-R reported: Bomb load 1 x 8000 lb. bomb, 90 x 4. Primary target: NUREMBURG. Crashed 2 miles south west of Waterbeach Aerodrome. Crew injured and suffered from shock and admitted Station Sick Quarters. Bomb Aimer (Sgt DA Pattison RCAF) and Mid Upper Gunner (Sgt J Shepherd) killed.
W/O WL McGown in LL683, JI-P reported: Bomb load 1 x 1000 lb. bomb, 96 x 30, 810 x 4, 90 x 4. Primary target: NUREMBURG. There was 9/10 cloud with tops 22,000 feet, with gaps. Bombed at 0126 hours from 20,000 feet. Many incendiaries scattered. Attack

very widespread. PFF not considered good. Crash landed on return at Sawbridgeworth. Three of crew baled out, one injured.

(Above) Sgts Robert Guy (left) and his twin brother Charles (right) served on 514 Squadron in 1944 as Air Gunner and Flight Engineer respectively. Robert lost his life on the night of 7th /8th June 1944 during an operation to Massy-Palaiseau with the crew of P/O WL McGown. Charles, who as Flight Engineer with P/O WE Chitty survived a crash landing returning from Nuremberg, was lost on 30th July 1944, operating against Caen. In the centre is their younger brother Colin, who spent two years with the Royal Artillery, surviving the war. Source: Guy family.

Combat Report:
Aircraft: DS633 'B2'
Captain: F/S CJ Johnson
Target: NUREMBURG
Whilst on bombing run, just about to drop bombs, flying on a course of 198 degrees M., at 20,500 feet, IAS 160. At 0129 hours in target area, Mid Upper Gunner reported a Ju88 lit up by glare of target on the starboard quarter slightly up at range of 700 yards which immediately opened fire on Lancaster, its trace passing underneath. Finally, on the instructions of the Rear Gunner, the Captain climbed into some vapour trail and changed course twice which effectively shook off E/A and it

was not seen again. There was very little flak at the time and no searchlights but numerous fighter flares.
MU Gunner – Sgt J Poad – 100 rounds.
Rear Gunner – Sgt RA Dymott RCAF – 50 rounds

Aircraft: LL733 'G'
Captain: F/S CJ Medland
Target: NUREMBURG
Homeward bound (bombs dropped), flying on a course of 294 degrees, IAS 160, height 20,000 feet. At 02.16 hours, Mid Upper Gunner reported unidentified twin engined aircraft on port quarter up at a range of 650 yards, behind another Lancaster and apparently about to attack it. Mid Upper Gunner opened fire in direction of E/A and at same time, gave order to corkscrew to port. E/A closed in on Lancaster 'G' to range of 200 yards without firing and broke away to port down and was not seen again, and the other Lancaster also started to corkscrew. Visibility was very good. There were numerous fighter flares, but no searchlights or flak at the time.
MU Gunner – Sgt CE Rose RCAF – 400 rounds.
Rear Gunner – Sgt BR Williams – Nil.

Aircraft: LL-739 'M'
Captain: P/O DA Woods RAAF
Target: NUREMBURG
Outward bound (bombs not dropped), flying on a course of 083 degrees T, IAS 155. At 0027 hours, Rear Gunner reported Me210 on starboard quarter down at 600 yards. Rear Gunner immediately gave order to corkscrew to starboard and pressed triggers but guns failed to fire. E/A was then temporarily lost to view. Approximately 2 minutes later, Rear Gunner reported Me210 on starboard quarter level at range of 700 yards. Rear Gunner gave order to corkscrew to starboard but again, guns failed to fire and enemy was lost to view. About 7 minutes later, E/A was again seen on starboard quarter down at 500 yards. Rear Gunner immediately gave order to corkscrew to starboard and at the same time, Mid Upper Gunner reported a fighter flare dropped by FW190 on starboard bow level. Me210 then came in to attack from starboard quarter below, closing to range of 400 yards and opening fire on Lancaster. Mid Upper Gunner fired a few rounds in direction of trace, before his guns failed. Lancaster sustained several hits on starboard wing. Me210 then broke away to port quarter up and was lost to view. About a minute later, Rear Gunner reported Me210 attacking from starboard quarter level at a range of 300 yards and gave order to

corkscrew to starboard. Mid Upper Gunner fired a 2 second burst from 1 gun, but did not observe any hits on E/A which closed to 150 yards and opened fire scoring hits on Lancaster starboard tail unit before breaking away. Lancaster went out of control in a spiral dive and recovered at 6,000 feet.

No flak was observed at the time, but there was numerous fighter flares on the port side. Visibility was very good with half-moon.

MU Gunner – Sgt WC Udell – 40 rounds.

Rear Gunner – Sgt HL Doherty – Nil.

Aircraft: LL731 'U'
Captain: P/O NW Thackray RAAF
Target: NUREMBURG

On the night of 30 / 31st March 1944 Lancaster 'U' of 514 Squadron was outward bound, bombs not dropped, flying 20,000feet, IAS 165. At 0123 hours just approaching target area, Bomb Aimer reported a Ju88 attacking another Lancaster on the starboard bow down at a range of 800 yards. Lancaster 'U' turned towards encounter to make an attack on E/A from astern and Bomb Aimer fired 2 or 3 long bursts. E/A immediately broke off the attack on the other aircraft and was last seen diving almost vertically through the clouds. Many hits were seen on E/A which is claimed as damaged. No return fire was observed from other Lancaster. Unfortunately the crew are now missing from an operation which took place a few days later, and fuller details of encounter are not available.

Bomb Aimer/Air Gunner: - F/S JR Moulsdale (since missing) – 100 rounds.

Target:	*Nuremberg Area*
Aircraft deployed total:	*795*
514 Squadron:	*19*
Aircraft lost total:	*95*
514 Squadron:	*4 plus 2 crashed on return.*

Comments: A tragic night for Bomber Command which suffered its worst losses of the war. It was a clear, moon-lit night and the aircrews were slaughtered as they fought their way through enemy night fighters and flak. In total 82 aircraft were shot down over the target and outbound, the remainder on the return leg. Due to the intensity of the battle, German fighters had to land, re-fuel, re-arm and return to the air. This left the surviving allied aircraft a safer run on the return to base. TIs were scattered and the raid considered unsuccessful.

(Above) A very narrow escape for the P/O DA Woods RAAF and the crew of LL739 JI-M. Outbound to Nuremberg the aircraft was attacked by Me210 and Me410 fighters on five occasions. Sustaining massive damage to its starboard wing and tail unit, the crew was forced to abandon the operation and return to the emergency airfield at Woodbridge, where the above photograph is believed to have been taken. LL739 was repaired and resumed operations on 18th April 1944 to Rouen. Her renaissance was short-lived, however, the aircraft being shot down on an op to Louvain on 11th May 1944 whilst in the care of P/O Bruce Cunningham whose crew fortunately survived the experience. F/O Woods and his crew were also lost, their aircraft LL620, JI-T being hit by flak attacking Villers Bocage on 30th June 1944. Source: F/L AH Morrison courtesy of Linda Miles.

Missing aircraft:

LL696, JI-A. 'Bomber Command Losses 1944' (WR Chorley) states 'Believed shot down while on final leg to target by Ju88 of Fw Emil Nonnenmacher, III./NJG2, crashing near Memmelsdorf', which is 6.5 km NE of Bamberg. According to 'Nachtjagd War Diaries' (Dr. Theo

Boiten) Fw. Nonnenmacher, who was actually with 9./NJG2, made no verified claim in that area; however, Lt. Achim Woeste, Stab III./NJG3 was credited with an unidentified 4-engined bomber in the Schesslitz area, 10 km NE of Bamberg at a time consistent with 514 Sqn. aircraft being in that area. It therefore more likely that LL696 was shot down by Lt. Woeste.

F/O PJK Hood	Pilot	POW
F/S HJ Cosgrove	Navigator	POW
F/O RJ Wilton	Bomb Aimer	POW
F/S VJ Rollings	WOP/Air	POW
Sgt CDF MacKenzie	MU Gunner	KIA
T/S M Lanthier USAAF	Rear Gunner	POW
Sgt HH Wickson	Flight Engineer	POW

Note: No record exists of why there was a USAAF Rear Gunner flying with 514 Squadron. However, T/S Lanthier was no doubt made very welcome.

LL738, JI-D. Shot down, possibly at 0020 hours by Lt. Hans Raum of 9./NJG3, whilst holding course at 21,000 feet and fell into outskirts of Sinzig at Westum.

P/O GS Hughes RAAF	Pilot	KIA
W/O AD Hall RNZAF	Bomb Aimer	POW
F/S LS Smith RNZAF	Navigator	KIA
W/O CJ Goddard RAAF	WOP/Air	KIA
Sgt GH Thornton	Rear Gunner	KIA
F/S LJH Whitbread	MU Gunner	KIA
Sgt H West	Flight Engineer	KIA

LL698, A2-J. Outbound, brought down by night-fighter, possibly flown by Uffz. Lorenz Gerstmayr of 4./NJG3 at 0038 hours, near Oberpleis, 12 km ESE of Bonn.

F/S F Gregory	Pilot	KIA
F/S CG MacDonald RCAF	Navigator	POW
F/S JD McCreary RCAF	Bomb Aimer	KIA
Sgt ER Pond	WOP/Air	KIA
Sgt R Byth	MU Gunner	KIA
Sgt A Cook	Rear Gunner	KIA
Sgt R Frith	Flight Engineer	KIA

DS836 JI-L. Whilst approaching turning point on to final leg at 22,000 feet, intercepted by a night-fighter, probably that of Lt. Wilhelm Seuss of 11./NJG5 at 0056 hours and coming down at Wulfershausen. The crew members who lost their lives are commemorated on the Runnymede Memorial.

P/O DCC Crombie RAAF	*Pilot*	*KIA*
F/O HG Darby	*Bomb Aimer*	*POW*
F/S A McPhee	*Navigator*	*POW*
Sgt MJ Tyler	*WOP/Air*	*KIA*
Sgt HR Hill	*Rear Gunner*	*KIA*
Sgt GC Payne	*MU Gunner*	*KIA*
Sgt J McGahey	*Flight Engineer*	*KIA*

31st March 1944.
Weather: Showers, colder.
Non-Operational Flying: No flying took place.

Monthly Summary for March 1944

Operational: (Compiled by F/Lt. JN Pollock.)

Enemy Aircraft:	1 plus 1 probable.
Enemy Aircraft Damaged:	1
Operational Flying Hours for March 1944:	866.20
Non-Operational Flying Hours for March 1944:	231.50
Total tons of bombs dropped in March 1944:	491
Cumulative tons of bombs dropped:	1411

Number of Sorties for March 1944: 125

Strength of Squadron as at 31st March 1944.
Aircrew: 58 Officers
191 SNCOs

Ground: 2 Officers
32 SNCOs.
331 other ranks
(Includes 12 WAAFs)

The Battle of Berlin was now over. Since 18th November 1943, Bomber Command dropped 78,477 tons of bombs. It flew 29,459 sorties on 100 night raids. Total losses amounted to 1,117 aircraft which represented 3.8% of those deployed.

April 1944

1st April 1944.
Weather: Overcast and cold.
Ground Training: A lecture at 14.00 hours on Flying Control was given for Crews not flying.
Non-Operational Flying: A limited amount of flying took place comprising an Air Test and Cross-Country Flights.

(Above) An unidentified 514 Sqn Lancaster Mk.II sits at dispersal. The absence of a squadron code suggests that the aircraft is being prepared for service in a different flight, or has recently arrived at the squadron. Source: Tracy Holroyd-Smith / Sgt George Henry.

2nd April 1944.
Weather: Rain all morning, clearing slightly later.
No flying took place all day.

3rd April 1944.
Weather: Overcast with some rain, visibility fair.
Ground Training: A lecture on Meteorology at 1400 hours was given for Crews not flying.
Non-Operational Flying: Air Tests were carried out.

4th April 1944.
Weather: Overcast, some rain.
Non-Operational Flying: Air Tests, Local Flying, Bombing Practice at sea and a Cross Country were carried out and 2 details of Fighter Affiliation.

5th April 1944.
Weather: Overcast, some rain in afternoon.
Ground Training: A lecture on Photographic Interpretation was given at 1030 hours for Crews not flying.
Awards: The immediate award of the DFC to Flying Officer HG Bryant was promulgated for his action on the night of 22/23rd, March, 1944, when on operations as Air Gunner, in dealing with 2 incendiaries.
Non-Operational Flying: Air Tests were carried out and 8 details of Fighter Affiliation.

6th April 1944.
Weather: Overcast.
Non-Operational Flying: Air Tests, Height and Load Tests, Air/Ground Firing at Lakenheath, Cross Country, Window exercises, and 12 details of Fighter Affiliation were carried out.
Movements: Flight Lieutenant JN Pollock, Squadron Gunnery Leader proceeded to GRU Exeter for interview. (Note: GRU was the Gunnery Research Unit).

7th April 1944.
Weather: Overcast.
Non-Operational Flying: Air Tests, Low Flying Practice and 8 details of Fighter Affiliation were carried out.

8th April 1944.
Weather: Fog early, improving later.
No flying took place. There was a stand-down in the afternoon.
Awards: The immediate award of the DFM to Flight Sergeant Windsor, BW, Pilot and Sergeant Dolamore, FL, Flight Engineer, was promulgated for their action on the night of 22nd. March, 1944, when on operations in bringing back their badly damaged Aircraft after both Gunners had been killed and other members of the Crew had baled out.
Movements: Flight Lieutenant JN Pollock, Squadron Gunnery Leader returned from interview at GRU Exeter.

9th April 1944.
Weather: Fair and Mild.
Non-Operational Flying: Air Tests and 2 'Bullseye' Exercises were carried out.
Operational Flying: BOMBING – VILLENEUVE.
2 aircraft were detailed to bomb the target and returned after completing their mission. Visibility was excellent. Photographs show one marker on the aiming point and another 2000 yards to the NE which attracted a considerable amount of attention. Some HF is reported.
F/S BW Windsor in DS822, JI-T reported: Bomb load 8 x 1000 lb bomb, 6 x 500 lb. bomb. Primary Target: VILLENEUVE MARSHALLING YARDS. Visibility clear. Bombed at 0001 hours from 13,000 feet. Good concentration of TIs and sticks of bombs seen exploding on yards. 1 x 1000 lb. bomb hung up, presence unknown until return. Bomb release faulty. Very successful attack. One very large explosion seen at 0002 hours.

Target:	*Villeneuve Railway Yards*
Aircraft deployed total:	225
514 Squadron:	2
Aircraft lost total:	Nil
514 Squadron:	Nil

Comments: Bomber Command's attention now turned away from German industrial targets as it set its sights on French infrastructure in preparation for the D-Day invasion. The attack on Villeneuve marshalling yards was a success, with no loss to bomber Command Aircraft.

10th April 1944.
Weather: Fair and mild, visibility good.
Non-Operational Flying: Air Tests, Height and Load Tests and an Air/Sea Rescue Search were carried out.
Operational Flying: BOMBING – LAON.
Nineteen aircraft were detailed to bomb the target. All took off and returned to Base after completion of their duty. Visibility was good, and the TIs were well concentrated and the operation should prove to have been successful. There was very little flak opposition, a few fighters were seen. The route was considered good.

F/L DAA Gray in LL670, A2-K reported: Bomb load 9 x 1000, 4 x 500 lb. bomb. Primary target: LAON. There was slight haze. Bombed at 0351 hours from 11,100 feet. Many TIs seen and bombing seemed to be concentrated. Railway line leading to yard seen. Attack quite successful.

Combat Report - Pro-forma:
Aircraft: LL732 'H2'
Captain: P/O Morgan-Owen
Target: LAON
At 0352 hours, height 12,500 feet, heading 022 degrees T., position 4937N, 0338E. Rear Gunner sighted Ju88 climbing from starboard to astern. Ordered Captain to corkscrew. Both Gunners fired at E/A, which broke away port up. Visibility was good. Moonlit. There was searchlights, and flak on the target.
MU Gunner – P/O Chapman – 120 rounds.
Rear Gunner – Sgt Hayward - 600 rounds.

Target:	*Laon Railway Yards*
Aircraft deployed total:	*163*
514 Squadron:	*19*
Aircraft lost total:	*1*
514 Squadron:	*Nil*

Comments: Another raid with little enemy resistance. A corner of the target was destroyed.

11th April 1944.
Weather: Fine and sunny.
Visits: Squadron Leader DB Keary DFC, Group Gunnery Leader, paid a visit to the Squadron.
Operational Flying: BOMBING – AACHEN.
Eleven aircraft were detailed to bomb the target. One is missing, the other ten carried out their mission and returned to Base. Weather was fair with some broken cloud. And the TIs were generally reported as being concentrated. Some crews saw a built up area. Opposition was less than expected.
F/S NR Wishart in LL728, JI-B reported: Bomb load 10 x 1000, 2 x 500 lb. bomb, 160 x 4, 20 x 4 incendiaries. Primary target: AACHEN. There was broken cloud. Bombed at 2240 hours from 20,000 feet. Red TIs concentrated and many good fires seen. Good successful attack. Route OK.

Combat Report:
Aircraft: LL620 'G2'
Captain: F/S LM Petry RNZAF
Target: AACHEN

Homeward bound (bombs dropped), flying on a course of 300 degrees M. IAS 180 at a height of 20,500 feet. At 23.19 hours in position 51.30N 04.40E, Mid Upper Gunner saw tracer coming from starboard quarter up, passing just beneath Lancaster, and immediately gave order to corkscrew to starboard. On commencement of corkscrew, Mid Upper Gunner saw unidentified twin engined aircraft on starboard quarter up at a range of 400 yards and fired several very long bursts at it. During corkscrew Rear Gunner saw E/A for the first time on port quarter up on breakaway and fired a 5 second burst. No hits were claimed on E/A and Lancaster sustained no damage. Visibility was fair. There were no fighter flares, searchlights or flak.
MU Gunner – F/Sgt RA Pitt RAAF – 200 rounds.
Rear Gunner – Sgt A McLean - 400 rounds.

Target:	*Aachen Area*
Aircraft deployed total:	*352*
514 Squadron:	*11*
Aircraft lost total:	*9*
514 Squadron:	*1*

Comments: A return to a German target as Aachen received its largest raid of the war. Considered an accurate raid causing widespread damage with many fires. Transport and infrastructure were extensively damaged.

Missing aircraft:

LL645, JI-R. Shot down, probably at 2315 hours 10km West of Roermond, by the Bf110 of Uffz. Hans Fischer of 12/NJG1. The crew members who were killed are buried at Heverlee War Cemetery.

P/O NWF Thackray RAAF	*Pilot*	KIA
Sgt EL Humes	*Navigator*	POW
F/S JR Moulsdale RAAF	*Bomb Aimer*	KIA
Sgt P Hughes	*WOP/Air*	KIA
F/S CH Henn RAAF	*MU Gunner*	KIA
F/S RE Bromley RAAF	*Rear Gunner*	KIA
Sgt CW Banfield	*Flight Engineer*	KIA

12th April 1944.
Weather: High cloud base.
Non-Operational Flying: Air Tests, 4 details of Air/Air Firing and an Air/Sea Rescue Search were carried out.

13th April 1944.
Weather: Fine and sunny all day.
Ground Training: A very interesting 'Escape' lecture was given to Squadron Aircrew by Flight Lieutenant HD Wardle.
Non-Operational Flying: Air Tests and 4 details of Air/Air Firing were carried out.

14th April 1944.
Weather: Cloudy, visibility good.
Operational Flying: 22 Aircraft were detailed for Operations, but the effort was cancelled.

15th April 1944.
Weather: Fine and sunny in the morning, cloudy later.
Non-Operational Flying: Air Tests, Air/Ground Firing at Lakenheath and Bombing Practices at Ebindon were carried out.

16th April 1944.
Weather: Overcast, visibility poor but improving slightly.
Operational Flying: 15 Aircraft were detailed for Operations but the effort was cancelled.
No flying took place all day.

17th April 1944.
Weather: Overcast, visibility poor but improving.
Non-Operational Flying: Air Tests were carried out.
Operational Flying: 16 Aircraft were required for Operational Flying but the effort was cancelled.

18th April 1944.
Weather: Fine and sunny.
Non-Operational Flying: Air Tests were carried out.
Operational Flying: BOMBING – ROUEN.
20 aircraft were detailed to bomb the target. All took off and returned to base after completing their duty. Weather was good with a small amount of haze. PFF markers were somewhat scattered. Fires and

smoke from the marshalling yards were seen by some crews. There was very little opposition over the target.

F/S RO Pick in LL696, JI-A reported: Bomb load 10 x 1000, 5 x 500 lb. Bomb. Primary target: ROUEN. There was some thin cloud. Bombed at 0043 hours from 12500 feet. Some fires seen as directed by M of C *(Master Bomber, also known as 'Master of Ceremonies')*. Too much conversation by M of C. Attack believed to fall too far west. Had combat with enemy aircraft.

Combat Report – Pro-forma:
Aircraft: LL696 'A'
Captain: F/S RO Pick
Target: ROUEN
At 0024 hours, height 14,000 feet, heading 110 degrees M, 4918N, 0009E. Rear gunner sighted unidentified S/E aircraft range 400 yards on starboard level. Rear Gunner ordered Captain to corkscrew port and opened fire. S/E broke away on port level. Visibility fair with starlight.
MU Gunner – Sgt Hanson. – Nil.
Rear Gunner – Sgt Aston - 160 rounds.

Target:	*Rouen Railway Yards*
Aircraft deployed total:	*289*
514 Squadron:	*20*
Aircraft lost total:	*Nil*
514 Squadron:	*Nil*

Comments: Another success for Bomber Command with widespread damage to the railway infrastructure, with no aircraft lost. A concentrated attack.

19th April 1944.
Weather: Fine and sunny, visibility fair. Rain in the evening.
Non-Operational Flying: Air Tests were carried out.
Movements: Wing Commander AJ Samson, DFC proceeded by air to RAF Cranwell for Junior Commanders' Course lasting 3 weeks.
Postings: Flight Lieutenant JN Pollock, Squadron Gunnery Leader proceeded on posting to GRU Wittering.
Operational Flying: 22 Aircraft were detailed for Operations but the effort was cancelled shortly after Briefing.

20th April 1944.
Weather: Fine and sunny.
Non-Operational Flying: Air Tests, Cross Country and Formation Practice were carried out.
Postings: Flight Lieutenant HH Wright, DFM, assumed duties of Squadron Gunnery Officer.
Operational Flying: BOMBING – KÖLN.
22 aircraft were detailed to bomb the target. All took off and returned to Base on completion of their duty with the exception of 1 which landed at Woodbridge. Weather outwards was clear but 10/10 cloud was encountered over the target. The PFF are reported as being from 6-12 minutes late and a number of crews bombed on ETA. Attack appears to have been scattered although some good fires were started which were visible from the English coast on the return trip. Opposition was negligible.
F/S EA Kingham in LL690, JI-J reported: Bomb load 1 x 1000, 1026 x 4, 108 x 30 lb. incendiaries. Primary target: KÖLN. There was 10/10 cloud. Bombed at 0213 hours from 20,000 feet. Cloud prevented sight of target. Defences lighter than expected. Good red glow seen below cloud as far away as the EC (home). Route good.

Target:	*Köln (Cologne) Area*
Aircraft deployed total:	*379*
514 Squadron:	*22*
Aircraft lost total:	*4*
514 Squadron:	*Nil*

Comments: A devastating raid with widespread destruction and severe casualties on the ground. Over 190 industrial buildings were destroyed along with heavy damage to 7 railway yards/stations. There were over 1290 fires and 46 Churches were destroyed. Deep penetrating bombs destroyed many underground bomb shelters. Around 660 people were killed. It is speculated that as many as 80% of those killed were in those shelters.

21st April 1944.
Weather: Overcast and cool all day, visibility good.
There was a general stand-down in the Afternoon.

22nd April 1944.
Weather: Fine and sunny, visibility excellent.

Non-Operational Flying: Air Tests were carried out.
Operational Flying: BOMBING – DÜSSELDORF.
22 aircraft were detailed to bomb the target. All took off, 2 returned early and 3 are missing. 1 of these sent an SOS giving position 5236N 0351E at 0256hours. No further news. Weather was clear with slight haze. TIs were seen on marshalling yards and the bombing was well concentrated. There was much smoke and many fires were seen. Flak was moderate with very active searchlights and many fighters. The attack was considered very successful.

(Above) Lancaster Mk.II JI-P (in background) believed to be LL624 at RAF Woodbridge for repair. Damage to the aircraft appears to involve the starboard wing and engines, this being consistent to that reported by W/O McGown above. Source: Garth Ridley

W/O WI McGown in LL624, JI-P reported: Bomb load 1 x 1000 lb. bomb, 26 x 30, 1140 x 4 incendiaries. Primary target: DÜSSELDORF. There was slight haze. Bombed at 0121 hours from 16,000 feet. Good fires were seen lighting up river. Starboard outer prop cowling u/s, both wings holed. Just before bombing aircraft damaged by falling bombs. Managed to get our run up and bombed as briefed. Fires had a good hold and were concentrated round the markers.

Target: *Düsseldorf Area*
Aircraft deployed total: *596*
514 Squadron: *22 (2 returned early)*
Aircraft lost total: *29*
514 Squadron: *3*

Comments: Stiffer opposition from night fighters penetrating the bombing stream, made this attack more difficult and losses were high. It was reported that 56 large industrial buildings were damaged with 7 being totally destroyed.

Missing aircraft:

DS682, JI-N. Crashed in the sea. Circumstances not stated. An SOS message was received at 0256hrs giving position 5236N 0351E. No night-fighter claim is recorded so it is likely that the aircraft sustained damage earlier in the raid and failed to make it home. Sgts Sadler and Tetley are buried in Sage War Cemetery, the rest of the crew are commemorated on the Runnymede Memorial.

(Left) F/O Maurice Morgan-Owen, pilot of DS682. Despite an SOS being sent by the WOP/AG, Sgt Sunny Gledhill, the aircraft was lost without trace. The story of the crew is told in the chapter 'War Stories' later in this book. Source: courtesy of Tracy Holroyd-Smith / Morgan-Owen family.

F/O ML Morgan-Owen	Pilot	KIA
F/S AW Green	Navigator	KIA
F/O P Jacobson	Bomb Aimer	KIA
Sgt E Gledhill	WOP/Air	KIA
Sgt DA Tetley	MU Gunner	KIA
Sgt S Hayward	Rear Gunner	KIA
Sgt P Sadler	Flight Engineer	KIA

DS828, JI-D. Believed to have been hit by flak, or possibly collided with DS669, crashing in the target area. Crew are buried at Reichswald Forest War Cemetery, except F/S Hudson and W/O Rolph, who are commemorated on the Runnymede Memorial.

F/S JG Hudson RNZAF	Pilot	KIA
F/S PM Constable	Navigator	KIA
Sgt G Goddard	Bomb Aimer	KIA
W/O HT Rolph	WOP/Air	KIA
F/S CA Campbell RCAF	MU Gunner	KIA
F/S WL Granbois RCAF	Rear Gunner	KIA
Sgt GR Jones	Flight Engineer	KIA

DS669, JI-C. Believed hit by flak or collided with DS828, crashing in target area at Ecke Rethel / Schubertstrasse. Crew buried at Reichswald Forest War Cemetery, with the exception of Sgt Nash, who is commemorated on the Runnymede Memorial.

F/S JD Harrison	Pilot	KIA
F/S E Wilde	Navigator	KIA
F/S PN Kirkpatrick RCAF	Bomb Aimer	KIA
Sgt FD Nash	WOP/Air	KIA
Sgt AG Buttling	Rear Gunner	KIA
Sgt W Wilson	MU Gunner	KIA
Sgt RWD Norris	Flight Engineer	KIA

23rd April 1944.
Weather: Cloudy, mild, visibility good.
There was a stand-down in the afternoon after 14.00 hours.

24th April 1944.
Weather: Fine and sunny, visibility good.
Non-Operational Flying: Air Tests were carried out.

Visits: Squadron Leader DB Keary DFC, Group Gunnery Leader, paid a visit to the Squadron.
Operational Flying: BOMBING – KARLSRUHE.
17 Aircraft were detailed for Operations. 1 was cancelled and 1 returned early, the remainder carried out their duty and returned to Base with the exception of 1 which landed at Woodbridge. The high cloud made it necessary to use sky markers as well as ground markers.
W/O WI McGown in DS822, JI-T reported: Bomb load 1 x 1000 lb. bomb, 1026 x 4, 114 x 30, 108 x 30 lb. incendiaries. Primary target: KARLSRUHE. There was 10/10 cloud over 17,000 feet, clear below. Bombed at 0055 hours from 15,000 feet. 1 x 1000 hung up. TIs concentrated. Fires seen in target area. Very successful attack. Route good. Flaps would not come down – caused Lancaster to land away from base, at Woodbridge.

Combat Reports – Pro-forma:
Aircraft: LL786 'F2'
Captain: F/S Gibson
Target: KARLSRUHE
At 2316 hours, height 16,000 feet, heading 103 degrees M., position 5215N, 0220E. Rear Gunner sighted an FW190 at 400 yards on the port quarter up and immediately ordered Captain to corkscrew to port and Rear Gunner opened fire. E/A broke away on the starboard beam down and was not seen again. No flak or searchlights.
MU Gunner – Sgt Kemp – Nil.
Rear Gunner – Sgt Gallagher - 600 rounds.

Aircraft: DS633 'B2'
Captain: F/S Johnson
Target: KARLSRUHE
At 0303 hours, height 12,500 feet, heading 318 degrees M., position 5058N, 0142E. Mid Upper Gunner sighted an Me210 coming from the port quarter up at 300 yards. Mid Upper Gunner ordered tight turn to port and fired at E/A. E/A broke away starboard beam down and was not seen again. Oxygen was unserviceable in rear turret. Visibility was clear.
MU Gunner – F/S RA Dymott – 200 rounds.
Rear Gunner – Sgt Poad - Nil.

Target: Karlsruhe Area
Aircraft deployed total: 637
514 Squadron: 16 (1 returned early)
Aircraft lost total: 19
514 Squadron: Nil

Comments: The accuracy of this large scale attack was diminished by heavy cloud and strong winds over the target. So much so that some aircraft dropped bombs on Mannheim some 30 miles north of the intended target.

25th April 1944.
Weather: Overcast and cold, visibility good.
Non-Operational Flying: Air Tests were carried out.
Operational Flying: 16 Aircraft were detailed for Operations but the effort was cancelled just after Briefing.

26th April 1944.
Weather: Fine and sunny, clear skies, warm, visibility good.
Non-Operational Flying: Air Tests were carried out.
Operational Flying: BOMBING – ESSEN.
10 aircraft were detailed to bomb the target, 2 were cancelled and 1 returned early. The remainder carried out their duty and returned to Base. Visibility was excellent. Markers were concentrated and bombing is believed to have been very good, leaving a big concentration of fires. A large explosion to the North of aiming point is reported. Opposition from flak and fighters was much less than expected, but searchlights were very numerous. The route was considered good.
S/L WG Devas in LL728, JI-B reported: Bomb load 1 x 8000 lb. bomb, 60 x 30, 405 x 4, 45 x 4 lb. incendiaries. Primary target: ESSEN. There was thin cloud with patches in layers. Bombed at 0135 hours from 21,000 feet. Good concentration of TIs and incendiaries, smoke column up to 15,000 feet. Considered very good raid. Slightly early. Target well alight as we left area.
F/S CF Prowles in LL734, JI-S reported: Bomb Load 1 x 2000 lb. bomb, 84 x 30, 945 x 4, 105 x 4lb incendiaries. Primary Target: ESSEN. Weather was clear. Bombed at 0140 hours from 19,000 feet. A large concentration of fires seen covered with smoke. Glimpse of river on approach. Attack seemed spread, markers were to the East of main concentration. Moderate heavy flak, no fighters.

(Above) A directed battery of 105mm Anti-Aircraft guns opens fire at night. German flak batteries were often radar-controlled or put up an intensive 'box barrage' at the height calculated to affect the most bombers. Aircraft on their bombing run had no choice but to attempt to fly through the potentially lethal barrage. Source: Airworx Gmbh Archive.

Combat Report – Pro-forma:
Aircraft: LL732 'H2'
Captain: F/S Gibson
Target: ESSEN
1st Encounter: At 0106 hours, height 20,000 feet, heading 150 degrees M., position 5320N 0625E. Bomb Aimer sighted an unidentified S/E (with nav. Lights on) approaching from the port bow level. Front Gunner and then Mid Upper Gunner opened fire at S/E aircraft, which

immediately broke away port bow down and was not seen again. Visibility was good but there was searchlight activity.

2nd Encounter: At 0135 hours, height 19,000 feet, heading 180 degrees M, position 5110N, 0640E. While being coned by searchlights, Rear Gunner sighted a Ju88 at a range of 500 yards astern down. Rear Gunner ordered corkscrew to port and opened fire on E/A which broke away starboard beam down.

3rd Encounter: At 0142 hours, height 19,000 feet, heading 240 degrees M., position 5110N, 0600E. Mid Upper Gunner sighted Me109 coming in from the port quarter up, and ordered Captain to corkscrew to port and opened fire. E/A broke away starboard beam down.

4th Encounter: At 0145 hours, height 18,000 feet, heading 240 degrees M., position 5040N, 0420E. Rear Gunner warned Captain of 2 unidentified T/E aircraft on the fine starboard quarter level, both with navigation lights on. Rear Gunner ordered corkscrew and fired and E/As where then lost to view and not seen again.

MU Gunner – Sgt P Kemp. – 160 rounds.
Rear Gunner – Sgt Gallagher - 1st Encounter - 400 rounds. (4th encounter)- 200 rounds
B/Aimer -Front Gunner – Sgt JL Dunbar - 400 rounds.

Target:	*Essen Industrial Plants*
Aircraft deployed total:	*493*
514 Squadron:	*8 (1 returned early)*
Aircraft lost total:	*7*
514 Squadron:	*Nil*

Comments: Good TI Marking by Pathfinders assisted in making this an accurate attack. This target was still considered to be of key industrial significance, and thus it continued to receive attention.

27th April 1944.
Weather: Fine and sunny, clear skies, strong westerly wind, visibility excellent.
Non-Operational Flying: Air Tests, Height and Load Tests and Air/Sea Firing were carried out.
Operational Flying: BOMBING – FRIEDRICHSHAVEN.
18 aircraft were detailed for operations. All took off and returned to base after completing their duty. Weather was very clear over the target, and markers are reported as being well placed. A very successful attack.

F/L RC Curtis in LL732, A2-H reported: Bomb load 1 x 4000, 2 x 1000, 1 x 500 lb. bombs. Primary target: FRIEDRICHSHAVEN. Weather was clear with slight haze. Bombed at 0205 hours from 19,000 feet. Fires were seen burning well among TIs. Green TIs seemed to go down before the reds, however a good attack developed. Two large orange explosions seen at 0205 hours. A good route. Had encounter with enemy aircraft.

Combat Reports – Pro-forma:
Aircraft: DS633 'R'
Captain: F/L Hay
Target: FRIEDRICHSHAVEN
At 0139 hours, height 20,000 feet, heading 118 degrees M, position 4814, 0807E. Rear Gunner sighted FW190, astern down at a range of 300 yards. Orders were given to corkscrew to port and Rear Gunner, followed by Mid Upper Gunner opened fire. E/A broke away on the starboard beam and was not seen again.
MU Gunner – Sgt Baldwin – 200 rounds.
Rear Gunner – Sgt Tate - 400 rounds.

Aircraft: LL731 'U'
Captain: P/O DA Woods RAAF
Target: FRIEDRICHSHAVEN
Homeward bound (bombs dropped), flying on a course of 296 degrees T. IAS (none stated), at a height of 17,000 feet. At 02.50 hours, in position 4810N 0645E, Captain saw trace coming from underneath Lancaster which seemed to be fired from starboard beam down, 'U' immediately corkscrewed to starboard. The Mid Upper Gunner and Rear Gunner fired 2 x 3 second bursts each in the direction of the trace which then ceased and was not seen again. No claims were made, as the E/A was not seen at all during combat. The Lancaster had 2 holes in the starboard main-plane. Visibility was good. There was no fighter flares, searchlights or flak.
MU Gunner – Sgt WC Udell – 200 rounds.
Rear Gunner – Sgt HL Doherty - 400 rounds.

Target:	*Friedrichshaven – Armament Works*
Aircraft deployed total:	*322 (321 Lancasters and 1 Mosquito)*
514 Squadron:	*18*
Aircraft lost total:	*18 (Lancasters)*
514 Squadron:	*Nil*

Comments: The location of important German tank making facilities and deep inside south Germany, this target was of strategic importance. German defences were hampered as the target was on the fringes of Luftwaffe coverage, thus night fighter opposition was minimal. Again with the assistance of a clear and moon-lit night and well placed TIs, the attack proved devastating, with approximately 2/3rds of the town being destroyed. After the war's end, this attack was described by German officials as 'the most damaging attack on tank production of the war'.

28th April 1944.
Weather: Scattered clouds, warm, visibility good.
Non-Operational Flying: Air/Sea firing were carried out.
There was a stand-down in the afternoon for Crews not flying.

29th April 1944.
Weather: Scattered clouds, clearing later. Visibility good.
Non-Operational Flying: Local Flying, Bombing practices, Air Tests and Fighter Affiliation were carried out.

30th April 1944.
Weather: Fine and sunny, clear skies, visibility good.
Non-Operational Flying: Local Flying, Bombing Practices, Air/Air Firing and Air Tests were carried out. 3 Aircraft were detailed for night flying exercises, which were carried out successfully. 3 aircraft were detailed for a 'Bullseye' Exercise. 1 crashed into the sea and all members of the Crew including 1 passenger are reported as missing.

Missing aircraft:

LL691, A2-D. Whilst on a training flight, crashed at 0015 hours in the English Channel off Dover. Crew commemorated on Runnymede Memorial. AC1 Robinson was a ground crewman, thought to be an Armourer, being carried as a passenger. This was a routine event on non-operational flights and was officially condoned, the passenger being officially recorded and issued with a parachute. Family sources suggest that the aircraft was shot down; however there is no record of a night fighter claim.

F/S N Turner	Pilot	KIA
Sgt PF Whale	Navigator	KIA
Sgt A Whitehead	Bomb Aimer	KIA
Sgt W Winkley	WOP/Air	KIA
W/O2 RF Easen RCAF	MU Gunner	KIA
Sgt VG Childs	Rear Gunner	KIA
Sgt WH Lamond	Flight Engineer	KIA
AC1 G Robinson	Supernumerary crew	KIA

(Above) F/O Stan Wright proudly shows off his car next to NF968, JI-L with F/O 'Chatty' Chatfield, P/O Jake Stansbury, Sgt John Jeffries, F/O Ken Ridley and Ken's brother Cecil. Cecil Ridley RCN was visiting for the day and was treated to a local flight with the crew in their Lanc. Source: Ken Ridley via Garth Ridley.

Monthly Summary for April 1944

Operational: (Compiled by F/Lt. JN Pollock and W/O. W.E. Egri)

Operational Flying Hours for April 1944: 670.50
Non-Operational Flying Hours for April 1944: 211.25
Total tons of bombs dropped in April 1944: 580 tons.
Cumulative tons of bombs dropped: 1990 tons.
Number of Sorties for April 1944: 166

Strength of Squadron as at 30th April 1944.

Aircrew: 73 Officers
218 SNCOs

Ground: 2 Officers
31 SNCOs
340 other ranks
(Including 12 WAAFs)

May 1944

1st May 1944.
Weather: Fine and sunny, visibility good.
Non-Operational Flying: Air Tests were carried out during the day.
Operational Flying: BOMBING – CHAMBLY.
Nineteen aircraft were detailed to bomb the target, all took off but one failed to return, the remainder carried out their duty and returned to Base. The weather was clear. The markers were bombed and the results appeared to be concentrated in the yards. The yards could be clearly identified by the light of the flares. Opposition was negligible over the target, but many fighters were encountered on the homeward journey.
S/L EGB Reid in LL728, JI-B reported: Bomb load 10 x 1000, 5 x 500 lb. bombs. Primary target: CHAMBLY. Weather was clear. Bombed at 0028 hours from 5000 feet. A good number of fires were seen in target area. Aircraft returned at 2000 feet to French coast – good attack. Route OK – no opposition over target. One fire seen south of target, either jettison or crashed aircraft.
F/S CF Prowles in DS816, JI-O reported: Bomb load 10 x 1000, 5 x 500 lb. bombs. Primary target: CHAMBLY. Weather was clear. Bombed at 0023 hours from 9000 feet. Saw bombs bursting around TIs inside railway yard. Chatter between M of C made it difficult to hear A/B's instructions. Had combat with enemy Aircraft.

Combat Reports:
Aircraft: DS786 'F2'
Captain: F/S WM Watkins.
Target: CHAMBLY
Homeward bound (bombs dropped), flying on a course of 325T, IAS 180, at a height of 10,000 feet. At 00.38 hours, in position 4910N 0150E, Rear Gunner reported an unidentified twin engined aircraft on the starboard quarter down at a range of 300 yards. The Rear Gunner immediately gave order to corkscrew to starboard and at the same time, opened fire with a 5 second burst at E/A, which closed in and broke away to port quarter up without firing. E/A ,then identified as a Ju88, then turned and came in from port quarter up and Rear Gunner ordered corkscrew to port and at the same time fired a 3 second burst and Mid Upper Gunner opened fire with a 7 second burst. E/A continued to close in and broke away to starboard beam down, still without firing. Lancaster resumed course but Captain then saw E/A coming in from starboard bow down and immediately corkscrewed to starboard and E/

A opened fire, to which Mid Upper Gunner replied with a 2 second burst and Rear Gunner fired a 3 second burst on the breakaway. In this attack R/T, intercom and electronics were shot away. E/A then stood off on port quarter and fired 3 bursts from about 800 yards which passed harmlessly over Lancaster. Visibility good. No cloud. Bright moonlight.
MU Gunner – Sgt P. Dawson – 400 rounds.
Rear Gunner – Sgt B Ferris - 1400 rounds.

Aircraft: LL695 'A'
Captain: F/S CJ Medland.
Target: CHAMBLY
1st Encounter: Homeward bound (bombs dropped), on a course of 329 M., at a height of 9,000 feet. At 00.29 hours in position 49.00N. 02.05E. Rear Gunner reported a twin engined aircraft (subsequently identified as a Ju88) on port quarter up at a range of 1,000 yards, and warned Captain to prepare to corkscrew to port. As E/A in to attack, Rear Gunner opened fire at a range of 700 yards with a 3 second burst., and Rear Gunner and Mid Upper Gunner continued with 4 further short bursts at E/A which opened fire at Lancaster at range of about 650 yards. At 600 yards, Captain was ordered to corkscrew to port and during this manoeuvre, E/A closed in, firing all the time to 50 yards, then breaking away to starboard quarter down. During the attack, the starboard inner motor was shot out of Lancaster, which commenced to fall out of control. Captain ordered crew to bale out, but subsequently countermanded order as he was able to resume control. Lancaster then resumed course, but as port outer engine was vibrating badly. It was feathered.
2nd Encounter: At 00.43 hours, in position 4910N 0157E, IAS 145 on course 329M at 6,000 feet, Rear Gunner sighted unidentified single engined aircraft at a range of 800 yards on port quarter up, closing in. E/A opened fire at 700 yards (the trace passing underneath Lancaster) and Rear Gunner replied at the same time ordering corkscrew to port. E/A continued to close in and at 200 yards broke away to starboard down.
3rd Encounter: At 00.48 hours in position 4925N 0140E, on course of 239 M. IAS 135, at 9,000 feet. Mid Upper Gunner sighted an unidentified single engined aircraft on the port beam at a range of 1,000 yards, closing in and firing at Lancaster. Mid Upper Gunner replied, firing and operating turret manually. The order was given at 600 yards to corkscrew to port and E/A broke away to starboard quarter down.

4th Encounter: At 00.48 hours in position 4937N 0130E on course of 329 M, IAS 145 at 9,000 feet. Rear Gunner reported an unidentified single engined aircraft at a range of 800 yards on port beam, firing at Lancaster, with trace falling short. Rear Gunner immediately gave order to corkscrew to port and at that moment, Captain saw unidentified single engined aircraft crossing over from port to starboard, 200 yards in front of Lancaster, then making steep turn to port and opening fire at a range of 1000 yards, the trace going past the nose of Lancaster. During Lancaster's corkscrew, both E/A were shaken off and were not seen again. The visibility throughout was good, with bright moonlight and no cloud. No searchlights or flak were in evidence prior to or during any of the combats. Lancaster sustained the following damage: Starboard inner motor shot away. Port outer motor damaged. Holes in starboard main-plane and engine nacelles.
MU Gunner – Sgt CE Rose RCAF – 520 rounds.
Rear Gunner – Sgt BR Williams – 1140 rounds.

Pro-forma:
Aircraft: DS816 'O'
Captain: F/S CF Prowles
Target: CHAMBLY.
At 0015 hours, position 4930N 0150E, at a height of 10,000 feet, a Monica warning sounded and Pilot was alerted to presence of E/A in the vicinity. Pilot called for both Gunners to search astern. Rear Gunner reported visual conformation of an FW190 approaching Lancaster from the port quarter down and closing from a range of 800 yards. Rear Gunner ordered corkscrew to starboard and opened fire with fairly uninterrupted fire with the E/A at 600 yards and closing rapidly. Rear Gunner continued firing as E/A followed the manoeuvre, E/A closing to 150 yards when the Mid Upper Gunner also identified the E/A and opened fire with several bursts. E/A closed to a range of 100 yards as it attempted to follow Lancaster's manoeuvre but broke away as it was under intense fire from both of the Lancaster's Gunners. Damage to E/A reported as unknown. There was no flak, fighter flares or searchlights and the visibility was good with bright moonlight.
MU Gunner – Sgt Holmes – 200 rounds.
Rear Gunner – Sgt Porrelli – 1000 rounds.

Target:	*Chambly – Railway Depot*
Aircraft deployed total:	*120*
514 Squadron:	*19*
Aircraft lost total:	*5*
514 Squadron:	*1*

Comments: Many of the following operations were aimed at targets in Northern France. This had two aims: disrupting German supplies in occupied France and a diversionary tactic to try fool the Germans into thinking the expected allied invasion would take place in the north, rather than Normandy further south. On this occasion, an extremely successful raid on what was considered the largest stores and repair depot in the North of France. Heavy damage was caused by some 500 HE bombs hitting the mark, which rendered the site inoperable for almost two weeks.

Missing aircraft:

LL732, A2-H. Shot down on the home leg by a night-fighter flown by Oblt. Jakob Schauss of 4./NJG4.   No survivors from the crew.   The pilot had previously flown a tour on Hampdens with 144 Sqn. and was on the 17th trip of his second tour.

F/L RJ Curtis DFM	*Pilot*	*KIA*
Sgt SF Martin	*Flight Engineer*	*KIA*
F/O WLW Jones	*Navigator*	*KIA*
F/S BG Green	*Bomb Aimer*	*KIA*
F/S RS Cole	*WOP/Air*	*KIA*
F/O HC Bryant DFC	*MU Gunner*	*KIA*
W/O RFJC Hall	*Rear Gunner*	*KIA*

2nd May 1944.
Weather: Fine and sunny, westerly wind, visibility good.
Non-Operational Flying: Air Tests and Bombing Practices were carried out, also 8 Exercises of Fighter Affiliation and 6 Exercises of Air to Air Firing.

3rd May 1944.
Weather: Scattered clouds, cold, visibility good.
Non-Operational Flying: Air Tests, Bombing Practices and 20 Exercises of Fighter Affiliation were carried out.

4th May 1944.
Weather: Overcast, cold strong westerly winds, visibility good.
Non-Operational Flying: Air Tests and Local Flying were carried out.
Defence: A Station Defence Exercise took place commencing at 1400hours. The Squadron Commander, Squadron Leader EGB Reid, for Wing Commander AJ Samson DFC, and the LDA Lieutenant Colonel W Jayne inspected defences.

5th May 1944.
Weather: Overcast, showers, cold strong westerly wind, visibility poor.
Non-Operational Flying: Air Tests were carried out in the morning. Remainder of the day was a stand-down.
Visits: Squadron Leader B Keary, DFC Group Gunnery Leader paid a visit to the Squadron.

6th May 1944.
Weather: Cloudy, strong winds visibility fair.
Non-Operational Flying: Local Flying, Air Tests, 24 Exercises of Fighter Affiliation and 9 Exercises of Air to Air Firing were carried out.

7th May 1944.
Weather: Fine and sunny all day, visibility good.
Non-Operational Flying: 3 Exercises of Air to Air Firing were carried out, also Local Flying and Air Tests.

Operational Flying: BOMBING – NANTES.
Ten aircraft were detailed to bomb the target, all took off and returned to Base after completing their duty. The weather was clear with good visibility. The attack appeared scattered at first but later became concentrated. Several explosions and fires were caused.
F/O TA Lever in LL652, JI-C reported: Bomb load 1 x 4000, 14 x 500 lb. bombs. Primary target: NANTES. Weather was clear. Bombed at 0306 hours from 9200 feet. Much smoke obscured target. One large explosion seen over target at 0305 hours. A good attack.
F/S CF Prowles in LL739, JI-M reported: Bomb Load 1 x 4000, 14 x 500 lb. Bombs. Primary target: NANTES. Weather was clear. Bombed at 0305 hours from 9700 feet. Bombs seen bursting on TIs. There was a heavy pall of smoke covering whole area. Raid appeared rather scattered. Route good.

Target:	*Nantes - Airfield*
Aircraft deployed total:	*99*
514 Squadron:	*10*
Aircraft lost total:	*1*
514 Squadron:	*Nil*

Comments: Another very successful raid for Bomber Commander, this time on the airfield at Nantes. Bombing was accurate with many hangers destroyed and runways damaged. This was achieved with the loss of only 1 aircraft.

8th May 1944.
Weather: Fine and sunny all day, visibility good.
Non-Operational Flying: 4 Exercises of Fighter Affiliation and 3 Exercises of Air to Air Firing were carried out.

Operational Flying: BOMBING – CAP GRIS NEZ.
Ten aircraft were detailed to bomb the target. All took off and returned to Base after completing their duty. Photographs show that most aircraft overshot. PFF were late and crews bombed visually in good visibility. There was no fighter opposition and very little flak.
S/L WG Devas in LL728 JI-B reported: Bomb load 14 x 1000 lb. bombs. Primary target: CAP GRIS NEZ. Weather was clear. Bombed at 2354 hours from 8000 feet. Smoke and small explosions seen also muzzle bursts from AA guns. Successful attack. Aircraft arrived in time and orbited to starboard before bombing. PFF markers first dropped at 2357 hours.

Target:	*Cap Gris Nez Coastal Gun Batteries*
Aircraft deployed total:	*38*
514 Squadron:	*10*
Aircraft lost total:	*Nil*
514 Squadron:	*Nil*

Comments: This attack was on gun batteries at Cap Gris Nez. The raid was unsuccessful and the guns left unscathed. Fortunately no Bomber Command Aircraft were lost.

9th May 1944.
Weather: Fine and sunny all day, visibility good.
Non-Operational Flying: Air Tests were carried out.
Lecture: An Operational Research for all Aircrew at 14.00 hours was given by Dr. Peters.

Movements: Wing Commander AJ Samson, DFC returned by air from RAF Cranwell on completion of the Junior Commanders' Course.

Operational Flying: BOMBING – CAP GRIS NEZ.
Nineteen aircraft were detailed to bomb the target. One failed to take off, the remainder returned to Base on completion of their duty. Weather was hazy but crews had visual of coastline and target. TIs appeared scattered and all bombing was corrected on instruction of Master Bomber, few crews having TIs in bomb sight. Target area was well covered with bombs, much smoke and dust being reported. One large bluish green explosion at 0414 hours. Opposition negligible. Two or three burst of H/F reported but no searchlights.
P/O R Langley in DS842, JI-F reported: Bomb load 1 x 1000 GP, 13 x 1000 MC. Primary target: CAP GRIS NEZ. Clear conditions, and visuals and red and green TIs were obtained. On instructions of Master Bomber, bombs were aimed to left of red TIs at 0413 hours from 6400 feet. For a small target, markers appeared scattered at beginning of raid but concentrated towards the end. Bombs were seen to burst in centre of TI concentration. Attack improved later and bombs appear to burst in area marked.

(Above) DS842 JI-F Fanny Firkin 2 landing at RAF Deenethorpe on lecture tour of USAAF bases, May 1944. Source: Marilyn Langley.

Target:	*Cap Gris Nez Coastal Gun Batteries*
Aircraft deployed total:	*414*
514 Squadron:	*18*
Aircraft lost total:	*1*
514 Squadron:	*Nil*

Comments: Bomber Command forces returned to the gun batteries for another attempt, this time being much more successful with four claimed to have been hit. A single aircraft was lost.

10th May 1944.
Weather: Fine and sunny, clear skies until evening, visibility good.
Non-Operational Flying: Air Tests and Cross Country Exercises were carried out.
Operational Flying: BOMBING – COURTRAI.
15 aircraft were detailed to bomb the target. All took off and returned to Base on completion of their duty. Weather was hazy but TIs of all colours were seen. The Master Bomber directed bombing operations and made favourable comments on results. Bomb bursts were concentrated around markers. Slight H/F but no searchlights. A few sightings of enemy aircraft were made but no combats.
F/S EHJ Shearing in LL728, JI-B reported: Bomb load 7 x 1000 GP, 6 x 1000 MC. Primary target: COURTRAI. Hazy conditions over target, but green and yellow markers seen. Bombed centre of green and yellow TIs at 2327 hours from 11,000 feet. Unable to hear Master Bomber. Target well illuminated. Sighted enemy aircraft (Me109) below.
F/S CF Prowles in DS816, JI-O reported: Bomb load 7 x 1000 GP, 7 x 1000 MC. Primary target: COURTRAI. There was no cloud but general mist. Bombed at 2337 hours from 11000 feet. Red glow seen in centre of target area. All bombs seen to fall in area indicated by Master Bomber.

Target:	*Courtrai Railway Yards*
Aircraft deployed total:	*506*
514 Squadron:	*15*
Aircraft lost total:	*13*
514 Squadron:	*Nil*

Comments: This was a combined raid on 5 separate targets, all of them railway marshalling yards. It was considered a success. Of the 13 Bomber Command aircraft lost, none were from the Courtrai raid.

11th May 1944.
Weather: Fine and sunny, visibility good, clear skies.
Non-Operational Flying: Air Tests were carried out, also Height and Load Tests.
Visits: Wing Commander M. Wyatt, DFC Headquarters No. 3 Group, who assumes command of the Squadron w.e.f. 15th. May, 1944, visited the Station. He attended the Main Briefing of the Operational Crews and witnessed the take-off. At the Main Briefing Wing Commander AJ Samson, DFC who leaves the Squadron on the 15th May 1944, to take over Command of the 1567 Con. Unit bade farewell to the Crews operating that night.
Administrative: Much against his better judgment and with an adequate measure of sympathy, Flight Lieutenant WAC Bowen DFC assumed responsibility for the compilation of the Squadrons Operations Record Book.
Operational Flying: BOMBING – LOUVAIN.
10 aircraft were detailed to bomb the target. All took off successfully, but one returned early owing to slight defect in port inner engine. 1 aircraft is missing. 1 aircraft brought its bombs back as no marker TI visible. The remaining seven aircraft attacked the primary target and returned to Base. Weather was clear with some haze. Target market was scattered and opinion varies as to success of raid. Result difficult to assess as smoke obscured vision in all cases. Flak was slight. Defences of Brussels and Antwerp in action. One aircraft had two combats.
P/O EA Greenwood RCAF in DS813, JI-H, reported: Bomb load 1 x 1000 GP, 5 x 1000 MC. Primary target: LOUVAIN. Clear conditions at target but ground haze. Bombed at 0022 hours from 8500 feet. Very few markers seen and bomb bursts scattered. Fuselage damaged by flak.
F/S CF Prowles in DS816, JI-O reported: Bomb load 5 x 1000 GP, 5 x 1000 MP, 5 x 500 MC. Primary target: LOUVAIN. Clear over target. Bombed as ordered by Master Bomber at 0018 hours from 8800 feet. TIs appeared concentrated and bombs fell in area marked. Large deep red explosion at 0014 hours.

Combat Report – Pro-forma:
Aircraft: LL733 'G'
Captain: P/O CJ Thomson RAAF
Target: LOUVAIN

1st Encounter: At 0024 hours, height 11,000 feet, heading 253 degrees M., position 5047N, 0450E. With Lancaster silhouetted against target and a fighter flare on port quarter, Rear Gunner sighted what he believed was a Ju88 approaching from the port quarter up to dead astern. Rear Gunner ordered corkscrew to port and both Gunners fired. E/A was then lost in corkscrew.

2nd Encounter: At 0032 hours, height 11,000 feet, heading 342 degrees M., position 5057N, 0404E. Visual Monica warning alerted crew to presence of A/C in vicinity. Mid Upper Gunner sighted S/E coming in from starboard quarter level. Mid Upper Gunner ordered for corkscrew to starboard and fired a short burst (but appears to have had a stoppage). E/A was lost in corkscrew.

MU Gunner – Sgt GR Lawrence – 40 rounds.   2nd Encounter – 12 rounds.
Rear Gunner – Sgt DA Gee - 160 rounds.

Target:	*Louvain Railway Yards*
Aircraft deployed total:	*110*
514 Squadron:	*10 (1 returned early)*
Aircraft lost total:	*4*
514 Squadron:	*1*

Comments: Another attack on railway marshalling yards was again successful with bombs hitting various buildings. Later reports stated that this was a major disruption at this site which did not fully recover full operations for over 6 months. Despite the best effort of crews, some civilian casualties were reported.

Missing aircraft:

LL739, JI-M. Aircraft attacked by an FW 190, possibly flown by Ofw. Vinzenz Glessübel, while leaving the target area. LL739 crashed in the Brussels area. Starboard inner engine caught fire which spread to entire wing. P/O Winterford was shot in the leg by German patrol who initially thought he was a saboteur. F/O Ramsey and Sgt Brown evaded for a while but were captured by the Gestapo. All crew members survived.

P/O AB Cunningham RNZAF	Pilot	POW
F/O RJ Ramsey	Navigator	POW
F/O R Brailsford	Bomb Aimer	Evaded
Sgt JW Stone	WOP/Air	Evaded

Sgt FW Brown *MU Gunner* *POW*
Sgt BL Roberts *Rear Gunner* *Evaded*
P/O DA Winterford *Flight Engineer* *POW*

12th May 1944.
Weather: Fine and sunny, visibility good.
Non-Operational Flying: Air Tests were carried out and Air to Sea Firing and Air to Air Exercises took place. 1 Cross Country Exercise was completed and 5 details of Fighter Affiliation.
Movements: All Aircrew personnel who were not operating on the previous night were assembled in the Briefing Room during the morning and Wing Commander AJ Samson, DFC, who leaves the Squadron to take command of No. 1657 Con. Unit w.e.f. 15th May 1944, said farewell to them.

13th May 1944.
Weather: Fine and sunny early, but dull and overcast later with rain during the evening.
Visits: Major General W Ogilvie, MCH, FRCS, Surgical Advisor to the Eastern Command, paid a visit to the Station and during the afternoon made a flight in one of the Aircraft engaged in the Fighter Affiliation detail.
Non-Operational Flying: Air Tests, Air to Sea Firing, Cross Country Exercises, 6 details of Fighter Affiliation and Formation Flying practices were carried out.
Operational Flying: 10 Aircraft were detailed for operations, but the effort was cancelled.

14th May 1944.
Weather: Dull and overcast for greater part of the day, with strong surface wind.
Non-Operational Flying: Air Tests were carried out, Formation Flying Practice and 8 details of Fighter Affiliation.
Operational Flying: 10 Aircraft were detailed for Operations, but the effort was cancelled during the course of Main Briefing.
Ground Training: Flight Lieutenant W.A.C. Bowen, DFC, gave a lecture during the morning to numbers of the Bomb Aimers and Wireless Operators, on the use of the Astro - compass.

15th May 1944.
Weather: Dull and overcast all day.
Non-Operational Flying: Air Tests were carried out, Formation Flying Practice and 14 details of Fighter Affiliation. 3 Aircraft were also engaged in a Special Night Navigation exercise in which was incorporated Infra-red Photography and Night Bombing at Rushford Range.
Ground Training: Further lectures were given to Bomb Aimers by Flight Lieutenant WAC Bowen, DFC, upon the use of the Astro-compass.

16th May 1944.
Weather: Dull and cloudy with occasional rain.
Non-Operational Flying: Air Tests were carried out, Air to Air Firing, Cross Country Exercises, Formation Flying and SBA Practice and 2 details of Fighter Affiliation.
Visits: During the afternoon Wing Commander H Mahaddie, DSO, DFC, AFC visited the Station and gave a lecture to all Squadron Aircrew Personnel upon the techniques and methods adopted by the Pathfinder Forces.
Movements: Flight Lieutenant M Stevens, Squadron Adjutant, was ordered to the Ely Hospital to undergo a throat examination.

17th May 1944.
Weather: Dull and cloudy with rain during the afternoon.
Non-Operational Flying: Air Tests were carried out and also some Air Firing and Formation Flying Practice. There was 1 Cross Country Exercise.
Awards: The immediate award of the DFM to Flight Sergeant CJ Medland was promulgated, for his action on the night of 1st May 1944, when on operations in bringing back his badly damaged aircraft on 2 engines.
Ground Training: Squadron Leader D Stafford Clark, the Medical Officer, gave a First - Aid lecture to the Aircrew.

18th May 1944.
Weather: Dull and overcast.
Non-Operational Flying: Air Tests were carried out.
Visits: The Squadron Commander paid a visit to No. 3 Group, Headquarters.
General: There was a general stand - down in the afternoon.

19th May 1944.
Weather: Heavy ground mist during morning, weather generally fair later.
Non-Operational Flying: Air Tests were carried out.
Operational Flying: BOMBING – LE MANS.
22 aircraft were detailed to bomb the target. All took off successfully but one returned early because of faulty equipment. Two others did not bomb through inability to identify target with certainty. The remaining 19 aircraft all attacked the primary target. 1 landed at Bourne on return and 1 at Gravely. 1 aircraft crashed on return near Newmarket, five members of the crew being killed. 10/10 cloud over target and all but one aircraft bombed below cloud. Attack appeared scattered towards the end. Two crews reported oil fires and one thought ammunition dump. Two enemy fighters were seen and one aircraft was engaged in combat which was claimed as damaged.

F/L LCA Taylor RAAF in LL652, JI-C reported: Bomb load 4 x 1000 USA, 5 x 1000 MC, 1 x 1000 GP, 4 x 500 GP. Primary target: LE MANS. Cloud base 8000 feet at target but clear below. Bombed markers at 0025 hours from 7500 feet, and bomb bursts seen. Was at target too early to form an opinion as to the effectiveness of the bombing.

F/S CF Prowles in DS222, JI-T reported: Bomb Load 4 x 1000 USA, 5 x 1000 MC, 1 x 1000 GP, 4 x 500 GP. Primary Target: LE MANS. 6-10/10ths cloud over target. Bombed on Master Bombers instructions at 0025 ½ hours from 8,000 feet. Large explosion seen near buildings. After bombing, second explosion seen giving a brilliant white flash. Attack appeared well concentrated. On return landed at Bourne in mistake.

Combat Report – Pro-forma:
Aircraft: DS842 'F'
Captain: F/O EA Campbell RCAF
Target: LE MANS
At 0015 hours, height 11,000 feet, heading 185 degrees M., position 4840N, 0010E. Rear Gunner sighted a Ju88 approaching from port quarter down at a range of 300 yards. Rear Gunner ordered corkscrew to port. Both Gunners opened fire as E/A broke away to starboard quarter up.
MU Gunner – Sgt Jones RCAF – 100 rounds.
Rear Gunner – Sgt SA Harvey RCAF – 500 rounds.

Target: Le Mans Railway Yards.
Aircraft deployed total: 116
514 Squadron: 22 (1 returned early)
Aircraft lost total: 3
514 Squadron: 1 (crashed on return near Newmarket)

Comments: This operation was to attack the railway yards at Le Mans. A very successful raid, with a large explosion as an ammunition carriage blew up. Two of the main lines were disrupted with trains and sheds also destroyed. In a tragic incident, the Master Bomber and his Deputy's aircraft collided in the air over the target.

Crashed aircraft:

LL641, JI-K. Bomb load 4 x 1000 USA, 5 x 1000 MC, 1 x 1000 GP, 4 x 500 GP. Primary target: LE MANS. Bombed markers at 0030 hours from 7500 feet. 1 x 1000 MC hung up and was jettisoned safe in the English Channel near French Coast. Aircraft crashed on return near Newmarket, trying to effect a forced landing after having earlier suffered battle damage. No night-fighter claims related to this loss; it is believed that the damage was due to flak. The Bomb Aimer baled out successfully and the Rear Gunner was thrown clear, but sustained injuries. All remaining members of the crew were killed.

F/S EHJ Shearing	*Pilot*	*KIA*
F/S VH Tayton	*Navigator*	*KIA*
F/O J Peake RCAF	*Bomb Aimer*	*Survived*
Sgt E Marshall	*WOP/Air*	*KIA*
Sgt JL Masson RCAF	*MU Gunner*	*KIA*
Sgt MH Smart RCAF	*Rear Gunner*	*Injured*
Sgt AT Blunden	*Flight Engineer*	*KIA*

20th May 1944.
Weather: Heavy ground mist during morning, generally overcast for remainder of day, with occasional sunny periods.
Non-Operational Flying: Air Tests were carried out.
Operational Flying: 24 Aircraft were detailed for Bombing Operations which were subsequently cancelled.
Awards: The award of the DFC to Pilot Officer ABL Winstanley was promulgated.

21st May 1944.
Weather: Dull and overcast all day, with strong surface winds.
Non-Operational Flying: Air Tests were carried out and some Air/Air Practices.
Operational Flying: BOMBING – DUISBURG.
23 aircraft were detailed to bomb the target and all took off successfully. 19 aircraft attacked the primary target and landed at Base on completion of the duty. 1 aircraft returned early as the pilot was sick and 3 aircraft were missing. Weather was 10/10 cloud with tops at 20,000 feet and consequently markers quickly disappeared into cloud. Many crews waited in target area to bomb on the markers which were not easily identified. Most crews reported sky markers as scattered and bombing therefore was widespread. Flak was in moderate heavy barrage, accurate at first but decreasing as attack progressed. Outward journey was uneventful but on homeward journey fighter activity was in evidence up to 4 deg E. One aircraft was attacked by a fighter up to 30 miles out to sea from the enemy coast.
F/L JG Timms in LL652, JI-C reported: Bomb load 1 x 2000 bomb, 120 x 30, 600 x 4 incendiaries. Primary target: DUISBURG. There was 10/10 cloud. Bombed red TI at 0123 hours from 21,000 feet. Opposition thought slight and searchlights ineffective. Arrived at DUISBURG at 0111 hours and orbited twice.
F/S CF Prowles in DS816, JI-O reported: Bomb Load 1 x 2000 lb. Bomb, 120 x 30, 600 x 4 incendiaries. Primary Target: DUISBURG. There was 10/10ths cloud with tops at 18.000 feet. Bombed markers at 0124 hours from 21,000 feet. Cloud prevented any visual. Fighter Flares seen from target to coast on homeward route. Sighted 4 E/As at 0026 hours which crossed above from port to starboard at 20,000 feet. At 0120 hours aircraft was fired on by unidentified E/A over target. Again at 0204 hours unidentified E/A approached from astern firing a short burst but Lancaster evaded.

Combat Report:
Aircraft: LL733 'S'
Captain: S/L. RC Chopping
Target: DUISBURG
Homeward bound (bombs dropped), flying on a course of 274 degrees T, IAS 180, at a height of 17,500 feet. At 02.04 hours in position 5250N 0314E Rear Gunner reported trace coming from dark part of sky passing 200-300 feet behind Lancaster and apparently fired at extreme range from fine starboard quarter down. Rear Gunner immediately gave order to corkscrew to starboard and no further

indication of E/A was experienced. The E/A was not observed by any member of the crew. Visibility was fair. No moon and 10/10ths cloud. Numerous fighter flares were burning in the vicinity but there were no searchlights or flak.
MU Gunner – Sgt LS Combe – Nil.
Rear Gunner – F/Sgt EJ Fox – Nil.

Target:	Duisburg Area
Aircraft deployed total:	532
514 Squadron:	23 (1 returned early)
Aircraft lost total:	29
514 Squadron:	3

Comments: The target area was covered with a blanket of cloud. However, the sky marking was excellent and the target was severely damaged.

Missing Aircraft:

DS633 A2-B. Circumstances unclear but Squadron ORB states aircraft is believed to have crashed in The Wash. A fix was obtained at RAF Waterbeach at 0303 hours and the crew was ordered to jettison its bombs. Possibly shot down by the Me410 intruder of Fw. Johann Trenke, who claimed three aircraft over Northern Norfolk between 0305 and 0322 hours.

F/S TL Gibson	Pilot	KIA
Sgt AH Freeburn	Navigator	KIA
Sgt JL Dunbar	Bomb Aimer	KIA
Sgt L Buxton	WOP/Air	KIA
Sgt GH Kemp	MU Gunner	KIA
Sgt J Gallagher	Rear Gunner	KIA
Sgt J Fraser	Flight Engineer	KIA

DS781 JI-R Crashed in the North Sea all crew KIA. There are several claims by night-fighter crews for Lancasters shot down as they left the Dutch coast and it is most likely that DS781 fell victim to one of these. MU Gunner Sgt Haigh is buried in Kiel.

P/O BW Windsor DFM RNZAF	Pilot	KIA
Sgt GK Woodward	Navigator	KIA
F/S WE Brown RCAF	Bomb Aimer	KIA
F/S RD Langford	WOP/Air	KIA
Sgt EW Haigh	MU Gunner	KIA
Sgt J Birch	Rear Gunner	KIA
Sgt FL Dolamore DFM	Flight Engineer	KIA

(Above) Hauptmann Martin Drewes claimed at least two 514 Sqn Lancasters amongst his 43 night victims. DS824, JI-K (P/O JK Williams) was brought down on 21st January 1944 on the op to Magdeburg whilst LL695, JI-A (F/S CJ Medland) was claimed on the Duisburg operation above. Martin Drewes survived the war, passing away in 2013 in Brazil. Source: Airworx Gmbh Archive.

LL695 JI-A. Shot down at 0138 hours by the night fighter (probably Bf110) of Hptm. Martin Drewes, Stab III./NJGI near Eindhoven.

F/S CJ Medland DFM	Pilot	POW
F/O D Walker	Navigator	Evaded
F/S LJ Venus	Bomb Aimer	POW
Sgt L Shimmons	WOP/Air	Evaded
Sgt CE Rose RCAF	MU Gunner	KIA
Sgt BR Williams	Rear Gunner	KIA
Sgt AR Sealtiel	Flight Engineer	KIA

22nd May 1944.
Weather: Dull in morning but broken cloud and sunshine later.
Non-Operational Flying: Air Tests were carried out.
Operational Flying: BOMBING – DORTMUND.
17 aircraft were detailed to bomb the target but only 16 took off, the seventeenth having its mid-upper turret u/s. Of the sixteen only 7 attacked the primary target, the other 9 being forced to return because of heavy icing conditions. 13 of the aircraft eventually landed at Base and the remaining three at Woodbridge. The Crew of 'S' which landed at Woodbridge were ordered to bale out and after doing so, the Pilot successfully landed the Aircraft. Rain and severe icing at take-off. Weather clear over target and all crews identified and bombed the markers. Fires numerous around the aiming point. Fighters were in evidence in target area only but no combats were reported. Defences were slight heavy flak with numerous searchlights acting aimlessly.
F/L LCA Taylor RAAF in LL652, JI-C reported: Bomb load 1 x 2000 lb. bomb, 96 x 30, 810 x 4, 90 x 4 incendiaries. Primary target: DORTMUND. Clear conditions over target. Bombed red and green markers at 0049½ hours from 17,000 feet. Bombing seemed accurate if markers correctly placed, but some severe undershoots noticed. Large explosion seen to north of aiming point. Fighter flares seen on whole route out to the target.

Combat Report – Pro-forma:
Aircraft: LL727 'C2'
Captain: F/O EA Campbell. RCAF
Target: DORTMUND
At 0125 hours, height 17,000 feet, heading 285 degrees T., position 5100N 0550E Monica warning caused Wireless Operator to alert

Captain of suspected E/A. Rear Gunner sighted unidentified E/A holding off at 500 - 550 yards on port quarter down. Corkscrew to port was ordered and Gunners Opened fire before E/A was lost in corkscrew.
MU Gunner – Sgt ER Jones RCAF – 150 rounds.
Rear Gunner – Sgt SA Harvey RCAF – 600 rounds.

Target: *Dortmund Area*
Aircraft deployed total: *375*
514 Squadron: *16*
Aircraft lost total: *18*
514 Squadron: *Nil*

Comments: This industrial target had not received Bomber Command attention for approximately a year. This would seem to have been a scattered raid with some severe under-shoots reported. Several 514 Squadron aircraft reported severe to extreme icing forcing 9 aircraft to return. This level of returns was unprecedented for 514 Sqn, which is a reflection of how hazardous the icing was. The majority of the bombs dropped landed in the south/eastern suburbs.

23rd May 1944.
Weather: Fair, slight haze during early part of the day, but clearing later. Sunny periods.
Non-Operational Flying: Air Tests were carried out.
General: During the afternoon there was a general stand - down.

24th May 1944.
Weather: Haze during early morning. Generally sunny.
Administrative: Wing Commander M Wyatt, DFC, arrived from Headquarters No. 3 Group and took over Command of the Squadron. Squadron Leader EGB Reid who has been acting Commander of the Squadron since the departure of Wing Commander AJ Samson, DFC, left to take up duties at Headquarters No. 3 Group.
Non-Operational Flying: Air Tests were carried out.
Operational Flying: BOMBING – BOULOGNE - GUN BATTERIES.
18 aircraft were detailed to bomb the target, but one failed to take off because of a fault in the mid-upper turret. The 17 aircraft which took off all bombed the primary target and on completion of their duty landed at Base. Cloudless conditions over target but a slight haze. Most crews saw the coastline but had other visuals. Bomb bursts were

well concentrated around green TIs. Very slight opposition encountered and no fighters.

F/O TA Lever in LL697, JI-E reported: Bomb load 9 x 1000 MC, 1 x 1000 GP, 1 x 1000 ANM, 4 x 500 GP. Primary target: BOULOGNE, GUN BATTERY. Haze over target. Bombed markers at 0115 hours from 8000 feet. Bombs seen to burst around TIs. Requests more trips like this one.

F/S CF Prowles in DS816, JI-O reported: Bomb load 9 x 1000 MC, 1 x 1000 GP, 1 x 1000 ANM, 4 x 500 GP. Primary target: BOULOGNE, GUN BATTERY. Very slight haze over target. Bombed at 0113 hours from 8100 feet. 1 searchlight and a few bursts of flak seen. No TI markers seen at first on arrival, only bomb bursts.

Target:	*Boulogne Gun Batteries*
Aircraft deployed total:	*224*
514 Squadron:	*17*
Aircraft lost total:	*Nil*
514 Squadron:	*Nil*

Comments: Small groups of aircraft from several Squadrons attacked the coastal batteries. Results are not reported.

25th May 1944.
Weather: Overcast all day with occasional light showers.
Non-Operational Flying: Air Tests were carried out.
Operational Flying: 19 Aircraft were detailed for Bombing Operations, but the effort was cancelled shortly after main briefing.

26th May 1944.
Weather: Overcast during the morning but sunny in the afternoon.
Non-Operational Flying: Air Tests, 1 Height and Load Test, Air/Sea Firing and Air/Air firing Exercises were carried out. There was also 14 details of Fighter Affiliation and some Practice Bombing at Gooderstone Range; a very full day's flying programme.

27th May 1944.
Weather: Bright and sunny, very warm.
Non-Operational Flying: Air tests were carried out and 1 Height and Load Test. Formation Flying and Air/Sea Firing Practice also took place.
Operational Flying: BOMBING – BOULOGNE - GUN BATTERIES.

9 aircraft were detailed to bomb the target. All took off, carried out their duty successfully and subsequently landed at base. Weather was clear and all crews clearly identified the markers, but no ground detail was seen other than the coastline. Two or three explosions seen in target area and attack believed successful. Flak was slightly heavier than before. Fighters were in evidence and one aircraft attacked an unidentified fighter near Dungeness which had been following for some time. Numerous fighter flares seen in target area from H hour onwards.

W/O CE Williams in LL728, JI-B reported: Bomb load 7 x 1000 MC, 4 x 1000ANM, 4 x 500 GP. Primary target: BOULOGNE, GUN BATTERIES. Clear at target. Bombed centre of the markers at 0116 hours from 10,000 feet. Flak slight and bursting beneath. Fighter flares seen on the run-in to the target.

Combat Report – Pro-forma:
Aircraft: DS826 'U'
Captain: F/O AP Fowke RCAF
Target: BOULOGNE
At 0131 hours, height 7,000 feet, heading 358 degrees T, position 5056N, 0055E, Mid Upper Gunner sighted Me210 at 300 yards, approaching from starboard beam up and he warned crew of S/E aircraft to starboard. Mid Upper Gunner ordered corkscrew to starboard and opened fire. E/A was subsequently lost in corkscrew. Visibility was fair. No searchlights fighter flares or flak.
MU Gunner – Sgt J Lewis – 120 rounds.
Rear Gunner – Sgt GR Murphy RCAF – Nil.

Target: | *Boulogne - Gun Batteries*
Aircraft deployed total: | *272*
514 Squadron: | *9*
Aircraft lost total: | *2*
514 Squadron: | *Nil*

Comments: The targets were 5 gun batteries. Weather was clear over target and results reported as being 'believed successful'. Flak was reported as being worse than on the previous occasion.

(Above) Aiming Point photo over the gun batteries at Boulogne, taken by the crew of P/O CB Sandland. Note the other Lancaster running the gauntlet of bombing by higher-flying aircraft (bottom left). Source: courtesy of Wendy Flemming, daughter of Sgt RA Flemming RCAF, Navigator in the Sandland crew.

BOMBING – AACHEN.
10 aircraft were detailed to bomb the target, and all took off. One aircraft was missing. The remaining nine completed their duty and landed successfully at Base. Weather at target was clear but hazy. Some visuals were obtained of river and built-up area and all crews saw the red and green markers. Bomb bursts were concentrated around these. Dense smoke obscured the markers at times. Two large explosions seen. Slight to moderate light and heavy flak. Only one searchlight seen. A few sightings of fighters were made and one combat occurred, although no claim was made. Fighter flares seen from target back to enemy coast.

F/S NR Wishart in LL697, JI-E reported: Bomb load 7 x 1000 MC, 4 x 500 MC. Primary target: AACHEN. Clear over target but 10/10 cloud over sea. Bombed TIs at 0228 hours from 14,000 feet. Visual seen of built up area by light of photo flash. Some heavy flak over target. Route good. Unidentified aircraft seen dropping flares on outward journey at 0212 hours.

F/S CF Prowles in DS816, JI-O reported: Bomb load 7 x 1000 MC, 4 x 1000 ANM, 4 x 500 MC. Primary target: AACHEN. Clear at target. Bombed markers at 0229 hours from 14000 feet. One stick seen to fall among red TIs but heavy smoke pall prevented visual. Flak moderate. Trouble free trip. Unidentified twin-engine aircraft approached at 0215 hours but Lancaster evaded.

Combat Report – Pro-forma:
Aircraft: DS795 'C2'
Captain: P/O RR Harvey.
Target: AACHEN
At 0230 hours, height 12,000 feet, heading 175 degrees T, position 5050N, 0604E Rear Gunner sighted FW190 on the port quarter down, at a range of 800 – 1000 yards, illuminated by a rocket flare. Rear Gunner ordered corkscrew and both gunners opened fire with a short burst. E/A was subsequently lost in corkscrew. Visibility was good. Quarter moon.
MU Gunner – Sgt DF Acaster. – 20 rounds.
Rear Gunner – F/S ED Reid RCAF – 60 rounds.

Target:	*Aachen Railway Yards*
Aircraft deployed total:	*170*
514 Squadron:	*10*
Aircraft lost total:	*12*
514 Squadron:	*1*

Comments: This was an unusual raid in that it only lasted around 12 minutes. A new tactic using delayed, action bombs continued to hamper rescue and repair efforts on the ground. Extensive damage was reported and the suburb of Frost was described as having been 'razed to the ground'.

Missing aircraft:
LL652 JI-C Shot down by a night fighter and crashed at Schendelbeke, which is 21 miles south west of Brussels. The aircraft possibly fell victim at 0256 hours to Hptm. Hans-Karl Kamp of Stab.III/NJG4.

F/L LCA Taylor RAAF	Pilot	KIA
Sgt V Vincent	Navigator	KIA
F/S CK Thomas RAAF	Bomb Aimer	KIA
F/S SW Newman RAAF	WOP/Air	KIA
F/O FB Hill	MU Gunner	KIA
Sgt R Gill	Rear Gunner	KIA
Sgt A Roderick	Flight Engineer	KIA

28th May 1944.
Weather: Clear and sunny; very warm.
Operational Flying: BOMBING – ANGERS.
21 aircraft were detailed to bomb the target. All took off and on completion of their duty landed successfully at Base. Hazy conditions existed over the target but the markers were seen and a visual of the river was obtained. Most crews bombed on yellow TIs as instructed. Bomb bursts were well concentrated around the markers. Much smoke and some small fires were visible. A large explosion was seen at 2354½s. There were a few bursts of light and heavy flak but no searchlights. Only two fighters were seen.
F/L JG Timms in DS842, JI-F reported: Bomb load 5 x 1000 MC 1 x 1000 USA, 4 x 500 MC. Primary target: ANGERS. Clear with slight haze. Bombed at 2357 hours from 8000 feet. Bombed as instructed by Master Bomber, bursts falling across TIs. Good effort. Trouble free route.
F/S CF Prowles in DS816, JI-O reported: Bomb load 5 x 1000 MC, 1 x 1000 USA, 4 x 500 MC. Primary target: ANGERS. Clear over target. Bombed at 23591/2 hours from 9000 feet. A good visual of target. Whole target area seemed covered with flames and smoke. Route satisfactory.

Target:	*Angers Railway Yards*
Aircraft deployed total:	*126*
514 Squadron:	*21*
Aircraft lost total:	*1*
514 Squadron:	*Nil*

Comments: Collateral damage and the subsequent unintended deaths of around 254 French citizens marred this operation. The railway marshalling yards were attacked. It was described as a concentrated attack, though local reports and the 254 unintended casualties suggested otherwise.

29th May 1944.
Weather: Bright sunshine all day; very warm.
Non-Operational Flying: Air Tests were carried out and some Practice Bombing.
General: There was a Squadron stand - down during the afternoon.

30th May 1944.
Weather: Bright sunshine all day; very warm.
Non-Operational Flying: Air Tests were carried out and also some Practice Bombing at Gooderstone Range and 2 details of Fighter Affiliation.
Visits: Flight Lieutenant RF Steele and Flying Officer G McGregor of No. 84 Wing visited the Squadron and had discussions with the Navigation Section upon matters arising out of the propagation of Gee signals by the type 7000 Stations. During the afternoon they made a flight in 1 of the Squadron Aircraft and later, with the consent of the Squadron Commander, attended the briefing for the night's operations and witnessed the take – off.
Operational Flying: BOMBING – BOULOGNE - GUN BATTERIES.
15 aircraft were detailed to bomb the target and all took off, but in the case of one aircraft, an engine out on take-off and after jettisoning out at sea, the aircraft returned safely. The others all landed at Base after completing their duty. Weather was clear at target with slight haze. TIs were well concentrated, with most bombs on them, but tending to be slightly to the North. There was a fair amount of smoke and no visuals were obtained, except of the coastline. Heavy and light flak was slight but a little more than on the previous occasion. Three fighters only were seen, two twin-engined and one single-engined.
W/O CE Williams in LL728, JI-A reported: Bomb load 6 x 1000 MC, 4 x 500 MC. Primary target: BOULOGNE GUN BATTERIES. Clear over target. Bombed red TIs at 0005 hours from 8000 feet. Light and heavy flak commenced as soon as TIs fell. Flak slightly more than on previous occasion.
F/S CF Prowles in DS816, JI-O reported: Bomb load 6 x 1000 MC, 4 x 500 MC. Primary target: BOULOGNE GUN BATTERIES. Clear over target. Bombed at 0005 hours from 7100 feet. Bomb bursts concentrated on TIs.

Target:	*Boulogne Gun Batteries*
Aircraft deployed total:	*54*
514 Squadron:	*15 (1 returned early)*
Aircraft lost total:	*Nil*
514 Squadron:	*Nil*

Comments: Probably a part of a series of diversionary raids in the north of France, intended to give the impression of a potential forthcoming invasion to the north, around Pas de Calais, instead of Normandy to the south.

31st May 1944.
Weather: Sunny during the morning, but becoming overcast later in the day.
Non-Operational Flying: Air Tests were carried out and in addition there was some Local Flying and Air Photography Practice.
Operational Flying: BOMBING – TRAPPES MARSHALLING YARDS.
18 aircraft were detailed to bomb the target. Only 16 took off and all bombed the primary target, landing successfully at Base on completion of their duty. Weather was clear over the target and all crews reported the marking as concentrated. The Master Bomber was clearly heard. All crews had perfect means of visual identification and reported the bombing as straddling the yards. Flak was reported as slight and accurate with one searchlight. Fighters were much in evidence 20 miles either side of the target and several aircraft were seen shot down in the area. No combats reported by the Squadron aircraft, but a few sightings.
F/S RC Pick in DS813, JI-H reported: Bomb load 8 x 1000 MC, 8 x 500 MC. Primary target: TRAPPES. Clear at target. Moon bright. Bombed at 0200 hours from 9500 feet, as directed by Master Bomber. Bomb bursts appeared to be on target but no big fires visible. Weather unexpectedly good.

Target:	*Trappes Marshalling Yards.*
Aircraft deployed total:	*219*
514 Squadron:	*16*
Aircraft lost total:	*4*
514 Squadron:	*Nil*

Comments: It was reported by crews that the target was clear and moon-lit. The railway yards were attacked in split waves, to fairly good effect. A satisfactory operation.

(Above) Off duty: a brief respite from the pressures of war for 514 Sqn's new commander, W/Cdr Mike Wyatt DFC. The location was possibly Great Ouse, Norfolk. Source: Garth Ridley.

Monthly Summary for May 1944

Operational: (Compiled by W/O WE Egri and F/Lt. AC Bowen)

Operational Flying Hours for May 1944:	778.45
Non-Operational Flying Hours for May 1944:	223.10
Total tons of bombs dropped in May 1944:	1,088 ¾ tons.
Cumulative total tons of bombs dropped:	3,078 ¾ tons
Number of Sorties for May 1944:	218

Strength of Squadron as at 31st May 1944.

Aircrew: 81 Officers
 227 SNCOs

Ground: 2 Officers
 31 SNCOs
 316 other ranks
 12 WAAFs

June 1944

1st June 1944.
Weather: Overcast all day with light showers in the afternoon.
Non-Operational Flying: Air Tests were carried out.
Operational Flying: 16 Aircraft were detailed for Bombing Operations, but the effort was subsequently cancelled.

2nd June 1944.
Weather: Generally dull and overcast with sunny periods.
Non-Operational Flying: Air Tests were carried out and 9 details of Fighter Affiliation took place. In addition there was some Air/Air Firing Practice, 1 Cross Country Exercise and 1 Aircraft engaged on Circuits and Landings.
Operational Flying: BOMBING – WISSANT GUN POSITIONS.
10 aircraft were detailed to bomb the target, but only nine took off. Of the nine, four only bombed the primary target. Weather was 10/10ths cloud with base at 4700 feet and the tops at 6000 feet. The four aircraft bombed on the markers but the red TIs were believed to be too inland. Only bomb bursts were seen. One crew went below cloud to bomb at 4700 feet and saw bomb bursts on the land. The five aircraft which did not attack the primary target were unable to identify the target and therefore jettisoned part of their bomb loads, bringing the remainder back to Base. Flak was reported as odd bursts of heavy. No fighters were seen. All nine aircraft landed successfully at Base.
S/L WG Devas in LL728, JI-B reported: Bomb load: 1 x 1000 GP, 10 x 1000 MC, 4 x 500 MC. Primary target: WISSANT GUN POSITIONS. 8/10ths cloud with a gap. Bombed between red and green TIs at 0214½ hours from 6000 feet. Success of attack difficult to ascertain but red TI believed to be too far inland.

Target: *Wissant Gun Positions*
Aircraft deployed total: *271*
514 Squadron: *9*
Aircraft lost total: *1*
514 Squadron: *Nil*

Comments: Another Northern diversionary raid. 4 separate gun batteries were attacked.

3rd June 1944.
Weather: Generally dull and overcast, with sunny periods and occasional light rain.
Non-Operational Flying: Air Tests were carried out, and also some Air/Air and Air/Sea Firing Exercises. A number of Aircraft took part in Cross Country Formation Flying and 1 Aircraft took part in Practice Bombing.

4th June 1944.
Weather: Dull and overcast all day.
Non-Operational Flying: Air Tests and Formation Flying Practice were carried out. Some Practice Bombing took place at Gooderstone Range, and some Air/Air Firing. In addition there was 7 details of Fighter Affiliation and 1 Aircraft was engaged in Night Circuits and Landings.
Operational Flying: 10 Aircraft were detailed for Bombing Operations which were however cancelled shortly before Main Briefing was due to take place.

5th June 1944.
Weather: Fine and sunny.
Non-Operational Flying: Air Tests were carried out, Formation Flying Practice, Air/Air Firing Exercises and 1 detail of Fighter Affiliation.
Operational Flying: BOMBING – OUISTERHAM.
22 aircraft were detailed to bomb the primary target at Ouisterham but only 21 aircraft took off. 1 aircraft had engine trouble. On completion of the duty 20 aircraft landed at Base and 1 at Woodbridge. Cloud over target was 3/10 – 10/10 with slight haze. All crews bombed on the markers which were reported as concentrated with a few red and green slightly to the East, believed to be in the sea, which attracted some bombing. Consensus of opinion was that the attack was good and concentrated bombing resulted on the land around the Aiming Point. Explosions were reported at 0510 hours in the target area. One fighter was seen in the target area and occasional bursts of H/F from Caen area. All aircraft carried a bomb load of 9 x 1000 MC and 2 x 500 MC. P/O CJ Thompson RAAF in LL692, JI-A reported: Broken cloud at target. Obtained visual of coast and target and bombed at 0507 hours from 9000 feet. Unable to assess results as little to be seen for ice on the panel.

Target:	Ouisterham Gun Batteries
Aircraft deployed total:	1012
514 Squadron:	21
Aircraft lost total:	3
514 Squadron:	Nil

Comments: Several gun batteries in the actual invasion area were targeted on the early morning of D-Day. Although shown in the ORB as 5th June 1944, F/L Alex Campbell recalls this raid as having taken place at dawn in 6th June. 514 Squadron was tasked to bomb Ouisterham. A record total of 5000 tons of bombs was dropped by BC in the one night.

6th June 1944.
Weather: Sunny periods during the morning, overcast in the afternoon and heavy rain during the evening. Strong winds all day.
Operational Flying: BOMBING – LISIEUX.
20 aircraft were detailed to bomb the primary target of Lisieux but only 17 aircraft succeeded in taking off. Aircraft 'K2', G2', 'F2', 'E2', 'C2' and 'J2' carried bomb loads of 16 x 500 MC Nose Inst. and 2 x 500 MC LD, whilst aircraft 'Q', 'T', 'S', 'O', 'L', 'J', 'G', 'F', 'R', 'E' and 'B' carried 16 x 500 MC tail fused and 2 x 500 MC LD. All aircraft landed at base on completion of their duty. Broken cloud down to 6000 feet at target and crews bombed below cloud. Red TIs seen until 0142 hours. Most of the time the Master Bomber was unintelligible because of other aircraft transmitting on the intercom. Many bomb bursts were seen on the town and a few fires. A little light flak only was seen and no searchlights. One Ju88 and 2 unidentified fighters were sighted. An aircraft on fire, believed hit by naval units, was also hit by Lancaster 'E2' of this Squadron. Some light flak on the coast and from the sea.
Note: No loss of German aircraft was noted in Nachtjagd War Diaries.
F/S CS Johnson in LL677, A2-E reported: Weather was clear below but cloud above. Bombed at 0139 hours from 2400 feet. Bombing seemed accurate but smoke obscured target area. Route quiet. Gunners assisted an Me110 into the sea, finishing a job apparently started by a Mosquito, although A/A fire was seen previously. Both F/Gunner and MU Gunner fired bursts and strikes were seen. Aircraft crashed and exploded in sea. Half claim made.

Combat Report:
Aircraft: LL677 'E2'
Captain: F/S CS Johnson.

Target: LISIEUX
At 0206 hours in position 5005 N 0053 E, (immediately after Captain had seen cannon fire to starboard beam and Mosquito in same direction). Front Gunner reported Me110 on starboard bow level at a range of 300 to 400 yards with port engine on fire. As E/A crossed in front of Lancaster from starboard to port, both Front and Mid Upper Gunners opened fire and strikes were observed on E/A by Gunners, W/Op and Captain. E/A was immediately enveloped in flames and exploded just before crashing in the sea where it continued to burn for a considerable period. E/A aircraft claimed as destroyed.
MU Gunner – Sgt J Poad – 200 rounds.
Rear Gunner - F/S RA Dymott. – Nil
Front Gunner – F/S E Lush - 60 rounds.

Target:	Lisieux Railway Yards and Lines
Aircraft deployed total:	1065
514 Squadron:	17
Aircraft lost total:	11
514 Squadron:	Nil

Comments: Bomber Command provided this massive effort, with a multitude of targets, in support of the D-Day invasion. With varying weather conditions over the different targets accuracy was always going to be compromised. Unfortunately this resulted in a number of civilian casualties in several locations. 6 aircraft were lost in the attack on Caen alone. Complications with TIs delayed the attack and gave time for defences to be readied. The crews were forced to bomb from 3000 feet and so experienced extraordinary amounts of flak and the losses that came with it. The railway yards in Lisieux were badly damaged. Sadly, the town was unfortunately also hit.

7th June 1944.
Weather: Overcast all day but clearing slightly towards the evening.
Non-Operational Flying: Air Tests were carried out.
Visits: Captain P Mansdorf of the United States Naval Air Corps paid a visit to the Station and attended the briefing of the Crews for the nights Bombing Operations and also the interrogation on the Crews' return.
Operational Flying: BOMBING – MASSEY PALAISEAU
18 aircraft were detailed to bomb the primary target of Massey Palaiseau and all aircraft took off, each carrying a bomb load of 18 x 500 MC. Two aircraft were missing and two returned early to Base due

to compass trouble. Of the remaining 14 aircraft, 13 landed at Base on return and one landed at Manston. Weather was clear below the cloud, the base of which was about 7500 feet. All aircraft bombed on the markers which were reported as concentrated and the result was concentrated bombing amongst the TIs. Huge columns of smoke were seen on leaving the target. Light flak was particularly vicious in the target area and two aircraft were damaged the rear gunner in each case being injured. Searchlights were few. Much fighter activity was experienced in target area and eight or nine aircraft were seen to be shot down.

P/O CJ Thomson RAAF in LL692, JI-A reported: Weather was clear below cloud, base at 7500 feet. Bombed green TI at 0213 hours from 6000 feet. Bomb bursts were seen and raid was thought satisfactory. Monica was u/s. Master Bomber was clear and precise.

P/O EJ Cossens RNZAF in LL624, JI-R, reported: Clear below cloud. Bombed as instructed by Master Bomber at 0216 hours from 5000 feet. Starboard wing damaged by light flak. Rear turret damaged due to a fighter attack. Rear Gunner seriously injured. Captain too busy elsewhere to pay attention to raid. Landed at Manston.

Combat Report:
Aircraft: LL624 'R'
Captain: P/O EJ Cossens. RNZAF
Target: MASSY PALAISEAU
On the night of 7 / 8th June 1944, Lancaster 'R' of 514 Squadron was in target area on bombing run flying on a course of 120 deg T at a height of 6000 feet IAS 180. At 0217 hours M/U Gunner and Captain simultaneously saw an Me109 at range of 300 yards on starboard beam level. Captain immediately corkscrewed to starboard and E/A closed in very fast and passed under Lancaster. As E/A passed under Lancaster, Mid Upper Gunner fired a 3 second burst and E/A broke away to port quarter down. E/A then attacked again at a very steep angle from dead astern below and fired a burst which shot off the Rear Gunner's leg and rendered the rear turret unserviceable. The E/A's breakaway was not seen owing to the Rear Gunners injuries.
MU Gunner – F/L HH Wright – 120 rounds.
Rear Gunner – Sgt PC Brown. – Nil

Aircraft: LL678 'L2'
Captain: P/O HS Delacour RAAF
Target: MASSY PALAISEAU

Outward bound (bombs not dropped), approaching target area, flying on a course of 092 degrees T, IAS 175 at height of 2000 feet. At 02.05 hours in position 48. 47N 01.55E, trace was seen by several members of the crew from port bow down. Almost immediately the W/Op. saw an unidentified S/E aircraft breaking away to starboard quarter up, at range of 400 yards. The Pilot, on seeing the trace, put Lancaster into diving turn to port into cloud, and E/A was not seen again.
MU Gunner – Sgt Williams RCAF – Nil.
Rear Gunner – F/S GD Savage.   - Nil.

Aircraft: LL677 'E2'
Captain: P/O LM Petry. RNZAF
Target: MASSY PALAISEAU
Homeward bound (bombs dropped), flying on a course of 005 degrees M at a height of 7,000 feet. At 0240 hours in position 4849N 0105E, Mid Upper Gunner reported a Do-217 on the starboard quarter level at range of 200 yards and ordered Captain to dive into cloud about 200 feet below. During the dive E/A opened fire, the trace passing fairly close behind Lancaster. Neither Gunners opened fire. The Mid Upper Gunner being unsighted and the Rear Gunner having previously having sustained severe injuries from flak and the rear turret having been rendered unserviceable. The E/A was lost to view in the cloud and was not seen again.
MU Gunner – F/S KA Pitt RAAF – Nil.
Rear Gunner – F/S A MacLean - Nil.

Aircraft: DS842 'F2'
Captain: F/S WM Watkins
Target: MASSY PALAISEAU
On bombing run over target area, flying on a course of 100 degrees T, IAS 180, at a height of 7000 feet. At 02.12 hours when just about to bomb, Mid Upper Gunner saw Ju88 on starboard quarter below at range of 50 to 100 yards in attacking position, and immediately ordered corkscrew to starboard as E/A opened fire to which Mid Upper Gunner replied with a 5 second burst and Rear Gunner a 1 second burst in direction of Mid Upper Gunners trace. E/As trace passed very close to Lancaster's rear turret but caused no damage. No hits were claimed on E/A which was lost to view in corkscrew.
2nd Encounter: At 02.58 hours, homeward bound flying on a course of 335 degrees T. in position 4955N 0030E, IAS 200 at a height of 7,000 feet, Rear Gunner reported Me410 dead astern below at a range of 300 yards and immediately ordered corkscrew to starboard. At the same

time, Rear Gunner opened fire with a 3 second burst but E/A did not reply and broke away below Lancaster and was not seen again. No hits were claimed on E/A
MU Gunner – Sgt P Dawson – 200 rounds.
Rear Gunner – Sgt B Ferries - 320 rounds.

Target:	*Massey Palaiseau Railway Targets*
Aircraft deployed total:	*337*
514 Squadron:	*18 (2 returned early)*
Aircraft lost total:	*27*
514 Squadron:	*2*

Comments: This turned out to be a costly raid, with the loss of 8.3% of the Force. The attack was split into two waves and delays proved deadly when enemy night fighters attacked with a vengeance taking a heavy toll. It is testimony to crews' commitment that under such extreme circumstances, the bombing remained accurate.

Missing aircraft:

LL727 A2-C. Set on fire by a night fighter over the target area, the crew escaped from their attacker, received further flak damage before finally being shot down by the Ju88 of Hptm. Herbert Lorenz of 1/NJG2 at 0255 hours. Crashed at St-Eusoye, 20 km NE of Beauvais.

F/O L Greenburgh	*Pilot*	*Evaded*
W/O LJW Sutton	*(2nd Pilot)*	*Evaded*
F/S R Fox	*Navigator*	*Evaded*
F/S EG Rippingale	*Air Bomber*	*Evaded*
F/S J Stromberg	*WOP/Air*	*KIA*
Sgt PJ Carey	*MU Gunner*	*POW*
Sgt RS Woosnam	*Rear Gunner*	*POW*
Sgt F Collingwood	*Flight Engineer*	*POW*

DS822, JI-T. Crashed at La Celle-les-Bordes. The aircraft is believed to have been coned and hit by flak leaving the target area. The Lancaster was then shot down by a Bf110 flown by Major Walter Borchers. German soldiers attempted to shoot at P/O McGown as he descended by parachute. On his return to England, he transferred to another squadron, flying Mosquitoes. Sgt Clarke was held as a POW at Buchenwald Concentration Camp until transferred to a POW camp. It is believed that Sgt Clarke and another airman were due to be executed by the SS, but a Luftwaffe officer intervened after being told this by another RAF officer, insisted that the RAF men were Luftwaffe prisoners and ensured that they were transferred to a Luftwaffe POW camp. It is recognised by many veterans that some Germans, at least, fought a decent war.

P/O WL McGown	Pilot	Evaded
W/O AN Durham RAAF	Navigator	Evaded
P/O LWC Lewis	Bomb Aimer	POW
W/O KE Bryan RAAF	WOP/Air	KIA
F/S JGS Boanson	MU Gunner	KIA
F/S RC Guy	Rear Gunner	KIA
Sgt J Clarke	Flight Engineer	POW

(Above) The tail section of DS822 photographed the morning after being shot down at La Celle les Bordes. The child in the picture is Francois Ydier, son of the Town Clerk. Source: Frank Corner / Jean Ronald.

8th June 1944.
Weather: Overcast all day with rain in the evening.

Non-Operational Flying: Air Tests and 1 Cross Country Exercise were carried out.
Movements: Flight Lieutenant LC Blomfield took over the duties of Squadron Adjutant vice Flight Lieutenant M Stevens who today proceeded to Headquarters, No 3 Group.
Operational Flying: BOMBING – FOUGERES.
10 aircraft were detailed to Fougeres and all took off successfully. Each aircraft carried a bomb load of 16 x 500 GP and 2 x 500 MC LD. All landed at Base on completion of their duty. Weather was much as forecast and clear over target. TIs were scattered. Crews bombed westerly white TIs on the instructions of the Master Bomber who, incidentally, ran out of markers at about 0025 hours and then gave instructions for bombs to be aimed at large yellow fire. One crew bombed from 4000 feet and saw trucks blown into the air as bombs fell on railway tracks. Clouds of billowing smoke up to 5000 feet and a large explosion at 0023 hours. Fires were seen 80 miles away. Flak was negligible.
F/L JG Timms in DS842, JI-F reported: Bombed as instructed by Master Bomber at 0019 hours from 7300 feet. TIs were scattered and a built-up area was seen to south-east of the TI dropped. Opposition slight. Weather as forecast.

Target:	*Fougeres Railway Lines*
Aircraft deployed total:	*483*
514 Squadron:	*10*
Aircraft lost total:	*4*
514 Squadron:	*Nil*

Comments: Another multi-target operation saw the Bomber Command force split into groups to bomb various railway targets. This was an attempt to prevent the Germans reinforcing their troops in Normandy.

9th June 1944.
Weather: Drizzle and Rain.
Non-Operational Flying: Air Tests and Cross Country Flights were carried out.
Operational Flying: Nil

10th June 1944.
Weather: Cloudy and dull with some rain.
Non-Operational Flying: Air Tests were carried out.
Operational Flying: BOMBING – DREUX.

19 aircraft were detailed to bomb the primary target at DREUX and all took off successfully. Each aircraft carried a bomb load of 16 x 500 GP and 2 x 500 LD. All landed at Base on completion of their duty. Weather was clear with some haze. Target well marked. Green TIs at first slightly to NE of target, yellows at 0101/2, white at 0103. Master Bomber corrected bombing in each case but there was much RT interference. Large orange flash was seen at 0056 hours. Large explosion at 0100 and 0110 hours and good fires. Generally the attack was considered good. Flak was negligible and there were no searchlights. There was much fighter activity. One Me109 was claimed as damaged by Lanc 'D'.

F/S RD Pick in LL666, JI-D reported: Bomb load 16 x 500 GP, 2 x 500 LD. Primary target: DREUX. Bombed as instructed by Master Bomber at 0056½ hours from 6000 feet. Many bomb bursts near TIs seen and smoke at end of yards. Weather clear, generally quiet trip.

F/S CF Prowles in DS816, JI-O reported: Bomb load 16 x 500 GP, 2 x 500 LD. Primary target: DREUX. Bombed to starboard of green TIs as instructed by Master Bomber at 0100 hours from 6000 feet. Bombs seen to burst across yards. No trouble experienced. Weather clear with slight haze.

W/O CE Williams in LL692, JI-A reported: Had combat with enemy aircraft.

F/S JA Whitwood in LL734, JI-G reported: Unidentified S/E aircraft claimed as destroyed.

Combat Report:
Aircraft: LL734 'G'
Captain: F/S JA Whitwood
Target: DREUX

At 0106 hours in position 4845N - 004 E. Rear Gunner saw an unidentified S/E) aircraft almost dead astern slightly to starboard at a range of 200 yards and immediately opened fire with a 2 second burst. M/U Gunner followed almost immediately with a 2 second burst. Rear Gunner then gave order to corkscrew to starboard and both Gunners continued to fire during this manoeuvre. E/A was temporarily lost in corkscrew and Lancaster had just resumed course when both Gunners and W/Op saw a ball of fire astern which fell rapidly to the ground and burst.

MU Gunner – F/O HCA Chapman – 150 rounds.
Rear Gunner – Sgt TA Rirch – Not Listed

Aircraft: LL677 'E2'
Captain: F/S CS Johnson
Target: DREUX
At 0109 hours in position 4842N 0050E. Rear Gunner reported another Lancaster on the starboard beam level at a distance of 300 yards and being attacked by an Me410 and warned Captain to stand by to corkscrew to starboard. Rear Gunner at the same time opened fire at E/A which immediately turned to attack Lancaster 'E2' from starboard quarter level. As E/A closed in Rear Gunner fired almost continuously and at range of 250 yards E/A also opened fire, the trace passing under nose of Lancaster. While E/A was firing its port engine was seen to catch fire but it still continued to attack on curve of pursuit. At this stage Mid Upper Gunner got in 2 short bursts. When E/A had come in dead astern and below Lancaster, Rear Gunner got in another long and accurate burst and E/A became enveloped in flames and started to fall. On hitting the ground (position logged by Navigator at 48.42 N. 00.47 E) E/A was seen to explode by several members of the crew and by other crews in the bomber stream. The E/A is claimed as definitely destroyed.
MU Gunner – F/S. Poad – 100 rounds.
Rear Gunner – F/S RA Dymott – 600 rounds

Aircraft: DS795 'J2'
Captain: P/O RR Harvey.
Target: DREUX

At 0109 hours in position 48.49 N – 0037E. Rear Gunner reported Ju88 on the starboard quarter (very fine) below at a range of 500 yards and immediately gave order to corkscrew to starboard. On commencement of corkscrew, E/A and Rear Gunner opened fire simultaneously at a range of about 400 yards and Lancaster was hit on starboard flap and wing-tip and the starboard tyre. E/A only fired one short burst but Rear Gunner continued to fire with a long burst of 5 seconds, though no hits were observed. Finally E/A was lost to view in the corkscrew and the breakaway was not seen. The Mid Upper Gunner was unable to see E/A, being dazzled by trace and subsequently unsighted. No casualties were sustained by the crew of Lancaster.
MU Gunner – F/S Acaster – Nil
Rear Gunner – W/O Reid - 400 rounds.

Pro-forma:
Aircraft: LL666 'D'

Captain: F/S RD Pick
Target: DREUX
Combat Report –Homeward bound, at 0153 hours, height 7,000 feet, heading 306 degrees T, position 4938N, 0220W, Rear Gunner sighted an Me109 at 500 yards on the fine starboard quarter up and ordered corkscrew as, simultaneously, both Gunners opened fire, observing probable hits to E/A. E/A was then lost in corkscrew and not seen again. Visibility was hazy and there were no fighter flares, S/Ls or flares.
MU Gunner – Sgt AW Hanson – 200 rounds.
Rear Gunner – Sgt W Aston - 400 rounds.

Aircraft: LL492 'A'
Captain: W/O CE. Williams.
Target: DREUX.
Homeward bound (bombs dropped), flying on a course of 194 degrees M. IAS 180 at a height of 8,000 feet. At 01.10 hours in position 48.47N. 00.32E. Pilot saw an unidentified twin engined aircraft on starboard bow level at a range of 300 yards and immediately warned the crew and dived to starboard. As Lancaster commenced dive E/A opened fire, the trace passing in front of and over Lancaster. The Mid Upper Gunner got in a short burst at E/A from a range of 200 yards, and Rear Gunner, who was waiting for the breakaway, fired a burst at very short range as E/A broke away to starboard quarter down. No hits were claimed on E/A which was not seen again.
MU Gunner – Sgt J Kelly – 60 rounds
Rear Gunner – W/O EE De Joux – 120 rounds

Target:	*Dreux Railway Facilities*
Aircraft deployed total:	*432*
514 Squadron:	*19*
Aircraft lost total:	*15*
514 Squadron:	*Nil*

Comments: Multiple targets were again on for operations tonight. The attacks were primarily on railway infrastructure at various locations. 'Nachtjagd War Diaries' states that a Ju88, one Me410, one Bf110 and 'two Me109s' were claimed as destroyed by bomber gunners with five other unspecified night fighters claimed as possibly shot down or damaged.

11th June 1944. Weather: Cloudy visibility moderate, improving towards evening.
Non-Operational Flying: Air Tests and a Cross Country were carried out.
Operational Flying: BOMBING – NANTES.
16 aircraft were detailed to bomb the primary target at Nantes but one failed to take off. All landed at Base on completion of their duty. There was 10/10ths cloud with tops 4/8000 feet, base down to 2500 feet. Most crews bombed below cloud on instructions of the Master Bomber, but a few did not hear and bombed glow of markers from above. Red and green TIs were close together. Yellows were seen later in the attack. No assessment of results could be made. There was moderate L/F and a few bursts of heavy. There were 2 or 3 S/Ls below clouds. 2 fighters only were seen and there were no combats.
W/O CE Williams in LL692, JI-A reported: Bomb load 16 x 500 GP, 2 x 500 LD. Primary target: NANTES. Bombed as instructed by Master Bomber at 0247 hours from 2300 feet. No visual obtained. Conditions hazy below cloud base of 2700 feet. Port outer engine u/s on return.

Target: *Nantes Railway Facilities*
Aircraft deployed total: *329*
514 Squadron: *15*
Aircraft lost total: *4*
514 Squadron: *Nil*

Comments: As in the previous raid, multiple railway targets were attacked.

12th June 1944.
Weather: Fair, Visibility good. Strong winds.
Non-Operational Flying: Air Tests were carried out.
Operational Flying: BOMBING – GELSENKIRCHEN.
17 aircraft were detailed to bomb the primary target at Gelsenkirchen. Two aircraft are missing and one returned early. One aircraft landed at Woodbridge with u/s ASI and the remainder landed at Base on the completion of their duty. The weather was clear over the target. The marking was exceptionally good with bombs concentrated on the markers and large fires and a thick pall of smoke were seen. H/F moderate to intense with much S/L activity. There were few sightings but two combats in one of which a twin-engined aircraft with light on the nose was claimed to have been destroyed by Lancaster K2.

F/S WM Watkins in LL670, A2-K reported: Bomb load 1 x 4000 HC, 12 x 500 GP, 4 x 500 MC. Primary target: GELSENKIRCHEN. Clear over target. Bombed red and green TIs at 0108 hours from 16,000 feet. Large explosion seen at 0105 hours and large fires with much smoke. Route quiet but track marked by succession of 4 red balls. Flak barrage and intense searchlights over target. Twin engined aircraft claimed destroyed.

F/S CF Prowles in DS816, JI-O reported: Bomb load 1 x 400 HC, 12 x 500 GP, 4 x 500 MC. Primary target: GELSENKIRCHEN. Clear over target. Bombed red and green TIs at 0108 hours from 19700 feet. Close concentration of bomb bursts seen in area of TIs with smoke and fires.

Combat Report:
Aircraft: LL670 'K2'
Captain: F/S W.M. Watkins
Target: GELSENKIRCHEN
At 0141 hours in position 5235N 0525E. M/U Gunner reported an unidentified twin-engined aircraft on starboard quarter above at range of 300 yards, and immediately ordered corkscrew to starboard and opened fire. E/A, which did not open fire throughout the combat, followed Lancaster through 3 complete movements of the corkscrew with M/U Gunner firing continuously for about 10 seconds, mostly with 1 gun, as a stoppage was experienced in the other. Rear Gunner also got in 1 short burst, when E/A closed in dead astern and slightly above. Previously E/A had been too far above for Rear Gunner to get guns to bear. Both Gunners saw numerous strikes on E/A which started to fall, leaving a trail of smoke, and they and other members of the crew observed E/A fall into the sea where it burst into flames and burnt there for a considerable period.
MU Gunner – Sgt R. Dawson – 400 rounds.
Rear Gunner – Sgt B Ferries – 100 rounds

Pro-forma:
Aircraft: LL694 'E'
Captain: F/Lt McFetridge
Target: GELSENKIRCHEN
At 0047 hours, outward bound, height 20,000 feet, heading 095 degrees T., position 5135N, 0415E, with flares on either side, Rear Gunner sighted an Me410 at 500 yards on the starboard quarter above. Corkscrew was ordered and Rear Gunner, followed by Mid Upper Gunner, opened fire. E/A then broke away to the port quarter below. Visibility was moderate, no flak or searchlights reported.

MU Gunner – Sgt WH Corney – 130 rounds.
Rear Gunner – Sgt R. Britnell – 300 rounds.

Target: *Gelsenkirchen – Nordstern Oil Plant*
Aircraft deployed total: *303*
514 Squadron: *17 (1 returned early)*
Aircraft lost total: *17*
514 Squadron: *2*

Comments: The target for this raid was an oil plant in Nordstern. This marked the start of the 'Oil Plan'. On this occasion, TIs laid by Pathfinders were extremely accurate. The oil plant was extensively damaged with local reports estimating some 1,500 bombs hit the target. This caused the loss of around 1000 tons of fuel per day, for a period of several weeks. Locals reported that 6 German schoolboy 'Flakhilfers' were killed whilst manning the anti-aircraft defences.

Missing aircraft:

LL678 A2-L. According to www.lostaircraft.com, shot down by night-fighter of Oblt. Dietrich Schmidt, II/NJG1, crashing at 0124 hours at Zuid Loo, 3km SE of Bathmen, where those who died are buried in the general cemetery. However, 'Nachtjagd War Diaries' credits Hptm Gerhard Friedrich, 1/NJG6, with shooting down LL678.

P/O HS Delacour RAAF	Pilot	KIA
F/O SA Phillips RCAF	(2nd Pilot)	KIA
F/O RG Picton	Navigator	KIA
F/S G Palamountain	Bomb Aimer	Evaded
Sgt AC Bentham	WOP/Air	KIA
F/S GD Savage	Rear Gunner	KIA
Sgt SF Williams RCAF	MU Gunner	Evaded
Sgt GE Martin	Flight Engineer	Evaded

DS818 JI-Q. Crashed at Nunspeet, Gelderland. Cause not stated. Possibly shot down by Hptm. Joachim Böhner, 2./NJG6 who claimed an unidentified 4-engine aircraft 20 km S of Deelen. Nunspeet is approx. 50 km north of that location. Those who died are buried at Ermelo (Nunspeet) New General Cemetery.

P/O DA Duncliffe	Pilot	Evaded
F/S G Lewis	Navigator	KIA
Sgt GK Brown	WOP/Air	KIA
F/S HJ Bourne	Bomb Aimer	POW
Sgt KR Baker	MU Gunner	KIA
Sgt WE Steger	Rear Gunner	KIA
Sgt PG Cooper	Flight Engineer	POW

13th June 1944.
Weather: Unsettled, with rain storms in morning and afternoon, improving towards evening, strong winds.
Non-Operational Flying: No flying took place, a stand-down being given to the Squadron in the afternoon.

14th June 1944.
Weather: Heavy clouds with fine intervals. Strong wind.
Non-Operational Flying: Air Tests, Fighter Affiliation, Air/Air firing Practice and Cross Country Exercises were carried out.
Operational Flying: BOMBING – LE HAVRE.
17 aircraft were detailed and took off to attack the docks at Le Havre. 17 aircraft attacked the primary target and returned to Base on completion of duty. Weather was clear and target well marked. All crews bombed on markers, chiefly red and green as instructed by Master Bomber. The dock area was illuminated by fires started in the northern part of the harbour earlier in the attack and by numerous explosions which lasted throughout the attacks, bombs were seen falling in the dock area. Flak was negligible and confined to light tracer. Four aircraft had combats, 1 enemy aircraft claimed destroyed and 2 damaged.
F/S CJ Johnson in LL677, A2-E reported: Bomb load 11 x 1000 MC, 4 x 500 GP. Primary target: LE HAVRE. Weather clear. Bombed at 0116 hours from 15,000 feet on green TI. 3 large fires seen burning on arrival. Good raid – markers concentrated. Defences seldom in action. Successful combat in Fecamp area.
F/S CF Prowles in DS816, JI-O reported: Bomb load 11 x 1000 MC, 4 x 500 GP. Primary target: LE HAVRE. Weather clear – much smoke. Bombed at 0116 hours from 15000 feet on green markers. Good concentration of bombs on markers. Big area of fire in docks and town to the North. One aircraft seen shot down.

Combat Reports:
Aircraft: LL677 'E2'

Captain: F/Sgt CJ Johnson
Target: LE HAVRE
At 0124 hours in position 4946N 0026 E, Rear Gunner saw an Me110 at range of 250 yards, attacking another Lancaster dead astern and below. Rear Gunner immediately opened fire with a short burst at E/A and ordered Captain to stand-by for corkscrew to starboard. The other Lancaster corkscrewed out of sight and E/A climbed to attack 'E2'. The Rear Gunner then ordered Captain to corkscrew to starboard and immediately afterwards E/A opened fire with 2 fairly long bursts, the trace passing very close under Lancaster 'E2'. Rear Gunner replied to E/A's fire with a number of short bursts on the fourth of which E/A burst into flames and started to head back towards the French coast. Rear Gunner continued to fire with further short bursts and E/A commenced to fall into a steep dive enveloped in flames. Both Gunners the W/Op, and the Flight Engineer saw E/A fall and hit the ground where it exploded. M/U Gunner was unable to bring guns to bear throughout the combat. While the Me110 was actually falling in flames, M/U Gunner saw unidentified T/E (Trailing Enemy) aircraft on starboard quarter level at range of 250 yards and immediately gave order to corkscrew to starboard. E/A then opened fire to which M/U Gunner replied with several bursts, but throughout the combat was unable to get guns to bear effectively. E/A broke away on port beam down and was not seen again.
MU Gunner – F/S J Poad – 200 rounds.
Rear Gunner – F/S RA Dymott - 500 rounds.

Aircraft: LL731 'L'
Captain: F/Lt M. Dods
Target: LE HAVRE
Flying over the target, on a course of 127 degrees M. at a height of 15,000 feet, at 01.15 hours, just as bombs were about to be released, Rear Gunner saw an Me110 at range of 700 yards dead astern and below, coming in very fast. At 600 yards, Rear Gunner opened fire as E/A continued to close in. At 400 yards Rear Gunner gave order to corkscrew to port. As Lancaster commenced to corkscrew E/A opened fire with a long burst, the trace passing close above Lancaster. All this time Rear Gunner had been firing continuously and only stopped after E/A had broken away to port quarter above. E/A then turned and came in to attack again from port quarter level, and as came in, Rear Gunner fired another long burst and ordered corkscrew to port. E/A also opened fire again as Lancaster commenced to corkscrew but then broke

away to starboard quarter down and was not seen again. In both attacks Rear Gunner saw numerous strikes and ricochets on E/A
MU Gunner – Sgt J Edwards – Nil.
Rear Gunner – Sgt RK Redfern - 1050 rounds.

Pro-forma Combat Report:
Aircraft: LL733 'S'
Captain: S/L RC Chopping.
Target: LE HAVRE
Over the target, at 0117 hours, height 15,000 feet, heading 540 degrees M. Both Gunners sighted an FW190 at 600 yards on the port quarter level, and ordered corkscrew and opened fire. E/A was subsequently lost to view and was not seen again. Visibility was good. No fighter flares, flak or searchlights were reported.
MU Gunner – Sgt JS Johnson – 80 rounds.
Rear Gunner – F/S PJ Fox – 200 rounds.

Target:	*Le Havre E-Boat Base*
Aircraft deployed total:	*234*
514 Squadron:	*17*
Aircraft lost total:	*1 (Lancaster)*
514 Squadron:	*Nil*

Comments: A notable raid for several reasons. Spitfires (of 11 Group) were used to escort the bombers. This was required because this raid took place in daylight, making it the first daylight raid since May of 1943. The aim of the attack was to neutralise German E-Boats some 30 miles from the beaches of Normandy. This was to prevent them from interrupting shipping movements of allied supplies. The raid was deemed a success, with good TIs and concentrated bombing. The raid effectively eradicated the E-Boat threat to supplies for the allied positions on the beach-head. No loss of enemy aircraft attributable to 514 Sqn. gunners was recorded in 'Nachtjagd War Diaries'.

15th June 1944.
Weather: Mainly fine and sunny all day. Some cloud.
Non-Operational Flying: Air Tests and Cross Country were carried out.
Operational Flying: BOMBING – VALENCIENNES.
20 aircraft were detailed and took off. 17 aircraft attacked the primary target, 1 aircraft was abortive owing to Navigational aid failures and returned early, 2 aircraft are missing. 10/10ths cloud at 10,000 feet was

encountered over the target, crews were instructed to bomb below cloud by the Master Bomber. Markers were scattered, but concentration was slightly improved by Master Bomber and bursts observed across marshalling yards. No flak or searchlights.

F/S RD Pick in LL666, JI-D reported: Bomb load 16 x 500 GP, 2 x 500 MC. Primary target: VALENCIENNES. Weather clear below cloud – base 1000 feet. Bombed at 0039 hours from 9000 feet on green TIs as instructed by Master Bomber. Good concentrated bombing. Much interference on R/T. Route very good.

Combat Report:
Aircraft: LL734 'G'
Captain: F/O M Jones
Target: VALENCIENNES
At 0043 hours in position 5012N – 0327E M/U Gunner reported a fighter flare on starboard beam, followed a few seconds later by a rocket projectile coming from the same direction which passed about 100 yards behind Lancaster. M/U Gunner ordered Captain to dive to starboard to avoid course of rocket, but E/A was not seen by any member of the crew.
MU Gunner – Sgt R Lane – Nil
Rear Gunner - Sgt AE Braine - Nil

Target:	*Valenciennes Railway Yards.*
Aircraft deployed total:	*224*
514 Squadron:	*20 (1 returned early)*
Aircraft lost total:	*11*
514 Squadron:	*2*

Comments: A return to rail transport infrastructure on this split two target raid. Both the Lens and Valenciennes targets were bombed accurately. Enemy fighter activity on the Valenciennes target was quite intense which saw the loss of 5 aircraft on this raid, 2 from 514 Squadron.

Missing aircraft:

LL790, JI-J. Shot down, probably at 0052 hours by a Bf110 flown by Oblt. Peter Ehrhardt of 9/NJG5. The aircraft came down between Iwuy (Nord) and Rieux-en-Cambresis, 9 km from Cambrai.

P/O EA Kingham	Pilot	KIA
F/S RH Hutt	Navigator	KIA
F/S FR Spencer	Bomb Aimer	KIA
F/S B Bloom	WOP/Air	KIA
Sgt FN Ansell	MU Gunner	KIA
Sgt DG Davis RCAF	Rear Gunner	KIA
Sgt J Black	Flight Engineer	KIA

DS816, JI-O. Shot down, probably at 0051 hours by Bf110 flown by Hptm Hubert Rauh of Stab II/\NJG4. Crashed at Croisilles (Pas de Calais) where those who died are buried in the British Cemetery.

F/S CF Prowles	Pilot	KIA
P/O AH Morrison RAAF	Navigator	Evaded
Sgt R Surtees	WOP/Air	KIA
F/S RB Spencer RAAF	Bomb Aimer	KIA
Sgt AA Holmes	MU Gunner	KIA
Sgt J Porrelli	Rear Gunner	KIA
Sgt HA Osborn	Flight Engineer	KIA

Sgt Porrelli was the grandfather of author Andrew Porrelli. RAAF Flight Lieutenant Arnold Hughes Morrison was awarded the DFC for evading capture. See 'War Stories' later in the book for a full story of this crew.

(Above) Some 2800 people of Croisilles turned out to honour the dead of DS816, JI-O after it was shot down over the town. The Germans did not intervene to stop this moving tribute to the loss of F/S Ted Prowles and his crew. Source: Linda Miles, daughter of P/O AH Morrison.

P/O Morrison later filed the following crash report for the RAAF. Arnold Morrison was discharged from the RAAF as a Flight Lieutenant on 30th May 1945.

'About eight minutes after bombing the target, we were attacked presumably by a night fighter. Cannon shell raked the port side and the port wing was set on fire. The aircraft was losing height rapidly and at about 8000 feet, the Captain ordered the crew to 'prepare to abandon'. By 2000 feet, the Air Bomber had not been able to remove the front escape hatch. I am not certain whether the Rear Gunner, Mid Upper Gunner or the WOP had baled out through the rear escape hatch but the remainder stayed in the aircraft. The pilot landed the aircraft on a fairly flat field and the aircraft disintegrated and was set on fire. I was unconscious for a while, and while still in a dazed condition looked without result to the numerous small fires for the remainder of the crew. I was informed by the Germans that their bodies were in the wreck and buried in the cemetery at Croisilles, France. The funeral was attended by about 2800.'

16th June 1944.
Weather: Overcast and cloudy all day.
Non-Operational Flying: Air Tests were carried out.
Operational Flying: 12 Aircraft were detailed for Bombing Operations, but the effort was cancelled at 16.00 hours.

17th June 1944.
Weather: Mainly fine and sunny with cloudy intervals. Very strong winds.
Non-Operational Flying: Air Tests and Bombing Practices were carried out.
Operational Flying: BOMBING – MONTDIDIER.
14 aircraft were detailed to bomb the target. 13 took off and reached the primary target. 3 attacked primary and 11 aircraft were abortive owing to instructions from Master Bomber. The three aircraft who attacked primary stated the Master Bomber was indistinct and no order was received until after bombing. 10/10ths cloud was encountered over target, there was no flak and no searchlights. Many aircraft saw 'Flying bombs' on the return route.
F/L PB Clay in LL666, JI-D reported: Bomb load 16 x 500 GP, 2 x 500 ANM 64 GP. Primary target: MONTDIDIER. Weather 10/10ths thin cloud. Bombed at 0258 hours from 10,000 feet red TIs. Arrived early

and did an orbit of target, voice heard instructing return to base but no call sign given at this period.

Target: *Montdidier Railway Facilities*
Aircraft deployed total: *317*
514 Squadron: *13*
Aircraft lost total: *1*
514 Squadron: *Nil*

Comments: This was another two target raid. The Montdidier raid was aborted after only 12 aircraft had bombed. 3 crews of 514 Squadron stated that the Master Bomber was indistinct and no order was received until after bombing. Some crews reported seeing flying bombs on the return route. This operation saw the first deployment by 514 Sqn of the Mk.III Lancaster, powered by Packard Merlins rather than the Bristol Hercules. PB143, JI-B was flown by W/O N Jennings and crew on this raid, returning safely.

18th June 1944.
Weather: Fine and sunny all day.
Non-Operational Flying: Air Tests, Fighter Affiliation details, Air to Air Firing Practices and a Cross Country were carried out.
Operational Flying: 17 Aircraft were detailed for Bombing Operations but the effort was cancelled at 16.00 hours.

19th June 1944.
Weather: Fine and sunny all day.
Non-Operational Flying: Air to Air Firing Practices, Fighter Affiliation details and Cross Countries were carried out.
Operational Flying: 19 Aircraft were detailed for Bombing Operations, but the effort was cancelled at 23.15 hours.

20th June 1944.
Weather: Fine, becoming fair.
Non-Operational Flying: 'A' and 'B' Flights practiced Formation Flying. Air to Air and Air to Sea Firing were carried out and Air Tests. 2 Aircraft went to East Kirkby to collect special incendiary bombs.
Operational Flying: Warned to stand-by for Operations, further instructions at 1300 hours. No Operations tonight, required for Goodwood effort tomorrow in daylight.

21st June 1944.
Weather: Cloudy with drizzle becoming fair.
Non-Operational Flying: 1 Air Test carried out. All Aircraft standing by for daylight operations.
Operational Flying: Squadron required to stand-by with Derby Figures for target in afternoon or evening.
BOMBING – DOMLEGER, FLYING BOMB INSTALLATIONS.
18 aircraft were detailed to make a daylight attack, all aircraft took off and 1 aircraft returned early with engine trouble. Weather over target was 10/10ths cloud and aircraft were ordered to return to Base by Master Bomber. All aircraft jettisoned part of load and landed safely at Base with remainder of load. Slight heavy flak encountered over target.
P/O CJ Thomson RAAF in PB142, JI-A reported: Bomb load 18 x 500 MC. Primary target: DOMLEGER. Returned to base as instructed by Master Bomber as TIs were not visible. Jettisoned safe 8 x 500 MC at 1943 hours from 12,000 feet 5013N 0123E.

Target: *Domleger Flying Bomb Installations*
Aircraft deployed total: *322*
514 Squadron: *18 (1 returned early)*
Aircraft lost total: *Nil*
514 Squadron: *Nil*

Comments: Cloud affected this raid. 3 targets were selected for this split raid, 2 of these raids were cancelled after only 17 aircraft had bombed. The cancellations were due to the cloud cover obscuring the TIs.

22nd June 1944.
Weather: Fair.
Non-Operational Flying: Air Tests were carried out in the morning. The Squadron was given a stand - down in the afternoon.
Operational Flying: Aircraft not required for Operations.

23rd June 1944.
Weather: Cloudy with showers, becoming fair.
Non-Operational Flying: 2 Cross Countries were carried out testing new Lanc. I/III. Air to Air Firing and Air Tests were carried out.
Visits: Wing Commander RD Max, DSO, DFC, GTI at 3 Group, visited 514 Squadron.

Operational Flying: BOMBING – L'HEY.   FLYING BOMB INSTALLATIONS.

20 aircraft were detailed and took off. 20 aircraft attacked Primary target successfully and returned to Base. Weather over target was 10/10ths cloud at 5000 feet. All crews bombed on the glow of red TIs and attack was reported concentrated. Flak over target was slight heavy and light and no combats were reported.

S/L PB Clay in PB143, JI-B, reported: Bomb load 11 x 1000 MC, 4 x 500 GP. Primary target: L'HEY. There was 10/10ths cloud, tops 4-5000 feet. Bombed at 0015 hours from 8090 feet glow of red TIs. Raid appeared concentrated, bomb bursts seen amid glow of red TIs. Heavy flak intense and fairly accurate.

Target:	*L'Hey Flying Bomb Installations*
Aircraft deployed total:	*412*
514 Squadron:	*20*
Aircraft lost total:	*5*
514 Squadron:	*Nil*

Comments: The 4 targets were all bombed successfully.

24th June 1944.
Weather: Fair to fine.
Non-Operational Flying: A Cross Country, Air Tests and Air to Sea Firing were carried out.
Operational Flying: BOMBING – RIMEUX - FLYING BOMB INSTALLATIONS.

20 aircraft were detailed and took off to bomb the primary target, and all returned to Base on completion of their duty. Weather was clear. Red TIs were concentrated, but green TIs fell wide. Crews report bombing concentrated. Slight heavy and light flak was encountered and intense searchlight activity. Several fighters and combats seen on return route. Good photos obtained.

P/O R Langley in DS842, JI-F reported: Bomb load 18 x 500 GP. Primary target: RIMEUX. Weather clear, a few patches of cloud. Bombed at 0033 hours from 11500 feet. Bomb bursts seen amongst red TIs, which were well concentrated. Numerous searchlights, flak negligible. Three small fires seen.

Target:	*Rimeux Flying Bomb Installations*
Aircraft deployed total:	*739*
514 Squadron:	*20*

Aircraft lost total: 22
514 Squadron: Nil

Comments: A large contingent was used for 7 targets. Although the raids all caused fresh damage, the cost was high due to it being a moon-lit night. Accurate searchlights assisted night fighters in causing most of the losses.

25th June 1944.
Weather: Fair.
Non-Operational Flying: Cross Countries, Air to Sea Firing and Air Tests were carried out.
Operational Flying: The Squadron was required to stand-by for target in Northern France when weather permitted, but was postponed later in the day.

26th June 1944.
Weather: Intermittent rain most of day and night.
Non-Operational Flying: Nil owing to weather.
Operational Flying: Operations postponed indefinitely.
Visits: Wing Commander ICK Swales, DFC, DFM, Officer Commanding 622 Squadron and Wing Commander WDG Watkins, DFC, DFM, 15 Squadron visited the Squadron to discuss Daylight Tactics.

27th June 1944.
Weather: Showery with Thunderstorms.
Non-Operational Flying: Air Test and Fighter Affiliation were carried out.
Visits: Wing Commander L.M. Hodges, DSO, DFC, Bomber Command Tactics Officer visited the Squadron and attended Briefing, Take - off, Landing and Interrogation. Air Commodore HJ Kirkpatrick, DFC, SASO 3 Group came to watch Landing and was present at Interrogation.
Operational Flying: BOMBING – BIENNAIS. FLYING BOMB INSTALLATIONS.
19 aircraft were detailed and took off. 19 aircraft attacked the primary target and returned to Base on completion of their duty. Weather was 10/10ths cloud over the target. Most crews bombed the glow of red TIs. One crew went below cloud and reported 2 red TIs close together, but greens scattered. Explosions were reported at 0111 hours, 0115 hours and 0117 hours. No flak or searchlights. 1 combat.

P/O LM Petry RNZAF in DS787, A2-D reported: Bomb load 16 x 500 GP, 2 x 500 ANM 64 GP. Primary target: BIENNAIS. There was 10/10ths cloud. Bombed at 0110 hours from 13,500 feet red glow. Combat with single-engined enemy aircraft; no claims.

Combat Report – Pro-forma:
Aircraft: DS787 'D2'
Captain: P/O LM Petry RNZAF
Target: BIENNAIS
At 0114 hours, height 13,000 feet, heading 262 degrees T., position 4934N, 0102E. Rear Gunner sighted unidentified S/E. Aircraft approaching from the starboard quarter down. Captain was ordered to corkscrew to starboard and Rear Gunner opened fire. S/E. Aircraft was subsequently lost in corkscrew and was not seen again. Visibility was good, with no flak, searchlights or flares.
MU Gunner – F/S KA Pitt RAAF – Nil.
Rear Gunner - Sgt WB Watt - 200 rounds.

Target:	*Biennais – Flying Bomb Installations*
Aircraft deployed total:	*721*
514 Squadron:	*19*
Aircraft lost total:	*3*
514 Squadron:	*Nil*

Comments: 6 separate targets were successfully attacked.

28th June 1944.
Weather: Cloudy with drizzle and rain.
Non-Operational Flying: Air Sea Firing and Air Tests were carried out.
Operational Flying: Squadron to stand-by for a tactical target in Northern France. Postponed later.

29th June 1944.
Weather: Cloudy all day, drizzle in morning, showers in the afternoon.
Non-Operational Flying: Air Tests and Circuits and Landings were carried out.
Operational Flying: Squadron to stand-by for Operations in the morning but was cancelled later owing to bad weather.

30th June 1944.
Weather: Cloudy all day, rain at night.

Non-Operational Flying: Cross Countries, Air/Sea Firing and Local Air Tests were carried out.

Operational Flying: 29 Aircraft took off to attack troop concentrations at Villers Bocage. 1 Aircraft collided with a Lancaster on the way out and exploded in the air (2 survivors). 1 Aircraft is missing, believed to have been shot down over target. 27 Aircraft landed at Base on completion of their duty.

BOMBING – VILLERS BOCAGE.

29 aircraft were detailed to make a daylight attack on troop concentrations, all aircraft took off, 27 aircraft bombed successfully. 'P'/514 collided with a 15 Squadron aircraft over Tangmere and blew up in the air. There were two survivors from the crash (Sgt TS Colbeck and Sgt CA Brown). Weather was 5/10ths cloud with good breaks over the target. Some crews bombed from high level, others obeyed the Master Bomber's instructions and came down to 3-4000 feet. Bombing was highly concentrated and large fires and smoke completely obscured the target. T/514 was seen shot down over target, no parachutes seen to open.

P/O CB Sandland in LL635, JI-M reported: Bomb load 10 x 1000 MC, 3 x 500 GP. Primary target: VILLERS BOCAGE. Bombed at 2000 hours from 4000 feet. Weather 4/10ths cloud at 6000 feet. Clouds of smoke obscuring target. The aircraft received damage by flak to nose, also on port and starboard side of mid-upper turret. Much heavy flak. Good photo taken. Lancaster aircraft just astern received direct hit by flak which broke tail off. Seen to hit ground no survivors, thought to be T/514.

Target: *Villers Bocage -Communication Lines*
Aircraft deployed total: *266*
514 Squadron: *29*
Aircraft lost total: *2*
514 Squadron: *2*

Comments: To stop the advance of a German Panzer (Tank) Division, a major road junction was bombed. Orders were received to bomb from 4,000 feet to ensure the bombs were correctly placed. 1,100 bombs hit the mark as a testament to their accuracy. This put an end to the chances of any Panzer involvement.

Missing aircraft:
PB178 JI-P. Collided with a Lancaster of 15 Sqn. at about 5000 feet and crashed at Pittsham Farm, near Midhurst, Sussex. The other aircraft landed safely at Ford.

F/S JEK Hannesson RCAF	Pilot	Killed
F/S BG Lee RAAF	Navigator	Killed
Sgt TS Colbeck	Bomb Aimer	Survived
Sgt BA Brown	WOP/Air	Survived
Sgt AL George	MU Gunner	Killed
Sgt HJ Morgan	Rear Gunner	Killed
Sgt KEA Fox	Flight Engineer	Killed

LL620 JI-T. Seen to be hit by flak over target, which broke tail off. Aircraft seen to crash without survivors.

P/O DA Woods RAAF	Pilot	KIA
F/O P Longson	Navigator	KIA
F/S ET Shanks	Bomb Aimer	KIA
Sgt KR Heron	WOP/Air	KIA
Sgt WT Udell	MU Gunner	KIA
Sgt HL Doherty	Rear Gunner	KIA
Sgt EC Coles	Flight Engineer	KIA

(Above) P/O CB Sandland and crew stand with their Lancaster Mk.II LL635 JI-M 'Minnie the Moocher'. The crew survived their tour of operations. Minnie was not so lucky, being damaged beyond repair on an operation to Vincly on 25th August 1944. Source: courtesy of Wendy Flemming.

Monthly Summary for June 1944

Awards:

1388280	F/Sgt HG Friend	Air Bomber	DFM 15/6/44
1368303	F/Sgt JC Wilson	WOP/Air	DFM 15/6/44
70126	A/Squadron Leader RC Chopping	Pilot	DFC 30/6/44
1334210	F/Sgt CS Johnson	Pilot	DFM 30/6/44
1870250	F/Sgt S Poad	M/U Gunner	DFM 30/6/44
1600884	F/Sgt RA Dymott	Rear Gunner	DFM 30/6/44

Operational:

Enemy Aircraft Destroyed (includes 1 shared with 100 Grp)	5
Operational Flying Hours for June 1944:	904.00
Non-Operational Flying Hours for June 1944:	147.10
Total tons of bombs dropped in June 1944:	1,069 tons.
Cumulative Total tons of bombs dropped:	4,147 ¾ tons.
Number of Sorties for June 1944:	281

Strength of Squadron as at 30th June 1944.

Aircrew: 86 Officers
                   241 SNCOs

Ground: 2 Officers
                   33 SNCOs
                   348 other ranks
                   (Includes 12 WAAFs)

July 1944

1st July 1944.
Weather: Raining most of day.
Non-Operational Flying: Two Air Tests were carried out.
Operational Flying: Squadron not required, standby for daylight early tomorrow.

2nd July 1944.
Weather: Low cloud, some drizzle and rain.
Non-Operational Flying: No flying owing to daylight operations.
Operational Flying: BOMBING – BEAUVOIR – FLYING BOMB SITE.
26 aircraft were detailed and took off. 25 aircraft attacked the primary target and returned to Base, having successfully completed their sortie. One aircraft returned early with engine trouble. Weather was 5-10/10ths broken drifting cloud. Most crews bombed on yellow TIs as instructed by the Master Bomber. Bombing on the whole was concentrated, but slightly scattered bombing extending to decoy airfield. One crew went down to 3000 feet and reported yellow TIs in NW corner of decoy airfield about 300 yards from Aiming Point.
S/L PB Clay in PB143, JI-B reported: Bomb load 11 x 1000 MC, 4 x 500 GP. Primary target: BEAUVOIR. Bombed at 1435 hours from 9000 feet on yellow TIs.

Target: *Beauvoir – Flying Bomb Site*
Aircraft deployed total: *374*
514 Squadron: *26 (1 returned early)*
Aircraft lost total: *Nil*
514 Squadron: *Nil*

Comments: This raid had 3 targets. Bombing was well concentrated despite the cloud cover.

(Above) A Lancaster of 514 Sqn attacks the flying bomb site at Beauvoir. Three separate aiming points were selected, requiring aircraft to approach from different directions. This photograph illustrates the risk of bombs from one aircraft striking another. Source: Airworx Gmbh Archive.

3rd July 1944.
Weather: Rain and low cloud.
Non-Operational Flying: Nil on account of weather.
Operational Flying: Squadron not required, standby for daylight tomorrow.

4th July 1944.
Weather: Fair
Non-Operational Flying: Air Tests and three Cross Countries carried out.
Operational Flying: Squadron not required today, required early tomorrow.

5th July 1944.
Weather: Fair.
Non-Operational Flying: Air tests, Air/Sea Firing and Cross Countries were carried out.
Investiture: His Majesty the King, who was accompanied by Her Majesty the Queen and Her Royal Highness Princess Elizabeth – in attendance Air Vice Marshall R Harrison, CBE, DFC, AFC, Air Officer Commanding No. 3 Group, and Group Captain HR Hills, OBE, Staff Officer i/c Administration, No. 3 Group, arrived at the Station at 1500 hours and proceeded to the Main Hangar, was there received by Air Commodore HH Down, AFC. The personnel of the Station, who were on parade in the Hangar, were called to attention whilst the Guard of Honour presented arms and the Station Band played the National Anthem.

(Above) King George VI, accompanied by Queen Elizabeth and Princess Elizabeth, visit RAF Waterbeach and 514 Sqn. The visit saw His Majesty confer awards on a selection of aircrew including squadron commander W/Cdr Mike Wyatt. HRH the Princess Elizabeth was apparently finding the windswept airfield somewhat trying. Source: Linda Miles.

His Majesty then invested the following Officers and Warrant Officer with the DFC and DFM respectively:-

70816	S/LDR EGB Reid	Pilot	DFC
115023	A/S/LDR AL Roberts	Pilot	DFC (Bar to)
37994	A/W/CDR M Wyatt	Pilot	DFC
70126	A/S/LDR RC Chopping	Pilot	DFC
148559	A/F/LT. C Payne	Pilot	DFC
170661	P/O ABL Winstanley	Pilot	DFC
132709	P/O KW Armstrong	Navigator	DFC
169554	P/O JM Hydes	WOP/AIR	DFC
138423	F/LT JN Pollock	Air Gunner	DFC
1378365	W/O PM Ashpital	Pilot	DFM

Their Majesties, after making a short tour of the Station, and taking tea in the information room, left again at 1615 hours.
Operational Flying: BOMBING – WATTEN CONSTRUCTIONAL WORKS.

22 aircraft were detailed, took off and attacked primary target. 22 aircraft returned to Base having successfully completed their sortie. Weather was clear. Red TIs were in a line of three clusters, east to West. Most crews bombed centre. Slight heavy flak, no combats.
W/C M Wyatt, DFC, in ME841, JI-H reported: Bomb load 11 x 1000 ANM 65, 4 x 500 GP. Primary target: WATTEN. Bombed at 0009 hours from 11,000 feet, red TIs.

Target:	*Watten Constructional Works*
Aircraft deployed total:	542
514 Squadron:	22
Aircraft lost total:	4
514 Squadron:	Nil

Comments: The conditions were clear and the night moon-lit. 2 storage depots and 2 launch sites were the targets of this raid. All targets were successfully bombed.

6th July 1944.
Weather: Fair.
Non-Operational Flying: Air tests and three cross countries were carried.

Operational flying: 21 aircraft detailed for Operations but this was cancelled later in the day.

7th July 1944.
Weather: Some rain, otherwise fair.
Non-Operational Flying: Local air tests were carried out.
Operational Flying: BOMBING – VAIRES MARSHALLING YARDS. 21 aircraft were detailed and took off, 2 aircraft returned early with engine trouble. 19 aircraft attacked primary target and landed safely having completed their duty. Weather was clear. TIs were well placed and bombing concentrated. Two large explosions were seen in yards. Five combats in target area.
F/S GC France in ME842, JI-K reported: Bomb load 11 x 1000 ANM 65. Primary target VAIRES. Weather 8/10ths cloud at 13,000ft. Bombed at 0134 hours from 12600 feet centre of a group of green TIs on edge of red markers as instructed by Master Bomber. Large fires started. Good trip, combat with FW190, no claims.

Combat Report:
Aircraft: DS826 'U'
Captain: F/O AF Fowke RCAF
Target: VAIRES MARSHALLING YARDS
At 0145 hours, in position 48.45N - 02.10E. Whilst Lancaster was weaving to avoid heavy flak from Paris defences, a burst of trace was observed to pass between Rear and Mid-upper Turrets. Immediately afterwards R/Gunner saw a T/E aircraft on starboard fine quarter above, closing in, and ordered corkscrew to starboard, at the same time opening fire with a 4 second burst. In this burst, many hits and ricochets were observed on E/A and its starboard wing was seen to burst into flames. At this moment, Mid Upper Gunner fired a 2 second burst at E/A which was starting a controlled dive to port and both Gunners fired a further short burst as E/A passed below the port. By this time the whole front of the E/A was enveloped in flames brightly lighting up the fuselage and fin (which appeared to be a silver colour) and identifying the E/A as a Ju88. Both Gunners and the Engineer Kept observations on the burning E/A as it was falling and saw it hit the ground where it burnt for a considerable period. On return it was found that the port outer engine nacelle of Lancaster had been shot away by a cannon shell and the oil system had been damaged. There were no casualties to the crew.
MU Gunner – F/O Chapman – 120 rounds.
Rear Gunner - F/O Murphy - 400 rounds.

Pro-forma:
Aircraft: LL733 'S'
Captain: S/L RC Chopping.
Target: VAIRES MARSHALLING YARDS
1st Encounter: At 0134 hours, height 12,000 feet, heading (not stated), position 4848N, 0121E, Rear Gunner sighted an unidentified S/E aircraft on the starboard quarter down at a range of 400 yards. Gunner ordered corkscrew to starboard and both Gunners opened fire as S/E broke away to starboard quarter up. Visibility was good, no searchlights, fighter flares or flak.
2nd Encounter: At 0148 hours, height 10,000 feet, heading 270 degrees, position 4845N, 0130E, Rear Gunner sighted Me109 at 300 yards, approaching from the starboard quarter up. Rear Gunner ordered corkscrew and opened fire as E/A broke away port down. Visibility was good, but there were some fighter flares and flak was moderate to heavy.
MU Gunner – Sgt JS Johnson. – 100 rounds. 200 rounds (2nd Encounter)
Rear Gunner - F/S PJ Fox - 150 rounds.

Aircraft: ME842, 'K'
Captain: F/S GC France
Target: VAIRES MARSHALLING YARDS
Fishpond system was u/s. At 0030 hours Lancaster ME842 'K' of 514 Squadron was outbound, on track, at 15,000 feet, heading 150 deg. Position 49.49N, 00.10E. Cloud 7/10ths below, moon ahead, visibility fair. Searchlights present, no flak. M/U Gunner saw an FW190, no lights, approaching from starboard beam up and gave warning. E/A broke away port quarter down at a range of 300 yards without opening fire. Intercom was u/s at this point. MU Gunner fired 200 rounds at 300 yards range. No claim made.
MU Gunner – Sgt Meredith - 200 rounds
Rear Gunner – Sgt Coles – Nil

Aircraft: LL728 'L2'
Captain: P/O BK McDonald
Target: VAIRES MARSHALLING YARDS
At 0224 hours, height 10,000 feet, heading 308 degrees T, position 5010N, 0005W, Visual Monica sounded and Captain and crew were warned. 2 minutes later Rear Gunner sighted Ju88 on the starboard quarter down at a range of 800 yards. Mid Upper Gunner then Rear

Gunner opened fire. E/A broke away to starboard quarter and was not seen again. Visibility was good with full moon. No S/Ls, flak or flares.
MU Gunner – Sgt DH Gardiner RCAF – 300 rounds.
Rear Gunner - Sgt HE Bentley - 200 rounds.

The following report was filed by the Station Intelligence Officer on 9th July 1944 and hand-marked 'This is the aircraft which reported being fired at over Luton'.

```
SECRET
From: RAF Station, Waterbeach.
To: Headquarters, No. 33 Base.
Date: 9/7/1944
Ref. WB/S. 1739/1/int.

With reference to paragraph 16 of Reid Report
No. 1139, Waterbeach, the crew of Lancaster
Mark II, 514 Squadron (Captain, F/O Fowke) A/C
'U' reports as follows:

Mission: VAIRES M/Y. 7/8th July 1944.
Position of our A/C: Outward 51.57N 00.20W.
Heading 213 degrees T., 11,000 feet, 3 miles to
starboard of bomber stream.
Time: 23.29 hours.
Observation: Stream of red tracer lasting 2 -3
seconds and fired almost vertically, 2 -3 miles
to port (presumably into bomber stream)
Remarks: No searchlight exposed at the time and
no indication of E/A

ME Clarkson, S/L
Station Intelligence Officer
R.AF. Station, Waterbeach.
```

Target: Vaires Marshalling Yards
Aircraft deployed total: 128
514 Squadron: 21 (2 returned early)
Aircraft lost total: Nil
514 Squadron: Nil

Comments: Railway infrastructure was targeted. The attack went off without a hitch, with no losses reported, despite Luton's AA defences allegedly firing at our own aircraft. Bombing was thought accurate.

8th July 1944.
Weather Fair,
Non-Operational Flying: Air tests and cross-countries carried out.
Operational Flying: Stand-down for the Squadron.

9th July 1944.
Weather: Slight rain.
Non-Operational Flying: Fighter affiliation, formation flying and air tests were carried out.
Operational Flying: Not required for operations today but required early tomorrow.

10th July 1944.
Weather: Cloudy with showers.
Non-Operational Flying: Air tests were carried out.
Operational Flying: BOMBING – NUCOURT CONSTRUCTIONAL WORKS.
26 aircraft detailed, one failed to take off. 25 aircraft took off, attacked the primary target and returned to Base on completion of duty. Weather was 10/10ths low cloud over the target, which made identification difficult and most crews bombed on GH. Most crew saw red TIs going down, but they quickly disappeared in cloud. Two crews bombed red TIs. Flak was slight heavy, no sightings.
F/S GC France in ME841, JI-H reported: Bomb load 11 x 1000 ANM 65, 4 x 500 GP. Primary target: NUCOURT. Bombed at 0607½ hours from 16,000 feet Gee Fix.

Target:	*Nucourt Constructional Works*
Aircraft deployed total:	*223*
514 Squadron:	*25*
Aircraft lost total:	*Nil*
514 Squadron:	*Nil*

Comments: This target was a flying bomb storage site. Bad cloud cover hampered the raid and bombing was reported as inaccurate.

11th July 1944.
Weather: Cloudy.
Non-Operational Flying: Fighter Affiliation, Air/Air Firing, Air/Sea Firing and Local Air Tests were carried out.
Operational Flying: Not required today, but required tomorrow daylight.

(Above) The G-H bombing technique required Lancasters to fly in close proximity on daylight raids. Here an unidentified 514 Sqn Lancaster formates on the aircraft of P/O CB Sandland on a daylight operation in Summer 1944. Source: Wendy Flemming.

12th July 1944.
Weather: Fair.
Non Operational Flying: Air tests were carried out.
Operational Flying: BOMBING – VAIRES – MARSHALLING YARDS.
23 aircraft were detailed and took off. 1 aircraft attacked primary, 1 aircraft attacked Bosville railway siding, 21 aircraft abandoned mission as instructed by Master Bomber. Weather was 8-10/10ths cloud over target.

P/O CJ Thomson RAAF, in PB142, JI-A reported: Bomb load 18 x 500 GP. Primary target: VAIRES. Weather 8/10ths cloud, one thin patch. Bombed at 2000 hours from 15,000 feet yellow TIs. Stream of aircraft port of track on run up to target. TIs clearly seen.

Target: *Vaires – Marshalling Yards*
Aircraft deployed total: *159*
514 Squadron: *23*
Aircraft lost total: *Nil*
514 Squadron: *Nil*

Comments: The target was an important railway yard near Paris. Cloud cover caused early cancellation of the raid. Only 12 aircraft had bombed.

13th July 1944.
Weather: Cloudy with intermittent rain.
Non-Operational Flying: Air Tests and Air/Sea Firing were carried out.
Operational Flying: 24 aircraft were detailed for operations but this was cancelled later in the day.

14th July 1944.
Weather: Cloudy.
Non-Operational Flying: Air Tests and a Navigational Exercise were carried out.
Operational Flying: Squadron required for operations tonight but this was cancelled later in the day.

15th July 1944.
Weather: Cloudy.
Non-Operational Flying: Navigation Exercises and Air Tests were carried out.
Operational Flying: BOMBING- CHALONS SUR MARNE – RAILWAY CENTRE.
24 aircraft detailed and took off, 18 aircraft attacked primary target, 5 aircraft abortive. 24 aircraft landed at Base. Weather was clear below cloud and target was clearly marked and bombing concentrated. Crews obtained good visuals of the yards and river. Bombs were seen bursting across the yards. Flak was negligible. 3 combats reported.
S/L PB Clay in PB143, JI-B reported: Bomb load 18 x 500 GP. Primary target: CHALONS SUR MARNE. Weather 5/10ths cloud below, 10/10ths above, clear for bombing. Bombed at 0134 hours from

12,000 feet green TIs. ASI u/s shortly after take-off also starboard engine out on route to target.

Combat Report – Pro-forma:
Aircraft: LL692 'C2'
Captain: F/O EA Campbell RCAF
Target: CHALONS SUR MARNE.
At 0130 hours, height 10,000 feet, heading 190 degrees, position 4035N, 0422E. Rear Gunner sighted Me410 on the starboard quarter up against the light sky at a range of 600 yards. Rear Gunner ordered corkscrew to starboard and opened fire. E/A broke away dead astern into cloud patch. Visibility was good. No searchlights, flares or flak encountered.
MU Gunner – Sgt Jones RCAF – Nil.
Rear Gunner - Sgt S Harvey RCAF – 200 rounds.

Aircraft: LL677 'E2'
Captain: W/O E Beaton.
Target: CHALONS SUR MARNE
1st Encounter: At 0100 hours, height 16,000 feet, heading 130 degrees T, position 4814N, 0112E Rear Gunner sighted unidentified E/A on the starboard quarter down at a range of 400 yards with its nose light on. Gunner ordered corkscrew and fired at E/A which was subsequently lost in corkscrew.
2nd Encounter: At 02.00 hours, height 15,000 feet, heading 130 degrees T., position 4818N, 0116E, Rear Gunner sighted unidentified E/A on the port quarter up at a range of 350 yards. Rear Gunner immediately opened fire and E/A broke away to the port quarter down. Visibility was good, with no searchlights, fighter flares or flak encountered.
MU Gunner – Sgt R Rutherford – Nil.
Rear Gunner - Sgt DM Temple - 800 rounds

Target: *Chalons-sur-Marne Railway Centre*
Aircraft deployed total: 229
514 Squadron: 24 (5 aborted)
Aircraft lost total: 3
514 Squadron: Nil

Comments: Two railway targets were both successfully bombed.

16th July 1944.
Weather: Mainly fine, fog after dawn.
Non-Operational Flying: Air tests were carried out.
Operational Flying: 24 aircraft required for operations tonight, but cancelled later in the day.

17th July 1944.
Weather: Cloudy.
Non-Operational Flying: Air Tests and Practice Bombing carried out.
Operational Flying: Not required for operations today, but required early tomorrow morning.

18th July 1944.
Weather: Fair to cloudy.
Non-Operational Flying: No non-operational flying took place today owing to operational flying.
Operational Flying: BOMBING – EMIEVILLE – TROOP CONCENTRATIONS.
26 aircraft were detailed to attack German troop concentrations at Emieville, taking off early in the morning. All took off and landed safely at base on completion of the duty. Weather was clear and target well marked. Bombing was highly concentrated.
F/S GC France in LM180, JI-G reported: Bomb load 11 x 1000 MC, 4 x 500 GP. Primary target: EMIEVILLE. Weather clear. Bombed at 0607 hours from 10,500 feet, South East corner of smoke as directed by Master Bomber. A good attack.

Target: *Emieville – Troop Concentrations.*
Aircraft deployed total: *942*
514 Squadron: *26*
Aircraft lost total: *6*
514 Squadron: *Nil*

Comments: This attack was in support of 'Operation Goodwood' a British Army attack in Normandy, 18th – 20th July 1944. By the raid's end, it was considered one of the most effective bombing operations in support of the Army of the whole war. Weather was clear for the raid, which included American aircraft in the early morning attacks. Support from Navy gunfire and Army artillery meant there were few reports of flak as they suppressed the AA guns. In total, Bomber Command dropped 5,000 of the 6,800 tons total for the raid. The result was that two whole German enemy divisions were severely affected.

(Above) 'A' Flight Lancasters of 514 Sqn at Waterbeach prior to the attack on German troop positions at Emieville, east of Caen. LM627, JI-D (nearest camera) survived the war with the squadron; however LM181, JI-E (centre of photo) was lost two days later on 20th July 1944 on the raid to Homberg. Source: Tracy Holroyd-Smith / Sgt George Henry.

BOMBING – AULNOYE – RAILWAY JUNCTION.
18 aircraft were detailed to attack the railway centre at Aulnoye, taking off at night. All took off and landed safely at base on completion of the duty. Weather was cloudless with slight haze. One Me.109 is claimed as destroyed, by the crew of A2-B.
F/Sgt GC France in ME818, JI-J reported: Bomb load 18 x 500 GP. Primary target: AULNOYE. Weather clear. Bombed at 0054hrs from 10,000ft red and green TIs. A quiet trip, weather good.

Aircraft: LL697 'B2'
Captain: F/Lt MR Head RNZAF

Target: AULNOYE – RAILWAY JUNCTION
At 0105 hours the MU Gunner reported an unidentified aircraft with navigation lights burning on the starboard beam up. A minute later the Rear Gunner reported a S/E fighter (later identified as an Me109) coming in from the starboard quarter down range about 300 yards. The Rear Gunner gave orders to corkscrew starboard, and at the same time the E/A opened fire, his trace passing well behind our A/C. The Rear Gunner returned fire with a 3 second burst, there was a small explosion and the E/A dived to the ground enveloped in flames where it was seen to burn for a considerable period by the Mid Upper Gunner and Rear Gunner. During the combat the aircraft burning navigation lights was kept under observation by the Mid Upper Gunner. As the Me109 dived to the ground the other aircraft switched off its lights and was not seen again.
MU Gunner – W/O R Craig – Nil
Rear Gunner - Sgt AF Backford - 500 rounds.

Target: *Aulnoye – Railway Junction*
Aircraft deployed total: 263
514 Squadron: 18
Aircraft lost total: 22
514 Squadron: Nil

Comments: Another split attack with 2 targets, Aulnoye and Revigny railway junctions. Both attacks were successful and both junctions destroyed. On the Revigny raid, the allied Lancasters were ambushed by Luftwaffe fighters, with the subsequent loss of 24 aircraft. This represented 22% of the crews involved in that raid. This was the second operation of the day for many of the crews.

19th July 1944.
Weather: Fair to cloudy.
Non-Operational Flying: Cross Countries and Air Tests were carried out.
Operational Flying: 22 aircraft detailed for ops but was cancelled later in the day.

20th July 1944.
Weather Fair to cloudy.
Non-Operational Flying: Cross-countries and air tests were carried out.
Operational Flying: BOMBING – HOMBERG – OIL PLANT.

24 aircraft were detailed to attack oil plant at Homberg. All took off, 17 attacked the primary target, 2 aircraft returned early and 1 aircraft (P/O Watkins' LL726) jettisoned in the target area due to fighter attack. 20 aircraft landed back at Base, 4 aircraft are missing. Weather was clear with a slight haze over the target. Red TIs were reported very concentrated. Large fires and explosions were seen and columns of black smoke. Enemy fighters were very active and moderate heavy flak experienced.

W/O CE Williams in LM206, JI-C reported: Bomb load 1 x 4000 HC, 2 x 500 MC, 14 x 500 GP. Primary target: HOMBERG. Weather slight haze. Bombed at 0120 hours from 20,000 feet red TIs. Satisfactory raid. Considerable number of fighters.

Combat Report:
Aircraft: LL726 'H2'
Captain: P/O W.M. Watkins
Target: HOMBERG
At 0120 hours, an unidentified aircraft was seen by the Rear Gunner to fall in flames astern and a Ju88 was silhouetted against the glare on the port quarter down. The Rear Gunner opened fire immediately at a range of 300 yards, and ordered the Pilot to corkscrew to port. The E/A opened fire as the Pilot commenced to corkscrew and the starboard outer engine of 'H2' was put out of action. During this time, the Rear Gunner continued to fire and observed hits on E/A, which pulled up as if to break away, rolled over on its back and started to spin down with a red glow., bursting into flames after the aircraft had spun for a few seconds. The E/A was observed by the Rear Gunner, Pilot and Mid Upper Gunner to hit the ground where it burst into a patch of flames.
MU Gunner – Sgt R Dawson – Nil
Rear Gunner – Sgt B Ferries - 800 rounds.

Aircraft: DS787 'D2'
Captain: F/S AJ Holland.
Target: HOMBERG
1st Encounter: Homeward bound (bombs dropped) on a heading of 280 degrees T, IAS 180 at a height of 15,000 feet. At 01.38 hours in position 5144N 0546E Rear Gunner reported a Ju88 coming in from the starboard quarter up, range 300 yards. Rear Gunner immediately gave order to corkscrew to starboard and opened fire with a short burst. E/A broke away to starboard quarter down and was not seen again.
 2nd Encounter: At 0147 hours, on a course of 258 degrees T, IAS 185, height 12,000 feet, in position 5142N 0505E, Rear Gunner reported an

E/A (later identified as an FW190) attacking from the port quarter up, range 500 yards. Rear Gunner immediately gave order to corkscrew port. Mid Upper Gunner opened fire immediately and E/A continued to close in, Rear Gunner opened fire from 450 yards. As Lancaster corkscrewed, E/A opened fire from 400 yards but Lancaster sustained no hits. Mid Upper Gunner claimed strikes on E/A which was seen to burst into flames and fall through the cloud.
MU Gunner - Sgt C O' Brian - 150 rounds.
Rear Gunner – Sgt W MacDonald – 350 rounds.

Note: There is a discrepancy between the ORB entry and the above combat report, the latter stating the aircraft serial as DS620.

Aircraft: LL697 'B2'
Captain: F/O BE MacDonald.
Target: HOMBERG.
Inward bound (bombs not dropped) on a heading of 059 degrees T, height 19,000 feet, IAS 160, in position 5115N 0600E. At 0115 hours, Rear Gunner reported a T/E unidentified aircraft passing from port to starboard above range, 700 yards. The E/A was next seen coming in from the starboard quarter level range 400 yards. The Rear Gunner immediately gave order to corkscrew starboard and as our Lancaster started to corkscrew the E/A opened fire with a short burst. The Mid Upper and Rear Gunners opened fire at 450 yards and observed their trace hitting the E/A, which burst into flames and fell away to the starboard quarter. The E/A was seen to fall in flames by the 2 Gunners and the Flight Engineer.
MU Gunner - Sgt DF Gardiner RCAF - 200 rounds.
Rear Gunner – Sgt HE Bentley - 400 rounds.

Pro-forma Report:
Aircraft DS786 'F2'
Captain: F/L Timms
Target: HOMBERG
0108 hours, Aircraft at 19,000 feet heading 105 deg T in target area, 5118N, 0636E. No moon, no cloud, good visibility. Fighter flares seen dead astern. One Ju88 seen above and astern, distance 200 yards. Corkscrew starboard undertaken. MU Gunner fired 100 rounds with E/A between 200 yards and 150 yards. E/A broke away starboard quarter down without opening fire.
MU Gunner: Sgt EH Bradshaw 100 rounds.
Rear Gunner: Sgt DE Holland – Nil.

Aircraft: DS826 'J'
Captain: F/S J Lawrie RNZAF
Target: HOMBERG.
At 0136 hours, height 12,000 feet, heading 280 degrees, position 5130N 0440E. 30 seconds after 'Monica' warning, Mid Upper Gunner sighted Me109 on the fine port quarter up at a range of 250-300 yards. Mid Upper Gunner ordered corkscrew to port and opened fire. E/A broke away on the port beam and was not seen again. Visibility was poor with no moon. There were no searchlights, fighter flares or flak encountered.
MU Gunner – F/S LR Burford RAAF – 100 rounds.
Rear Gunner - F/S R Chester-Masters RAAF - Nil.

Aircraft: LL677 'E2'
Captain: W/O D Beaton
Target: HOMBERG.
1st Encounter: Homeward bound (bombs dropped), position 5126N 0632E, height 17,500 feet, heading 058T. IAS 160. At 0123 hours, the Mid Upper Gunner observed trace coming from the starboard quarter down range about 800 yards. He warned Captain to stand by to corkscrew and at that moment trace stopped and nothing more was seen.
2nd Encounter: Lancaster 'E2', position 5133N 0525E, height 17,000 feet, heading 276 T. IAS 160. At 01.27 hours the Bomb Aimer sighted an Me109 on the port bow level, range 300 yards. He immediately gave orders to corkscrew port and at that moment the E/A fired a short burst which passed harmlessly above our A/C. The E/A then broke away to the starboard bow up and was not seen again.
MU Gunner – Sgt T Rutherford - Nil.
Rear Gunner – Sgt EM Temple - Nil.

Aircraft: DS813 'N'
Captain: F/S E Richardson.
Target: HOMBERG
1st Encounter: Outward bound, heading 065 degrees M., height 19,500 feet, position 5110N 0550E. At 0110 hours, the Rear Gunner sighted an FW190 flying in the opposite direction astern up. Shortly afterwards, Rear Gunner reported trace coming from starboard quarter down, 600 yards and immediately gave order to corkscrew starboard. E/A closed in to 400 yards, fired another short burst and was lost during the second part of the corkscrew.

2nd Encounter: Lancaster nearing target on a heading of 065 degrees M, height 18,000 feet, position Homberg, 10 miles S.W. At 0118 hours, the Mid Upper Gunner reported a T/E unidentified E/A attacking from starboard beam level, range 500 yards, and immediately gave order to corkscrew starboard. Mid Upper Gunner opened fire at 400 yards with a 1 second burst. At the same time, E/A opened fire but Lancaster sustained no damage. E/A closed in to 350 yards and was lost in 2nd part of corkscrew.

3rd Encounter: Lancaster 'N' in target area, (bombs dropped), height 18,000 feet, heading 057 degrees M, position target area, time 0123 hours. Pilot reported E/A attacking dead ahead at 800 yards, firing rockets. He immediately corkscrewed starboard and lost E/A in corkscrew. Lancaster sustained no damage.

4th Encounter: Lancaster 'N' was homeward bound on a heading of 285 degrees M, height 15,000 feet position 5135N 0540E. At 01.30 hours. Pilot reported E/A attacking dead ahead 750 yards, and immediately corkscrewed to starboard. E/A fired 2 rockets but Lancaster sustained no damage. E/A was lost in corkscrew.

MU Gunner – Sgt B Vince – 40 rounds (in 2nd combat)
Rear Gunner – Sgt PR Smith – Nil.

Target: *Homberg – Rhein-Preussen Oil Plant.*
Aircraft deployed total: *158*
514 Squadron: *24 (2 returned early)*
Aircraft lost total: *20*
514 Squadron: *4*

Comments: Although this raid achieved its objective of disrupting the supply of aviation fuel, for 514 Squadron, this first visit to Homberg proved to be a costly operation. 7 of the Squadron's aircraft reported combats, not including the 4 aircraft that were lost, a total surpassed only on the night of the Nuremberg raid. 75 (NZ) Squadron also suffered badly, losing 7 of its 25 aircraft. Heavy damage was caused to the oil plant which caused disruption to the supply of fuel from 6000 tons, down to under 1000 tons per day. Homberg was to feature significantly on the casualty lists of both squadrons in the future. Night fighters were a significant problem on this op. F/S Richardson, pilot of DS813, reported 'We had five fighter attacks within 30 miles of target'. F/S John Lawrie, flying DS826 early in his tour, reported a combat with an enemy fighter, whilst W/O Boston in LL677 noted a 'Head on attack by single engine fighter just after leaving the target area'. Seven crews reported combat with enemy fighters, in addition to the four crews posted missing.

Missing Aircraft:

HK570 JI-P.   Shot down, possibly by either Hptm. Heinz-Martin Hadeball, 3./NGr.10, or Hptm. Ernst-Wilhelm Modrow, 1./NJG1. HK570 crashed at 0159 in the sea off the Dutch coast (presumably on return leg as the squadron aircraft bombed between 0119hrs and 0125hrs).

W/O JL Lassam	Pilot	KIA
Sgt WC Taylor	Navigator	KIA
Sgt WJ Anthony	Bomb Aimer	KIA
F/S AR Hope	WOP/Air	KIA
Sgt BH Cooper RCAF	MU Gunner	KIA
Sgt DP Manchul RCAF	Rear Gunner	KIA
F/S EJ Hack	Flight Engineer	KIA

HK571 JI-L Probably shot down by Hptm. Hermann Greiner, 11./NJG1, crashing at 0124 at Daubenspeckhof 1 km W of Moers (in target area).

P/O SM Anderson	Pilot	KIA
WO2 WOD Larmouth RCAF	Navigator	KIA
Sgt KE Rhodes RCAF	Bomb Aimer	KIA
Sgt RP Whitehall	WOP/Air	KIA
Sgt KA Jeffrey RCAF	MU Gunner	KIA
Sgt CN Samson RCAF	Rear Gunner	KIA
Sgt A Wilson	Flight Engineer	KIA

LM181 JI-E Probably shot down by Fw. Klaus Moller, 12./NJG3, or Ofw. Heinrich Schmidt, 2./NJG6. LM181 crashed at 0122 in the target area. No further details.

F/O LW McLean RNZAF	Pilot	KIA
F/S AT Stone RNZAF	Navigator	KIA
F/S WS McIlraith RNZAF	Bomb Aimer	KIA
F/S TK Durie RNZAF	WOP/Air	KIA
Sgt M Duncan	Rear Gunner	KIA
Sgt RE Digby	MU Gunner	KIA
Sgt GW Bumstead	Flight Engineer	KIA

ME858 JI-J. Shot down at 0114 hours by the Bf 110G-4 of Uffz. Gustav Sarzio, 6./NJG1. The aircraft crashed at 0116hrs at Limburg (approaching the target). The aircraft was lost on its way to the target. The Lancaster's complete bomb load was on board when it crashed. Only a few bombs exploded in the open field outside the village of Hunsel. The Lancaster was also carrying a large 4000 HC (Cookie) bomb which did not explode. According to an eye-witness, 'the aircraft was hit in one of the wings and exploded high in the air. None of the crew members was able to leave the Lancaster. Parts of the plane are laying in a circle of 500 meters around the crash site.' (Source: Balfour Collegiate, Regina, Saskatchewan, Canada)

(Above) Uffz. Gustav Sarzio and his crewman pose with their Bf110 night fighter. Uffz. Sarzio claimed five victories before being wounded in a Mosquito attack on 4th/5th November 1944. Source: Airworx GmbH Archive.

F/O D Millar	Pilot	KIA
F/O DO Brown RCAF	Navigator	KIA
Sgt HM Glansford	Bomb Aimer	KIA
Sgt GH Holt	WOP/Air	KIA
Sgt WE Blore	MU Gunner	KIA
Sgt HE Long	Rear Gunner	KIA
Sgt N Derham	Flight Engineer	KIA

21st July 1944.
Weather: Cloudy with intermediate drizzle.
Non-Operational Flying: Formation flying and Air/Sea firing were carried out.
Operational Flying: 20 aircraft were detailed to stand by for daylight targets. The effort was cancelled later in the day.

22nd July 1944.
Weather: Cloudy with intermittent drizzle.
Non-Operational Flying: Formation flying and fighter affiliation were carried out.
Operational Flying: 19 aircraft were detailed for operations but the effort was cancelled later in the day.

23rd July 1944.
Weather cloudy.
Non Operational Flying: Fighter affiliation and air tests carried out.
Operational Flying: BOMBING - KIEL - WAREHOUSES AND DOCKS.
22 aircraft were detailed to attack Kiel harbour installations. All aircraft took off. 20 aircraft attacked the primary target. 2 aircraft returned early, the remainder landed safely at base after completion of the duty. Weather was 10/10ths thin cloud over the target. Sky marking was good but bombing scattered. Flak over target moderate to heavy, few searchlights and fighters.
F/S GC France in PB143, JI-B reported: Bomb load 10 x 1000 MC, 5 x 500 GP. Primary target Kiel. Weather 10/10ths cloud. Bombed at 0120hrs from 20,000 feet, centre of red and green TIs. Large explosion giving an orange glow at 0121hrs.

Combat Report:
Aircraft: PB185 'F2'
Captain: F/S AJ Holland.

Target: KIEL
In the target area (bombs not dropped), height 20,000 feet IAS 180, heading 170 degrees T. At 0125 hours the Rear Gunner saw a S/E unidentified A/C attacking a Lancaster on the starboard beam, range 700 yards. The Mid Upper and Rear Gunners opened fire, as did 3 other Lancasters in the vicinity. The E/A was last seen falling in flames, stern down.
MU Gunner – Sgt C O' Brian – 80 rounds.
Rear Gunner – Sgt W MacDonald – 160 rounds.
Several crews noted carrying 'special nickels'.

Target: *Kiel – Warehouses and Docks*
Aircraft deployed total: *629*
514 Squadron: *22 (2 returned early)*
Aircraft lost total: *4*
514 Squadron: *Nil*

Comments: This operation went much more smoothly, with over 600 aircraft dropping their bomb loads in a mere 35 minutes. This was the first time in 2 months that an operation was carried out on a German target and the largest attack on Kiel of the war. Damage was extensive and the U-Boat facilities and the port were heavily bombed. 500 pound delayed action bombs ensured that recovery operations were made more difficult for the enemy. F/S John Lawrie and crew returned early due to intercom problems whilst F/O BK Richardson had a u/s rear turret.

24th July 1944.
Weather: Cloudy.
Non-Operational Flying: Cross countries and air tests were carried out.
Operational Flying: BOMBING – STUTTGART.
18 aircraft were detailed to attack Stuttgart. All took off and 12 attacked the primary target. Five aircraft returned early, one aircraft is missing. Weather was 10/10ths cloud, tops at 5-7000 feet. Red TIs quickly disappeared into cloud. Master bomber gave instructions to bomb on sky markers. Attack believed scattered.
F/S GC France in PB143, JI-B reported: Bomb load 7 x 1000 MC and 4 x 500 GP. Primary target: STUTTGART. Weather 10/10ths cloud. Bombed at 0148hrs from 20,000 feet south east corner of green and yellow star sky markers. Glow seen beneath cloud.

Combat Reports – Pro-forma:
Aircraft: ME841 'H'
Captain: W/O N Jennings.
Target: STUTTGART
At 0204 hours, height 19,000 feet, heading 285 degrees T., position, 4840N 0635E, Mid Upper Gunner sighted FW190 at 700 yards on port beam level. Rear Gunner ordered corkscrew and opened fire at E/A, which was subsequently lost in corkscrew. Visibility was moderate, with no moon. No fighter flares, searchlights, of flak was experienced.
MU Gunner – Sgt HJ Ball – Nil.
Rear Gunner - Sgt CF Haslam - 150 rounds.

Aircraft: LL 716 'G2 '
Captain: F/O W.M. Watkins.
Target: STUTTGART.
At 23.39 hours, height 17,500 feet, heading 133 degrees T, 4840N, 0010E, Rear Gunner sighted unidentified T/E at 400 yards range on the port quarter level against the dark sky. Rear Gunner ordered Captain to corkscrew and simultaneously opened fire with a short burst. E/A was lost in corkscrew and was not seen again. Visibility was hazy with no moon or cloud. No searchlights, fighter flares or flak were encountered.
MU Gunner – Sgt P Dawson – Nil
Rear Gunner – Sgt B Ferries - 200 rounds.

Target:	*Stuttgart Area*
Aircraft deployed total:	*614*
514 Squadron:	*18 (5 returned early)*
Aircraft lost total:	*21*
514 Squadron:	*1*

Comments: This raid was to be the first of three raids on the city, planned over the next five nights and caused the most serious damage of the war to the city. Many of the city's public buildings in the city centre were destroyed.
F/S John Lawrie reported this as a 'moderate attack', having bombed at 0149 from 19,000 ft onto green and yellow sky markers.
W/O Jennings and F/O Watkins both reported combats with enemy aircraft.

Missing Aircraft:

PB185 A2-F. Probably shot down at 0233 hours by Hptm. Paul Zorner of Stab III./NJG5 in the vicinity of Trier, returning from the target. All crew lost. Despite Sgt Stafford being identified at the time he, along with the rest of the crew, are commemorated on the Runnymede Memorial, for aircrew with no known resting place.

F/O TJ Middleton	Pilot	KIA
F/O FK Beers RCAF	Navigator	KIA
F/O AG Burgess	Bomb Aimer	KIA
F/S TD Jones	WOP/Air	KIA
Sgt ABE Booth	MU Gunner	KIA
Sgt C Brown	Rear Gunner	KIA
Sgt RW Stafford	Flight Engineer	KIA

25th July 1944.
Weather: Cloudy with intermittent drizzle.
Non-Operational Flying: Cross countries and air tests were carried out.
Operational Flying: BOMBING - STUTTGART.
18 aircraft were detailed, 17 aircraft took off, 13 aircraft attacked the primary target and 4 aircraft returned early. 3 aircraft landed away from Base on return, short of petrol. Weather was 10/10ths cloud, tops up to 22,000 feet for most of route with a break over target. Bombing started early on scattered marking. Slight to moderate heavy Flak was encountered. 3 combats were reported.
P/O PF Carter RNZAF in ME841, JI-H reported: Bomb load 7 x 1000 MC, 4 x 500 GP. Primary target: STUTTGART. Weather clear. Bombed at 0216 hours from 14,000 feet centre of fires. Very large fire in centre of target, smaller fires covering an area approx. radius 5 miles.
F/L Dods reported: Large red glow seen in sky 80 miles away.

Combat Report:
Aircraft: LL697 'B2'
Captain: F/S MR Oliver RNZAF
Target: STUTTGART
1st Encounter: Outward bound, height 18,000 feet, heading 150 degrees T, IAS 150, position 4740N 0140E. At 0012 hours the W/Operator warned the Captain and Gunners of an E/A on the starboard quarter. The Captain commenced to corkscrew and shortly afterwards the Rear Gunner sighted an Me110 coming in from the starboard

quarter down, range 800 yards. At 500 yards, the E/A opened fire with a short burst. A minute later, a fighter flare was seen astern down and the Rear Gunner had a good view of the E/A closing in from astern, range 250 yards. The Rear Gunner opened fire immediately and observed the aircraft to fly through his arc of fire. The Mid Upper Gunner opened fire as the E/A was breaking away starboard beam down, range 250 yards. No strikes were seen and contact with E/A was lost.

2nd Encounter: Lancaster 'B2' was at position 4745N 0240E, heading 099 degrees T, height 18,000 feet. At 00.20 hours, W/Operator warned crew that an E/A was 1500 yards starboard quarter level. Gunners did not observe E/A at that range. E/A closed range, to about 500 yards and opened fire. The Captain immediately corkscrewed to starboard, Gunners had not sighted E/A at that time. E/A pressed home his attack and was not observed until he reached 200 yards, when both Gunners opened fire. E/A broke away to port quarter up and was the recognised as a Ju88. No strikes were observed.

3rd Encounter: Lancaster 'B2', heading 093 degrees T., position 4780N 0320E, height 18,000 feet. At 00.30 hours, W/Operator warned crew that 2 E/A was coming in, 1 dead astern, the other on the port beam. The E/A (S/E unidentified) dead astern opened fire at 1000 yards. Trace was observed to pass the Lancaster above at 200 yards range. Rear Gunner ordered Captain to corkscrew to port, as the other E/A (S/E unidentified) was on the port side, presumably waiting for Lancaster to give away its position, by firing at attacking E/A The E/A dead astern was then lost to view. As Lancaster corkscrewed to port, the other E/A was seen to close in from the port quarter at a range of 200 yards. Both Gunners opened fire, no strikes were seen. E/A broke away starboard quarter up and was not seen again. During the 3 attacks, Lancaster sustained no damage.

MU Gunner – F/S WJ Larter – 300 rounds.
Rear Gunner – F/S JT Mephan RNZAF – 350 rounds.

Target:	*Stuttgart Area*
Aircraft deployed total:	*550*
514 Squadron:	*17 (4 returned early)*
Aircraft lost total:	*12*
514 Squadron:	*Nil*

Comments: 12 Aircraft lost on this return raid to Stuttgart. Further damage was done to the target. Most of 514 Sqn bombed between

0150hrs and 0155hrs, apart from P/O Carter and F/S Williams who turned up some twenty minutes later.
F/O R Harvey returned early when his port inner engine suffered a rapid drop in oil pressure and caught fire.
On what was not a good night for port inner engines, F/S Holland's aircraft also suffered a failure and landed at Ford, where it overran the runway sustaining damage to the fuselage.
F/S Wilson's engines were all working correctly but unfortunately his mid-upper turret wasn't, necessitating an early return.

26th July 1944.
Weather: Fair to cloudy.
Non-Operational Flying: Air / Sea firing and practice bombing were carried out.
Operational Flying: Not required for operations today.

27th July 1944.
Weather: Cloudy with some showers.
Non-Operational Flying: Air tests were carried out.
Operational Flying: BOMBING - LES CATELLIERS FLYING BOMB SITE.

(Above) 514 Sqn Lancasters attack Les Catelliers. The bombs are probably 500 lb GP. Source: Wendy Flemming

12 aircraft detailed and took off. 11 aircraft attacked primary and 12 aircraft landed back at Base on completion of sortie. Weather over the

target was 6-7 10ths cloud. All crews bombed on leading Mosquito, bombs seen to straddle target. 1 aircraft had to jettison owing to engine trouble.

F/S SE Wilson in FS726, JI-J reported: Bomb load 18 x 500 GP. Primary target: LES CATELLIERS. Bombed at 1851 hours from 16,000 feet on Mosquito.

Target:	Les Catelliers Flying Bomb Site
Aircraft deployed total:	*72*
514 Squadron:	*12*
Aircraft lost total:	*Nil*
514 Squadron:	*Nil*

Comments: This series of split raids introduced the first use of the 'GH Leader technique' in which following aircraft would release their bombs when they saw the Leading GH equipped aircraft doing so. 5 separate targets were on for Bomber Command for tonight. Cloud cover hampered efforts, making the bombing scattered. Use of this equipment, of course, became a speciality of 514 Squadron and is reflected in the squadron crest. The aircraft with engine trouble was flown by F/L McDonald. No further details given and all crew reports simply gave time of release without further observations.

28th July 1944.
Weather: Cloudy, few showers.
Non-Operational Flying: Fighter affiliation and cross-countries were carried out.
Operational Flying: BOMBING – STUTTGART.
20 aircraft were detailed, 18 took off, 14 attacked the primary target, 1 abortive sortie - jettisoned. 3 aircraft missing. Weather was 10/10ths thin layer of cloud over the target. TM was scattered. Several clusters of green and red TIs seen and Master Bomber was not always specific as to which cluster should be bombed. Consequently bombing was scattered. Little evidence of bombing, although reflection of fires seen through cloud.

F/S DC Gordon, RAAF in PB142, JI-A reported: Bomb load 7x 1000 MC, 2x500 GP. Primary target: STUTTGART. Weather 8/10ths cloud. Bombed at 0157 hours from 19,000 feet green TIs as instructed. Much fighter activity. Should be a good attack.

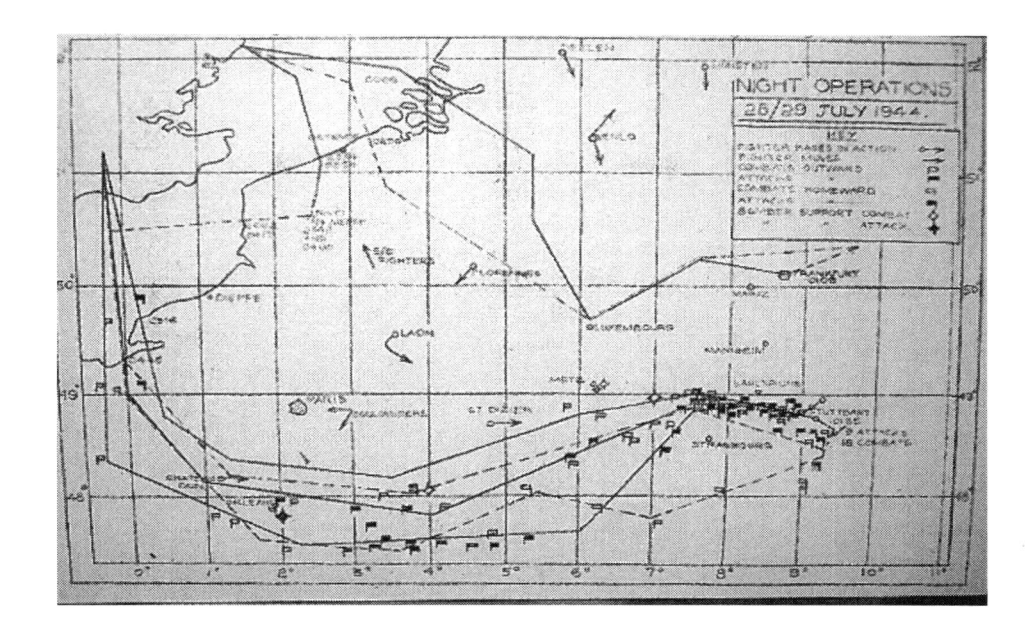

(Above) Chart for the Stuttgart operation on 28th / 29 July 1944. Black flags indicate losses of Bomber Command aircraft; white flags indicate combats with night fighters. Source: Ron Pickler.

F/S GC France in PB143, JI-B reported: Bomb load 7x 1000 MC, 2x500 GP. Primary target: STUTTGART. Weather 9/10 thin layer of cloud. Bombed at 0200hrs from 20,000 feet glow of green TIs. Uneventful trip.

F/S Oliver: Abortive sortie. Starboard outer fluctuating, temperature and pressure oil leak on port inner.

Combat Report -Pro-forma:
Aircraft: LM 180 'G '
Captain: F/S JA Whitwood.
Target: STUTTGART
At 0215 hours, height 19,000 feet, heading 282 degrees, position 4832N, 0815E. Rear Gunner sighted Ju88 on the port quarter down at 1000 yards visible against the light sky. Rear Gunner ordered corkscrew and both Gunners opened fire. E/A was subsequently lost in corkscrew and was not seen again. Visibility was clear, with cloud tops at 7,000 feet. No fighter flares, searchlights or flak were experienced.
MU Gunner – Sgt JV Gillespie RCAF – 200 rounds.
Rear Gunner – Sgt RA Birch - 400 rounds.

Target: *Stuttgart Area*
Aircraft deployed total: *496*
514 Squadron: *18*
Aircraft lost total: *39*
514 Squadron: *3*

Comments: The final in the series of attacks on this target. A bad night for Bomber Command, saw the loss of 39 aircraft. Night fighters infiltrated the return stream of bombers which led to the high losses. The combined damage over the 3 raids was extensive, with the central areas of the city badly affected.

Missing Aircraft:

LM206 JI-C. Shot down by a Ju88 flown by Oblt. Heinz Roekker of 2./NJG2 at 0117 hours, 7 km NW of Neufchateau, en route to target.

F/O R Jones	*Pilot*	*KIA*
Sgt GF Robinson	*Navigator*	*POW*
F/O KH Loder	*Bomb Aimer*	*KIA*
F/S FS Jones	*WOP/Air*	*KIA*
Sgt R Lane	*MU Gunner*	*KIA*
Sgt AR Braine	*Rear Gunner*	*KIA*
Sgt TH Harvell	*Flight Engineer*	*Evaded*

DS813 JI-N. Crashed at Deinvillers, near St. Die, circumstances not known. Possibly shot down by Offzr. Walter Swoboda, 2./NJG6, who claimed a Lancaster in the St. Die area at 0130 hours. F/L Chapman was Gunnery Leader for the squadron.

F/L AF Fowke RCAF	*Pilot*	*KIA*
F/O JT Daly	*Navigator*	*KIA*
F/O RJ Bennett RCAF	*Bomb Aimer*	*KIA*
Sgt SA Picton	*WOP/Air*	*KIA*
F/L HCA Chapman	*MU Gunner*	*KIA*
F/O GR Murphy	*Rear Gunner*	*KIA*
Sgt HG Carter	*Flight Engineer*	*KIA*

(Above): P/O E Greenwood and crew, including MU Gunner Sgt George Henry, stand with 'their' Lancaster Mk.II, DS813. Whilst in the care of P/O Greenwood's crew, DS813 was part of 'A' Flight, bearing the code JI-H. In mid-June 1944 the aircraft was transferred to 'B' Flight as JI-N, being lost on her 56th operational sortie whilst so marked. Source: Tracy Holroyd-Smith / Sgt George Henry.

LL692 A2-C. The first aircraft to be shot down on this night, LL692 was brought down at 0001 hours by the Ju88 G1 4R+AK flown by Lt. Johannes Strassner of 2./NJG2. The location was 4 km. East of Chateaudun. F/L Campbell and most of his crew fortunately survived and their tale is told in a short film produced by his son.

F/L EA Campbell RCAF	Pilot	Evaded
F/O RR Griffin	Second Pilot	KIA
F/S EF Garland RCAF	Navigator	Evaded
F/O JE Chapman RCAF	Bomb Aimer	Evaded
Sgt AR Lyons	WOP/Air	Evaded
F/S ER Jones	MU Gunner	Evaded
F/S SA Harvey	Rear Gunner	Evaded
Sgt WA Donaldson	Flight Engineer	Evaded

F/O RR Griffin is not listed in the ORB as part of the crew of LL692 but was part of the crew on this flight, on a 'second dickey' trip. F/O

Griffin was able to leave the stricken aircraft but his parachute had deployed inside and was bundled up by the Flight Engineer and handed to F/O Griffin who then baled out. It appears to have failed as he was found dead on the ground.

(Above) F/L EA Campbell RCAF and crew. Inset: F/S ER Jones, RCAF (MU Gunner), Back row: F/S WA Donaldson (Flight Engineer), F/L EA Campbell RCAF (Pilot), F/O JE Chapman RCAF (Bomb Aimer), F/S B Lyons (W/OP). Front row: F/S SA Harvey RCAF (Rear Gunner), F/S ER Garland RCAF (Navigator)

29th July 1944.
Weather: Cloudy with rain in the afternoon.
Operational Flying 11 aircraft were detailed for operations but the effort was cancelled later in the day.

30th July 1944.
Weather: Cloudy with light rain at first.
Non-Operational Flying: Air to Sea firing and air tests were carried out.

Operational Flying: BOMBING: CAEN 'B'.
18 aircraft were detailed, 17 aircraft took off. 16 aircraft attacked the primary target, 1 aircraft is missing. 8 aircraft landed at Woodbridge, 1 aircraft at Bassingbourne and 1 at Debash due to low cloud over base on return. Weather over target - low cloud. Master Bomber gave instructions re: cloud base at 3000 feet then 2000 feet and instructed to bomb on red TIs and southern edge of smoke from same. Master

Bomber also instructed not to bomb yellow markers dropped to the North of the target, presumably in our own lines. Most crews identified the main road and the village in the North part of the target area.

F/S GC France in LM180, JI-G reported: Bomb load 18 x 500 GP. Primary target: CAEN 'B'. Weather 10/10ths cloud. Bombed at 0749 hours from 2000 feet, red TIs as instructed. Clouds of yellowish smoke. Bomb bursts seen across the reds. A good trip. Damage to the fuselage from bomb bursts. Landed at Woodbridge.

F/S LR Campbell noted 'much jamming on RT' whilst F/L BK McDonald noted 'port inner u/s at 0835 and starboard inner u/s at 0852', and landed at Bassingbourne.

Target: *Caen – Aiming Point 'B'.*
Aircraft deployed total: *692*
514 Squadron: *17*
Aircraft lost total: *4*
514 Squadron: *1*

Comments: Cloud cover hampered this multi-target raid on 6 gun positions near Villers Bocage. Cloud was so restrictive that only 377 aircraft dropped their bombs, with the result that only 2 of the targets were bombed successfully.

Missing Aircraft:

LL733 JI-S. Lost without trace with all crew. A 75(NZ) Sqn. Lancaster, HK558, AA-D, was seen to crash in the sea after colliding with another Lancaster, possibly LL733 whose loss was unobserved.

F/L WE Chitty RAAF	*Pilot*	*KIA*
W/O LA Ding	*Navigator*	*KIA*
F/O WS Bonell RCAF	*Bomb Aimer*	*KIA*
F/S JE Richardson	*WOP/AG*	*KIA*
F/S EW Jenner	*MU Gunner*	*KIA*
F/S GC Wells	*Rear Gunner*	*KIA*
Sgt CM Guy	*Flight Engineer*	*KIA*

Note: F/L Chitty and Sgt Guy had survived an earlier crash returning from Nuremburg on 30/31st March 1944. Sgt Charles M. Guy was the twin brother of Sgt Robert C. Guy, killed in action June 8th, 1944 when DS 822 of 514 Squadron was shot down over France.

31st July 1944.
Weather: Overcast becoming fine in afternoon and evening.
Non-Operational Flying: Air to Sea firing and air tests were carried out.
Operational Flying: Squadron not required for operations today.

(Above) Lancasters of 514 Sqn en-route to Emieville on 18th July 1944, part of the squadron's effort in support of Operation Goodwood. Source: Airworx GmbH Archive.

Monthly Summary for July 1944

Awards:

131030	Acting Flight Lieutenant DAA Gray,	Pilot DFC 4/7/44
172535	Pilot Officer R Langley,	Pilot DFC 4/7/44
740534	Warrant Officer CE Williams,	Pilot AEA 13/7/44
177638	Pilot Officer DG Hughes,	F/Engineer DFC
1420245	F/Sergeant CB Williams	DFC

Operational:

Enemy Aircraft Destroyed: 2 plus 2 probable.

Operational Flying Hours for July 1944:   1336.10
Non-Operational Flying Hours for July 1944:   206
Total tons of bombs dropped in July 1944:   1,229 ¼ tons
Cumulative total tons of bombs dropped: 5,377 tons
Number of sorties for July 1944: 280

Strength of Squadron as at 31st July 1944.

Aircrew: 92 Officers
     266 SNCOs

Ground: 1 Officer
     33 SNCOs
     355 other ranks
     (Includes 12 WAAFs)

August 1944

1st August 1944.
Weather: Fog early then slight drizzle becoming fair.
Non-Operational Flying: Air tests were carried out.
Operational Flying: BOMBING - DE NIEPPE CONSTRUCTIONAL WORKS.
19 aircraft detailed. 18 aircraft took off. 12 aircraft attacked the primary target. 6 aircraft were abortive. 18 aircraft returned safely to base. Weather was 10/10ths cloud over the target, tops about 3000 feet. The aircraft who bombed early did so on leading aircraft and the order to 'abandon mission' was not heard until late into the attack.
F/S DC Gordon RAAF in PB142, JI-A reported: Bomb load 11 x 1000 MC and 4 x 500 GP. Primary target: DE NIEPPE. Bombed at 2045 hours at 12,000 feet smoke from red TIs.

Target: De Nieppe Flying Bomb Constructional Works
Aircraft deployed total: 777
514 Squadron: 18
Aircraft lost total: Nil
514 Squadron: Nil

Comments: Numerous targets were on for this attack. It would seem this raid was weather affected, as only 79 of the 777 aircraft were able to Bomb. The logbook of F/S Geoff France records this op as being on 2nd August. He states that the raid was abandoned on the Master Bomber's orders and he jettisoned some of his bombs.

2nd August 1944.
Weather: Low cloud, and slight drizzle in the morning. Fair in afternoon. Low cloud in the evening.
Non-Operational Flying: Special Navigation exercise and air tests were carried out.
Operational Flying: Squadron not required for operations today but required tomorrow.

3rd August 1944.
Weather: Low cloud with slight drizzle in the morning, fair in afternoon and evening.
Non-Operational Flying: Air tests were carried out.

Operational Flying: BOIS DE CASSON FLYING BOMB SUPPLY DEPOT

19 aircraft were detailed and took off. 18 aircraft attacked primary target. 1 aircraft is missing, the remainder returned to base safely. Weather was 2-3/10ths low cloud over the target, all crews identified visually and some good photographs were obtained. Bombing was concentrated.

Squadron will not be required before midday tomorrow. 18 aircraft required for operations. Zero hour 18.15 hours tomorrow.

F/S GC France in PB142, JI-A reported: Bomb load 11 x 1000 MC, 4 x 500 GP. Primary target: BOIS DE CASSON. Bombed at 1406hrs from 16,000 feet on smoke of yellow TI.

Target: *Bois de Casson Flying Bomb Supply Depot*
Aircraft deployed total: *1,114*
514 Squadron: *19*
Aircraft lost total: *6*
514 Squadron: *1*

Comments: With much improved weather, raids were carried out on 3 separate flying bomb stores sites. The attack was a success.

Missing Aircraft:

LL716 A2-G. This was the only aircraft lost on the Bois de Casson raid. It had just bombed the target when it was hit by at least one bomb, which passed through the aircraft's wing. The pilot, F/O John Topham, managed to crash-land successfully, the aircraft coming down at about 1410 hours, some 10km South of Beaumont (Oise). F/S Dennehy was flying as mid-under gunner, a role unique to the Mk.II Lancs.

F/O JB Topham	*Pilot*	*Evaded*
F/O S Baxter	*Navigator*	*POW*
F/S JR McClenaghan	*Air Bomber*	*POW*
F/S H Gilmore	*WOP/Air*	*POW*
F/S FW Dennehy	*Air Gunner*	*Evaded*
Sgt J Scully	*MU Gunner*	*POW*
WO2 WE Egri RCAF	*Rear Gunner*	*POW*
Sgt JD Reid	*Flight Engineer*	*POW*

4th August 1944.
Weather: Fog early then low cloud during the morning. Fair in afternoon and evening. Low cloud at night.
Non-Operational Flying: None noted.
Operational Flying: BOMBING - BEC D'AMBES DEPOT.
16 aircraft were detailed and 16 took off and attacked the primary. Weather was clear and crews identified the target visually. Bombs were seen straggling the target and oil tanks. The whole target was covered with flames and palls of smoke. Attack was considered successful. Occasional LF. No enemy aircraft seen. One aircraft went down after bombing to 2000 feet and took great delight in shooting up a couple of tankers in the estuary. All aircraft returned safely to base.
W/O WD Brickwood in DS786, A2-H reported: Bomb load 5 x 1000 MC, 2- x 500 GP. Primary target: BEC D'AMBES DEPOT. Weather clear. Bombed at 1802 hours from 8000 feet. Storage tanks south of fires. Master Bomber instructed crews to bomb yellow TIs which were not visible. Column of black smoke up to 8000 feet.

(Above) A 514 Sqn Lancaster over the Bec d'Ambes oil depot. Source: Airworx Gmbh Archive.

F/S Richardson in JI-T HK572 reported 'Aircraft orbited target after bombing. Rear Gunner and Mid Upper Gunner fired burst at two tankers in the river at 2000 feet.' The gunners were Sgt RR Smith (rear) and Sgt B Vine (MU). This is a rare example of the Lancaster being used in a ground attack / anti-shipping role. All crews were pleased with the results. F/S John Lawrie commented 'Bang on, couldn't have been better.'

Target: *Bec d'Ambes Oil Storage Depot*
Aircraft deployed total: 288
514 Squadron: 16
Aircraft lost total: Nil
514 Squadron: Nil

Comments: For the first time, 'Serrate'- equipped Mosquitoes were used as escorts, on this attack on an oil storage depot. Serrate equipment detected and homed in on the Liechtenstein radar fitted to German night fighters. No combats were reported.

5th August 1944.
Weather: Low cloud during the morning. Fair afternoon and evening. Low cloud late at night.
Non-Operational Flying: Air tests were carried out.
Operational Flying: BOMBING - BORDEAUX - BASSEN OIL DEPOT.
14 aircraft were detailed and took off, 13 aircraft attacked the primary target, one aircraft attacked 'Blaye at Lt. Luce' *(sic)* in error. All crews identified the target visually by the river and fires. Large fires and explosions were reported in the target area, with black smoke rising up to 3/4000 feet. All aircraft returned safely.
S/L PB Clay in PB143, JI-B reported: Bomb load 8 x 1000 MC 2 x 500 GP. Primary target: BASSEN DEPOT. Weather: cum nimbus, 7000 feet over target. Bombed visually at 1902 hours from 6000 feet oil storage tanks. Two large explosions seen with flames up to 800/1000 feet followed by dense black smoke. Bombing concentrated.
P/O Carter (LM627 JI-D) reported: Hit by heavy flak over the target with the main plane holed.
F/S Drew (LM277 JI-F) reported: Hit by Flak over the target, rear turret u/s, hydraulics and oxygen system.
P/O Hebditch (DS786 A2-H) reported: Blae et St. Luce attacked in error. Bombed at 1903 hours from 8000 feet, yellow TIs as per Master Bomber's instructions. Flames and smoke seen in target area. Altering course as TIs were seen to go down plus hearing Master Bomber's instructions to bomb at 8000 feet caused error in bombing target.'

Target: *Bordeaux -Bassen Oil Depot.*
Aircraft deployed total: *306 (Lancasters)*
514 Squadron: *14*
Aircraft lost total: *1*
514 Squadron: *Nil*

Comments: 3 oil storage depots on the River Gironde were attacked with excellent results.

6th August 1944.
Weather: Low cloud with slight drizzle during morning. Fair in afternoon and evening. Fog towards midnight.
Non-Operational Flying: Special Navigational exercises, fighter affiliation, bombing and air tests were carried out.
Operational Flying: Squadron not required today. 15 aircraft will be required for an Army target tomorrow night.

7th August 1944.
Weather: Fog and low cloud until mid-morning then fair to fine.
Non-Operational Flying: Fighter affiliation and air tests were carried out.
Operational Flying: BOMBING - MANE DE MAGNE TROOP CONCENTRATIONS.
15 aircraft took off, attacked the primary target and returned safely to base. Weather was clear over the target with slight haze. Red TIs were dropped in the identical position of the red star shells fired by our own troops to mark the aiming point. 5 combats with 1 FW190 shot down and confirmed were reported.
F/O CJ Thomson RAAF in PB142, JI-A reported: Bomb load 11 x 1000 MC and 4 x 500 GP. Primary target: MANE DE MAGNE. Weather clear, slight haze. Bombed at 2339 hours from 9000 feet centre of red TIs. Bursts seen across and around TIs.
Major General F. Crawford CB, MC, passenger in ME841 JI-H with F/L Prager and crew commented: 'On approach to target I noticed gun flashes and gun fire on ground and Bofors tracer very clearly. Searchlights appeared after bombing, Red TIs dropped in identical position as red star shells. Bombing very concentrated.
Combat Report:
Aircraft: LL728 'L2'
Captain: F/O JH Harland.
Target: MARE DE MAGNE

Homeward bound (bombs dropped) in position 4955N, 0000E, height 7,000 feet, heading 344T, IAS 190. At 0015 hours the Mid Upper Gunner sighted an FW190 coming in from the port quarter up, range 400 yards. He reported it to the Rear Gunner who saw it and immediately gave orders to corkscrew to port and at the same time fired a 4 second burst. The M/U Gunner fired a 2 second burst. The E/A burst into flames and dived straight into the sea where it was seen to burn by the Gunners and the rest of the crew. The E/A was also seen to dive into the sea and burn by the crew of Lancaster 'O2' of 514 Squadron.

MU Gunner – Sgt SD Lucans – 50 rounds.
Rear Gunner – Sgt L Slocombe – 700 rounds.

Aircraft: DS826 'C2'
Captain: F/S MR Oliver RNZAF
Target: MARE DE MAGNE.
1st Encounter: Homeward bound (bombs dropped), in position 4930N 0000E, height 7,500 feet, heading 043 degrees T., IAS 200. At 23.51 hours, the W/Operator warned the Rear Gunner of an E/A on the starboard quarter. The Rear Gunner searched in that area and shortly afterwards sighted a S/E unidentified E/A coming in from the starboard quarter down range 800 yards. The E/A opened fire and the Rear Gunner gave orders to corkscrew starboard and replied with 2 short bursts, the E/A dropped a scarecrow and then broke away to the port quarter up and was not seen again.
2nd Encounter: Lancaster 'C2' in position 4935N 0020E, height 7,500 feet, heading 043 degrees T, IAS 200. At 23.57 hours, the W/Operator warned the Rear Gunner of an E/A astern down. The Rear Gunner searched and shortly afterwards sighted a S/E unidentified E/A coming in from astern down range 500 yards. He immediately gave orders to corkscrew port and opened fire with 2 short bursts. The E/A replied with a long burst and then broke away to the port beam down and was not seen again. Our aircraft suffered no damage or casualties during the 2 attacks.
MU Gunner – F/S W.J. Larler. – 100 rounds.
Rear Gunner – F/S J.T. Maphan. RNZAF – 150 rounds.

Aircraft: LM 265 'E'
Captain: P/O DC Gordon RAAF
Target: MARE DE MAGNE
Homeward bound (bombs dropped), in position 4915N 0015E, height 8,000 feet, heading 045 degrees T., IAS 190. At 23.53 hours the Rear Gunner observed trace coming from the starboard quarter down, range about 300 yards. He immediately gave order to corkscrew starboard and opened fire with a 3 second burst. The trace ceased and nothing more was seen.
MU Gunner – F/S Burke RNZAF – Nil.
Rear Gunner – Sgt B Robinson – 250 rounds.

Pro-forma Report:
Aircraft: LM286 'F2'
Captain: F/O FF Hebditch.
Target: MARE DE MAGNE
At 00.20 hours, height 9,000 feet, heading 350 degrees, position 5015N 0003E. Bomb Aimer sighted Me410 on starboard bow up at a range of 500 yards. Bomb Aimer ordered corkscrew and Mid Upper Gunner opened fire as corkscrew was initiated. E/A was lost in corkscrew manoeuvre and was not seen again. Visibility was hazy, with moon on starboard side. There was fighter flares astern, no searchlights or flak.
MU Gunner – Sgt CA Clarke – Nil.
Rear Gunner – F/O SE Jones - 50 rounds.

Target:	*Mane de Magne Troop Concentrations*
Aircraft deployed total:	*1,019*
514 Squadron:	*15*
Aircraft lost total:	*10*
514 Squadron:	*Nil*

Comments: This attack was in support of allied ground troops. Fighter opposition claimed 7 Lancasters, with 2 lost to flak. Of the 1,019 aircraft, only 660 aircraft dropped their bombs. The results were good with German positions being significantly damaged.

8th August 1944.
Weather: Fog till mid-morning then fair.
Non-Operational Flying: 3 aircraft were flown to Farnborough and staying for special equipment to be fitted. Air tests were carried out.

Operational Flying: BOMBING - FORET DE LUCHEUX PETROL DUMP.

17 aircraft detailed, took off, attacked primary target and returned safely to base. Weather was clear over target and early arrivals found the target well illuminated by flares. Bombing commenced on green TIs and reds were dropped slightly later, instructions being given by the Master Bomber to bomb red TIs. Target left well ablaze with large column of black smoke rising up to 7/8000 feet. One combat reported, FW190 claimed destroyed. (Note: No combat report has been found to verify this claim).

F/O R Limbert in PB142, JI-A reported: Bomb load 18 x 500 GP. Primary target: FORET DE LUCHEUX. Weather clear. Bombed at 2349 hours, 12,000 feet, red TIs. Fires and much black smoke, good, concentrated attack.

Combat Report - Pro-forma:
Aircraft: LM265 'E'
Captain: F/S S Wilson
Target: FORET DE LUCHEUX.

At 2349 hours, height 12,000 feet, heading 108 degrees T, position 5013N 0225E. Rear Gunner sighted an FW190 at 500 yards range approaching from the starboard quarter up. Rear Gunner ordered to corkscrew and opened fire. E/A was subsequently lost in manoeuvre and was not seen again. Visibility was good with moon on starboard quarter. No searchlights, fighter flares or flak were encountered.

MU Gunner – Sgt R Cooper – Nil.
Rear Gunner – Sgt J Golden - 400 rounds.

Target:	*Foret de Lucheux Petrol Storage.*
Aircraft deployed total:	*180*
514 Squadron:	*17*
Aircraft lost total:	*1*
514 Squadron:	*Nil*

Comments: 2 oil storage depots were attacked on this raid. The attack was successful.

9th August 1944.
Weather: Fine becoming fair.
Non-Operational Flying: Special Navigation Exercise, Fighter Affiliation, Air Tests also 2 aircraft returned from Farnborough.

Operational Flying: BOMBING – FORT D'ENGLOS. PETROL DUMP.
13 aircraft took off at night to attack petrol installations at Fort D'Englos. 12 aircraft attacked primary target, one aircraft returned early. Weather clear. Two crews bombed early and reported white flashes of flames, crews attacking later saw no sign of the success of the attack. One combat reported but no claims. All aircraft returned safely to base.
P/O J Whitwood in PB143, JI-B reported: Bomb load 14 x 1000 MC. Primary target: FORT D'ENGLOS. Weather clear. Bombed at 2313½ hours, 12,000 feet. Red TIs. Very good concentration of bomb bursts just short of red TIs. Orange coloured fires seen as aircraft left target.

Combat Report - Pro-forma:
Aircraft: ME841 'H'
Captain: W/O N Jennings.
Target: FORT D'ENGLOS
At 2315 hours, height 12,500 feet, heading 180 degrees, position 5040N 0256E. Rear Gunner sighted a Ju88 at 700 yards range on the starboard quarter up. The sighting was followed by a Monica warning 2 to 3 seconds later. Rear Gunner ordered for corkscrew to starboard and opened fire with a short burst. E/A was subsequently lost in corkscrew manoeuvre and was not seen again. Visibility was good, with moon on starboard and no cloud. Searchlights were moderate, fighter flares numerous and light flak was experienced.
MU Gunner – Sgt H Ball – Nil.
Rear Gunner – Sgt C Haslam - 100 rounds.

Target:	*Fort d'Englos Petrol Storage*
Aircraft deployed total:	*311*
514 Squadron:	*13 (1 returned early)*
Aircraft lost total:	*Nil*
514 Squadron:	*Nil*

Comments: 4 flying bomb launch sites and the Fort d'Englos petrol depot were successfully attacked with no losses.

10th August 1944.
Weather: Cloudy becoming clear.
Non-Operational Flying: Formation flying and practice bombing were carried out.

Operational Flying: Squadron not required tonight but required for daylight tomorrow.

11th August 1944. Weather: Fine becoming fair.
Non-Operational Flying: Air tests were carried out.
Operational Flying: BOMBING - LENS MARSHALLING YARDS.
14 aircraft detailed, 13 took off and 13 attacked primary target. 12 aircraft returned to base. One aircraft landed at Woodbridge with the nose of the aircraft blown off (by bomb dropped from above) and the Bomb Aimer missing. Weather was 3-5/10ths patchy cloud over target. Master Bomber clear and concise, bombing reported very concentrated. Flak negligible.
F/L TA Lever in LM288, JI-C reported: Bomb load 11 x 1000 MC, 4 x 500 GP. Primary target: LENS. Weather 5/10ths cloud. Bombed at 1633 hours from 14500 feet, cluster of red TIs. Sticks of bombs seen to burst on target.
F/S AJ Holland reported: Bombed at 1633 hours from 14,000 on red TIs. Bomb bursts well concentrated in yards.
F/S Lawrie reported: Clouds up to 10,000 feet, no opposition, appeared good attack.
W/O W Brickwood in LL697, A2-B reported: Bombed at 1633hrs, 14,000 feet. Bomb Aimer had given 'Steady' when Lancaster was hit in nose by bombs from Lancaster above. The bomb aimer and equipment were hurled from aircraft. Pilot tried to jettison bombs but believed already gone. All instruments on panel u/s except altimeter. Aircraft was assisted back to Woodbridge by 'E2'. The Bomb Aimer was F/O H Crampton RNZAF who was killed and is buried in Loos British Cemetery.

Note: It is possible that the bombs that hit A2-B were dropped by PB142, JI-A flown by F/S T Charlton. This aircraft bombed at 1633hrs from 14500 feet. No report was made concerning this however.

Target: *Lens Marshalling Yards*
Aircraft deployed total: *459*
514 Squadron: *13*
Aircraft lost total: *1*
514 Squadron: *Nil (1 Bomb Aimer was killed)*

Comments: A bridge and 3 railway yards were the targets on this raid. After a good start, smoke obscuring the target affected the precision of the bombing.

12th August 1944.
Weather: Cloudy in morning with slight drizzle, becoming fair.
Non-Operational Flying: Air tests were carried out.
Operational Flying: BOMBING - BRUNSWICK.
5 aircraft were detailed, 5 aircraft took off. One returned early and jettisoned total load. 3 aircraft attacked the primary target. One aircraft attacked the eastern tip of Terschelling. Weather was 10/10ths cloud and success of attack was difficult to ascertain. Flak over the target was moderate heavy. 2 aircraft damaged by flak. Fighters were active.

F/S GC France in LM286, A2-F reported: Bomb load 1 x 2000 HC 12 x 500 J type clusters. Primary target: BRUNSWICK. Weather 10/10ths cloud. Bombed at 0005 hours, 20,000 feet. Glow of fires seen through cloud. Bombing appeared rather scattered. Black smoke up to 6/8000 feet. Good trip. NB: F/S France's logbook notes that the crew bombed on H2S.

W/O C Williams (JI-C, LM288) reported port inner seized and feathered after leaving target.

W/O N Jennings (JI-B. PB143) jettisoned at 2246hrs due to insufficient fuel pressure, starboard outer engine.

F/S HT Prager (JI-H, ME641) reported flak damage to aircraft over target.

F/L G Bradford (JI-A, PB142) reported: Bombed last resort target, eastern tip of Terschelling, at 0118 hours from 5000 feet. Bomb doors would not open over target. Photo flash taken of Brunswick. Fuselage and hydraulic (sic) shot away.

Target:	*Brunswick Area (H2S attack)*
Aircraft deployed total:	*379*
514 Squadron:	*5 (1 returned early)*
Aircraft lost total:	*27*
514 Squadron:	*Nil*

Comments: This raid was an experiment to test the accuracy of H2S by not providing Pathfinder support. Crews relied on their own H2S equipment, with less than acceptable results. Towns around 20 miles away were mistakenly bombed. The bombing was very scattered and losses quite heavy, proving this tactic very unsuccessful.

BOMBING - RUSSELHEIM.

12 aircraft detailed, 12 aircraft took off. 9 attacked primary target, 1 landed at Woodbridge, 2 aircraft missing. Weather was clear and crews identified the Rhine. Markers were scattered, thus creating fires over a wide area. Master Bomber instructed to bomb centre of the fires. Fighters very active. Success of attack doubtful.

F/S AJ Holland in LM285, JI-H reported: Bomb load 1 x 400 HC, 6 x 500 No. 14 Cluster, 6 x (150 x 4) 10% XIB. Primary target: RUSSELHEIM. Weather clear. Bombed at 0019, 18,000 feet. Red TIs. Bombing seemed concentrated. Master Bomber heard talking to Deputy but no instructions heard.

F/L M Head reported an FW190 claimed as destroyed by his rear gunner, F/S A Beckford.

Target:	*Russelheim*
Aircraft deployed total:	*297*
514 Squadron:	*12*
Aircraft lost total:	*20*
514 Squadron:	*2*

Comments: A return to PPF marking didn't fair too well on this attack on the Opel motor factory. Many bombs fell in open fields with only minor damage to the target.

Missing Aircraft:

LM180, JI-G. Shot down at 0130hrs by night-fighter, probably flown by Uffz. Hermann Moeckel of 2./NJG4. This was Moeckel's only victim in his career as a night fighter pilot. He was himself shot down by an Allied night fighter on 29-30/12 1944, surviving as a POW F/S John Lawrie sacrificed his life by remaining at the controls in order to allow his crew to escape.

F/S J Lawrie RNZAF	*Pilot*	*KIA*
F/S DR Orth RAAF	*Navigator*	*Evaded*
Sgt MJ Carter	*Bomb Aimer*	*Evaded*
Sgt EG Durland	*WOP/Air*	*Evaded*
F/S LR Burford RAAF	*MU Gunner*	*Evaded*
F/S RC Chester-Masters RAAF	*Rear Gunner*	*Evaded*
Sgt TD Young	*Flight Engineer*	*Evaded*

LM265, JI-E. Cause not stated. The aircraft crashed at 0030 hours on the 13th August, in the village of Engegstadt, about 10 miles south west of Mainz, Germany. Possibly shot down by Lt. Otto Teschner, 11./NJG1, who claimed a 4-engine aircraft at 0030 hours in the Bad Kreuznach area, which is in the appropriate vicinity.

F/S E Richardson	Pilot	KIA
P/O HF Roome RAAF	(Second Pilot)	KIA
F/S WJ McIntosh	Navigator	KIA
Sgt GH Trigwell	Bomb Aimer	KIA
F/S CB Robertshaw	WOP/Air	KIA
Sgt LD Vince	MU Gunner	KIA
Sgt PR Smith	Rear Gunner	KIA
Sgt GM Holt	Flight Engineer	POW

13th August 1944.
Weather: Mainly fair.
Non-Operational Flying: Air tests and practice bombing carried out.
Operational Flying: 8 aircraft were required for operations but were cancelled later in the day. Aircraft are now to stand down until tomorrow morning.

14th August 1944.
Weather: Fine to fair.
Non-Operational Flying: Formation flying by all flights and special navigation exercises were carried out.
Operational Flying: BOMBING - HAMEL TROOP CONCENTRATIONS.
8 aircraft were detailed, took off and attacked primary target and returned safely to base. Weather was no cloud but slight haze. All crews identified targets by TIs. The attack appeared successful though a pall of smoke obscured the target.
F/O R Edmundson in ME841, JI-H reported: Bomb load 11 x 1000 MC and 4 x 500 GP. Primary target: HAMEL. Weather clear. Bombed at 1555 hours, 8,600 feet red TIs. Bomb bursts well concentrated around TIs which were well placed.

Target:	Hamel - Troop Concentrations
Aircraft deployed total:	805
514 Squadron:	8
Aircraft lost total:	2
514 Squadron:	Nil

Comments: Another tactical raid to support the Allied ground offensive, most of the bombing was effective but mid-way through the attack, Canadian troop positions in a large quarry received the inadvertent and unwelcome attention of approximately 70 aircraft, resulting in the loss of 13 troops. It is thought that yellow flares ignited by Canadian troops were mistaken for the yellow target indicators dropped by PFF.

15th August 1944.
Weather: Fine to fair.
Non-Operational Flying: Special navigation exercises and practice bombing carried out.
Operational Flying: BOMBING – ST. TROND AIRFIELD.
12 aircraft took off to attack ST. TROND airfield. 12 aircraft attacked the primary target and returned to base. Weather was perfect and crews visually identified intersection of runways. Bombing was very concentrated and later reports state all runways u/s.
S/L PB Clay in PB149, JI-B reported: Bomb load 11 x 1000 MC, 4 x 500 GP. Primary target: ST. TROND A/F. Weather perfect. Bombed at 1209 hours, 17,000 feet, red TIs and intersection of runways. Very successful attack, accurate bombing.
P/O LJ Saltmarsh in LL624, JI-R reported: Bomb load 11 x 1000 MC, 4 x 500 GP. Primary target: ST. TROND A/F. Weather clear, slight haze. Bombed at 1209 hours, 17000 feet between red TIs and intersection of runways. Starboard outer feathered 15 miles before target, attacked target and returned on three engines which were giving trouble. Very concentrated attack.

Target:	*St. Trond Airfield*
Aircraft deployed total:	*1,004*
514 Squadron:	*12*
Aircraft lost total:	*3*
514 Squadron:	*Nil*

Comments: Bomber Command's attention was about to return to Germany itself. In preparation for upcoming attacks, 9 German airfields in Belgium and Holland were targeted. The attacks were successful, aided by excellent weather conditions.

16th August 1944.
Weather: Fine.
Non-Operational Flying: Special navigation exercises carried out.
Operational Flying: BOMBING – STETTIN.
10 aircraft were detailed, took off. 9 aircraft attacked primary target, one aircraft returned early with generator trouble. Weather was 6-9/10ths broken drifting cloud over the target, making sighting and run-up on the target very difficult. Bombing and subsequent fires somewhat scattered, and the dummy 5 miles N of target collected several loads. No combats are reported, defences slight to moderate. 1 aircraft landed at Woodbridge on two engines. 1 aircraft landed at Foulsham short of fuel. The remainder landed safely at base.
F/O E Cossens in LL635, JI-M reported: Bomb load 1 x 2000 HC, 9 x 500 'J' type clusters. Primary target: STETTIN. Weather 7/10ths cloud. Bombed at 0107 hours from 17,000 feet centre of red and green TIs. Bomb bursts seen across TIs.
F/S Holland reported: Bombed centre of concentration of fires from 19,000 feet, no markers being visible. Large L shaped fire seen in built up area.

Target:	*Stettin – Industry and Docks*
Aircraft deployed total:	*461 (Lancasters)*
514 Squadron:	*10 (1 returned early)*
Aircraft lost total:	*5*
514 Squadron:	*Nil*

Comments: This raid on industrial and port facilities was a complete success. 8 ships were damaged and 5 ships sunk and considerable damage was caused to the port and factories.

17th August 1944.
Weather: Fair.
Non-Operational Flying: Formation flying, practice bombing and special navigation exercises.
Operational Flying: 8 aircraft required to standby for tonight. Cancelled later in the day.

18th August 1944.
Weather: Fair.
Non-Operational Flying: Formation flying and special navigation exercises were carried out.
Operational Flying: BOMBING – BREMEN.

17 aircraft detailed and took off. 16 aircraft attacked the primary target, one aircraft attacked Emden. There was no cloud over the target but slight haze. The Aiming Point was well marked with flares and TIs and bombing was well concentrated around markers, the whole area left a mass of flames with smoke rising up to 10,000 feet. All aircraft returned safely to base.

F/S RM Coyle in LL726, A2-H reported: Bomb load 1 x 8000 HC, 40 x 30 lb inc. 350 x 4.40 x 4 inc. Primary target: BREMEN. Weather clear. Bombed at 0015 hours, 18,000 feet, centre of red TIs. Searchlights very accurate but did not seem to hold.

W/O D Beaton in LL677 A2-E reported: Navigation trouble caused us to be late over BREMEN. Nothing in view and all quiet so set course and bombed first flak area – EMDEN at 0042 hours from 19,000 feet.

F/O F Hebditch in LL728 A2-L reported: Fires seen 80 miles away at 4000ft.

Target:	*Bremen -Area*
Aircraft deployed total:	*288*
514 Squadron:	*17*
Aircraft lost total:	*1*
514 Squadron:	*Nil*

Comments: This was a demonstration in precision bombing. With excellent marking and fine weather conditions, the end results were to be the most destructive attack on Bremen of the war. A fire-storm was started and over 8,500 homes and apartments were destroyed. Over 60 ships were damaged and 18 ships destroyed. 1,100 tons of bombs were dropped by 274 aircraft. Bremen was devastated.

19th August 1944.
Weather: Fair in morning, slight rain until evening.
Non-Operational Flying: Special navigation exercises were carried out.
Operational Flying: Squadron not required for operations.

20th August 1944.
Weather: Low cloud with drizzle and rain.
Non-Operational Flying: No exercises took place today.
Operational Flying: Squadron not required for operations today or tonight.

21st August 1944.
Weather: Low cloud with rain, fair in the afternoon.
Non-Operational Flying: Air tests were carried out.
Operational Flying: Squadron not required for operations today or tonight.

22nd August 1944.
Weather: Low cloud and slight drizzle.
Non-Operational Flying: No non-operational flying today.
Operational Flying: 12 aircraft required for operations tonight. Operations cancelled at 1815 hours.

23rd August 1944.
Weather: Low cloud, drizzle and fog, fair in the afternoon.
Non-Operational Flying: Formation flying and Special navigation exercises in the afternoon.
Operational Flying: Squadron not required for operations.

24th August 1944.
Weather: Slight rain early, thunder and rain later.
Non-Operational Flying: Special navigation exercises were carried out.
Operational Flying: 14 aircraft detailed for operations but was (sic) cancelled later in the day.

25th August 1944.
Weather: Mainly fair.
Non-Operational Flying: Special navigation exercises. Deliveries of Mk.II Lancasters to Bottesford, practice bombing and formation flying were carried out.
Operational Flying: BOMBING – VINCLY.
9 aircraft detailed, 7 aircraft took off to attack VINCLY flying bomb site. Patchy cloud over target hampered clear visual of attack. All aircraft bombed on visual of GH Leaders bombs. Several bomb aimers appeared to think attack was an overshoot but claim several hits on target area. All aircraft returned safely.
F/L TA Lever in LL731, JI-U reported: Bomb load 11 x 1000 MC, 2 x 500 GP Mk IV, 2 x 500 GP Mk IV LD. Primary target: VINCLY. Weather, cloud patches. Bombed at 2030 hours from 15,300 feet, visual of GH Leader. Flak over target area.

F/O EJ Cossens in LL635 JI-M reported being damaged by Flak over the target with no injuries. Note: LL635 was deemed to be damaged beyond repair, after her 39th operational sortie.

Target: *Vincly – Flying Bomb Sites*
Aircraft deployed total: *161*
514 Squadron: *7*
Aircraft lost total: *3*
514 Squadron: *Nil*

Comments: There were 5 targets chosen for today's raids, 514 Squadron attacking Vincly.

BOMBING – RUSSELHEIM.
13 aircraft were detailed, 12 aircraft took off to attack RUSSELHEIM. 1 aircraft failed to take off. 1 aircraft could not identify target. Weather was clear and several crews identified river. Bombing was concentrated among TIs, but many loads of incendiaries fell wide of markers. No combats. All aircraft returned safely.
F/S HC Richford in PB426, JI-J reported: Bomb load 1 x 4000 HC, 11 x 500 LB Clusters. Primary target: RUSSELHEIM. Weather, clear. Bombed at 0100 hours from 17,000 feet centre of red TIs. TIs well scattered by bomb bursts. Should be a god attack.
F/S LR Campbell in PB419 JI-N reported: Starboard inner engine feathered. No oil pressure. Coned on run up.
P/O GW Smith in HK572 JI-T reported: Perspex blown from mid-upper turret by flak over target.

Target: *Russelheim – Opel Motor Factory*
Aircraft deployed total: *421 (Lancasters)*
514 Squadron: *12*
Aircraft lost total: *15*
514 Squadron: *Nil*

Comments: This raid saw a return to the Opel Factory. Marking was accurate. Bombing was completed in a mere 10 minutes and was concentrated. A successful raid.

26th August 1944.
Weather: mainly fair.
Non-Operational Flying: Special navigation exercises and Formation Flying carried out.

Operational Flying: BOMBING - KIEL.
17 aircraft were detailed and all took off. 15 attacked the primary target, 1 abortive due to hang up (electrical fault). 1 aircraft is missing. Weather clear with slight haze. Two areas of fire which joined and gained a good hold. Several explosions in target area. General opinion tends towards a successful raid. F/O Uffindell's HK577, JI-P, was attacked on the run in by two Me109s. One Me109 shot down by F/S AE Clark, Rear Gunner and seen to crash by crew.
F/S WM Coyle in LL666, A2-K reported: Bomb load 1 x 8000 HC, 180 x 4 IB, 16 x 30 IB. Primary target: KIEL. Weather clear. Bombed at 2315 hours, from 17800 feet red TIs. Bombing well concentrated round TIs.

Combat Report:
Aircraft: HK577 'P'
Captain: P/O ADJ Uffindell
Target: KIEL
1st Encounter: At the target area (bombs not dropped), course 012 degrees, height 19,000 feet, IAS 180. At 2308 hours, the M/U Gunner reported an Me109 flying on opposite course, range 300 yards port beam level. The E/A turned in to attack and the M/U Gunner gave order to corkscrew port and opened fire with a 5 second burst. The Rear Gunner noted position of end of trace, and fired a 1 second burst. E/A closed to 150 yards, then broke away starboard down and was not seen again.
2nd Encounter: As the first E/A broke away the Rear Gunner sighted another E/A, recognised as an Me109 attacking from the fine port quarter down range 600 yards. Pilot was still corkscrewing from first attack and was going down port in this instance. The Rear Gunner opened fire immediately, firing until a burst of flames was seen coming from the nose of the E/A. The E/A continued to close in, Rear Gunner firing throughout attack. The E/A then dropped away on its port wing and dived to the ground in flames. The M/U Gunner and Rear Gunner saw the E/A burning on the ground.
MU Gunner - Sgt JF Wilson - 200 rounds.
Rear Gunner – F/S AE Clark - 500 rounds.

Target:	*Kiel - Area*
Aircraft deployed total:	*382*
514 Squadron:	*17*
Aircraft lost total:	*17*
514 Squadron:	*1*

Comments: Fires created from heavy bombing were enhanced by strong winds. Smoke from this obscured the PFF markers, but bombing was fairly concentrated none the less. The town hall as well as many other public buildings were destroyed. Local reporting described the attack as a very serious raid, suggesting that it was effective.

Missing aircraft:

LL728 A2-L (above right, on an earlier operation to Emieville. Source:Airworx GmbH Archive). Shot down by night-fighter of Fw. Gottfried Schneider, 1./NJG3, crashing near Kleve at 2345hrs, 10 km SSE of Friedrichstadt. LL728, one of three successes for Fw. Schneider that night, was lost on its return from the target area.

F/O FF Hebditch	Pilot	KIA
Sgt CG Washington	Navigator	KIA
F/O KS Robinson	Bomb Aimer	POW
W/O JP Edwards	WOP/Air	KIA
Sgt CA Clarke	MU Gunner	KIA
F/O SE Jones	Rear Gunner	KIA
Sgt JR Plant	Flight Engineer	KIA

27th August 1944.
Weather: Mainly fair.
Non-Operational Flying: Special navigation exercises, bombing and air tests were carried out.
Operational Flying: Squadron not required for operations tonight.

28th August 1944.
Weather: Cloudy early, slight rain mid-morning then mainly fair.
Non-Operational Flying: Special navigation exercises, fighter affiliation, formation flying and practice bombing were carried out.
Operational Flying: Stand down for 3 Group.

29th August 1944.
Weather: Fair with occasional rain.
Non-Operational Flying: Air tests were carried out. 17 aircraft required for operations. All Mk.II Lancasters withdrawn later in the day.
Operational flying: BOMBING – STETTIN.
10 aircraft were detailed to attack STETTIN, 9 aircraft took off. 8 aircraft attacked, 1 aircraft is missing. Weather, a thin layer of cloud about 5/10ths, did not hamper crews. TIs were clearly seen and by visuals, appeared to be in two areas, one to N of old town amongst docks and other area stretching to SW part of town. Explosions seen at 0206 hours with a mushroom of black smoke. No combats. 8 aircraft landed safely. Number of aircraft seen to go down on route.
S/L H Dods in LM685, JI-Q reported: Bomb load 1 x 4000 HC, 52 x 30, 468 x 4, 54 x 4 LB incendiaries. Primary target: STETTIN. Weather, clear. Bombed at 0206 hours from 17,000 feet, red and green TIs. 0205 hours large column black smoke following an explosion. Very good attack. Master Bomber enthusiastic.

Target:	*Stettin*
Aircraft deployed total:	*403*
514 Squadron:	*9*
Aircraft lost total:	*23*
514 Squadron:	*1*

Comments: Despite the losses to the attacking force, further extensive damage was caused to Stettin, much of it to areas previously untouched. Sips were sunk in addition to the damage on land.

Missing aircraft:

PB143 JI-B. Shot down at 0012 hours en route to the target, by Oblt. Fritz Brandt of Stab II./NJG3. PB143 crashed into the sea off the village of Estruplund, Denmark. There were no survivors amongst the crew.

F/S TT Charlton	*Pilot*	*KIA*
Sgt N Stevens	*Navigator*	*KIA*
Sgt KM Goodman	*Bomb Aimer*	*KIA*
F/O RF Dell RCAF	*WOP/Air*	*KIA*
Sgt PT Delvin	*MU Gunner*	*KIA*
F/O WE Gibbs	*Rear Gunner*	*KIA*
Sgt RW Pomroy	*Flight Engineer*	*KIA*

30th August 1944.
Weather - Rainy during early part then cloudy.
Non-Operational Flying: Special navigational exercises and air tests were carried out.
Operational Flying: Squadron not required for operations today.

31st August 1944.
Weather: Cloudy with strong winds and occasional showers.
Non-Operational Flying: Special navigation exercises and air tests were carried out.
Operational flying: BOMBING – PONT REMY (DUMP).
16 aircraft (including 4 GH aircraft) were detailed and took off and all bombed the primary target. Cloud over target varying from 5/10ths to 8/10ths made identification of target difficult. Six crews bombed on Gee-H and remainder on visual. General opinion tends towards undershoots.
F/O CJ Thomson RAAF in PB142, JI-A reported: Bomb load 11 x 1000 MC, 4 x 500 GP Mk IV LD. Primary target: PONT REMY. Weather, cloudy. Bombed at 1807 hours from 16,000 feet on Leader's release of bombs. Slight flak.

Target:	*Pont Remy (V2 Rocket Storage)*
Aircraft deployed total:	601
514 Squadron:	16
Aircraft lost total:	6
514 Squadron:	Nil

Comments: The targets were 9 sites believed to be storing V-2 rockets. 8 of these were successfully bombed.

Monthly Summary for August 1944

Awards:

CAN J.27538	A/F/L BK McDonald	Pilot	DFC 11/8/44
177530	A/F/O NR Wishart	Pilot	DFC 16/8/44
174576	A/F/O LJ Saltmarsh	Pilot	DFC 25/8/44
105193	A/S/L PB Clay	Pilot	DFC 25/8/44

Operational:

Enemy Aircraft Destroyed:	3
Operational Flying Hours for August 1944:	1178.05
Non-Operational Flying Hours for August 1944:	327.30
Total tons of bombs dropped in August 1944:	1158 ¾ tons
Cumulative total tons of bombs dropped:	6535 ¾ tons.
Number of Sorties for August 1944:	250

Strength of Squadron as at 31st August 1944.

Aircrew: 106 Officers
                                                                          247 SNCOs

Ground: 1 Officer (Adjutant)

September 1944

1st September 1944.
Weather: Fine becoming cloudy.
Non-Operational Flying: No flying took place.
Operational Flying: 15 aircraft were required for operations but the effort was cancelled later in the day.

2nd September 1944.
Weather: Cloudy with thundery rain.
Non-Operational Flying: Practice bombing, special navigation exercises and air tests were carried out.
Operational Flying: Not required for operations today but required tomorrow.

3rd September 1944.
Weather: Fine becoming cloudy with some rain.
Non-Operational Flying: Practice bombing, special navigation exercises, fighter affiliation and air tests were carried out.
Operational Flying: BOMBING – EINDHOVEN.
10 aircraft detailed, 10 aircraft took off to attack Eindhoven and 7 aircraft attacked the primary target. 2 aircraft returned early. 1 aircraft attacked Gilze-Ripen airfield. Weather was troublesome. Cloud up to 20,000 feet, over target 5/10ths patchy cloud. Red TIs seen dead to north of airfield, Master Bomber instructed to bomb south of airfield. Crews bombed visually on red TIs. A good concentration of bombing was seen, the opinion is that the airfield was well pranged. 8 aircraft landed safely at base on completion of their duty.
F/L G Bradford in PD265, JI-G reported: Bomb load 11 x 1000 MC, 4 x 500 GP. Primary target: EINDHOVEN. Bombed at 1730 hour from 18,500 feet, red TI.

Target: *Eindhoven – Luftwaffe Airfields*
Aircraft deployed total: *675*
514 Squadron: *10 (2 returned early)*
Aircraft lost total: *1*
514 Squadron: *Nil*

Comments: *The fifth anniversary of the outbreak of the war was celebrated by heavy raids on 6 airfields in Southern Holland.*

4th September 1944.
Weather – Cloudy with occasional rain.
Non-Operational Flying – No flying took place.
Operational Flying – Not required for operations today but required tomorrow.

5th September 1944.
Weather – Cloudy with some rain, becoming fair.
Non-Operational Flying – Practice bombing, special navigation exercises, air/sea firing and air tests were carried out.
Operational Flying: BOMBING – LE HAVRE.
19 aircraft were detailed, took off, attacked the primary target and landed safely at base on completion of their duty. The weather was clear and the target well-marked. Bomb bursts and fires were observed close to aiming point. No fighters encountered, some flak on run in to target.
F/O LS Drew in LM627, JI-D reported: Bomb load 11 x 1000 MC and 4 x 500 GP. Primary target: LE HAVRE. Bombed at 1923 hours from 13,000 feet red TI.

Target:	Le Havre – German Defences
Aircraft deployed total:	348
514 Squadron:	19
Aircraft lost total:	Nil
514 Squadron:	Nil

Comments: The first of a series of heavy raids against the beleaguered German garrison was accurate with good visibility.

6th September 1944.
Weather: Fine becoming cloudy.
Non-Operational Flying - Special navigation exercises, air/sea firing and air tests were carried out.
Operational Flying: BOMBING – LE HAVRE.
16 aircraft were detailed, took off and attacked the primary target. Cloud base 8000 feet. Master Bomber ordered aircraft to come down below cloud base to bomb Red TIs. All crews bombed red TIs and checked position visually. All aircraft landed safely at base on completion of their duty. Attack was considered successful.
P/O CJ Thomson in PB142, JI-A reported: Bomb load 11 x 1000 MC, 4 x 500 GP. Primary target: LE HAVRE. Bombed at 1839 hours from 7000 feet. Overshot on green TIs.

Target: *Le Havre – German Defences*
Aircraft deployed total: *344*
514 Squadron: *16*
Aircraft lost total: *Nil*
514 Squadron: *Nil*

Comments: A further raid against the German fortifications and transport was carried out without loss to the 344 attacking aircraft.

7th September 1944.
Weather: Cloudy with rain.
Non-Operational Flying: No flying took place.
Operational Flying: No operational flying today but required early tomorrow.

8th September 1944.
Weather: Cloudy with some thundery rain.
Non-Operational Flying: Practice bombing, special navigation exercises and air tests were carried out.
Operational Flying: BOMBING – LE HAVRE.
14 aircraft were detailed, 14 took off, 5 aircraft attacked primary, 1 aircraft returned early and the others abandoned mission on instructions of Master Bomber. 1 aircraft, 'H' (F/L Prager) was hit by Flak in the target area, much flame and smoke. Fire extinguished by Navigator (F/L Trick) and MU Gunner (Sgt Watt). 10/10ths cloud down to 3000 feet. Master Bomber gave varying instructions for bombing TIs, then abandon mission. Attack was scattered - much smoke and one fire in area. Some fires in North part of town. Red explosion at 0806 hours. Slight to moderate Flak. No fighters seen. Five Lancasters seen shot down. 1 aircraft returned early with starboard outer engine u/s. 1 aircraft (LL677, A2-E) was hit by flak and crash-landed at Tangmere, the pilot (F/O D Beaton) and engineer (Sgt J Sherry) being seriously injured and the navigator (P/O Nye) slightly injured. 12 aircraft landed safely at base on completion of their mission.
F/O DC Gordon RAAF in PB142, JI-A reported: Bomb load 11 x 1000 MC, 4 x 500 GP. Primary target: LE HAVRE. Bombed at 0755 hours from 3000 feet, green TI.
F/O D. Beaton in LL677, A2-E reported: Bomb load 11 x 1000 MC, 4 x 500 GP. Crash landed at Tangmere. Primary target: LE HAVRE. Bombed at 0805 hours from 4,500 feet, 400 yards short of TIs.

Aircraft damaged by flak. Pilot and Engineer seriously injured, Navigator slightly injured.

Target: Le Havre – German Defences
Aircraft deployed total: 333
514 Squadron: 14 (1 returned early)
Aircraft lost total: 2
514 Squadron: Nil (1 a/c crash landed at Tangmere)

Comments: This was the final raid in which Bomber Command Stirlings were to participate. In bad weather, only about 1/3 of the force was able to drop their bombs.

9th September 1944.
Weather – Fine to fair.
Non-Operational Flying: Practice bombing, special navigation exercises, fighter affiliation and cross countries were carried out.
Operational Flying: Not required for operations today, but will probably be required tomorrow.

10th September 1944.
Weather – Fair with morning fog.
Non-Operational Flying: Special navigation exercises and air tests were carried out.
Operational Flying: BOMBING – LE HAVRE.
12 aircraft detailed. 12 aircraft took off and attacked primary. All crews undershot TIs by about 200 yards and attack was very concentrated. There was much smoke. No fighters were seen. All aircraft landed safely at base on completion of their mission.
F/O N Jennings in LM277, JI-F reported: Bomb load 11 x 1000 MC, 4 x 500 GP. Primary target: LE HAVRE. Bombed at 1739 hours from 11,000 feet. Undershot red TIs by 200 yards.

Target: Le Havre – German Defences
Aircraft deployed total: 992
514 Squadron: 12
Aircraft lost total: Nil
514 Squadron: Nil

Comments: 8 separate strong points were targeted with great success due to the accurate marking. The Germans surrendered the next day.

11th September 1944. Weather – Mainly fine.
Non-operational Flying – Practice bombing, special navigation exercises and air tests were carried out.
Operational Flying: BOMBING - KAMEN (synthetic oil plant).
13 aircraft detailed. 13 aircraft took off. 12 aircraft attacked primary. 1 aircraft is missing, weather was clear. Target marking and Master Bomber good. Bombing exceedingly good, this was endorsed by Master Bomber. Several very large fires seen, possibly oil. Smoke rising to 12,000 feet. Large explosion at 1841 hours. Large fires and much smoke and a smoke screen over the Ruhr. 3 aircraft were seen going down, 1 hit by bomb.
F/O GC France (JI-F, LM277) reported: Bomb load 1 x 4000 HC, 16 x 500 GP, bombed 1842½ hours from 16500 feet on red fires per Master Bomber's instructions.

Target:	*Kamen (synthetic oil plant).*
Aircraft deployed total:	*379*
514 Squadron:	*13*
Aircraft lost total:	*8*
514 Squadron:	*1*

Comments: 26 Squadrons of fighters escorted the bombers on this raid, with no enemy fighters seen. All the aircraft lost were from flak or friendly bombs from aircraft above. The targets were synthetic oil plants. The Kamen plant was bombed successfully.

Missing Aircraft:

DS787, A2-G. Crashed at 1842 hours onto a road at Lerche, 5 km from the centre of Kamen. This was the only aircraft lost on the Kamen raid and it is believed to have been hit by a bomb from another aircraft.

W/O RJ Thornton RNZAF	*Pilot*	*KIA*
F/O PB Baley	*Navigator*	*KIA*
Sgt GA Hubbard	*Air Bomber*	*KIA*
W/O JW Hall	*WOP/Air*	*KIA*
Sgt CL Robison RCAF	*MU Gunner*	*POW*
F/S DR Burns	*Rear Gunner*	*POW*
Sgt GF Good	*Flight Engineer*	*POW*

12th September 1944.
Weather: Fair to fine.
Non-Operational Flying: Practice bombing and special navigation exercises were carried out.
Operational Flying: BOMBING – FRANKFURT-MAIN.
14 aircraft detailed. 12 aircraft primary, 1 aircraft is missing, 1 aircraft returned early. Weather was clear over the target and all crews bombed on the markers which were reported as concentrated. Target area on leaving was one large mass of fires and palls of black smoke. Flak reported as slight to moderate. HF barrage with numerous searchlights on the target stretching as far South as Mannheim. 4 aircraft had combats and 1 aircraft believed jet-propelled destroyed. 1 aircraft had 5 successive attacks by Me109 and an unidentified aircraft.
F/O GC France in LM277, JI-F reported: Bomb load 1 x 4000 HC, 14 x 500 clusters 41B. Bombed at 2258½ hours from 16,000 feet on red and green TIs. Accompanied by P/O DW Parks as 'second dickey', F/O France later recollected that an FW190 fighter had passed within a hair's breadth of the cockpit of his Lancaster. Miraculously there was no collision.

Combat Report:
Aircraft: LL666 'K2'
Captain: F/O WM Coyle.
Target: FRANKFURT
Homeward bound, position 5014N 0833E, course 250 degrees T, height 12,000 feet, IAS 190 M.P.H. At 25.10 hours, Lancaster K2 was coned in searchlights and remained in them for 6 minutes, corkscrewing throughout. During the 6 minutes whilst coned, the bomber was subjected to 5 attacks, by E/A identified as Me109.
1st Encounter: W/Operator standing in astro-dome reported first attack from astern and above, range 200 yards. Rear Gunner opened fire with a 2 second burst and E/A broke away port quarter down.
2nd Encounter: Rear Gunner reported Me109 coming in to attack from astern up, range 200 yards. He opened fire with a 1 second burst, and E/A broke off attack.
3rd Encounter: Mid Upper Gunner reported Me109 coming in to attack from starboard quarter up, range 200 yards. Mid Upper Gunner opened fire with a 2 second burst. E/A broke off attack.
4th Encounter: Mid Upper Gunner saw line of trace coming from starboard quarter up and fired in that direction. E/A was not seen.

5th Encounter: Rear Gunner saw line of trace coming from port quarter down. E/A was only visible when breaking away port bow down. Gunners did not fire.

Throughout these attacks, gunners were blinded by flare of searchlights and could only see E/A when at close range.

MU Gunner – Sgt WH Fuller – 300 rounds.
Rear Gunner – F/S GC MacPhee - 400 rounds.

Aircraft: PB142, JI-A
Captain: F/O DC Gordon RAAF
Target: FRANKFURT
Outward bound (bombs not dropped), in position 4914N 0815E, heading 008 degrees height 17,500 feet, IAS 165. At 2239 hours the Wireless Operator warned the Captain and Gunners of an E/A closing from dead astern. A minute later the Rear Gunner reported a red glow astern. The Captain immediately commenced to corkscrew and the Rear Gunner opened fire with a 3 second burst. As the glow closed in the M/U Gunner fired a 4 second burst and the Rear Gunner another burst. The glow then seemed to glide down to the ground and burst into very white flames.

MU Gunner – F/S G Burke – 200 rounds.
Rear Gunner – Sgt H Dobinson - 500 rounds.

Aircraft: DS786 'L2'
Captain: F/O R Hardwick
Target: FRANKFURT
Homeward bound (bombs dropped), in position 5014N 0840E, heading 030T, height 16,000 feet, IAS 180. At 23.06 hours, the Bomb Aimer saw a S/E E/A attacking a Lancaster on the starboard bow up range 400 yards. He immediately opened fire with a short burst. The E/A immediately broke off attack on other Lancaster and dived away to the starboard bow down.

Front Gunner – F/O TB Searles RCAF - 50 rounds.

Aircraft: LM275 'E'
Captain: F/Lt G Bradford
Target: FRANKFURT
Outward bound (bombs not dropped), in position 50N 03E, heading 037 degrees T., height 17,000 feet, IAS 165. At 22.53 hours, Lancaster 'E' was coned in searchlights. The Captain immediately commenced to corkscrew and as he did so the Mid Upper Gunner reported trace coming from the starboard quarter up. This continued for about 3

seconds and then ceased and nothing more was seen. During the attack, the Rear Gunner received head injuries and the rear turret rendered unserviceable. There were also numerous holes in the fuselage and tailplane.
MU Gunner – Sgt AC Potipher – Nil.
Rear Gunner – W/O WS Nicol - Nil.

Target:	*Frankfurt - Main*
Aircraft deployed total:	*388*
514 Squadron:	*14 (1 returned early)*
Aircraft lost total:	*17*
514 Squadron:	*1*

Comments: This attack was carried out with great success. In the west of the city, there was severe damage. A troop train was also hit. It was the last major raid on this target of the war. In LM275, JI-E, rear gunner W/O WS Nicol was wounded by a fighter attack 10 NM SW of Frankfurt.

Missing Aircraft:

LL731 JI-U Shot down by Lt. Fred Hromadnik of 9./NJG4, LL731 crashed at 2330 hours at Kordel 8km NW of Trier.

F/O WD Brickwood	*Pilot*	*KIA*
F/S KV Stafford RNZAF	*Navigator*	*KIA*
F/S RJ Rigden	*Air Bomber*	*POW*
F/S RG Collender RNZAF	*WOP/Air*	*KIA*
Sgt WP Blake	*MU Gunner*	*KIA*
P/O JS Lupton RAAF	*Rear Gunner*	*KIA*
P/O CO Turner	*Flight Engineer*	*POW*

13th September 1944.
Weather – Mainly fair, fog around dawn.
Non-Operational Flying – Practice bombing, fighter affiliation, special navigation exercises and air tests were carried out.
Operational Flying – Not required for operations today but will be required tomorrow.

14th September 1944.
Weather – Fog, becoming cloudy.
Non-Operational Flying – Special navigation exercises, fighter affiliation and air tests were carried out.
Operational Flying: BOMBING – WASSENAAR.
10 aircraft were detailed, 10 aircraft attacked primary. Weather was good, nil cloud. Master Bomber instructed first of all to bomb 100 yards to port of red TI and then 100 yards to starboard later and finally on centre of smoke. All these positions were duly bombed by our aircraft without sensational incidents. Target was left with clouds of smoke obscuring the A/P. There was flak from 1 gun crossing enemy coast and Rotterdam defences were in action. No enemy aircraft were seen. 10 aircraft landed safely at base on completion of their duty.
F/O DW Parks in LM274, JI-B reported: Bomb load 11 x 1000 MC, 4 x 500 GP. Primary target: WASSENAAR. Bombed at 1430 hours from 12,000 feet, red TI.

Target:	*Wassenaar -V2 Storage Facility*
Aircraft deployed total:	*45*
514 Squadron:	*10*
Aircraft lost total:	*Nil*
514 Squadron:	*Nil*

Comments: This target was suspected to be the site of a V-2 rocket storage facility. Smoke obscured the target after a successful beginning to the operation, reducing the impact of the attack.

15th September 1944.
Weather – Cloudy with showers, becoming fine.
Non-Operational Flying – Special navigation exercises, formation flying, fighter affiliation and air tests were carried out.
Operational Flying – Not required for operations today or tonight.

16th September 1944.
Weather – Fine becoming cloudy.
Non-Operational Flying – Special navigation exercises, practice bombing and air tests were carried out.
Operational Flying – Not required for operations today.

17th September 1944.
Weather: Fair to fine with fog around dawn.
Non-Operational Flying - Fighter affiliation, air tests and cross country were carried out.
Operational Flying: BOMBING – BOULOGNE AIMING POINT 2.
18 aircraft detailed, 17 aircraft took off. 5 primary. 1 aircraft failed to take off. Weather (clear) below cloud. Crews orbited target area awaiting instructions from Master Bomber who gave instructions to bomb red TIs. Bombing appeared concentrated. At 1215 hours, abandon mission was given. Therefore 12 crews did not bomb.

AIMING POINT 3.
3 aircraft detailed and 3 took off and attacked primary. Weather clear below cloud. Crews orbited target area while waiting for instructions from Master Bomber who gave instructions to bomb red TI in NW corner of target. Bombing appeared concentrated. 1 aircraft received slight flak damage to starboard fin. No fighters seen.
F/L G Bradford in LM627, JI-D reported: Bomb load 11 x 1000 MC, 4 x 500 GP. Primary target: BOULOGNE, Aiming Point 2. Bombed at 1216 hours from 4000 feet, starboard of red TI, which were port of target.

18th September 1944.
Weather: Fine with morning fog, becoming cloudy.
Non-Operational Flying: Practice bombing, fighter affiliation, Special navigation exercises, formation flying and cross countries.
Operational Flying: Not required for operations today, but required tomorrow.

19th September 1944.
Weather: Cloudy with some rain.
Non-Operational Flying: Air tests were carried out.
Operational Flying: Not required for operations today, 25 aircraft required for operations tomorrow.

20th September 1944.
Weather: Cloudy with rain, becoming foggy then fair.
Non-operational Flying: Air tests were carried out.
Operational Flying: BOMBING - CALAIS.
25 aircraft detailed, 24 attacked primary. 1 aircraft is missing. Weather was clear over target. Some crews orbited owing to congestion of aircraft. One crew saw many trenches while orbiting

which were craters on second run. All crews were enthusiastic about the concentration. A Lancaster was seen to spin into the sea off Calais, with its wings on fire preceded by bombs which exploded before the aircraft.

S/L PB Clay in LM274, JI-B reported: Bomb load 11 x 1000 MC, 4 x 500 GP. Primary target: CALAIS. Bombed at 1605 hours from 3000 feet, red TIs.

Target: *Calais – German Garrison*
Aircraft deployed total: *646*
514 Squadron: *25*
Aircraft lost total: *1 (Lancaster)*
514 Squadron: *1*

Comments: The target was another German Garrison in the Calais area. Bombing was accurate, with the crews being 'enthusiastic' about the concentration of the attack.

(Above) Calais target photo on 20th September 1944 from PB426, JI-T flown by F/O N Jennings RCAF who bombed at 1602 hours from 2500 feet. Source: Crown Copyright / National Archive.

Missing aircraft:

LM277 JI-F. This was the only aircraft lost on the Calais raid, which involved 646 aircraft in total. It is clear that this was the aircraft reported to have crashed into the sea off Calais. It is not clear from the description in the ORB (above) whether JI-F was in fact hit by flak or bombs from another aircraft. Sadly there were no survivors from the crew.

F/O LN Arkless	*Pilot*	KIA
F/O L Partington	*Navigator*	KIA
F/O AJD Teece	*Air Bomber*	KIA
Sgt TE Jones	*WOP/Air*	KIA
Sgt J Harman	*MU Gunner*	KIA
Sgt RDD Shields	*Rear Gunner*	KIA
Sgt AH White	*Flight Engineer*	KIA

21st September 1944.
Weather: Fog, becoming cloudy from afternoon.
Non-Operational Flying – No flying took place.
Operational Flying – Not required for operations today or tonight.

22nd September 1944.
Weather: Cloudy with morning fog, some rain.
Non-Operational Flying – Practice bombing, formation flying, special navigation exercises.
Operational Flying – Squadron not required for operations today or tonight.

23rd September 1944.
Weather: Mainly cloudy.
Non-Operational Flying – Practice bombing, special navigation exercises and cross countries were carried out.
Operational Flying: BOMBING – NEUSS.
22 aircraft detailed, 22 aircraft took off. 18 attacked primary, 3 abortive, 1 circled target but did not bomb as target not sighted. Weather was 10/10ths cloud over target, tops 8/10,000 feet. Markers were just visible and all crews bombed on the glow of the markers as they disappeared into cloud. Result of raid difficult to assess as no visual means of identification possible. Of the 2 A/Ps the northerly one seemed more than 1000 yards away which did not attract much bombing. Bombing appeared fairly well concentrated on the southerly

A/P as photo flashes and bomb bursts seen in the target area. Flak reported as light to moderate HF, barrage bursting about 15,000 feet. Some fighter flares seen and sighting of Me109 but no combats. 19 aircraft landed safely at Base on completion of their mission.

F/O RF Limbert in LM288, JI-C reported: Bomb load 11 x 1000 ANM 59, 4 x 500 GP. Primary target: NEUSS. Bombed at 2123 hours from 20,000 feet slightly to port of red glow of red TIs.

Target: *Neuss - Area*
Aircraft deployed total: *549*
514 Squadron: *22*
Aircraft lost total: *7*
514 Squadron: *Nil*

Comments: Over 10 public buildings, 600 houses, the factory areas and the dock were all bombed and destroyed or severely damaged in this raid. This raid was the last time the Lancaster Mk.II was used by 514 Sqn. 'C' Flight's DS826, A2-C (F/O MR Oliver), DS842, A2-J (F/O TC Marks) and LL666, A2-K (F/O WM Coyle) all returned safely, after which the type was retired by the squadron.

24th September 1944.
Weather: Cloudy with rain.
Non-operational Flying – No flying took place.
Operational Flying – Not required for operations today or tonight but 22 aircraft will be required tomorrow morning.

25th September 1944.
Weather: Mainly cloudy with some rain.
Non-Operational Flying – Formation flying and air tests were carried out.
Operational Flying: BOMBING – CALAIS.
21 aircraft were detailed, 21 took off. 21 aircraft abortive. Abandoned mission on instructions from Master Bomber. All aircraft returned safely to Base.

Target: *Calais – German Garrison*
Aircraft deployed total: *872*
514 Squadron: *21*
Aircraft lost total: *Nil*
514 Squadron: *Nil*

Comments: Cloud affected the raid, so only 278 aircraft were able to drop their bombs. The target was the site of German defensive positions around the port. 514 Squadron's effort was aborted as instructed by Master Bomber.

26th September 1944.
Weather: Fair to cloudy becoming fine.
Non-Operational Flying: Special navigation exercises and air tests were carried out.
Operational Flying: BOMBING – CALAIS.
19 aircraft detailed, 19 aircraft took off and attacked the primary target. All aircraft returned safely. Weather was clear below cloud which was 3500 feet. Master Bomber was good and instructed crews to overshoot red TIs by one second. Later crews were told to wait until smoke and dust cleared. No flak or fighters.
F/O DC Gordon RAAF in PB142, JI-A reported: Bomb load 11 x 1000 MC, 4 x 500 GP. Primary target: CALAIS. Bombed at 1244 hours from 3400 feet on TI red + ½ second.

Target:	*Calais – German Garrison*
Aircraft deployed total:	*722*
514 Squadron:	*19*
Aircraft lost total:	*2 (Lancasters)*
514 Squadron:	*Nil*

Comments: 722 aircraft carried out 2 simultaneous raids on a total of 7 targets. The bombing was accurate and concentrated on all targets. 2 Lancasters were lost.

27th September 1944.
Weather: Fine then cloudy with some rain, fine later.
Non-Operational Flying: Special navigation exercises, practice bombing, formation flying, air tests and a Bulls Eye were carried out.
Operational Flying: BOMBING – CALAIS.
13 aircraft detailed, 13 aircraft attacked the primary target, all returned safely. Cloud 5500 feet 10/10ths. Red and green TIs corrected for bombing by Master Bomber. Bombing concentrated. Slight to moderate LF. No fighters. All aircraft carried bomb load of 11 x 1000 MC, 4 x 500 GP.
F/O SE Wilson in LM724, JI-B reported: Primary target: CALAIS. Bombed at 0843½ hours from 5500 feet on port of green TI.

Target:	Calais – German Garrison
Aircraft deployed total:	341
514 Squadron:	13
Aircraft lost total:	1 (Lancaster)
514 Squadron:	Nil

Comments: Accuracy was improved by bombing from below the cloud cover on this attack.

28th September 1944.
Weather: Fine becoming cloudy.
Non-Operational Flying: Formation flying, special navigation exercises, practice bombing were carried out.
Operational Flying: BOMBING – CALAIS.
12 aircraft detailed, 6 attacked the primary target, 6 abortive, instructions from Master Bomber. Weather 8/10ths cloud at 3000 feet. After orbiting early aircraft bombed on red TIs. Remaining aircraft told to orbit and after trying to re-mark the target a second time the Master Bomber gave abandon mission at 0928. No flak. No fighters. All aircraft landed safely at Base on return.
F/O RF Limbert in LM288, JI-C reported: Bomb load 11 x 1000 MC, 4 x 500 GP. Primary target: CALAIS 19. Bombed at 0920 hours from 9500 feet red TI.

Target:	Calais – German Garrison
Aircraft deployed total:	494
514 Squadron:	12
Aircraft lost total:	Nil
514 Squadron:	Nil

Comments: With around 50 aircraft in each group, attacks on 10 positions in the Calais area were undertaken. The Master Bomber called a close to proceedings after cloud cover worsened, many of the bombers having not dropped their bombs. Although this hampered the effort considerably, it proved successful, as the Germans surrendered to the Canadian Forces shortly afterwards, leaving all French ports in Allied hands, if somewhat damaged.

29th September 1944.
Weather: Cloudy with occasional rain.
Non-Operational Flying: Fighter affiliation, practice bombing and special navigation exercises were carried out.

Operational Flying: Squadron not required for operations today.

30th September 1944.
Weather: Fair becoming cloudy with rain after dusk.
Non-Operational Flying: Fighter affiliation, bombing, special navigation exercises were carried out.
Operational Flying: Squadron not required for operations today.

(Above) An 8000lb 'Blockbuster' bomb is carefully manoeuvred under the open bomb bay of 514 Sqn Lancaster. Because of their immense explosive power, such bombs were usually confined to 'area' targets such as industrial plants in Germany, where collateral damage was not a particular worry. Source: Airworx GmbH Archive.

Monthly Summary for September 1944

Awards:

179980	A/F/O D Beaton	Pilot	DSO 28/9/44
CAN J25414	F/L EA Campbell	Pilot	DFC 28/9/44
1821127	Sgt WA Donaldson	F/Engineer	DFM 28/9/44

Operational:

Enemy Aircraft Destroyed:	3
Operational Flying Hours for September 1944:	774.50
Non-Operational Flying Hours for September 1944:	421.20
Total tons of bombs dropped in September 1944:	1041 tons
Cumulative total tons of bombs dropped:	7,576 ¾ tons
Number of Sorties for September 1944:	242

Strength: Strength of Squadron as at 30th September 1944.

Aircrew: 112 Officers,
                                                                             246 SNCOs

Ground: 1 Officer (Adjutant)

(Above) Less well-known than other night fighters, the Messerschmitt 210 features frequently in the squadron's combat reports. Source: Airworx GmbH Archive.

October 1944

1st October 1944.
Weather: Fair becoming cloudy with some showers. Fine after dusk.
Non-Operational Flying: GH and H2S training carried out, also formation flying.
Operational Flying: 10 aircraft to be bombed up and available at 3 hours' notice. Crews standing by may stand down, aircraft to remain bombed up.

2nd October 1944.
Weather: Fine becoming cloudy.
Non Operational Flying: GH and H2S training carried out, also air tests.
Operational Flying: 10 aircraft to stand by for daylight target. Crews may stand down but aircraft must remain bombed up. 10 aircraft to be ready to take off at 3 hours' notice. 9 aircraft are to be bombed up in addition to the 10 aircraft, to attack Westkapelle tomorrow morning.

3rd October 1944.
Weather: Mainly cloudy with rain after dusk.
Non Operational Flying: Air to Sea firing and bombing at Rushford.
Operational Flying: Operation on Westkapelle confirmed. 3 Group will not be required tonight.
BOMBING – WESTKAPELLE.
19 aircraft detailed. 19 aircraft took off and attacked primary. Target was covered with patchy-scattered cloud and aircraft were told base was 5,000 feet. Most crews made dummy runs before identifying target. Cloud obscured vision. The second wave of aircraft claim to have straddled the wall which some crews identified as large brown embankment – some bombing to the north of the target. The fourth wave of aircraft reported many bombs seem to fall in the sea and Master Bomber commented on bombing as lousy. The bombing improved later in the attack, and was reported fairly concentrated. 1 aircraft bombed after 5 dummy runs and flew down the wall. Several craters seen on the wall and although nothing spectacular to report in the way of a breach, markers reported as well placed. All aircraft returned safely to base.
F/O GC France in LM733, JI-F reported: Bomb load 1 x 4000 MC, 6 x 1000MC, 1 x 500 GP L/Delay. Primary target: WESTKAPELLE. Bombed at 1357½ hours, 5,700 feet, undershot red TI on instructions.

Target: *Westkapelle – Gun Batteries*
Aircraft deployed total: *259 (7 Mosquitoes)*
514 Squadron: *19*
Aircraft lost total: *Nil*
514 Squadron: *Nil*

Comments: The force attacked the sea walls of Walcheren island in an attempt to flood out the coastal gun batteries preventing the Allies from controlling access to the port of Antwerp. The target for the first in a series of raids was the sea wall at Westkapelle, which was successfully breached. (Author's note: The water marks on local buildings were still visible in 1969 when the author visited the island on a school trip).

4th October 1944.
Weather: Cloudy with rain - becoming fine.
Non Operational Flying: Air tests.
Operational Flying: Not required today.

5th October 1944.
Weather: Fine to fair with some slight rain.
Non-Operational Flying: Air to Sea firing and H2S training.
Operational Flying: 28 aircraft required for tonight.
BOMBING – SAARBRUCKEN.
28 aircraft detailed. 27 aircraft took off to attack Saarbrucken. 10 aircraft attacked primary target. 1 attacked alternative and 16 aircraft were abortive. 514 Sqdn. 'F' (F/O GC France) attacked rail tracks 5-6 miles East of Saarbrucken at 2034hrs from 15,000 feet dropping 11x1000 MC, 1x500 GP, 1x500 GP l/delay. Weather was clear over target and red TIs were seen but Master Bomber was heard to say they were unable to locate target and called 'Abandon Mission – Our troops in vicinity'. At 2033 hours some crews bombed on TIs Green before this and bomb bursts were seen after the cancellation. No fighters or searchlights -slight to moderate HF. Reddish explosion seen in centre of group of 5 tall chimneys at 2036 hours. All aircraft returned safely to base.
F/O AJ Holland RAAF in NG141 A2-J reported: Bomb load 11x1000 MC, 1x500 GP. Primary target: SAARBRUCKEN. Bombed at 2032½ hours at 13,500 feet on green TIs. Defences fairly heavy, searchlights not in action. Master Bomber gave instructions not to bomb as we bombed.

Target: Saarbrucken – Supply Lines
Aircraft deployed total: 551
514 Squadron: 27
Aircraft lost total: 3 (Lancasters)
514 Squadron: Nil

Comments: This attack was to block supply routes and sever rail-lines in the area and was requested by the American Third Army. It was the first return to the target since September 1942, and crews reported very accurate bombing with severe damage caused in the main town, which was on the Siegfried Line.

6th October 1944.
Weather: Fair to cloudy.
Non-Operational Flying: H2S training and air tests.
Operational Flying: BOMBING – DORTMUND.
29 aircraft detailed. 26 aircraft took off. 25 attacked primary target. 1 attacked Bremen (F/O RF Limbert, LM288, JI-C). 3 aircraft failed to take off. Weather over the target was clear with slight ground haze. All crews identified target with red and green TIs and bombing was reported as concentrated amongst the markers. Numerous large fires seen and much smoke. The raid can be considered successful although no crews could identify ground details. Flak was moderate, heavy barrage with no searchlights exposing until 2028 hours. They then exposed to the west from Bochum-Laastrap Rauxel area north of the target, but were described as aimless. Two combats reported and 1 Me410 claimed damaged and 1 single engine fighter - no claim. Fighter flares seen in target area. All aircraft returned safely to Base.
F/S WR Foreman in PB142, JI-A reported: Bomb load 1 x 4000 MC, 12 x No.14 clusters. Primary target: DORTMUND. Bombed at 2029 hours from 20,000 feet on green TIs. Smoke and fires. Good raid.
F/O RW Vickers in NF968 JI-L reported bombing without use of bomb sight due to evading a fighter.

Combat Report:
Aircraft: LM728 'U'
Captain: F/O F Stephens. RAAF
Target: DORTMUND
Homeward bound (bombs dropped), in position 5115N 0530N, height 10,000 feet, heading 230 degrees T, IAS 190. At 21.00 hours, the Rear Gunner sighted a single engined unidentified E/A on the starboard quarter up, range 900 yards. He immediately gave orders to corkscrew

starboard and at that moment the E/A opened fire with a short burst which passed harmlessly astern or our aircraft. The E/A then broke away to the starboard quarter level and was not seen again.
MU Gunner – Sgt MH Hanley – Nil.
Rear Gunner – Sgt PE Steele - Nil.

Aircraft: PB482 'P'
Captain: F/O AD Uffindell. RNZAF
Target: DORTMUND
Homeward bound (bombs dropped), in position 1536N 0725E, height 20,000 feet, heading 346T, IAS 220. At 2028 hours the Rear Gunner sighted an Me410 coming in from the port quarter up, range 700 yards. He immediately gave orders to corkscrew port and at the same time opened fire with a 2 second burst. The E/A continued to close and at 500 yards the M/U Gunner opened fire. The Rear Gunner continued firing throughout the attack. At 400 yards the E/A broke away to the starboard quarter down with a small fire burning in his port wing. The E/A was then lost to view and was not seen again.
MU Gunner – F/S JF Wilson. RCAF - 200 rounds.
Rear Gunner – P/O AE Clark - 600 rounds.

7th October 1944.
Weather: Fair to cloudy. Fog near midnight.
Non-Operational Flying: Air tests carried out.
Operational Flying: BOMBING – EMMERICH.
27 aircraft detailed. 2 aircraft failed to take off. 24 aircraft attacked primary target. 1 aircraft 'G2' F/S Gilchrist – MISSING. Weather was clear with cloud at 13,000 feet. Very few crews saw red TIs on account of huge pall of smoke, and all bombed according to master bomber's instructions. Fires were spread over a large area including railway siding west of the harbour. No fighters seen. 24 aircraft landed at Base. F/O AJ Whitwood in PD265, JI-G reported: Bomb load 1 x 4000 MC, 10 x No.14 clusters, 4 x (150 x 4). Primary target: EMMERICH. Bombed at 1428 hours from 13,000 feet on North of smoke as ordered by the Master Bomber. 1 cluster of incendiaries fell 50 miles East of Southwold when checking the bombing doors.

Target: *Emmerich – Supply Lines*
Aircraft deployed total: *350*
514 Squadron: *25*
Aircraft lost total: *3 (Lancasters)*
514 Squadron: *1*

Comments: A successful raid was carried out on the town, with nearly 2,500 buildings destroyed leaving an estimated 680,000 cubic meters of debris.

Missing Aircraft:

LM735, A2-G. Circumstances are not known. All are buried in Reichswald Forest War Cemetery, except for Sgt Sheehy who has no known grave, and is commemorated on the Runnymede Memorial.

F/S T Gilchrist	*Pilot*	*KIA*
W/O GJ Manlow	*Navigator*	*KIA*
Sgt T Fenwick	*Air Bomber*	*KIA*
F/S S McLean RAAF	*WOP/AG*	*KIA*
Sgt PJ Sheehy	*MU Gunner*	*KIA*
Sgt BL Roberts	*Rear Gunner*	*KIA*
Sgt HR Knight	*Flight Engineer*	*KIA*

8th October 1944.
Weather: Fog, becoming cloudy with drizzle. Fair after dusk.
Non-Operational Flying: Air tests carried out.
Operational Flying: Today's attack postponed 1 hour. Operation postponed 1 further hour. Aircraft to remain on the ground until a further decision is made. Operation cancelled. Attack planned will take place at earliest possible opportunity, aircraft are to remain bombed up and crews are to stand by.

9th October 1944.
Weather: Cloudy.
Non-Operational Flying: Air tests carried out.
Operational Flying: Squadron are to continue to stand by.
No operation laid on for tonight but crews are to be available early tomorrow morning. 14 aircraft required for a GH target tomorrow.

10th October 1944.
Weather: Cloudy with fog at dawn.
Non-Operational Flying: Air / sea firing and H2S training.
Operational Flying: 2 aircraft required for minelaying tonight. Minelaying cancelled.

11th October 1944.
Weather: Cloudy with some rain in the evening, becoming fine.
Non-Operational Flying: Air tests carried out.
Operational Flying: 15 GH aircraft required for target today. Operation cancelled. All aircraft to remain bombed up.

12th October 1944.
Weather: Fine becoming cloudy with showers.
Non-Operational Flying: Air tests carried out.
Operational Flying: Aircraft bombed up are to stand by for further instructions.
All available aircraft are to be bombed up, but Squadron is not required today or tonight.

13th October 1944.
Weather: Fine becoming cloudy with rain in the afternoon. Fine after dusk.
Non-Operational Flying: Formation flying and GH training.
Operational Flying: 31 aircraft required for daylight tomorrow.

14th October 1944.
Weather: Cloudy to fair, becoming fine after dusk.

Non-Operational Flying: H2S training and air tests.
Operational Flying: BOMBING – DUISBURG.
31 aircraft detailed, 29 aircraft took off. 2 aircraft failed to take off. Weather – patchy cloud with gaps for bombing, some scattered TIs were seen, but the Master Bomber gave 'free hand' and all crews bombed visually except one which bombed on H2S. Bombing concentrated on built up area from docks to airport. Direct hit on barge on river with ensuing large explosion. Bridge to East of docks straddled. No enemy aircraft seen. All aircraft returned safely.
F/O AJ Whitwood in PD265, JI-G reported: Bomb load 11 x 1000 MC, 4 x 500 GP Long Delay. Primary target: DUISBURG. Bombed at 0907 hours from 18,200 feet. Built up area north of docks.

Combat Report:
Aircraft: NF966 'R'
Captain: F/O F Stephens RAAF
Target: DUISBURG
1st Encounter: Outward bound (bombs not dropped), in position 5020N 0325E, height 16,000 feet, heading 088T, IAS 155. At 0052 hours, The

Mid Upper Gunner sighted an Me410 coming in from the port quarter down, range 600 yards. He immediately gave orders to corkscrew port and then fired a 1 second burst. The E/A fired a short burst which passed harmlessly beneath our aircraft and then broke away to the starboard quarter down and was not seen again.

2nd Encounter: At 0123 hours, the Mid Upper Gunner sighted an unidentified E/A with a greenish blue flame appearing to come from underneath, turning in to attack from the port quarter up, range 500 yards. He immediately gave order to corkscrew port and opened fire with a long burst. The E/A closed in very fast and at 400 yards fired a long burst which passed harmlessly above our A/C. The Mid Upper Gunner continued firing and at 500 yards the E/A broke away to the starboard quarter down and was not seen again.

MU Gunner – F/S Davies - 600 rounds.
Rear Gunner – Sgt PE Steele - 100 rounds.

Target:	*Duisburg – Area (1st attack)*
Aircraft deployed total:	*1,013 Bombers escorted by fighters.*
514 Squadron:	*29*
Aircraft lost total:	*14*
514 Squadron:	*Nil*

Comments: The raid was part of Operation Hurricane, intended to demonstrate to the Germans the overwhelming superiority of the Allied Air Forces over Europe. The first raid was mounted soon after dawn. 3,574 tons of high explosives and 820 tons of incendiaries were dropped on Duisburg with the loss of 14 aircraft before the flak defences were subdued. The American Eighth Air Force followed up the raid with a daylight attack on Cologne by 1,251 of their own bombers escorted by 749 fighters. 5 American bombers and 1 fighter were lost. The Luftwaffe did not attend the event.

BOMBING – DUISBURG.
30 aircraft detailed. 30 aircraft took off and attacked the primary target. Weather was clear with small amount of cloud over the target. PFF marking reported as very good. Bombing reported as good and concentrated. Last crews to leave reported fires seen from 100 miles. Searchlight activity on small scale but aimless. 1 aircraft had two combats with believed jet-propelled aircraft (F/O F Stephens, NF966 JI-R). No claims. Decoys to north-west in action but attracted no bombing. All aircraft returned safely.

S/L Clay in LM724, JI-B reported: Bomb load 11 x 1000 MC, 4 x 50 GP Long delay. Primary target: DUISBURG. Bombed at 0130 hours from 19,000 feet. Red TI. S/L Clay, 'A' Flight Commander, was carrying William Troughton, a correspondent from the Daily Express. A full report appeared in the Daily Express on 16th October 1944.

Target: Duisburg - Area (2nd attack)
Aircraft deployed total: 1,005
514 Squadron: 30
Aircraft lost total: 7
514 Squadron: Nil

Comment: A night raid followed the earlier effort, featuring 1,005 aircraft attacking in two waves, separated by two hours. Only 7 aircraft were lost. Nearly 9,000 tons of bombs had fallen on Duisburg in less than 48 hours and local reports were understandably less than comprehensive.

15th October 1944.
Weather: Fine becoming cloudy. Fine after dark, fog after midnight.
Non-Operational Flying: Air tests.
Operational Flying: BOMBING – WILHELMSHAVEN.
13 aircraft detailed. 13 aircraft took off and attacked the primary target. Weather – haze and thin cloud at first with thick cloud later. Target marking seemed concentrated at first, scattered later. Difficult to assess bombing results although crews claim to have bombed on TIs (one on H2S). Few small fires reported. One combat 514 'N' – No claim. All aircraft returned safely.
F/O GD Orr in LM719, A2-E reported: Bomb load 11 x 1000 MC, 4 x 500 GP. Primary target: WILHEMSHAVEN. Bombed at 1955 hours from 17,000 feet. Flames.

Combat Report:
Aircraft: PB419 'N'
Captain: F/O IR Campbell. RAAF
Target: WILHELMSHAVEN
On the night of 15th October 1944, Lancaster N of 514 Squadron was homeward bound, bombs dropped in position 5429N 0538E. Height 12,000ft, heading 275, IAS 190. At 2018 hours, the Rear Gunner observed trace coming from the starboard quarter. He immediately gave orders to corkscrew starboard and at that moment sighted an FW190 coming in from the starboard quarter down at a range 500

yards. The Rear Gunner opened fire immediately and continued firing throughout the attack. The M/U Gunner fired a 2 second burst as the E/A became visible over the tailplane. The E/A closed in to 100 yards range, firing the whole time and then broke away to the starboard beam down and was not seen again.
MU Gunner – W/O NF Cook RCAF - 80 rounds.
Rear Gunner – Sgt E Langlands - 300 rounds.

Target:	*Wilhelmshaven - Area*
Aircraft deployed total:	*506*
514 Squadron:	*13*
Aircraft lost total:	*Nil*
514 Squadron:	*Nil*

Comment: This was the last of 14 major RAF raids on Wilhemshaven since 1941. Severe damage was claimed, and the Rathaus destroyed.

16th October 1944.
Weather: Fog becoming cloudy with some rain.
Non-Operational Flying: Nil on account of weather.
Operational Flying: Make and Mend. 16 GH aircraft required for daylight tomorrow.

17th October 1944.
Weather: Fair to cloudy with rain in the afternoon.
Non-Operational Flying: H2S training carried out.
Operational Flying: GH attack confirmed.   Operation cancelled. Operation detailed for today will take place tomorrow.

18th October 1944.
Weather: Fair with showers, becoming cloudy, rain in evening.
Non-Operational Flying: Formation flying and H2S training.
Operational Flying: BOMBING – BONN.
16 aircraft detailed. 16 aircraft took off and 15 aircraft attacked primary target. 1 aircraft 'B' jettisoned and landed at Woodbridge after being hit by heavy Flak, Bomb Aimer injured. 'O' landed Lille Veneville partly owing to Flak damage and severe icing experienced on leaving target and shortage of petrol. Weather – varying cloud 2-7/10ths with break for bombing. 5 crews bombed on GH, the rest visually. Bombing was accurate around the A/P by evidence of thick smoke, some bombs seen to fall on built up area, East bank of the river.

Three of our aircraft hit by Flak, no fighters. 14 aircraft landed back at Base.

F/O GC France in PD265, JI-G reported: Bomb load 1 x 4000 HC, 5 x 12 x 30 - 2 x 12 x 30 modified, 9 x No. 14 clusters. Primary target: BONN. Bombed at 1101 hours from 19,000 feet. West Side of bridge.

F/O GW Smith in LM684 JI-O reported: 1 x 4000 HC fell out due to heavy flak burst 15 miles short of target when bomb doors were opened, bomb doors battered, slight damage to starboard wing. Aircraft landed at Lille-Vendeville.

P/O AE Williams in LM734, JI-B reported: Aircraft jettisoned on approaches to target when direct hit by heavy flak. Peeled off immediately. Numerous flak holes in fuselage and starboard wing. Bomb Aimer fractured leg. Heavy damage to aircraft. Landed at Woodbridge.

Target: *Bonn Area. Assessment of GH effectiveness.*
Aircraft deployed total: *128 (Lancasters)*
514 Squadron: *16*
Aircraft lost total: *1*
514 Squadron: *Nil*

Comment: *3 Group commenced a new independent role due to their use of GH which enabled targets to be accurately attacked over 10/10ths cloud not exceeding 18,000 feet. 128 Lancasters were dispatched with the loss of only a single aircraft and the raid was considered a success. The heart of Bonn was destroyed though the former home of the composer Beethoven was saved by 'the courageous actions of its caretakers.'*

19th October 1944.
Weather: Fair, with few showers becoming cloudy.
Non-Operational Flying: Air/ Sea Firing and H2S training.
Operational Flying: BOMBING: STUTTGART Aiming Point 'D' 1st attack.
12 aircraft detailed. 12 aircraft took off and 11 attacked the primary target. 1 aircraft returned early 'U' (oxygen failure to rear turret) jettisoned safe in sea. Weather 10/10ths cloud which broke to 6/10ths at the end of the period. Most crews bombed on sky markers, 1 on Gee. Air to air tracer seen. 4 aircraft seen shot down. (All 514 aircraft returned safely).

F/L MR Head in PD324, A2-B reported: Bomb load 1 x 4000HC, 3 x 500 clusters, 7 x 150 x 4lb and 1 x 90 x 4lb incendiaries. Primary target: STUTTGART. Bombed at 2032 hours from 17,500 feet. Red flares with yellow stars. Checked by H2S.

BOMBING – STUTTGART Aiming Point 'E' 2nd attack.
12 aircraft detailed. 12 aircraft took off and attacked primary target. Weather was 10/10ths low cloud over target and all crews arrived late owing to winds not as forecast. All crews bombed on sky markers, but results difficult to assess. Flak was heavier than usual. Defences of Saarbrucken-Strasbourg and Karlsruhe in action. Some fighter activity. 2 combats reported. 1 twin-engine, 1 FW190 – no claim. 1 aircraft damaged by heavy Flak. 12 aircraft landed safely at Base.
F/O GC France, LM733, JI-F, reported: Bomb load 1 x 4000HC, 6 x 1000MC, 1 x 500GP. Primary target STUTTGART. Bombed at 0110 hours from 20,000 feet. Estimated position of Wanganui flares, which died out ½ minute before aircraft bombed.
F/O AD Uffindell in PB842, JI-P reported markers as 'Red flares with yellow stars. Combat with twin-engine aircraft over target 0110 hours. Rear gunner could not fire.'
F/O DW Parks in PB426, JI-J reported: 'Bombed at 0112 hours from 18500 feet. Port inner damaged by Flak. Hydraulics to mid upper turret severed – direct hit by flak at 48.33N 05.35E at 0156 hours. Combat with FW190 at 0047 hours 49.08N 06.50E 19,000 feet – Rear gunner fired 3 long bursts. MU gunner long burst – no claim. MU Gunner (Sgt IR Clarke) wounded.

Combat Reports:
Aircraft: PB482 'P'
Captain: F/O AD Uffindell RAAF
Target: STUTTGART
Over target area, in position 4838N 0911E, height 18,000 feet, heading 101T, IAS 240. At 0110 hours the Rear Gunner sighted a T/E unidentified aircraft coming in from the port quarter level, range 700 yards. He immediately warned Captain to stand by to corkscrew and at that moment the E/A opened fire, the trace passing astern of our aircraft. The Rear Gunner then gave orders to corkscrew and opened fire with a 2 second burst. The E/A continued to close and was then lost in the corkscrew and was not seen again.
MU Gunner – F/Sgt JF Wilson RCAF - Nil.
Rear Gunner – P/O AE Clark - 200 rounds.

Aircraft: PB426 'J'
Captain: P/O DW Parks.
Target: STUTTGART
At 0047 hours, height 19,000 feet, heading 099 degrees, position 4908N 0650E. Rear Gunner sighted an FW190 at 700 yards approaching to attack from astern and below. Gunner ordered corkscrew and both Gunners opened fire. E/A was subsequently lost in corkscrew and was not seen again. Visibility was clear, with no fighter flares, searchlights or flak encountered.
MU Gunner – Sgt HC Taylor - 100 rounds. .
Rear Gunner – Sgt IR Clark - 200 rounds.

Target: *Stuttgart - Area*
Aircraft deployed total: *583 (in two waves)*
514 Squadron: *12 (1 returned early)*
Aircraft lost total: *6*
514 Squadron: *Nil*

Comment: The raid took place in two waves, separated by 4½ hours. Despite the bombing not being concentrated, serious damage was caused and the important Bosch factory was hit.

20th October 1944.
Weather: Cloudy with rain, becoming continuous after dusk.
Non-Operational Flying: Nil owing to weather.
Operational Flying: No operations today or tonight. Maximum effort required tomorrow. 25 aircraft to be bombed up. Target in Flushing area to be attacked tomorrow morning.

21st October 1944.
Weather: Cloudy with light rain. Fog at dawn. Fair after dusk.
Non-Operational Flying: Air tests and Air/Sea Firing.
Operational Flying: BOMBING: FLUSHING 'B'.
25 aircraft detailed. 25 aircraft took off and attacked primary target. Weather was clear and all crews were able to identify land marks and A/P. Average of bombing – good. The land as a whole was described as flooded. One of our aircraft was hit by flak on the run up, and bombs fell on the oil refinery. Other crews saw flames and smoke. A small ship was hit – a large ship berthed North end of Haren. Flak slight, although two of our aircraft were hit. No enemy fighters seen. All aircraft landed safely at Base.

F/O GC France in LM733, JI-F reported: Bomb load 12 x 1000 MC, 2 x 500 GP. Primary target: FLUSHING 'B'. Bombed at 1230 hours from 5,000 feet. Coastal tip of target area.

Target: *Flushing – Gun Batteries, Aiming Point 'B'.*
Aircraft deployed total: *75 (Lancasters)*
514 Squadron: *25*
Aircraft lost total: *1 (Lancaster)*
514 Squadron: *Nil*

Comments: Gun batteries covering the river Schelde near Flushing, were the aim of this raid. Damage to a ship was reported as well as to an oil refinery.

22nd October 1944.
Weather: Fog at first becoming cloudy.
Non-Operational Flying: Air tests carried out.
Operational Flying: BOMBING - NEUSS.
10 aircraft detailed. 10 aircraft took off and attacked primary target. Weather – 10/10ths cloud over target. Formations appeared to be flying in all directions and consequently bombing was scattered. 5 aircraft bombed on Gee-H. 3 aircraft bombed on Gee-H leader. Defences moderate. Two aircraft had small flak holes in mid upper turrets. No fighters seen. All aircraft returned safely to Base.
F/O GC France in PD265, JI-G reported: Bomb load 1 x 4000HC, 6 x 1000 MC, 6 x 500GP. Bombed at 1557½ hours from 16,400 feet. Following aircraft 'E2'.

Target: *Neuss - Area*
Aircraft deployed total: *100 (Lancasters)*
514 Squadron: *10*
Aircraft lost total: *Nil*
514 Squadron: *Nil*

Comment: A GH raid. Bombing was scattered on this occasion.

23rd October 1944.
Weather: Cloudy with rain in afternoon, becoming fine after dark.
Non-Operational Flying: Air tests.
Operational Flying: BOMBING - ESSEN.
26 aircraft detailed. 26 aircraft took off and 25 aircraft attacked primary target. 1 aircraft abortive sortie, jettisoned bombs 40 miles

East of Southwold (F/O RW Vickers, NF968 JI-L with ASI and port engine unserviceable). Weather 10/10ths over target – tops 12/14,000 feet with most appalling weather en route – cloud up to 23,000 feet. Most crews bombed on the sky markers. 4 on Gee-H and 1 on H2S. The four Gee-H crews considered the markers coincided with the Gee-H position. Little evidence seen of the attack. Red glows seen below cloud. Bombing reported as fairly concentrated. Flak moderate, Düsseldorf and Cologne defences in action. 1 combat reported – no claim. A few sightings of Me190s. Severe electrical storms encountered. All aircraft landed at Base.

F/O SG Wright RCAF in LM719, JI-B reported: Bomb load 1 x 4000 HC, 6 x 1000 MC, 6 x 500 GP. Primary target: ESSEN. Bombed at 1932 hours from 18,000 feet. Port of Red flares. Attacked by fighter at 5145N 0640E at 1940 hours at 14,000 feet. MU Gunner fires 1 burst. Rear turret guns frozen and rear turret unserviceable by flak.

Combat Report:
Aircraft: LM719 'B'
Captain: F/O SG Wright RCAF
Target: ESSEN

On the night of 23rd October 1944, Lancaster 'B' of 514 Squadron was homeward bound, bombs dropped, in position of 5145N 0640E, height 14,000 feet, heading 230T, IAS 240. At 1940 hours, the Mid Upper Gunner sighted a T/E unidentified E/A coming in from the starboard beam up, range 600 yards. He immediately gave order to corkscrew starboard and fired a three second burst. The E/A fired a short burst at 600 yards and then turned off and passed astern of our A/C, the Rear Gunner firing a long burst manually (hydraulics u/s due to flak damage) as E/A passed through his sights. The E/A then dived away to the port quarter down and was not seen again.

MU Gunner – P/O WW Maynes RCAF - 120 rounds.
Rear Gunner – P/O AJ Stansbury RCAF - 200 rounds.

Target:	*Essen - Area*
Aircraft deployed total:	*1,055*
514 Squadron:	*26*
Aircraft lost total:	*8*
514 Squadron:	*Nil*

Comments: This was the heaviest attack to date on the city, involving 1,055 aircraft which itself was a new record for numbers in any raid. The proportion of HE to incendiaries, at more than 90%, was higher than previously as it was considered that most burnable buildings had by now been destroyed. A further 607 buildings were destroyed on this visit.

24th October 1944.
Weather: Cloudy with rain, fog after dusk.
Non-Operational Flying: Air / Sea Firing and H2S training.
Operational Flying: 25 aircraft required for night attack. Operation cancelled. 26 aircraft required for daylight tomorrow.

25th October 1944.
Weather: Fog, becoming fair at noon. Further fog after dusk.
Non-Operational Flying: Air tests.
Operational Flying: BOMBING - ESSEN.
26 aircraft detailed. 26 aircraft took off and 25 attacked primary target. 1 aircraft abortive 'E2' (starboard outer u/s), jettisoned 40 miles East of Southwold. Weather over target 10/10ths low cloud with one clear patch which appeared to fill up later in the attack. Earlier crews identified built up area and Red TIs and crews were instructed to bomb them. Bombing described as concentrated. Considerable haze and smoke quickly accumulated and the raid was described as successful. No enemy fighters seen.
F/O GC France, LM733 JI-F, reported: Bomb load 1 x 4000 HC, 6 x 1000 MC, 6 x 500 GP. Bombed at 1532 hours from 21500 feet. White smoke as ordered by Master Bomber.

Target:	*Essen - Area*
Aircraft deployed total:	*771*
514 Squadron:	*26*
Aircraft lost total:	*4*
514 Squadron:	*Nil*

Comment: Using sky-markers as the target was cloud-covered, the bombing was scattered. A further 1,163 buildings were destroyed and there was severe damage to the remaining industrial plants in the city, including the vital Krupps steelworks. Much of Essen's industries were by now dispersed and the city lost its important role in German war production.

26th October 1944.
Weather: Fog, becoming cloudy with fog after dusk.
Non-Operational Flying: Air tests.

Operational Flying: BOMBING – LEVERKUSEN.
10 aircraft detailed. 10 aircraft took off and attacked the primary target. Weather over target and en route was 10/10ths cloud. 8 aircraft bombed on GH and two, whose GH was unserviceable, bombed on the leading aircraft. Formation and bombing was reported as very good, all bombs falling within a radius of 200 yards. No results seen due to cloud. No fighters seen or aircraft damaged.
F/O GW Smith, PB419, JI-N, reported: Bomb load 1 x 4000 HC, 6 x 1000 MC, 4 x 500 GP, 2 x 500 GP long delay. Primary target: LEVERKUSEN. Bombed at 1530 hours from 17,500 feet on GH.

Target: *Leverkusen – Chemical Works*
Aircraft deployed total: *105 (Lancasters)*
514 Squadron: *10*
Aircraft lost total: *Nil*
514 Squadron: *Nil*

Comments: A GH raid on the chemical works. Cloud prevented an assessment of the results.

27th October 1944.
Weather: Fog and rain, becoming fair.
Non-Operational Flying: Air/Sea firing and H2S training.
Operational Flying: 25 aircraft required for night attack. All operations cancelled. 12 aircraft required for tomorrow morning.

28th October 1944.
Weather: Fine early, cloudy and showers later.
Non-Operational Flying: Air/Sea firing and fighter affiliation.
Operational Flying: BOMBING - FLUSHING.
12 aircraft detailed, 12 aircraft took off and 11 attacked the primary target. 1 aircraft hit by heavy Flak over the target - wing petrol tank holed and intercom unserviceable. Could not bomb accurately and therefore jettisoned off Southwold. Weather over the target quite clear and conditions perfect although believed to be only local, and some low cloud approaching. All crews clearly identified the A/P and the jetty, and bombing was reported as concentrated. All aircraft landed at Base.
F/O AJ Holland in NG141, A2-J reported: Bomb load 1 x 4000 HC, 6 x 1000 MC, 4 x 500 GP. Primary target: FLUSHING. Bombed at 1016hrs from 10,000 feet, A/P.

Target: Flushing – Coastal Gun Batteries
Aircraft deployed total: 277
514 Squadron: 12
Aircraft lost total: 2
514 Squadron: Nil

Comments: The force attacked gun positions with apparent success. The aircraft hit by flak was F/O MR Oliver's LM734, A2-C. The crew appears to have emerged unscathed.

BOMBING - COLOGNE.
12 aircraft detailed. 12 aircraft took off and 11 attacked the primary target. 1 aircraft abortive sortie. Weather over the target was clear and aircraft easily identified the target by visual means and red and yellow TIs. Master Bomber instructed to bomb on the red markers and on the up wind edge of the smoke. Markers were scarcely necessary. The target on leaving was described as one large concentrated mass of brown smoke rising up to 1000 feet. Flak reported as moderate to intense, predicted, accurate for height with tracer destroying at 10,000 feet. No enemy aircraft seen.
P/O AD Uffindell in PB482, JI-P, reported: Bomb load 1 x 4000 HC, 8 x 150 x 4. Primary target: COLOGNE. Bombed at 1547 hours from 20,000 feet. Smoke trails as instructed.

10 aircraft were required for a further operation tonight, but this was cancelled. 10 aircraft required for tomorrow morning.

Target: Cologne - Area
Aircraft deployed total: 733
514 Squadron: 12
Aircraft lost total: 7
514 Squadron: Nil

Comments: A two-wave attack. There was, reportedly, massive damage caused, with the destruction of 2,239 blocks of flats as well as other buildings. There was damage to the power and transport infrastructure as well.

29th October 1944.
Weather: Fog early, followed by slight rain becoming fine.
Non-Operational Flying: GH training and fighter affiliation.
Operational Flying: BOMBING – FLUSHING.

10 aircraft detailed. 10 aircraft took off and attacked the primary target. Weather was clear over the target and all crews after circling for 4/5 minutes were able to identify the target by the markers, which were described to be dropped in a line along the coast. The first markers were not accurately placed. The target was remarked and the Master Bomber was helpful in instructing the crews how to bomb. Although the actual gun position may have been hit, the attack in general tended to be scattered. No Flak at all and no fighters. All aircraft landed at Base.

F/O GC France in NG203, JI-A reported: Bomb load 11 x 1000 ANM59, 4 x 500 GP MC. Bombed at 1137 hours from 7000 feet. Starboard of Green TI as instructed.

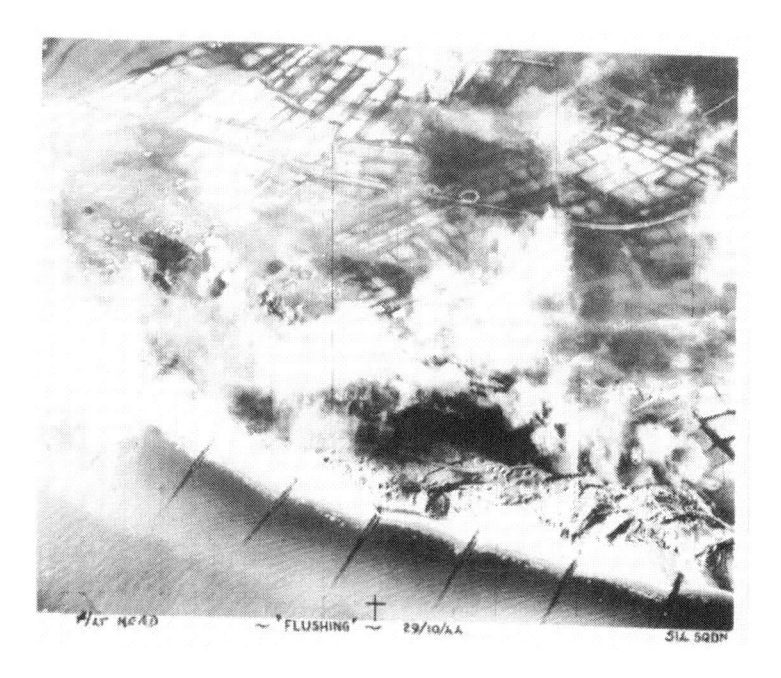

(Above) Target photo of Flushing from NG142, A2-H flown by F/Lt MR Head, who bombed at 1137 hours from 5800 feet. Source: Crown Copyright / National Archive.

Target:	*Flushing – Coastal Gun Batteries*
Aircraft deployed total:	*358*
514 Squadron:	*10*
Aircraft lost total:	*1*
514 Squadron:	*Nil*

Comments: The aircraft attacked 11 different German positions. With good visibility it was believed that all the targets were hit.

30th October 1944. Weather: Fine becoming cloudy towards evening.
Non-Operational Flying: GH training and air tests.
Operational Flying: BOMBING – WESSELING.
24 aircraft detailed. 24 aircraft took off and attacked primary target. Weather was 10/10ths cloud – tops about 7000 feet. The attack was scattered and at least 2 areas of bombing. Some black smoke seen rising above the clouds on the 1st A/P. Flak described as slight to moderate. No enemy fighters seen. All aircraft landed at Base.
F/O SG Wright in NG121, JI-H reported: Bomb load 1 x 4000 HC, 16 x 500 GP. Primary target: WESSELING. Bombed at 1159 hours from 19,000 feet on release of GH Leader's bombs.

Target:	*Wesseling – Oil Refinery*
Aircraft deployed total:	*102 (Lancasters)*
514 Squadron:	*24*
Aircraft lost total:	*Nil*
514 Squadron:	*Nil*

Comments: 102 Lancasters mounted a GH attack on the refinery. Cloud prevented an assessment but bombing was believed to be accurate, and no aircraft were lost.

31st October 1944.
Weather: Fair but cloudy.
Non-Operational Flying: H2S training and air tests.
Operational Flying: BOMBING – BOTTROP.
24 aircraft detailed. 23 aircraft took off and attacked primary target. 1 aircraft 'N' failed to take off – engine failure. 10/10ths cloud over target. 9 aircraft bombed on GH. The remainder as followers. Most crews reported that bombing and red flares were concentrated and accurate. Flak was moderate predicted. Four of our aircraft were hit.
F/O GC France in JI-K, LM285, reported: Bomb load 1 x 4000 HC, 15 x 500 GP. 1 Flare. Primary target: BOTTROP. Bombed at 1500 hours from 18,000 feet on GH.

Aircraft damaged:

F/O RH Edmundson JI-M LM275 – MU turret and starboard outer damaged.

F/O RW Vickers A2-G PB423 – Starboard fin and rudder damaged.
F/O IJ Bittner JI-U LM728 – Fuselage damaged.
F/O F Heald A2-H NG142 – Bomb Aimer's panel damaged.

Target: *Bottrop – Oil Refinery*
Aircraft deployed total: *101 (Lancasters)*
514 Squadron: *23*
Aircraft lost total: *1*
514 Squadron: *Nil*

Comments: 101 Lancasters carried out a good GH attack on the oil plant with the loss of 1 aircraft.

(Above) An unidentified Mk.I or III Lancaster awaits her next task at her RAF Waterbeach dispersal. Source: Airworx GmbH Archive.

Monthly Summary for October 1944

Award:

1825315 Sgt Sherry, J F/Engineer (award not stated) 5/10/44

Operational:

Enemy Aircraft Destroyed:	Nil
Operational Flying Hours for October 1944:	1632.30
Non-Operational Flying Hours for October 1944:	177.30
Total tons of bombs dropped in October 1944:	1946 tons
Cumulative total tons of bombs dropped:	9522 ¾ tons
Number of sorties for October 1944:	395

Strength of Squadron as at 31st October 1944.
Aircrew: 111 Officers,
250 SNCOs

Ground: 1 Officer (Adjutant).

November 1944

(Above) Squadron members assemble for a photo opportunity at Waterbeach in November 1944. Source: Airworx Gmbh Archive

1st November 1944.
Weather: Cloudy becoming fair.
Non-Operational Flying: H2S Training and GH bombing at Rushford.
Operational Flying: No operations today or tonight. 19 aircraft (9 GH and 10 followers) required early tomorrow. 514 Squadron now offer 23 aircraft.

2nd November 1944.
Weather: Fair to cloudy. Some fog after dawn, showers in afternoon.
Non-Operational Flying: Air tests.
Operational Flying: BOMBING – HOMBERG.
19 aircraft required tomorrow morning. 23 aircraft detailed. 23 aircraft took off and attacked primary target. Weather: there was variable cloud but clear for bombing. 4 aircraft bombed on instruments, 6 on Green flares, remainder visually. The target was obscured by a pall of smoke rising to 10,000 feet. Some fires. Bombing concentrated. Flak - moderate to intense, accurate heavy flak. 5 of our aircraft slightly damaged. Photographs doubtful on account of evasive action. All aircraft landed at Base.
F/O GC France in JI-G, PD265 reported: Bomb load 1 x 4000 HC, 6 x 1000 ANM59, 6 x 500 MC. Primary target: HOMBERG. Bombed at 1406hrs from 20,000 feet, on instruments.

Aircraft damaged:

F/O AJ Holland, NG141, A2-J – MU turret and flap on port wing damaged.
F/O CIM Nicholl, PD233, A2-K – Pilot's windscreen and Air Bomber's panel damaged, also tail plane.
F/O RW Vickers, PB482, JI-P – Bomb doors hit by Flak.
F/O DC Gordon, LM719, JI-B – Aircraft hit by Flak.

Target:	*Homberg -Rhein-Preussen Oil Plant*
Aircraft deployed total:	*184 (Lancasters)*
514 Squadron:	*23*
Aircraft lost total:	*5*
514 Squadron:	*Nil*

Comment: A GH attack on the Rhein-Preussen synthetic oil plant at Meerbeck, Homberg. Large fires were started with a thick column of smoke.

3rd November 1944.
Weather: Fog, becoming cloudy with rain. Fair after dusk.
Non-Operational Flying: Nil on account of weather.
Operational Flying: Operations cancelled. 20 aircraft required tomorrow morning.

4th November 1944.
Weather: Fair to cloudy.
Non-Operational Flying: H2S and GH training.
Operational Flying: BOMBING – SOLINGEN.
20 aircraft detailed. 20 aircraft took off. 1 aircraft abortive. 19 aircraft attacked primary target. Weather was 8/10ths – 10/10ths low cloud. Red flares reported as concentrated. Bombing in accordance. Results were chiefly unobserved, but some crews obtained visuals through gaps in cloud and reported some bombs falling in open country and some on built up area, and brownish smoke seen rising. The attack believed generally satisfactory. No Flak reported over the target but a number of scarecrow flares seen which was a matter of speculation as to whether aircraft falling or scarecrows. No fighters. All aircraft landed at Base.
F/O GC France in LM719, JI-B reported: Bomb load 1 x 4000 HC, 6 x 1000 ANM9, 4 x 500 GP, 2 x 500 MC (L/Delay), 3 flares. Primary

target: SOLINGEN. Bombed at 1406½ hours from 20,000 feet on red flares.

Target: *Solingen – Area*
Aircraft deployed total: *176 (Lancasters)*
514 Squadron: *20*
Aircraft lost total: *4 (Lancasters)*
514 Squadron: *Nil*

Comments: Bombing was badly scattered and the raid not successful. 'Bomber Command Losses' notes that two aircraft exploded over target area, which would almost certainly account for the 'scarecrow shell' sightings. These Lancasters were HK458, A4-C and NG219, JE-T, both aircraft being with 195 Sqn, which lost 3 Lancasters on this raid. 195 Sqn was based at this time at RAF Witchford. Witchford was also part of 33 Base along with Waterbeach and Mepal.

5th November 1944.
Weather: Fair to cloudy, with rain in the afternoon.
Non-Operational Flying: GH training and air tests.
Operational Flying: BOMBING – SOLINGEN.
23 aircraft detailed. 22 aircraft took off and 21 attacked primary target. 1 aircraft returned early – supercharger disintegrated (F/O Geoff France in A2-G, PB423). 1 aircraft failed to take off – starboard outer unserviceable. Weather over target – 10/10ths cloud. 10 aircraft bombed on instruments, some on flares and the remainder on the leading aircraft. One burst of Flak over the target. No fighters. All aircraft landed at Base. 3 Group will not be required until after 0930 hours tomorrow.
F/L RA Pickler in PB482, JI-P reported: 'Bomb load 1 x 4000 HC, 6 x 1000 ANM59, 4 x 500 GP, 2 x 500 GP (L/Delay), 3 flares. Primary target: SOLINGEN. Bombed at 1306 hours from 17,000 feet on instruments.

Target: *Solingen – Area*
Aircraft deployed total: *173*
514 Squadron: *22 (1 returned early)*
Aircraft lost total: *1*
514 Squadron: *Nil*

Comments: On this occasion the force achieved much better accuracy and concentration. German records show this raid to have been an outstanding success.

6th November 1944.
Weather: Fine to fair, becoming cloudy with rain in the evening.
Non Operational Flying: GH training and fighter affiliation.
Operational Flying: BOMBING - KOBLENZ.
19 aircraft detailed. 19 aircraft took off and 17 aircraft attacked the primary target. 2 aircraft returned early, one with port inner engine unserviceable, the other with rear turret unserviceable. Weather was clear over the target. 5 aircraft bombed on GH, the remainder on TIs. All crews were enthusiastic about the results. Marking was concentrated. Better than PFF. Large fires spreading over a wide area in loop of river junction. Flak was slight to moderate. Few fighters seen. No combats. No searchlights. All aircraft landed.
F/O JF Ness in NG203, JI-A reported: Bomb load 1x4000 HC, 2100 x 4 lb IB. Primary target: KOBLENZ. Bombed at 1935 hours from 18,000 feet on centre of fires.

Target:	*Koblenz - Area*
Aircraft deployed total:	*128 (Lancasters)*
514 Squadron:	*19 (2 returned early)*
Aircraft lost total:	*2*
514 Squadron:	*Nil*

Comments: The GH raid was successful with over 300 acres were destroyed by a large area of fire, representing 58% of the town's built up area.

7th November 1944.
Weather: Fair to fine.
Non-Operational Flying: GH and H2S training.
Operational Flying: Squadron not required today. 18 aircraft required tomorrow morning.

8th November 1944.
Weather: Fair to cloudy.
Non-Operational Flying: GH training and air tests.
Operational Flying: BOMBING - HOMBERG.
18 aircraft detailed. 18 aircraft took off and attacked primary target. Weather was clear. Some aircraft bombed on instruments, some

visually and some on leading aircraft. Flak was moderate to intense predicted. 8 of our aircraft were damaged slightly. 1 aircraft had 3 engines damaged. No fighters. All aircraft landed.

F/O GC France in ME841, JI-J reported: Bomb load 1 x 4000 HC, 12x No. 14 Clusters, 2x150x4. Primary target: HOMBERG. Bombed at 1031 hours from 17,500 feet on instruments.

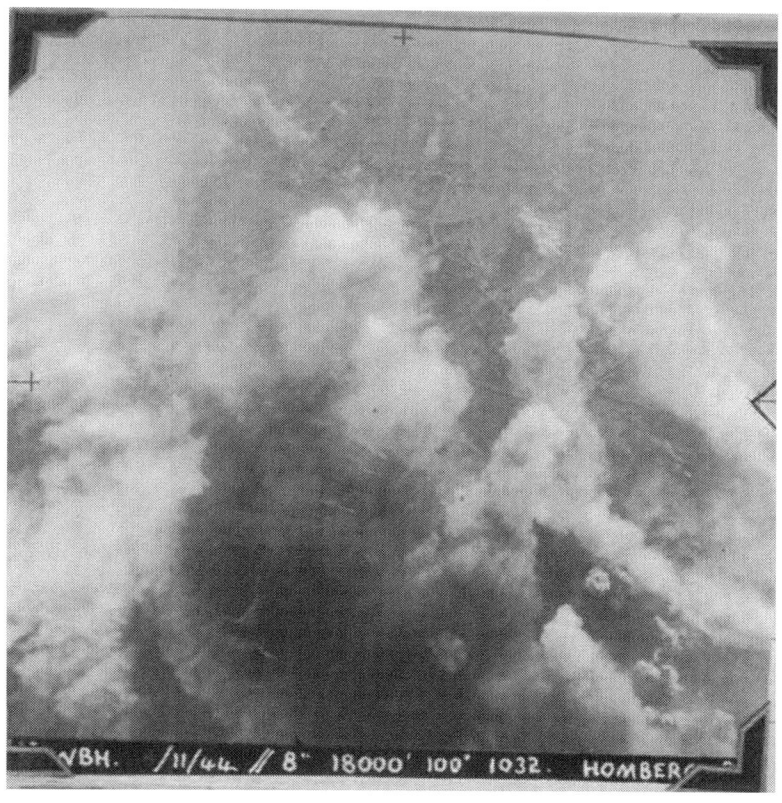

(Above) Aiming point photograph of the Rhein-Preussen synthetic oil plant at Meerbeck, Homberg on 8th October 1944. The bombing time (1032 hours) and height (18000 feet) match those of either F/O JHG Harland in PD333, A2-K, or F/O SE Wilson in LM285, JI-K. Photo courtesy of Victoria RSL.

Target: Homberg – Rhein-Preussen Synthetic Oil Plant
Aircraft deployed total: 136
514 Squadron: 18
Aircraft lost total: 1
514 Squadron: Nil

Comments: The force attacked the Rhein-Preussen plant again using GH. Bombing was initially accurate causing two large fires, but then smoke obscured the target and bombing became more scattered.

9th November 1944.
Weather: Mainly fair, becoming cloudy with rain in the evening.
Non-Operational Flying: GH training and bombing.
Operational Flying: No operations in Command today or tonight. 22 aircraft to be bombed up for tomorrow morning.

10th November 1944.
Weather: Fine becoming cloudy.
Non Operational Flying: Air to sea firing and GH training.
Operational Flying: Operation cancelled. Same operation will be laid on tomorrow.

11th November 1944.
Weather: Cloudy becoming fair.
Non-Operational Flying: Air tests and flight affiliation.
Operational Flying: BOMBING – CASTRAP RAUXEL.
18 Aircraft required from the squadron. 18 Aircraft took off to attack Castrap Rauxel, 1 Aircraft returned early. 14 Aircraft attacked primary target, 3 Aircraft attacked last resort (Wuppertal). Weather was 10/10 through cloud. 7 Aircraft bombed on GH, 4 Aircraft bombed on GH leaders and 3 Aircraft bombed flares. The attack was believed concentrated. Flak was slight to moderate, no fighters. All Aircraft landed at base. Derby figures of Aircraft are to be bombed up. 514 Squadron offers 24 Aircraft.
F/O LS Drew in LM627, JI-D reported: Bomb load 1 x 4000 HC, 15 x 500 GP, 1 Flare. Primary target: CASTRAP RAUXEL. Bombed at 1106 hours from 19,000 feet.

Target:	*Castrap Rauxel - Synthetic Oil Plant*
Aircraft deployed total:	*122 (Lancasters)*
514 Squadron:	*18 (1 returned early)*
Aircraft lost total:	*Nil*
514 Squadron:	*Nil*

Comments: Another accurate GH raid on a synthetic oil plant.

12th November 1944.
Weather: Fair becoming cloudy with rain and fog.
Non-Operational Flying: GH training and air tests.
Operational Flying: No operations for 3 Group today or tonight. Two targets laid on for tomorrow. The alternative target is cancelled.
Administration: A Ceremonial parade was held in 'A' Hangar at 1600 hours when Air Vice Marshal R Harrison CBE, DFC, AFC Air Officer Commanding No. 3 Group, presented the Squadron Badge to Wing Commander M Wyatt DFC, who received it on behalf of 514 Squadron.

13th November 1944.
Weather: Fog until dawn becoming fair.
Non-Operational Flying: H2S Training and Air Tests.
Operational Flying: Operation cancelled. 514 Squadron are not required today or tonight. 25 Aircraft will be required for a target tomorrow morning.

14th November 1944.
Weather: Cloudy with intermittent rain, becoming continuous.
Non-Operational Flying: Air tests.
Operational Flying: Operation cancelled. No operations tonight. 30 aircraft to stand by for tomorrow.

15th November 1944.
Weather: Cloudy with rain, becoming fair.
Non-Operational Flying: Air tests.
Operational Flying: BOMBING – HOESCH-BENZIN DORTMUND.
30 aircraft detailed. 29 aircraft took off to attack Dortmund. 1 aircraft failed to take off. 1 aircraft 'C' F/O Limbert landed at Woodbridge on 2 engines. Weather over target was 10/10ths cloud. Red flares were well concentrated and raid believed successful. Flak was reported as slight to moderate. 2 aircraft reported shot down (presumably by flak) which formated on 514/'D'. One of our own aircraft damaged by flak. No enemy fighters seen and our fighter escort reported as good. 25 aircraft required tomorrow. All aircraft landed at Base except the one landing at Woodbridge.
P/O R Limbert, LM288 JI-C, reported: Bomb load 1x4000 HC, 15x500GP, 1 Red with green star flare. Primary target: HOESCH-BENZIN DORTMUND. Bombed at 1540hrs from 17,000 feet on GH. 1540 hours port outer engine smashed by falling bomb also port inner engine damaged. Another bomb came through the fuselage beside

main spar remaining there until landing at Woodbridge. Yet another bomb struck the starboard outer engine. Crew behaved admirably.

Target: *Dortmund Hoesch- Benzin Plant*
Aircraft deployed total: *117 (Lancasters)*
514 Squadron: *29*
Aircraft lost total: *2*
514 Squadron: *Nil*

Comments: A GH attack on the oil plant. It is believed that the raid was accurate. The 514 Sqn. aircraft damaged was a GH Leader, LM627, JI-D, flown by F/O LS Drew. The Bomb Aimer, F/S RS Williams, was wounded in the head. The two aircraft seen to be shot down whilst formatting on JI-D over the target were probably Lancasters HK595, KO-A and NN706, KO-B, both of 115 Sqn. at Witchford. 115 Sqn was part of 33 Base along with 514 Sqn and 75(NZ) Sqn. They were the only two aircraft lost from this operation. There were no survivors from either crew.

16th November 1944.
Weather: Fine with fog until noon.
Non-Operational Flying: Nil owing to weather.
Operational Flying: BOMBING – HEINSBURG
25 aircraft detailed. 25 aircraft took off and 24 attacked the primary target. 1 aircraft did not bomb owing to hang up. Jettisoned 40 miles East of Southwold. There was no cloud over the target but slight haze. Our aircraft attacked the town visually or on the upwind edge of the smoke. The attack was considered successful and the target left one mass of smoke and flames. Flak was slight to moderate heavy. 3 aircraft were damaged. No fighters seen. All aircraft landed at base. 25 aircraft required for tomorrow.
F/O GA Wark in PD325, A2-L, reported: Bomb load 1 x 4000 HC, 6 x 1000 MC, 6 x 500 GP. Primary target: HEINSBURG. Bombed at 1536 hours from 9,000 feet. Smoke.

Target: *Heinsburg – German Defensive Positions*
Aircraft deployed total: *1,188*
514 Squadron: *25*
Aircraft lost total: *4*
514 Squadron: *Nil*

Comments: The attack focused on 3 targets about to be attacked by the American First and Ninth Armies. 514 Sqn joined the 182 Lancasters that attacked communication lines behind Heinsburg. The raids caused massive damage to the three towns targeted; however the American attack suffered from problems unrelated to this operation.

17th November 1944.
Weather: Cloudy with rain.
Non-Operational Flying: Nil on account of weather.
Operational Flying: Operation cancelled. Squadron to stand-by for a target tonight.
No targets tonight, all available aircraft required tomorrow. Operation cancelled.

18th November 1944.
Weather: Cloudy with intermittent rain.
Non-Operational Flying: Nil on account of weather.
Operational Flying: No operations today or tonight.

19th November 1944.
Weather: Fair becoming cloudy with rain.
Non-Operational Flying: Air tests and beam approach practice.
Operational Flying: 26 aircraft required today. Operation cancelled. 514 Squadron is required tomorrow afternoon.

20th November 1944.
Weather: Cloudy with intermittent rain.
Non-Operational Flying: GH Training and Air Tests.
Operational Flying: BOMBING – HOMBERG
26 aircraft detailed. 26 took off and 23 attacked the primary target. 2 abortive sorties. 1 aircraft missing. 1 aircraft landed at Woodbridge on return. 23 aircraft landed at base. Weather over the target was 10/10ths cloud. 9 aircraft bombed on GH, the remaining 13 on leading aircraft. Bombing appeared concentrated. No results seen due to cloud. Flak reported as slight. Scarecrows seen. Our missing aircraft believed hit by falling bombs and the explosion damaged 3 of our aircraft formating. No hostile fighters seen.
F/O GC France in LM733, JI-F reported: 1 x 4000 HC, 12 x 500 MC, 4 x 500 GP. Primary target: HOMBERG. Bombed at 1514½ hours from 19,000 feet on GH Leader.
F/L LL Currie in NF966 JI-R reported 'Damage to fuselage due to aircraft exploding.'

F/O SG Wright in PB756, JI-B reported: Bomb load 1 x 4000 HC, 12 x 500 GP, 4 x 500 MC. Primary target: HOMBERG. Bombed at 1515 hours from 20,000 feet on GH.

Target: *Homberg–Rhein-Preussen Synthetic Oil Plant*
Aircraft deployed total: *183 (Lancasters)*
514 Squadron: *26*
Aircraft lost total: *5 (Lancasters)*
514 Squadron: *1*

Comments: A GH raid in stormy weather on the robustly-defended oil plant. Many aircraft were unable to formate on GH leaders and the bombing was scattered. The 'Scarecrows' might refer to the explosion of 75(NZ) Sqn's PB689, AA-X, near the target, one of three aircraft lost by that unit on this raid.

(Above) Taken on either Nov. 20 or 21 1944, both days flying ops to Homberg, F/O Stan Wright RCAF and crew pose happily in front of Lancaster PB756, JI-B. Back row, left to right: Ground crew known only as Jock, Shag and Taffy, are the three ground crew; P/O WW 'Curly' Maynes (Mid-Upper Gunner), F/O Ken Ridley Navigator, F/O Stan Wright, Pilot and P/O Jake Stansbury Rear Gunner. Front row, left to right: Ground crew known as 'Yorkie', F/S LE 'Pete' Jewell Air Bomber Sgt Nick Andreashuk WOP/Air Sgt Joe Dibley Flight Engineer. Source: Ken Ridley via Garth Ridley.

Missing aircraft:

LM286 A2-F. The aircraft crashed in the target area, possibly as a result of being struck by bombs. There is an uncorroborated suggestion that the aircraft exploded over the target (probably as mentioned by F/L Currie).

F/O JHG Harland	*Pilot*	*KIA*
F/Sgt RI Gray	*Navigator*	*KIA*
F/O TGH Adams RNZAF	*Bomb Aimer*	*KIA*
W/O MG George	*WOP/AG*	*KIA*
Sgt SD Lucas	*MU Gunner*	*KIA*
Sgt G Slocombe	*Rear Gunner*	*KIA*
Sgt R McK Paterson	*Flight Engineer*	*KIA*

21st November 1944.
Weather: Mainly fair.
Non-Operational Flying: Air Tests.
Operational Flying: BOMBING – HOMBERG.
22 aircraft detailed. 22 aircraft took off to attack the primary target at Homberg. 1 aircraft attacked last resort. 2 aircraft missing. 1 aircraft crash landed in Belgium after bombing the target. Weather about 5/10ths cloud but clear for bombing. Five aircraft bombed on GH. Ten aircraft bombed visually and one on markers. Two aircraft bombed on GH leaders. Target markers were concentrated. Attack mainly concentrated with fires and much thick brown smoke. Large explosion at 1510 hours. Some bombs fell to the South West and some near bridge over river - believed hit. Flak was moderate and accurate heavy. Estimated 4 aircraft were shot down. 7 of our aircraft were damaged by Flak. 19 aircraft landed at base, one aircraft crash landed 5 miles South of Antwerp, the Rear Gunner having baled out, the rest of the crew were uninjured.
F/O JF Ness in JI-A, NG203, reported: Bomb load 1x4000 HC, 16x500 GP. Primary target: HOMBERG. Bombed at 1506½ hours from 20,000 feet on GH leader.
F/O TGN Trask in NG118, A2-E reported: Jettisoned at 10 seconds before GH indicated time owing to aircraft being out of control over target area. Aircraft dived steeply to starboard, pulled out at 17,000 feet.

Target: *Homberg – Rhein-Preussen Synthetic Oil Plant*
Aircraft deployed total: *160 (Lancasters)*
514 Squadron: *22*
Aircraft lost total: *3*
514 Squadron: *2 plus 1 crash-landed.*

(Above) The Rhein-Preussen plant had proved a hard nut to crack. Repeated attacks by Bomber Command cost numerous aircraft and their crews. The operation on 21st November 1944 finally put the plant out of action for the remainder of the war. Source: Airworx GmbH Archive.

Comments: 3 Group again carried out a GH attack on the Rhein-Preussen plant, with the loss of 3 aircraft. The bombing was scattered at first but then became very concentrated, culminating in a vast sheet of yellow flame followed by black smoke rising to a great height, according to the raid report. The raid was very satisfactory and finally put the plant permanently out of action. It is possible that the loss of control reported by F/O Trask was due to LM684 exploding. At least one other aircraft, NF968 JI-L, also released its bombs early, probably as a result of NG118, a GH Leader, doing so. According to Axel Heyermann in Moers, 'Nov. 21. 1944 became notorious as Black Tuesday. In the morning 160 Lancaster bombers of 3 Group took off from their bases in Eastern England. The bomb run began at approximately 15.00 hrs. Exactly above Kamp-Lintfort Lancaster LM 684 of 514 Sqn., flown by F/O Limbert, was hit by flak. The bomb aimer jettisoned the bomb load in emergency and the bomber crashed. The whole crew died. These bombs fell into residential area of Kamp-Lintfort. Some following bombers were misled and dropped their bomb load into the city as well. 74 civilians died within the destroyed buildings. Yet most of the bombers found their target and damaged the plant repeatedly.'

In addition to LM684 and PD265, a third aircraft, NG121, JI-H, flown by F/O JH Tolley, was also badly damaged and crash-landed near Antwerp. The rear gunner baled out. He was Sgt WH Ellis, who survived as a POW. F/Lt. Harry Yates DFC of 75(NZ) Squadron from Mepal, described the loss of the three 514 Sqn aircraft in his book 'Luck and a Lancaster' (Airlife Publishing 1999):

'The familiar shell-bursts began to hang in the sky, multiplying every few seconds. An aircraft about a mile in front of us was hit, and then a second. Both began to trail smoke and flame. Their noses turned slowly, irrevocably downwards and their fate was sealed. A third aircraft, again about a mile ahead, took a direct hit, obviously in the bomb bay. The prodigious explosion distributed hundreds of burning fragments across the sky. There could be no parachutes but, sickened, I searched for them all the same.'

A more detailed account can be found in 'War Stories – Sgt Peter Gosnold' below.

Missing Aircraft:

LM684, JI-C was seen to explode as the aircraft approached the target. It is believed that it was hit by Flak, as described above. There were no survivors from the crew. The aircraft crashed next to a heavy flak emplacement named 'Grossbatterie Daubenspeckhof' on a farm approximately 1 km NW of Moers City Centre.

F/O RF Limbert	Pilot	KIA
F/O HL Hallam	Navigator	KIA
F/O ARL Lundie	Bomb Aimer	KIA
Sgt D Bolton	WOP/Air Gunner	KIA
Sgt AI Prescott	MU Gunner	KIA
Sgt C Stepney	Rear Gunner	KIA
Sgt R Scott	Flight Engineer	KIA

(Above) F/O Geoff France and his crew at RAF Waterbeach with an unidentified Lancaster prior to an earlier non-operational flight. L-R F/O Fred Eisberg (Navigator), F/Sgt Lewis Shaw (MU Gunner from another crew), Sgt Pete Coles (Rear Gunner), F/O Geoff France (Pilot), F/O Ken Barker (Bomb Aimer), Sgt Pete Gosnold (Flight Engineer), Sgt Ron Harding (WOP/AG). Photo courtesy of Rachel Rhodes, daughter of F/O France.

PD265, JI-G. After bombing the target the aircraft was hit by flak between the starboard inner engine and the cockpit, killing the flight engineer, Sgt Pete Gosnold, and injuring the pilot, F/O Geoff France, in the thigh. F/O France believed the aircraft was also hit in the tail as it became uncontrollable. He remembered bracing his feet on the instrument panel whilst attempting to pull the aircraft out of its dive. Baling out at more than 20,000 feet, F/O France saw another parachute, the navigator F/O Frederick Eisberg having also been thrown clear, fortunately wearing his parachute. F/O France noted the tail becoming detached, and the aircraft eventually exploding though whether this was on or above the ground he does not know. He landed in a cabbage field, breaking his left leg, so was unable to effect an escape. F/O Eisberg also landed in farmland whilst the aircraft came down in the moat surrounding the Grafschafter Castle in the centre of Moers. Both were captured, although separately. F/O

France subsequently lost his right leg due to untreated wounds turning gangrenous.

F/O GC France	*Pilot*	*POW*
F/O FJ Eisberg	*Navigator*	*POW*
F/O KH Barker RCAF	*Bomb Aimer*	*KIA*
Sgt RWI Harding	*WOP/Air Gunner*	*KIA*
F/O P Slater	*MU Gunner*	*KIA*
Sgt RP Coles	*Rear Gunner*	*KIA*
Sgt PA Gosnold	*Flight Engineer*	*KIA*

22nd November 1944.
Weather: Cloudy with occasional rain.
Non-Operational Flying: Fighter Affiliation and Air Tests.
Operational Flying: 514 Squadron is not required today or tonight. 19 aircraft required tomorrow.

23rd November 1944.
Weather: Cloudy with some rain.
Non-Operational Flying: Air to sea firing.
Operational Flying: BOMBING – NORDSTERN
19 aircraft airborne to attack Nordstern. Weather over target was 10/10ths cloud. Markers were concentrated but no results observed. 8 aircraft bombed on GH, 5 on GH leaders and 6 on flares. Slight to moderate heavy Flak - scattered. No fighters.
P/O SG Wright in JI-B, PB756, reported: Bomb load 1 x 4000 HC, 16 x 500 GP. Primary target: NORDSTERN. Bombed at 1521 hours from 18,000 feet on GH leader.

Target:	*Nordstern – Oil Plant*
Aircraft deployed total:	*168 (Lancasters)*
514 Squadron:	*19*
Aircraft lost total:	*1*
514 Squadron:	*Nil*

Comments: An accurate GH raid was carried out on the Nordstern plant at Gelsenkirchen.

24th November 1944.
Weather: Cloudy with drizzle. Fog after dusk.
Non-Operational Flying: Air Tests.
Operational Flying: No operations today or tonight.

25th November 1944.
Weather: Cloudy with rain, becoming fair.
Non-Operational Flying: GH bombing at Rushford and H2S Training.
Operational Flying: No operations today or tonight.

26th November 1944.
Weather: Mainly fine, becoming cloudy with rain.
Non-Operational Flying: 6 aircraft on 'Remould' exercise. GH Training and H2S Training. Note: 'Remould' exercise is not defined.
Operational Flying: No operations today or tonight. 22 aircraft required tomorrow.

27th November 1944.
Weather: Low cloud early then fair. Fog after dusk.
Non-Operational Flying: GH and H2S Training.
Operational Flying: BOMBING – COLOGNE.
22 aircraft took off to attack Cologne/Kalk Marshalling Yards. Weather was clear with haze over target. 4 aircraft bombed on GH, 11 aircraft on GH leaders and 7 aircraft bombed visually. Bombing was concentrated but there was scattered bombing to West and South-west. Much smoke seen over target. Five large explosions seen, 1 on West bank of the Rhine at 1506 hours and large fires. No fighters. Flak moderate to intense, predicted heavy Flak, accurate for height. 21 aircraft landed at base, 1 aircraft landed at Woodbridge with Rear Gunner wounded and severe flak damage.
F/L Ron Pickler in A2-G, PB423, reported: Bomb load 1 x 4000 HC, 15 x 500 GP, 1 Red/Green star flare. Primary target: COLOGNE. Bombed at 1504 hours from 19,800 feet on red TI. Flare brought back as GH unserviceable. At 1501 hours aircraft hit by flak making it very difficult to control. Bombing run completed and aircraft kept under control and flown back by combined efforts of pilot, engineer, air bomber, navigator and rear gunner on stick plus a length of rope. Mid upper gunner (F/S G Coulson RCAF) wounded in the head by Flak. Captain comments that the crew behaved splendidly.

Target: *Cologne – Kalk Nord Railway Yards*
Aircraft deployed total: *169 (Lancasters)*
514 Squadron: *22*
Aircraft lost total: *1*
514 Squadron: *Nil*

Comments: This GH raid on the Kalk Nord railway yards had good results, although one aircraft was lost. F/L Pickler received a DFC for his actions.

28th November 1944.
Weather: Low cloud, rain and drizzle, fair later.
Non-Operational Flying: Air Tests.
Operational Flying: 19 aircraft required early tomorrow morning for operations.

29th November 1944.
Weather: Fine becoming fair in the evening.
Non-Operational Flying: Flight Affiliation, GH and H2S Training.
Operational Flying: BOMBING – NEUSS
19 aircraft detailed. 18 aircraft took off and attacked primary target. 1 aircraft failed to take off (throttle jammed). Marking was fairly concentrated and several large explosions and glow of fires seen through cloud. 5 aircraft bombed on GH, 12 aircraft bombed on flares and 1 on H2S. Flak was negligible. 2 Fighters seen. 18 aircraft returned to base having completed their sortie. Weather was 10/10ths cloud over the target but the glow of fires was seen through cloud.
17 aircraft required tomorrow.
F/O AD Uffindell in JI-P PB482 reported: Bomb load 1 x 4000 HC, 6 x 1000 MC, 6 x 500 GP, 3 x flares red with green stars. Primary target: NEUSS. Bombed at 0535 hours from 19,000 feet on GH. Bright glow seen through cloud.

Target:	*Neuss - Area*
Aircraft deployed total:	*145*
514 Squadron:	*18*
Aircraft lost total:	*Nil*
514 Squadron:	*Nil*

Comments: This was a mainly GH raid without loss. Modest property damage was noted locally.

30th November 1944.

Weather: Fine.

Non-Operational Flying: GH bombing at Rushford, Fighter Affiliation, H2S Training.

Operational Flying: BOMBING – OSTERFELD

17 aircraft detailed. 17 aircraft took off and attacked the primary target. Weather was 10/10ths cloud, tops to 10,000 feet. 7 aircraft bombed on GH, 8 aircraft bombed on GH Leaders and 2 on flares. Bombing was fairly concentrated and a large pall of smoke was seen rolling up through the cloud. Flak was slight heavy. One of our aircraft (NG350, JI-C) hit over target - slightly damaged. All aircraft landed at base. 19 aircraft required tomorrow.

P/O AE Munro RAAF in NG350, JI-C reported: Bomb load 1 x 4000 HC, 16 x 500 GP. Primary target: OSTERFELD. Aircraft slightly damaged by flak.

Target:	*Osterfeld – Benzol Plant*
Aircraft deployed total:	*60 (Lancasters)*
514 Squadron:	*17*
Aircraft lost total:	*2*
514 Squadron:	*Nil*

Comments: 60 Lancasters attacked the benzol plant with the loss of 2 aircraft.

Monthly Summary for November 1944

Awards:

Aus/411168	F/O Morrison AH	Navigator	DFC	11/11/44
Aus/420266	F/O Pritchard K	Air Bomber	DFC	11/11/44
Can J9067	F/L Hoffman JW	Wireless Operator	DFC	11/11/44
132602	A/S/L Stewart DWA	Pilot	DFC	14/11/44
151536	A/F/L Hay ICS	Pilot	DFC	14/11/44
51634	F/O Grinter PAE	Navigator	DFC	14/11/44
151336	F/O MacLennan HC	Navigator	DFC	14/11/44
Aus/413783	F/O Mayes WG	Navigator	DFC	14/11/44
1175873	F/S Hounsome RA	Wireless Operator	DFM	14/11/44
Can J/18874	F/O Sauve AM	Air Gunner	DFC	18/11/44
Aus/423963	F/O Williams EE	Pilot	DFC	18/11/44
182447	A/F/O Merrett HL	Pilot	DFC	19/11/44
NZ/422315	A/F/O Petry LM	Pilot	DFC	19/11/44
178795	P/O Pick RO	Pilot	DFC	19/11/44
179615	A/F/O Watkins WM	Pilot	DFC	19/11/44
179828	P/O Hargreaves B	Wireless Operator	DFC	19/11/44
1592295	Sgt Dawson P	Air Gunner	DFM	19/11/44
1623889	Sgt Ferries B	Air Gunner	DFM	19/11/44
143269	F/O Limbert RF	Pilot	DFC	30/11/44
106323	F/O Hallam HL	Navigator	DFC	30/11/44

Operational:
Enemy Aircraft Destroyed: Nil
Operational Flying Hours for November 1944:   286.53
Non-Operational Flying Hours for November 1944: 186.26
Total tons of bombs dropped in November 1944: 1,451 tons.
Cumulative total tons of bombs dropped: 10,973 ¾ tons.
Number of sorties for November 1944:   302 carried out
                                                3 failed to take off
                                                6 early returns
                                                3 missing

Strength of Squadron as at 30th November 1944.

Aircrew: 118 Officers,
                                                264 SNCOs
Ground: 1 Officer (Adjutant)

December 1944

1st December 1944.
Weather: Slight rain during morning, otherwise fair.
Non-Operational Flying: Air/Sea Firing and Air Tests.
Operational Flying: No operations today or tonight, aircraft will be required tomorrow.
Tomorrow's operation cancelled, aircraft to remain bombed up.
2nd December 1944. Weather: Fair - fine with rain early.
Non-Operational Flying: G.H and H2S Training.
Operational Flying: 15 Aircraft required for a daylight target.
BOMBING – DORTMUND.
15 aircraft took off to attack Dortmund. Weather was 10/10ths cloud. Six aircraft bombed on GH, 8 on GH leaders and 1 on flares. Marker flares reported as well grouped. 5 aircraft were hit by Flak which was moderate/heavy accurate. 5 aircraft hit. No fighters seen. All aircraft landed.
No daylight target tomorrow for 3 Group.
S/L JG Timms, A2-L PD325, reported: 'Bomb load 14 x 1000 HC. Primary target DORTMUND. Bombed at 1456 ½ hours from 20,000 feet on leading aircraft. Aircraft hit by Flak. Mid upper turret and starboard inner and outer engines damaged. Mid Upper Gunner (W/O J Moran) wounded by flak.

Target:	*Dortmund – Hansa Benzol Plant*
Aircraft deployed total:	*93 (Lancasters)*
514 Squadron:	*15*
Aircraft lost total:	*Nil*
514 Squadron:	*Nil*

Comments: The force attacked the Hansa benzol plant, probably using GH. As was usual for 3 Group, the target was covered in cloud but this did not prevent the attack being carried out accurately.

3rd December 1944.
Weather: Some rain and drizzle, low cloud early.
Non-Operational Flying: Air tests carried out.
Operational Flying: No operations today or tonight. 20 aircraft are required for tomorrow.

4th December 1944.
Weather: Fine.
Non-Operational Flying: GH Training and Air tests.
Operational Flying: BOMBING – OBERHAUSEN.
20 aircraft detailed. 20 aircraft took off and attacked the primary target. Weather was 10/10ths cloud. Flares well grouped also aircraft when bombing. Very good attack. Flak slight, Heavy Flak. No fighters. 1 aircraft seen to be blown up by its own 4000 lb bomb. All aircraft landed safely at base.
F/O JF Ness in JI-E, NN717 reported: 'Bomb load 1 x 4000 HC, 6 x 100 MC, 6 x 500 GP. Primary target OBERHAUSEN. Bombed at 1408 hours from 20,000 feet on upwind edge of red flares.'
Derby figures will be required for tomorrow.

Target: *Oberhausen - Area*
Aircraft deployed total: *160 (Lancasters)*
514 Squadron: *20*
Aircraft lost total: *1*
514 Squadron: *Nil*

Comments: No results of this GH raid could be observed. However local reporting mentions heavy damage in the centre of the town, around the railway station.

5th December 1944.
Weather: Fine.
Non-Operational Flying: GH bombing carried out and Air Tests.
Operational Flying: BOMBING – HAMM - MARSHALLING YARDS.
21 aircraft detailed. 20 aircraft attacked the primary target. 1 returned early 1 aircraft returned early on account of oxygen failure but jettisoned load on Bochalt as last resort. Weather was 10/10ths cloud over the target but otherwise varying from 6-10/10ths. A good concentration of bombing was achieved. GH leader enthusiastic. Slight to nil heavy flak. No fighters. All aircraft landed.
F/O DC Gordon RAAF in JI-C, NG350 reported: Bomb load 1 x 4000 HC, 1950 x 4lb incendiaries. Primary target: HAMM. Bombed at 1130 hours from 20500 feet on GH Leader.

Target:	Hamm – Marshalling Yards
Aircraft deployed total:	94 (Lancasters)
514 Squadron:	21 (1 returned early)
Aircraft lost total:	Nil
514 Squadron:	Nil

Comments: This GH attack destroyed nearly 40 percent of Hamm's built up area. All our aircraft returned safely.

6th December 1944.
Weather: Fair, but cloudy in afternoon with light rain.
Non-Operational Flying: Air Tests carried out.
Operational Flying: BOMBING – MERSEBURG.
19 aircraft detailed. 15 attacked primary target and 4 returned early, one of these landing at Oakington. Weather was 10/10ths cloud with odd breaks. Electrical storm and icing over France. Master Bomber not helpful – reception poor. Clouds were lit up by searchlights and red glow. Large explosion at 2058 hours and another described as terrific at 2052 hours. Moderate to intense heavy Flak below. Fighter flares seen from front line to target and an occasional fighter. No combats.
All aircraft landed at base.
F/L Ron Pickler in PA186, A2-G, reported: Bomb load 1 x 4000 HC, 8 x 500 GP, 1 x 500 GP Long Delay. Primary target: MERSEBURG. Bombed at 2046 hours from 22500 feet on centre of Wanganui flares.

Target:	Merseburg – Leuna Oil Plant
Aircraft deployed total:	487
514 Squadron:	19 (4 returned early)
Aircraft lost total:	5
514 Squadron:	Nil

Comments: This target was in Eastern Germany, near Leipzig. Despite considerable cloud in the target area, considerable damage was recorded by post-raid photographs.

7th December 1944.
Weather: Fair.
Non-Operational Flying: GH Training and Air Tests.
Operational Flying: No operations today or tonight. 18 aircraft required tomorrow.

8th December 1944.
Weather: Fair, with rain in afternoon.
Non-Operational Flying: Air Tests.
Operational Flying: BOMBING – DUISBURG.
18 aircraft detailed. 18 aircraft attacked primary target. Weather 10/10ths cloud. Target marking good. Aircraft well together at bombing although adverse weather made formation keeping difficult. 17 aircraft landed at base, 1 aircraft landed at Woodbridge with flaps unserviceable. 15 aircraft required for tomorrow night.
F/O IJ Bittner RCAF in JI-L, NF966 reported: 'Bomb load 13 x 1000 ANM59, 1 red/green flare. Primary target DUISBURG. Bombed at 1105 hours from 21,000 feet.'

Target: *Duisburg – Railway Yards*
Aircraft deployed total: *163 (Lancasters)*
514 Squadron: *18*
Aircraft lost total: *Nil*
514 Squadron: *Nil*

Comments: *The Lancasters used GH to attack the cloud-covered railway yards, without loss.*

9th December 1944.
Weather: Fair with rain.
Non-Operational Flying: Nil on account of weather.
Operational Flying: Operation cancelled. 17 aircraft required for tomorrow.

10th December 1944.
Weather: Fair with rain in evening.
Non-Operational Flying: Fighter Affiliation and Air Test.
Operational Flying: No operations today or tonight. 17 aircraft required for tomorrow.

11th December 1944.
Weather: Fair to cloudy with some showers.
Non-Operational Flying: GH Training and Fighter Affiliation.
Operational Flying: BOMBING – OSTERFELD
17 aircraft took off to attack Osterfeld, Weather was 10/10ths cloud, tops up to 16,000 feet. Few marker flares were seen, but aircraft were in good formation while bombing. 2 aircraft were seen to blow up over

target. 1 aircraft 'C' F/O Hill is missing. 16 aircraft landed at base. 16 aircraft required tomorrow.

F/O D Crome, JI-A, NG203 reported 'Bomb load 1 x 4000 HC, 14 x 500 GP Long Delay, 1 flare. Primary target OSTERFELD. Bombed at 1108 hours from 20,000 feet on green flares.'

Target:	Osterfeld – Benzol Plant and Railway Yards
Aircraft deployed total:	150 (Lancasters)
514 Squadron:	17
Aircraft lost total:	1
514 Squadron:	1

Comments: This GH raid attacked the railway yards and 52 bombing the benzol plant. The only aircraft lost was from 514 Sqn.

Missing aircraft:

NG 350, JI-C. Hit by Flak and fell into a built up area of Sterkrade, destroying several houses. Sadly none of the crew survived. Sgts Balman and Bowen were 19 years old.

F/O E Hill	Pilot	KIA
F/O E Cowells	Navigator	KIA
F/S F Guest	Bomb Aimer	KIA
Sgt C Atter	WOP/AG	KIA
Sgt JH Balman	MU Gunner	KIA
Sgt AG Bowen	Rear Gunner	KIA
Sgt TA Readman	Flight Engineer	KIA

12th December 1944.
Weather: Fair.
Non-Operational Flying: H2S Training, GH Training and Fighter Affiliation.
Operational Flying: BOMBING – WITTEN.
16 aircraft detailed. 15 aircraft attacked primary target, 1 aircraft returned early. Weather 10/10ths cloud, tops 14/16,000 feet. Bombing reported as slightly scattered at first improving towards the end of the attack when the flares and bombing were reported as very concentrated. Results unobserved due to cloud. Enemy fighters seen but no contact with 514 Squadron. All aircraft landed.

F/L R Pickler in LM627, A2-H, reported: Bomb load 1 x 4000 HC. 5 x 500 GP. 6 x 500 ANM 58, 4 x 500 ANM 64. Primary target WITTEN. Bombed at 1405½ hours from 20,000 feet on GH.

Target: *Witten – Ruhrstahl Steel Works*
Aircraft deployed total: *140 (Lancasters)*
514 Squadron: *16 (1 returned early)*
Aircraft lost total: *8*
514 Squadron: *Nil*

Comments: On this GH raid the stream was attacked by night-fighters and 8 bombers were lost. This was the town's first major raid of the war and bombing missed the steelworks but was scattered all over the town.

13th December 1944.
Weather: Foggy.
Non-Operational Flying: Nil on account of weather.
Operational Flying: No operations today or tonight.

14th December 1944.
Weather: Early fog, Fair later.
Non-Operational Flying: H2S Training and Air Tests.
Operational Flying: 19 aircraft required for tonight.
Operation cancelled. 19 aircraft required tomorrow.

15th December 1944.
Weather: Misty with much cloud.
Non-Operational Flying: H2S Training and Air Tests.
Operational Flying: BOMBING – SIEGEN
19 aircraft took off. All aircraft recalled as fighters were unable to take off. All aircraft landed. 21 aircraft required for tomorrow.

16th December 1944.
Weather: Misty, otherwise fair.
Non-Operational Flying: GH bombing and Air Tests.
Operational Flying: BOMBING – SIEGEN.
21 aircraft detailed. 21 took off and 16 attacked the primary target. 5 aircraft returned early due to severe icing, 2 aircraft landed at Woodbridge. Weather was 7-10/10ths cloud, with very bad icing. Formation was ragged until just before the target where the concentration improved. Attack seems to have been good. A number of

Me109s were seen. No flak over target. Flak slight – heavy from Bonn and front line. 2 of our aircraft were hit. All aircraft landed.
F/L RA Pickler in PA186, A2-G reported: Bomb load 1 x 4000 HC, 5 x 1000 MC, 7 x 500 GP, 1 Flare. Primary target: SIEGEN. Bombed at 1500 hours from 18,000 feet on GH Leader. Aircraft hit by flak, bomb doors damaged.

Target:	*Siegen – Railway Yards*
Aircraft deployed total:	*108 (Lancasters)*
514 Squadron:	*21 (5 returned early)*
Aircraft lost total:	*1*
514 Squadron:	*Nil*

Comments: Most of the bombs from this GH attack hit the town itself and neighbouring Weidenau, most having missed the railway yards.

17th December 1944.
Weather: Rain early, fair later.
Non-operational Flying: GH and H2S Training and Air Tests.
Operational Flying: No operations today or tonight. 21 Aircraft required tomorrow

18th December 1944.
Weather: Fine, visibility poor later.
Non-Operational Flying: GH and H2S Training. Bombing at Holbeach.
Operational Flying: Today's target cancelled. No operations today or tonight. 21 Aircraft required tomorrow.

19th December 1944.
Weather: Foggy.
Non-Operational Flying: Nil on account of weather.
Operational Flying: Operations cancelled. Same aircraft required for tomorrow.

20th December 1944.
Weather: Foggy.
Non-operational Flying: Nil on account of weather.
Operational Flying: All Aircraft to take off if possible. Crews to stand by till further notice.
Attack now cancelled. 14 Aircraft required for same target tomorrow.

21st December 1944.
Weather: Foggy. Lifting during afternoon.
Non-operational Flying: Air Tests carried out.
Operational Flying: Attack is confirmed for this afternoon.
BOMBING - TRIER.
14 aircraft detailed. 14 aircraft took off. 1 abortive - bombs would not release. Weather 10/10 cloud, tops 6/9000 feet. Formation was good at bombing, smoke seen rising through cloud. Flak moderate, heavy at first, dwindling to Nil. Believed 4 fighters seen. 1 of our aircraft was hit by Flak. Richard Dimbleby from the B.B.C. flew in 'G2' with F/L RA Pickler, DFC. All aircraft landed safely at base. 14 aircraft required tomorrow.
F/L RA Pickler DFC in A2-G reported: Bomb load 1x 4000 HC, 10 x 500 GP, 2x 250 GP, 4 x 250 TI Red. Primary target: TRIER. Bombed at 1458 hours from 18,000 feet on GH.

Target:	*Trier – Railway Yards*
Aircraft deployed total:	*113 (Lancasters)*
514 Squadron:	*14*
Aircraft lost total:	*Nil*
514 Squadron:	*Nil*

Comments: No results were observed because of cloud though smoke was noted. Heavy casualties were reported by ground sources but there are no other details available.

22nd December 1944.
Weather: Fog, with drizzle and low cloud.
Non-Operational Flying: Nil on account of weather.
Operational Flying: Attack will now be for GH aircraft only.
Attack cancelled on account of weather, crews are to standby. 14 aircraft required tomorrow.

23rd December 1944.
Weather: Foggy early, cloud later.
Non-Operational Flying: GH and H2S Training.
Operational Flying: BOMBING – TRIER.
14 aircraft detailed. 14 aircraft attacked primary. Weather, clear over target and the Red markers were reported as concentrated over the town, and the MB gave precise instructions as to bombing. The place was easily identified and the town on leaving was one mass of brown smoke rising up to 8,000 feet and the attack was an unqualified

success. Numerous explosions were reported. Flak was reported as moderate H/F. No enemy fighters seen. All aircraft returned safely to Base. 14 aircraft required tomorrow.

F/O DW Parks in NG203, JI-A, reported: Bomb load 1 x 4000 HC, 10 x 500 GP, 2 x 250 GP, 4 x 259 TI Red. Primary target: PRIER. Bombed at 1429 hours from 18,000 feet visually.

Target:	*Trier – Railway Yards*
Aircraft deployed total:	153 (Lancasters)
514 Squadron:	14
Aircraft lost total:	1
514 Squadron:	Nil

Comments: Another attempt, probably using GH, to bomb the railway yards through cloud, losing a single aircraft in the process. On this occasion, bombing appeared to be concentrated and accurate but the only local report just states that this was the town's worst raid of the war.

24th December 1944.
Weather: Foggy.
Non-Operational Flying: Nil on account of weather.
Operational Flying: Operation postponed until this evening.
Operation cancelled. Another target received, 14 aircraft to stand by to take off at the shortest possible notice.

25th December 1944.
Weather: Foggy.
Non-Operational Flying: Nil on account of weather.
Operational Flying: Operation cancelled owing to dense fog. No operations today or tonight. 14 aircraft required for tomorrow.

26th December 1944.
Weather: Foggy.
Non-Operational Flying: Nil owing to weather.
Operational Flying: Operation cancelled, on account of weather. 14 aircraft required for tomorrow.

27th December 1944. Weather: Foggy
Non-Operational Flying: Nil, on account of weather.
Operational Flying: BOMBING - RHEYDT.

7 aircraft detailed, 1 was withdrawn iced up and batteries low. Ready too late. 6 aircraft took off to attack Rheydt Marshalling Yards. Weather was clear and target well marked. Yards were left a mass of billowing smoke and attack was thought highly successful. Flak practically nil. No fighters. All aircraft landed safely at base in spite of bad weather conditions. 14 aircraft required tomorrow.
F/O F Stephens, RAAF, in PD325, JI- L2, reported: Bomb load 7 x 1000 MC, 6 x 500 GP, 3 x 250 GP. Primary target: RHEYD. Bombed at 1500 hours from 20,000 feet. Centre of Red TIs.

Target: *Rheydt – Marshalling Yards*
Aircraft deployed total: *211*
514 Squadron: *6*
Aircraft lost total: *2*
514 Squadron: *Nil*

Comments: No details are available, other than the 514 Sqn report above. So according to us the raid was an outstanding success, and no one has said differently.

28th December 1944.
Weather: Fog early, then almost cloudless with haze. Severe frost.
Non-Operational Flying: Extensive GH and H2S. Training
Operational Flying: BOMBING KÖLN GREMBERG.
14 aircraft detailed, 14 aircraft took off and attacked primary target. Target was obscured by 10/10ths cloud and fog. Aircraft were so close together at bombing as to risk collision. Although two or three lots of flares seen 3 minutes before ETA, large plumes of smoke seen to rise above undercast. Flak negligible. No fighters. All aircraft landed. 14 aircraft required for operations for tomorrow.
F/O D Crome in NG203, JI-A, reported: Bomb load 7 x 1000 MC, 6 x 500 GP, 2 x 250 GP, 1 Flare. Primary target: KÖLN GREMBERG. Bombed at 1506 hours from 20,000 feet on GH.

Target: *Köln Gremberg – Marshalling Yards*
Aircraft deployed total: *167 (Lancasters)*
514 Squadron: *14*
Aircraft lost total: *Nil*
514 Squadron: *Nil*

Comments: The force, using GH, carried out an accurate attack on the railway yards, without loss.

29th December 1944.
Weather: Hazy early. Severe frost.
Non-Operational Flying: Extensive GH and H2S. Training.
Operational Flying: 'L2' blew up on dispersal. 7 other aircraft seriously damaged and casualties amongst ground personnel. Station Commander cancelled operations, on account of danger of long delay bombs on remainder of aircraft exploding.

PD325, A2-L. PD325 was bombed up with a 4000 lb. cookie and a mixture of 500 lb. and 250 lb. bombs, totalling 11,000 lbs. It is thought that the cause might have been one of the 250 lb. bombs, many of which were well past their best, detonating and taking the rest with it. NG141, PD324, NG118 and LM727 were amongst those seriously damaged. The following 514 Squadron ground crew lost their lives when PD325 exploded:

Cpl J Westgarth
LAC DG Bichard
LAC S Bolton
AC2 DV Brewer
LAC R Davies
LAC GG Hayden
AC1 HG Leach
LAC L Smales
LAC FC Watson

30th December 1944.
Weather: Fine, with keen frost.
Non-Operational Flying: GH and H2S. Training.
Operational Flying: No bombing today or tonight. 10 aircraft required for tomorrow.

31st December 1944.
Weather: Fine with keen frost.
Non-Operational Flying: GH and H2S. Training.
Operational Flying: BOMBING – VOHWINKEL.
10 aircraft detailed, 10 aircraft took off and attacked primary target. The weather on approaching target was 10/10 cloud although the target itself was clear. There were at least two bomber streams, one stream at least ½ mile to starboard and consequently at least two areas of bombing. Consensus of opinion was the raid was scattered with the Northern part of Vohwinkel receiving some of the bombs and the area

containing the marshalling yards the other. Marshalling yards reported as covered in smoke. Winds were troublesome and navigation difficult. Flak over the target was negligible and no fighters seen.

F/O D Crome in NG203, JI-A, reported: Bomb load 1 x 4000 HC, 3 x 1000 M65, 2 x 500 GP, 2 x 500 ANM58, 2 x 500 GP L/Delay, 4 x 250 GP. Primary target: VOHWINKEL. Bombed at 1440 hours from 20,000 feet on GH.

(Above) The crew of F/O F Stephens RAAF with their Lancaster LM685, JI-K completing their tour after returning from the op to Vohwinkle on New Year's Eve 1944. Crew: F/O Frederick Stephens (Pilot), Sgt DJ Taylor (Flight Engineer), Sgt WO Harradine (Navigator), Sgt FWP Daldry (Bomb Aimer), F/S AW Bennington (W/Operator), Sgt MH Hanley (MU Gunner), Sgt PE Steele (Rear Gunner). LM685 (as JI-B by then) was lost over Dortmund on 3rd February 1945, with F/O Fisher and crew. Source: courtesy of Sam Stephens, great nephew of F/O F Stephens.

Target: *Vohwinkel – Railway Yards.*
Aircraft deployed total: *155 (Lancasters)*
514 Squadron: *10*
Aircraft lost total: *2 (Lancasters)*
514 Squadron: *Nil*

Comments: 3 Group carried out a GH attack on the railway yards at Vohwinkel, near Solingen, though strong winds resulted in much of the bombing being south of the target. 2 Lancasters failed to return.

Monthly Summary for December 1944

Awards:

66013	A/S/L Dods M	Pilot	DFC	4/12/44
138695	A/S/L Prager HET	Pilot	DSO	4/12/44
185934	A/F/O Tolley JH	Pilot	DFC	7/12/44
128922	F/Lt Pickler RA	Pilot	DFC	10/12/44
178865	A/F/O Topham JB	Pilot	DFC	23/12/44
176513	F/O Smith GW	Pilot	DFC	28/12/44
183874	A/F/O Marks TC	Pilot	DFC	28/12/44

Operational:

Enemy Aircraft Destroyed:	Nil
Operational Flying Hours for December 1944:	999.20
Non-Operational Flying Hours for December 1944:	95.20
Total tons of bombs dropped in December 1944:	1,086 tons.
Cumulative total tons of bombs dropped:	12,059 ¾ tons.
Number of Sorties for December 1944:	193 carried out
	1 failed to take off
	11 early returns
	1 missing

Strength of Squadron as at 31st December 1944.

Aircrew:	144 Officers
	288 SNCOs
Ground:	1 Officer (Adjutant)

January 1945

1st January 1945.
Weather: Fine, becoming foggy, with slight rain at night.
Non-Operational Flying: GH and H2S. Training.
Operational Flying: 11 Aircraft required to attack Vohwinkel.
BOMBING- VOHWINKEL.
10 aircraft detailed. 1 aircraft failed to take off. 9 aircraft attacked the primary target. Weather was clear, and marking reported as concentrated. Bombing reported as accurate. Flak over target slight. Searchlights not troublesome though numerous. Combats nil. 2 Me109s sighted. All aircraft landed.
F/O SG Wright in NF968, JI-B reported: Bomb load: 1 x 4000 HC, 12 x 500 GP, 4 Red Tis. Primary target: VOHWINKEL. Bombed at 1945 hours from 20,500 feet on GH.

Target: *Vohwinkel – Railway Yards*
Aircraft deployed total: *146*
514 Squadron: *9*
Aircraft lost total: *1*
514 Squadron: *Nil*

Comments: 3 Group returned to successfully attack the railway yards using GH, 1 aircraft being lost.

2nd January 1945.
Weather: Fog early, then fine.
Non-Operational Flying: GH and H2S. Training.
Operational Flying: 10 Aircraft required to attack Nuremburg. 4 Aircraft required for target tomorrow.
BOMBING – NUREMBERG.
10 aircraft detailed. 10 aircraft took off and attacked the primary target. Weather was clear. Marking concentration and Master Bomber clear and concise. Slight inaccurate heavy Flak. Few searchlights and few fighters seen. Ju88 and Me410. One Rear Gunner 514/J2 fired 2 bursts at twin-engine fighter. No claim. All aircraft landed.
F/O LP Baines in NF968 JI-B reported: Bomb load 1 x 4000 HC, 7 x 500 Clusters. Primary target: NUREMBERG. Bombed at 1937 hours from 18,000 feet. Undershot TIs on Master Bomber's instructions.

Combat Report - Pro-forma:
Aircraft: 'J2'
Captain: F/O CIM Nicholl RCAF
Target: NUREMBERG
At 1844 hours, height 12,000 feet, position 4535N 0903E. Rear Gunner sighted T/E unidentified A/C at 800 yards. Gunner ordered corkscrew and simultaneously opened fire with a short burst. Aircraft was lost in corkscrew manoeuvre and was not seen again. Visibility was good, with no moon. There were a series of fighter flares astern up. No searchlights or flak reported.
MU Gunner – Sgt T Smyth - Nil.
Rear Gunner – Sgt EB Dobbin - 100 rounds.

Target:	*Nuremberg - Area*
Aircraft deployed total:	*519*
514 Squadron:	*10*
Aircraft lost total:	*6*
514 Squadron:	*Nil*

Comments: PFF produced good marking in clear visibility, the city centre being destroyed. The Rathaus, castle and some 2,000 preserved medieval buildings succumbed to the attack, along with 4,640 dwellings, mostly flats, and industrial premises including those of MAN and Siemens.

3rd January 1945.
Weather: Fair at first, slight rain later.
Non-Operational Flying: Fighter Affiliation and GH Training at Holbeach. 13 Aircraft required for target tomorrow.
BOMBING – DORTMUND-HUCKARDE.
4 aircraft detailed. 4 aircraft took off and bombed the primary target. Weather over target 10/10ths cloud. Formations over target reported as good although slightly elongated. Bombing concentrated and also Red and Green flares. Results entirely unobserved. Moderate heavy Flak barrage over target. No fighters seen. All aircraft landed.
F/O SG Wright in NF968, JI-B reported: Bomb load 1 x 4000 HC, 12 x 500ANM58 or 64, 3 x 500 GP, 1 Flare. Primary target: DORTMUND. Bombed at 1533 hours from 19,100 feet on GH.

Target:	*Dortmund – Huckarde Benzol Plant*
Aircraft deployed total:	*99*
514 Squadron:	*4*
Aircraft lost total:	*1*
514 Squadron:	*Nil*

Comments: This was a two-pronged GH attack on the Dortmund and Castrop-Rauxel benzol plants. Bombing was assessed as accurate, with a single Lancaster being lost from the Dortmund raid.

4th January 1945.
Weather: Fair early, then snow showers later.
Non-Operational Flying: GH and H2S. Training, also Fighter Affiliation.
Operational Flying: Operation cancelled. Nothing further today or tonight. 14 Aircraft required for target tomorrow.

5th January 1945. Weather: Snow showers early, then mainly fair.
Non-Operational Flying: GH and H2S. Training.
Operational Flying: BOMBING – LUDWIGSHAVEN.

14 aircraft detailed, 14 aircraft took off and 13 attacked primary target, 1 attacked last resort. Weather was clear over target. Marshalling Yards easily identified. Bombing was scattered at first, later tended to improve and the Marshalling Yard was definitely hit, although cannot be classified as a first class effort. Flak was moderate to intense, accurate and predicted, and split up the formation and affected the bombing. 11 aircraft damaged by Flak. No enemy fighters seen. 7 Aircraft required to attack Neuss tomorrow. All aircraft landed safely, 1 at Woodbridge.
F/O JN Gallicano RCAF in PD334 A2-D reported: Bomb load 1 x 4000 HC, 10 x 500 ANM58 or 64, 2 x 500 GP, 1 Flare. Primary target: LUDWIGSHAVEN. Bombed at 1508 hours from 21,000 feet on leading GH aircraft. Aircraft hit by Flak- Mid-upper turret damaged.

Target:	*Ludwigshaven – Railway Yards*
Aircraft deployed total:	*160 (Lancasters)*
514 Squadron:	*14*
Aircraft lost total:	*2*
514 Squadron:	*Nil*

Comments: In this GH attack, the yards were hit along with surrounding residential and industrial areas.

6th January 1945.
Weather: Fog early, then slight drizzle - becoming fine later, but only moderate visibility.
Non-Operational Flying: GH and H2S Training.
Operational Flying: Today's target cancelled. Same target for tonight.
BOMBING NEUSS.
7 aircraft detailed, 7 took off and attacked primary target. Weather 8-10/10ths low cloud over target. Target reported to be well marked with Red Tis and sky markers very concentrated and all crews reported a good concentration of bombing. Ground identification impossible due to cloud. Few results seen apart from explosion at 1850 hours. Flak slight to moderate, accurate for height. No enemy aircraft seen. All aircraft landed.
P/O AE Munro RAAF in PB902 JI-A reported: Bomb load 1 x 4000 HC, 2 x 500 ANM58, 12 x 500 ANM64. Primary target: NEUSS. Bombed at 1848 ½ hours from 20,000 feet on Red and Green flares.

Target:	*Neuss- Railway Yards*
Aircraft deployed total:	*147 (Lancasters)*
514 Squadron:	*7*
Aircraft lost total:	*1*
514 Squadron:	*Nil*

Comments: Lancasters attacked railway yards with one Lancaster crashing in Belgium. Most bombing was scattered over surrounding districts with damage to residential and public buildings.

7th January 1945.
Weather: Fair early, slight rain in the morning. Snow showers in the afternoon. Then fine.
Non-Operational Flying: GH and H2S Training.
Operational Flying: 11 Aircraft required for target tonight.
BOMBING – MUNICH.
11 aircraft detailed. 10 aircraft took off and 8 attacked primary target, 2 aircraft returned early. Weather was 10/10ths cloud over target 6-8000 feet with a thin layer altitude 16,000 feet. Target marking began punctually at 2228 hours and reported as an average concentration of Red and Green markers, although intervals occurred where none were seen. All crews bombed on flares, no TIs seen. Reflection of fires seen below clouds. Flak was slight to moderate. Occasional sighting of enemy aircraft. No combats. All aircraft landed.

F/L RH Marks in LM724, JI-H, reported: Bomb load 1 x 1000 ANM65, 1 x 500 ANM58, 1080 x 4 lb. IB, 120 x 4 X IB. Primary target: MUNICH. Bombed at 2243½ hours from 20,200 feet on Red and Green flares.

Target: *Munich - Area*
Aircraft deployed total: *654*
514 Squadron: *10 (2 returned early)*
Aircraft lost total: *15*
514 Squadron: *Nil*

Comments: In what was the last major raid on Munich, a successful area raid was claimed with the centre and some industrial areas being severely damaged.

8th January 1945.
Weather: Fine early, then snow and hail showers and fine periods.
Non-Operational Flying: Air Tests and GH Training.
Operational Flying: No operations today or tonight. 12 Aircraft to be bombed up.

9th January 1945.
Weather: Snow during morning, fog in afternoon. Further snow showers later.
Non-Operational Flying: Nil on account of weather.
Operational Flying: No operations today or tonight.

10th January 1945.
Weather: Snow showers and fog early - thin cloud - then further snow showers in the afternoon and evening.
Non-Operational Flying: Nil owing to weather.
Operational Flying: No operations today or tonight. 11 Aircraft required to attack Krefeld tomorrow.

11th January 1945.
Weather: Mainly fair until evening, then snow.
Non-Operational Flying: GH and H2S Training.
Operational Flying: BOMBING – KREFELD MARSHALLING YARDS.
12 aircraft detailed. 11 aircraft took off and attacked primary target. 1 failed to take off. Weather 10/10ths cloud above and below. Visibility poor. Crews had the impression that the attack was concentrated

although some aircraft were seen to bomb above 20,000 feet. Flak slight. No fighters. All aircraft landed. 13 Aircraft required for target tomorrow.
F/O LP Baines RNZAF in PB902, JI-A, reported: Bomb load 1 x 4000 HC, 10 x 500 ANM64, 4 x 250 GP. Primary target: KREFELD. Bombed at 1516 hours from 20,000 feet on GH Leader.

Target: *Krefeld – Marshalling Yards*
Aircraft deployed total: *152*
514 Squadron: *11*
Aircraft lost total: *Nil*
514 Squadron: *Nil*

Comments: This GH raid on the railway yards was locally described as a 'large attack', though no further details are available. No aircraft were lost.

12th January 1945.
Weather: Slight sleet early, then rain and drizzle and low cloud persisting.
Non-Operational Flying: Nil on account of weather.
Operational Flying: Todays operation cancelled. 13 Aircraft required for target tonight.
3 Group not required tonight. 13 Aircraft required for tomorrow.

13th January 1945.
Weather: Cloudy with low cloud and almost continuous drizzle.
Non-Operational Flying: GH Bombing at Holbeach and H2S Training.
Operational Flying: BOMBING - SAARBRUCKEN MARSHALLING YARDS.
13 aircraft detailed. 13 aircraft took off and 12 attacked primary target. 1 returned early. All aircraft were diverted on return to Exeter as weather at Base was unfit to land. Weather 3-5/10ths cloud, tops 4/5,000 feet. 2 aircraft bombed on GH, the rest on leaders. All crews could check visually position of Marshalling Yards. On leaving the target was covered with smoke. Blue puffs reported as excellent means of marking. Flak almost non-existent. No fighters seen.
F/S CG Fiset, NG298, JI-E, reported: Bomb load 1 x 4000 HC, 10 x 500 ANM58 or 64, 4 x 250 GP. Primary target: SAARBRUCKEN. Bombed at 1522 hours from 20,000 feet on leading aircraft.

Target:	*Saarbrucken – Marshalling Yards*
Aircraft deployed total:	*158*
514 Squadron:	*13 (1 returned early)*
Aircraft lost total:	*1*
514 Squadron:	*Nil*

Comments: This GH attack on the railway yards was apparently accurate though with some overshooting. 1 Lancaster crashed in France.

14th January 1945.
Weather: Cloudy.
Non-Operational Flying: Air Sea Firing, GH Training and Air Tests.
Operational Flying: No operations today or tonight. Derby Aircraft to be bombed up for target tomorrow.

15th January 1945.
Weather: Fog early and slight rain or drizzle - fair in the afternoon - fog at night.
Non-Operational Flying: GH and H2S. Training.
Operational Flying: BOMBING – LAGENDREER.
14 aircraft detailed, 14 aircraft took off, 13 attacked primary target, 1 aircraft landed at Manston. Weather 10/10ths cloud. Formation good en route and at bombing. After leaving the target, stream turned off early and passed over North Ruhr defences and too far eastwards. Flak over target slight to moderate heavy flak. 5 aircraft hit by Ruhr defences. No enemy aircraft seen. Derby figures to be bombed up for target tomorrow.
F/O LJW Sutton in PB419, JI-J, reported: Bomb load 1 x 4000 HC, 10 x 500 ANM64, 4 x 250 GP, 1 Flare. Primary target: LAGENDREER. Bombed at 1500 hours from 19,000 feet on GH Leader.

Target:	*Lagendreer – Robert Muser Benzol Plant*
Aircraft deployed total:	*63 (Lancasters)*
514 Squadron:	*14*
Aircraft lost total:	*Nil*
514 Squadron:	*Nil*

Comments: The Lancasters carried out a GH attack without loss on the Robert Muser benzol plant in the suburb of Lagendreer, Bochum. There was no assessment available.

16th January 1945.
Weather: Fog and slight drizzle, cloudy later.
Non-Operational Flying: Nil on account of weather.
Operational Flying: Today's (daylight) target cancelled. 14 aircraft required for a target tonight.
BOMBING – WANNE-EICKEL.
14 aircraft detailed, 14 aircraft took off, 13 attacked the primary target, 1 aircraft missing. 10/10ths thin low cloud. Most aircraft arrived late on the target. Marking being spread out in time in consequence. Bombing appeared concentrated. Slight/moderate heavy flak barrage over target with DÜSSELDORF defences in action. 1 Ju88 seen in target area, but no combats seen.
F/O LJW Sutton in NG203, JI-C, reported: Bomb load 1 x 4000 HC, 10 x 500 ANM58, 4 x 250 GP. Primary target: WANNE-EICKEL. Bombed at 0222 hours from 20,000 feet on GH.

Target:	*Wanne-Eickel Benzol Plant*
Aircraft deployed total:	*138 (Lancasters)*
514 Squadron:	*14*
Aircraft lost total:	*1*
514 Squadron:	*1*

Comments: The benzol plant was the target with our Lancaster being the only loss. No results are recorded.

Missing aircraft:

PB906 A2-B. Lost without trace. All crew commemorated on the Runnymede Memorial. This was the only aircraft lost in action on this raid and RAF reports (mentioned in 'Nachtjagd War Diaries') note that it 'exploded'. There is no record of Nachtjagd claims of specific aircraft shot down though there were clearly night fighters active, as mentioned in the summary above. It is therefore considered likely that PB906 was lost to an unidentified night fighter at an unknown location. F/O GD Orr had previously been disciplined for failing to fly at a specified altitude, which had been due, he explained, to icing conditions.

F/O GD Orr	*Pilot*	*KIA*
F/S J Bryson	*Navigator*	*KIA*
F/S TF Wilcox	*Air Bomber*	*KIA*
Sgt A McGlone	*WOP/Air*	*KIA*
F/S HE Bishop	*MU Gunner*	*KIA*
F/S G Spencer	*Rear Gunner*	*KIA*
Sgt R Werrill	*Flight Engineer*	*KIA*
F/O ML Matkin RCAF	*Second Pilot*	*KIA*

17th January 1945.
Weather: Mainly cloudy.
Non-Operational Flying: GH and H2S. Training.
Operational Flying: No operations today or tonight. Derby aircraft to be bombed up for tomorrow.

18th January 1945.
Weather: Cloudy with occasional slight rain.
Non-Operational Flying: GH and H2S Training.
Operational Flying: No operations today or tonight.

11 Aircraft required tonight.
Operation cancelled.

19th January 1945.
Weather: Snow showers early, otherwise fair.
Non-Operational Flying: Nil on account of weather.
Operational Flying: 11 Aircraft required for tonight.
Operation cancelled.

20th January 1945.
Weather: Fair till noon, then continuous snow showers.
Non-Operational Flying: GH and H2S Training.
Operational Flying:
11 Aircraft required tonight.
Operation cancelled.

21st January 1945.
Weather: Mainly fair.
Non-Operational Flying: GH and H2S. Training.
Operational Flying: 12 Aircraft required tonight.
Operation cancelled.
12 Aircraft required for daylight tomorrow.

22nd January 1945.
Weather: Fine early, snow showers in afternoon.
Non-Operational Flying: GH and H2S Training, and Air Sea Firing.
Operational Flying: Operation cancelled.
12 Aircraft required tonight.
BOMBING – THYSSEN WORKS AT HAMBORN.
12 aircraft detailed. 12 aircraft took off and attacked primary target. Weather over target was clear and almost as bright as day. All crews identified target by the concentration of Red and Green TIs which were reported as U concentrated and correctly placed. Bombing reported as good and the target on leaving was covered with smoke and fires, and numerous heavy explosions were heard. Flak slight to moderate, heavy flak, decreasing as attack progressed. No fighters seen. All aircraft landed at Base.

(Above) Target photo of Hamborn suburb of Duisburg from PB902, JI-A flown by F/O LP Baines, bombing at 2006½ hours from 20000 feet. Photo dated 1944 in error. Source: Crown Copyright / National Archive.

F/L JF Ness RCAF in PB426 JI-D reported: Bomb load 1 x 4000 HC, 7 x 500 ANM58 or 64, 2 x 500 GP (L/Delay) 3 x 250 GP. Primary target: HAMBORN. Bombed at 2009 ½ hours from 19,000 feet. (Bomb sight not used as aircraft had to take evasive action from flak)

Target: *Hamborn – Thyssen Steel Works*
Aircraft deployed total: *302*
514 Squadron: *12*
Aircraft lost total: *2*
514 Squadron: *Nil*

Comments: The aircraft were tasked with attacking the benzol plant in the Bruckhausen district, resulting in much damage. By misidentification of the target, or scattering of the attack, bombing spread to the nearby Thyssen steelworks, which received 500 high explosive bombs. However it is, perhaps, significant that the author of the 514 Sqn ORB listed the Thyssen steelworks as the specific target.

23rd January 1945.
Weather: Snow showers, cloudy to fair in afternoon.
Non-Operational Flying: Formation Flying, GH and H2S Training.
Operational Flying: No operations today or tonight. Derby Aircraft to be bombed up for tomorrow.

24th January 1945.
Weather: Cloudy, with fog and snow.
Non-Operational Flying: Nil on account of weather.
Operational Flying: Operation cancelled. No operations today or tonight. 13 Aircraft required tomorrow.

25th January 1945.
Weather: Thick fog all day.
Non-Operational Flying: Nil owing to weather.
Operational Flying: Operation cancelled. No operations today or tonight.

26th January 1945.
Weather: Fog, with slight clearance in afternoon.
Non-Operational Flying: Nil owing to weather.
Operational Flying: No operations today or tonight. 14 Aircraft required for tomorrow.

27th January 1945.
Weather: Fog during morning, snow showers later.
Non-Operational Flying: Air tests.
Operational Flying: Operation cancelled. No operations tonight. 14 Aircraft required tomorrow.

28th January 1945.
Weather: Slight snow, fair during afternoon.
Non-Operational Flying: GH and H2S. Training.
Operational Flying: BOMBING – KÖLN-GREMBERG MARSHALLING YARDS.
14 aircraft detailed. 14 aircraft took off and 13 attacked the primary target. Weather 10/10ths cloud en route clearing on approach to target where visibility was good and nil cloud. Bombing at first reported as scattered but later improved and the Marshalling Yards were straddled the whole length. . The attack became concentrated in later stages and the Marshalling Yards well straddled. Flak slight/moderate, accurate. 8 Aircraft were damaged. No enemy fighters seen. All Aircraft landed. 13 Aircraft required for tomorrow.
F/L R Worthing in PB 902, JI-A, reported: Bomb load, 10 x 500 ANM64, 1 x 4000 HC, 2 x 500 GP, 3 x 250 GP. Primary target: KÖLN-GREMBERG. Bombed at 1411 ½ hours from 20,000 feet on GH Leader.

Target:	*Köln-Gremberg Marshalling Yards*
Aircraft deployed total:	*153 (Lancasters)*
514 Squadron:	*14*
Aircraft lost total:	*4*
514 Squadron:	*Nil*

Comments: Lancasters attacked the railway yards in good visibility with mixed results. 1 Lancaster crashed in France.

29th January 1945.
Weather: Fair during morning, fog and slight snow later.
Non-Operational Flying: GH Bombing at Holbeach and H2S. Training.
Operational Flying: BOMBING – KREFELD.
13 aircraft detailed. 12 aircraft took off – 10 attacked primary target and 2 could not release bombs over target. Weather 10/10ths low thin cloud over target although clear patches en-route. Bomber stream and bombing reported as very concentrated and the attack should prove a success. Brownish smoke seen rising above the cloud. Only slight heavy flak over target. Trip very uneventful. All aircraft landed.
F/O JF Ness RCAF in NF968, JI-B, reported: Bomb load 1 x 4000 HC, 10 x 500 ANM64, 2 x 500 GP, 4 x 250 GP. Primary target: KREFELD MARSHALLING YARDS. Bombed at 1359½ hours from 19,700 feet on GH.

Target: *Krefeld – Uerdingen Railway Yards*
Aircraft deployed total: *148*
514 Squadron: *12*
Aircraft lost total: *Nil*
514 Squadron: *Nil*

Comments: Although bombing was claimed as accurate, a local report suggested otherwise.

30th January 1945.
Weather: Fog and snow, fair in the afternoon, fog later.
Non-Operational Flying: Nil on account of weather.
Operational Flying: No operations today or tonight. 14 Aircraft required tomorrow.

31st January 1945.
Weather: Fog at first, low cloud and rain later.
Non-Operational Flying: Nil on account of weather.
Operational Flying: Operation cancelled. 14 Aircraft required tomorrow.

Monthly Summary for January 1945

Awards: Nil

Operational:

Enemy Aircraft Destroyed:	Nil
Operational Flying Hours for January 1945:	787.45
Non-Operational Flying Hours for January 1945:	388.55
Total tons of bombs dropped in January 1945:	583¼ tons
Cumulative total tons of bombs dropped:	12,643¼ tons

Number of Sorties for January 1945: 151 carried out
4 failed to take off
3 early returns
1 missing

Strength of Squadron as at 31st January, 1945.
Aircrew: 128 Officers
254 SNCOs
Ground: 1 Officer (Adjutant)

Total: 383

February 1945

1st February 1945.
Weather: Occasional rain and drizzle.
Non-Operational Flying: GH Bombing, H2S and GH Cross Countries, and Air Tests.
Operational Flying: BOMBING – MUNCHEN-GLADBACH MARSHALLING YARDS.
14 aircraft detailed. 14 aircraft took off and attacked primary. Formation arrived late and the bomber stream rather long. All results unobserved. Results difficult to ascertain, probably scattered. Flak slight. All aircraft landed at Base. 14 Aircraft required for tomorrow.
F/O HC Mottershead in PB423, A2-L, reported: Bomb load 1 x 4000 HC, 14 x No. 14 Clusters. Primary target: MUNCHEN-GLADBACH. Bombed at 1633 hours from 17,600 feet on leading aircraft.

Target: *Mönchengladbach Marshalling Yards*
Aircraft deployed total: *160 (Lancasters)*
514 Squadron: *14*
Aircraft lost total: *1*
514 Squadron: *Nil*

Comments: The force of Lancasters attacked the town using GH through almost complete cloud cover. Results are not known. 1 aircraft crashed in France.

2nd February 1945.
Weather: Rain and drizzle early, fine later.
Non-Operational Flying: GH Bombing and H2S and GH Training Flights.
Operational Flying: BOMBING – WIESBADEN.
14 aircraft detailed. 1 aircraft failed to take off – Radar trouble. 13 aircraft took off, 1 aircraft missing. 12 attacked primary target. 'C2' F/O WE McLean missing. Weather 10/10ths cloud. Winds very erratic. Attack believed to cover a large area, and 1 Aircraft which was forced down to 3,000 feet in an explosion, reported the built up area a mass of flames. Flak reported as slight. No combats, but a few sightings of Me109 and Ju88. 2 aircraft damaged by heavy flak and 1 aircraft seen to explode in target area. 11 aircraft landed at Base.
F/L TW Hurley in PB209, JI-A reported: Bomb load 1 x 4000 HC, 10 x 500 ANM64, 2 x 500 GP, 4 x 250 GP. Primary target: WIESBADEN. Bombed at 0001 hours from 18,700 feet on Gee fix.

Target: Wiesbaden - Area
Aircraft deployed total: 507
514 Squadron: 13
Aircraft lost total: 3
514 Squadron: 1

Comments: This was Bomber Command's only large raid on the town, with most of the bombing, through complete cloud cover, hitting the area including the railway station. Approximately 1,000 people on the ground were killed in the raid. 3 Lancasters crashed in France.

Missing Aircraft:

NN772 A2-C. The aircraft was hit by flak, just after releasing its bomb load. The aircraft came down at Springen, 6km W of Bad Schwalbach. Casualties are now buried at Durnbach War Cemetery. Although shown as Killed in Action, in fact Sgt AT Blackshaw parachuted from the aircraft and was captured. He was then murdered by his captor, Heinrich Hanke, who was himself later convicted and hanged for this war crime. A detailed account of the last minutes of this aircraft was recorded by Squadron Commander, W/C PLB Morgan as follows:

'On the night of the 2nd/3rd February 1945, the above named officer was detailed as pilot and captain of a four engined heavy bomber to attack Wiesbaden.
The target was a heavily defended one, and just after the bombs had been released there was a loud explosion in the aircraft. Flying Officer McLean was then heard to ask the Flight Engineer if the starboard inner engine had been hit. He got no reply but almost immediately he himself confirmed that it was the starboard inner engine and that it was now out of action. At this moment the Mid-Upper Gunner saw that the starboard inner engine was on fire.
The air bomber, who was down in the bomb aimer's position when the explosion occurred, then came up to see if he could give any assistance. At this moment, a large piece of white-hot metal came into the aircraft and lodged between the pilot's feet just aft of the rudder bar. The Air Bomber attempted to remove this with the aid of a flying jacket, but was unable to do so. Seeing this, Flying Officer McLean ordered the crew to carry out the emergency procedure for abandoning the aircraft.

Flying Officer McLean continued to control the aircraft in spite of the white hot metal, which by now was quickly setting fire to everything in its vicinity, including Flying Officer McLean's boots and clothing.

Just prior to leaving his turret, the Mid-Upper Gunner saw that the whole of the front part of the aircraft was on fire but the aircraft was still being kept steady which enabled him to reach the emergency exit and abandon the aircraft.

The Air Bomber, on his way to the emergency exit, noticed the Flight Engineer lying on the floor, apparently wounded or killed, so he called for a parachute pack, which he fastened to the Flight Engineer's harness. The pilot then told them to get out quickly. The Air Bomber then noticed that Flying Officer McLean was enveloped from head to foot in flames and that the whole cockpit was on fire. He then received a blow to the stomach and fell out of the aircraft.

The Air Bomber and the Mid-Upper Gunner were the only two survivors of the crew but they undoubtedly owe their lives to the outstanding bravery of the captain, Flying Officer McLean, who remained at the controls in order to steady the aircraft sufficiently to let his crew abandon it, completely disregarding his own safety and enduring what must have been extreme agony. Had he chosen, Flying Officer McLean was in a position to save himself but, crippled as the aircraft was, it is unlikely that any other members of the crew would have survived.

By his action, Flying Officer McLean set the highest example for outstanding bravery and courage, sacrificing his own life in attempting to save the lives of his crew and comrades.

It is very strongly recommended that this outstanding example of heroism be recognised by the posthumous award of the Victoria Cross to Flying Officer W.E. McLean.'

F/O McLean RCAF received a Mention in Despatches.

F/O WE McLean RCAF	*Pilot*	*KIA*
Sgt NM Nightingale	*Navigator*	*KIA*
Sgt SW Moore	*Air Bomber*	*POW*
Sgt AT Blackshaw	*WOP/AG*	*KIA*
Sgt GHS Berridge	*MU Gunner*	*POW*
Sgt W Harvey	*Rear Gunner*	*KIA*
Sgt FG Maunder	*Flight Engineer*	*KIA*

3rd February 1945.
Weather: Fair.
Non-Operational Flying: GH and H2S. Training Flights.
Operational Flying: BOMBING DORTMUND-HUCKARDE COKING PLANT.

11 aircraft detailed. 11 aircraft took off and 9 attacked primary target. 1 abortive sortie and 1 aircraft missing, 'B2' F/O WJK Fisher. Weather was clear with slight haze. Target marking reported as good and bombing concentrated. No ground identification possible due to smoke. Few fires were seen and some explosions. Slight to moderate heavy flak from Dortmund and the Ruhr area, with terrific searchlight activity throughout the Ruhr. Many fighter flares seen in target area, although only 1 Ju88 identified, occasional sightings of single-engined aircraft. No combats. 2 aircraft damaged by flak. 9 aircraft landed at Base.
S/L KG Condict in NP968, JI-B reported: Bomb load 1 x 4000 HC, 2 x 500 MC, 2 x 500 MC L/Delay, 6 x 500 ANM64, 2 x 500 GP, 3 x 250 GP, 1 Red/Green flare. Primary target: DORTMUND-HUCKARDE. Bombed at 1946 hours from 19,600 feet on GH. Good concentration of TIs.

Target:	*Dortmund-Huckarde Coking Plant*
Aircraft deployed total:	*149 (Lancasters)*
514 Squadron:	*11*
Aircraft lost total:	*4*
514 Squadron:	*1*

Comments: This is described in Bomber Command records as an attack on the Hansa benzol plant. 514 Sqn records show it as a coking plant. In any event the attack was not accurate.

Aircraft missing:

LM685 A2-B. 'Nachtjagd War Diaries' states 'Two Lancasters, HK688 (AP-W of 186 Sqn.) and LM685, were lost during the run up to the target, probably to the Flak, in combination with the searchlights' though the same source notes that the aircraft was possibly shot down by Maj. Heinz-Wolfgang Schnaufer of Stab NJG4. There were no survivors from the crew, who are buried in Reichswald Forest War Cemetery.

F/O WJK Fisher RCAF	Pilot	KIA
F/O AQ Downward RCAF	Navigator	KIA
F/O DE Stephens RCAF	Air Bomber	KIA
F/S R Hardy RAAF	WOP/Air	KIA
Sgt AR McWhinney RCAF	MU Gunner	KIA
Sgt AH Morrison RCAF	Rear Gunner	KIA
F/S WB Warr	Flight Engineer	KIA

4th February 1945.
Weather: Rain early, fair later.
Non-Operational Flying: Fighter Affiliation, H2S. Bombing, H2S and GH Training Flights and Cross Country.
Operational Flying: No Operations today or tonight. 14 Aircraft required for tomorrow.

5th February 1945.
Weather: Fair early, fine later.
Non-Operational Flying: H2S., GH Bombing and Training Flights.
Operational Flying: Operation cancelled.

6th February 1945.
Weather: Fine early, rain later.
Non-Operational Flying: Bombing and H2S and GH Training Flights.
Operational Flying: No Operations today or tonight. 12 Aircraft required for tomorrow.

7th February 1945.
Weather: Drizzle early, fine later.
Non-Operational Flying: Fighter Affiliation, GH Bombing, H2S and GH Training Flights.
Operational Flying: 33 Base withdrawn from Operations.
12 Aircraft required for tactical target tomorrow.

Wing Commander Michael Wyatt DFC today relinquished his post, being posted to the Air Ministry. He survived the war. Command of 514 Squadron passed to Wing Commander Peter Morgan, who remained in post for the rest of the unit's existence.

8th February 1945.
Weather: Fine at first, light rain in afternoon and evening. Thick medium cloud at mid-day.
Non-Operational Flying: H2S. Bombing, GH Exercises and Cross Country.
Operational Flying:
0135 hrs: Target cancelled.
1045 hrs: 12 Aircraft required for tonight.
1405 hrs: Operations cancelled.
1755 hrs: 12 Aircraft required tomorrow.

9th February 1945.
Weather: Fine Afternoon, rain morning and night.
Non-Operational Flying: GH Exercises and GH and H2S. Bombing.
Operational Flying: Note: This operation is shown in other sources as night of 8th/9th February, but aircraft left Waterbeach after 0300hrs on 9/2/45.
BOMBING – HOHENBUDBERG MARSHALLING YARDS. (Krefeld).
12 aircraft detailed, 11 aircraft took off, 10 aircraft attacked primary target and returned to base on completing sortie. 1 aircraft failed to take off, 1 aircraft returned early. Weather was 8/10ths cloud over the target. Bombing was well concentrated and TIs clearly visible. Slight flak, no enemy fighters. Searchlights ineffective. 10 aircraft landed at Base.
F/L JF Ness RCAF in PB426, JI-D reported: Bomb load 1 x 4000 HC, 2 x 500 MC, 2 x 250 GP, 4 x 500 GP, 6 x 500 ANM64, 2 x 250 Red TIs. Primary target: HOHENBUDBERG. Bombed at 0622 hours from 18,500 feet on Red TIs. TIs brought back. GH unserviceable. Few markers visible.

Target: *Krefeld – Hohenbudberg Marshalling Yards*
Aircraft deployed total: *151 (Lancasters)*
514 Squadron: *11 (1 returned early)*
Aircraft lost total: *2*
514 Squadron: *Nil*

Comments: No new damage was noted as a result of this GH raid.

10th February 1945.
Weather: Rain early, fine later.
Non-Operational Flying: H2S and GH Bombing, H2S and GH Exercises and Fighter Affiliation.
Operational Flying: No Operations today or tonight. The Squadron will not be required tonight but other Base Squadrons will.

11th February 1945.
Weather: Fine early, rain in afternoon, fog later. Thick medium cloud most of the day.
Non-Operational Flying: H2S and GH Bombing and GH Exercises.
Operational Flying: No Operations today or tonight.

12th February 1945.
Weather: Fog and drizzle in the morning, fair later.
Non-Operational Flying: GH and H2S. Bombing and Cross Countries.
Operational Flying: Squadron to stand-by for a possible tactical target. 12 Aircraft required for daylight tomorrow. 14 Aircraft required from this Squadron.

13th February 1945.
Weather: Rain during late morning.
Non-Operational Flying: H2S and GH Bombing.
Operational Flying: Daylight operations cancelled. 13 Aircraft required tonight.
BOMBING - DRESDEN.
13 aircraft detailed, 12 aircraft took off. 1 failed to take off – intercommunication failure in both turrets. 11 aircraft attacked primary target. 1 landed at Manston on return - short of fuel, oil leak and Gee unserviceable. Weather 5/10ths cloud over target. Target marking reported as good and Master Bomber clear and precise. The whole area on leaving was reported as one mass of flames and smoke, all crews highly delighted. A few enemy aircraft seen and two combats reported, one in the target area – Ju88 and an Me410 in the Mainz area, no claims. None of our aircraft sustained damage. Flak was slight, heavy in target area. 11 aircraft landed at Base.
F/L BA Audis in PB482, A2-K reported: Bomb load 1 x 500 MC, 15 x No.14 Clusters. Primary target: DRESDEN. Bombed at 0136 hours from 20,000 feet on Red TIs. Aircraft attacked by fighter on outward journey.

Combat Report - Pro-forma:
Aircraft: NN782 'F'
Captain: F/O H MacLean RCAF
Target: DRESDEN
At 0110 hours, height 20,000 feet, heading 036 degrees T., position 6030N 1130E. Rear Gunner sighted Ju88 at a range of 500 yards astern and below visible against the light sky. Rear Gunner ordered corkscrew and opened fire but E/A was subsequently lost to sight in the corkscrew. Visibility was good. No moon. No searchlights, fighter flares or flak reported.
MU Gunner – Sgt JM Moses - Nil.
Rear Gunner – Sgt EV Flatekval RCAF – 500 rounds.

Aircraft: PB482 'K2'
Captain: F/L. BA Audis
Target: DRESDEN
Outward bound (bombs not dropped), in position 4952N 0758E, height 17,000 feet, heading 106 degrees T, IAS 160. At 0035 hours the Engineer sighted an Me410 on the port bow up, range 800 yards. The E/A dived beneath Lancaster and started to attack from starboard quarter up, range 600 yards. The Rear Gunner gave order to corkscrew. The fighter opened fire when starting its attack and continued to do so until breakaway, range 250 yards. The Rear Gunner and Mid Upper Gunner opened fire at 500 yards and continued firing until breakaway of fighter at 250 yards. Me410 broke away port quarter down and then turned in and attacked again. Lancaster continued to corkscrew with Rear Gunner and Mid Upper Gunner firing throughout. Fighter did not fire on second attack, but just broke away starboard quarter down and was not seen again.
MU Gunner – Sgt AJ Mackness - 150 rounds.
Rear Gunner – Sgt A Kallick - 300 rounds.

Target: *Dresden – Communications and Supply Lines*
Aircraft deployed total: 805
514 Squadron: 12
Aircraft lost total: 6
514 Squadron: Nil

Comments: Much has been written about the series of raids on Dresden in the closing stage of the war, part of Operation Thunderclap. The cataclysm that befell those present in the city was not known to the crews, several of whom simply noted that this was 'a good effort'. On this occasion, two waves of aircraft three hours apart totaled 805 aircraft, dropping between them 1,478 tons of HE and 1,182 tons of incendiaries. 514 Sqn took part in the second wave, itself consisting of 529 Lancasters. The ensuing firestorm is believed to have resulted in up to 50,000 deaths on the ground, nearly equal to the total number of aircrew lost by Bomber Command in the whole campaign against Germany. 6 Lancasters were lost with another 3 crashing in the combined attack.

(Above) An iconic wartime image of the aftermath of the Dresden bombing raid. The crews, carrying out their orders, knew nothing of the cataclysm on the ground or of the enduring controversy that would follow. Source: Airworx GmbH Archive.

14th February 1945.
Weather: Fine early then fair.
Non-Operational Flying: GH and H2S. Exercise.
Operational Flying: BOMBING – CHEMNITZ.
14 aircraft detailed. 14 aircraft took off and 12 attacked primary target, 2 attacked last resort. Weather 8-10/10ths cloud, tops 15-16,000 feet with occasional breaks. There were at least two areas of bombing and it is believed that the bulk of the attack was NW of Chemnitz, probably on the existing fires at Rositz. Marking not good but occasional clear patches indicated that the built up areas in Chemnitz area were well ablaze. Flak nil to slight, heavy with many scarecrows in evidence. No combats reported or aircraft damaged.
W/C PLB Morgan in PB423, A2-L reported: Bomb load 1 x 500 MC, 15 x No.14 Clusters. Primary target: CHEMNITZ. Bombed at 0037½ hours from 20,000 feet on centre of fires.

Target:	*Chemnitz - Area*
Aircraft deployed total:	*617*
514 Squadron:	*14*
Aircraft lost total:	*13*
514 Squadron:	*Nil*

Comments: Operation Thunderclap continued as 617 bombers took part in a two-wave attack. Due to cloud cover, sky-marking was employed and most of the bombing fell outside the city.

15th February 1945.
Weather: Fair early, then foggy.
Non-Operational Flying: Nil.
Operational Flying: Nothing today or tonight for No. 33 Base. 13 Aircraft required from this Squadron for a target tomorrow.

16th February 1945.
Weather: Fog or mist till late in night.
Non-Operational Flying: Nil.
Operational Flying: BOMBING – WESEL.
13 aircraft detailed. 13 aircraft took off, 12 attacked primary target, 1 abortive sortie. Weather clear, and crews reported marking clear and concentrated. Bombing accurate among the built up area. Fires reported on the Railway Marshalling Yards in the Northern part of Wesel. Undoubtedly Wesel has 'had it'. Formation good. Flak slight

to moderate, very accurate. 3 aircraft being hit over the target. No enemy fighters seen. All aircraft landed safely.

S/L KG Condict in NF968, JI-B reported: Bomb load 1 x 4000 HC, 4 x 500 GP, 2 x 500 MC L/Delay, 3 x 250 GP, 6 x 500 ANM64, 1 Red Puff. Primary target: WESEL. Bombed at 1600 hours from 20,000 feet on GH.

Target: *Wesel – Supply Lines*
Aircraft deployed total: *101*
514 Squadron: *13*
Aircraft lost total: *Nil*
514 Squadron: *Nil*

Comments: The target lay near the front line by now. The town and railway were apparently well hit in this GH raid with, it is presumed, heavy casualties on the ground.

17th February 1945.
Weather: Mist and occasional rain.
Non-Operational Flying: Nil.
Operational Flying: Make and Mend today and tonight. 13 Aircraft required to attack Wesel tomorrow.

18th February 1945.
Weather: Mist and rain during morning, fair later.
Non-Operational Flying: H2S and GH Bombing. H2S and GH Training Flights.
Operational Flying: BOMBING – WESEL.
13 aircraft detailed. 12 aircraft took off. 1 failed to take off ICC unserviceable port inner engine. Weather 10/10ths cloud. Bombing appeared scattered but results unobserved due to cloud. Green puffs reported as concentrated. Flak slight. No hostile aircraft seen in target area. All aircraft landed. 21 Aircraft required from the Squadron to attack Wesel tomorrow.

F/O G Robertson in PB902, JI-A reported: Bomb load 1 x 4000 HC, 4 x 500 GP, 2 x 500 MC L/Delay, 4 x 250 GP, 6 x 500 ANM64. Primary target: WESEL. Bombed at 1525 hours from 20,000 feet on leading aircraft.

Target: *Wesel – Supply Lines*
Aircraft deployed total: *160 (Lancasters)*
514 Squadron: *12*
Aircraft lost total: *Nil*
514 Squadron: *Nil*

Comments: A further GH attack behind the front line, in support of the forthcoming Rhine crossing.

19th February 1945.
Weather: Cloudy early, fog at dawn, with poor visibility throughout the day.
Non-Operational Flying: GH Training Flights.
Operational Flying: BOMBING – WESEL.
21 aircraft detailed. 21 aircraft took off. 7 aircraft landed at Base, 14 aircraft landed at Morton-in-the-Marsh. Weather over target 5/10ths – 7/10ths cloud. Clear patch just port on run in. Bombing reported as very concentrated as were the Red puffs. Bombs seen to straddle the town and rail Marshalling Yards to the East of the town. Red puffs not as distinguishable as blue and green. Flak nil to slight with 1 Scarecrow seen over the target. No hostile aircraft seen.
F/O WG Gibson in NG142, JI-J reported: Bomb load 1 x 4000 HC, 6 x 500 MC, 6 x 500 ANM64, 4 x 250 GP. Primary target: WESEL. Bombed at 1635 hours from 18,500 feet on leading aircraft.

(Above) NG142, JI-J, seen taxying at Waterbeach, enjoyed a long and successful career with 514 Sqn, completing over 50 ops and surviving the war. Originally with 'C' Flight as A2-H, she moved to 'A' Flight in early 1945. Source: Airworx GmbH Archive.

Target: *Wesel – Supply Lines*
Aircraft deployed total: *162 (Lancasters)*
514 Squadron: *21*
Aircraft lost total: *1*
514 Squadron: *Nil*

Comments: *The same again for Wesel with 3 Group's Lancasters carrying out a concentrated raid on the railway area in what was considered a good attack overall. It is possible that the 'Scarecrow' seen over the target was Lancaster PD336, WP-P, of 90 Sqn. The aircraft crashed at Xanten which is near the target area. The aircraft was flown by W/C PF Dunham DFC who lost his life along with his crew.*

20th February 1945.
Weather: Misty early, slight rain during morning, then fair.
Non-Operational Flying: GH and H2S. Training Flights and Cross Countries.
Operational Flying: BOMBING – DORTMUND.
10 aircraft detailed. 10 aircraft took off, 1 aircraft returned early with starboard outer engine unserviceable – 'E', jettisoned in sea. 9 aircraft attacked primary. There was 8/10ths – 10/10ths thin cloud at about 5,000 feet. Target marking well grouped, bombing mostly concentrated, with some scattered. 7 aircraft bombed TIs, 2 on flares. Some fires, large explosion at 0109 hours. Slight to moderate heavy flak, bursting well below. Searchlights under cloud ineffective. Ruhr defences generally quiet. Several fighters seen, 'G' had three combats, Me109, Me110, Ju88, no claims. 4 aircraft shot down over target, 2 over France.
F/O CIM Nicholl in PD389, A2-J reported: Bomb load 1 x 2000 HC, 12 x 750 Type 15 Clusters. Primary target: DORTMUND. Bombed at 0107 hours from 21,000 feet on centre of Red/Green TIs.

Combat Report:
Aircraft: PB142 'G'
Captain: F/L JDK Crooks
Target: DORTMUND
On the night of 20th February 1945, Lancaster 'G' PB142 of 514 Squadron was homeward bound, bombs dropped, in position 5125N 0730E height 20,000 feet. Heading 030T. IAS 240 mph.

1st Combat: At 01.11 hours, Mid Upper Gunner sighted an Me109 attacking from the port bow down. Range 450 yards. The E/A opened fire immediately and the Mid Upper Gunner gave orders to corkscrew port and returned enemy E/As fire. The Me109 dived underneath our aircraft and broke away to the starboard quarter down, and was not seen again.

2nd Combat: At position 5158N 0720E. Height 15,000 feet. Heading 072T. IAS 240. At 0114 hours Rear Gunner sighted an Me110 on the starboard quarter level, flying on a parallel course and silhouetted against the bank of cloud. E/A came in to attack at 300 yards range. Rear Gunner gave order to corkscrew starboard and opened fire. E/A opened fire and continued to close. At this moment, all 4 guns stopped firing (due to insufficient recoil from faulty tracer ammunition). The Rear Gunner informed Captain that guns had jammed., and the Mid Upper Gunner who had been searching on port side then engaged the E/A, until it broke away to the port quarter down, range 50 yards. The Me110 climbed up then turned in and attacked from the port quarter up range 350 yards. Our Lancaster continued to corkscrew, and the Mid Upper Gunner opened fire, observing hits and parts of the aircraft breaking off. E/A did not open fire, but dived into a cloud bank on the starboard quarter down and was not seen again.

3rd Combat: At position 5145N 0638E. Height 12,000. Heading 233T. At 0123 hours the Engineer reported a Ju88 coming in from the port bow up range 600 yards. The Bomb Aimer give orders to corkscrew port and opened fire (guns jammed after short burst, due to faulty tracer ammunition). The Mid Upper Gunner also opened fire. The E/A did not fire but broke off to starboard bow down, and was not seen again.

MU Gunner – Sgt J Deighton - 900 rounds.
Rear Gunner – W/O GW Copland - 50 rounds.
Front Gunner - F/O WL Combs RNZAF - 20 rounds.

Target: Dortmund - Area
Aircraft deployed total: 518
514 Squadron: 10 (1 returned early)
Aircraft lost total: 14
514 Squadron: Nil

Comments: The force attacked the city in what was its last large Bomber Command raid of the war. There were no details recorded locally but Bomber Command considered that it had achieved its aim of destroying the southern half of the city.

21st February 1945.
Weather: Fog at dawn, medium cloud increasing during day.
Non-Operational Flying: GH and H2S bombing, GH and H2S Training Flights and Cross Countries.
Operational Flying: Make and Mend for No. 3 Group tonight. 21 Aircraft required from this Squadron to attack Osterfeld tomorrow.

22nd February 1945.
Weather: Misty early, fair during morning and cloudy later.
Non-Operational Flying: Bombing and GH Training Flights.
Operational Flying: BOMBING – OSTERFELD.
21 aircraft detailed. 21 aircraft took off. 19 attacked primary, 1 aircraft attacked secondary target, 1 aircraft abortive. Target clear of cloud but hazy. Blue smoke puffs were seen. Bomb bursts, fires and much smoke, which later obscured the aiming point. Accurate heavy flak, moderate to intense, caused much evasive action over target, which in turn increased the risk from falling bombs. 9 aircraft damaged by flak. No fighters seen. 19 Aircraft landed at Base, 1 landed at Woodbridge - no flaps.
S/L KG Condict in LM724, JI-H reported: Bomb load 1 x 4000 HC, 9 x 500 ANM64, 2 x 500 MC, 3 x 250 GP, 1 x 250 Blue Puff. Primary target: OSTERFELD. Bombed at 1601 hours from 19,500 feet on GH.

Target:	*Osterfeld – Oil Refinery*
Aircraft deployed total:	*167 (Lancasters)*
514 Squadron:	*21*
Aircraft lost total:	*1*
514 Squadron:	*Nil*

Comments: A joint attack saw 85 Lancasters deployed to Gelsenkirchen and 82 to Osterfeld. Both targets were accurately bombed, with the single aircraft lost failing to return from Gelsenkirchen.

23rd February 1945.
Weather: Low stratus all day, till late in the evening.
Non-Operational Flying: GH Bombing.
Operational Flying: BOMBING – GELSENKIRCHEN.
14 aircraft detailed. 14 aircraft took off, 10 aircraft diverted on return because of weather. 1 aircraft landed at Woodbridge ASI unserviceable. 6 landed at Acklington,

1 at Hutton Cranswick, 1 at Chipping Ongar, 1 at Witchford and 1 at Stradishall. Weather 10/10ths cloud. Formation straggly up to 0300E then good. 2 bursts Flak. Flak slight.
8 Aircraft required for an attack tomorrow.
F/L MD Muggeridge in ME354, JI-M reported: Bomb load 1 x 4000 HC, 9 x 500 ANM64, 2 x 500 MC, 3 x 250 GP, 1 Green Puff. Primary target: GELSENKIRCHEN. Bombed at 1459 hours from 19,500 feet on GH.

Target:	*Gelsenkirchen – Alma Pluto Benzol Plant*
Aircraft deployed total:	*133 (Lancasters)*
514 Squadron:	*14*
Aircraft lost total:	*Nil*
514 Squadron:	*Nil*

Comments: No results were seen from this GH attack.

24th February 1945.
Weather: Fog early, with thick medium cloud later.
Non-Operational Flying: Fighter Affiliation, GH and H2S Bombing, GH Training Flights and exercises.
Operational Flying: No. 3 Group attack cancelled. Nothing further today or tonight. 14 Aircraft required for an attack tomorrow.

25th February 1945.
Weather: Cloudy at medium levels with light rain at noon.
Non-Operational Flying: GH and H2S Bombing and Cross Country.
Operational Flying: BOMBING – KAMEN.
14 aircraft detailed. 13 aircraft took off and attacked primary target. 1 failed to take off. Weather 6 – 8/10ths cloud. The Canal and Forest North of the target identified and bombing reported as concentrated in the factory area. Clouds of black smoke seen billowing through the haze, and crews confident that attack was successful. Flak slight on outward route and over target, but the defences of Solingen and Köln were in action and 4 aircraft were damaged by heavy flak. Blue puffs not seen until after bombing. No enemy fighters seen. All aircraft landed at base. 18 Aircraft required for an attack tomorrow.
F/O JN Gallicano in NN781, A2-D reported: Bomb load 1 x 4000 HC, 2 x 500 GP, 9 x 500 ANM64, 3 x 250 GP and Smoke Puff. Primary target: KAMEN. Bombed at 1246½ hours from 19,000 feet on GH Leader.

Target: *Kamen – Synthetic Oil Plant*
Aircraft deployed total: *153 (Lancasters)*
514 Squadron: *13*
Aircraft lost total: *1*
514 Squadron: *Nil*

Comments: No results are recorded relating to this raid.

26th February 1945.
Weather: Fair.
Non-Operational Flying: GH and H2S. Cross Countries.
Operational Flying: BOMBING – DORTMUND –HOESCH BENZIN.
18 aircraft detailed. 18 aircraft took off. There was 10/10ths cloud, tops 8/10,000 feet. A few Red Puffs seen. General impression that aircraft were concentrated at bombing. GH good. No enemy fighters, but fighter cover well in evidence. Flak moderate, accurate between 18,000 and 21,000 feet. 1 aircraft hit by falling bombs - 'J' tailplane. 1 aircraft hit by flak. All aircraft landed at Base. 21 Aircraft offered for target tomorrow.
F/O WG Gibson in NG142, JI-J reported: Bomb load 1 x 4000 HC, 2 x 500 MC L/Delay 37B, 9 x 500 ANM64, 4 x 250 GP. Primary target: DORTMUND HOESCH BENZIN. Bombed at 1406½ hours from 17,000 feet on GH Leader.

Target: *Dortmund – Hoesch Benzol*
Aircraft deployed total: *149 (Lancasters)*
514 Squadron: *18*
Aircraft lost total: *Nil*
514 Squadron: *Nil*

Comments: This GH attack appeared to be concentrated on the target, the Hoesch benzol oil plant.

27th February 1945.
Weather: Fair.
Non-Operational Flying: GH Bombing.
Operational Flying: BOMBING – GELSENKIRCHEN.
21 aircraft detailed. 21 aircraft took off and 20 aircraft attacked primary target. 1 aircraft attacked Solingen (last resort). 10/10ths cloud, 6/10,000 feet tops. Blue puffs marking concentrated.

Formation good at bombing. Stream narrow but long. Better on return than way out. Slight to moderate heavy flak, accurate. No fighters. One aircraft shot down over target at 1429 hours. 1 parachute. All aircraft landed. 10 Aircraft required for target tomorrow.
F/O JH Tolley DFC in NN775, A2-F reported: Bomb load 1 x 4000 HC, 2 x 500 MC L/Delay 37B, 9 x 500 ANM64, 4 x 250 GP. Primary target: GELSENKIRCHEN. Bombed at 1428½ hours from 20,000 feet on GH Leader.

Target: *Gelsenkirchen – Alma Pluto Benzol Plant*
Aircraft deployed total: *149 (Lancasters)*
514 Squadron: 21
Aircraft lost total: 1
514 Squadron: Nil

Comments: 3 Group used GH to attack the Alma Pluto benzol plant through cloud. 1 aircraft was lost. As reported above, this was over the target, the Lancaster being NG175, AP-J, of 186 Sqn based at Stradishall. There were two survivors, believed to be the Bomb Aimer and WOP/Air.

28th February 1945.
Weather: Fair.
Non-Operational Flying: GH Bombing.
Operational Flying: BOMBING – NORDSTERN.
19 aircraft detailed. 19 aircraft took off and attacked primary target. Weather 10/10ths cloud. Fairly good formation. Squadron formation improved. Bombing and marking concentrated. Greyish smoke seen rising above cloud. Slight heavy flak over target. No enemy aircraft seen. All aircraft landed. 19 Aircraft required for target tomorrow.
F/O HC Snow in LM275, JI-C reported: Bomb load 1 x 4000 HC, 9 x 500 ANM64, 2 x 500 MC L/Delay, 4 x 250 GP. Primary target: NORDSTERN. Bombed at 1205 hours from 20,500 feet on GH.

Target: *Gelsenkirchen – Nordstern Synthetic Oil Plant*
Aircraft deployed total: 156 (Lancasters)
514 Squadron: 19
Aircraft lost total: Nil
514 Squadron: Nil

Comments: No results are noted from this GH attack.

Monthly Summary for February 1945

Awards:

119080	A/S/L JG Timms	Pilot	DFC	16/2/45
Can J/16632	F/Lt MC Smith	Air Bomber	DFC	16/2/45
Can J/10772	F/Lt JD Trick	Navigator	DFC	16/2/45
Can J/16828	F/O AH Fallis	Navigator	DFC	16/2/45
Can J/29859	F/O J Frieson	Navigator	DFC	16/2/45
1867675	F/S TA Rirch	Air Gunner	DFM	16/2/45
1582472	F/S AB Foster	Air Bomber	DFM	16/2/45
Aus/429215	F/S AW Cassidy	Navigator	DFM	16/2/45
146376	F/O KW Hall	Navigator	DFC	20/2/45
175191	F/O B Haslam	Pilot	DFC	20/2/45
182006	A/F/O R Hardwick	Pilot	DFC	20/2/45
178864	A/F/O JA Whitwood	Pilot	DFC	20/2/45
182344	A/F/O CE Williams	Pilot	DFC	20/2/45
183647	P/O AE Clark	Air Gunner	DFC	20/2/45
1549561	F/S JA Peduzie	Navigator	DFM	20/2/45
1566160	F/S RJ Wilson	Navigator	DFM	20/2/45
NZ/421683	A/F/O ET Cossens	Pilot	DFC	20/2/45

Operational:

Enemy Aircraft Destroyed:	Nil
Operational Flying Hours for February 1945:	1,474.15.
Non-Operational Flying Hours for February 1945:	427.15.
Total tons of bombs dropped in February 1945:	1,060 ½ Tons.
Cumulative tons of bombs dropped:	13,703 ¾ tons.

Number of Sorties for February 1945:   229 carried out
4 failed to take off
7 early returns
2 missing

Strength of Squadron as at 28th February 1945:

Aircrew:

127 Officers.
233 SNCOs

Ground: 1 Officer (Adjutant)
Total: 361

March 1945

1st March 1945.
Weather: Fair.
Non-Operational Flying: H2S and Air Tests.
Operational Flying: 1110 hrs: 2 Aircraft required from 514 Squadron for special target tonight.
1427 hrs: Tonight's target cancelled.
BOMBING – KAMEN.
18 aircraft detailed. 18 aircraft took off and attacked primary target. Formation became disorganised at 0700E when leading formation failed to turn to starboard for run in to target. These aircraft turned later and bombed on various headings. Risk of falling bombs was great and some of our Aircraft had to orbit to avoid them. Attack would seem to be scattered. No flak. No fighters. 18 Operational aircraft landed safely.
F/L JF Knight RCAF in NF968, JI-B reported: Bomb load 1 x 4000 HC, 10 x 500 ANM64, 2 x 500 MC L/Delay, 1 Blue smoke puff. Primary target: KAMEN. Bombed at 1505 hours from 18,600 feet on leading GH aircraft.

Target:	*Kamen – Oil Plant*
Aircraft deployed total:	*151 (Lancasters)*
514 Squadron:	*18*
Aircraft lost total:	*Nil*
514 Squadron:	*Nil*

Comments: 3 Group attacked the oil plant through the usual cloud cover, killing 9 people on the ground but with no other results noted.

2nd March 1945.
Weather: Fine to fair.
Non-Operational Flying: H2S, GH, Cross Country and Air Tests.
Operational Flying: BOMBING – KÖLN.
19 aircraft detailed. 18 aircraft took off. 8 attacked primary, 1 attacked BONN, 9 abortive sorties. Weather over Köln 10/10ths cloud. South and South-East of Köln clear. No aircraft bombed on GH, probably Ground Station failure. Three of our aircraft (D2, T, F2) bombed on P whose own GH was unserviceable, but all four crews identified the South-East part of Köln on the Gremberg Marshalling Yards area. Flak was slight Heavy flak – accurate. Two aircraft damaged around the bomb release point. No fighters seen. All 514 Squadron Operational

aircraft landed safely. No further instructions until 0930 hours tomorrow.
F/L JF Knight RCAF in NF968, JI-B reported: Bomb load 1 x 4000 HC, 11 x 500 ANM64. Primary target: KÖLN. Bombed at 1603 hours from 19,800 feet. Visual of Southern end of town on edge of River.

Target: *Köln – German Defences and Supply Lines*
Aircraft deployed total: 885
514 Squadron: 18
Aircraft lost total: 9
514 Squadron: Nil

Comments: There were two prongs to this raid on Köln (Cologne) which, by now, was almost on the front line. The second was a GH raid by 155 Lancasters of 3 Group, including 514 Sqn. Whilst the first raid was highly destructive, the second raid was less so due to GH transmitter problems, with only 15 aircraft bombing. At least 160 German soldiers, mostly SS men, were killed. Köln fell to the Allies 4 days later.

3rd March 1945.
Weather: Fine becoming cloudy.
Non-Operational Flying: ASF
Operational Flying: Make and Mend for 3 Group today and tonight.

4th March 1945.
Weather: Cloudy, rain in evening.
Non-Operational Flying: H2S and Cross Country and GH
Operational Flying: 514 Squadron not required today. 20 Aircraft required from 514 Squadron tomorrow.
1 Aircraft withdrawn. 514 Squadron now offer 19 Aircraft.

5th March 1945.
Weather: Fine becoming cloudy with rain in afternoon.
Non-Operational Flying: H2S and GH Training.
Operational Flying: BOMBING – GELSENKIRCHEN.
19 aircraft detailed. 19 aircraft took off. 16 attacked primary target, 2 last resorts, 1 missing. All 514 Squadron Aircraft landed except F.E. F/O Kerr (missing). Weather over target 10/10ths cloud with cirrus cloud at bombing height. Formation reported good to the target. Bombing reported as concentrated with three Red Puffs. All results unobserved. Flak slight to moderate, Heavy flak, accurate for height. Two aircraft

damaged. One aircraft seen shot down over the target at 1404 hours. Five parachutes seen (NF972, OJ-H, of 149 Sqn. at Methwold). No enemy aircraft seen. 17 Aircraft required from 514 Squadron to attack a target tomorrow.

F/O WG Gibson in LM285, JI-A, reported: Bomb load 1 x 4000 HC, 12 x 500 ANM64. Primary target: GELSENKIRCHEN. Bombed at 1408 hours from 21,000 feet on leading aircraft.

Target: *Gelsenkirchen – Consolidation Benzol Plant*
Aircraft deployed total: *170 (Lancasters)*
514 Squadron: *19*
Aircraft lost total: *2*
514 Squadron: *1*

Comments: By now the residents of Gelsenkirchen were probably beginning to regret the number of oil plants that had been set up in their town, as it was the turn of the Consolidation benzoyl plant to receive a visit. No results were noted.

Missing aircraft:

NN775, A2-F. *No survivors from crew when aircraft crashed at Bunsbeek, province of Brabant, Belgium. Circumstances of loss not stated but most likely due to flak or 'friendly bomb' damage as no fighter activity was noted on this daylight raid. Crew members are buried at Heverlee War Cemetery, 30 km from Brussels.*

F/O HGS Kerr	*Pilot*	*KIA*
F/S S Smith	*Navigator*	*KIA*
F/O F Clarke	*Air Bomber*	*KIA*
F/S A Olsen RAAF	*WOP/Air*	*KIA*
Sgt CG Hogg	*MU Gunner*	*KIA*
Sgt HP Thomas	*Rear Gunner*	*KIA*
Sgt W Marsden	*Flight Engineer*	*KIA*

6th March 1945.
Weather: Cloudy with some intermittent drizzle.
Non-Operational Flying: H2S. Training and Cross Country.
Operational Flying: BOMBING – SALZBERGEN.
17 aircraft detailed. 17 aircraft took off. 16 attacked primary target. 1 'T' missing. Crews attacked in 10/10ths cloud, tops 10,000 feet. GH Navigators exceptionally enthusiastic over the success of the bombing

run. Clusters of four blue sky markers drifted rather to starboard as crews attacked. Formation of 33 Base reported as good and the whole stream rather better than usual. One aircraft 514/'T' seen to explode over the target when its bombs had dropped 20/30 feet. Flak over target slight. No fighters seen.

F/S S Abel in LM285, JI-A reported: Bomb load 1 x 4000 HC, 12 x 500 ANM64, 2 x 500 MC. Primary target: SALZBERGEN. Bombed at 1214 hours from 21,000 feet on GH Leader. Whole Squadron compact over target.

Target: *Salzbergen – Wintershall Oil Refinery*
Aircraft deployed total: *119 (Lancasters)*
514 Squadron: *17 Aircraft lost total:*
514 Squadron: *1*

(Above) F/O Leslie Flack's crew was the last from 514 Squadron to be killed in action. Front row, right, is F/O Roy Young RCAF. The crew rest in Reichswald Forest War Cemetery with many of their comrades from Bomber Command. Source: Young family, enhanced by Roger Guernon.

Comments: Once again 3 Group used GH to attack the Wintershall oil refinery through cloud, losing one aircraft, which was from 514 Sqn. Although no results were noted, the GH Navigators believed the raid to be successful.

Missing aircraft:

ME365, JI-T. Seen to explode over target at 1204 hours. No survivors from the crew who are buried at Reichswald Forest War Cemetery. It is not known if the aircraft was hit by flak or by bombs. This was the last 514 Sqn crew lost in action.

F/O L Flack RCAF	Pilot	KIA
F/O RA Young RCAF	Navigator	KIA
F/S RA Wall	Air Bomber	KIA
F/S PF O'Donohue RAAF	WOP/Air	KIA
Sgt A Reilly	MU Gunner	KIA
Sgt D Heeley	Rear Gunner	KIA
Sgt JW Watson	Flight Engineer	KIA

3 GH Aircraft required from 514 Squadron to attack target tonight. All Aircraft that have landed and can be made serviceable, are to be bombed up immediately. 7 GH Aircraft required from 514 Squadron for dawn attack on Wesel.
Evening Operation: BOMBING – WESEL.
3 aircraft detailed. 3 aircraft took off and attacked primary target. Weather 10/10ths cloud, tops 16,000 feet preventing visual. Several large explosions reported in target area between 21.03 and 21.05 hours with an extra-large explosion at 2111 hours. H/F was slight but accurate for height. Two crews reported Jet propelled fighters.
F/L MD Muggeridge RNZAF in ME354, JI-M reported: reported: Bomb load 1 x 4000 HC, 13 x 500 ANM64, 2 x 500 MC. Primary target: WESEL. Bombed at 2110 hours from 18,000 feet on GH. Bombing concentrated.

Night Operation: BOMBING – WESEL.
8 aircraft detailed. 7 aircraft took off and attacked primary target. 1 aircraft withdrawn. Weather 10/10ths cloud, thin in places. All crews reported good GH run and flashes of bomb bursts concentrated also glow of fires. Flak slight. Explosion at 0246. Twin engine fighter seen. No combats.

F/O H MacLean RCAF in LM285, JI-A reported: Bomb load 1 x 4000 HC, 13 x 500 ANM64, 2 x 500 GP. Primary target: WESEL. Bombed at 0531 hours from 17,800 feet on GH. Bomb bursts appeared concentrated judging by flashes seen in cloud.

Target: *Wesel – German Troop Concentrations*
Aircraft deployed total: *138*
514 Squadron: *3*
Aircraft lost total: *Nil*
514 Squadron: *Nil*

Comments: A night attack was carried out in two waves on German troops believed to be gathering in Wesel.

7th March 1945.
Weather: Cloudy with light rain, becoming fair.
Non-Operational Flying: GH Training. Cross Country and ASF.
Operational Flying: BOMBING – DESSAU
18 aircraft detailed. 15 aircraft took off and attacked primary target. 5/10ths to 10/10ths thin cloud. Marking concentrated. Most crews bombed on sky markers, but some crews arrived on the wrong heading, had to orbit and due to strong following wind were late in getting back and bombed fires. Fires and explosions covered a large area. Master Bomber was enthusiastic about results. Very large explosion at 2217 hours. Slight to moderate heavy flak. Several fighters seen in target area and Magdeburg. Many fighter flares seen between Ruhr and Magdeburg. 'Q' fired two bursts at M.E. 109 over target. No claims. Much activity over Ruhr, Magdeburg, Brunswick and Wuppertal. New kind of scarecrow seen in several places. All 514 Squadron aircraft landed.

F/O LJ Sutton in NN773, JI-K reported: Bomb load 1 x 500 ANM64, 15 x No.15 Clusters. Primary target: DESSAU. Bombed at 2206 hours from 20,000 feet on Red/Green flares.

Combat Report - Pro-forma:
Aircraft: ME442 'Q'
Captain: F/O CA Dunn RCAF
Target: DESSAU
At 2017 hours, height 20,000 feet, heading 035 degrees T, position 5105N 0701E. Rear Gunner sighted Me109 at 400 yards flying astern level against the light sky. Rear Gunner ordered for corkscrew manoeuvre and both Gunners opened fire. First the Rear Gunner, then

the Mid Upper Gunner got the E/A in his sights. E/A was subsequently lost in corkscrew. Visibility was good, with no reports of searchlights, fighter flares and flak.
MU Gunner – Sgt WH Wylie RCAF - 500 rounds.
Rear Gunner – F/S IP Cahill RCAF – 100 rounds.

Target:	*Dessau - Area*
Aircraft deployed total:	*536*
514 Squadron:	*15*
Aircraft lost total:	*18*
514 Squadron:	*Nil*

Comments: This was a new target in Eastern Germany, and there was considerable damage to the town and its facilities. It is possible that this was intended to support the approaching Soviet Army.

8th March 1945.
Weather: Fair becoming cloudy and later fine.
Non-Operational Flying: H2S and GH Training and Cross Country.
Operational Flying: 3 Group Make and Mend today and tonight. 16 aircraft required from 514 Squadron to attack Datteln tomorrow.

9th March 1945.
Weather: Fine becoming cloudy.
Non-Operational Flying: H2S and GH Training.
Operational Flying: BOMBING – DATTELN.
16 aircraft detailed. 15 aircraft took off and attacked primary target. 1 aircraft withdrawn. 10/10ths cloud, tops 8-10,000 feet. Bombing appears to have been concentrated, the blue smoke puffs being close together. Flak nil to slight. No enemy fighters. All 514 Squadron aircraft landed. 13 Aircraft required from 514 Squadron to attack Gelsenkirchen tomorrow.
F/O PG Dean RAAF in NN782, JI-F reported: Bomb load 1 x 4000 HC, 13 x 500 ANM64, 2 x 500 MC L/D.37. Primary target: DATTELN. Bombed at 1400 hours from 20,700 feet on GH Leader.

Target:	*Datteln – Emscher Lippe Benzol Plants*
Aircraft deployed total:	*159 (Lancasters)*
514 Squadron:	*15*
Aircraft lost total:	*1*
514 Squadron:	*Nil*

Comments: A GH attack was made on two Emscher Lippe benzol plants through cloud. The attack appeared to be accurate.

10th March 1945.
Weather: Cloudy.
Non-Operational Flying: H2S and GH Training, ASF, Cross Country.
Operational Flying: BOMBING – GELSENKIRCHEN.
13 aircraft detailed. 13 aircraft took off and attacked primary target. Weather at target 10/10ths cloud, tops 8,000 feet. A cluster of blue puffs varying from 5/8 in number showing concentration of bombing. Formation rather straggling, closing up on the run-up. Flak over target was slight heavy flak, increasing to moderate. Two aircraft were hit over target. No fighters seen. All 514 Squadron aircraft landed.
1900 hrs: 16 Aircraft required to attack Essen tomorrow.
F/L JF Ness RCAF in PB142, JI-G reported: Bomb load 1 x 4000 HC, 2 x 500 MC, 13 x 500 ANM64, 1 Sky-marker Blue Puff. Primary target: GELSENKIRCHEN. Bombed at 1536 hours from 19,000 feet on GH. Bomb Aimer's panel damaged by flak.

Target:	*Gelsenkirchen – Scholven / Buer Oil Refinery*
Aircraft deployed total:	155 (Lancasters)
514 Squadron:	13
Aircraft lost total:	Nil
514 Squadron:	Nil

Comments: Another oil plant in Gelsenkirchen received attention in a very effective and accurate GH raid without loss.

11th March 1945.
Weather: Cloudy becoming fair.
Non-Operational Flying: H2S and GH Training. ASF and Cross Country.
Operational Flying: BOMBING – ESSEN.
16 aircraft detailed. 15 aircraft took off and attacked primary target. 1 aircraft withdrawn. Weather was 10/10ths cloud, tops 7/8000 feet. The formation was good, and the bombing, as indicated by well clustered blue puffs, was concentrated. All enthusiastic on success of attack. Flak nil. Fighters nil. 15 aircraft landed.
F/O PG Dean RAAF in LM275, JI-C reported: reported: Bomb load 1 x 4000 HC, 13 x 500 ANM64, 2 x 500 MC. Primary target: ESSEN. Bombed at 1525 hours from 19,300 feet on GH Leader.

Target:	*Essen – Supply Lines*
Aircraft deployed total:	*1079*
514 Squadron:	*15*
Aircraft lost total:	*3*
514 Squadron:	*Nil*

(Above) A Lancaster explodes over Essen on 11th March 1945. It is possibly NG201, P4-T of 153 Sqn from Scampton. F/O EW Gribbins and his crew were regrettably, though unsurprisingly, KIA. Source: Airworx GmbH Archive.

Comments: The largest force of aircraft to hit a target so far dropped 4,661 tons of bombs through complete cloud cover ahead of Allied ground forces. The bombing was accurate, effectively taking Essen out of the war, and the city fell to the Allies shortly afterwards. 3 aircraft were lost. Needless to say, this was the last of many attacks on the city of Essen and its war industries.

12th March 1945.
Weather: Fine with fog after dawn. Fair later.
Non-Operational Flying: H2S and GH Training.
Operational Flying: BOMBING – DORTMUND.
15 aircraft detailed. 15 aircraft took off and attacked primary target. Weather over target was 10/10ths cloud, tops 6/10,000 feet. 514 Squadron formation was good. GH Navigators report good GH runs. Technically the attack was successful. An enormous circular patch of black smoke was seen mixed with cloud over A/P 'Q'. A smaller one developed over A/P 'P' and merged with the larger. H2S was in no case switched on before 05 East. Flak – slight accurate heavy flak over the target area. Fighters – 1 FW190 seen over target, 3 Mustangs on his tail. All 514 Squadron aircraft landed. No further instructions until 0930 hours tomorrow.
F/L LR Worthing in LM724, JI-H reported: Bomb load 1 x 4000 HC, 13 x 500 ANM64, 1 Sky marker Red Puff. Primary target: DORTMUND. Bombed at 1658 hours from 19,000 feet on GH.

Target:	*Dortmund - Area*
Aircraft deployed total:	*1,108*
514 Squadron:	*15*
Aircraft lost total:	*2 (Lancasters)*
514 Squadron:	*Nil*

Comments: This was the largest raid to a single target in the war, the GH-guided force attacking Dortmund through cloud. The record tonnage of bombs, 4,851, fell mainly in the centre and south of the city and, as with Essen the previous day, effectively stopped all production in the city.

13th March 1945.
Weather: Fine becoming mainly fair.
Non-Operational Flying: H2S and GH Training and Cross Country.
Operational Flying: 17 Aircraft required from 514 Squadron for target tonight.
1645hrs: Tonight's target cancelled. 19 Aircraft required from 514 Squadron for target tomorrow.

14th March 1945.
Weather: Fine, with fog around dawn.
Non-Operational Flying: H2S and GH Training and Cross Country.
Operational Flying: BOMBING – HEINRICHSHUTTE.
19 aircraft detailed. 19 aircraft took off and 17 attacked primary target. 2 aircraft returned early. Weather was 10/10ths cloud, tops 7/12,000 feet visibility. Formation poor. Skies were clear before and after the target, and flak moderate to intense but slight over target. 4 aircraft damaged. Wireless Operator of 514/'H' killed. No fighters seen. 1 aircraft seen shot down. All 514 Squadron aircraft landed.
S/L KG Condict in LM724, JI-H reported: reported: Bomb load 1 x 4000 HC, 11 x 500 ANM64, 1 Sky marker Red Puff. Primary target: HEINRICHSHUTTE. Bombed at 1640 hours from 18,500 feet on GH. 1 Red smoke puff as we bombed. At 1642 hours North of Hattingen, a burst of heavy flak caught the aircraft killing the Wireless Operator (F/S WJ Sparkes) instantly. Squadron formation good.

Target: *Hattingen – Heinrichshutte Benzol Plant*
Aircraft deployed total: *169 (Lancasters)*
514 Squadron: *19 (2 returned early)*
Aircraft lost total: *1*
514 Squadron: *Nil*

Comments: 3 Group mounted a joint attack on benzol plants at Datteln and Hattingen. Using GH through the cloud cover, the bombing appeared accurate. 1 aircraft was lost from the Hattingen raid.

15th March 1945.
Weather: Fine, with fog around dawn.
Non-Operational Flying: H2S and GH Training, ASF and Cross Country.
Operational Flying: No Operations for 3 Group today.
1600 hrs: Derby offers required – 17.
1900 hrs: Target for tomorrow.

16th March 1945.
Weather: Cloudy with rain at dawn becoming fine.
Non-Operational Flying: H2S and GH Training and ASF.
Operational Flying: Today's Operation cancelled. Same target to be attacked tomorrow. 514 Squadron offer 21 Aircraft.

17th March 1945.
Weather: Cloudy.
Non-Operational Flying: H2S and GH Training.
Visits: The Secretary of State for Air, The Rt. Hon. Sir Archibald Sinclair, Bt., KT, CMG, MP, visited 514 Squadron on the 17th March 1945, arriving in a Grumman Goose at 17.36 hours. After talking to the Aircrew Personnel in the briefing room he took off again at 1836 hours.
Operational Flying: 16 Aircraft required from 514 Squadron for target tomorrow.
BOMBING – AUGUST VIKTORIA.
21aircraft detailed. 21 aircraft took off and 18 attacked primary target. 3 abortive sorties. Weather 10/10ths cloud, tops and contrails up to 23,000 feet. Aircraft flying in and out of cloud and contrails much congested over target. GH Leaders frequently lost, assessment of attack impossible. Slight to nil heavy flak. No fighters. 1 Scarecrow. V2 trail reported by 7 crews between 1517 and 1519 hours. All 514 Squadron aircraft landed.
F/L JF Ness RCAF in NF968, JI-B reported: reported: Bomb load 1 x 4000 HC, 13 x 500 ANM64, 2 x 500 MC. Primary target: AUGUST VIKTORIA. Bombed at 1506½ hours from 20,500 feet on GH.

Target: *Hüls – August Viktoria Benzol Plant*
Aircraft deployed total: *167 (Lancasters)*
514 Squadron: *21*
Aircraft lost total: *Nil*
514 Squadron: *Nil*

Comments: This was part of a two-pronged assault on benzol plants, at Dortmund and Hüls (August-Viktoria), involving 167 Lancasters guided by GH. 514 Sqn participated in the latter raid. Both attacks were subsequently believed to be accurate.

18th March 1945.
Weather: Mainly fair becoming cloudy.
Non-Operational Flying: H2S and GH Training and Cross Country.
Operational Flying: BOMBING – BRUCHSTRASSE COKING PLANT.
16 aircraft detailed. 16 aircraft took off and attacked primary target. Weather 10/10ths cloud, tops between 6,000 and 12,000 feet. Two to four blue smoke puffs were seen and aircraft concentrated at bombing. GH runs satisfactory. Slight accurate heavy flak. No fighters. All 514

Squadron aircraft landed. No further instructions until 0930 hours tomorrow.
F/O LC Baines RNZAF in LM285, JI-A reported: Bomb load 1 x 4000 HC, 13 x 500 ANM64, 2 x 500 MC. Primary target: BRUCHSTRASSE. Bombed at 0505 hours from 19,000 feet on GH.

Target:	*Lagendreer – Bruchstrasse Coking Plant*
Aircraft deployed total:	*100 (Lancasters)*
514 Squadron:	*16*
Aircraft lost total:	*Nil*
514 Squadron:	*Nil*

Comments: Hattingen and Langendreer were the targets for 100 Lancasters in a GH attack. The targets are described in Bomber Command records as Benzol plants. Both attacks appeared to be accurate with no losses. The coking plant described in the ORB as 'Bruchstrasse' was at Langendreer.

19th March 1945.
Weather: Cloudy with rain.
Non-Operational Flying: H2S and GH Training.
Operational Flying: No Operations for 33 Base today. 21 Aircraft required from 514 Squadron tomorrow.

20th March 1945.
Weather: Fine - becoming fair.
Non-Operational Flying: H2S and GH Training.
Operational Flying: 17 Aircraft required from 514 Squadron for target tomorrow.
BOMBING – HAMM MARSHALLING YARDS.
21 aircraft detailed. 21 aircraft took off. 20 aircraft attacked primary target, 1 aircraft returned early with engine trouble and landed at Manston. Weather 5/10ths cloud. Leading Squadrons took stream 8-10 miles to starboard 20 miles from target. This was eventually corrected. 514 Squadron in tight formation over the target. Bomb bursts and smoke seen on Marshalling Yards and results should be good. Slight to moderate accurate heavy flak. Mulheim, Hamm and Haltern. 9 aircraft hit. No fighters. All 514 Squadron aircraft landed.
F/L JF Knight RCAF in LM285, JI-A reported: reported: Bomb load 7 x 1000 ANM59, 8 x 500 ANM64, 1 Sky marker Green Puff. Primary target: HAMM. Bombed at 1315½ hours from 17,800 feet on GH.

Partial failure of GH resulting in bombs falling on North-east part of town.

Target: Hamm – Marshalling Yards
Aircraft deployed total: 99 (Lancasters)
514 Squadron: 21 (1 returned early)
Aircraft lost total: Nil
514 Squadron: Nil

Comments: Bombs were seen to hit the target of this GH attack by 3 Group.

21st March 1945.
Weather: Fair - Becoming fine.
Non-Operational Flying: H2S and GH Training.
Operational Flying: BOMBING – MUNSTER VIADUCT.
17 aircraft detailed. 17 aircraft took off and 16 attacked primary target. 1 aircraft bombed built up area near Dorstern. Cloud nil to 2/10ths. In some cases GH run was cut short by aircraft being off track just before last leg. Bombing was well concentrated in Viaduct area and to North on Marshalling Yards. One crew reported viaduct hit by 1 x 4000 HC. Slight to intense accurate heavy flak. 8 aircraft hit. No enemy fighters. Apart from avoiding action photos should be good. 2 aircraft seen shot down. 4 to 6 parachutes. All 514 Squadron aircraft landed safely. No further Operations for 33 Base till 09.30 hours tomorrow.
F/O JN Gallicano RCAF in NN776, A2-D reported: reported: Bomb load 1 x 4000 HC, 13 x 500 ANM64, 2 x 500 MC. Primary target: MUNSTER VIADUCT. Bombed at 1308 hours from 18,000 feet on GH aircraft and visuals. 1 x 4000 HC seen to hit a bridge.

Target: Münster – Viaduct and Marshalling Yards
Aircraft deployed total: 160 (Lancasters)
514 Squadron: 17
Aircraft lost total: 3
514 Squadron: Nil

Comments: All casualties in this GH attack occurred over the target area and were from 33 Base's 75(NZ) Sqn. Flak was very heavy and there was the ever-present possibility of being hit by bombs from higher-flying colleagues.

22nd March 1945.
Weather: Mainly fair - becoming fine.
Non-Operational Flying: H2S and GH Training. Cross Country.
Operational Flying: Bomb load for tomorrow. 514 Squadron offers 14 Aircraft. Only 10 Aircraft required from 514 Squadron.

23rd March 1945.
Weather: Fine.
Non-Operational Flying: H2S and GH Training. A.S.F.
Operational Flying: BOMBING – WESEL.

(Above) Wesel claimed to be the most intensively-bombed bombed town of its size in Germany. This photo tends to support the residents' perception. Source: Airworx GmbH Archive.

10 aircraft detailed. 10 aircraft took off and 9 attacked primary target. 1 aircraft abortive sortie. Weather was perfect and GH sets worked well. All crews checked visually and reported all bombs falling on Eastern bank of Rhine and the town completely obliterated by brown smoke. Flak was negligible and no trouble experienced by any of the crews. No fighters seen. All 514 Squadron aircraft landed.
F/O LC Baines RNZAF in LM285, JI-A reported: reported: Bomb load 13 x 1000 MC. Primary target: WESEL. Bombed at 1738½ hours from 19,500 feet on GH. All bombs appeared to fall in town.

Target: *Wesel – Supply Lines.*
Aircraft deployed total: *218*
514 Squadron: *10*
Aircraft lost total: *Nil*
514 Squadron: *Nil*

Comments: This was the last bombing raid to be suffered by Wesel, which claims to be the most intensively-bombed town of its size in Germany. As a result of Bomber Command's attention, which was in preparation for and support of the Rhine crossing, 97 percent of the main town area had been destroyed and the population reduced from 25,000 to less than 2,000.

24th March 1945.
Weather: Fine - Becoming fair.
Non-Operational Flying: GH Training.
Operational Flying: Derby Signals to be bombed up. 514 Squadron offers 18 Aircraft. No further instructions until 09.30 hours tomorrow.

25th March 1945.
Weather: Cloudy - With occasional rain.
Non-Operational Flying: H2S and GH Training.
Operational Flying: 3 Group to stand by for possible tactical target. 3 Group required tomorrow morning.

26th March 1945.
Weather: Cloudy - with rain.
Non-Operational Flying: H2S and GH Training. Cross Country.
Operational Flying: Operations cancelled. Same target laid on for tomorrow morning - 18 Aircraft required from 514 Squadron.

27th March 1945.
Weather: Mainly cloudy - but fair in afternoon.
Non-Operational Flying: H2S and GH Training.
Operational Flying: Derby signals to be bombed up as soon as possible.
BOMBING – HAMM SACHSEN.
18 aircraft detailed. 18 aircraft took off and attacked Primary target. 10/10 cloud. Formation good on way out and at bombing. Green smoke puffs well together. Black smoke seen rising through cloud after leaving, also from other target. Nil to slight Heavy Flak, mainly

from Hamm itself. No fighters. Uneventful trip. All 514 Squadron aircraft landed. 19 Aircraft required for target tomorrow.
F/L FW Morrish in LM627, JI-D reported: Bomb load 1 x 4000 HC, 13 x 500 ANM64, 2 x 500 MC. Primary target: HAMM SACHSEN. Bombed at 1404 hours from 18,000 feet.

Target:	Hamm – Sachsen Benzol Plant
Aircraft deployed total:	150 (Lancasters)
514 Squadron:	18
Aircraft lost total:	Nil
514 Squadron:	Nil

Comments: This was part of a GH attack on 2 benzol plants through cloud cover without loss. No results were observed but dense smoke rose from both targets.

28th March 1945.
Weather: Cloudy - With occasional drizzle.
Non-Operational Flying: H2S and Cross Country.
Operational Flying: Todays target cancelled. 17 Aircraft required from 514 Squadron for target tomorrow.

29th March 1945.
Weather: Cloudy with rain early morning and evening.
Non-Operational Flying: H2S and GH Training, ASF and Cross Country.
Operational Flying: BOMBING – SALZGITTER.
17 aircraft detailed and took off. 16 attacked Primary target, 1 abortive sortie 'L2'. 10/10th Cloud. Formation good until 50 miles short of target when high icing cloud experienced causing formation to go hay wire. Result difficult to ascertain as Green puff immediately lost in cloud and the followers had consequently great difficulty in identifying. No results observed. Flak was slight to mod: accurate. Four aircraft damaged. Defences of Hamm in action. No enemy fighters seen. All 514 Squadron aircraft landed. No further instructions until 09.30 hours tomorrow.
F/L LC Baines RNZAF in LM285, JI-A reported: reported: Bomb load 1 x 4000 HC, 8 x 500 ANM64. Primary target: Salzgitter. Bombed on GH Leader at 1643½ hours from 22,500 feet.

Target: *Salzgitter – Hermann Goering Benzol Plant*
Aircraft deployed total: *130 (Lancasters)*
514 Squadron: *17*
Aircraft lost total: *Nil*
514 Squadron: *Nil*

Comments: *The unfortunate choice of name for the benzol plant probably made no difference to its being selected as a target for this GH attack.*

30th March 1945.
Weather: Showers and fair periods.
Non-Operational Flying: H2S and GH Training.
Operational Flying: Aircraft to be bombed up - but no target laid on at present - Crews to stand by.
No target today or tonight - but we are to stand by for tomorrow morning. No further information until 09.30 hours tomorrow.

31st March 1945.
Weather: Cloudy - intermittent rain after 18.00 hours.
Non-Operational Flying: H2S and GH Training, ASF and Cross Country.
Operational Flying: Make and Mend for 3 Group today and tonight - Stations are to change A/C instruments from miles to knots by dusk. 17 Aircraft required for target tomorrow.

Monthly Summary for March 1945

Awards:

156933	A/F/L G Bradford	Pilot	DFC	23/3/45
Aus/418944	F/O DC Gordon	Pilot	DFC	23/3/45
172604	F/O RH Edmundson	Pilot	DFC	27/3/45
179940	A/F/O ST Wilson	Pilot	DFC	27/3/45
Aus/424481	F/O RW Vickers	Pilot	DFC	27/3/45
Aus/418521	F/O IR Campbell	Pilot	DFC	27/3/45
Aus/427474	F/OAJ Holland	Navigator	DFC	27/3/45
J88101	A/P/O GA Wark	Pilot	DFC	27/3/45
NZ/425302	A/P/O DJ Uffindell	Pilot	DFC	27/3/45
NZ/42705	P/O MR Oliver	Navigator	DFC	27/3/45
179987	A/P/O P Heald	Pilot	DFC	27/3/45

Operational:

Enemy Aircraft Destroyed:	Nil
Operational Flying Hours for March 1945:	1,707.25.
Non-Operational Flying Hours for March 1945:	378.25.
Total tons of bombs dropped in March 1945:	342¼ tons.
Cumulative tons of bombs dropped:	14,046 tons

Number of Sorties for March 1945: 269 carried out
6 early returns
1 failed to take off
2 missing

Strength of Squadron as at 31st March 1945:
Aircrew: 157 Officers
NCOs 279

Ground: 1 Officer
Total: 437

April 1945

(Compiled by F/Lt AG Rhodes)

1st April 1945.
Weather: Cloudy with slight rain early and late.
Non-Operational Flying: GH and H2S Training, altitude tests.
Operational Flying: Today's Operation cancelled. No further instructions until 09.30 hours tomorrow.

2nd April 1945.
Weather: Rain and low cloud early, then fair.
Non-Operational Flying: GH and H2S Training, Cross Country.
Operational Flying: No Operations for 3 Group today. 19 Aircraft required from 514 Squadron for a target tonight.
Tonight's Operations cancelled.

3rd April 1945.
Weather: Occasional showers, otherwise fine.
Non-Operational Flying: GH and H2S Training, Fighter Affiliation and Cross Country.
Operational Flying: We are to stand by for a tactical target.
19 Aircraft required to attack a target tomorrow.
Tomorrows target cancelled.

4th April 1945. Weather: Fair.
Non-Operational Flying: GH and H2S Training, Fighter Affiliation.
Operational Flying: BOMBING – MERSEBERG.
21 Aircraft detailed. 20 Aircraft took off. 1 returned early (internal defect). 14 attacked primary target. 3 attacked last resort (J2, F and J). 3 abortive (B2, C2 and K). Weather 5/10 – 10/10ths thin cloud. PFF marking over Merseberg began late. TI Markers, Red, green were dropped over a wide area from the target to 50 miles NW with quite a large concentration over the Magdeburg area, which attracted some bombing. Over Merseberg, consensus of opinion was 10/10ths cloud and most crews bombed on Sky Markers. Fires seen reflected on clouds and moderate heavy flak experienced. Patchy cloud around the target and in the Magdeburg area where the ground TIs were quite visible. Result of raid very scattered. MB heard faintly, who gave varying instructions. Fighters were in evidence and some jet propelled. Our aircraft had two combats in target area. Ju88, Me109. No claim.

Fighter flares followed stream back to the English Channel. All operational aircraft landed safely.

F/O H MacLean in ME530, JI-C reported: Bombed Primary Target. Bomb load 1 x 4000 HC and 6 x 500 ANM 64. 5/10th to 10/10th thin cloud. Glow of fires and bursting bombed. Bombed at 2246 from 20,000 feet. Bombed glow of fires, Red and Green Decoy Markers seen to port of track near target. W/T U/S and H2S U/S. Fires seen at Magdeburg on leg into target. No markers seen in our A/P as orbited on glow of fires.

Target:	*Merseberg – Leuna Synthetic Oil Plant*
Aircraft deployed total:	*341*
514 Squadron:	*20*
Aircraft lost total:	*2*
514 Squadron:	*Nil*

Comments: This attack was not particularly effective with scattered bombing.

5th April 1945.
Weather: Rain early, then occasional showers.
Non-Operational Flying: GH Training only.
Operational Flying: 16 Aircraft required to attack a target tonight.
18 Aircraft now required from 514-C Squadron.
Tonight's Operations cancelled. No further instructions until 09.30 hours tomorrow.

6th April 1945.
Weather: Fine at first, but rain after mid-day till late.
Non-Operational Flying: GH and H2S Training, Fighter Affiliation, Low Level and Cross Country.
Operational Flying: No Operations today or tonight. 21 Aircraft required from 514 Squadron for target tomorrow.

7th April 1945.
Weather: Fog early, then cloud with low stratus.
Non-Operational Flying: Low Level Flying, H2S and GH Training.
Operational Flying: 21 Aircraft required for target tonight.
Tonight's target cancelled. No further information until 0930 hours tomorrow.

8th April 1945.
Weather: Cloudy early, then fine.
Non-Operational Flying: GH and H2S Training, Fighter affiliation, A-S Firing, Low Level Cross Country.
Operational Flying: Make and Mend for 3 Group today. No further information until 09.30 hours tomorrow.

9th April 1945.
Weather: Fog at dawn and early in the morning then fair.
Non-Operational Flying: Cross Country.
Operational Flying: BOMBING – KIEL.
26 aircraft detailed. 1 A/C 'L2' failed to take off, fuel pumps, starboard inner u/s. 1 A/C 'S' returned early W/T U/S – 1 x 4000 HC 12 x 500 ANM 64. Jettisoned 7 x 500. 2 A/C attacked last resort, (PFF Marking in Hamburg area). 22 attacked primary target between 2237 / 2244½ hours from 19,000 ft to 20,300 feet dropping 22 x 4000 HC and 264 x 500 ANM 64.
Weather was clear with slight haze. Crews report both sets of markings well placed by visuals of harbour and canal. Majority of crews bombed on green TIs with undershoots as ordered by MB. Bombing appeared very accurate on TIs and many fires were left burning red – seen as far away as Sylt on homeward trip. Crews enthusiastic on success of raid. Flak. Much light flak bursting at 15,000 feet. Mod. HF decreasing to slight towards end of attack. Fighters – 2, 190'3. 4000s jettisoned across N. Sea. All 514 Squadron aircraft landed.
F/L LC Baines RNZAF in LM285, JI-A reported: Bombed Primary Target - KIEL. Bomb load 1 x 4000 HC and 12 x 500 ANM 64. Bombed at 2238 hours from 20,000 feet on centre red/green TIs. Explosion seen in target 1 and 2. Great number of 4000 lb seen to fall in the sea area from 0300 E. Six were seen to fall at one time. Rear turret u/s oil had drained out. Good attack. Release of 4000 lb increased in frequency as dusk fell. Gee faded from 0500 E. H2S u/s over target.

Target: *Kiel – Harbour, Deutsche Werke U-Boat Yard.*
Aircraft deployed total: *599*
514 Squadron: *25*
Aircraft lost total: *3*
514 Squadron: *Nil*

Comments: This was an accurate attack on two aiming points in the harbour area of the port. The Deutsche Werk U-Boat yard was severely damaged, whilst warships Admiral Scheer, Admiral Hipper and Emden were put out of action.

10th April 1945.
Weather: Dawn fog dispersing during the morning.
Non-Operational Flying: H2S. Training, Fighter Affiliation, Cross Country and Low Level Flying.
Operational Flying: Make and Mend for 3 Group today. No further instructions until 09.30 hours tomorrow.

11th April 1945.
Weather: Slight rain early, fair around mid-day, then further slight rain.
Non-Operational Flying: GH and H2S Training, Fighter Affiliation, Low Level Flying and Cross Country.
Operational Flying: No Operations for 3 Group today or tonight. 21 aircraft required for target tomorrow.
Operation cancelled. Reason: our troops are too near the target.

12th April 1945.
Weather: Fair, with slight rain in the morning.
Non-Operational Flying: GH Training, Fighter Affiliation and Low Flying.
Operational Flying: 21 Aircraft required for a target today.
Today's Operation cancelled.
Make and Mend today and tonight for 3 Group. No further instructions until 09.30 hours tomorrow.

13th April 1945.
Weather: Fair.
Non-Operational Flying: GH and H2S, Low Flying, Fighter Affiliation and Cross Country.
Operational Flying: BOMBING – KIEL.
21 aircraft detailed. 21aircraft took off. One aircraft 514/M abortive 1 engine u/s 2nd partially u/s. 1 x 4000 HC and 12 x 500 ANM 64 jettisoned in sea. 20 aircraft attacked primary target dropping 12 x 4000 HC, 284 x 500 ANM 64, between 2327 and 2339 hours from 18,000 to 21,000ft. Weather – 10/10ths cloud low and thin. Marking was fairly well concentrated, Green TIs following Reds closely. At one time there were 2 or 3 areas of green glow through cloud. MB was clear and most crews bombed to his instructions with concentrated results. Large fire area indicated by glow through cloud. Large explosion at 2330. Flak slight heavy. Few S/Ls but ineffective. S/Ls

and LF from Sylt and Frisians. Several fighters seen in target area. Me109, Ju88, FW190, 2 jet. No combats. All 514 Squadron aircraft landed safely.

F/L JK Crooks in NF968, JI-B reported: Bombed primary target, KIEL. Bomb load 1 x 4000 MC and 12 x 500 ANM 64. Bombed centre of green glow on M/B instructions at 2331½ hours from 19,000 feet. Glow of fires seen through cloud. Two targets separately marked. Merged into one large glow after bombing. H2S u/s. Very good attack. Marking concentrated. M/B clear and helpful.

Combat Report - Pro-forma:
Aircraft: ME422 'Q'
Captain: F/L. RH Marks
Target: KIEL.
At 2344 hours, height 17,500 feet, heading 256 degrees, position 5413N 0954E. Mid Upper Gunner sighted a Ju88 at a range of 700 yards on the port beam down against the light sky. Mid Upper Gunner immediately opened fire with a short burst, to which E/A broke away to the starboard beam down, without firing. Visibility was good, with no searchlights, fighter flares or flak reported.
MU Gunner – Sgt GR Morgan - 60 rounds.
Rear Gunner – Sgt. R Vipond - Nil.

Target: *Kiel – U-Boat Yards*
Aircraft deployed total: *475 (Lancasters and Halifax)*
514 Squadron: *21*
Aircraft lost total: *2 (Lancasters)*
514 Squadron: *Nil*

Comments: Notwithstanding 514 Sqn's reports above, this attack on the port was considered 'poor' by Bomber Command with scattered bombing. However, an ammunition depot was hit.

14th April 1945.
Weather: Fair.
Non-Operational Flying: GH and H2S Training.
Operational Flying: 21 Aircraft required from 514 Squadron for target tonight.
514 Squadron will not be required tonight.

15th April 1945.
Weather: Cloudy, with low stratus early. Fair later.
Non-Operational Flying: H2S and GH Training, Low Flying, Fighter Affiliation, A-G Firing and Cross Countries.
Operational Flying: Make and mend today and tonight for 3 Group. 21 Aircraft required from 514 Squadron for target tonight.
Tonight's target cancelled. No further instructions until 09.30 hours tomorrow.

16th April 1945.
Weather: Fair.
Non-Operational Flying: H2S and GH Training, Low Flying.
Operational Flying: Make and Mend today. 24 Aircraft required from 514 Squadron to attack a target tomorrow.

17th April 1945.
Weather: Fair.
Non-Operational Flying: Cross Country.
Operational Flying: Todays target cancelled. 25 Aircraft required from 514 Squadron to attack a target tomorrow.

18th April 1945.
Weather: Fair.
Non-Operational Flying: GH and Low Flying.
Operational Flying: BOMBING – HELIGOLAND.
25 aircraft detailed, 25 took off to attack Heligoland. 25 aircraft attacked Primary target, dropping 143 x 1000 MC, 6 x 1000 GP, 246 x 500 ANM 64 between 1307½ and 1310 hours from 16,500 feet to 19,000 ft. No cloud, slight haze. Whole target area obscured by smoke and flame, few markings seen, but M/B was heard and most crews bombed on up-wind edge of smoke. Only the north east tip of island was visible. Evidence of a large oil fire and a very large explosion at 1327 hours. Many bombs seen to overshoot as our Squadron left. No flak. No fighters. All 514 Squadron aircraft landed safely. 20 Aircraft from 514 Squadron to stand-by for a probable daylight operation tomorrow.
F/O W Allan in PB426 (no code) reported: Bombed primary target, Heligoland. Bomb load 6 x 1000 MC, 10 x 500 ANM 64. Bomb visually at 1308 from 18,500 ft. Whole island obscured by smoke, 1 x 1000 MC hang up. Very good effort. Flame seen from the submarine harbour.

F/L ES Henderson in LE358 (no code) reported: Bombed primary target: Heligoland. Bomb load 4 x 1000 MC, 2 x 1000 GP, 10 x 500 ANM 64. Bombed visually up-wind edge of smoke at 1309 from 18700. Island obscured with flames and smoke. Wizard effort no troubles.

Target: *Heligoland – Naval Base, Airfield and Area*
Aircraft deployed total: 969
514 Squadron: 25
Aircraft lost total: 3 (Halifax)
514 Squadron: Nil

Comments: The bombing was assessed as accurate and resulted in intensive cratering of the target areas.

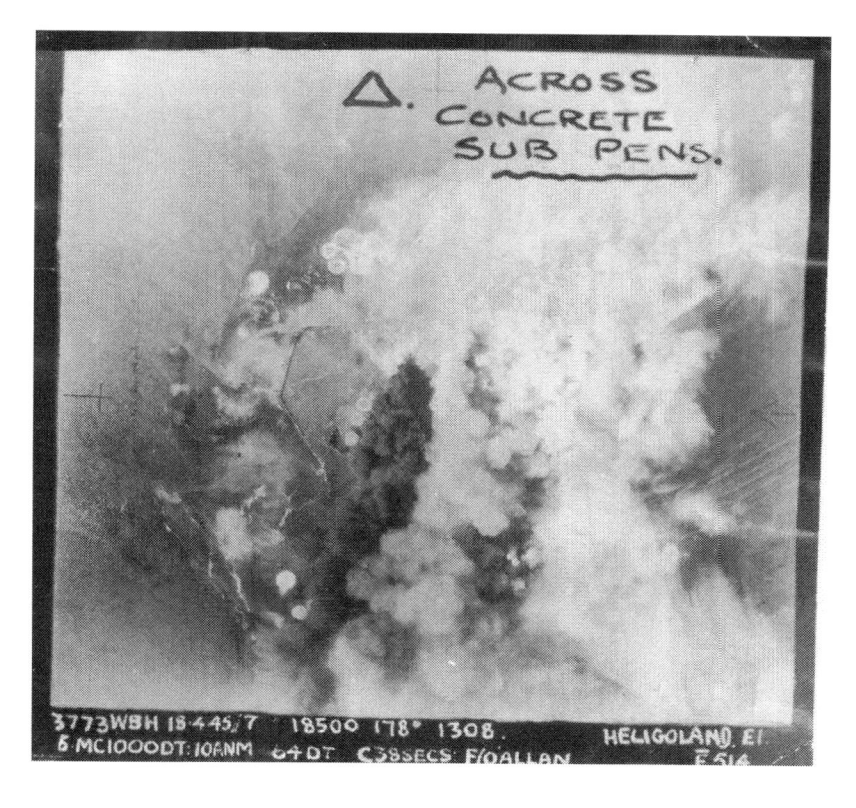

(Above) Bombs from F/O Allan's aircraft PB426 straddle the U-Boat pens at Heligoland. Source: Alcan ManOne.

19th April 1945.
Weather: Fine.
Non-Operational Flying: Cross Country and GH Training.
Operational Flying: We are to continue to stand-by with Aircraft bombed up. 20 Aircraft required from 514 Squadron to attack target tomorrow.

20th April 1945.
Weather: Fine then fair, thunderstorm at mid-night.
Non-Operational Flying: GH and H2S Training, A-S Firing, Fighter Affiliation, Cross Country and Low Flying.
Operational Flying: BOMBING – REGENSBURG.
20 aircraft detailed, 20 aircraft took off, 19 aircraft attacked primary target, dropping 293 x 500 ANM 64 and 8 blue smoke puffs between 1355½ and 1407 hours from 18500/19500 ft. One aircraft 514/J2 brought back 16 x 500 ANM 64 which hung up after every effort to release after orbiting. 10 aircraft detailed to bomb on GH. 6 bombed on GH and 3 on GH leaders. 10 aircraft bombed visually. Weather was clear over target and whole route. GH runs were good. Bombing concentrated, but appears to have overshot and undershot, in effect straddling target. Fires and smoke seen. Railway bridge seen hit. Large fire and column of smoke 10-15 miles east of target, and another 10-15 miles south west. Flak was nil increasing to slight. No enemy fighters seen. One aircraft seen shot down at 1400hrs (Lancaster I PA285, GI-O of 622 Sqn was the only aircraft lost on this raid). All 514 Squadron aircraft landed. No further instructions until 09.30 hours tomorrow.
F/O WA Winkworth in LM724 (no code) reported: Bombed primary target, Regensburg. Bomb load 15 x 500 ANM 64. Bombed GH and visual. GH Tracking pulse. Released visually as release pulse was unsatisfactory. At 1355½ from 19,000ft. Bomb bursts seen across target. Some undershooting seen. Formation poor although the attack should be successful.

Target: *Regensburg – Fuel Storage Depot*
Aircraft deployed total: *100 (Lancasters)*
514 Squadron: *20*
Aircraft lost total: *1*
514 Squadron: *Nil*

Comments: The final birthday of the German Führer was marked by 3 Group mounting Bomber Command's final operation in its ten-month campaign against oil targets. 3 Group's Lancasters bombed the fuel storage depot at Regensburg accurately. It was assessed that the reduction in oil and fuel supplies had, despite the great cost to Bomber Command, been of considerable assistance to the war effort against the Germans on all fronts.

21st April 1945.
Weather: Thunderstorms early, drizzle and low cloud at dawn then fair.
Non-Operational Flying: GH Training, Fighter Affiliation, Low Flying and Cross Country.
Operational Flying: Make and Mend tonight for 3 Group. Bomb up for Derby figures. 21 Aircraft required from 514 Squadron for target tomorrow.

22nd April 1945.
Weather: Fair.
Non-Operational Flying: GH and H2S Training, Low Flying.
Operational Flying: BOMBING – BREMEN.
21 aircraft detailed. 21 aircraft took off. 18 attacked primary target (BREMEN). 1 aircraft outstanding, 'A' crash landed Venlo. 2 aircraft abortive C2 and K2. 18 attacked primary dropping 18 x 4000 HC, 36 x 500 HC, 252 x 500 ANM 64 between 1840 and 1847 hours from 18200 t0 19500 feet. 11 a/c detailed to bomb on GH. 7 a/c bombed on GH. 11 bombed on Leaders. Weather on approaching target 4/10 – 5/10ths clouds. Formation good and good concentration of bombing on NE bank of Weser around the A/P. Much smoke seen, appeared to be a successful raid. Flak reported as slight to moderate: on target and at Wilhelmshaven, and accurate in both cases. 11 aircraft damaged by flak. No enemy a/c seen.
F/O S Abel in LM285, JI-M reported: Bombed Primary Target. BREMEN. Bomb load 1 x 4000 HC and 2 x 500 MC, 14 x 500 ANM 64. Bombed on leading aircraft 'M' 514 at 1842 from 19,000. Structural damage at Wilhelmshaven. Rear turret damaged. Port wing petrol tank holed. Hole in fuselage. Starboard wing damaged. A/C Cat: A1. Sustained damage at Wilhelmshaven on outward journey and further damage on the run up to the target. Port inner engine feathered. A/c finally crash landed near Venlo, due to loss of control about 1930 hours on 22.4.45. Crew returned Waterbeach evening 25th April 1945. (Aircraft was escorted by JI-D and JI-N).

Aircraft: LM285, JI-M
Captain: F/O S Abel
Target: BREMEN

This aircraft took off on a bombing operation at 1504 from Waterbeach and was flying as a follower in a vic of three formation, the leader carrying blind bombing equipment. While near Wilhelmshaven in clear weather at 17,000 ft. aircraft sustained damage from H/F fragments, one of which smashed the windscreen near Flight Engineer, and others caused damage to fuselage. A piece of flak passed through Pilot's sleeve without causing injury and grazed Flight Engineer's hand. This did not affect control of aircraft and formation was maintained as well as possible until approaching target at 1839, but while on run up, aircraft encountered more heavy flak. Rear Gunner reported a piece of flak had passed through bottom of rear turret – upwards to the rear, exploding some rounds of ammunition, and the turret was filled with smoke. At this time, Pilot noticed rudders were at fault, and it is believed controls had been affected by explosion in turret. By the time Rear Gunner had got out of his turret to use the fire extinguisher the smoke had cleared, but at almost the same time another flak shell burst at 50 feet away, slightly below on port side. A fragment from this hit No.2 tank on the port side and petrol began to come out immediately. Aircraft continued on bombing run and just before releasing bombs, (1x 4000, 16x 500lb.) 1841 hours, 19,000 feet, 3 heavy bursts were felt below. One of these shook the aircraft violently and splinters were heard rattling on the underside of the aircraft. After bombing two small holes were noticed in starboard wing.

It was impossible to keep in formation after this and aircraft staggered round in a half circle on to a course heading west. Gee and H2S. Were found to be u/s. and it was very cold inside the aircraft. As petrol was leaking fast from port tank and Captain decided he couldn't make base, port inner engine was feathered to reduce the risk of fire.

A course to steer – 325 degrees – was passed on request by Lancaster 'D' – 514, which was following closely. Aircraft gradually lost height and when at 15,000 feet Pilot noticed something wrong with ailerons. Rudder and aileron trim were u/s. and aircraft made a gentle turn to port at about 30 degrees which Pilot could not correct for some time, but eventually it came back on course, the Bomb Aimer in his hatch holding back the right rudder, and this approximate course was maintained. The Captain in the meantime ordering crew to put on parachute. Aircraft was then flying above 7-10 cloud and Captain was able to descend through a hole in this cloud and came out below cloud at 2,000 feet. Continuing at this height aircraft flew through a storm shower and then through some convection cloud when it was thrown about violently. Aircraft was then crossing the River Maas. Controls were extremely sluggish and pilot had to use full right rudder, full right aileron.

'Darkie' was called 3 times, but although an American voice was heard on this frequency there was no reply to call. On approaching Venrai, aircraft banked to port 30 degrees and pilot could not control it. Crew were ordered to crash positions but Flight Engineer remained by side of Captain. Aircraft was stopped from turning by closing throttle of starboard inner engine, and straight approach was made for pre-selected field, airspeed being 110-115 knots. A successful approach was made the wing being picked up by using engine, the ailerons and rudders were definitely jammed.

At 150 feet Pilot selected 'Wheels Down' to give cushioning effect on landing. They came down about half way. Aircraft made a normal final approach without flaps, the Engineer controlling throttles, and touched down at 1930 – 3 km E of Venrai, rolling on the wheels for some distance when the starboard wheel collapsed. Aircraft skidded rather sharply to port then stopped suddenly, the inside being filled with dust. Crew were uninjured and got out in 9 seconds, the Flight Engineer put switches off and Captain followed pulling off main cocks. Starboard inner engine caught fire and Captain tried to extinguish it with small fire extinguisher, but it eventually died out not spreading any further although there seemed to be leaking petrol about. Aircraft was placed under a guard and was not structurally damaged on landing, believed Category A.C. by C.T.O. from nearby aerodrome.

CREW: All survived.

F/O S Abel	*Pilot*
F/O JV Francis	*Navigator*
F/S DD Cramp	*Air Bomber*
F/S TF O'Neil	*WOP/AG*
Sgt R.O.Thomas	*Flight Engineer*
Sgt CA Cook	*Rear Gunner*
Sgt FG Gillett	*MU Gunner*

Target:	*Bremen – Supply Lines and Defences*
Aircraft deployed total:	*767*
514 Squadron:	*21*
Aircraft lost total:	*2 (Lancasters)*
514 Squadron:	*Nil*

Comments: Bomber Command despatched a large force to soften up the areas of the city due to be attacked by British ground forces. However, bombing was affected by cloud and smoke, with the Master Bomber ordering the attack to stop after 195 aircraft had bombed. The first major German port to be captured, Bremen surrendered after 3 days of ground attack, with 6,000 German troops deciding that, for them, the war was now over.

23rd April 1945.
Weather: Fair.
Non-Operational Flying: GH and Cross Country.
Operational Flying: Make and Mend today and tonight. Derby Figures required from 514 Squadron for target tomorrow. 514 Squadron offer 13 Aircraft.

24th April 1945.
Weather: Fine at first, then fair.
Non-Operational Flying: H2S and GH Training, Cross Country and A-S Firing.
Operational Flying: BOMBING – BAD OLDESLOE.
Thirteen aircraft detailed. Thirteen aircraft took off, all attacked primary target, dropping 78 x 1000 ANM 65 and 130 x 500 ANM 64 and 3 smoke puffs, between 1043 hours and 1046 hrs, from 16,900/18,700 ft. Five out of seven detailed to bomb on GH (2 GH u/s), 7 bombed on GH leaders, one bombed visually. 3/10ths to nil cloud. Very good GH runs. Rail and road junction and M/Y clearly visible, and bombing was concentrated on them, producing fires and smoke and explosions (especially at 1045). No fighters stop. No flak except over Dutch coast where one a/c was hit. All 514 Squadron aircraft landed.
F/O JH Tolley in RE123, A2-K reported: Attacked primary target: Bad-Oldesloe. Bomb load 6 x 1000 ANM 65 and 10 x 500 ANM 64. Bombed on GH 1054½ from 17,300ft. Good GH run. Heavy smoke over centre of target area, and explosions along rail tracks. Good concentration in centre of M/Y some bombs fell along residential area. Smoke and fires on junction. Bang on. Formation good but our followers not with us over target.
Squadron to stand-by for supply dropping tomorrow if ordered. No further instructions until 09.30 hours tomorrow.

Target: *Bad Oldesloe – Railway Yards*
Aircraft deployed total: *100 (Lancasters)*
514 Squadron: *13*
Aircraft lost total: *Nil*
514 Squadron: *Nil*

Comments: This was the final bombing raid for 514 Sqn, as they attacked the railway yards without loss. The town, between Hamburg and Lübeck, was described as 'unprepared for air attack' and its precautions were 'slack'.

Author's note: Perhaps they had believed their leaders' propaganda but in reality, one would have thought that the town's civic leaders would have noticed what had been going on around them, and been prepared for the eventuality of an air raid.

(Above) Assuming the recorded time is correct, F/O Tolley and his crew arrived over the target some nine minutes after the rest of 514 Squadron and, in doing so, dropped the squadron's last operational bomb load. Source: courtesy of Victoria RSL

25th April 1945.
Weather: Dawn mist then fair.
Non-Operational Flying: H2S and GH, Low Flying and Cross Country.
Operational Flying: 8 Aircraft required from 514 Squadron for supply dropping tonight. 8 Aircraft required from 514 Squadron for supply dropping tomorrow.
Tonight and tomorrows Operation cancelled.

26th April 1945.
Weather: Dawn mist then fair, cloudy with slight rain early in evening.
Non-Operational Flying: GH Training, Low Flying, Fighter Affiliation and Cross Country.
Operational Flying: Make and Mend today for 3 Group. No further information until 09.30 hours tomorrow.

27th April 1945.
Weather: Rain early, cloudy with showers during evening.
Non-Operational Flying: GH and H2S. Training, Fighter Affiliation and Cross Country.
Operational Flying: Aircraft loaded with rations, may be required today.
6 Aircraft required from 514 Squadron for supply dropping tonight.
Tonight's Operation cancelled. 14 Aircraft required from 514 Squadron for supply dropping.

28th April 1945.
Weather: Rain early, slight showers in later afternoon, otherwise fair.
Non-Operational Flying: GH Training, A/S Firing.
Operational Flying: Tonight's Operation cancelled. Today's Operation laid on for tomorrow.

29th April 1945.
Weather: Fair early, slight rain during morning, cloudy in afternoon, snow showers in evening.
Non-Operational Flying: Cross Country.
Operational Flying: There will be another attack for Aircraft who failed to take off at 12.20 hours. 14 Aircraft airborne for supply dropping in Holland. All 14 Aircraft landed. 514 Squadron offer 16 Aircraft for supply dropping.
2 Operations for tomorrow, we are on both attacks.

Both targets cancelled. Given a different target, which we are to go to twice tomorrow.

THE HAGUE – FOOD DROPPING.

Fourteen aircraft detailed. Fourteen aircraft took off, dropping 64 Packs between 1347/1403 hours on the dropping zone. Weather was broken cloud above and clear below. Dropping zone identified by red TIs dropped slightly to the Port and White Cross. Red TIs burnt out before the attack finished, and later crews saw only the White Cross. Food Packs sometimes only released with difficulty and some crews made 2 or 3 orbits in order to release. Bomb doors of several a/c suffered slight damage due to release of Food Packs. All crews reported a cheering populace delighted to receive the food. People on house tops waving flags.

F/L JA Chadwell in ME364, JI-P reported: Dropping area The Hague. Dropped 5 packs on red TI to port of airfield and white cross at 1352½ hours. Thousands of cheering civilians gave hearty welcome.

(Above) Food sacks are loaded into the bomb bay of a 514 Sqn Lancaster at Waterbeach prior to delivery to starving Dutch citizens. Source: Airworx Gmbh Archive.

30th April 1945.
Weather: Snow in morning. Cloudy afternoon, fine at night.
Non-Operational Flying: Cross Country.
Operational Flying: First attack cancelled, still standing by for second attack. 16 Aircraft airborne for dropping food in Holland.
All 514 Squadron Aircraft landed.
ROTTERDAM FOOD DROPPING.
16 Lancasters detailed. 16 took off. 16 dropped 62 out of 80 packs between 1810½ and 1830 hours. There were intermittent showers and low cloud. No TIs seen, only white cross. Dropping on the whole was concentrated. Some bags fell in water, some on marshy ground. People were picking up bags almost as they fell. Great enthusiasm from the populace. House on fire. (May have been caused by a Red TI according to F/L HC Mottershead in ME225, A2-L).

(Above) Ground crew, including Electrician LAC Frederick Blencowe, in front of an unidentified 514 Sqn Mk.I or III Lancaster. Too often overlooked, except by aircrew, the ground staff worked in often horrible conditions to keep the squadron operational. Source: Paul Blencowe.

Monthly Summary for April 1945

Awards:

1567211	F/Sgt J McGilmour	DFM
J9582	F/L LL Currie	DFC
J86219	F/O IJ Bittnor	DFC
146719	F/O TB Carpenter	DFC
153454	F/O RW Hemmings	DFC
169025	A/F/O DW Parks	DFC
183028	A/F/O WH Coyle	DFC
186325	A/F/O D Crome	DFC
165740	A/F/O HC Richford	DFC
187032	P/O JS Thomas	DFC
636773	W/O GB Stratford	DFC
1685202	Sgt L Woodroofe	DFC
A/419921	F/O TGN Trask	DFC
A/424502	F/O DL Wright	DFC

Operational:

Enemy Aircraft Destroyed:	Nil
Operational Flying Hours for April 1945:	990.5
Non-Operational Flying Hours for April 1945:	430.10
Total tons of bombs dropped in April 1945:	606½ tons
Cumulative tons of bombs dropped:	14,652½ tons
Number of sorties for April 1945:	136 carried out.
	8 early returns
	1 failed to take off
	1 crash landed

30 Sorties carrying Food Packs to Holland (Operation Manna): 62 tons.

Strength of squadron as at 30th April 1945:

Officers:	173
Aircrew:	276
Ground:	1 Officer
Total:	450

May 1945

1st May 1945.
Weather: Misty, then fair, with hail showers in afternoon.
Non-Operational Flying: Air Tests and Cross Country.
Operational Flying: 16 Aircraft airborne dropping food in The Hague. Weather clear. Bags dropped well together. Usual flag-waving crowds seen.
All 514 Squadron Aircraft landed. 17 Aircraft required for food dropping tomorrow.

2nd May 1945.
Weather: Misty early, then fair.
Non-Operational Flying: Air - Sea Firing, Air Tests, GH Bombing and Cross Country.
Operational Flying: 18 Aircraft airborne dropping food in The Hague. Weather clear. All 514 Squadron Aircraft landed. 12 Aircraft required for food dropping tomorrow.

3rd May 1945.
Weather: Fair with some drizzle, then cloudy with rain.
Non-Operational Flying: H2S and Cross Country, GH Bombing and Photo Bombing.
Operational Flying: 12 Aircraft airborne dropping food in The Hague.
All 514 Squadron Aircraft landed. 12 Aircraft required for food dropping tomorrow.

4th May 1945.
Weather: Snow and rain early, then fair with some showers.
Non-Operational Flying: H2S Exercises and Cross Country, GH Bombing and Photo Bombing.
Operational Flying: Only 6 Aircraft now required from 514 Squadron. 6 Aircraft airborne dropping food in The Hague.
All 514 Squadron Aircraft landed.

5th May 1945.
Weather: Misty early, rain during afternoon.
Non-Operational Flying: Nil.
Operational Flying: 6 Aircraft airborne dropping food in The Hague. All 514 Squadron Aircraft landed. 20 Aircraft required from 514 Squadron tomorrow.

6th May 1945.
Weather: Drizzle early, then fair.
Non-Operational Flying: Air - Sea Firing and Cross Country.
Operational Flying: Todays Operation cancelled. It will be repeated tomorrow.

(Above) This widely-circulated photograph shows a 514 Sqn Lancaster (JI-C, D or O) dropping food parcels as part of Operation Manna. The photo clearly demonstrates the low level at which the crews had to operate, over occupied territory whilst the war was still on. The operation depended on the German anti-aircraft defences honouring the agreement to let the Lancasters drop food supplies without being shot down. Source: Airworx Gmbh Archive.

7th May 1945.
Weather: Foggy early, then fair.
Non-Operational Flying: Air Tests, Air - Sea Firing and Cross Country.
Operational Flying: 20 Aircraft airborne dropping food in The Hague.
All 514 Squadron Aircraft landed. 24 Aircraft required from 514 Squadron tomorrow.

8th May 1945.
Weather: Slight rain at dawn then fair.
Non-Operational Flying: Nil.
Operational Flying: 8 Aircraft airborne dropping food in Rotterdam.
All 514 Squadron Aircraft landed. 10 Aircraft required from 514 Squadron to pick up POWs tomorrow.

9th May 1945.
Weather: Cloudy, slight rain at 13.00 hours.
Non-Operational Flying: Nil.
Operational Flying: 10 Aircraft airborne to pick up POWs at Juvincourt. 1 Aircraft 'B' F/C Beaton crashed 1 mile ESE of Roye Amy. 26 bodies recovered from Aircraft. 8 Aircraft landed at Base. (POWs dropped at Ford).
'E' landed at Base. 18 Aircraft required for picking up POWs tomorrow.

Crashed Aircraft:

RF230 JI-B. The aircraft took off at 0726 hours from Juvincourt in France at 1215 hours. A message giving their estimated time of arrival was received at RAF Waterbeach at 1219 and shortly afterwards the pilot reported he was experiencing trouble with the controls and was putting back to Juvincourt. A further message sent by the aircraft at 1225 stated that it was making a forced landing. Flares were fired off from an airfield on route indicating permission to land but no acknowledgment was received.

At 1230 hours RF230 was seen by a number of witnesses on the ground to approach Roye Ami airfield from the west. After circling the airfield twice the aircraft was seen to go into a steep bank to port, before going into a flat spin and crashing into the ground one mile east of Roye Ami. On investigation the aircraft seemed to be fully serviceable and it was not possible to establish the cause of the crash. The position of the passengers to the rear of the fuselage however indicated that the aircraft may have been tail heavy which could have resulted in the pilot believing that there was something seriously wrong with the aircraft, subsequently losing control and crashing. Whether the passengers' positions were taken up before or after difficulties arose could not be determined.

All the passengers and crew lost their lives and were buried at Clichy Northern Cemetery, which is on the northern boundary of Paris.

F/L D Beaton DSO	*Pilot*	*Killed*
F/O RB Hilchey RCAF	*Navigator*	*Killed*
F/S JG Brittain	*WOP/AG*	*Killed*
F/S RH Toms RCAF	*MU Gunner*	*Killed*
F/S OC Evers RCAF	*Rear Gunner*	*Killed*
F/S A McMurrugh	*Flight Engineer*	*Killed*

Passenger list – all killed.

Capt RW Wheeler	*Royal Engineers*
Lt PAT Campbell	*Royal West Kent Regt.*
Lt ETT Snowdon	*Royal Artillery*
Sgt RA Adams	*Royal Warwickshire Regt*
Cpl EL Belshaw	*East Surrey Regt*
Cpl AG Thompson	*Worcestershire Regt*
L/Cpl GW Franks	*Kings Royal Rifle*
Fus H Cummings	*Lancashire Fusiliers*
Fus O Parkin	*Lancashire Fusiliers*
Gdsm J Roe	*Irish Guards*
Gunner AJS Crowe	*Royal Artillery*
Gunner AN Labotake	*SAA*
WL Lindhelmer	*PAL*
M Maschit	*PAL*
Pte T Anderson	*Cameron Highlanders*
Pte WL Ball	*Queens Royal Regt*
Pte SJ Bayston	*Green Howards*
Pte RA Betton	*KSLI*
Pte RE Clark	*Royal Scots*
Pte W Croston	*Pioneer Corps*
Pte R Danson	*East Surrey Regt*
Pte R Turnbull	*Durham Light Infantry*
Pte P Yates	*Leicestershire Regt*
Rfn TJ Edwards	*Regiment not stated.*

10th May 1945.
Weather: Misty early then fair with slight rain.
Non-Operational Flying: Air Tests and Cross Country.
Operational Flying: 15 Aircraft airborne for Juvincourt to pick up POWs.
All 514 Squadron landed at Base. POWs dropped at Ford.

11th May 1945.
Weather: Fair, visibility moderate.
Non-Operational Flying: Air Tests.
Operational Flying: 15 Aircraft airborne for Juvincourt to pick up POWs.
All 514 Squadron Aircraft landed. (POWs dropped at Tangmere)
5 Aircraft took off for Juvincourt and picked up POWs.
5 Aircraft landed at Base (POWs dropped at Wing).

12th May 1945.
Weather: Misty at first then fair.
Non-Operational Flying: Air Tests only.
Operational Flying: 9 Aircraft airborne for Juvincourt to pick up POWs.
9 Aircraft landed at Base. (POWs dropped at Wing). 10 Aircraft airborne for Brussels, repatriating Belgian refugees and picking up POWs on return.
10 Aircraft landed at Base. 2 Aircraft returned empty. POWs dropped at Tangmere.

13th May 1945.
Weather: Fair slight rain and showers in afternoon.
Non-Operational Flying: Air Tests, Local Flying and Cross Country.
Operational Flying: 9 Aircraft airborne for Juvincourt to pick up POWs.
The weather at Juvincourt is unsuitable for landing and Aircraft are being told to return to Base on R/T. All 514 Squadron Aircraft landed at Base. No POWs picked up.

14th May 1945.
Weather: Fair at first then cloudy.
Non-Operational Flying: Fighter Affiliation, Air Tests.

Operational Flying: 14 Aircraft airborne for Juvincourt to pick up POWs.
All 514 Squadron Aircraft landed at Base. (POWs dropped at Oakley).

15th May 1945.
Weather: Fair.
Non-Operational Flying: Air Tests, Fighter Affiliation, H2S. Exercises, Local Flying.
Operational Flying: 5 Aircraft airborne for Juvincourt picking up POWs.
All 514 Squadron Aircraft landed. (POWs dropped at Wing).

16th May 1945.
Weather: Fair.
Non-Operational Flying: Fighter Affiliation, Air Tests, GH Bombing, H2S Exercises, A.S.F.
Operational Flying: 5 Aircraft airborne for Brussels, repatriating Belgian refugees and bringing back POWs.
All 514 Squadron Aircraft landed. (POWs dropped at Westcott).

17th May 1945.
Weather: Fine then fair.
Non-Operational Flying: Cross Country and Air Tests.
Operational Flying: 21 Aircraft airborne for Brussels, repatriating Belgian refugees and bringing back POWs.
All 514 Squadron Aircraft landed. (POWs dropped at Westcott).

18th May 1945.
Weather: Cloudy with drizzle early.
Non-Operational Flying: Air - Sea Firing, H2S Exercises, Air Tests, Cross Country.
Operational Flying: 20 Aircraft airborne for Brussels repatriating Belgian refugees and bringing back POWs.
All 514 Squadron Aircraft landed at Base. (POWs dropped at Oakley).

19th May 1945.
Weather: Fair and cloudy.
Non-Operational Flying: Cross Country.
Operational Flying: 20 Aircraft airborne for Brussels, repatriating Belgian refugees and bringing back POWs.
All 514 Squadron Aircraft landed at Base. (POWs dropped at Oakley).

20th May 1945.
Weather: Fair at first, rain during afternoon.
Non-Operational Flying: Nil.
Operational Flying: Today's Operation cancelled. 23 Aircraft required for tomorrow.

21st May 1945.
Weather: Fair.
Non-Operational Flying: Local Formation, Air Tests, Air -Sea Firing, Circuits and Landings.
Operational Flying: Todays Operation cancelled. 17 Aircraft required for tomorrow.

22nd May 1945.
Weather: Fair or cloudy, with slight rain.
Non-Operational Flying: Air Tests.
Operational Flying: Todays Operations cancelled. 16 Aircraft required from 514 Squadron tomorrow.

23rd May 1945.
Weather: Fog at sunrise, then cloudy with showers.
Non-Operational Flying: H2S. Exercises and Local Flying, GH Bombing.
Operational Flying: 16 Aircraft airborne for Brussels, repatriating Belgian refugees and bringing back POWs.
5 Aircraft required from 514 Squadron to view bomb damage in Germany tomorrow, also 14 Aircraft required for repatriating Belgian refugees and bringing back POWs. All 514 Squadron Aircraft landed at Base. (POWs dropped at Oakley).

24th May 1945.
Weather: Cloudy mostly.
Non-Operational Flying: Local Flying and H2S Exercises.
Operational Flying: Aircraft to view bomb damage cancelled. 14 Aircraft airborne for Brussels, repatriating Belgians and bringing back POWs.
All 514 Squadron Aircraft landed. No POWs brought back. 2 Aircraft required from 514 Squadron to view bomb damage in Germany tomorrow, also 14 Aircraft to repatriate Belgians and bring back POWs.

25th May 1945.
Weather: Fine at first, later cloudy with slight rain.
Non-Operational Flying: Taking spares to Juvincourt. H2S, Cross Country and Air Tests.
Operational Flying: 2 Aircraft airborne on tour over Germany. 14 Aircraft airborne repatriating Belgians and bringing back POWs.
All 514 Squadron Aircraft landed at Base. No POWs brought back. 2 Aircraft landed from the tour. 15 Aircraft required from 514 Squadron to repatriate Belgians and pick up POWs tomorrow, also 2 Aircraft required to view bomb damage in Germany.

26th May 1945.
Weather: Rain during morning and evening.
Non-Operational Flying: Air Tests, Air Sea Firing.
Operational Flying: 2 Aircraft airborne on tour over Germany. 14 Aircraft airborne repatriating Belgians and bringing back POWs.
2 Aircraft landed from the tour. All 514 Squadron Aircraft landed at Base. (POWs dropped at Ford). 2 Aircraft required tomorrow to view bomb damage over Germany.
3 Group standing down tomorrow.

27th May 1945.
Weather: Cloudy with showers and thunderstorms in evening.
Non-Operational Flying: Nil.
Operational Flying: 2 Aircraft airborne on tour over Germany. 12 Aircraft from 514 Squadron to stand by for further instructions.
2 Aircraft landed from tour. 2 Aircraft required to view bomb damage over Germany tomorrow.

28th May 1945.
Weather: Fog, becoming fair, then cloudy with slight rain.
Non-Operational Flying: Cross Country.
Operational Flying: Todays tour over Germany cancelled. The Aircraft will be required tomorrow.

29th May 1945.
Weather: Cloudy with slight rain, becoming fine after dark.
Non-Operational Flying: Nil.
Operational Flying: 2 Aircraft airborne on tour over Germany.
Both 514 Squadron Aircraft landed at Base. 2 Aircraft required again tomorrow, also 12 Aircraft are to stand by to bring POWs from Belgium.

30th May 1945.
Weather: Fine becoming cloudy, slight rain in afternoon and evening.
Non-Operational Flying: Nil.
Operational Flying: 2 Aircraft airborne on tour over Germany.
Both 514 Squadron Aircraft landed at Base. Our 12 Aircraft standing by may now stand down. 514 Squadron will not be required tomorrow.

31st May 1945.
Weather: Fair apart from slight showers in late afternoon.
Non-Operational Flying: Nil.
Operational Flying: Nil. 4 Aircraft required from 514 Squadron for tour over Germany tomorrow.

(Above) The Brewery Tap pub in Waterbeach had close ties to the RAF Station and, later, the RE barracks. It would have been a favoured retreat for squadron personnel. Source: Garth Ridley.

Monthly Summary for May 1945

Enemy Aircraft Destroyed: Nil
Operational Flying Hours for May 1945: 203.10
Non-Operational Flying Hours for May 1945: 20.40
Cumulative tons of bombs dropped: 14,652½ tons.

Number of Sorties for May 1945:

Operation Manna — 96 carried out, 2 brought back load.

Operation Exodus — 171 carried out, 14 abortive, 1 crashed.

Strength of Squadron as at 31st May 1945:

Officers: 152
Airmen: 242
Total: 394

June 1945

Compiled by F/Lt AJ Talbot.

1st June 1945.
Weather: Fair to cloudy; occasional showers.
Non-Operational Flying: None.
Operational Flying: 12 Aircraft, 514 Squadron to stand by for repatriating POWs. 4 Aircraft airborne on tour over Germany.
4 Aircraft landed from tour. 2 Aircraft from 514 Squadron required for tour tomorrow.

2nd June 1945.
Weather: Fair to cloudy, occasional showers.
Non-Operational Flying: Air Tests.
Operational Flying: 2 Aircraft airborne on tour.
2 Aircraft landed from tour. 2 Aircraft required for tomorrow.

3rd June 1945.
Weather: Fair, with some light rain.
Non-Operational Flying: None.
Operational Flying: 0938 hrs: Both Aircraft on tour.
1407 hrs: 2 Aircraft landed from tour. 2 Aircraft required for tomorrow.

4th June 1945.
Weather: Fair.
Non-Operational Flying: Cross Countries, Bombing details, GH Exercises, Circuits and Landings. A/T's, Night Flying, Circuits and Landings.
Operational Flying: Tour postponed, Take off now 16.30 hours.
1648 hrs: 2 Aircraft airborne on tour. 2 Aircraft required tomorrow for tour over Germany.
2112 hrs: 2 Aircraft landed from tour.

5th June 1945.
Weather: Cloudy with occasional rain.
Non-Operational Flying: Air Tests, GH Details, Air to Sea Firing.
Operational Flying: 2 Aircraft airborne on tour.
2 Aircraft landed from tour. 3 Aircraft to stand by to take Bomber Command Personnel on tour tomorrow in addition to the usual 2 Aircraft.

6th June 1945.
Weather: Rain and low cloud.
Non-Operational Flying: Night Flying - Circuits and Landings and High Level Bombing.
Operational Flying: Tour cancelled owing to bad weather. Same 5 Aircraft required for tour tomorrow.

7th June 1945.
Weather: Cloudy with some slight rain and drizzle.
Non-Operational Flying: Formation Flying - Air Tests and Air to Sea Firing - Bombing Details.
Operational Flying: Tour cancelled. 5 Aircraft required from No. 514 Squadron for tour tomorrow. Also 6 Aircraft to stand by for repatriating POWs

8th June 1945.
Weather: Fair.
Non-Operational Flying: Bombing Details - Cross Countries - Air Tests and Air to Sea Firing - Night Flying, Cross Countries.
Operational Flying: 2 Aircraft airborne on tour.
2 Aircraft landed from tour. 3 Aircraft with Bomber Command Personnel airborne on tour.
3 Aircraft landed from tour. 2 Aircraft required from 514 Squadron for tour tomorrow.

9th June 1945.
Weather: Fair.
Non-Operational Flying: Bombing Details.
Operational Flying: 2 Aircraft airborne on tour.
2 Aircraft landed from tour. 514 Squadron will not be taking part in the tour tomorrow.

10th June 1945.
Weather: Cloudy with rain at mid-day.
Non-Operational Flying: Nil.
Operational Flying: 7 Aircraft from 514 Squadron to stand by for repatriating POWs from 23.59 tonight. 2 Aircraft required for tour tomorrow.

11th June 1945.
Weather: Cloudy.
Non-Operational Flying: Air Tests - GH Details - Bombing Details - Night Flying - Circuits and Landings.
Operational Flying: Tour cancelled today owing to bad weather over the Continent. 2 Aircraft from 514 Squadron required for tour tomorrow.

12th June 1945.
Weather: Fair, slight showers in afternoon.
Non-Operational Flying: GH Details and Bombing Details, Night Flying, Circuits and Landings, High Level Bombing.
Operational Flying: Take off time for tour postponed.
1223 hrs: 2 Aircraft airborne on tour.
1726 hrs: 2 Aircraft landed from tour. 2 Aircraft required for tour tomorrow.

13th June 1945.
Weather: Fair.
Non-Operational Flying: High Level Bombing - GH Details - Fighter Affiliation. Night Flying - High Level Bombing and Cross Countries.
Operational Flying: 2 Aircraft airborne on tour.
2 Aircraft landed from tour. 2 Aircraft required from 514 Squadron for tour tomorrow. Also 7 aircraft to stand by to repatriate POWs.

14th June 1945.
Weather: Fair.
Non-Operational Flying: Fighter Affiliation and Air to Sea Firing. Night Flying. Cross Countries and High Level Bombing.
Operational Flying: 2 Aircraft airborne on tour.
2 Aircraft landed from tour. 3 Aircraft required from 514 Squadron for tour tomorrow, to carry Bomber Command Personnel.
3 Aircraft required from 514 Squadron; now not required.

15th June 1945.
Weather: Fair to cloudy.
Non-Operational Flying: Formation Flying and Air Tests.
Operational Flying: Nil.

16th June 1945.
Weather: Fair to cloudy.
Non-Operational Flying: Nil.
Operational Flying: 6 Aircraft required from 514 Squadron to stand by to repatriate POWs tomorrow. Also 3 Aircraft required for tour plus 3 Aircraft to carry Bomber Command Personnel on tour.

17th June 1945.
Weather: Fair.
Non-Operational Flying: Night Flying, Cross Countries and Fighter Affiliation.
Operational Flying: Only 2 Aircraft required for Bomber Command Party on tour today.
5 Aircraft airborne on tour.
5 Aircraft landed from tour. 2 Aircraft required from 514 Squadron for tour tomorrow.

18th June 1945.
Weather: Fair.
Non-Operational Flying: GH Bombing - High Level Bombing - Air Tests.
Night Flying - Circuits and Landings and Night Exercises.
Operational Flying: 2 Aircraft airborne on tour.
2 Aircraft landed from tour. 3 Aircraft required from 514 Squadron for tour tomorrow also 9 Aircraft required for a special daylight exercise.

19th June 1945.
Weather: Fair.
Non-Operational Flying: GH Bombing and High Level Bombing. Night Flying High Level Bombing, Circuits and Landings.
Operational Flying: 9 Aircraft airborne on special exercise. 3 Aircraft airborne on tour. 2 Aircraft required from 514 Squadron for Bullseye tonight.
3 Aircraft landed from tour. 9 Aircraft landed from exercise. Bullseye tonight cancelled. 5 Aircraft required from 514 Squadron for tour tomorrow. 3 Aircraft to carry Bomber Command Personnel.

20th June 1945.
Weather: Fair.
Non-Operational Flying: GH Bombing and Air Tests. Night Flying and Cross Countries.
Operational Flying: 2 Aircraft airborne on tour.

Tour for Bomber Command Personnel cancelled.
2 Aircraft Landed from tour. 2 Aircraft required for tour tomorrow, also 3 Aircraft to stand by to take Bomber Command Personnel. 9 Aircraft required for a special daylight exercise.

21st June 1945.
Weather: Fair, slight rain at mid-day.
Non-Operational Flying: High Level Bombing, Air Tests and Local Flying. Night Flying, Cross Countries.
Operational Flying: 9 Aircraft airborne on exercises. Tour cancelled today.
9 Aircraft landed from exercises. 9 Aircraft required from 514 Squadron for special daylight exercises tomorrow. 5 Aircraft required for tour and 3 Aircraft for Bomber Command Personnel tomorrow.

22nd June 1945.
Weather: Fair.
Non-Operational Flying: High Level Bombing and Air Tests. No Night Flying.
Operational Flying: 8 Aircraft airborne on exercise (1 failed to take off).
8 Aircraft landed from exercises. 2 Aircraft airborne on tour.
2 Aircraft landed from tour. 7 Aircraft required from 514 Squadron to stand by to repatriate POWs. 3 Aircraft airborne on tour.
2 Aircraft required from 514 Squadron for tour tomorrow. 3 Aircraft landed from tour.

23rd June 1945.
Weather: Cloudy with rain early.
Non-Operational Flying: High Level Bombing and Air Tests. Night Flying, Circuits and Landings and High Level Bombing.
Operational Flying: 2 Aircraft airborne on tour.
2 Aircraft landed from tour. 514 Squadron not required for tour tomorrow.

24th June 1945.
Weather: Fair.
Non-Operational Flying: Nil.
Operational Flying: 18 Aircraft required for special exercise tomorrow.

25th June 1945.
Weather: Fair.
Non-Operational Flying: Air Tests. Night Flying. Cross Countries.
Operational Flying: 16 Aircraft airborne on special exercises. 2 Aircraft failed to take off. 2 Aircraft required from 514 Squadron for Bullseye tonight. 10 Aircraft required from 514 Squadron for special exercises tomorrow. All 514 Squadron Aircraft landed from special exercises. 2 Aircraft required for tour tomorrow. 2 Aircraft airborne on Bullseye.
2 Aircraft landed from Bullseye.

26th June 1945.
Weather: Cloudy with drizzle during morning.
Non-Operational Flying: Formation Flying.
Operational Flying: Special exercises for today cancelled. 2 Aircraft airborne on tour.
Both Aircraft landed from tour. 10 Aircraft required from 514 Squadron for special exercises tomorrow. Also 2 Aircraft for tour.

27th June 1945.
Weather: Fair at first, showers and thunder storms in afternoon.
Non-Operational Flying: GH Details and Local Flying. Formation Flying, Night Flying and Cross Countries.
Operational Flying: Special exercises for today cancelled. Tour today cancelled. 5 Aircraft required for tour tomorrow. 3 to carry Bomber Command Personnel. Also 10 Aircraft required for special exercises.

28th June 1945.
Weather: Fair during day, with cloud and some rain at night.
Non-Operational Flying: Air Tests, Formation and Air to Sea Firing. No Night Flying.
Operational Flying: Special exercises for today cancelled.
6 Aircraft airborne on tour.
12 Aircraft required from 514 Squadron for special exercises tomorrow. 6 Aircraft landed from tour.

29th June 1945.
Weather: Misty early, with showers due in evening.
Non-Operational Flying: GH Bombing and Fighter Affiliation. No night flying.
Operational Flying: There will be a tour today.
Tour cancelled. 12 Aircraft airborne on special exercises.

No Bullseye tonight. 10 Aircraft required from 514 Squadron for special exercises tomorrow. All 514 Squadron Aircraft landed from special exercises. 3 Aircraft from 514 Squadron required for tour tomorrow.

30th June 1945.
Weather: Fair to cloudy.
Non-Operational Flying: GH Details, Air Tests and Local Flying.
Operational Flying: Special exercises postponed. 3 Aircraft airborne on tour.
Special exercises cancelled. 2 Aircraft required for tour, and 10 Aircraft for special exercises tomorrow.

(Above) A sense of scale is given to this 4000lb 'Cookie' by the author's son. William Hepworth had been reassured that the bomb was not live before he agreed to stand next to it. The location is the Lincolnshire Aviation Heritage Centre at East Kirkby, home of Lancaster 'Just Jane'. Photo: Simon Hepworth.

Monthly Summary for June 1945

Operational: (compiled by F/Lt. AJ Talbot - Adjutant, 514 Squadron)

Enemy Aircraft Destroyed:	Nil
Non-Operational Flying Hours for June 1945:	1184.35
Cumulative tons of bombs dropped:	14,652½ tons.

Number of Sorties for June 1945:

Operation Baedeker:	66 carried out.
	3 returned early.
Operation Dodge:	7 carried out.
	1 A/C u/s in Italy.
Operation Post Mortem:	33 carried out.

Strength of Squadron as at 30th June 1945:

Officers:	134
Aircrew: SNCOs	196
Ground:	1 Officer
Total:	331

July 1945

1st July 1945.
Weather: Fine a.m. Cloudy and thunderstorm in afternoon -showers.
Non-Operational Flying: Air Tests. Local and formation flying.
Operational Flying: Tour cancelled. 10 Aircraft airborne on special exercises.
2 Aircraft required from 514 Squadron for tour tomorrow. 1 Aircraft returned early from exercises on account of weather.
9 Aircraft landed from exercise.

2nd July 1945.
Weather: Fair during day. Slight rain at night.
Non-Operational Flying: Nil.
Operational Flying: Tour cancelled. 10 Aircraft required from 514 Squadron for special exercises tonight. 514 Squadron allocated for tour tomorrow - 2 Aircraft and 1 Aircraft for Base personnel and 3 Aircraft for Bomber Command Party.
Special exercises cancelled.

3rd July 1945.
Weather: Cloudy morning; Fair evening. Fine at night.
Non-Operational Flying: Air tests and local flying.
Operational Flying: 3 Aircraft airborne on tour. Stand by for Special Exercises. Take off at 14.00 hours. 3 Aircraft landed from Tour. 3 Aircraft for Bomber Command Personnel cancelled. 12 Aircraft airborne on special exercises.
All Aircraft landed from special exercises.

4th July 1945.
Weather: Fog after dawn, then cloud, slight drizzle in the evening.
Non-Operational Flying: Nil
Operational Flying: Squadron stood down today. 11 Aircraft required from 514 Squadron for special exercises. 3 Aircraft are required for tour in morning and 3 Aircraft for Bomber Command Personnel in the afternoon.

5th July 1945.
Weather: Cloudy morning. Slight drizzle towards noon.
Non-Operational Flying: Air Tests.
Operational Flying: No Bullseye tonight. 11 Aircraft airborne on special exercises. 3 Aircraft airborne on tour. 3 Aircraft airborne on

tour with Bomber Command Personnel. 14 Aircraft required for special exercise tomorrow.
2 Aircraft required for tour tomorrow. 11 Aircraft landed from special exercise. 3 Aircraft landed from tour. 3 Aircraft landed from tour with Bomber Command Personnel. Exercise tomorrow is cancelled.

6th July 1945.
Weather: Fine morning. Fair afternoon. Cloudy at night.
Non-Operational Flying: Fighter Affiliation, Air tests and Formation Flying.
Operational Flying: 2 a/c airborne on tour. No Bullseye tonight. 2 Aircraft required from 514 Squadron for tour tomorrow.
2 Aircraft landed from tour. No special exercises tomorrow.

7th July 1945.
Weather: Mainly fair during day. Fine in evening.
Non-Operational Flying: High Level Bombing, H2S, Cross Country, GH and Air Tests.
Operational Flying: 2 airborne on tour.
2 Aircraft landed from tour. 2 Aircraft required for tour tomorrow and 2 Aircraft for Bomber Command Personnel.

8th July 1945.
Weather: Mainly fair.
Non-Operational Flying: High Level Bombing, Formation Flying. Fighter Affiliation and GH Bombing.
Operational Flying: 2 Aircraft airborne on tour.
2 Aircraft landed from tour. 3 Aircraft required from 514 Squadron for tour tomorrow. 3 Aircraft airborne on tour with Bomber Command Personnel.
3 Aircraft landed from tour with Bomber Command Personnel.

9th July 1945.
Weather: Fair early - then cloudy. Slight rain and showers in evening.
Non-Operational Flying: GH Bombing, Air/Sea Firing, H2S., Cross Country, GH Photo and Local Flying.
Operational Flying: 2 Aircraft airborne for Italy. 3 Aircraft airborne on tour.
No bulls eye tonight. 3 Aircraft landed from tour. 2 Aircraft required for tour tomorrow.

10th July 1945.
Weather: Cloudy early, then low cloud and slight rain or drizzle.
Non-Operational Flying: Nil
Operational Flying: Tour cancelled today. 9 Aircraft required for Bullseye tonight. Owing to weather, no orders for tomorrow until 1800 hrs. Bullseye tonight cancelled.
1640 hrs: No operations tomorrow.

11th July 1945.
Weather: Drizzle and fog till early afternoon then cloud. Fine later.
Non-Operational Flying: Nil
Operational Flying: 2 Aircraft required for tour tomorrow.

12th July 1945.
Weather: Mainly fair.
Non-Operational Flying: GH Bombing and Photo High Level Bombing. H2S, Cross Country, and H.L. Bombing.
Operational Flying: 2 Aircraft airborne on tour.
4 Aircraft required for Bullseye tonight. 2 Aircraft landed from tour. 3 Aircraft required for tour tomorrow - Also 3 Aircraft to carry Bomber Command Personnel in afternoon. 514 Squadron will not be required to participate in special exercises tomorrow.
4 Aircraft airborne on Bullseye.
4 Aircraft landed from Bullseye.

13th July 1945.
Weather: Cloudy early, then fine to fair.
Non-Operational Flying: Nil
Operational Flying: 3 Aircraft airborne on tour. 3 Aircraft landed from tour.
3 Aircraft airborne on tour with Bomber Command Personnel. 2 Aircraft required for tomorrow. 'E' landed from Italy. 3 Aircraft landed from tour with Bomber Command Personnel.

14th July 1945.
Weather: Cloudy with slight rain during morning, fair afternoon. Cloudy with thunder and slight rain at night.
Non-Operational Flying: High Level Bombing, Air to Sea Firing and Local Flying.
Operational Flying: 2 Aircraft airborne on tour.

2 Aircraft landed from tour. 'J2' landed from Italy. 2 Aircraft required for tour tomorrow.

15th July 1945.
Weather: Thunder early, then mainly fair till evening, when showery.
Non-Operational Flying: GH Bombing, Air to Sea Firing, Local Flying and Fighter Affiliation.
Operational Flying: 2 Aircraft airborne on tour.
2 Aircraft landed from tour. 2 Aircraft required for tour tomorrow. 9 Aircraft required for special exercise tomorrow.

16th July 1945.
Weather: Showers and slight rain during morning, then cloudy becoming fair later.
Non-Operational Flying: Air to Sea Firing and Air Tests.
Operational Flying: Special exercises today cancelled. We are to be prepared to do the special exercise tomorrow. 2 Aircraft airborne on tour. No Bullseye tonight.
2 Aircraft landed from tour. 5 Aircraft for tour tomorrow. 3 for Bomber Command Passengers.

17th July 1945.
Weather: Fine very early, thin fog. Fog clearing and generally cloudy, thin evening then fine.
Non-Operational Flying: Air Test, Local Flying.
Operational Flying: 2 Aircraft airborne on tour. 1 Aircraft airborne on special exercise. 3 Aircraft required for Bullseye tonight.
2 Aircraft landed from tour. 3 Aircraft airborne on tour with Bomber Command Personnel. 3 Aircraft required for tour tomorrow. 3 Aircraft landed from tour. 2 Aircraft airborne on Bullseye, 1 Aircraft failed to take off.
2 Aircraft landed from Bullseye.

18th July 1945.
Weather: Fine early then cloudy, slight rain in evening.
Non-Operational Flying: Air Tests, High Level Bombing and Local Flying.
Operational Flying: 3 Aircraft airborne on tour.
3 Aircraft landed from tour. 2 Aircraft required for tour tomorrow, also 3 Aircraft for Bomber Command Passengers.

19th July 1945.
Weather: Slight rain early, then fair to cloudy. Slight showers and slight rain in evening.
Non-Operational Flying: GH Bombing.
Operational Flying: 2 Aircraft airborne on tour.
2 Aircraft landed from tour. 3 Aircraft airborne on tour, with Bomber Command Passengers. 3 Aircraft required for tour tomorrow. 3 Aircraft landed from tour.

20th July 1945.
Weather: Slight rain early, cloudy with slight showers during afternoon. Fair at night.
Non-Operational Flying: Air to Sea Firing.
Operational Flying: 3 Aircraft airborne on tour.
There will be a Bullseye tonight, 514 Squadron will supply 4 Aircraft.
3 Aircraft landed from tour. 2 Aircraft required for tour tomorrow, also 3 Aircraft to carry Bomber Command Passengers.
4 Aircraft airborne on Bullseye.
4 Aircraft landed from Bullseye.

21st July 1945.
Weather: Slight drizzle early, then cloudy to fair.
Non-Operational Flying: Air to Sea Firing and Air Tests.
Operational Flying: This morning's tour cancelled.
3 Aircraft airborne on tour with Bomber Command Personnel. 2 Aircraft required for tour tomorrow. 3 Aircraft now required for tour.
1950 hrs: 3 Aircraft landed from tour.
2345 hrs: 'D' RE137 crashed on Night Cross Country - crew OK.
Note: There is no other record of this loss.

22nd July 1945.
Weather: Fair to cloudy during day, fine at night
Non-Operational Flying: HL Bombing and jettisoning of incendiaries.
Operational Flying: 'Q' W/Cdr Morgan airborne for Italy. 3 Aircraft airborne on tour.
3 Aircraft landed from tour. 2 Aircraft required for tour tomorrow, also 3 Aircraft for Bomber Command Party. 'Q' landed in Italy.

23rd July 1945.
Weather: Fair to fine.
Non-Operational Flying: Jettisoning of incendiaries.
Operational Flying: 2 Aircraft airborne on tour.

5 Aircraft required to go to Italy tomorrow. 2 Aircraft landed from tour. 3 Aircraft airborne on tour with Bomber Command Passengers. 2 Aircraft required for tour tomorrow.
3 Aircraft landed from tour.

24th July 1945.
Weather: Mainly cloudy, hazy in afternoon and evening.
Non-Operational Flying: Jettisoning incendiaries.
Operational Flying: 3 Aircraft airborne for Italy. 2 Aircraft airborne on tour.
2 Aircraft landed from tour. 2 Aircraft required for tour tomorrow.

25th July 1945.
Weather: Mainly cloudy, occasional slight rain in early evening.
Non-Operational Flying: Jettisoning of incendiaries and Air Tests.
Operational Flying: 2 Aircraft airborne on tour.
2 Aircraft landed from tour. 3 Aircraft required for tour tomorrow, also 3 Aircraft required to carry Bomber Command Passengers.

26th July 1945.
Weather: Cloudy with slight rain till late afternoon, then cloudy to fair.
Non-Operational Flying: Air Tests.
Operational Flying: 3 Aircraft airborne on tour.
3 Aircraft landed from tour. 5 Aircraft landed from Italy. No tour tomorrow.

27th July 1945.
Weather: Slight rain in early morning, then cloudy to fair.
Non-Operational Flying: High Level Bombing.
Operational Flying: No Bullseye tonight. 3 Aircraft required for tour tomorrow morning.

28th July 1945.
Weather: Fine early, then fair to cloudy.
Non-Operational Flying: Air to Sea Firing.
Operational Flying: 3 Aircraft airborne on tour.
3 Aircraft landed from tour. 2 Aircraft required from 514 Squadron for tour tomorrow.

29th July 1945.
Weather: Mainly fair.
Non-Operational Flying: Air to Sea Firing, Formation Flying and Air Tests.
Operational Flying: 2 Aircraft airborne on tour. 2 Aircraft required from 514 Squadron in the morning for tour and 3 Aircraft in the afternoon for Bomber Command Personnel.
2 Aircraft landed from tour.

30th July 1945.
Weather: Cloudy early, then slight drizzle - cloudy to fair.
Non-Operational Flying: High Level Bombing and Air Tests.
Operational Flying: Tour postponed to this afternoon. No Bullseye tonight.
2 Aircraft airborne on tour. 3 Aircraft airborne on tour with Bomber Command Personnel.
1 Aircraft returned early from tour. 2 Aircraft from 514 Squadron required for tour tomorrow. 2 Aircraft landed from tour. 2 Aircraft returned from tour with Bomber Command Personnel.

(Above) Battle of Britain Memorial Flight Lancaster PA474 overflies the main runway at RAF Waterbeach for the 2002 reunion of 514 Sqn. Source: Garth Ridley.

31st July 1945.

Weather: Mainly cloudy, occasional light drizzle in the morning and evening.

Non-Operational Flying: High Level Bombing, GH Exercise and Local Flying.

Operational Flying: 2 Aircraft airborne on tour.

2 Aircraft returned early from tour on account of bad weather. 2 Aircraft plus 1 Aircraft for Base Personnel in the morning and 3 Aircraft for Bomber Command Personnel in the Afternoon required tomorrow. No Bullseye tonight. No tour tomorrow either morning or afternoon.

(Above) This simple memorial to 514 Squadron's lost crews is in the Parish Church of St John the Evangelist in Waterbeach. The squadron Roll of Honour is displayed beneath it. Photo: Simon Hepworth.

Monthly Summary for July 1945

Operational: (compiled by F/Lt AJ Talbot - Adjutant, 514 Squadron)

Enemy Aircraft Destroyed:	Nil
Non-Operational Flying Hours for July 1945:	1184.35
Cumulative tons of bombs dropped:	14,652½ tons.

Number of Sorties for July 1945:

Operation Baedeker:	66 carried out.
	3 returned early.
Operation Dodge:	7 carried out.
	1 A/C u/s in Italy.
Operation Post Mortem:	33 carried out.

Strength of Squadron as at 31st July 1945:

Aircrew:	
Officers:	134
SNCOs	196
Ground:	1 Officer
Total:	331

August 1945

1st August 1945.
Weather: Cloudy with intermittent rain. Good visibility.
Non-Operational Flying: Air Tests, GH Bombing, Night Cross Countries.
Operational Flying: 2 Aircraft required from 514 Squadron for Baedeker tour tomorrow.
9 Aircraft required for Operation Dodge tomorrow.

2nd August 1945.
Weather: Cloudy becoming fine, good visibility.
Non-Operational Flying: GH Exercises.
Operational Flying: 9 Aircraft for Italy. 2 Aircraft on Baedeker tour. 8 Aircraft offered for Bullseye tonight.
2 Aircraft landed from Baedeker tour. 8 Aircraft airborne on Bullseye.
2 Aircraft required for Baedeker tomorrow. 2 Aircraft landed early for Bullseye. Remaining 6 Aircraft landed from Bullseye.

3rd August 1945.
Weather: Fine but fog after dawn. Poor to good visibility.
Non-Operational Flying: Air Tests, Night Cross Countries and Bombing.
Operational Flying: 2 Aircraft airborne on Baedeker.
2 Aircraft landed from Baedeker. There is no Baedeker tomorrow.

4th August 1945.
Weather: Fine to fair. Moderate to good visibility.
Non-Operational Flying: Formation Flying and Night Local Flying.
Operational Flying: 8 of our Aircraft will be returning from Italy today.
All Aircraft landed from Italy except 'U' which is u/s at Foggia, Italy.

5th August 1945.
Weather: Fine becoming cloudy with thunderstorms during evening. Good visibility.
Non-Operational Flying: Nil
Operational Flying: 9 Aircraft required for Dodge Operation tomorrow from 514 Squadron, tomorrow.

6th August 1945.
Weather: Fair becoming cloudy with showers. Good visibility but misty at dawn.
Non-Operational Flying: Nil
Operational Flying: 9 Aircraft airborne for Italy.

7th August 1945.
Weather: Mainly cloudy with some rain. Good visibility.
Non-Operational Flying: Air tests, Bombing and Air to Sea Firing.
Operational Flying: No Bullseye tonight due to bad weather conditions. There will be no Baedeker tomorrow, weather u/s, but 3 Aircraft required for Dodge Operation.

8th August 1945.
Weather: Cloudy to fair. Moderate to good visibility.
Non-Operational Flying: GH Exercises, Bombing and Formation Flying.
Operational Flying: Operation Dodge cancelled. Our Aircraft will not be returning from Italy today. 3 Aircraft required for Dodge tomorrow.

9th August 1945.
Weather: Fine but cloudy with rain after dawn. Poor to moderate visibility. Fog at dawn.
Non-Operational Flying: Local Flying.
Operational Flying: Operation Dodge cancelled. No Bullseye tonight. 6 Aircraft required from 514 Squadron for Dodge tomorrow. Take off postponed for Italy trip tomorrow.

10th August 1945.
Weather: Cloudy with rain becoming fair to fine. Moderate to good visibility.
Non-Operational Flying: 2 Aircraft delivered to Hullavington 10.10 Kemble.
Operational Flying: Operation Dodge cancelled. Crews to stand by for Dodge to take off about 11.30 hours. No Bullseye tonight.
Dodge Operation cancelled. Crews to stand by for Dodge tomorrow as for today. Baedeker tomorrow, 2 Aircraft from 514 Squadron.
Dodge Operation confirmed tomorrow. 2 of our Aircraft are returning from Italy tonight.
 2 Aircraft have been diverted to Glotton as we cannot land them here due to bad weather.

11th August 1945.
Weather: Cloudy with some drizzle. Poor visibility, becoming good.
Non-Operational Flying: Nil
Operational Flying: All 6 Aircraft airborne for Italy, but 'H' had to land at Ford, engine u/s. Our other 7 Aircraft are returning from Italy today. Baedeker cancelled because of bad weather. Baedeker tomorrow, 2 Aircraft and 2 Aircraft for Bomber Command Personnel required from 514 Squadron.
All Aircraft landed from Italy.

12th August 1945.
Weather: Cloudy with drizzle, becoming mainly cloudy. Poor to moderate visibility.
Non-Operational Flying: Air Tests.
Operational Flying: Baedeker confirmed today, 1 more Aircraft for Bomber Command Personnel. Warning order for Operation Dodge tomorrow, 6 Aircraft. 2 Aircraft airborne on Baedeker. 3 Aircraft airborne on Baedeker with Bomber Command Personnel.
Baedeker tomorrow, 3 Aircraft required. 2 Aircraft landed from Baedeker. 3 Aircraft returned from Baedeker with Bomber Command Personnel.

13th August 1945.
Weather: Cloud with drizzle near midnight. Moderate to good visibility.
Non-Operational Flying: Nil
Operational Flying: Operation Dodge is postponed for 3 hours and is subject to cancellation.
Operation Dodge cancelled.
Baedeker cancelled.
Stand by with 6 Aircraft for Operation Dodge. There will be no Baedeker tomorrow. All Aircraft returned from Italy except 'R'.

14th August 1945.
Weather: Cloudy with continuous drizzle becoming fine. Fog at dawn otherwise moderate visibility.
Non-Operational Flying: Nil
Operational Flying: Operation Dodge postponed for 3 hours.
Operation Dodge postponed for a further hour.

Operation Dodge cancelled. 2 Aircraft required from 514 Squadron for Baedeker tomorrow. No Aircraft required from 514 Squadron for Operation Dodge tomorrow.

VJ Day. Confirmed throughout official channels. (Note: VJ Day is celebrated on 15th August everywhere except 514 Sqn).

15th August 1945.
Weather: Cloudy with some rain in afternoon. Moderate to good visibility.
Non-Operational Flying: Air Tests.
Operational Flying: Operation Baedeker cancelled. 514 Squadron standing by with 15 Aircraft for Operation Dodge.

16th August 1945.
Weather: Fair to cloudy, good visibility.
Non-Operational Flying: Nil
Operational Flying: 14 Aircraft airborne for Italy - 1 Aircraft went u/s.
Operation Baedeker: 3 Aircraft required, 1 for Group Personnel.
All Aircraft landed safely at Bari, Italy. 514 Squadron not required for Dodge Operation.

17th August 1945.
Weather: Fine becoming cloudy with rain in evening, moderate visibility.
Non-Operational Flying: Air Tests and 1 delivery to Kemble.
Operational Flying: Operation Baedeker cancelled owing to weather. No Bullseye tonight. 514 Squadron have offered 3 Aircraft Crews for tomorrows Dodge Operation.
No Operation Dodge tomorrow. Baedeker: 3 Aircraft required tomorrow, 1 for Base Personnel.

18th August 1945.
Weather: Cloudy with intermittent drizzle. Moderate to good visibility.
Non-Operational Flying: Air Tests.
Operational Flying: 2 Aircraft airborne on Baedeker, the other Aircraft went u/s owing to PO and PI magneto drops. Warning for Operation Dodge tomorrow. Squadron may be required to produce up to their maximum effort. Our Aircraft will not be coming back from Italy today.
2 Aircraft required from 514 Squadron for Baedeker tomorrow. 514 Squadron not required for Operation Dodge tomorrow. 2 Aircraft landed from Baedeker Operation.

19th August 1945.
Weather: Cloudy with intermittent drizzle becoming cloudy, good visibility.
Non-Operational Flying: Nil
Operational Flying: There will be no Aircraft returning from Italy tomorrow. Baedeker scrubbed on account of weather.
2 Aircraft for Baedeker tomorrow. 2 Aircraft returning from Italy tomorrow afternoon.

20th August 1945.
Weather: Cloudy, moderate to good visibility.
Non-Operational Flying: Air Tests.
Operational Flying: It is now confirmed Aircraft are returning from Italy. No Bullseye tonight.
2 Aircraft airborne on Baedeker.
All Aircraft landed at Base from Italy. No Baedeker tomorrow. 2 Aircraft landed from Baedeker. No Operation Dodge for 514 Squadron tomorrow.

21st August 1945.
Weather: Cloudy with rain in forenoon and showers late evening. Moderate to good visibility.
Non-Operational Flying: 2 Aircraft delivered to Aston Down.
Operational Flying: No Bullseye tomorrow.

22nd August 1945
514 Squadron has now disbanded. Aircrew Personnel have been posted according to instructions, and remainder have been sent on leave to await instructions.

PLB Morgan,
Wing Commander,
Commanding,
514 Squadron, RAF Waterbeach.

Note: There is no monthly summary for August 1945.

514 Squadron Operational Record

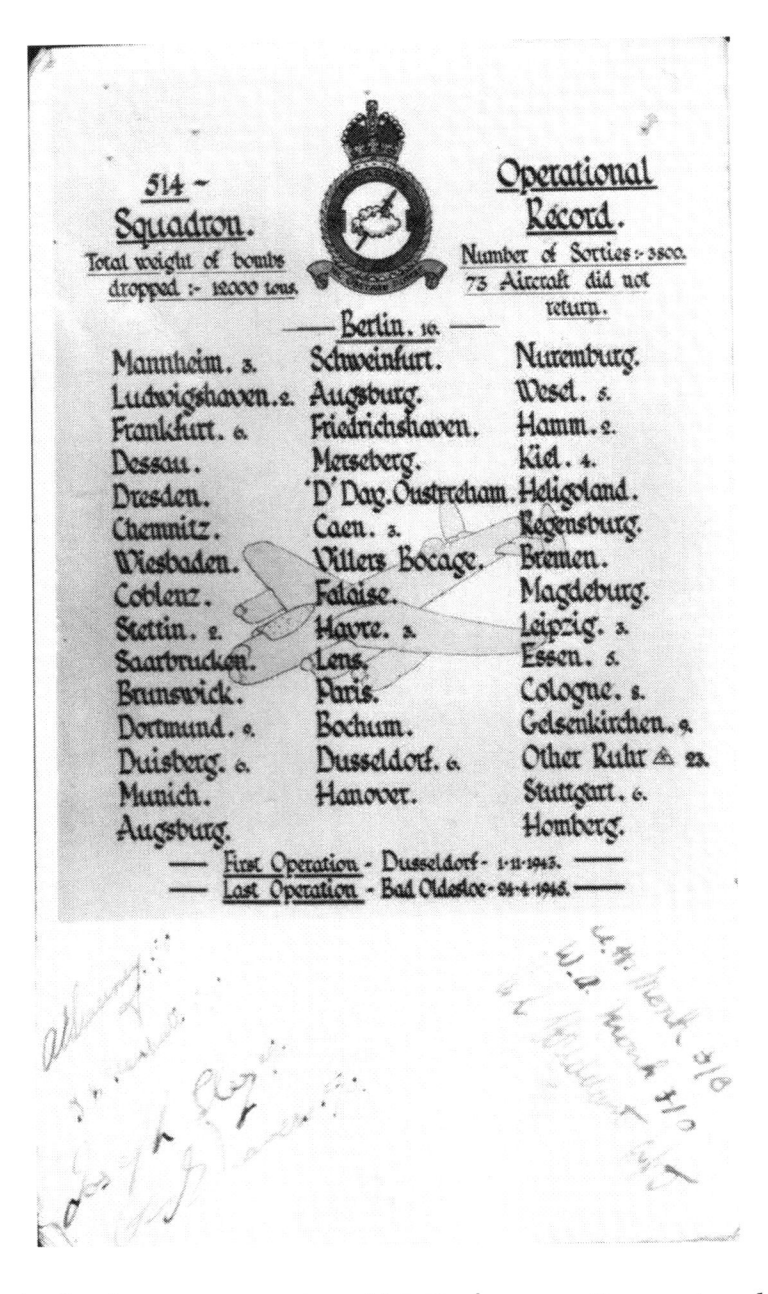

Total weight of bombs dropped :- 18,000 tons.

Number of Sorties :- 3800.
73 Aircraft did not return.

— Berlin. 10. —

Mannheim. 3.	Schweinfurt.	Nuremburg.
Ludwigshaven. 2.	Augsburg.	Wesel. 5.
Frankfurt. 6.	Friedrichshaven.	Hamm. 2.
Dessau.	Merseberg.	Kiel. 4.
Dresden.	'D' Day. Oustreham.	Heligoland.
Chemnitz.	Caen. 3.	Regensburg.
Wiesbaden.	Villers Bocage.	Bremen.
Coblenz.	Falaise.	Magdeburg.
Stettin. 2.	Havre. 3.	Leipzig. 3.
Saarbrucken.	Lens.	Essen. 5.
Brunswick.	Paris.	Cologne. 5.
Dortmund. 9.	Bochum.	Gelsenkirchen. 9.
Duisberg. 6.	Dusseldorf. 6.	Other Ruhr. 23.
Munich.	Hanover.	Stuttgart. 6.
Augsburg.		Homberg.

— First Operation - Dusseldorf - 1-11-1943. —
— Last Operation - Bad Oldesloe - 24-4-1945. —

(Above) Card commemorating 514 Sqn's operations, signed by a number of surviving members. Some frequently-visited targets have the number of raids noted alongside them; Homberg is mentioned just once but this single target, visited on five occasions, accounted for eight aircraft, the highest number of all. Source: Garth Ridley.

(Above) Still going strong in 2007. The 514 Squadron Association was reformed in 1988 by Hugh Woodcraft. Reunions at Waterbeach have subsequently been organised by Clive Hill, great nephew of Sgt Clive Banfield, KIA on 11th April 1944 attacking Aachen. The 514 Squadron Association in Canada is run by Wendy Flemming, daughter of Sgt Ross Flemming, who survived the war. Source: Wendy Flemming.

(Above) An unidentified 514 Sqn crew sits on the wing of their Mk.II Lancaster. Source: Linda Miles.

(Above) Derelict and unreachable, the former Watch Office at RAF Waterbeach is fenced off, along with the rest of the airfield. Instead of Lancasters, it now keeps watch over mountains of straw, fuel for a nearby power station. The Ministry of Defence wants to sell the land to property developers. It is hoped that the Memorial Garden will be preserved. Photo: William Hepworth.

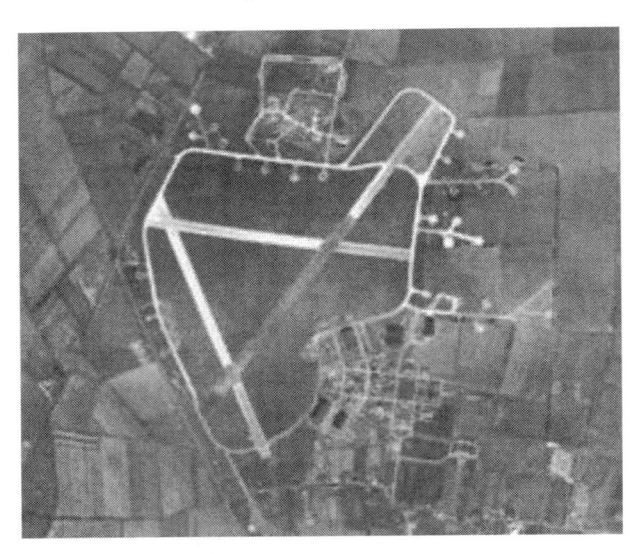

(Above) An aerial photograph of RAF Waterbeach in 1945. Source: Airworx GmbH Archive.

War Stories

Sgt Ernest 'Sunny' Gledhill
by Tracy Holdroyd-Smith

Sunny Gledhill joined up on 5th October 1941, joining 10RC on 19th January 1942. Whilst in this training school, he was photographed on the 25th of April. One photograph included two training school friends; F Betson (1682564) from Feltham, Middlesex and SD Cook (1580183) from Scunthorpe, Lincolnshire. It appears that both these men survived the war.

(Above) Sunny Gledhill with F Betson and SD Cook.

Entering 2 Signals School at RAF Yatesbury, Wiltshire, on 14th May 1942, Sunny then endured a succession of postings, before training as an Air Gunner. It was usual in Bomber Command for Wireless Operators to act as the crew's reserve air gunner on heavy bombers, ensuring a certain degree of resilience.

His gunnery training was at 7 Air Gunners School at Stormy Down, Wales and involved flying in Whitley bombers. Sunny gained his Sergeant's stripes on the 9th of June, after gaining 78% in his training.

The next move was to 9 OAFU (Observer Advanced Flying Unit), at RAF Llandwrog, near Caernarfon, Wales, training on Avro Ansons shortly after his 22nd birthday. RAF Llandwrog was considered a very pleasant base, being positioned on the coast directly next to the beach and in the shadow of the mountains of Snowdonia.

In July 1943 Sunny joined 12 Operational Training Unit. This training unit was re-organised as 1657 Conversion Unit, based at RAF Stradishall, Suffolk. Sunny remained there until 6th of December 1943, becoming part of a crew. These were:

Sergeant John Clare Gilbertson-Pritchard (1084862), Pilot.
Sergeant Gordon Kenneth Woodward (1549227), Navigator, from Ardwick, Manchester.
Sergeant Jack Birch (1600760), Rear Gunner, from Chesham, Buckinghamshire.
Sergeant James McGahey (1421544), Flight Engineer, from Exeter.
Sergeant Ernest Walter Haigh (811039), Mid Upper Gunner, from Speke in Liverpool, at 28 years old the 'Grandpa' of the crew.

Back Row, Left to Right: Sunny, William Brown, John Gilbertson-Pritchard, Jack Birch. Front Row, Left to Right: Ernest Haigh, Gordon Woodward, Jim McGahey. Source: Frederick McGahey.

Sunny and his new crew joined 218 Squadron at RAF Downham Market, Norfolk on 6th December 1943. Joined by Flight Sergeant William Earle Brown (CAN R155985) from Calgary, Alberta, Canada, the Bomb Aimer, they became a full seven man crew.

Operations Flown with No. 218 Squadron:

16th December 1943, Mining (Off Frisian Islands) Short Stirling MkIII HA-S LJ452. Take-Off 17.05hrs-Landed 20.05hrs Comments: 2 x B204 + 2 x B218 mines dropped in allotted area, nothing of interest to report.

22nd December 1943, SPECIAL TARGET, ABBEVILLE Short Stirling Mk.III, HA-R, EF124. Take-Off 21.05hrs-Landed 00.05hrs. Crew unchanged. Comments: "Bombs were dropped on T.I Markers, light flak experienced. Uneventful trip." Notes: Only squadron aircraft detailed to bomb target that night.

14th January 1944, SPECIAL TARGET, SOUTH CHERBOURG, (4935N 01381/2W). HAZEBRUCK Construction Works. Short Stirling MkIII HA-M EH942. Take-Off 18.00hrs. Landed 21.45hrs. Crew unchanged. Comments: Bombed primary target from 14,000ft on Red TI markers. No built up area seen. Bombing very concentrated on T.I's.

21st January 1944, SPECIAL TARGET (BLACKCAP) Pas-de-Calais Short Stirling Mk.III HA-P 'Peter' BF504. Take-Off 18.10hrs. Landed 21.10hrs. Crew unchanged. Comments: Bombed target from 9000ft, bombs were seen to burst near TI Markers. 18x500lb brought back due to hang-up.

On the 23rd January 1944, the whole crew were transferred to 1678 Conversion Flight at RAF Waterbeach, Cambridgeshire. 218 Squadron historian, Steve Smith, gave this explanation.

'A possible reason the crew of Sgt Gledhill were posted so soon into their operational tour could have been the disbandment of No.623 Squadron on December 6th 1943. No.623 Squadron was formed from No.218 Squadron in August 1943, like 218 it operated from RAF Downham Market. On the squadron's disbandment, a number of former squadron crews were posted back to No.218. Another factor was that at the time No.218 Squadrons losses were exceptionally low, between December 1st 1943 and February 1st 1944 only one crew

were lost. This meant that the squadron had its full complement of crews, plus spares. Thankfully the Stirling equipped squadrons of No.3 Group were not participating in the bloodbath over Berlin. This was left to the Avro Lancaster equipped squadrons, one of which was No. 514 Squadron. During the period December 1943 to February 1944 No.514 Squadron lost I believe 12 crews. On the January 21/22nd attack on Berlin 514 Sqdn lost 4 crews in one night. I feel it is a combination of 218 having too many crews, and losses suffered by No. 514, which saw Sgt Gledhill posted.'

Sunny's crew joined 514 Squadron en masse on 4th February 1944, moving to the squadron's base at RAF Waterbeach in Cambridgeshire.

Operations Flown with No. 514 Squadron:

1st / 2nd March 1944, STUTTGART Avro Lancaster Mark II, 'P' LL683

Take-Off 23.41hrs-Landed 02.05hrs CREW Only change was the Mid Upper Gunner, who was Sergeant George A. Henry COMMENTS "Bomb load 1 x 2000, 1 x 500 lb bomb, 40 x 30, 900 x 4 incendiaries. Returned early. Furthest point reached on course - Cambridge. W/T receiver U/S. Jettisoned bombs to reduce load for landing."

15th / 16th March 1944, STUTTGART Avro Lancaster Mark II, 'S' LI734

Take-off 19.14hrs-Landed 02.39hrs CREW The Mid Upper Gunner of this mission is not known. COMMENTS "Bomb load 1 x 1000 lb bomb, 72 x 30, 1050 x 4, 90 x 4, incendiaries. There was very thin cloud. Bombed at 23.20 hours from 21000 feet. Attack not concentrated. Holes in fuselage due to flak on homeward near French coast."

18th / 19th March 1944, FRANKFURT Avro Lancaster Mark II, 'T' DS821

Take-Off 19.30hrs-Landed 01.04hrs CREW Sergeant E.W. Haigh was the Mid Upper Gunner this time. COMMENTS "Bomb load 1 x 4000lb. bomb, 1350 x 4, 90 x 4, 32 x 30 incendiaries. Weather hazy. Bombed at 22.04 hrs from 21000 feet. Incendiaries scattered round TIs.

Fires to South and East. Monica and Gee u/s homeward. Holes in port wing by heavy flak.

18th / 19th April 1944, ROUEN Avro Lancaster Mark II 'T' DS882

Take-Off 22.41hrs-Landed 03.10hrs CREW Flying Officer M.L. Morgan-Owen, Captain Flight Sergeant A.W. Green, Navigator Flying Officer G.A. Jacobson, Bomb Aimer Sergeant E. Gledhill, Wireless Operator and Air Gunner Sergeant A.D. Tetley, Mid Upper Gunner Sergeant H.S. Hayward, Rear Gunner Sergeant H. Sadler, Flight Engineer. This is the first mission Sunny flew with F/Officer Morgan-Owen's crew. Comments: Bomb load 10 x 1000 MC, 5 x 500 MC lb bombs. Weather was clear, good visibility. Bombed at 00.52 hours from 13500 feet. Target identified visually. TIs markers were scattered. Bombing was well concentrated. 1 x 1000 bomb hung up and brought back. A successful mission. Good weather on route."

22nd / 23rd of April 1944, DÜSSELDORF Avro Lancaster Mark II, DS682, JI-N. Take-Off 22.58hrs CREW Flying Officer M.L. Morgan-Owen, Captain, Flight Sergeant A.W. Green, Navigator Flying Officer G.A. Jacobson, Bomb Aimer Sergeant E. Gledhill, Wireless Operator and Air Gunner Sergeant A.D. Tetley, Mid Upper Gunner Sergeant H.S. Hayward, Rear Gunner Sergeant H. Sadler, Flight Engineer Comments: Bomb load 1 x 8000lb. bomb, 48 x 30, 486 x 4, 54 x 4 incendiaries. Aircraft Missing.

The circumstances of the loss are not known. An SOS message was received from the aircraft at 0256 hours, giving its position as 5236N 0351E, the time suggesting that it was returning to base. There was intensive night fighter activity over and around the target area, and it is possible that the aircraft was damaged, either in combat or by flak, being unable to make it home. The bodies of Sgts Tate and Sadler were subsequently washed ashore and buried in Holland. Sunny and the other members of his crew are commemorated on the Runnymede Memorial.

The mission in which Sunny went missing was the second he had ever flown without his regular crew and also the second time he had flown with F/O Morgan-Owen's crew. The reasons for this, I think, are twofold. Firstly, on the 19th of April 1944 Sunny's pilot, Flight Sergeant John Clare Gilbertson-Pritchard was posted to the NE Strength of No.33 Base. Previous to this, Sunny's flight engineer and best friend, Sergeant James McGahey had died on the 31st of March 1944 whilst on a mission to Nuremberg with another crew. His aircraft was shot down by a night fighter as it turned on to the base leg towards the target. Two of the crew had time to bale out, but not Jim.

(Above) Sgt. Jim McGahey, Flight Engineer and Sunny's best friend, lost on the Nuremberg raid of 30th / 31st March 1944.

One of the survivors of the crew, Harry Darby, the Bomb Aimer, later recounted the events of that night. Jim died going to the aid of the rear gunner, Sgt Roy Hill, who was trapped in his turret after the Lancaster was attacked by a night fighter. The plane crashed with a full bomb load just outside the Bavarian village of Eichenhausen, district of Bad Neustadt. In 1984, the local German parishioners erected a stone memorial with a bronze cross and plaque bearing the names of the five men who died.

The fate of the remaining members of Sunny's original crew is a little confused. Sergeant Jack Birch, Sergeant Gordon Kenneth Woodward, Warrant Officer Class II William Earle Brown and Sergeant Ernest Walter Haigh, all died on 22nd May 1944 as part of the crew of Lancaster DS781, JI-R, bombing Duisburg. The aircraft is thought to have been attacked by night fighters, crashing in the North Sea. Several aircraft were lost without trace, with claims for unidentified four motor aircraft being made by a number of night fighter pilots. Sergeant Haigh is buried in Kiel War Cemetery in Germany, Sergeant Woodward and W/Officer Brown's bodies were never found. The crew in which Sergeant Birch died is a little unclear, due to incorrect records at the Public Records Office. However, it appears that he was also in Lancaster DS781 and perished with his fellow crew members.

Warrant Officer John Clare Gilbertson-Pritchard, died on 31st March 1945. Having been promoted through the ranks, he was in 154 Squadron, based at RAF Hunsdon, Hertfordshire by the time of his death. This squadron was in fighter command. At the time of his death, Warrant Officer Gilbertson-Pritchard was a fighter pilot flying Mustang Mark IVs.

Postscript: on the 24th & 25th of February 1944. Sunny's pilot, Flight Sergeant Gilbertson-Pritchard, was the second pilot with a crew on a mission to Schweinfurt. Just after bombing the target, 'A 4lb incendiary dropped from above into the aircraft by the Navigator's table and was thrown to safety by WOP. Pilot's nerves affected by falling incendiary. Slight damage to Navigator's table.' I'm not surprised his nerves were affected..!

Tracy Holroyd-Smith

Sgt Bill Saddler
by John Saddler

The photo above shows my uncle, Bill Saddler, with members of his crew at the time they joined 514 Sqn which was then based at Foulsham, Norfolk. From second on the left: Bill Saddler (Navigator), Eric Michell (Wireless Operator), Maurice Cantin (Pilot), Neville Walne (Air Gunner), Stuart Smith (Air bomber). The figure on the left named Jock was not one of the crew on the night the plane was lost. In fact a different Engineer flew with the crew on their only earlier mission and was replaced for Berlin so he escaped death that night only to be killed on a later mission. It is thought that the photo was taken by the seventh crew member, William Mitchell, and that the location was RAF Foulsham. The crew spent only three days at RAF Waterbeach.

The listings below are of the seven crew members of Lancaster DS814 that took off from RAF Waterbeach. They never returned and were only the second crew lost from 514 Squadron. The names and other details are exactly as recorded in the cemetery register at the British and Commonwealth Second World War Cemetery in Berlin which I visited last year for the first time and again this year.

DS814 was one of eight aircraft from the squadron to take off at around 5.50pm on 26 November 1943 to join a total force of 443 Lancasters in one of the biggest raids on Berlin to that point. They initially headed for Frankfurt on a decoy run before turning towards the German capital where weather conditions were unexpectedly clear with a great deal of activity from anti-aircraft flak stations and night fighters.

My uncle's plane was on its way home when it was coned by searchlights to the northwest of the city. Unable to escape, it was eventually hit by anti-aircraft fire, exploded and came down in pieces in woods close to the village of Germendorf.

The next morning villagers found the wreckage strewn over a wide area. The bodies of all seven crew were retrieved and taken for burial in the churchyard at Germendorf where they lay until after the war when they were exhumed and reburied in the Berlin war cemetery.

I of course never knew Uncle Bill, and never had a chance to call him by that or any other name. But as I find out more about him, he becomes more familiar and I feel I can refer to him in that way. This was the crew's first major operation and their last. All their months of training came to this – one bomb-load dropped successfully, or as far as can be told, on target. They were all very young men in their late teens and early twenties apart from the middle upper gunner Leslie Eyre, a 36 year-old with a wife and family.

Uncle Bill was 20 when he died and my father, his eldest brother and older than him by 10 years, never once spoke of him in my hearing. So it wasn't explained to me as a boy what a hero Bill had been simply to pull on his flight hat and headset, step into that Lancaster and take off into a dark Cambridgeshire night. No doubt there were back slaps and good lucks said among the crew before they climbed on board. This was the test they'd been waiting for, but they must have known there was a fifty-fifty chance they wouldn't come back.

My father never told me about any of this because I don't think he could face it. But on the 26th November 1983, he and my Uncle Norman placed an 'In Memoriam' notice in the Daily Telegraph to mark the 40th anniversary of their younger brother's death. I found that notice cut out and placed in a brown envelope in an old leather suitcase that was among my father's possessions when he died. I think that says it all about how my father felt. That's why 30 years later I'm doing the same thing and using this opportunity to pay tribute to my Uncle Bill, to his crew and to all the brave airmen of 514 Squadron commemorated here. I'm also now doing what I can to find out more about Bill's story and what the young man that you see in these photographs was really like.

If any relatives of any of the crew members named below read this, please contact me through the 514 Squadron RAF Facebook page. I'd really like to hear from you or anybody else who can give me any information at all about my uncle or any family background about members of the crew. Similarly do get in touch if you'd like to follow up anything that you have come across in what I have written here.

(Above) Sgt Bill Saddler and his crew mates from Lancaster Mk.II DS814 rest in the Berlin War Cemetery, along with many other Bomber Command aircrew. Source: John Saddler.

CANTIN, Flying Officer (Pilot) MAURICE RAOUL, J/20214, 514 (R.A.F.) Sqdn., Royal Canadian Air Force, 26 November 1943. Age 21. Son of Amedee J. Cantin, and of Julienne M. Cantin (nee Daudin), of McCreary, Manitoba, Canada. Grave Ref. 9, D.16.

SMITH, Flight Sergeant (Air Bomber), STUART ELMER, R/161620 514 (R.A.F.) Sqdn., Royal Canadian Air Force. 26 November 1943. Grave Ref. 9.D.17

EYRE, Sergeant (Air Gnr,) LESLIE FRANK, 928328, 514 Sqdn., Royal Air Force Volunteer Reserve. 26 November 1943. Age 36. Son of Frank E. Eyre and Ada R. Eyre; husband of Catherine Beckett Eyre, of Framlingham, Suffolk, Grave Ref.9.D.18.

WALNE, Sergeant (Air Gnr.) ROBERT NEVILLE, 1287750, 514 Sqdn., Royal Air Force Volunteer Reserve, 26 November 1943. Age 20, Son of Capt. H. A. Walne, Mrs. Walne, of Framlingham. Suffolk. Grave Ref. 9, D.19.

KING, Sergeant (Flt. Eng.,) KERRY GEORGE, 57708, 514 Sqdn., Royal Air Force, 26 November 1943. Age 19. Son of Francis P. King and Henrietta Mary King, of Yiewsley, West Drayton, Middlesex. Grave Ref. 9, D.20.

MICHELL, Sergeant (W.Op./Air Gnr.) WILLIAM ERIC THOMAS, 1388185, 514 Sqdn. Royal Air Force Volunteer Reserve. 26 November 1943. Age 22. Son of Nellie Michell, of Tunbridge Wells, Kent. Grave Ref. Joint Grave 9.D.21-22.

SADDLER, Flight Sergeant (Nav.) WILLIAM GEORGE FYFE, 1346909, 514 Sqdn., Royal Air Force Volunteer Reserve, 26 November 1943. Age 20. Son of Archibald and Helen Gordon Fyfe Saddler, of Forfar, Angus. Grave Ref. Joint grave 9.D. 21-22.

Sgt Peter Gosnold
by Simon Hepworth

(Above) Left to right: Sgt. Ron Harding (WOP/AG), Sgt. Pete Coles (Rear Gunner), Sgt. Pete Gosnold (Flight Engineer), F/O Geoff France (Pilot), F/O Ken Barker RCAF (Bomb Aimer), Sgt. Bill Meredith (MU Gunner - left crew 31/10/44), F/O Fred Eisberg (Navigator). The note 'Peter' was on the original photograph. Not shown: P/O Pete Slater, replacement MU Gunner. Source: Simon Hepworth

One Christmas, when I was about six years old, my grandparents bought me an Airfix model of a Wellington bomber. Looking at the picture on the box, which showed the aircraft flying through a flak barrage, my mother commented that her uncle, only eight years her senior, had flown in bombers but had been shot down and killed. She knew no more than that his grave was in Germany. Pete Gosnold was twenty years old when he died.

Decades later, the Commonwealth War Graves Commission launched their website with its search engine. This gave me Peter's service number and thus, through the Air Historical Branch, his service record. He served in only one operational squadron, as a Flight Engineer with 514 Squadron. The internet, an awesome facility that made research immeasurably easier than before, led me to Wendy Flemming in Canada, thence to Ron Pickler, Joe Dibley and others who had served or knew much more about 514 Squadron. With their help and other research I came to learn what had happened to Peter and others in the crew of F/O Geoff France when their Lancaster PD265, JI-G, was shot down over Homberg on 21st November 1944.

I was helped by a number of fortuitous discoveries and contacts. One afternoon whilst killing time in a bookshop I chanced upon a copy of 'Luck and a Lancaster' by Harry Yates, DFC. Harry, a pilot with 75(NZ) Sqn, had written a well-structured and detailed account of his operations, including a chapter on Homberg, which he described as a 'jinx' target. Harry told of the operation on 21st November 1944 in which he witnessed the loss of all three Lancasters. I knew, therefore, that Peter's aircraft was hit by flak in the vicinity of the target. The publishers were kind enough to put me in touch with Harry and I was able to make the most of his incredible recollection after more than sixty years.

Wendy Flemming then passed on a message from a collector of militaria who had obtained the log book and uniform of F/O Geoff France. He was, for a price, willing to part with these items, and they are now securely in my possession. Peter having left no personal record of his service, these are of immense personal value.

In 2011, I set up a Facebook community page for 514 Sqn, with the intention of sharing personal recollections and photographs from veterans and their families. This in turn put me in contact with Rachel Rhodes, daughter of Geoff France, and other members of the France family. I was also able to contact members of the family of Bill Meredith, mid-upper gunner in their crew until a rearrangement of the crew meant that he swapped places with F/O Pete Slater. The switch saved Bill's life. Finally, after years of searching for the family of the crew's Navigator, F/O Fred Eisberg, I made contact with his son Neil.

Neil referred me to a book by Mel Rolfe, 'Hell on Earth' (Grub Street, 1999). This contained a full chapter being Geoff France's story of the crew, their time on the squadron and their demise over Homberg.

The definitive story, which I was able to share with Pete's surviving brothers, was of immense comfort even after so many years. Sadly I was not in time to speak with Geoff, Fred or Bill, all of whom have passed on. Their story, however, has survived.

Pete Gosnold joined the RAF in 1943, at the age of eighteen. From Hornsea, on the east coast of Yorkshire, he was working as an apprentice turner in a foundry in Hull when he decided to join up. Originally 'not recommended for aircrew duties' at his initial medical, according to his personnel record, Pete was re-interviewed by the Air Crew Selection Board and recommended for training as a Flight Mechanic, potential Flight Engineer.

A year older than Pete, Sgt Geoff France was at university but interrupted his studies in 1941 to join the RAF. Selected for pilot training, he was sent to Clewiston, Florida, for training, a far cry from his home in Bolton, before returning to England in 1943.

The crew's navigator, F/O Fred Eisberg, was from Plaistow in East London. He suffered, according to his family, from airsickness but was determined to stay with his crew. Remaining at his desk throughout each flight, he paid the ground crew to clear up after he had been sick at his desk.

(Above) The crew attend the October 1944 wedding of F/O Ken Barker and Doris Brown. It is believed that Doris Brown was, in fact, an SOE agent. L-R F/O Fred Eisberg, F/O Geoff France, Sgt Ron Harding, F/O and Mrs. Ken Barker, Sgt Pete Coles, Sgt Pete Gosnold. Source: France family.

Bomb Aimer F/O Ken Barker was one of many RCAF members attached to British bomber squadrons. He was from Killdeer, Saskatchewan. Whilst in England, however, he met and married Doris Brown, from Essex, the whole crew attending the wedding in October 1944. Five weeks later, tragically, Doris Barker would be left a widow. Sgt Ron Harding, the wireless operator, came from Barry Island in South Wales. Along with the mid upper gunner, Sgt Bill Meredith, he was one of two Welshmen in the crew.

Sgt Pete Coles, the crew's rear gunner, was from London and, at 19, only slightly younger than Pete Gosnold.

Sgt Meredith had to contend with a serious illness in the family and was granted special leave towards the end of October 1944. He was replaced by F/O Pete Slater, at 22 and married, considered the 'old man' of the crew.

The crew had, by prevailing standards, a fairly uneventful tour of operations. They came close to attack by an FW190 fighter on an early operation to Vaires, whilst Geoff France recalled on an op to Frankfurt another such fighter skimmed perilously close to their Lancaster, passing just in front of the cockpit canopy. Their aircraft was hit by flak on a number of occasions, but such occurrences were so commonplace as to be considered scarcely worthy of note in the official records. One notable incident, however, saw their fuselage damaged by the blast from their bombs as they attacked German positions near Caen from 2000 feet. The damage was sufficient to see their aircraft divert to the emergency runway at RAF Woodbridge on its return.

For a while, the France crew was allocated LM277, JI-F until the aircraft was lost with the crew of F/O Arkless attacking Calais. LM733 was assigned the code JI-F and the France crew continued to use that aircraft intermittently. For the most part, however, they seem to have taken different aircraft on each operation. The crew was trained in the use of G-H special equipment, acting as G-H Leader on a number of flights.

The crew was told that they would be screened off operations after 35 ops. Their 34th was on 21st November 1944. The target, once again, was the Rhein-Preussen synthetic oil plant at Homberg, on the outskirts of Moers and just across the Rhine from Duisburg. The oil plant was strenuously defended, with heavy flak units being deployed around the area. In particular, the Grossbatterie Daubenspeckhof unit was sited 1 km NW of Moers and close to the run in to the target.

G-H bombing required a long and steady approach to ensure accuracy, making the approaching aircraft more vulnerable to flak defences. To make matters worse, the promised cloud cover cleared as the force approached the target. The France crew, in PD265, JI-G on this occasion, had just bombed when a flak shell exploded on the aircraft's starboard side, killing Sgt Pete Gosnold almost instantly. More shells hit the Lancaster which was critically damaged, going immediately into a dive. Geoff France remembered bracing his feet against the instrument panel as he tried to pull the aircraft back onto an even keel, but without success. Fortunate to be wearing their parachutes when the aircraft was hit, Geoff France and Freddie Eisberg were thrown clear, the pilot watching on as his aircraft, by now missing its tail unit, plummeted to earth. The pilot and navigator were the only survivors.

The aircraft, according to local historian Axel Heyermann in an e-mail to the author, crashed into the moat surrounding the Grafschafter Castle in the centre of the city of Moers. Those of the crew who lost their lives are buried in Reichswald Forest War Cemetery, in a communal grave with members of the crew of JI-C, also shot down approaching the target.

F/O Geoff France spent the rest of the war as a POW. He had sustained an injury to his right leg from flak shrapnel, passed out during his descent and broke his left femur on landing in a cabbage field. He regained consciousness to find himself guarded by a member of the local defence forces who promptly stole his cigarettes. He was given inadequate medical care and eventually his left leg was amputated. He carried a piece of shrapnel in his thigh ever after. After leaving the RAF he returned to Manchester University, qualified as an architect and in 1959 was ordained as a clergyman.

Fred Eisberg landed on farmland nearby and was also captured. He went to a separate POW camp and did not apparently meet up with his pilot. He was liberated by Russian forces, but was chilled by the behaviour of the Soviet forces, considering it an ill-omen for the future. After his release F/O Eisberg wrote to Peter Gosnold's family, explaining what had happened and apologising for not having been able to save the other crew members, but everything had happened very quickly. He told his family that he felt tremendously guilty that he had survived whilst his mates died, though of course his fate was not in his own hands once the aircraft broke up.

Sgt Bill Meredith, flying in JI-A on this op, was unfortunate enough to witness the loss of his former crew. Sgt Meredith survived the war, returning to South Wales where he worked as fireman in a colliery.

Rachel Rhodes, daughter of Geoff France, relates that her father never forgot his crew. When his own father died, he wrote on a floral tribute 'Give my love to my mother, and say hello to my crew'.

No. 514 Squadron,
Royal Air Force Station,
Waterbeach, Cambs.

Reference:
514/C.2050/64/P.1.

23rd November, 1944.

Dear Mr France.

Prior to the receipt of this letter, you will have received a telegram informing you that your Son 179705 Flying Officer Geoffrey Charles France is reported missing as the result of an Operational Flight which took place on the afternoon of the 21st November, 1944.

At 12.28 hours on Tuesday last, an aircraft Piloted and Captained by your Son took off to carry out a bombing attack on HOMBERG. This attack was one of the many essential, courageous and fighting efforts now called for from the Royal Air Force, from this flight your Son's aircraft failed to return.

I sincerely hope that we shall hear that your Son and the other members of the crew are prisoners of war, but it is of course too early yet for any information to come through from enemy sources. Any further information which we may receive will of course be passed on to you immediately.

A Committee of Officers, known as a Committee of Adjustment, has gathered your Son's personal belongings together and will communicate with you in the near future.

May I express my personal sympathy with you and that of the entire Squadron in what I know must be a great anxiety for you.

Yours sincerely,

M. Wyatt

Wing Commander, Commanding,
No. 514 Squadron. R.A.F.

Mr. A. France,
46 Brighton Avenue,
Bolton,
LANCS.

(Above) Letter from W/Cdr Michael Wyatt to the father of F/O Geoff France. Such letters were intended to be a more personal follow up to the formal telegram notifying families of their loss. In this case, there was to be good news that F/O France had survived, albeit as a POW. Source: France family.

P/O Bob Langley

All information courtesy of Marilyn Langley.

(Above) P/O Bob Langley DFC. Source: Marilyn Langley

Sgt (later P/O) Bob Langley, from Ferryhill, County Durham, was one of the first pilots to join 514 Sqn, arriving at RAF Foulsham and making his first familiarisation in DS787, JI-F, on 25th September 1943. The squadron was still in its infancy and was more than a month away from being operational.

His crew was Sgt RC Parker (Flight Engineer), Sgt FR Jones (Navigator), Sgt DT Bradsell (Air Bomber), Sgt CF Wakeling (WOP/AG), Sgt SR Smith (MU Gunner) and Sgt HG Oliver (Rear Gunner).

Training continued throughout October and on 3rd November 1943 Sgt Langley and his crew took part in the squadron's first operation, dropping sea mines off the Frisian Islands. Sgt Langley recorded in his logbook concise observations after most of his operational flights which tell a succinct story of his tour.

3rd November 1943   DS787 JI-F   Mining   Frisian Islands
'Wizard night, never saw a thing'.

11th November 1943 DS787 JI-F   Mining La Rochelle 'Heavy flak damage to aircraft over Nantes'.

26th November 1943 DS787 JI-F   Bombing   Berlin 'Flaps U/S. Had to make flapless landing'.

2nd December 1943   DS787 JI-F   Bombing   Berlin (Returned) 'Excessive engine icing. Brakes failed on landing due to ice on linings. Ran through fence. No damage'.

20th December 1943 DS787 JI-F   Bombing   Frankfurt (Returned away) '2 engines U/S. Bombed enemy aerodrome. 2 engine landing at Woodbridge. Overflared'.

14th January 1944   DS786 JI-E   Bombing   Brunswick

20th January 1944   DS842 JI-F   Bombing   Berlin 'Returned – Compasses U/S'.

21st January 1944   LL624 JI-B   Bombing   Magdeburg 'Intercom U/S'.

15th February 1944 DS842 JI-F   Bombing   Berlin 10th (operation).

19th February 1944 DS820 JI-A   Bombing   Leipzig 'Returned – Compass U/S 130 deg out. P4 U/S'.

20th February 1944 DS820 JI-A   Bombing   Stuttgart 11th (operation).

24th February 1944 DS842 JI-F   Bombing   Schweinfurt Bombing concentrated, clear night, good prang, trip very quiet.

1st March 1944   DS813 JI-H   Bombing   Stuttgart. Bert's oxygen mask U/S. Does trip with tube in his mouth. Fred gets frostbite'.

26th March 1944   LL733 JI-G   Bombing   Essen 'Happy Valley quiet'.

11th April 1944   DS842 JI-F   Bombing
Aachen   'Quite a good prang'.

18th April 1944   DS842 JI-F   Bombing   Rouen 'Bandits. Circled base for an hour'.

20th April 1944   DS842 JI-F   Bombing   Cologne
'Bombing very scattered. PFF boobed and were late'.

22nd April 1944   DS842 JI-F   Bombing   Düsseldorf 'Happy Valley in all its glory'

9th May 1944 DS842 JI-F   Bombing   Cap Gris Nez. 'Good prang, good photo'.

11th May 1944   DS842 JI-F   Bombing   Louvain 'PFF boob. Brought back Aiming Point'.

21st May 1944   DS842 JI-F   Bombing   Duisberg 'Not so good, flak moderate, bags of NF flares'.

22nd May 1944   DS842 JI-F   Bombing   Dortmund
'Boomerang – excessive icing. Aircraft damaged by ice'.

30th May 1944   DS842 JI-F   Bombing   Boulogne
'Bombing very concentrated, but PFF off'.

12th June 1944   DS842 JI-F   Bombing   Gelsenkirchen
'Good prang – Happy Valley very happy'.

14th June 1944   DS842 JI-F   Bombing   Le Havre 'Good prang – very concentrated'.

15th June 1944   DS842 JI-F   Bombing   Valencienne 'Very concentrated bombing – good photo'.

17th June 1944   DS842 JI-F   Bombing   Montdidier
'Ordered to bring bombs back. Sortie was abortive due to 10/10 Sc (Strato-cumulus cloud)'.

21st June 1944   DS842 JI-F   Bombing   Domleger / Pas de Calais 'Ordered to bring bombs back. Sortie was abortive due to 10/10 Sc'.

23rd June 1944   DS842 JI-F   Bombing   L'Hey (Doodle-Bugs) 'PFF OK. Bombed glow as instructed'.

24th June 1944   DS842 JI-F   Bombing   Rimeux (Doodle-Bugs) 'Clear night. PFF OK. Bombing concentrated'.

25th June 1944   DS842 JI-F   Bombing   Biennais. No.30 '10/10 Sc. Bombed glow of TIs. FINIS'.

(Above) P/O Bob Langley and his crew are believed to be the first from 514 Sqn to complete a full tour of thirty operations.
Back row, L-R: Sgt RR Smith (MU Gunner), Sgt CF Wakeling (W/OP), Sgt R Parker (Flight Engineer), Sgt H Oliver (Rear Gunner).
Front Row, L-R: Sgt FR Jones (Navigator), Sgt R Langley (Pilot), Sgt DT Bradsell (Air Bomber). Source: Marilyn Langley.

By now having been promoted and commissioned as a Pilot Officer, Bob Langley and his colleagues became the first 514 Sqn crew to complete a full tour of thirty operations. On July 3rd 1944 he was awarded the Distinguished Flying Cross (DFC). This was confirmed by Postagram from Air Chief Marshal Sir Arthur Harris to RAF Waterbeach, the news reaching P/O Langley the following day when Wing Commander Mike Wyatt, 514 Squadron Commander, sent a telegram to his home. The citation read:

'This officer is a most efficient captain and pilot of aircraft. He has completed a noteworthy tour of operations, including 6 attacks on Berlin. On 1 occasion when detailed to attack a target in Germany 2 engines became useless. Nevertheless Pilot Officer Langley released his bombs over an enemy airfield and afterwards flew the aircraft home. This officer has invariably displayed a high degree of determination and devotion to duty;'

DS787, the original JI-F, had transferred to 'C' Flight. Sadly the aircraft was lost on 11th September 1944, crashing in the target area whilst attacking Kamen. It is believed that the aircraft was hit by bombs from another aircraft. Five of the crew, including the pilot W/O RJ Thornton, lost their lives. DS842, JI-F was christened 'Fanny Firkin 2' and took part in a tour of USAAF bases to show off the Lancaster to American forces. The aircraft has been immortalised as one of the markings available for the 1:72 scale Airfix model of the Lancaster Mk.II.

Pilot Officer Bob Langley DFC survived the war. After the end of his tour of duty he was seconded to BOAC and then flew as a pilot in civil aviation for the rest of his flying career. Whilst working for BOAC he had to make a forced landing in the Sahara Desert; that event was made into a programme in the BBC series 'Meet the Ancestors', called Desert Rescue. He was offered a job by Freddie Laker. He then worked with Fred for many years and they only parted company when Fred left to start up Laker Airways. Laker wanted Bob to go with him, but he didn't have any jets on his licence and felt he was too old to start again on new aircraft. He stayed connected with aviation in one way or another literally up until he died in February 1999 at the age of 77. As with many who served, he never spoke of his experiences, and his daughter remembers that a school friend once asked him how he got his DFC and was told it was for making jam butties for the rest of the crew.

Sgt John Porrelli and F/L Arnold Morrison
by Andrew Porrelli

I've known all my life I didn't have a 'Granddad', and through those young years, my Nan (Mabel) never spoke of him that much. I guess, in the back of her mind, she never really got over him leaving her with two young children (Bernard and John - my Dad) and going off to volunteer. He worked for the GPO as a Telephone Cable Joiner. He was, by all accounts, one of the best in the business, which meant he was classified as 'position 3 – Skilled Workmen' on the official 'Exempt from Service' List. After several rejected attempts to join up, he finally got accepted. I guess he felt it was his duty. My family emigrated to Australia in 1975 when I was nine. As I got older I was aware of Anzac Day every year and so I started asking my father and uncle about Granddad, finding we actually had quite a full story of his service. Over the past ten years our family interest has continued to grow, especially as the internet revealed more details. My father also had a lengthy exchange of correspondence with that most wonderful lady, Wendy Flemming in Canada.

'Feadora': DS816, JI-O, painted by a Waterbeach artist in 1944. Photo courtesy of Linda Miles, daughter of F/L AH Morrison.

I knew there were two Aussies in the crew of DS816, the aircraft in which my Granddad was killed and the sole survivor, F/L Arnold

Hughes Morrison DFC, was Australian. It bothered me that service personnel who, like him, had survived, really didn't seem to get the same recognition as the ones who had died. Sadly it turned out that F/L Morrison had passed away some 10 years earlier, around 1989. This moved me incredibly in a way words can't adequately describe. I was too late to tell him that I, and many others, consider him to be a hero. His daughter told my father that he had never forgotten the 'lads of DS816' and that he was sad he had little contact from the families, as the Air Ministry didn't give F/L Morrison the addresses of the crews' families. This meant he was out of contact for nearly 70 years. The story of my Granddad came full circle when, in 1998, my Father interred my Nan's ashes with my Granddad, according to her wishes.

My interest in researching my Granddad's story never lessened as I became more determined to pass it to my sons. Off work with a medical condition, and at a loose end, I revisited my father's own research. 12 months ago I contacted Wendy Flemming in Canada and she, in turn, introduced me to the 514 Squadron Face-book page along with others such as Simon Hepworth and Robert Guy. Each of us has a personal connection with 514 Squadron and therefore a shared interest, leading to some most wonderful friendships. When Simon mentioned he was working on transcribing the ORBs I simply offered to help. The project was his inspiration, which he was so generous to share with me. This gave me an opportunity to see that not only my Granddad, but all who served in 514 Squadron, were remembered. This, I hope, will go a long way to showing the other survivors how much we value their own contribution. My efforts have been driven by these circumstances.

I am the grandson of the Rear Gunner and, some 70 years since my 'Pops' first mission, I feel it incumbent on me to make my best effort, regardless of my worthiness for such a task, to tell the story of his crew. Ultimately, this story is only made possible with the kind permission and assistance of Linda Miles, (daughter of A H Morrison DFC), for being so kind as to provide photos and text from her father's estate.

OPERATIONS
22/23 April 1944   DS826. JI-L DUSSELDORF.
(No Sgt. Porrelli, Sgt. RD Keen)
26/27 April 1944   LL -734. JI-S ESSEN.
(Sgt. Porrelli joins crew)

1st May 1944	DS816. JI-O	CHAMBLY.
7th May 1944	LL739, JI-M	NANTES.

(Sgt Porrelli Rear Gunner from now on)

10th May 1944	DS816, JI-O	COURTRAI.
11/12th May 1944	DS816 JI-O	LOUVAIN.
19th May 1944	DS222 JI-T	LE MANS.
21-22nd May 1944	DS816 JI-O	DUISBURG.
24/25th May 1944	DS816 JI-O	BOULOGNE GUN BATTERY.
27/28th May 1944	DS816 JI-O	AACHEN.
28/29th May 1944	DS816 JI-O	ANGERS.
30/31st May 1944	DS816 JI-O	BOULOGNE GUN BATTERIES.
10/11th June 1944	DS816 JI-O	DREUX.
12/13th June 1944	DS816 JI-O.	GELSENKIRCHEN.
14th June 1944	DS816 JI-O	LE HAVRE.
15/16th June 1944	DS816 JI-O	VALENCIENNES Aircraft Missing.

(Above) The people of Croisilles turned out to honour the six crew of DS816 who lost their lives. Some 2800 ensured that a proper funeral was held. The German occupiers did not intervene. Source: F/L Arnold Morrison via Linda Miles.

The crew, like most others who flew Lancasters, comprised seven men, six of whom were sadly killed in action.
F/S CF Prowles   Pilot - KIA, P/O AH Morrison RAAF Navigator - EVADED, Sgt R Surtees   WOP/Air – KIA, F/S RB Spencer RAAF

Bomb Aimer - KIA, Sgt AA Holmes MU Gunner - KIA, Sgt J Porrelli Rear Gunner - KIA, Sgt HA Osborn Flight Engineer – KIA. The sole survivor was the crew's Australian Navigator, P/O Arnold Hughes Morrison, RAAF, who was later awarded the DFC following his success in evading capture.

The crew's graves lie in a special section of Croisilles British Cemetery. (Left to right) Holmes, Porrelli, Osbourne, Surtees, Prowles, Spencer.

PILOT: P/O. Charles. Frank. (Ted) Prowles, 177531,
Son of Charles Walter and Dorothy Eveline Prowles, of Southampton. Despite being only 21 years of age, Ted was highly regarded and as talented as any Pilot in the Squadron.

The above photo is believed to be of Ted Prowles whilst undergoing his pilot training. Source: Linda Miles.

FLIGHT ENGINEER: Sgt. Henry Albert (Harry) Osborn, 1715000.
Son of Henry John and Grace Osborn, of Plumstead, London.
Another very young member of the crew, at only 20 years of age. His abilities are best described by the words of Arnold Morrison, who commented in a letter to Harry's parents on 11th November 1944.

'I honestly think that Harry was the coolest member of the crew. On our first trip - to the Ruhr - we ran into some trouble and had to come home on 3 engines, and Harry's prompt and efficient handling of the matter undoubtedly saved us from having an engine on fire. He was always such a great source of help to the pilot, particularly during landings, that Ted never had to worry about or question the engine settings etc., and believe me that was very important'(courtesy of Linda Miles).

WIRELESS OPERATOR: Sgt. Raymond Surtees, 1670154.
It is with great sadness that I am unable to provide further details of this serviceman.

BOMB AIMER: F/S. Ronald Bernard Spencer. (RAAF), (AUS) 425771
Born on the 9th August 1914 in Zeehan, Tasmania. He enlisted on the 26th April 1942 at Brisbane, Queensland, Australia. Son of Cyril Robert Holtum Spencer and Evangeline Holtum Spencer (CWGC) E. Hall. (WW2 Australian Nominal Roll). Aged 29.
On operations on Schweinfurt on the 24th/25th of February 1944 – Their aircraft was struck by 4 incendiaries near the Navigators Station, F/S Spencer picked them up and threw them out of the Aircraft.

MID UPPER GUNNER (REAR GUNNER): Sgt. Arthur Albert (Bert) Holmes, 519212
Son of John Joshua Holmes, his mother remarried after his death (in the Somme) and became Mrs. Bartrup. Aged 30, 'Bert' as he was known, was a career Serviceman. He enlisted in 1935 at RAF Hendon North London and went to Iraq. His death notice in the paper stated he was in Egypt where he captained the RAF cricket team and from there he was in British India (now mostly Pakistan) until he was shipped back to England in about May of 1943 when he must have signed for Bomber Command work. Bert was probably the Rear Gunner for the crews first 3 missions

Information and photograph of Bert Holmes (above) courtesy of Robert Fleatcher and Ingatestone Boys' Own Club.

REAR GUNNER: Sgt. John (Jack) Porrelli 1594519
Born on the 3rd January 1909 in Bradford, Yorkshire, he volunteered and enlisted on 26th May 1943 it is thought in Hull, Yorkshire. Son of Carmine and Lilly, Husband of Mabel Elizabeth Porrelli. Father of Bernard and John Porrelli, of Bradford.

Sgt John 'Jack' Porrelli (above) was a first class cable joiner for the G.P.O. Telecommunications section. He was 'exempt from service' –

being at position 3 for 'skilled workmen'. He was undertaking reconnection of telecommunications all over England. After several failed attempts to enlist, he was finally accepted (in fact his boss tried to reverse his enlistment).

He volunteered to join this crew (as a gunner) on their 2nd mission (replacing a sick airman) and then volunteered for the Rear Gunner position on his 3rd operation, the attack on Nantes (As Bert Holmes had a very young baby). He remained as the Rear Gunner and was lost with 5 of the 6 other crewmen, in the crash at Crosilles (Valenciennes raid). Jack Porrelli is commemorated on the GPO War Memorial in Bradford (below).

NAVIGATOR: F/L. Arnold Hughes Morrison, RAAF, DFC (AUS) 411168

Born on the 15th November 1917 in Canley Vale, N.S.W., Australia. He enlisted on the 26th April 1941 in Sydney, N.S.W., Australia. The son of James Herbert Morrison and Margaret Ellen Morrison (nee Eaton). His wife, who he loved very much, was Edith Morrison (nee Thornton). They met when she was nursing in the RAAF hospital at Jervis Bay, where he was recuperating after the war. They had two children, Ian and Linda Morrison and a granddaughter, Selina Miles.

An amazing navigator and absolutely outstanding serviceman. The only survivor of the crash of DS816 'JI-O'. Obviously a larger than life 'Aussie', who went to extraordinary efforts to contact his crew-mates families after his repatriation to share photographs of the funeral of the lost crew that he had acquired whilst evading capture.

F/L Arnold Morrison, RAAF, DFC.   Photograph courtesy of Linda Miles and Australian War Memorial.

The following record was written by F/L Arnold Hughes Morrison, RAAF, DFC who had, at the start of this account, already completed 12 ops. It is reproduced with the most kind permission of his daughter, Linda Miles.

'After seven days leave we came back to start again on 10/6/1944 with a trick on Dreux - had 2 combats with fighters on this one (no. 13). Next was no. 14 - Gelsenkirchen and then no. 15 - Le Havre where we dropped an 8000 pounder on the shipping in the harbour. No 16 was the unlucky one for us - on Valenciennes near the French Belgian frontier.
We ran into the target beautifully. It was a black night with just a little bit of light in the top sky from the Northern Lights. The bombing went well and old Spence as usual dropped them smack on the T.I.s. Just after turning for home old Ted decided to climb into a thin layer of cloud above us to get some reflected light from the cloud under our tail He stopped the banking search - our usual practice - to start the climb

and just at that moment all hell broke loose. Cannon fire just about chopped front wing to pieces and fire poured out of it. The fighter must have been following us and waited until we were level. The gunners didn't see him at all.

Ted started avoiding manoeuvres when he saw the trace on the port side and we lost a lot of height when the port wing went down. I think the control surfaces must have been shot away. When he got the kite somewhat level he decided that we would have to bail out. He gave the order but Spence could not open the hatch. I don't know whether he was wounded or whether the hatch was jammed. I stood up and put my pack on and then helped Harry fix Ted's pack. By that time we were down to a few thousand feet and the airspeed was about 280. Then Spence turned around and by his attitude we or rather I gathered that he could not do anything with the hatch. So I just decided that it was the finish and I might as well get used to the idea of being dead in a few minutes. We hit pretty steeply at about 300 indicated. I remember my last thoughts - will we hit the deck before that bloody wing tank blows up? What the heck difference it made then I can't remember.

Anyway I saw a bright red flash in front of my eyes and that was all I knew for the next 2 hours. I woke up lying in a field on my parachute pack with my face in the dirt. I stood up, instinctively I suppose, and then had a look around. I was very groggy, and anything I write here is only what I can remember now (some five months later). I took a long time getting any thoughts in my head at - it was like being hopelessly blind drunk. I tried to walk but found that the parachute silk had fallen out in a big roll and it tripped me. I bent down to pick it up and then discovered that I had no boots on. Then I tried to think why I was standing up in an open field on a black night like that with no boots - it seemed damned silly. Then I saw lots of fires around me and wondered what they were.

After what seemed hours of standing there, swaying about and trying to think, I suddenly remembered that I was in an aeroplane shortly before and slowly all the stuff about the fighter attack came back to me. I didn't stop to think about how I got out of the crash - I figured in my dim way that some or all of the boys might be lying around somewhere so I set off to walk towards a large piece of fire. The chute worried me so I took the pack off the harness and smashed the catch on the front of the harness and let it fall to the ground. That was stupid because the Huns found it later and were looking for the bloke who owned it.

I then started out again but after wandering around for a long time I gave it up because every few minutes I would get a dizzy spell and would wander in a daze - usually in a different direction from the one I wanted to go. I got so mad because I couldn't find any of the crew or any wreckage of the plane that I started to howl like a kid. Must have been shock I guess. I must have wandered around for several hours before I noticed that the first light of dawn was showing - very faintly but it served to stir me into getting the hell out of there. I figured that the Huns would be arriving soon and they could look after any of the lads who were still alive. So I started this wandering stuff again and after falling over a few hedges and down a sunken road (which shook me up a good deal) I eventually reached the edge of a wood.

I instinctively crawled into it in what I imagined to be a stealthy manner - probably I was making a heck of a noise - and found a level spot amongst some weeds. I had a check over on my head and hands to see if I was badly injured and found that my forehead was bleeding a fair bit and the rest of my face felt as if the skin was mostly missing. The condition of my hands and wrists was about the same - one finger - index on my right hand - was rather badly split. I was pretty sure no bones were broken and my head - although very sore and still like Big Ben was not deeply cut I left my helmet on though - just in case.

I unrolled the parachute and wrapped myself in it. I had a terrific yearning for a cigarette so I pulled the silk over my head and lit a Pall Mall. I had to smoke it with my face down in the grass to hide the light, and I got numerous stings from the nettles but despite all that I have never enjoyed a smoke more. After a while I started getting dizzy again so I rolled up tight in the chute and passed out. After several hours I woke to find that it was fully light and though I still felt dizzy and had a bad headache I decided to get up and look around.

I discovered I was still wearing my 'Mae West' and took it off. Couldn't think of any use for it so removed the torch and battery and hid the rest under a thick bunch of undergrowth. I cautiously examined the wood and found that it was only a circular patch of trees about 100 yards in diameter and had numerous trenches and earth barricades through it - apparently constructed by the Bosche. This served to stir me into some action. First I cut some panels out of the parachute canopy and wrapped these around my feet. Then I checked the contents of my pockets and found the razor blades, nail file, cigarettes, matches, wallet of foreign currency (1000 francs French and 1000 francs Belgian - also the silk maps) and escape kit intact, but I had lost the Air Force watch - I was wearing it on my left wrist which was scratched about a good deal, so I presumed it had been torn off - but my own watch was still on my right wrist and working OK.

I opened the escape kit and checked the contents for future reference. My Bendix photographs were OK, then I laid out the map and by some 'mental dead reckoning' established my position as somewhere near Arras. I then cut the cords off my chute and stowed them in my pockets, rolled the silk into a bundle and tied it for carrying (it would be useful covering at night) and hid the remainder of the chute cover etc. under another bush. From the edge of the wood I could see that the areas of wooded country were very scattered and was undecided about the safest way to cross the intervening fields. The country was undulating agricultural stuff and afforded very little cover so, after some indecision, I consulted the compass from the escape kit and set off along the most southerly road. I first had a look north to see if I could identify the wreckage of the aircraft but there was no sign of it - this puzzled me a great deal and worried me too. (In view of what I was told later, it was obvious that the aircraft was very thoroughly broken up and scattered over half a mile and the small pieces of wreckage would not be easily seen from a distance).

I could see what appeared to be some sort of military buildings on the crest of the next low hill and I figured it was time to get away from that area. Soon after starting out I could see a small village below the crest of the rise, and this scared me a bit, but I figured that if anyone was watching me and saw me hesitate or turn back, they would be suspicious, so I kept right on. The first thing I came to was a little building by the roadside with a shrine for any passersby to use. I gave my thanks while walking past and this little act gave me a certain help along.

I soon reached the edge of the village and could see nobody at all in the road, but at the fork of the first road into the main street I looked up at the corner house and got a great shock to see a chap in peasant clothes regarding me in what seemed a suspicious or surprised manner. My morale at this stage was rather lousy and after the initial suspense my first impulse was to seek the help of this chap - he was the first person I had seen since the crash - in the foregoing period I have never felt so lonely, depressed and forsaken in my life and I hope never to feel like that again - the feeling is impossible to describe.

To resume, I walked into the front yard of this house and spoke to the man in English. He didn't answer - just stared. Then I said R.A.F. but all he did was to look scared. Maybe I did present a weird sight - no shoes and all bloody and dirty. He directed me to walk along the arm of the V-junction of the roads which led back on the other side of the wood I had left just before and I guess that one effect of the shock was to obey any order without reasoning. Anyway, I started off and had walked about 200 yards or so before I realised that this road led me back near the scene of the crash, whereupon I retraced my steps. I was going to keep walking south, my original direction. When I reached the house again this chap was in the front yard again - now with his wife and several sons. Madame made signs for me to come in - that was OK by me. When we were safely inside she started to talk at machine gun speed to the old boy - apparently tearing him off a strip for sending me away. Next she gave me water to wash the blood and dirt off my face and hands and started to natter in French. I said 'Pas parlez Francais' and that stopped her. Then she said something in what I took to be Polish (this was correct - they were Polish immigrants in France). I shook my head then set about trying to explain. I can't remember details of the conversation or how I made them understand but I told them I had crashed about 2 kilometres north of there and that I was an Aussie in the R.A.F. They identified the village as Mory and showed its position on the map in relation to Bapaume and Arras - the village was not shown. Then I was given 'cafe et pain et beurre' - and felt a lot better for it.

They produced some civvy clothes - brown coat, brown striped trousers, black beret and white sandals. I had black socks and a khaki bush shirt on and I kept these as well as my silk flying scarf. They told me that the Belgian notes were of no use so I told them that they could keep them. They kept the German silk map (I wish I hadn't been so silly in the head - I would certainly have kept that). I told them to burn my battledress and the parachute - also the helmet

After a lot of chatter about 'Bosche' and a lot of pointing at the map, I figured out that the Huns were just about everywhere and my safest course was to walk openly along the main road (what an optimistic mug - if I had known that day about the periodic identity card checks). After a while the people wrapped some bread and butter in a handkerchief then arranged my clothing to conform to the then 'fashionable' set of muffler, shirt, etc. for farm workers. I thanked them profusely and ventured out again with a lot more confidence. I soon had a chance to test my disguise. I passed a group of chaps in the centre of the village who were just harnessing some horses ready for the day's work and they just regarded me with, I hoped, normal curiosity for village folk seeing a stranger in their town.

I walked right through the village without being spoken to and then checked on my beret to make sure it was pulled well down over the deep cut in my forehead. I put dust on my face again to cover the patches where the skin had been wiped off and let the trousers down as far as possible - they were far too short. I walked for a long time before I saw anybody - not until I reached the railway crossing just outside Bapaume. Several civilians looked at me very curiously but did not speak. Walked into the centre of Bapaume, passing a doctor's surgery. I considered going in to have my damages examined but something prompted me to keep going. When I reached the centre of the town there was a junction of about five roads and I was not sure which one led to the south, i.e. to Albert, so I walked right on down a road so that I could read the signs as I passed. I figured the main southern road was the one I had crossed and did a detour around some back streets, to emerge on the main road near the railway line on the far side of town. When I saw some Frenchmen drinking beer in an estaminet I considered going into one myself to quench my thirst - it was rather considerable by this time. It was a strong temptation but the possibility of the natives not being friendly ruled it out.

When I was crossing the railway line there was a chap standing in the doorway of a house a little bit back from the road who yelled something while looking straight at me. I was in a bit of a panic, but fortunately ignored him - it was OK - a woman behind the house answered him a bit later. I was feeling very sick and had some difficulty keeping going. Had to sit down to rest at times and wait until my head quit swimming. I was afraid to force myself too far with the possibility of passing out on the road - I'd be a certainty to be picked up then.

Once while walking, two Hun officers in a small car passed me and seemed to stare at me rather hard, but I looked straight ahead and they didn't stop. Once I walked into a farmhouse and asked for water but was simply greeted with scared looks and a lot of 'no' and head-shaking. Boy, was I mad at them. Another time I started to turn off the road into a big farmhouse and then noticed a big circular sign on the gatepost, the principal feature of which was a large swastika in the middle, upon which I changed my mind about going in.

I passed though several villages and lots of people stared very curiously but nobody spoke to me. Also saw a number of workmen repairing the road and tried saying 'bon jour' to some of them - they all answered very civilly but did not attempt to strike up any conversation - to my relief. Just outside Pozieres I sat down for a long time as I was feeling rather sick. I ate one of my pieces of bread and butter and was appreciating the rest when two lads started to dig a hole by the roadside just a few yards away. They looked as if they were going to speak to me, so I thought it wise to push off. (I learned later that they were ordered by the Huns to dig these holes as part of a roadside defence system - all able-bodied men in the villages etc. had to help).

Eventually I reached Pozieres and was then very sick and weak - had walked 25 kilometres or so - and decided I would have to rest for that night. I figured that the church was the best spot so whilst approaching the village I picked out the spire and kept it in my sight until I reached the correct street. There were some people in the main street but fortunately nobody in the side street near the church. I went straight to the door which was fortunately not locked, and went straight in. I sat down on a pew and pretty soon passed out and stayed that way for quite a long time until I woke to find the priest, dressed in his long black frock, looking down at me. It gave me quite a shock and I was too scared to say anything, but he smiled and I was reassured enough to start to talk to him - in English.

He grasped that I was an Allied airman, whereupon he took my arm and led me down the aisle and into a little room at the back. He then went away and got some food - brawn sandwiches and a bottle of 'biere' and told me to set about these until he brought assistance. He left after putting me in the room on the opposite side of the altar and locking me in. I enjoyed the food and especially the beer, and settled down for a long wait, as he had to cycle to Albert - about 5 kilos to bring the head of the local Resistance group. Some chap was cutting grass in the churchyard but I kept out of sight and he didn't notice me. The cure had left about 2.30 and it was almost 4 before I heard footsteps in the church and my door was unlocked. Two chaps came in - one was a (different) cure and a civilian. They both spoke English, the civvy very well. They were a little reserved until they finished asking me a lot of questions and definitely checked my identity and that I was a member of the R.A.F.

They then became very friendly and enquired about any injuries I might have. Both M. Deflandre and M. l'abbe Damoulin had bicycles and the cure and I rode ahead with M Deflandre walking. We turned down the side road to Ovillers (Ovillers la Boiselle) and turned down to the village. We waited at the outskirts until M. D. caught up, and the cure pointed out some of the local landmarks, including the Thiepval Monument (the largest British Commonwealth memorial to those missing soldiers who fought in World War I) and the Pozieres cemetery which we had just passed. When M. Deflandre caught us up we walked along right to the edge of the village and then waited with the bicycles while M. D went ahead and made sure the coast was clear. Then the cure and I rode and went straight to the front door of a farmhouse which was right on the street. The cure rang the bell twice and the door was opened immediately.

I found the whole family assembled. M and Mme Jouane, Gran'mere (Mme Jouane's mother), and four sons - Henri 22, Eve 16, Guy 15, and Michel 13 years old. They were all very curious but I found that only

Mme Jouane could speak or understand any English. Our first talk was conducted by using M. Deflandre as interpreter. He told me that he had an English wife, who kept his English up to the mark, and that he was in charge of the 'underground' movement in the Somme.

We had some coffee and something to eat and after the cure and Leandre Deflandre had left, (after promising to come back to see me and taking my identity photos for an identity card) I asked Mme Jouane for some water and a towel to wash myself properly. They did not own a bath so I had to stand the basin on the floor and pour the water over myself with the aid of a cup. I felt a lot better after this wash and went downstairs again and Mme Jouane put some sulphanilamide powder on my finger and on the scratches on my face and legs. Incidentally this powder healed all the cuts etc. perfectly - there was no sign of any scar tissue on my face at all when got back to England. I found out from Mme J. that Henri was actively engaged in the resistance work - was a sergeant - major in fact.

I was shown to my bedroom. It was on the top floor of the house on the right hand side and had a small window on the sloping section of the roof. The bed was very comfortable and clean and there was a small cupboard affair with the 'can' inside and my dish and water jug on top. Life in the farmhouse could be described as mainly boring with occasional interesting periods. I had to remain indoors most of the time and if anybody came to the house (which was quite often) I had to retire to my room and remain dead quiet because the fewer people that knew about my being there, the safer it would be. There was a very cunning hideout built into the attic. Part of the floor had been pulled up and made into a door, which was hinged to the floor on one side and had a catch to fasten it down securely. This was done after I had crawled in, from the inside. The free space was only 10 inches and about 4 feet wide and, although it was very cramped and uncomfortable, was very safe from detection. It was for the use of Henri originally. He had been ordered to Germany to work in a factory but had forfeited his identity card (which had to be handed in to the Hun authorities) and had obtained a false carte d'identite.

Rationed food was on very short supply and most of the meat we ate was from the black market, as well as coffee and most essentials such as salt and matches, The farmers were more fortunate than the town or city folks - they could retain some of their crops and produce by giving false returns to the Huns. Also Mme J. had a large vegetable patch and we had lots of strawberries, black and red currants, lettuce, onions, cabbage, raspberries and some fruit and in addition we had lots of hens and rabbits. All this meant that in addition to the vegetables and fruits we ate, and the milk and butter from the three cows, we could swap them to the black market operators for meat (usually pork) and forged or scrounged bread coupons. M. Jouane was an 'agricultural controller' for the village and had quite a lot of visitors, including local gendarmes, so that I had to spend quite a lot of time in my room. I helped Mme J. As much as I could with the housework - dishwashing, butter-making, collecting firewood and sweeping etc. etc. I got hold of a French - English dictionary and tried to improve my vocab. a little, but could not make much progress with French grammar. M. le cure Bartolomeus brought me some ancient English novels and these kept me amused for a few days. I tried to translate some French novels and magazines but did not have much success. Occasionally some trusted friend of Henri visited and I would be permitted to show myself. Their amazement on being told who I was very amusing.

Almost every day there was aerial activity in the vicinity - usually strafing of railways by Thunderbolts, Lightnings or Mustangs and occasionally Spitfires, which helped to pass the hours. The railway line from Albert to Bapaume passed within 2 kilometres or so of the farm and we could usually see the kites all the way down on their strafing run, and hear both their firing and the return fire of Hun light flak. On July 13 a big train of 47 petrol wagons was caught by some boys in Thunderbolts. Some of them were carrying incendiaries and after an hour or so of nipping around they destroyed the whole train and left a column of dirty black smoke rising through the cloud base 3 or 4 thousand feet up. I had a small pair of opera glasses and could see most of what was going on.

With these glasses I could watch the Hun traffic along the Route Nationale and for a while I kept a tally of all the different types of vehicles and convoys passing along the road. On July 17 I saw a flight of about 5 or 6 Messerschmitt 109s circle around Albert and once they passed right over the house. They landed at Meault which I could see beyond la Boselle (Ovillers la Boiselle). The next day a single ME109 circled around and unfortunately for him there was a train standing in the station at Albert which had a flak car attached. The light flak opened up with a terrific clatter. He came down in a long glide and hit just beyond la Boselle. All the Frenchmen grabbed their pistols and set off on bicycles to finish off the pilot but unfortunately there was a lorry load of Wehrmacht passing who immediately made a detour and formed a cordon around the kite. Everything was OK though - the pilot was shot in the head and stomach and had one hand knocked off and he died later.

The RAF cooperated very well with the Frenchmen and dropped lots of Stens and 9 mm ammunition in our area. Henri brought home about 2 dozen Stens and I had a job for a while showing a select number of the FFI (a total of about 20 originally) how to clean and maintain and how to use the small arms. The language problem was overcome by a screed written in English and French describing the Sten and I was able to pick out the various names for the parts and I had sufficient knowledge of the Sten from the old Battle School days in England to put the boys right.

Henri and M. Damoulin together with 2 or 3 other Frenchmen went out one night and blew up a lock in the Somme canal. This piece of work was very effective - it stopped all traffic in the canal until the Huns left. They had some explosive in a petrol tin with a long fuse attached They made the guard on the lock see reason with the aid of a Sten and then the cure climbed out and deposited the charge, lit it and scrambled back. The fuse was faulty and suddenly burnt with a fierce light and then died right out. This light attracted the attention of a Hun searchlight crew not far away and they put their beam parallel with the ground and started to sweep it around. The cure had climbed back to replace the fuse and the beam caught him on top of the lock, but he kept perfectly still and apparently the Huns didn't see him. They finished setting the charge and by the time it went off they were on their way per bicycle. I went on another 'do' a few nights later. We went to the cemetery near Pozieres and the boys climbed the high walls and cut down about 300 yards of 20 - 30 telephone lines. I stood guard with my 'Sten gun mob' and we all helped to roll up the wire and cart it away. There was one scare halfway through - a Hun truck came along the road and if he had stopped we were all set to shoot anybody who climbed out - but it was OK - he didn't notice anything and kept going.

Several times the gendarmes came to the house and each time there was a bit of a panic which meant that I had to retire to my hideout. Also there were several occasions when Huns came though the village and I had to beat it. Every night, with few exceptions, a number of JU88s would fly right over the house on a heading of 260 or so and about 50 feet or less above the ground. It made me as mad as hell to see them so close and not be able to do anything about it. Towards the end of my stay I was able to venture out into the fields by day, and help with the harvesting - but if anyone came along the roads into the village, I'd have to beat it back to the house.

There was occasional news of other airmen, generally American, in hiding in the area. I had a letter carried in the fake heel of a couriers shoe, from 2 Yanks - Graham Sweet (pilot) and Willie Neal (gunner) of a Fortress crew who were in a pretty shaky hiding place and expected to be moved at any time because of the gestapo's increased activity. We were visited by them one day, on their way north. I was hustled into the attic when the visitors arrived and a little later Madame Jouane called me down 'to meet some friends'. I thought it was the usual introduction to FFI members and in walking into the room saw two Frenchmen sitting there and greeted them with the usual 'Bon jour messieurs'. Was very surprised indeed to hear the biggest bloke (Graham Sweet) reply 'Bon jour yourself old boy. How are you?' Much nattering followed. They could not tell me where they were being shifted to, but I had another letter from Willie (Neal) several days later saying that they were a lot of searches on in his new spot also and he had spent a lot of time out in the woods. Willie came from Mississippi in the 'deep south' and claimed to be the only man in France who spoke French with a Southern drawl. He had, like most of us, a dictionary of commonly used words and phrases, written first in French, with the English equivalent, then a phonetic pronunciation. Willie's version of this latter made highly amusing reading.

At this time M Deflandre was denounced and shot by the gestapo and it was decided to move me also. The air was full of rumours at the time, constant false alarms about an aeroplane coming from England to pick up a bunch of evaders. I wrote many messages which would be transmitted to England, but apparently never were. There was supposed to be a Fortress hidden in a forest somewhere and it only needed a crew to be assembled and we would be off for home. All of these things of course came to nothing, but at least they gave me something to think about. There had been an American general in Graham Sweet's aircraft and he was being held in captivity not far away so the story went. Great plans were laid to rescue him, but unfortunately nothing came of it. Much activity in Albert when 60 gestapo were brought in, after Mme Jouane's nephew, a member of the Milice Francaise (French Nazi outfit) (Vichy police) was found with his feet sticking out of a wheat field. The FFI had caught up with him. At this time I learned that the rest of my crew had bought it in the prang. The news did nothing to build up my morale.

The wheat crop was due to be harvested and the old mowing machine was patched up once more and the horses put to work to cut it. I got some time out of doors, stacking the sheaves into stooks and the aching back was overlooked in the pleasure of being out in the sun for a day or two. The garden produced a good crop of strawberries, gooseberries and red currants. Mme Jouane made a pastry effort which through lack of fat and sugar was pretty dry, but much improved by having the above fruits spread over it before cooking. The geese in the yard were fairly well fed because gran'mere would shepherd them continually around the roads. The fowls were not so lucky and were perpetually hungry. If Mme Jouane happened to leave the kitchen door open to the backyard, there would be a sudden influx of fowls who would storm out and snatch every crumb or scrap of food in sight. The broom would then be brought into use and the lot swept out. The kitchen floor was laid in a 'mosaic design' in small tiles. The village was completely destroyed in the 14/18 war - I was shown a photograph which showed a great pile of bricks and rubble with the base of one chimney still standing. When the rebuilding was started a large number of Italian artisans and workmen were imported to do the work - hence the tiled floors.

There was a great fear of reprisals against the FFI sabotage etc. about this time. The usual practice of the methodical Hun was to throw a cordon around a village or town at 4am (always at this time). They would then search every building and collect every male from 16 to 60, and if their identity card and carte de travail were not in order they were put straight onto trains for Germany for forced labour. Any FFI evidence found would lead to quick work by the Gestapo and Abwehr. This meant a roster of early morning watches from the loft of the barn, and also the stuffing of beds - if the Huns found an unoccupied bed with the blankets still warm, then the pressure was on.

The elder of the two priests was M. l'Abbe Bartolomeus, a beaut type. He rode a bicycle to Orleans (through Paris) and back, a distance of about 200 miles on a mercy mission to his sister, and brought back a stack of stuff for all sorts of people. For me he brought a French-English dictionary, some English novels, road maps, and most wonderful of all, a small packet of French Indo-Chinese tea (I still have the packet). After the usual beverage of ersatz 'coffee', made from roasted wheat grains, with 3 or 4 coffee beans to a kilogram of wheat, this was a treat beyond description.

We had a small party in the garden one day, with me dressed in Henri's best suit. We took photographs and when I got some prints of these I wrote a letter to mother and together with the pictures buried them in a bottle. Eventually they reached home after the liberation. Another walk Mme Jouane and I took was to the cemetery to visit the grave of her daughter Micheline, the twin sister of Michel. Since none of the villagers knew I was there, when we met two people I was introduced by Mme J. As her 'cousine Belgique', and hurried off before the talk became embarrassing.

On 10th August (Thursday) Henri was called away. The Resistance was being mobilised and were to live 'in the field', to finish their training for work in hampering the Hun retreat which was expected. Then on 11th August Henri called in a truck with stacks of packing cases (empty) in the back. I was to be moved north, which was the wrong direction for me, but the golden rule was do as you are told, smartly, and don't argue. I said my farewells to the rest of the family and owing to my poor French, I felt my thanks were quite inadequate. I climbed in under the cases, Henri stacked some more on top and away to Ecoust-St-Mein. On the way (not sure where) we picked up Willie Neal and another Yank. When we arrived at E St M we were taken to Marc Harlet's house. Marc was a Captain and was responsible for arranging the funeral of the rest of my crew. He gave me the face of my altimeter and also showed me the remains of my Dalton computer which he promised to sent to me in Aussie 'après la guerre'. Marc showed me the pictures of the funeral and graves and these were given to me later by Mimi at Sallaumines.

False identity card - for Arnold Morrison

Had a cup of coffee and shortly after M. Bodani called in a car to take 3 of us to Billy Montigny. We stopped at one town (Douai I think) and had a drink in a boozer. B. had the popsy behind the bar teed up to keep a conversation going and all we had to do was to say or no at the right moments. Nearly caught at Vitry-en-Artois. The road leads straight through the town with a humpback bridge over a canal at the far end. The streets were full of Hun troops and as we approached the bridge we saw a staff car on the roadside, troops across the road with an officer in front of them. Bodani blew his horn loud and long and barely slowed down whereupon the officer apparently assumed that we were gestapo or something (the windscreen was liberally plastered with stickers of various sorts - swastikas and eagles all over). He hopped to the side of the road and barked an order to his troops who smartly cleared the road leaving us to sail though in state.

We then started skirting the Vitry aerodrome (loaded with FW 190s and traversed the coal mining country to the north of BM (The Huns at Vitry would have been interested to know that none of the three evaders had identity cards or papers of any sort and car priorities were forged. Arrived at Bodani's house and he drove on with the strange Yank (X) and Willie and I walked till we came to his house. We said ' good day ' in French to X and stood around smoking Caporals till Bodani came out and walked along to Mme Heller's photographic shop and studio. B. Stopped several times and we had to stop too about 25 metres behind and look unconcerned until he went on.

Eventually reached the shop and went in, and after being talked to by Mme Heller about our alleged appointments, were taken into a back studio and then promptly rushed upstairs. Met another Yank, Bill du Bose up there - Lightning pilot - bailed out at 800 feet - chute just opened in time - broken ankle and laid up for two months. American X decided that as he had got as far as Ecoust St Mein on a bicycle from Brussels (crossed the border with a gendarme escort) he was going further south. He got a carte d'identite and a carte du travail and pushed off disguised as a miner (I believe he eventually made it to the allied lines). While at Heller's we met the excitable popsy Mimi. More of her later.

Was taken to Octave Perroy's house and met John Cullity (another Aussie). Been there 5 weeks. Not a good hiding place - had to talk quietly, nothing to read, nothing to smoke - good food though - Octave conducted a 'Dairy Foods Store'. Was introduced to fromage blanc avec caramel sauce- very super. Also tasted liquor called Angelique - very insidious. Eldest son Jacques was adjutant (Sar-major) in FFI - always bringing pistols home. Keen type. Youngest son Jean proper twerp. John Cullity spoke excellent French and had lots of arguments with Jean. Breakfast 8am in our room - could not go downstairs until 12 noon because of the maid - she knew John was there. Mme. Perroy said that he was a miner on night shift and could not be disturbed during the day. After lunch with the family we had to go upstairs again until about 5pm. Then we couldn't talk loudly or go out into the backyard for fear of neighbours seeing us. John had an escape route worked out- climb onto the roof of the outhouse, and up to the second story roof in case of a quick search by the Hun.

Jacques Perroy told us of an incident. A collaborator in a nearby cafe was going to denounce 5 patriots so two blokes cycled up and went in for a drink. When the bod went to get some glasses, one chap shot him twice in the head and then walked out leaving him for dead. However he recovered somewhat and was taken to hospital and looked like getting better. Later the Resistance bod called at the hospital and asked to see the collaborator. The nurse showed him into the ward and pointed out this chap swathed in bandages and said he was going to recover, whereupon the Resistance bod produced a pistol again and finished him off properly, then walked calmly out without interference. This bit of work caused some consternation around the district and as the Perroys were rightly afraid of reprisals we were shifted. The Polish lass Leonie Simoniak called and we were guided - John and I - to the Heller's. While there I got my identity card and John arranged for his to be delivered.

Set off for Mama Dernancourt's shop with Leonie walking in front pushing her bicycle (air let out of tyre to fake a puncture). Arrived after detour, Leonie signalled from the doorway and John and I walked into the shop. In back met Bill du Bose, Pat Brophy (Canadian rear gunner), Cliff Williams (American fighter pilot and extra good bloke), Danny Murray (Canadian), Maurice Bemrose (Benny - RAF - gunner - ex RAF Regiment and later my offsider in FFI stooging). Most of the blokes had been there for about 9 weeks. Met Mama and Papa Dernancourt, Leonie and the 11 year old Rouge (Red) Mama's grandson and beaut lad. Met Mme Quiquampaux later - another patriot with a house - full of evaders.

Mama and Papa came from Martinique and were the most loveable people one could ever meet. Papa was awarded the Croix de Guerre at Verdun and when any heartening news arrived per radio, he would stand erect and sing the Marseillaise, and would not be hushed by anyone. Mama would smile at the mob sitting around and say how nice it was to have such a beautiful big family. A truly saintly woman.

We had rooms upstairs and a small yard for exercise. The upstairs windows had lace curtains and we spent a fair bit of time looking at the people walking in the street, and feeling quite useless when we saw the Bosche strutting around. Had a radio and kept track of the war's progress towards us. Bill du Bose got hold of a small scale map and kept the frontline marked with pins. (We would periodically throw him into a rage by pulling them out and rearranging them in some fantastic positions.

Papa had a pig in a shed which was to be done over 'après le liberation' and it was the alleged duty of the 'orderly officer' to read the war news to the pig. Benny Bemrose drew up a daily copy of DROs (Daily Routine Orders) and it was really funny - sometimes screamingly so. Benny fell for Leonie and when he wanted some time with her (undisturbed) he would confine all ranks to quarters for a specified time.

The intruder and medium bomber boys flew over our town on their way to targets and we got an idea of their objectives by timing them out and back. One day they came in from the SW and we were all in the yard watching. Somebody saw what they thought was a 'window' falling. The mob said phooey - there's no ack-ack or radar here and everyone woke up it was bombs we saw. We achieved the impossible - 7 bods went through the cellar door simultaneously. The rail junction at Henin-Lietard - (11/2 Km, east) copped it.

Bath night was fun. Only one bloke at a time could go to the laundry (down the yard) to collect water from the copper. We set up the tub in the kitchen and went to work. The soap was like pumice - no lather. Benny overdid the hot water and soap and came out all over in a red rash and we had to get some black salve delivered by M. le medicin to take the resultant fever down. We were able to do very little to help Mama - mainly cutting up food ration coupons. Spent a lot of time playing dominoes (Papa was pretty good), also in arguing and laughing about Mme Heller and Mimi - 'He is a bad man - some of my chaps has told me he will sprang my house. He must be killed.' (He was). Food was reasonably plentiful - all 'marche- noir'. Meat 5 times per week, bags of pommes frits.

We had all sorts of plans about our defences if the Huns came snooping in the house. We had no firearms at this stage but all were armed with loaded hose pipes. One day the boys were hopping mad- saw hostages collected in the street. The tardy ones were assisted forcibly into the back of the high truck with rifle butts. Bastard Bosche. We had a visitor for lunch one day - a bod arrived in a truck driven by producer gas which he parked in the street outside. During lunch he said that he would be around until dark. He would then be going westward along the Route Nationale to blow up a bridge using unexploded RAF bombs. When we asked where he had the bombs hidden he said they were in the truck outside. The boys promptly rushed upstairs and peered through the curtains. Sure enough the truck had a stack of stuff covered with a tarpaulin. We told him about delay fusing but he shrugged it off - 'c'est ne faire rien'. Anyway he shoved off at nightfall, picked up some mates and carried out the job OK. Various Resistance bods called and promised that when the expected Hun retreat was on, that we would be given arms and allowed to join the fun. An air raid destroyed a petrol plant not far away, and the FFI successfully sabotaged a petrol tanker in the street and also a static storage tank we could see several blocks behind the house.

Good news at last. The retreat was finally on, after the usual spate of rumours. The Route Nationale was crammed with Huns in all manner of vehicles and on foot. Even farm carts (with civilian drivers) wheelbarrows etc., all with weapons at 'ready' for ack ack. Big show of Typhoons shooting up road transport just south of us - full squadron 'do' - peeling off in turn - creating havoc with cannon fire. By the night of Thursday 31st August (1944), retreat had nearly finished. FFI erected a barricade just down the street. A Hun truck ran the gauntlet - sounds of firing from away along the road - rifles, automatic weapons and finally a bod near our house gave them both barrels of a 12 gauge shot gun. Sounded quite funny. The truck arrived at the railway level crossing just down the road at the same moment as a truck was rolled out by the FFI boys. Quite a pile up - the Huns took to the surrounding house and it was 24 hours or so before they winkled them out.

Lots of excitement. Immediate round up of 'collaborators' and 'feld Deutsch'. We were taken into the street and put on display then taken into the cafe across the road and plied with drinks. Tried dancing with some of the local frippets to the music of prewar records, but not much success. The local celebrations were on in a big way. It transpired that there were, in all. 21 Allied evaders hidden in the town and a civic reception was in the town square and we were all presented to the crowd from the balcony above M. Heller's shop - 'Ici deux aviateurs Australiens etc.' Then a round of visits to various houses of FFI stalwarts with magnums of champagne being produced all over. Dinner at the doctor's house a big success with due honours being paid to Mama and Papa Dernancourt, Mme Quicampoix, M. and Mme Heller and all the rest. Cliff Williams and I talked for quite a while on the significance of what was then happening. Another dinner at Octave Perroy's house. Highly successful. A further dinner at Colonel Ami's house (CO of Resistance).

A party of us visited Vimy Ridge Canadian War Memorial - no damage to memorial except several bullet scars and tank tracks across the lawns. Saw the bomb damage at Arras - the railway station completely destroyed (one engine still vertical and rails looked like a stack of twisted wire.) Houses and shops on the other side of the streets barely touched. On the way home we again passed Vitry aerodrome, now stacked with Typhoons, Dakotas and Mustangs. Quite a pleasant change.

On the 8th September we set for a stooge with the FFI. Benny and I went to Lille where we met Col. Ami for lunch in a restaurant. Later we watched a group of British armour arriving. Had some fun by standing near a Pongo sergeant and when he wasn't looking said 'got a smoke, chum?' Then looked elsewhere when he wheeled around. Finally introduced myself and had smokes thrust on me. We then shoved off and inspected some Hun prisoners Ami had cooped up (about 40 of them). Asked Ami what would be done with them? He shrugged his shoulders and said 'no need to worry about them'. (Don't quite know what he meant but had a fair idea). Went to St Omer - saw several (German) Tiger tanks knocked into the ditch. On arriving in St Omer walked straight into a ruckus. Some 'feld Deutsch' were parked in a cellar with pavement height windows and were sniping at English troops going past. We were issued with two grenades - French type - but Benny and I were very suspicious of them and gave them to some FFI bods. We could at least depend on the German service rifles we had not blowing up in our face. The fun was short and sweet and the sniping types were soon done over

We had a large German staff car that Ami had souvenired - complete with a cocktail cabinet and cigar cabinet. Nice smokes too. Pretty thirsty for gasoline and we spent a lot of time trying to scrounge gas from the Pommy bods - no dice. Saw a RAF reconnaissance car outside a cafe so Benny and I went in. There were several F/Os, an F/L and an S/Ldr (Flying Officers, Flight Lieutenant, Squadron Leader) having a drink at one table. They were making facetious remarks in French to the lass serving them then engaging in ribald banter in English. We edged a little closer and then I remarked to Benny 'One would imagine that if one was an officer and a gentleman, it would be a good idea to act as such and not annoy innocent girls.' The Squaddo gave a look and said 'Blimey, you can always find a bloody Australian wherever you go'. Much nattering all round, questions galore from the boys. They wanted to take us back to an AOB right away and shoot us off to England, but we said no dice, we were having too much fun They said we were nuts but OK - then we scrounged all the spare gas they had. Ami very pleased

Then went to a forest near St Omer with 40 of the troops to rout out 200 SS troops who were cutting up rough, some shooting, but the darkness beat us. 'Terry', a very small FFI bloke, didn't have a chance to cut loose with his Boyes anti-tank rifle. He toted this thing - which was about a foot longer than he was - and a whacking great pannier of ammunition, all over. Used it to good effect during the retreat at Billy Montigny. The sound of the armour piercing bullets ricocheting off buildings was enough to scare any Hun. We proceeded towards Lens and got mixed up with several convoys at a cross roads.

Several incidents while scrounging gasoline. One truck load of bods told about a solitary Hun prisoner they had handed over to an FFI bloke at a cross roads (he was just a nuisance to them). The Frenchman marched him off across a field and they disappeared behind a hedge. They heard a Sten chatter and the bloke came back. When asked what happened to the Hun, the bloke shrugged his shoulders and said 'Il mort, m'sieur'.

Got a fair haul of gas but struck a snag with a Pongo Intelligence bloke in a Jeep. He demanded to know who I was - showed him dog-tags but he was not convinced - reckoned I was a 5th columnist - and demanded more proof. Whistled up Ami who put the bloke straight. I then told him about the 200 SS who were sniping the column. He said he knew all about it and pointed to a bullet hole in the front of his Jeep and said that the pontoon bridge that was holding up the convoy was blown up by them.

Eventually arrived back at Resistance HQ and found that there was not much work to do anyway, so back to Sallaumines. Collected my gear and said my farewells to the Dernancourts - Mama and Papa just about upset as I was. Benny decided to stick around for a while longer but Pat Brophy had come back at the same time so we set off for Vitry aerodrome and bludged a ride in a Dakota to England, where we were debriefed and re-kitted before sailing for home.'

F/L Arnold Morrison, RAAF, DFC (front row, second from right) with other evaders after their liberation. Out of uniform the very young age of many aircrew is clearly apparent. Source: Linda Miles.

Finally, I owe so many thanks to my friends Simon, his partner Mandy and son William, my wife Leeanne and boys Aaron and Jayden, My dad John, my mum Irene, my Uncle Bernard, Wendy Flemming, Linda Miles (nee Morrison), and in memory of my Nanna, Mabel Elizabeth Porrelli, who stayed devoted to her husband till death, never re-marrying. When her time came, her ashes were interred with my granddad, re-uniting them once more.

I hope that this record that we have created will help to ensure the memory of those who served in 514 Squadron RAF and their most outstanding efforts are never forgotten. 'We Will Remember Them'.

Andrew Porrelli
Nymboida, NSW, April 2014

Sgt Ross Flemming
by Wendy Flemming

When I think back to the first time that I was truly interested in my parents' Airforce careers, I guess it would have to been on January 10, 1977. My husband and I and my parents were on a holiday in England, my Mum's home country, and were at the train station in Southwick, Sussex when my Mum had a massive heart attack, and died immediately. She was only 53 years old and I was 24. We were on our way up to Scotland, where my parents were going to take us to the cities that they used to go to when they were on leave from the airforce during WW2. Needless to say, that day changed my life forever. We were all in shock as she was a young, vibrant woman with so much more living to do. My Dad was so devastated. After that day, he couldn't talk about Mum without breaking down, so I never pushed him for answers.

My Dad was an RCAF navigator who was attached to 514 Squadron RAF, based in Waterbeach, Cambridgeshire, England. While he was stationed there, a beautiful, young lady caught his eye as he was eating his meal that was served to him and the crew before they went on night bombing raids. They dated for a few months, but never got engaged till after Dad was finished his 'tour' of 31 operations over enemy territory. I guess they wanted to make sure that he would return alive and not leave a widow behind.

The only thing that we knew about their relationship was when we asked them how they met- Dad said 'I had a 5 speed bike and your Mum only had a single speed.' Mum's version was 'He told me that he owned a Gopher Ranch in Alberta' and apparently all I heard was the word 'RANCH'; I never had a clue what a gopher was.'

Over the next few years, I asked my Dad questions about the airforce and about their life while serving in it but he wouldn't say much. I bought him all the airforce books that I could get my hands on. I thought that would make him feel more comfortable about talking about his time in England, but it didn't seem to. So I bought him all the books that I could find on Lancaster bombers, books on life in the RAF and others about Canadians who served in the RAF and then some more about Lancasters. All the while I was hoping that something would start him talking but it didn't. One thing that I noticed is that he would talk a bit to other veterans about the airforce in general, but nothing too specific. He used to attend all the Airforce Reunions which were held in Canada, but was disheartened when he got there and never found anyone that he knew. As we were growing up, though, there was a photo that stood proudly on a shelf in the living room of our home. It was of Dad and the crew in front of their aircraft 'Minnie the Moocher'.

Mary Flemming (above, left) met her future husband Ross (right) when both served at RAF Waterbeach. Source: Wendy Flemming.

The one thing that stands out in my mind was one day when I was pestering him for information and he said 'It wasn't all good times.' He told me how the aircrew of 7 that they were a part of would never mix much with the other crews, as they never knew who would be coming back. Many crews were lost. He said there were many times when he would come back to the Nissen hut after an op and find a row of 7 beds cleaned and bags packed. It must have been a horrible feeling.
The turning point in my quest came one Remembrance Day in Camrose. The guest speaker was Rev. Brian Hunter, who said the veterans needed to talk to their children and tell them about their life in WW2 and what it was like. After all, it had shaped them into what they were today. I nudged my Dad and said 'See; that is what I am asking!!!' From that time on, my Dad was a bit more open, but still reluctant to talk about that time of his life.

One of the things that I remember my Dad mentioning later in his years was that he wondered what had happened to his crew. His pilots name was 'Sandy'; I never knew a last name. But other than that he never mentioned any other names. I never even knew the squadron number. Heavens, at that time I didn't even know that they had numbers. But I did know that they were married at Waterbeach, England on September 7th 1944 in St. John the Evangelist Church.

My Dad passed away in 1997, about 6 months after I got my first computer. I started to search for information for him; he had told me that the squadron number was 514 and that was all I needed. I found out some info on the web, but it was sparse. I found another daughter of a 514 Squadron Bomb Aimer, Karen Russell in Keene, Ontario, who was looking for the same thing; answers to lots of questions about her Dad's time at Waterbeach. We searched and searched and both of us found little bits of information on the internet. But we needed more. Then about 6 months after my Dad died, my step mother got a call from a fellow who was looking for my Dad. It was his reargunner, Doug, from Ontario. Well, I called him immediately. Sadly, I had to tell him that Dad was gone but that I would be delighted to keep in contact with him and eventually meet him. He, too, was excited about that prospect and over the next few years we became the closest of friends. We kept in very close contact and were both excited about meeting one another, so in 2001 I went to Ontario, armed with a videocamera and many tapes, ready to get some answers.

I wasn't disappointed. He spent an entire day answering my questions and filling me in on their life in the RAF at Waterbeach.

He was a great fellow who, sadly, passed away with cancer.

I learned so much from him and there was a bonus; he also knew my Mum, because he too was served meals in the Sergeants' Mess by her. She was a 20 year old WAAF (Womens' Auxiliary Air Force) at that time. He told me that he met hundreds of women while at Waterbeach and my Mother was the only one he could remember. She had an infectious smile and beautiful olive coloured skin. She was always happy. He told me that he and my Mum had gone on some walks down by the river Cam.

Dad had a few pictures of his RCAF/RAF days and I took them along with me to Ontario. Doug was able to tell me all the names of the crew except the pilot- his last name was Sandland and "Sandy" was just a nickname like so many men had back then. But now I had some names to go on, I started searching the web. I connected with the RAF 514 Squadron Association in England but was unable to find any of the crew.

Because of the internet, I left my name and address at many websites, asking anyone who served with 514 Sqn to get in touch with me. I was surprised at the response. With the help of the internet and Dad's rear gunner, I was able to locate my Dad's flight engineer and Bomb Aimer, both living in England.

You can imagine their shock when I telephoned them. They were very excited to hear from me and had also wondered what had happened to the crew after they were done their operations. It was such an emotional time in my research. I was ecstatic; I couldn't believe that I had managed to track some of the crew. I was also able to trace the daughter of Dad's Wireless operator- he had died in 1997.

The pilot was an Englishman, and to this day I have not been able to trace him. Also his Midupper Gunner was a Canadian from Toronto and I haven't been able to find him either. His name is Ernie Gordon and because Gordon is such a common name, I have been unable to locate him or his family.

I began getting requests for information about fellows from the squadron looking for some of their mates and as I knew the feeling that I had when I saw my Dad's gunner for the first time, I wanted other people to have that same feeling. I started trying to match up people that had emailed me for help with the people that
I had in my database. With the help of a couple of fellows in England, I was able to create a database of about 300 names and addresses of men who had served with 514 Sqn. I remember well the first time that I matched up a couple of fellows living in Ontario- and they only lived about 30 miles apart. You can just imagine the excitement for the two of them!!!

Then I found out that there has been a yearly reunion held each June at Waterbeach for many years. I wanted to meet some of the English people that I had been corresponding with over the past 6 years. So in June of 2002, my sister, Laurie and I headed for the Waterbeach reunion. It was amazing to say the least. One great story involving an Edmonton man comes out of that trip to England.

While I was pondering over some photos at the reunion, I came across a name, Joe Speare. He was one of the fellows that I have lunch with in Edmonton every couple of months. Incidentally I have found 2 fellows in Edmonton that served with 514 Squadron and they have been so much of a help, it is amazing.

I told my sister 'I know that fellow!!!!' Right behind me was an Englishman and he overheard me say the name 'Joe Speare'. He tapped me on the shoulder and asked me if he had heard right and I said 'Yes, I have lunch with this fellow every couple of months.' Well, his mouth dropped open and he gasped. He was Joe Speare's pilot from 58 years ago!!! Joe attended the reunion last year and was reunited with his pilot and from what Joe told me it was like they had never been apart for all those years. Just like two young fellows talking about the flights, the pubs and the life at Waterbeach.

(Above) LL635 JI-M 'Minnie The Moocher' Lancaster Mk II crew, 514 Squadron 1944. LL635 was damaged beyond repair by flak on an operation to Vincly on 25th August 1944, whilst in the care of another crew. L to R back: Sgt Herbert Thornley (Bomb Aimer), P/O Bert Sandland (Pilot), Sgt Ross Flemming (Navigator), Sgt Ernie Gordon (MU Gunner). Front row: Sgt Stan Sedgwick (Flight Engineer), P/O Michael Shingleton (WOP/AG), Sgt Doug MacLaughlin (Rear Gunner). Source: Wendy Flemming.

While we were at the reunion at Waterbeach we got to go to the church where Mum and Dad were married and they even searched and dusted off the register, showing us where Mum and Dad had signed some 58 years earlier. The church was built in 1677 and not much had changed I don't think.

One of the highlights of the reunion was the flypast of the RAF's Lancaster bomber, one of only two flying in the world today. The hair stood up on my arms as it roared by us again and again. Seeing the tears in the men's eyes, knowing how much it meant to them, I knew that my quest for reuniting crews had just begun.

In 2003, I had ten fellows in Ontario that served with the squadron, but for one reason or another (mostly health) were unable to attend the reunions in Waterbeach. So I thought "Why not have a reunion in Ontario, where the other flying Lancaster bomber makes its home. In the summer of 2003 - I organised a reunion in Hamilton, Ontario and attended by these ten fellows and their families making fifty people in all. They were so tickled to get together and reminisce about their time in England and at Waterbeach. I took the photos from the reunion in England, and we had a guest speaker Floyd Williston who had written a book on his brother Albert, who was killed while serving with 514 Sqn.

The plan was to watch the Lancaster do a take off and a fly by that day, but it was pouring rain, and they scrapped the idea of a flight. I spoke to the pilot of the Lancaster, who kindly let each of the men and their families go inside the Lanc and sit in the same spot that they would have some 60 years before. The response from the veterans was great- but the response from the family members was even more heart-touching. Many of them were surprised that their fathers were talking about 'those days'. Like with my father, they had rarely spoken about their experiences and everyone respected their feelings. They weren't there to brag, just to help their kids understand what it must have been like. To see the sparkle in their eyes as they took their position and tried to explain to their families what it was like; that was worth all the time that I spend on this 'operation' of mine.

And so my quest for connection of the crew members goes on and every week I receive requests from either veterans or their children wanting information on those years. I see such a need for men and women that served with RAF 514 Squadron to come together and find crew mates, friends, and families from so long ago. I have reunited about 25 crews- not all from every crew- but 2 or 3. To hear the excitement in their voices when they have spoken to one another is my reward!And as these fellows/ladies get on in years, with most of them are in their late 80's and early 90's, I feel that time is so precious.

If we don't preserve this history for them, I am afraid that it will be lost. I want our children and future generations, never to forget the sacrifices that were made by all the veterans who fought for our country in every way. If it wasn't for them, we surely wouldn't have the freedom that we have today.

Lancaster pilot F/L Ron Pickler DFC, Wendy Flemming and Rear Gunner Sgt Don Gardiner, Milestones Restaurant, June 2009. Photo courtesy of Garth Ridley.

My niece Sarah Atchison wrote a lovely poem in remembrance of these special men and women (it follows the dedication at the start of this book).
I feel that I am living my Dad's dream and will continue as long as I can- to help others understand what a great sacrifice these veterans made for us. We were lucky; our parents survived the war and came home, had a family and life carried on for them. I think that there was such a great strong bond between my parents because they had seen the worst and survived. I think that is why my Dad found it so hard to talk about Mum after she passed away. His love ran deeper than we will ever know.

Move of No. 514 Squadron to RAF Waterbeach

SECRET
HEADQUARTERS NO. 3 GROUP
ADMINISTRATIVE INSTRUCTION NO. 89

MOVE OF NO. 514 SQUADRON

INFORMATION

In connection with the re-organisation of No. 3 Group it is necessary to move No. 514 Squadron from R.A.F. Station Foulsham to R.A.F. Station Waterbeach

2. This will be carried out on November 23rd 1943 and all moves will be by road. No. 2 M.T. Company will send an Officer to Foulsham immediately to assess the requirements of transport, and it may be possible for certain vehicles to arrive at Foulsham prior to the date of move for the purpose of loading some of the heavy equipment. It is necessary, however, for the program to be carried out as speedily as possible so that the operational effort of the Squadron receives the minimum of interference.

3. A separate Instruction will be issued regarding No. 1678 Conversion Flight.

INTENTION

4. To move No. 514 Squadron from Foulsham to Waterbeach on 23rd November 1943.

EXECUTION

5. (a) PERSONNEL – The Squadron will move to the old establishment (WAR/BC/336) (this Headquarters signal 0374 dated 13.11.43 applies); and all personnel on the posted strength will move with the Squadron. It is essential that all personnel possible are moved on the 23rd as the vehicles are required for another move on the 25th. The rear party can be moved by Squadron transport on the 24th if necessary.

(b) TRANSPORT - All transport will be supplied by No. 2 M.T. Company, Cambridge, and as stated above, an Officer from that Unit will attend at Foulsham immediately to assess requirements and arrange routes etc.

(c) CRANES – It will be necessary to ensure that sufficient cranage facilities are available at Foulsham and Waterbeach for loading and unloading purposes during the period of the move, and the Group Transport Officer will arrange to have sufficient cranes at each place.

(d) AIRCRAFT – Aircraft on charge of No. 514 Squadron will be rendered serviceable and ready to fly from Foulsham to Waterbeach on 23rd November 1943 or afterwards as weather permits.

(e) EQUIPMENT – The Squadron will move with equipment according to War Schedule, with the addition of special items peculiar to Lancaster Aircraft. No barrack equipment will be taken from Foulsham.

(f) M.T. - All vehicles on charge of 514 Squadron will move in convoy from Foulsham to Waterbeach. These should move under the charge of an Officer and the regulations regarding convoys will be carried out. It may be possible to convoy certain of the Squadrons personnel in these vehicles.

(g) – MARCHING OUT – Officer Commanding R.A.F. Station Foulsham will arrange
for a Marching Out Inspection of all buildings occupied by No. 514 Squadron to be carried out.

(h) – MOVEMENT ORDER – A Movement Order will be prepared immediately by Officer Commanding No. 514 Squadron, copies to be forwarded to : -

Headquarters No. 3 group	1 copy
Headquarters Bomber Command	1 copy
Headquarters No. 33 Base	1 copy
No. 2 M.T. Company	1 copy
Air Officer i/c Records	1 copy

(I) – COMPLETION OF MOVE SIGNAL – No. 514 Squadron will advise this Headquarters by signal when the movement has been carried out.

ACKNOWLEDGE.

1st November 1943.

Group Captain,
Staff Officer i/c Administration.

DISTRIBUTION.

Headquarters No. 33 Base. (2 copies)
R.A.F. Station Foulsham. (2 copies – 1 for 514 Squadron)

No. 2 M.T. Company.
Headquarters, Bomber Command.
Air Officer i/c Records.

Internal Distribution.

A.O.C.	M.T. G.B.L.	ENG.	P.R.O.	SIGS. SEC.
S.A.S.O.	P.T.I.	NAV.	EQUPT.	C.R. P.STAFF.
OPS.	PHOTOS.	NAV.G.	W.A.A.F.	D.R.L.S.
S.O.A.	G.G.O.	M.T.O.	S.M.O.	MET.
INT.	G.G.F.O.	DEF.	C&D.	SIGS.

From:- 514 Squadron, R.A.F. Station, Foulsham.
To:- Distribution List Below.
Date:- 16th November 1943.
Ref:- 514/8.1712/1/Org.

NO. 514 SQUADRON MOVEMENT ORDER.

1. INFORMATION.

No 514 Squadron has been ordered to move to the old establishment (WAR/BC/336) from R.A.F. Station, Foulsham, to R.A.F. Station, Waterbeach on 23rd November 1943, Authority:- Postagram 3G/S.8004/19/Org. dated 14th November, 1943.

2. INTENTION.

To move the Squadron with all Aircraft M.T., and equipment on the Squadron charge (other than Barrack Equipment) by air and road by the 24th November, 1943.

3. EXECUTION.

The movement will be carried out as follows: -

(i) ADVANCE PARTY. Personnel detailed in Appendix 'A' will proceed by road on the 18th November, 1943, to prepare for the reception of the main body.

(ii) MAIN PARTY.
(a) Road Party. Personnel detailed in Appendix 'B' will proceed by road on 23rd November 1943.

(b) Air Party. Personnel detailed in Appendix 'C' will proceed by air on 23rd November 1943.

(iii) REAR PARTY. Personnel detailed in Appendix 'D' will proceed by road on completion of handing over, Barrack Equipment etc. to R.A.F. Station, Foulsham.

4. ADMINISTRATION.

   1. EMBUSSING PARADE.

   (a) Advance Party. Personnel detailed in Appendix 'A' will parade 0900 hours on the road between the two main hangers on the 18th November 1943.

   (b) Main Party. Personnel detailed in Appendix 'B' (i.e. Road party) will parade on the road between the two main hangers on the 18th November 1943.

   (c) Personnel detailed in Appendix 'C' (i.e. Air party) will proceed to Squadron Navigation Block on 23rd November 1943, for instructions by their Flight Commanders.

   (d) Rear Party. Personnel detailed in Appendix 'D' will proceed to R.A.F. Station Waterbeach on completion of the handing over to R.A.F. Station Foulsham.

   2. KIT.
All kit will be securely packed and labelled and clearly marked with Rank, Name and Number of owner. Kit will be collected as follows: -
(a) Advance Party. - If dry outside the Gymnasium, if wet, inside the Gymnasium by 0815 hours.
(b) Main Party and Air Party.-
(i) Officers. - Outside their respective quarters at 0815 hours.
(ii) Senior N.C.O.s. - Outside the picket posts on their respective Sleeping Sites.
(iii) Other Ranks. - If dry, outside the Gymnasium dumped in alphabetical order, if wet, inside the Gymnasium.
(c) Rear Party. The Officer or N.C.O. i/c of the rear party will be responsible for the completion of handing-over.

3. RATIONS.
The Senior N.C.O. in charge of each party will be responsible for the collection of the unconsumed portion of the day's rations and disassemble the messes at 0815 hours and that the rations be transferred to respective messes at R.A.F. Station, Waterbeach

4. NOMINAL ROLLS.
Senior N.C.O.s. In charge of sections will check all nominal rolls and report any absentees immediately to the Squadron Orderly Room.

5. EQUIPMENT.
(a) Flights and sections are to pack all equipment on their charge; all packing cases and items must be clearly marked with Squadron, Flight and Section.
(b) Loading parties will be detailed by the Squadron Engineer Officer. (See Appendix 'B').

6. SECRET and CONFIDENTIAL PUBLICATIONS.
Will be handed to Cypher Officer by holders before 1700 hours on 22nd November 1943.

7. DRESS.
(a) Advance party – Full marching order.
(b) Main road party – Full marching order.
(c) Air party – Working dress.
(d) Rear party – Full marching order.

8. MARCHING-OUT INSPECTION.
(a) **Sleeping Sites and Blocks of Officers**. Will be carried out by the officer detailed in charge of Rear party, in conjunction with the Station Equipment Officer, when a list of damages and deficiencies will be agreed upon and forwarded to Officer Commanding 514 Squadron.
(b) **Technical Buildings such as Hangars etc.** Will be carried out by the Squadron Engineer Officer (or somebody detailed by him) in conjunction with the Equipment warrant Officer and a list of damages and deficiencies agreed upon forwarded to Officer Commanding 514 Squadron.

9. MARCHING-IN INSPECTION.

F/O Bower in conjunction with the Barrack Warden of R.A.F Waterbeach will inspect all domestic and technical buildings when a list of damages and deficiencies agreed upon will be handed to the Officer Commanding 514 Squadron.

10. KEYS.

All keys of safes, doors, cupboards etc. are to be clearly labelled and handed over to the Equipment Officer.

11. TRANSPORT.

Squadron transport will allotted as detailed in Appendix 'C'. Transport will also be supplied by No. 2 M.T. Company, Cambridge.

12. BICYCLES.

All personnel having bicycles on their charge are to hand them in to Squadron Discip. N.C.O. complete and in good running order by 1200 hours on 22nd November 1943. Those failing to produce bicycles on their charge by the hour stated will have action taken.

13. W.A.A.F. PARTY.

The W.A.A.F. Party consisting of 11 Cooks, 1 Safety Equipment Assistant and 6 Waitresses as detailed in Appendix 'B' will parade with kit outside the N.A.A.F.I. Headquarters at 0900 hours on 23rd November 1943, and proceed in transport detailed to R.A.F. Station Waterbeach with the main party. The W.A.A.F. Corporal in charge of this party will receive orders direct from the Squadron Adjutant. Any W.A.A.F. Personnel being in possession of cycles must hand them in to Station Headquarters complete and in working order by 1200 hours on 22nd November 1943.

14. ACKNOWLEDGE RECEIPT.

AJ Samson,
Wing Commander, Commanding
No. 514 Squadron.   R.A.F.

DISTRIBUTION : -

Headquarters Bomber Command.
Headquarters No. 3 Group.
Headquarters No. 33 Base.
No. 2 Motor Transport Company.
Air Officer i/c Records, Gloucester.
H.Q.   R.A.F. Station, Foulsham.
Accts. Officer, R.A.F. Station, Foulsham.
Equipment Officer R.A.F. Station, Foulsham.
Squadron Leader Admin. R.A.F. Station, Foulsham.
Messing Officer, R.A.F. Station, Foulsham.
Transport Officer, R.A.F. Station, Foulsham.
Officer Commanding, 514 Squadron.
Officer Commanding 'A' and 'B' Flights 514 Squadron.
Adjutant, 514 Squadron.
Engineer Officer, 514 Squadron.
Armament Officer, 514 Squadron.
Officers Mess, R.A.F. Station, Foulsham.
Sergeants Mess, R.A.F. Station, Foulsham.
Station warrant Officer, R.A.F. Station, Foulsham.

APPENDIX 'A'
ADVANCE PARTY.

OFFICERS.

Flight Lieutenant J.N Pollock. Flying Officer W.A.C. Bowen DFC.

344913.	F/Sgt	Spinks, W.V.	A.C.H./G.D.
651830.	Cpl.	Walton, G.C.	Armourer.
653467.	L.A.C.	Hume, W.S.	Armourer.
850238.	A.C.2.	Bennett, T.J.	F/Amourer.
924430.	Cpl.	Crossingham, M.J.	Inst/Repairer (Grp 1).
1022052.	L.A.C.	Davies, L.S.	F.M.A.
1213890.	A.C.1.	Oldin, V.E.A.	F.M.A.
1289280.	A.C.2.	Denny, E.	F/Armourer.
1298130.	A.C.1.	Gillett, R.G.	W/Mechanic.
1512023.	Cpl.	Mercer, J.S.W.	RADAR/Mechanic.
1680864.	A.C.2.	Blaikie, J.	Arm/Assistant.
1680875.	A.C.2.	Coombe, J.I.	Arm/Assistant.
1692636.	A.C.1.	Antrobus, J.E.	Main/Assistant.
1694623.	A.C.1.	Minta, J.T.	Main/Assistant.
1694659.	A.C.2.	Mac Arthur, A.W.	Armourer.
1232525.	Cpl.	Bloomfield, J.H.	Electrician.

LOADING PARTY FOR KIT.

1233628.	Cpl.	Blackwell, C.F.	Fitt. II. A.
1636610.	A.C.1.	Sizmur. A.G.	Main/Assistant.
1636670.	A.C.1.	Shorey, E.C.	Main/Assistant.

PARTY FOR TECHNICAL BUILDINGS.

523992.	Sgt	Millar, W.G.	Fitt. II.E.
628188.	A.C.1.	Lewis, A.W.	F.M.A.
633941.	Sgt	Coulson, A.G.	Fitt. II.E.
654539.	L.A.C.	Evans, C.E.	F.M.E.
916000.	L.A.C.	Chapman. L.G.	Fitt. II.E.
1184425.	A.C.2.	Allnutt, H.	Fitt. II.A.
1254019.	L.A.C.	Powell, J.R.	Main/Assistant.
1615704.	A.C.2.	Bullimore, B.J.	Fitt. II.A.
1637888.	A.C.2.	Gaimster, W.	Main/Assistant.

1680876.	A.C.2.	Hamill, J.	Main/Assistant.
1797266.	A.C.2.	Fitzgerald, G.P.	Main/Assistant.
1797356.	A.C.2.	Flynn, A.	Main/Assistant.
1820131.	A.C.2.	Hughes, J.	Main/Assistant.
3010425.	A.C.2.	Halford, W.	Main/Assistant.

PARTY FOR SQUADRON STORES.

746088.	Cpl.	Smith, H.F.	Equip/Assistant.
1659414.	A.C.1.	Phillips, W.H.	Main/Assistant.
1873639.	A.C.2.	Marshall, A.C.	Main/Assistant.

NUMBERS:-   <u>Officers</u>   <u>S.N.C.O.s.</u>   <u>Other Ranks</u>.
                2   3   33

APPENDIX 'B'.
MAIN ROAD PARTY.

Wing Commander AJ Samson, D.F.C.

Flight Lieutenant M.J. Stevens	Flight Lieutenant S.P. Wond
Flight Lieutenant H. Beckett	Flight Lieutenant P.R. Thompson
Flight Lieutenant H. Hall	Flight Lieutenant J. Angus.
Pilot Officer J.D. Groston.	Flying Officer J.D. Trick.

Headquarters.

549584.	Cpl. Stewart, J.	A.C.H./G.D.
621208.	Cpl. Lavelle, S.G.G.	A.C.H./G.D.
626308.	Cpl. Morrison, H.J.	A.C.H./G.D.
1026725.	Cpl. Weston, J.	Clerk/G.D.
1500842.	A.C.1. Taylor, E.A.	Clerk/G.D.
1647545.	A.C.1. Harris, E.M.	Clerk/P.A.
1831504.	A.C.2. Pearcey, A.W.	A.C.H./G.D.
1831507.	A.C.2. Wild, C.	A.C.H./G.D.
1832762.	L.A.C. Hancock, J.H.	Clerk/G.D.
1870249.	A.C.1. Golding, R.W.	Clerk/G.D.

ARMOURY.

640091.	Cpl. Spring, R.H.	Fitt/Armourer.
946235.	A.C.2. Gilby, T.W.	Fitt/Armourer. (Bomb).
1044684.	Cpl. Collier, B.	Fitt/Armourer. (Bomb).
1093623.	A.C.2. Timberlake, A.S.	Fitt/Armourer. (Bomb).
1149557.	A.C.1. Stokes, B.	Fitt/Armourer. (Bomb).
1442306.	A.C.1. Gautier, D.	Fitt/Armourer. (Bomb).
1484680.	A.C.1. Moody, E.	Fitt/Armourer. (Bomb).
1513919.	A.C.2. Benson, V.H.	Fitt/Armourer. (Bomb).
1540902.	A.C.1. Hardaker, J.A.	Fitt/Armourer. (Gun).
518850.	F/Sgt Jeckells, H.	Armourer.
634345.	Cpl. Stephen, W.P.	Armourer.
644178.	Cpl. Brownsword, H.	Armourer.
643438.	L.A.C. Ayres, J.	Armourer.

942346.	L.A.C.	Stabler, J.H.	Armourer.
1008493.	Cpl.	Beavis, H.S.	Armourer.
1095519.	Cpl.	Barrowclough, F.	Armourer.
1148514.	A.C.2	McCready, B.	Armourer.
1176251.	L.A.C.	Johnson, E.C.	Armourer.
1272650.	L.A.C.	Carnell, B.	Armourer.
1295190.	A.C.1.	Bradford, A.H.	Armourer.
1326454.	L.A.C.	Stoneman, A.E.	Armourer.
1367272.	A.C.1.	Maynell, E.J.	Armourer.
1389255.	A.C.2.	Chanter, R.V.	Armourer.
1428241.	L.A.C.	Wilson, D.N.H.	Armourer.
1545171.	A.C.1.	Bretherton, F.	Armourer.
1551686.	A.C.1.	Scott, J.G.	Armourer.
1575528.	A.C.1.	Bradbury, D.W.	Armourer.
1611116.	A.C.1.	Hermes, V.G.	Armourer.
1615911.	A.C.1.	Brown, K.G.	Armourer.
1629739.	A.C.1.	Downes, L.	Armourer.
1641943.	A.C.2.	Rhodes, J.R.	Armourer.
1642780.	A.C.2.	Goraghty, R.J.	Armourer.
1646948.	A.C.1.	Lee, W.H.	Armourer.
1647323.	A.C.1.	Smith, W.G.	Armourer.
1667638.	A.C.1.	Pratley, W.J.	Armourer.
1669987.	A.C.2.	Killmaster,	Armourer.
1679810.	A.C.2.	Hunter,	Armourer.
1680737.	A.C.2.	Sansbury,	Armourer.
1680797.	A.C.1.	Searle, V.	Armourer.
1682958.	A.C.2.	Osborne, D.F.	Armourer.
1683078.	A.C.2.	Silverman, D.	Armourer.
1698414.	A.C.2.	Williamson, H.V.	Armourer.
1710276.	A.C.2.	Flight, G.	Armourer.
2263262.	A.C.2.	Goodchild, F.D.	Armourer.
1229715.	L.A.C.	Taylor, R.	Armourer. (Gun).
1338295.	A.C.2.	Philp, H.V.	Armourer. (Gun).
1534213.	L.A.C.	Crosby, W.F.	Armourer. (Bomb).

SQUADRON M.T.

520774.	A.C.1	Colne, C.W.R.	D.M.T.
532212.	Cpl.	Woodman H.W.	D.M.T.
643167.	Cpl.	Stark, T.	D.M.T.
1750283.	L.A.C.	Alder, O.	D.M.T.
1142078.	L.A.C.	Knight, H.	D.M.T.
1160811.	L.A.C.	Cole, L.F.	D.M.T.
1285004	L.A.C.	Jolleys, H.W.	D.M.T.
1406227.	L.A.C.	Davies, N.J.	D.M.T.
1440713.	L.A.C.	Pollard, E.W.	D.M.T.
1467774.	A.C.1.	Hillard, L.C.	D.M.T.
1610543.	Cpl.	Spalding, A.	D.M.T.
1617999.	L.A.C.	Balchin, C.H.	D.M.T.
1637849.	A.C.1.	Green, E.E.	D.M.T.
1666404.	A.C.1.	Attwood, W.J.	D.M.T.
1158435.	L.A.C.	Cox,	D.M.T.
1102181.	Cpl.	Whitely,	D.M.T.
1077334.	Cpl.	Faulkner,	D.M.T.

W.A.A.F. PERSONNEL.

437247.	A.C.W.1.	Lawrence, J.	D.M.T.
2003106.	Cpl.	McIntosh, A.A.	D.M.T.
2005988.	L.A.C.W.	Burgess, E.M.	D.M.T.
2006818.	L.A.C.W.	Plunden, E.G.	D.M.T.
2008024.	L.A.C.W.	Lusher, M.R.	D.M.T.
2010784.	L.A.C.W.	Shannan, B.	D.M.T.
2011154.	L.A.C.W.	Hockley, K.E.	D.M.T.
2036525.	L.A.C.W.	Prior, J.W.	D.M.T.
2060860.	L.A.C.W.	Burton,	D.M.T.
2132034.	L.A.C.W.	Ingram, M.	D.M.T.
2140996.	A.C.W.2.	Morris, E.F.P.	D.M.T.
2140858.	A.C.W.2.	Briggs, V.E.	D.M.T.
2141771.	A.C.W.1.	Otton,	D.M.T.

ELECTRICAL.

328262.	F/Sgt	Long, E.C.	Elect.	I.
535412.	Sgt	Henry, R.W.	Elect.	I.
618289.	Cpl.	Kerr, J.M.	Elect.	I.
620614.	Cpl.	Wilson, D.F.D.	Elect.	I.
1121643.	A.C.1.	Griffiths, V.J.	Elect.	I.
1290121.	A.C.1.	Rogers, A.E.	Elect.	I.
1401549.	Cpl.	Powell, D.	Elect.	I.
1431425.	Cpl.	Collins, C.	Elect.	I.
1483684.	A.C.1.	Cresswell, E.	Elect.	I.
1621144.	A.C.1.	Hopkins, R.	Elect.	I.
905441.	A.C.1.	Woodley, M.	Elect.	II.
1035276.	L.A.C.	Griffiths, W.J.	Elect.	II.
1066902.	L.A.C.	Thomas, E.C.	Elect.	II.
1204870.	L.A.C.	Forster, A.	Elect.	II.
1131692.	A.C.1.	Hammond, F.	Elect.	II.
1221634.	L.A.C.	Burroughs, L.	Elect.	II.
1245444.	A.C.1.	Muttock, F.W.	Elect.	II.
1433544.	A.C.2.	Lester, M.	Elect.	II.
1457814.	L.A.C.	Thomas, T.O.	Elect.	II.
1472333.	A.C.1.	Wendon, J.F.C.	Elect.	II.
1474395.	L.A.C.	Blencowe, F	Elect.	II.
1494322.	L.A.C.	Keynes, J.	Elect.	II.
1549084.	L.A.C.	Howard, S.T.	Elect.	II.
1663498.	A.C.2.	Barnes, A.V.	Elect.	II.

ARMOURY (Contd).

1057191	A.C.1.	Farrow, R.C.	Arm/Assist.
1636121.	A.C.1.	Cliff, T.	Arm/Assist.
1651218.	A.C.1.	Powell, T.	Arm/Assist.

SQUADRON STORES.

634317.	L.A.C.	Reay, R.G.	Equip/Assist.
1007409.	L.A.C.	Frizzel, A.	Equip/Assist.

MAINTENANCE FITT. II. A.

314940.	Sgt	Leadbetter, H.	523763.	Sgt	Hawcroft, A
539987.	Cpl.	Bush, K.J.	560514.	W/O.	Atkinson, T.W.
643943.	LAC.	McLaughlin, J.W.	746196.	Cpl.	Hill, F.W.
901515.	Cpl.	Gower, D.	921104.	Sgt	Addison, L.W.
938048.	AC1.	Sinclair, L	981523.	LAC.	Jones, W.R.
995879.	Sgt	Jones, J.	1014961.	Cpl.	Lockhart, R.
1062484.	LAC.	Potts, T.W.	1062665.	Cpl.	Spence, A.
1066027.	Cpl.	Jones, G.G.	1074168.	LAC.	Rich, F.J.
1085221.	AC2.	Adams, A.L.	1090467.	LAC.	Blenkin, H.
1095500.	AC1.	Hobbs-Hurrell, AJ	1096736.	LAC.	White, C.H.
1100439.	LAC.	Mace, B.	1175175.	LAC.	Newton, K.R.
1190654.	AC1.	Milton, R.G.	1208439.	AC1.	Sudds, L.
1262435.	LAC.	Pavall, J.L.	1272535.	LAC.	Harlow, D.C.
1357457.	AC2.	Thomas, K.R.	1357471.	LAC.	Snowin, J.P.
1456043.	AC1.	Kirby, R.	1481798.	AC1.	Maycock, H.
1485312.	AC1.	Read, R.J.	1582980.	AC2.	Howard, R.J.

FITT. II. B.

90224.	Cpl.	Pollett, J.L.	348723.	Sgt	Sherwood, W
525921.	LAC.	Stoan, W.A.	536467.	Sgt	Sheldon, T.J.
539255.	Sgt	Rawley, W.J.	543578.	AC2.	Smith, H.F.
614784.	Sgt	Simpson, H.E.	643376.	AC1.	Howard, W
651426.	LAC.	Fenlon A.W.	752411.	Cpl	Penny, R.J.
906359.	Cpl.	Horseman L.	920813.	Sgt	Bugg, R.H.
955871.	AC1.	Burton C.W.	954803.	LAC.	Round, A.A.
959447.	L.A.C.	Evans D.V.	960511.	LAC.	Evans, W.J.
1047982.	L.A.C.	Buxton C.W.	1081065.	Sgt	Giles, J.E.
1097566.	L.A.C.	Wood, C	1136052.	AC2.	Yeomans, G.H.
1237913.	L.A.C.	Pickering, L.	1260657.	LAC.	Wonnacott A.A.
1278272.	L.A.C.	Peacey, J.	1383576.	AC1.	Spencer, J.C.
1394029.	L.A.C.	Cowling, R.	1452667.	LAC.	Gray, W.N.
1460524.	AC1.	Popham, J.B.	1582524.	AC1.	Staniforth, S.
1685311.	AC2.	Trueman, H.	1808377	AC2.	Chapman, L.C.

'A' and 'B' FLIGHTS.

F.M.A.

632188.	LAC.	Montgomery, H.	639772.	LAC.	Wincott, W.H.
652699.	LAC.	Smith, A.W.	756753	AC1.	Lewis, S.

861123. Cpl.	Harris, A.E.	
963453. LAC.	Dodd W.C.	
1049518. LAC.	Doughty, XX	
1064553. LAC.	Hogg, C.M	
1093841 LAC.	Alanson, S.E	
1147204. LAC.	Pickard, J.	
1181968 LAC.	Winch xx	
1197927. LAC.	Green H.	
1284622. LAC.	Prescott C.J.	
1409892. AC1	Phillips, C.H.	
1418492. LAC.	Bateman, P.J.	
1445211. AC1.	Lebborn, A.W.	
1480085. LAC.	Thompson, P.	
1518656. AC1.	Harrison E.R.	
1553908. AC1.	Cameron, G.	
1621436. LAC.	Scales L.	
2202055 AC2.	Collison, J.	

944339 LAC.	Lane, C.E.	
973957. LAC.	Griffiths, K.J.	
1054321. LAC.	(Illegible), E.R.	
1083550 LAC.	Bonsall, J.O.	
1102939. LAC.	Tidyman, G.	
1180355. LAC.	Putman, S.F.	
1189679. LAC.	Broomfield, C.H.	
1230605. LAC.	Guilford, W.	
1389888. LAC.	Marriott, AJ	
1411922. AC2.	Morgan, R.	
1418725. LAC.	Harding, D.G.	
1445944. LAC.	Field, E.F.	
1508748. AC1.	Hough, H.	
1533715. LAC.	Curphey, F.R.	
1572162. AC2.	McNicoll, J.	
1638785. AC2.	Bolton, S.	

F.M.E.

549869. AC2.	Martin, L.J.	
615524. LAC.	Allen, J.S.	
644773. AC1.	(Illegible)	
933313. AC2.	Field, J.K.	
979517. LAC.	Davies, J.A.	
1016299. LAC.	Kelly, M.J.	
1064392. AC1.	Caulie, H.	
1126887. AC2.	Thomas, H	
1134947. LAC.	Biggin F.A.	
1155267. AC2.	Birch, C.S.	
1161657 XXX	Webster, J.E.	
1237794 AC1.	Conan F.C.	
1252984 AC1.	Dodd, F.W.	
1355924. AC2.	Crocker, D.H.	
1414605. LAC.	Hanson, AJ	
1454356. LAC.	Mills, K.R.	
1482410. AC1.	Wilkinson, J.A.	
1584159. AC2.	Silverstone, S.J.	
1698962. AC2.	Stevenson, R.	
1777051. AC1.	McLeod, V.	
1810490. AC2.	Fitzsimins AJ	
1835435 AC2.	Brind, F.N.	

559223. AC2.	Stephenson, J.S.	
640991. LAC.	Hoyle, A	
906910. AC2.	Hutchings, N.	
959345. AC2.	Puckingham, F.J.	
1015976. LAC.	Lewis, J.E.	
1063429. LAC.	Chanley, R.	
1067179. LAC.	Trimnell, J.E.	
1132793. LAC.	Kershaw, J.J.S.	
1149439. LAC.	Robinson, R.E.	
1178122. LAC.	Clarke, F.	
1232734. LAC.	Jermy S.	
1247011. AC1.	Mayes, R.S.	
1343913. AC2.	Watson, J.M.	
1370347. LAC.	Lamont, W.A.	
1452437. AC2.	Stiling, H.W.	
1473400. AC2.	Holloway, R.A.	
1536218. AC2.	Roberts, R.M.	
1606769. AC2.	Charlton, C.J.	
1676269. AC2.	Foulkes, V.	
1798500. AC2.	Moore, W.M.	
1818176. AC2.	Cruckshaw, R.J.	
1865543. AC2.	Fyson, A.W.	

1871280.AC2.Flockney, F.C.   1871313. AC2. Carvosso. F.S.
1871317.AC2.Arkley, S.H.   1872606. AC2. Brackpool, H.N.
1872813.AC2.Reeve, L.W.   1872877. AC2. Webb, C.W.
2201657.AC2.Heckler, K.   2208156. AC1. Parker, W.
2208687.AC2.Pike, E.G.   2208007. AC2. Jones, J.
2202961.AC2.Gauterin, O.

MAINTENANCE ASST.

1820134.AC2.Burns, J.M.O.

COMPASS/ADJ.

1589236. SgtHamblin, J.   Comps/Adj.
1676078. SgtLock, A.   Comps/Adj.

INSTRUMENT SECT.

571219.F/Sgt   Musgrave, J.H.   Inst/Maker
1005314.A.C.1. Bradney, W.G.   Inst/Rep.1
1044478.A.C.1. Fox, W.J.H.   Inst/Rep.1
1076787.L.A.C. McGowan, F.   Inst/Rep.1
1270750.A.C.1. Ouston, N.L.   Inst/Rep.1
1391737.Cpl.   Gillingham, J.W.   Inst/Rep.1
1528246.Cpl.   Miller, R.E.   Inst/Rep.1
1138042.A.C.1. Harriman, S.   Inst/Rep.2
1291286.A.C.1. Seaks, H.   Inst/Rep.2
1295110.L.A.C. Hobbs, D.E.F.   Inst/Rep.2
1352824.A.C.2. Johnson, H.C.   Inst/Rep.2
1385659.L.A.C.Mortimer, F.   Inst/Rep.2
1441082 L.A.C. Newitt, E.E.H.   Inst/Rep.2
1444192.L.A.C.Evered, J.W.   Inst/Rep.2
1465672.L.A.C.French, H.J.   Inst/Rep.2
1472936 A.C.1.Smith, A.G.   Inst/Rep.2
1475251.A.C.1. Vardy, T.L.   Inst/Rep.2
1475393.L.A.C.Davis, G.   Inst/Rep.2
1511389.A.C.1.Ware, J.   Inst/Rep.2
1669520.A.C.2.Vermore, C. G.   Inst/Rep.2
1720252.A.C.2.Hay, AJ   Inst/Rep.2

MEDICAL.

| 900413. | Cpl. | Hughes, N. | N/Orderly. |
| 1875758. | A.C.1. | Heath, D.H. | N/Orderly. |

PHOTOGRAPHY.

236377.	Sgt	Tilley, S.C.	Photo.
1183209	L.A.C.	Lang, T.	Photo.
11810576	A.C.1.	Palmer, A.F.	Photo.

R AND I. SECTION.

R94395	Cpl.	Blair, H.G.	RADAR/Mech
847686.	A.C.1.	Cooke E.T.	RADAR/Mech
1196399.	L.A.C.	Taylow, W.	RADAR/Mech
1404813.	F/Sgt	Phillips, J.	RADAR/Mech
1417140.	Cpl.	Taylor, D.L.S.	RADAR/Mech
1453427.	Sgt	Batchelor, K.	RADAR/Mech
1521288.	A.C.1.	Hawkins, J.B.	RADAR/Mech
1521502.	A.C.2.	Garrod, J.D.	RADAR/Mech
1614280.	A.C.1.	Tidy, F.G.	RADAR/Mech
1616420.	A.C.2.	Edwards, V.H.	RADAR/Mech
1688039.	L.A.C.	Henshaw, D.	RADAR/Mech
1698614.	A.C.2.	Davies, J.H.	RADAR/Mech
1832206.	A.C.2.	Harrison, K.F.	RADAR/Mech
1863381.	A.C.1.	Hayden, G.G.	RADAR/Mech
1863388.	A.C.2.	Brown, P.F.	RADAR/Mech

WIRELESS SECTION.

550157.	F/Sgt	Barry, W.H	W.E.M.
921007.	Cpl.	Meddermen, J.L.	W.O.M.
902097.	A.C.1.	Fennings, J.M.D.	W/Mech.
1172771.	A.C.2.	Hall, T.L.	W/Mech
1257272.	Cpl.	Calder, R.	W/Mech
1310691.	Cpl.	Wilson. G.N.	W/Mech
1394567.	A.C.1.	Smith, L.E.	W/Mech
1451610.	L.A.C.	Lockie, J.A.	W/Mech
1458589.	A.C.1.	Doe, K.P.	W/Mech
1467744.	L.A.C.	Gaze, F.H.	W/Mech
1509055.	A.C.2.	Cowley, C.	W/Mech
1785059.	L.A.C.	Gibb, R.W.	W/Mech

SAFETY EQUIPMENT SECTION.

1229026. A.C.1. Rigden, H.   S.Eq/Worker.
2095867. A.C.F2 Reedman, M.   S.Eq/Asst.

W.A.A.F PERSONNEL.

COOKS.

424035. LACW. White,G.E.M.	462973. ACM2.	Callaghan, M.
464350. ACW1. Ward,V.	2008019.ACW1.	Worsdale, M.
2011021.ACW1. Frost,A.E.	2052790.LACW.	Moffat, N.
2056277.ACW1. Roche,M.	2092647.LACW.	Urran, J.
2105780.ACW1. Elliott,J.M.	2105776.ACW1.	Lewis, W.A.
2148747.ACW2. Cooper,R.M.		

WAITRESSES.

425981.	Cpl. Jackson, D.R.	455970. ACW1.	Wright, K.A.M.
476876.	ACW2.Brown, V.M.	2025221.ACW1.	Sprules, P.M.
2066779.	ACW1.Pilgrim, xx.	2084580.ACW1.	Alexander, W.

KIT LOADING PARTY.

531475.	F/Sgt	Kershaw, F.	Fitt.II.E.
541142.	L.A.C.	Turner, J.	F.M.E.
457682.	Cpl.	Williams, J.I.	Fitt.II.A.
628438.	Cpl.	Murphy, K.	Fitt.II.E.
808212.	Cpl.	Hogarth, F.	Fitt.II.A.
1250325.	A.C.1.	Foetham, J.	Main/Asst.
1268267.	L.A.C.	Parry, D.V.	Fitt.II.A.
1280988.	A.C.2.	Green, H.F.C.	F.M.E.
1342023.	A.C.2.	Carroll, J.K.	Fitt.II.E.
1457929.	L.A.C.	Hawkins, C.	Main/Asst.
1666689.	A.C.2.	Ball, G.	F.M.E.
1724308.	A.C.2.	Lawrence, E.L.	Fitt.II.A.
1735506.	A.C.2.	Brown, AJL.	F.M.E.
1818151.	A.C.1.	Hill, J.C.	F.M.E.
1818180.	A.C.2.	Mills, R.C.	F.M.E.
1873445.	A.C.2.	Owen, W.C.	F.M.E.

AIR CREW.

133610.	F/O	Kingwell. L.J.	Pilot
1396522.	Sgt	Knight, G.E.	Nav.
Aus.409037.	F/S.	Fidge, H.S.	A/C.
1821145.	Sgt	Newbury, D.W.	F/Eng.
1330751.	Sgt	Wyer, W.H.	A/Bomber.
1076809.	Sgt	Hydes, J.M.	WOP/AG.
1399608.	Sgt	Loseby, S.	A/G

J20915.	F/C.	Peake, J.	A/Bomber.
1220052.	Sgt	Whichelow, H.M.	WOP/AG.
1581481.	Sgt	Taylor, H.	A/G.
1579592.	Sgt	Davies, P.C.	Nav.
1238470.	Sgt	Clewlow, G.	A/G.
1393193.	Sgt	Winterford, D.A.	F/Eng.

DETATCHED ON COURSE.

1127807.   Sgt   Blamries,   A.W/Mech.
To R.A.F. Station Watchfield, WEF 14/11/43.

1020630.   LAC.   Miller A.G.   Arm/Gun.
To 10 S of T.T. Kirkham, WEF 17/11/43.

542060.   LAC.   Senior, G.K.   Elect.1.
To 2 S of T.T. Cosford, WEF 16/11/43.

1528331.   AC2.   Cooper, S.F.   Fitt. II.N.
To 2 S of T.T. Cosford, WEF 16/11/43.

NUMBERS: -

Officers.	S.N.C.O.s	Other Ranks	W.A.A.F.s
11	33	312	31

APPENDIX 'C'

AIR PARTY

Officer In Charge:- Squadron Leader EGB Reid. D.F.C. Pilot.

'A' FLIGHT.

70816.	S/Ldr.	EGB Reid D.F.C.	Pilot.
1585089.	Sgt	Meade, V.E.D.	A/Bomber.
155676.	F/O	James, H.	Navigator.
Aus10114.	F/S.	Williams, G.G.	A/Gunner.
Aus425845.	F/S.	White, R.H.	A/Gunner.
1608232.	Sgt	O'Donnell, R.J.	F/Engineer.
NZ114385.	F/S.	Mack, W.T.L.	WOP/A.G.
156310.	P/O.	Thomas, S.P.I.	Pilot.
1612568.	Sgt	Brent, S.L.	Navigator.
1043366.	Sgt	Thomas, F.	WOP/A.G.
1334943.	Sgt	Fontaine, R.W.	A/Bomber.
1818663.	Sgt	Lucas, H.A.	A/Gunner.
Aus415979.	F/S.	Haines, B.S.	A/Gunner.
1332705.	Sgt	Stagg, H.	F/Engineer.
1291787.	Sgt	Samuels, K.F.	Pilot.
1454683.	Sgt	Martindale, B.	A/Bomber.
1600694.	Sgt	Adkin, L.S.J.	Navigator.
1311211.	Sgt	Muskett, W.	WOP/A.G.
1128920.	Sgt	Murphy, K.E.	A/Gunner.
981549.	Sgt	Nicholson, A.	A/Gunner.
1815316.	Sgt	Webb, P.W.	F/Engineer.
R85412.	W/O.	Greenwood, E.	Pilot.
147709.	P/O.	Nicol, D.A.	Navigator.
121738.	F/O	Lang, D.K.	B/Aimer.
R128609.	W/O.	Bourne, E.W.	A/Gunner.
143911.	P/O.	Dawes, J.K.	WOP/A.G.
1629747.	Sgt	Thornton, F.J.	F/Engineer.

J21428.	P/O.	Chequer, C.J.	Pilot.
1391232.	Sgt	Wallington, E.J.	A/Bomber.
1437368.	Sgt	Mortimer, K.	Navigator.
2366420.	Sgt	Montgomery, R.	WOP/A.G.
Aus418509.	F/S.	Robertson, AJ	A/Gunner.
Aus425740.	F/S.	O'Brian, J.L.	A/Gunner.
575828.	Sgt	Carey, J.S.	F/Engineer.
1040312.	Sgt	Langley, R.	Pilot.
928520.	Sgt	Bradsell, D.	A/Bomber.
1455046.	Sgt	Jones, F.R.	Navigator.
1450246.	Sgt	Wakeling, C.F.	WOP/A.G.
1813263.	Sgt	Oliver, F.G.	A/Gunner.
1821995.	Sgt	Smith, R.R.	A/Gunner.
573999.	Sgt	Parker, B.O.	F/Engineer.
Aus413614.	F/S.	Hughes, G.S.	Pilot.
NZ427199.	Sgt	Hall, A.D.	A/Bomber.
NZ416587.	F/S.	Smith, L.S.	Navigator.
Aus421267.	F/S.	Goddard, O.J.	WOP/A.G.
1618730.	Sgt	Thornton, G.H.	A/Gunner.
1105921.	Sgt	Moorhouse, E.G.	A/Gunner.
1523926.	Sgt	West, H.	F/Engineer.
80476.	F/Lt.	Hinde, G.H.D.	Pilot.
Aus422366.	Sgt	Alford, G.D.	A/Bomber.
143850.	P/O.	Emery, M.S.C.	Navigator.
1578078.	Sgt	Thom, D.	WOP/A.G.
1568236.	Sgt	Curle, R.	A/Gunner.
1672756.	Sgt	Galloway, R.	A/Gunner.
1566577.	Sgt	Stephen, W.J.	F/Engineer.
1020779.	W/O.	Williams, J.K.	Pilot.
151014.	P/O.	Henshaw. D.P.	A/Bomber.
1374196.	Sgt	Millis, L.N.	Navigator.
Aus427457.	F/S.	Chapman, W.H.	WOP/AG.
911246.	Sgt	Pratt, A.	A/Gunner.
932746.	F/S.	Lane, E.A.	A/Gunner.
1670438.	Sgt	Koenen, J.R.	F/Engineer.

1064854.	Sgt	Knights, J.	A/Bomber.
1503843.	Sgt	Vickers, A.	Navigator.
1025462.	Sgt	Scott, G.E.	WOP/AG.
1417820.	Sgt	Salt, C.A.	A/Gunner.
1424478.	Sgt	McAllister, R.V.	A/Gunner.
1579492.	Sgt	Bennett, E.C.K.	F/Engineer.
149539.	F/L.	Payne, C.	Pilot.
1324883.	Sgt	Young, G.C.	A/Bomber.
132709.	F/O	Armstrong, K.W.	Navigator.
978911.	Sgt	Robinson, J.B.	WOP/AG.
1396800.	Sgt	Twinn, P.A.S.	A/Gunner.
Aus421309.	F/S.	Bennett, D.N.	A/Gunner.
1336682.	Sgt	Gilbert, A.	F/Engineer.
R190270.	Sgt	McNeill, J.J.	A/Gunner.
R165360.	Sgt	Wilton, L.	A/Gunner.

AIR PARTY

'B' FLIGHT.

115023.	S/Ldr.	A.L.Roberts, D.F.C.	Pilot.
939667.	Sgt	Foggin, R.	A/Bomber.
1319583.	Sgt	Bell, A.	Navigator.
1336538.	Sgt	Upton, P.W.	WOP/AG.
R119782.	Sgt	Dahle, H.J.	A/Gunner.
940758.	Sgt	Kilfoyle, F.G.	A/Gunner.
951033.	Sgt	Bannister, R.A.	F/Engineer.
J20214.	F/O	M.R. Cantin.	Pilot.
R161620.	Sgt	Smith, S.E.	A/Bomber.
1287750.	Sgt	Walne, B.N.	A/Gunner.
1821076.	Sgt	Lonnigan, W.	A/Gunner.
1346909.	Sgt	Saddler, W.G.F.	Navigator.
1388185.	Sgt	Mitchell, W.E.	WOP/AG.
577808.	Sgt	King, K.G.	F/Engineer.

131090.	F/L.	D.A.A. Gray.	Pilot.
1315709.	Sgt	Brazier. E.W.R.	A/Bomber.
1610618.	Sgt	Brown, R.R.	Navigator.
1175873.	Sgt	Hounsome, R.A.	WOP/AG.
R142559.	F/S.	Sharp, H.G.	A/Gunner.
1283278.	Sgt	Hoddle-Wrigley, R.A.	A/Gunner.
1002381.	Sgt	Helliwell, R.	F/Engineer.
134092.	F/L.	C.W. Nichol.	Pilot.
523133.	P/O.	K.D. Deans.	A/Bomber.
1324521.	Sgt	Hoare, P.S.	Navigator.
1179569.	F/S.	Elliott, AJ	WOP/AG.
1262356.	Sgt	Fearman, G.C.	A/Gunner.
1377495.	Sgt	Jackson, A.V.	A/Gunner.
1615097.	Sgt	Townshend, F.	F/Engineer.
1118708.	F/S.	McGown, W.L.	Pilot.
1337757.	Sgt	Lewis, L.C.W.	A/Bomber.
Aus413305.	F/S.	Durham, A.N.	Navigator.
Aus410529.	F/S.	Bryan, K.E.	WOP/AG.
1590234.	Sgt	Tanney, J.O.	A/Gunner.
1873573.	Sgt	Boanson, J.G.S.	A/Gunner.
1581581.	Sgt	Clarke, J.	F/Engineer.
Aus414654.	F/S.	Crombie, C.C.G.	Pilot.
137547.	P/O.	H.G. Darby.	A/Bomber.
1392000.	Sgt	McPhee, A.	Navigator.
1323746.	Sgt	Tyler, M.J.	WOP/AG.
1579675.	Sgt	Hill, H.R.	A/Gunner.
1811733.	Sgt	Jenner, E.W.	A/Gunner.
1509891.	Sgt	Le-Neve Foster, B.P.	F/Engineer.
1378365.	F/S.	Ashpitel, P.M.	Pilot.
1450549.	Sgt	Green, B.G.	A/Bomber.
135670.	F/O	Jones, W.L.W.	Navigator.
1387235.	Sgt	Cole. R.S.	WOP/AG.
976475.	F/S.	Hall, R.	A/Gunner.
143598.	P/O.	H.C. Bryant.	A/Gunner.
1032632.	Sgt	Martin, S.F.	F/Engineer.

1345806.	Sgt	Henry, W.	Pilot.
R120852.	F/S.	Ball, W.S.	A/Bomber.
1323954.	Sgt	Ricketts, S.W.	Navigator.
1576668.	Sgt	Vallance. F.B.	WOP/AG.
928328.	Sgt	Eyre, L.F.	A/Gunner.
542541.	Sgt	Kenny, D.	A/Gunner.
1063741.	Sgt	Bennett, A.E.	F/Engineer.
1333416.	Sgt	Steed, F.C.B.	Pilot.
1389896.	Sgt	Bulled, M.J.	A/Bomber.
1433260.	Sgt	Watts, A.	Navigator.
651820.	F/S.	Robertson, A.N.	WOP/AG.
1651741.	Sgt	Sweet, W.H.	A/Gunner.
R78082.	Sgt	Forsythe, C.A.	A/Gunner.
1566622.	Sgt	Cumming, J.	F/Engineer.
Aus409973.	F/S.	Thackray, N.W.F.	Pilot.
642170.	Sgt	Humes, E.L.	A/Bomber.
Aus415482.	Sgt	Moulsdale, G.R.	Navigator.
1575442.	Sgt	Hughes, P.	WOP/AG.
Aus424001.	Sgt	Henn, C.H.	A/Gunner.
Aus424363.	Sgt	Bromley, R.E.	A/Gunner.
1832773.	Sgt	Banfield, C.W.	F/Engineer.
1553150.	F/S.	Davies, G.J.	Pilot.
1445550.	Sgt	Seddon, R.	A/Bomber.
14527782.	Sgt	Roberts, E.J.	Navigator.
1334931.	Sgt	Morris, H.	WOP/AG.
Aus418558.	Sgt	O'Dea, W.D.B.	A/Gunner.
1407182.	Sgt	Bird, A.R.	A/Gunner.
1062645.	Sgt	Smethurst.	F/Engineer.

MECHANIC FOR EACH AIRCRAFT BY AIR.

'A' FLIGHT.

366332.	F/S	Keenan, G.J.	Fitt. II .E.
405673.	Sgt	George, C.H.	Fitt. II .E.
572357.	Sgt	Burton, H.	Fitt. II .A.
636886.	Cpl.	Melluish, E.	Armourer.
1063899.	LAC.	Jamieson, J.	F.M.E.
1087038.	LAC.	Bell, W.	F.M.E.
1242999.	AC1.	Ellwood, J.W.	F.M.E.
1249454.	AC2.	Griffin, J.C.	F.M.E.
1146839.	LAC.	Nash, A.T.	F.M.A.
1423925.	LAC.	Head, L.F.	Elect. II.
1530890.	LAC.	Marriott, P.	Inst/Rep.II.
1637713.	AC1.	Burtt, F.H.	F.M.E.

MECHANIC FOR EACH AIRCRAFT BY AIR.

'B' FLIGHT.

535829.	Sgt. Brown, J.O.	Fitt II. A
527270.	Sgt Mayes, J.H.	Fitt II. E
651058.	Cpl.Evans, A.R.	Fitt II. E
803161.	Sgt Palmer, F.G.	Inst/Rep.I.
903077.	LAC.Pritchard, V.	F.M.E.
994088.	LAC.Trickett, W.A.	F.M.E.
1000399.	LAC.Blenkinship, T.A.	Elect.II.
1272427.	AC1.Argent, J.E.	F.M.A.
1503008.	AC2.Moss, W.	F.M.E.
2208005.	AC2.Revell, G.E.	F.M.E.
2208140.	AC2.Jordan, J.J.R.	F.M.E.

NUMBERS :- Officers: 20 S.N.C.O.s: 139 Other Ranks: 18

APPENDIX 'D'.

REAR PARTY.

Officer in charge:- 86817. P/O. H.C.A. Chapman - A/G.

(Sgt Self, Station Headquarters, Foulsham)

338376.	LAC.	Bass, F.	Fitt.II.A.
623033.	Cpl.	Hirst, J.	ACH/G.H.
905085.	Sgt	Pratt, D.A.	Fitt.II.A.
1001511.	AC2.	Marshall, S.R.	F.M.A.
1011179.	AC1.	Robinson, H.	Armourer.
1290867.	AC1.	Friendship, J.L.	Armourer.
1314470.	AC1.	Huggins, F.G.	Inst/Rep.
1447578.	AC2.	Davies, D.J.	Elect II.
1462029.	AC1.	McCombie, S.E.	Elect. II.
1631231.	AC1.	Cable J.H.I.	W/Mech.
1634698.	AC2.	Howard, A.S.	Main/Asst.
1643063.	AC2.	Graham, B.	Armourer.
1652691.	AC2.	Mugford, W.E.J.	F.M.A.
1690316.	AC1.	Jardine, J.F.B.	Armourer.

NUMBERS :- Officers :- 1 S.N.C.O.s :- 1 Other Ranks :- 13

APPENDIX 'E'.

SLEEPING ACCOMMODATION.

Officers:- Officer's Mess and Annex. Block.
Block.
Block.
Block.
Sergeants'Mess.
W.A.A F.s. Amendment to follow.

APPENDIX 'F'.

MESSING.

Officers:- Officer's Mess.
Sergeants:- Sergeant's Mess.
Other Ranks:- Downstairs Airmen's Dining Hall.
W.A.A.F.s :- Amendment to follow.

APPENDIX 'G'.

TRANSPORT.
Officer in charge to be detailed later.

ADVANCE PARTY. (By Station M.T. Officer).
Date:- 18th November,1943.
Time:- 09.00 hours.
Place:- On road between two Main Hangars.
Personnel :- 2 Officers. 3 S.N.C.O.s. 33 Other Ranks.
Kit :- 08.15 hours Gymnasium. Numbers – 38.

MAIN PARTY. (By No. 2 M.T. Coy. Cambridge and Squadron Transport).
Date :- 23nd. November, 1943.
Time :- 09.00 hours.
Place :- On road between two Main Hangars.
Personnel :-9 Officers, 23 SNCOs, 312 Ors, 31 WAAFs.
Kit :- 08.15 hours. Officer's Quarters, Nos. 2 and 5 Picket Post. Gymnasium.

NUMBERS :- 33 Officers, 162 SNCOs, 330 ORs, 31 W.A.A.Fs.

AIR PARTY.
Heavy kit to accompany the Main Party.

REAR PARTY.
Personnel :- 1 Officer. 1 S.N.C.O. 13 O.Rs.
Date :- November, 1943. To be arranged by Officer in charge and M.T. Officer.

W.A.A.F. PARTY.
Date:- 23nd. November, 1943.
Time:- 09.00 hours.
Place:- N.A.A.F.I. Headquarters.
Personnel :- 18 Other ranks.
Kit: - Numbers —31.

APPENDIX 'H'

BEDDING.
ADVANCE PARTY.
The Station Warrant Officer will detail a collecting party to check in all bedding which will be handed in by all Senior N.O.O.s. And Other Ranks at the gymnasium by 08.5 hours. This applies to Advance, Main and Rear Parties, including Air Party on dates stated.

APPENDIX 'J'

SENIOR N.C.O.s. IN CHARGE OF PARTIES.

ADVANCE PARTY.
Technical Buildings:- Sgt Miller.
Domestic Buildings:- F/Sgt Spinks.
Kit Loading Party Squadron Stores:- Cpl. Blackwell.

MAIN ROAD PARTY. W/O. Atkinson.
Orderly Room Equipment:- Cpl. Weston and Orderly Room personnel.
Technical:
Kit Loading Party:- F/Sgt Kershaw.

Rear Party. Sgt Self, Station Headquarters, Foulsham.

Glossary

A/Bomber	Air Bomber Bomb Aimer
A/C	Aircraft
A/C Instruments	Aircraft Instruments
AC1	Aircraftman - 1st Class
AC2	Aircraftman - Class
ACH/GD	Aircrafthand – General Duties
ACW1	Aircraftwoman – 1st Class
ACW2	Aircraftwoman – 2nd Class
Adj/Adjutant	The Administrative Officer of the Squadron
AFC	Air Force Cross
AFM	Air Force Medal
A - G Firing	Air to Ground Firing
A/G	Air Gunner
Air Tests	Test flight after maintenance or prior to an operational flight
A/G/C	Acting Group Captain
AOC	Air Officer Commanding
ASF	Air to Sea Firing
Assist	Assistant
Astro - Compass	Navigational instrument to obtain a position fix by sighting stars.
A/Ts	Air Tests
ATC Cadets	Air Training Corps Cadets
Baedeker Operation	After hostilities ended, ground crew were flown over bombed German cities so that they could see the results of bombing operations, in which they had also played a vital part. These are referred to in the 514 Sqn ORB as 'Baedeker Tours' after the travel guide. They were more commonly referred to as 'Cooks Tours', whilst 'Baedeker Raids' referred to bombing raids by the Luftwaffe on historic British cities and towns such as York and Canterbury.
BC	Bomber Command
Beam Approach Training	Training in instrument approach to landing.
Beam sorties	Training flights involving beam approaches.

535

Bombed - up	Aircraft loaded with bombs, awaiting an operation.
Bomb loads	The Avro Lancaster was designed for one purpose; delivering as many bombs as possible to enemy targets. Whilst special variants of the Lanc could carry a bomb load of up to 22,000 lbs, in the form of a single 'Grand Slam' bomb, the standard aircraft generally carried up to 14,000 lbs in a variety of configurations. Bomb loads were described in the individual sortie reports in the format number x weight of each bomb type. Incendiary bombs were small and clustered in packs, so the description was number of packs x bombs in each pack x weight of individual bombs. See 'Bomb Types' at the end of the Glossary.
Bullseye	A navigational sortie where the crew was required to navigate to a spot point, be observed and logged by ground observers.
CB	Companion of the Order of the Bath
CBE	Commander of the Order of the British Empire
CO	Commanding Officer
Cpl	Corporal
Cross Country/ies	Non-operational flights away from the home airfield, usually for navigational practice.
Derby Figures	The maximum effort from operational squadrons excluding crews which have operated on both of the two previous nights and crews screened for training, re-equipping or for any similar purpose.
Derby Signal	Instruction to bomb up 'Derby' number of aircraft.
DFC	Distinguished Flying Cross
DFC and Bar	An award of a further DFC to a person already holding this award.
DFM	Distinguished Flying Medal (Other Ranks equivalent of DFC).
Discip	Discipline
Ditch	Land aircraft in the sea.

DR Navigation	Dead Reckoning Navigation. Calculating the aircraft's position without use of radio aids or other external assistance.
DSC	Distinguished Service Cross
DSO	Distinguished Service Order
ENSA	Entertainments National Service Association. Organisation providing entertainment to military personnel.
Eric Exercise	Non-operational flights to provide practice for Home defences.
ETA	Estimated Time of Arrival
F/Eng	Flight Engineer
Fighter Affiliation	Mock attacks by 'friendly' fighter aircraft to train crews in fighter evasion.
Fighter Flares	Flares dropped by enemy aircraft to mark and illuminate the bomber stream.
Flak	Anti-aircraft fire (also AA, ack-ack). Flak was described by its intensity (slight, moderate or intense) and its calibre (light, medium or heavy).
Flak Suits	Body armour for aircrew to protect them from shrapnel. Heavy and cumbersome, they had to be removed prior to putting on a parachute, so were not adopted by the RAF.
F/L or F/LT	Flight Lieutenant
F/O	Flying Officer
F/Sgt or F/SGT	Flight Sergeant
Formation Flying	Flying in a tight group, either for protection against fighters or to drop bombs in a concentrated pattern.
FW190	Focke-Wulf 190, a German single-engined fighter aircraft.
Gardening Exercises	Dropping of sea mines
Gee Signals	Radio signals used by RAF to establish the aircraft's position.
GH / Gee-H	A more accurate development of Gee, more resistant to jamming. 3 Group squadrons were specialists in the use of GH as a blind-bombing aid. It allowed the aircraft's position to be pin-

	pointed with sufficient accuracy to allow bombing through 10/10ths cloud cover with a great degree of confidence that the target would be hit. A proportion of aircraft and their crews were designated 'GH Leader'. These would bomb using GH and other aircraft, formating closely on them, would release their own bombs as soon as they saw the GH Leader's bombs falling. The close proximity of aircraft in a tightly-packed stream, with aircraft at different heights, often led to aircraft being hit by 'friendly' bombs. Several 514 Sqn aircraft, possibly up to ten percent of losses, are believed to have been lost due to being hit by falling bombs and others were damaged.
Goodwood (figures)	The maximum possible effort from Operational Squadrons, including all suitable 'freshmen'. All crews whether screened for training, re-equipping or for any similar purpose, irrespective of the number of previous consecutive nights on which they have operated are to be employed.
Goodwood (Operation)	British Army operation in Normandy, 18th – 20th July 1944.
GRU	Gunnery Research Unit
H and L Tests	Height and load tests. Training in flying heavy aircraft at high altitude.
HF	Heavy flak
High-level Bombing	Tactic of dropping bombs from high altitude, as opposed to ground attack or dive-bombing.
HQ	Headquarters
HRH	His/ Her Royal Highness
H2S	Airborne radar navigation and target location system
Ic	Aircraft on the squadron's operational strength.
Incendiaries	Bombs designed to burst into flames on impact, starting fires.
Inst	Instrument/s
Ir	Aircraft in reserve.

Ju88	Junkers 88, a German twin-engined night-fighter aircraft.
KIA	Killed In Action. Death due directly or indirectly to contact with the enemy, as opposed to in an accident.
LAC	Leading Aircraftman
LACW	Leading Aircraftwoman
Local Flying	Non-operational flying in the vicinity of the home airfield.
Lt	Lieutenant
Lt Col	Lieutenant Colonel
Luftwaffe	German Air Force
Make and Mend	Kit and equipment repairs and modification.
M/B	Master Bomber. Experienced pilot and crew directing aircraft on where to release their bombs. This was to improve accuracy and prevent bombing becoming too dispersed.
Me/Bf109	Messerschmitt Bf-109, a single-engined German fighter aircraft. Particularly famous for its role opposite the Spitfire and Hurricane during the Battle of Britain, the Me109 was later used in a night-fighting role.
Me/Bf110	Messerschmitt Bf110, a German twin-engined fighter aircraft. Designed and deployed as a fighter/bomber in the Battle of Britain, the Bf110 was not particularly successful against Spitfires and Hurricanes. However, when used as a night-fighter against heavy bombers, the aircraft proved extremely deadly and Bf110 crews accounted for many 514 Sqn aircraft.
Me210 / Me410	Messerschmitt 210 and 410, twin-engined German fighters, used for night-fighting or intruder role.
Mech	Mechanic
Monica	A warning radar fitted to RAF bombers to warn of approaching night-fighters. However, the Germans developed their own radar device, Flensburg, to home in on Monica signals leading

	night-fighters to the bomber. It was withdrawn in July 1944.
MUG	Mid Upper Gunner
Nav	Navigator/Navigation
Nav Table	Navigators' Table
NCOs	Non – Commissioned Officer. For aircrew, these were Sergeants, Flight Sergeants and Warrant Officers.
No 3 Group	Bomber Command was organised into a number of 'Groups', each of which consisted of airfield clusters ('Bases') at which the operational squadrons were based. No. 3 Group in 1945 comprised 11 squadrons, which operated from 27 airfields at various times. RAF Waterbeach was the base station for 33 Base, which also included RAF Mepal and RAF Witchford.
OBE	Order of the British Empire
Operation Dodge	Deployment of Lancasters after the end of hostilities to bring home members of the British Eight Army from Italy. Many had been away from home for four or five years.
Operation Manna	Flights over German-occupied Holland to drop food parcels to starving residents. These were undertaken with the agreement of the German forces in the area.
Operation Post Mortem	Flights undertaken to measure and assess the performance of German radar systems.
OPS	Operations
ORB	Operational Record Book
ORs	Other Ranks
Pathfinders / PFF	Path Finder Force was a specific group within Bomber Command tasked with finding and marking targets for 'main force' squadrons to bomb. From mid-1944, 3 Group mostly operated independently of PFF once GH was fully operational. As with all 'elite' forces, any shortcomings in their performance was noted by those not considered elite, hence the numerous

PFF Flares	comments in crew reports concerning PFF timeliness and accuracy. Target-marking flares dropped by PFF to indicate where the main force aircraft should drop their bombs. The flares were used for ground marking, i.e. burning on the ground (Parramatta marking) or sky-marking, i.e. burning as they dropped (Wanganui marking). Wanganui marking was used if the target was obscured by cloud.
P/O	Pilot Officer
POW	Prisoner of War
PRANG	Attack or crash.
RAF	Royal Air Force
RAAF	Royal Australian Air Force
RCAF	Royal Canadian Air Force
RDF Methods	Radio Direction Finding (Radar).
RG	Rear Gunner
RN	Royal Navy
RNZAF	Royal New Zealand Air Force
SASO	Senior Air Staff Officer
SBAs	Standard Beam Approaches. Approach to landing using radio aids.
Scarecrow	Believed by crews to be a special shell fired by German anti-aircraft defences to simulate a bomber exploding, thereby demoralising the crews and disrupting the bombing effort. Whilst this explanation was never officially quashed, there is no evidence that such devices existed, and almost every report of a scarecrow did, in fact, relate to the explosion of an aircraft.
Serrate	Airborne radar detection equipment designed to home in on Luftwaffe *Liechtenstein* radar fitted to night fighters.
Sgt	Sergeant
Sky Markers	See PFF flares above.
S/LDR or S/L (as rank)	Squadron Leader. Rank usually held by the Flight Commander.
S/L (in raid reports)	Searchlights
SNCOs	Senior Non – commissioned Officers

Special Exercises / Training	Training for a specific operational purpose, e.g. navigation. In the case of 514 Sqn, although no details are given due to secrecy, this was probably GH training.
Sun Ray Treatment	Use of ultraviolet lamps to counteract vitamin deficiency.
Tame Boar	Night fighters acting on the directions of ground controllers. To a certain extent these could be confounded by jamming of their communication channels, or misdirection by German-speaking RAF controllers issuing spurious commands.
TIs	Target Indicators. Long-lasting incendiaries to mark the aiming point.
Up with the lark	A very early start, particularly after an evening in the pub or bar.
U/s	Unserviceable.
USAAF	United States Army Air Force (predecessor of USAF).
Vegetable planting	Laying Sea Mines (see also Gardening).
Very / Verey Light	An emergency signalling light stowed with the inflatable raft
VJ Day	Victory over Japan Day. The end of the Second World War.
WAAF	Women's Auxiliary Air Force
W/Cdr	Wing Commander. Rank held by the squadron's Commanding Officer.
W/O	Warrant Officer. The highest non-commissioned rank.
W/OP	Wireless Operator
W/OP/AG	Wireless Operator/Air Gunner
W/T	Wireless Telegraphy. Radio transmission by Morse code.
Wild Boar	Freelancing (undirected) night fighter. Usually single-engined aircraft such as Me109 or FW190, these aircraft did not rely on control from the ground. See also *Tame Boar*.

Bomb Types:

GP (General purpose)	Heavy-cased bombs for general use. These ranged in weight from 40lb to 4,000 lb and, as the name suggests, were used for general bombing purposes. They had a low charge/weight ratio, typically less than 20%.
MC (Medium Capacity)	Designed for general purpose use, MC bombs had a significantly higher proportion of explosive, typically 50%, meaning that they were more destructive than their GP equivalents. Typical weights ranged from 250 lbs to 4,000 lbs.
HC (High Capacity)	HC bombs were thin-walled with a high charge/weight ratio, typically 70%. In 514 Sqn use these bombs were 2,000 lbs, 4,000 lb 'Cookies' or 8,000 'Blockbusters'. The larger HC bombs were intended to break down large buildings, especially factories or housing, for incendiary bombs to ignite.
ANM	ANM bombs were American in origin and used for exactly the same purpose as British bombs. L/D bombs had Long Delay fuses, to cause inconvenience to the enemy in their attempts to clear up the damage caused by the raid.

Royal Air Force Ranks in Ascending Order   Luftwaffe Equivalent

Abbreviations are as per ORB, where applicable.

Non-Commissioned (Ground Crew)

AC2	Aircraftman Second Class	Flieger / Gefrieter
AC1	Aircraftman First Class	Obergefrieter
LAC	Leading Aircraftman	
SAC	Senior Aircraftman	
Cpl	Corporal	Unteroffizier

Non-Commissioned Officers (Air or Ground Crew)

Sgt	Sergeant	Feldwebel (FW)
F/S	Flight Sergeant	Oberfeldwebel
WO	Warrant Officer	Oberfeldwebel (Ofw)

Commissioned Officers (Air or Ground Crew)

PO	Pilot Officer	Leutnant (Lt)
FO	Flying Officer	Oberleutnant
F/Lt	Flight Lieutenant	Hauptmann (Hptmn)
S/L	Squadron Leader	Major
W/C	Wing Commander	Oberstleutnant
Gp Capt	Group Captain	Oberst
Air Cdre	Air Commodore	Generalmajor
AVM	Air Vice-Marshal	Generalleutnant
Air Mshl	Air Marshal	General
Air Chf Mshl	Air Chief Marshal	Generaloberst
MRAF	Marshal of the Royal Air Force	Generalfeldmarschall

Printed in Great Britain
by Amazon